A.J.P. TAYLOR

A.J.P. TAYLOR

Radical Historian of Europe

Chris Wrigley

I.B. TAURIS

LONDON · NEW YORK

Published in 2006 by I.B. Tauris & Co. Ltd
6 Salem Road, London W2 4BU
175 Fifth Avenue, New York NY 10010
www.ibtauris.com

In the United States and Canada distributed by Palgrave Macmillan,
a division of St. Martin's Press, 175 Fifth Avenue, New York NY 10010

ISBN 10: 1 86064 286 1
ISBN 13: 978 1 86064 286 9

A full CIP record for this book is available from the British Library
A full CIP record for this book is available from the Library of Congress
Library of Congress catalog card: available

Typeset in Caslon by Dexter Haven Associates Ltd, London
Printed and bound in Great Britain by TJ International Ltd, Padstow, Cornwall

CONTENTS

ILLUSTRATIONS

PREFACE AND ACKNOWLEDGEMENTS

Alan Taylor has been the subject of two good biographies, written by Adam Sisman and Kathleen Burk. Perhaps, in the centenary year of his birth, there is room for a third.

Initially I had intended writing about his historical and current affairs work but I found it unwise not to relate his early publications to his unusual home background and his evolving political views. I was urged to write a biography, and this is the result. I felt I had certain advantages in so doing, not least in having spoken with many who played parts in his earlier life and are now long dead. I had gathered much information for the biographical introduction to my bibliography of his writings, published in 1980, and also for a 'Memoir' published after his death in *The Proceedings of the British Academy* (1992). Although much younger, I had got to know Alan Taylor reasonably well during his later years. I first met him in 1968. Later, in the mid- to late 1970s, he and his first wife, Margaret, spoke to me several times about his various publications and aspects of his life when I was preparing the bibliography. They were very happy for me, indeed even encouraged me, to take notes of what they said. In turn, some of the factual details I found for that book (such as the venues of CND lectures) were helpful for his autobiography. Subsequently, I saw much of him and his third wife, Dr Éva Haraszti-Taylor.

In writing this biography I have been helped by many people, most of whom are recorded in the references at the end. I have long known Professor Kathy Burk. She recently reminded me that I had given her my large A.J.P. Taylor bibliography (1980) as a wedding present! I came to know Adam Sisman when he prepared his biography and I am grateful to him for his kind and generous help. Professor Robert Cole, the author of a study of Taylor's writings, generously shared his correspondence with Alan Taylor with Éva Taylor and me. I am very grateful to Giles and Sebastian Taylor for letting me interview them. I am also very grateful for much valuable information and advice from Professor Douglas Farnie, whose knowledge of Manchester, Manchester business history and Manchester University is encyclopaedic. I am also grateful to Professor Brian Harrison for permitting me to use his interview with Alan Taylor. I have also benefited from many conversations over thirty years with Della Hilton.

I am also grateful for the assistance of Jacqueline Kavanagh and her colleagues at the BBC Written Archives Centre, Caversham, as well as to the BBC for granting me permission to quote substantial amounts of its copyright material. I am also grateful to the archivists at Bristol University Library, The John Rylands Library, Manchester, The Hallward Library, Nottingham, The Modern Records Centre, Warwick University, The Harry Ransom Research Center, University of Texas at Austin, The Working Class Movement Library, Salford, The House of Lords Record Office and The National Archives, Kew.

Above all, I have been helped and encouraged by Éva Haraszti-Taylor. Sadly, she died on 29 October 2005. Fortunately, she read the whole book some six months earlier and I was pleased that she greatly liked it (though feeling I was sometimes too critical of her second husband). She was an able scholar and a major contributor to Anglo-Hungarian cultural relations. I miss her.

In preparing the book I am heavily in the debt of Su Spencer, who has typed it and revised it with the patience of a saint. My wife, Professor Margaret Walsh, has also shown immense patience while it has been researched and written. I am also grateful for the encouragement and patience of Dr Lester Crook and Elizabeth Friend-Smith of I.B. Tauris, and to Robert Hastings of Dexter Haven Associates for getting the book into final shape.

INTRODUCTION

During his lifetime Alan John Percivale Taylor (1906–90) was a controversial yet much-admired historian. He succeeded in being respected by much of the academic history profession as well as appealing to a wide readership beyond the bounds of higher education. A decade and a half after his death much of his work remains in print, mostly in paperback and available in small town bookshops as well as large city stores across the country. This book provides a biographical study of his career as a historian and radical intellectual.[1]

Over the years Alan Taylor developed his own distinctive style. This included much use of paradox as well as epigrams and wit. His own life was also full of paradoxes and contrasts. He began as something of a gentleman scholar but became almost obsessively anxious to be recognised as a professional scholar. He saw himself as the no-nonsense northern nonconformist yet in Oxford he soon cast off his northern accent and, appointed to an academic post in the prestigious history department at Manchester University, he was very quick to try, with eventual success, to return to Oxford. He saw himself as the sturdy outsider fighting the Establishment, yet he thrived within Magdalen College and was something of a stickler concerning observation of its traditions. He stood as a 'man of the people', a modern 'Trouble Maker' (to use the title of his 1956 Ford Lectures), yet he was a friend of Lord Beaverbrook and, following the lead of his friend Lord Berners, he even dined with 'Tom' Mosley. However, when all is said, he belonged to the radical side of British public life.

Indeed, Taylor's life and career are a part of the mainstream British Left culture of the mid-1930s to late 1950s. This was a British democratic socialism which readjusted from the post-First World War pacifism and dewey-eyed optimism concerning Bolshevik Russia prevalent in 1917–20 and after. It was anti-fascist, anti-appeasement and critically supportive of Labour in office (in coalition and then on its own) in 1940–51. It was in favour of 'the Great Alliance', with Soviet Russia, prone to 'Englishness' (as exemplified by George Orwell) and supportive of Labour's nationalisation and welfare state programmes. Alan Taylor was a major contributor to the *New Statesman* during much of its most influential period.

Taylor became a national radio and television performer immediately after the Second World War. Indeed, he was one of Britain's first 'TV personalities'. This came about from his willingness, even eagerness, to participate in current affairs programmes. He was a vigorous member of panels discussing politics and international issues. By his later years, he was sufficiently a 'personality' to be on discussing almost any aspect of life. For instance, on 14 May 1983 he was on 'The Late Clive James' show on Channel 4 with the writers John Mortimer and Edna O'Brien, discussing 'childhood'. A month later, on 27 June, he appeared with Barbara Castle on 'Private Lives' on BBC2, in which Maria Aitken interviewed them about their private lives. He cultivated his role as a television personality with his own distinctive style, encompassing his bow tie to his persona of prickly dissenter.

While a person of the Left, he was also very much an English partisan. This was especially so concerning Germany and, to a lesser degree, the United States. He travelled fairly swiftly from a teenage espousal of Marxist views to his own often idiosyncratic mix of political dissent. Kenneth O. Morgan has observed that Taylor was 'a little-England socialist of a kind who defied all orthodox categories'. In his day, he was one of Britain's best-known intellectuals, even coming first in a *Times* informal poll to ascertain the most influential British intellectual since the Second World War.[2]

However, though he made a name for himself as a prominent intellectual of the Left, Alan Taylor believed deeply in the historian's task being to seek for the truth about the past and to present that truth clearly, even if the findings were inconvenient to his or her own political views. He also believed in the central importance of history to the humanities as a subject which enhanced both individuals' and national understanding. From early on in his career he aspired to write history which would be read by a large section of the public. In this he sought to emulate the success of great figures of the past, such as Edward Gibbon and Thomas Babington Macaulay, as well as of the generation before his, such as George Macaulay Trevelyan. His output of historical writing was immense. His career brings to mind the artist Matisse's aphorism: 'Without hard work, talent is not enough.'

Well before his death he was undoubtedly one of the best-known historians of his time. Professor D.C. Watt, for example, observed in 1977, in a special A.J.P. Taylor issue of an American academic journal, that Taylor's television lectures had made him 'the sole British historian whose name is a household word'.[3] This continued to be the case, both before and since his death, even to an amusing extent. A cursory look at references to his name on CD-ROMs of the *Independent* newspaper of the early 1990s produced a sports page with a footballer being referred to as the A.J.P. Taylor of the pitch, apparently denoting a virtuoso performer. Another instance of the widespread recognition of his name was a spoof on the almost obligatory use of favourable A.J.P. Taylor quotations by publishers on book covers: Paula Yates' book *Sex With Paula Yates* (London, Sphere, 1987) having on its back cover 'A definitive work – A.J.P. Taylor'. More seriously, quotations from his writings have launched a thousand articles or reviews in the British quality press. He also became the historian of first resort for the cultured who wished to be informed quickly about historical events. He was also drawn on by major writers. For instance, those enjoying Tom Stoppard's superb play *Travesties* (1975) who know Taylor's *The First World War* (1963) have heard one speech on the events at Sarajevo in June 1914 which summarises Taylor's opening page. He was also sufficient of an immediately recognisable public figure for his face to be one of those of several celebrities who appeared on advertisements in the London underground and elsewhere which made a financial appeal to support research to seek a cure for Parkinson's disease.

He had a strong 'middle Britain' constituency of support. His books, his television appearances and his public lectures appealed to many of the comfortably off professional classes, especially graduates and especially those retired. These were the people who were the backbone of local history, local archaeology and local drama societies as well as of voluntary bodies such as the National Trust. Part of this support was that British middle-class radicalism that expressed itself through the Fabian Society, Christian Socialism and the Campaign for Nuclear Disarmament (CND), but more of it was Conservative in politics. For such Conservatives Alan Taylor, though often a fiery radical in politics, was acceptable in much the same way as J.B. Priestley was. Both men were a part of a much-admired pantheon of 'characters' who presented their subjects with panache as well as insight; a group which included John Betjeman on places, Alec Clifton-Taylor and Sir Nicholas Pevsner on buildings, Arthur Negus on antiques, Kenneth (Lord) Clark on art, Sir Mortimer Wheeler on archaeology, Jacob Bronowski on science and Malcolm Muggeridge on Muggeridge and much else.

His style has had an impact on historians and journalists alike. In particular, as Professor Avner Offer has observed, Alan Taylor has had a huge effect on the style of many British and some American historians. The short, sharp sentence, the love of paradox and epigrams and other features of his style had become common among these historians, a contrast to the style of continental European historians. Taylor was also sufficiently a familiar public figure for his style to attract comment in the British press. For instance, a columnist in the *Huddersfield Daily Examiner* in 1970 commented,

> He is the most irritating of British historians. Just when he has made some apparently outrageous remark he provides an authoritative foot-note in support of his contention.

But it's his style that worries me most – for...when I've been reading him I find that unconsciously I ape him. I find that I begin to write like this. In very short sentences. I make assertions which I do not qualify. I leave out words such as 'perhaps' or 'probably' or 'maybe'. I set myself up as the great know-all of the Press...

I regard him as a dangerous influence, especially for someone as susceptible as myself. He must not be allowed to infiltrate his method into the column. He must be resolutely resisted. I will not read him again for at least a week.[4]

He was a very English writer. His roots were very much in Lancashire. His feelings of 'Northernness' and 'Englishness' stemmed in large part from his pride in his family's involvement in the great Lancashire cotton trade and its associations with radicalism in politics from the time of his grandfather J.T. Taylor onwards. This 'Northernness' was painfully thrown into relief with the industrial calamities of Lancashire and elsewhere from 1921 onwards.[5] His roots are important in understanding the man.

– 1 –

ROOTS

Alan Taylor stemmed from a wealthy, intellectual, nonconformist background. The wealth had been accumulated in the cotton trade. This was the archetypal background for English individualistic radicalism, associated with Richard Cobden and John Bright in the days of the Anti-Corn Law League (1839–46) and after, and with many of the victors of the Liberal Party's January 1906 general election landslide victory. This background explains much about Taylor's views, both when moulded by his home and later in life when he had become an irreverent and opinionated maverick, yet still essentially of the Left.

Alan John Percivale Taylor was born on 25 March 1906 at 29 Barrett Road and grew up at 18 Crosby Road, Birkdale, then in Lancashire. This was not long after the Liberal Party's triumph. Seventy-five years later, with some glee, he recalled that his mother had gone daily to the *Southport Guardian* offices to see the Liberal victories being displayed on a screen: 'It is true that she was heavily gone with child and had to go in a bath-chair; but I can say that I witnessed the greatest Liberal triumph of all time – if from a privileged position!' More seriously, as he added then of the Liberal victory, 'I was brought up on it as a story.'[1]

Alan Taylor's family background is interesting, being of typical Lancashire entrepreneurial stock yet with marked radical political views in generations. Even more interesting are the nuances he saw, or imagined, between his northern middle-class relatives. His father, Percy Lees Taylor (1874–1940), was a second-generation cotton merchant in the firm James Taylor and Sons, founded in 1870. James Taylor (1848–1933) had become rich quickly in the boom of the early 1870s. His capital had probably come in part from the Quaker family of his wife, Amelia Lees, and perhaps in lesser part from his own efforts in dealing in cotton waste and running a soap warehouse. He had successfully developed his business of selling cotton piece goods, primarily to India, in the last three decades of the nineteenth century, when such trade was growing rapidly. To favourable trading opportunities he added hard work, tough bargaining and avoiding speculation in cotton futures. As he was not tied to a manufacturing base, a feature of his business was that he moved his offices and his warehouses frequently in pursuit of lower rents, so cutting overall costs. Percy, his eldest son, joined his father in his Manchester office in Bull's Head Chambers in 1890, becoming senior partner in effect from 1898, when James retired. Under his leadership the business diversified, acquiring a spinning mill at Blackburn and one at Preston. In 1914 the business's offices were at Calcutta House, 50 Princess Street, Manchester, with much of the firm's cotton piece trade being with India, Burma and China. According to Alan, Percy Taylor earned £5000 or more each year from when he was in his early twenties.[2] This was a very large income then and among his relatives he was deemed to be 'a very rich man'.[3]

Percy Taylor enjoyed reading and was interested in politics. He had stayed at Preston Grammar School until the then late age of sixteen and thereafter had continued to read English literature and history for pleasure. His misfortune was very poor hearing. He was a short man, a little on the plump side. He was good-natured and generally very well liked. He and his wife lived in Southport. On his return journey from six months in India, after his marriage in 1900, he contracted typhoid fever. He regularly suffered from bronchitis and, not long before his son Alan was born, one of his lungs was damaged by tuberculosis. Southport was famous as a health resort, with claims to being especially beneficial for those with bronchitis.

While Alan Taylor's grandfather was a stern Victorian paterfamilias, domineering over his wife and children, his father was a gentle person, notably – even excessively – considerate to his wife and very fond of children. Taylor later observed of his father that he 'adored kids more than anyone I've ever known'.[4] Unlike his father and son, Percy was generous with money. Alan Taylor was to fear that he was being too like his father when his first wife continued to subsidise Dylan Thomas regardless of his protests and he became excessively anxious about money as he became older in inflationary times, careful to avoid Percy's free-spending ways.

Alan Taylor's mother was Constance Sumner Thompson (1878–1946). She was the third daughter in a Methodist family linked to warehousing on one side and the corn trade on the other. Her father, William Henry Thompson (c.1830–1904), who was born out of wedlock to a woman with the surname Martin, ran a wholesale grocery business in Preston. No one of Alan Taylor's generation knew why he was given the surname Thompson. After a first wife died in childbirth, William Henry Thompson married Martha Thompson, and they had seven children: Florence (1876–1939),

Sally (c.1877–c.1892), Constance (1878–1946), who married Percy Taylor, Kate (1880–1906), who married Gustav Juhlin, John (1883–1939), who married Sarah Fraser, William Henry, 'Harry' (1886–1947), who married Joan Beauchamp, and Madge (1887–1965), who married William Sinclair. William Henry Thompson was a 'pro-Boer' during the Boer War; so both of Alan Taylor's grandfathers had radical political views.

Connie's mother, Martha, was the daughter of John Thompson, who as a boy had walked with his mother from Brampton, Cumberland, to Preston. He had been a handloom weaver and then an owner of several handlooms, selling out as handloom weaving collapsed in the face of steam-powered factory production. He became a miller, making much money from grain. He married a Sumner from Blackburn and they had

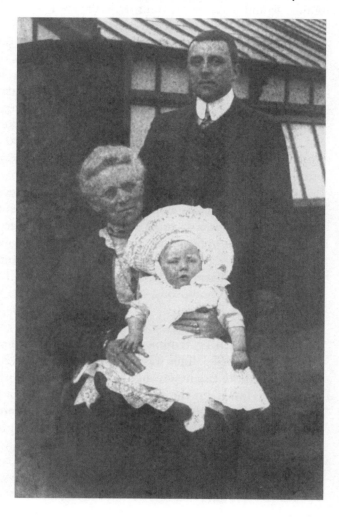

Three generations of Taylors: Alan Taylor with his father and grandmother.

three boys (John, William and Joseph) and two girls (Martha and Matilda, 'Taidy'). He established his family as among the wealthiest in Preston. When he died his widow, according to Alan Taylor, was the only one in their area, Ashton on Ribble, 'who kept her own carriage...in which she drove out every afternoon'. John Thompson was also radical, at least when young. He voted for Henry ('Orator') Hunt in Preston in the 1830 general election, receiving afterwards a commemorative medal. In turn his eldest son, John, was also radical, working as a journalist on the *Preston Herald*, in which he denounced the Anti-Corn Law League. The other sons, William and Joseph, were very successful solicitors. William Thompson was an alderman and in the early 1860s a leading figure of Preston's guild. According to Alan Taylor he was responsible for clearing many medieval buildings and also for creating between 1861 and 1867 Avenham Park, where formerly there had been mostly market gardens.[5]

Martha was the toughest of the Thompsons. Her three brothers ruined their health by excessive drinking, John apparently dying young in the Preston workhouse hospital. Martha and her children were vehemently anti-alcohol and had in them a stern streak of Puritanism. One niece recalled of Harry Thompson and another of his nieces, 'Puritanical in the extreme Thompson way, he once washed the make-up off Joy's face. She was eighteen at the time.' Alan Taylor recalled Martha as 'a hard woman...a terrible woman'. She was the only person who struck fear into Harry.[6]

Alan Taylor was always very sensitive to the nuances of class, especially among the middle class. For instance, he made a distinction between his public school (Bootham) and Michael Foot's (Leighton Park), arguing that Foot's was more upper crust and his own barely counted as such; even though both were Quaker. In the case of his grandparents he felt there was a social divide between the blunt, no-nonsense, Lancashire-accented Taylors and the Thompsons, who were closer to the landed interest and who spoke 'best English'.

He elaborated the social differences between the Taylors and the Thompsons when he reminisced about family history to his Thompson relatives in late 1973. This was in spite of both families living very close to each other in the late nineteenth century: the Thompsons living at Beech Grove, the Taylors in the next parallel road, Victoria Parade (with Percy and Connie Taylor returning close to these streets after the First World War). Martha Thompson's second and third brothers, Joseph and William, were both successful solicitors. According to Alan Taylor,

> There were two societies in Preston. One was the wealthy society but vulgar, of the mill owners and cotton men, who were rich but, like my

grandfather Taylor...spoke broad Lancashire. James Taylor spoke real thick Lancashire. It wasn't just an accent. But the Thompsons – I can remember from my grandmother – they spoke beautiful English...

And to be a solicitor in Preston was to put you up in the society of the earls of Derby and people like that. If you go back to the eighteenth century you'll find that the two Members [of Parliament for Preston], one was always a Stanley, the Derby family, and the other was nearly always a Fazackerley, who were hereditary solicitors...

[The Fazackerleys] handled all those north Lancashire, Roman Catholic landowners of the eighteenth century...They were...the Derby's solicitors, they handled people like the Welds and the Blundells who owned all the land of North Lancashire.

...There were these two separate societies and the Thompsons, because of the two uncles, belonged to this different society.[7]

One of Alan Taylor's nieces was less convinced of this Taylor–Thompson contrast, at least in accents, observing in 1985: 'My memory of aunts and uncles was of a fairly strong Lancashire accent.'[8]

This is suggestive of Alan Taylor's self-image, at least part of the time, as a no-nonsense, bluff Lancashire man, a chip off the block of his grandfather, 'JT'. In his memoirs he depicts JT as a male chauvinist and a successful entrepreneur who, unlike Alan's father Percy, took care of the pence as well as the pounds. Alan Taylor's JT became, at least in his grandson's depictions, an heroic radical figure of the Richard Cobden and John Bright kind. Cobden and Bright had argued the Corn Laws out of existence, in Taylor's much-favoured simplification of the history of the repeal of the Corn Laws in 1846. Alan Taylor could similarly engage in politics in such a way; not in grass-roots slog and anonymity. Perhaps his adoption of an identity through his initials – AJP – echoed his grandfather as JT, as well as then being an academic norm.

His near hero-worship of his Taylor grandfather appears to be a balance to his downgrading of his mother. This was due partly to the lesser financial prowess of his Thompson grandparents and partly to what he felt to be a harsher side of some of the Thompsons. While his Thompson grandfather was alive, he and Martha lived in grand style. After his death in 1904 Martha lived with her eldest daughter, Florence, in Blackton Road, Preston, and money was very tight. They were helped financially at one point by a legacy from Martha's brother Joe, who like her other brothers died early due to alcoholism. Percy Taylor funded Martha and he also paid for Harry's articles. He probably paid for the wedding of Madge, the youngest daughter (and sister of Connie). When Martha died in 1921 Percy provided a generous lump sum for Florence, part of which was used to buy a bungalow, which she named 'Brampton', and Florence's brother Harry provided her with a small annuity. She lived frugally until she died in 1939. Alan Taylor was not at ease with his father's generosity. As late as 1973 he was wanting to know how much money Florence had left. 'But there must have been some capital...somewhere [remaining of that] my father gave her,' he was insisting in 1973, with the implication that it should have returned to him, not been left to his Thompson cousins.[9]

In his autobiography Alan Taylor divided the children of his grand-parents, William Henry and Martha Thompson, between those who took after William Henry, who were 'soft and kind', and those who took after Martha, who were 'sharp-tongued and arrogant'. He had no hesitation in placing his mother in the second category. Whereas he deemed Florence 'the sweetest of the lot' he observed of his mother that she 'was hard and intellectually sharp, which made her aggressive'.[10] Connie Thompson stayed at school until seventeen and was pushed into elementary school teaching. She taught for only eighteen months. Given her well-remembered dislike of children, marriage provided a welcome escape from this work. Alan Taylor recalled, 'My mother often told me she married without love and only to get away from her elementary school.'[11] This was not something many would choose to tell, let alone reiterate, to their only child. It may have been the cause of Alan Taylor's occasional breathtaking frankness on personal matters, which could be notably insensitive to others' feelings.[12]

For some of their time in Southport, Connie had her youngest sister living with them – one aspect of his youth Alan Taylor omitted from his autobiography. Madge Thompson was a very lively, bright young woman. However, Alan Taylor later recalled, 'When Madge was quite a girl she had an affair with a married man...and when I was a tiny boy she was dumped on us for about two years.' Although recognising she was 'very sharp', he observed in 1973, 'All the Thompsons were tiresome with the exception of Florence and John, but Madge was the only one who was really a bitch.' Madge left to train as a nurse, later marrying a house surgeon at Lancaster hospital. The marriage took place from Percy and Connie Taylor's home in Preston.[13]

Connie Taylor was a powerful influence on her son, though, like several others, one that was understated in his autobiography. Eunice Holliday, née Blackwell, in old age recalled of Mrs Taylor, 'She was tall, quite arrogant, very smart – she had very good taste in clothes...Rather a masculine type. Very outspoken. Women used to kiss a lot in those days. Mrs Taylor always put her hand up. She didn't want to be kissed. She was strong-minded. But she liked straightforward, honest type of people.'[14]

Yet, although Connie Taylor was often reticent in showing her feelings, she clearly cared greatly for Alan. Her first child, Miriam, born in November

1902, died of tubercular meningitis after fifteen months. When Alan was sickly she sought the help of her friend Mrs Mary Ann ('Polly' or 'Mab') Blackwell, who was a firm believer in homeopathic medicine, as had been her mother and grandmother. She was deemed to have ensured the survival of her own daughter, Eunice, and several other delicate children by arranging for them to be treated by a Dr Wheeler. After the frail young Alan received homeopathic treatment Connie and the Blackwells came to believe that this had saved Alan's life, or at least enabled him to live the life of a normal child. Connie Taylor, who was an excellent needlewoman, spent many months preparing a huge tablecloth for afternoon tea, with a five to six foot centre of linen and great borders on which she crocheted butterflies. When this magnificent work was finished she presented it to Mrs Blackwell, saying: 'Every butterfly is a thank-you.' She gave Eunice beautiful editions of books such as *The Wind in the Willows*, also, Eunice felt, as a thank-you to her mother. In 1913 she was to know the heartbreak of the birth of a stillborn child It is very difficult to see her as the hard-hearted mother of Taylor's autobiography, at least not in his early years.

Alan Taylor appears to have eagerly sought more outward signs of motherly love and, later, her intellectual approbation. While his mother had other interests – she was an excellent golfer and a skilful needlewoman, and enjoyed playing bridge – she was (as Eunice Holliday recalled) 'very politically minded and strong in her views'. Given her apparent distaste for young children and her love of political argument, Alan soon learnt that the way to gain his mother's attention and interest was through intellectual precocity. In his autobiography Taylor perceptively commented, 'Books for me were real life,' though adding less accurately, 'people were an interruption and hardly even that'.[15] He probably did read at an early age, but in some of his claims of being a child prodigy he was assuming an early heroic character, inviting comparisons with John Stuart Mill, William Morris and others.

His early years were spent in a comfortable and secure, somewhat closed world and he was very much a spoilt child. His father, dressed in a blue serge suit and a bowler hat, smoking a Havana cigar, went every day to Manchester by train to work at the family firm's main offices in Calcutta House near the city centre.[16] His mother ran the home. She also played much golf, winning numerous trophies, including at county championships. Golf offered exercise, a break from the domestic scene and, in Edwardian England, participation in a very popular and socially respectable game among the middle class.[17] She had the benefit of Southport, one of the better of the many courses recently established by the coast. Beyond these patterns of life, the Taylors lived in a small community of similar interests, based primarily around the Southport Congregational Chapel and to a lesser extent the local Liberal Party.

The Southport Congregational Chapel provided a focus for much of the Taylors' social life. They were loyal to it, though the Taylor family background included Quaker and Baptist allegiances and on the Thompson side there had been strict Methodism. Congregationalism was more flexible in doctrine and often had a Liberal or radical edge. In the case of Southport, two of its leading figures were Joshua and Mary Anne Blackwell. Like Percy Taylor, Joshua Blackwell had been a Manchester businessman, selling food on the Manchester Exchange, but had retired and was superintendent and secretary of the Sunday school. He was a very strong Labour Party supporter. Percy Taylor supported the Sunday school work financially, including giving generously to the fund for the annual Christmas 'poor children's treat' (for those from the nearby very poor area within Southport), but not actively. He and his wife were friends of the Blackwells and participated in political discussions held at the Blackwells' house. Sometimes there were visiting national political figures, including quite probably George Lansbury.[18]

At this time the Taylors were still Liberals, ones who identified with the radical David Lloyd George. They supported the local Liberals by holding garden parties at their home. Connie, who was active in the local Liberal women's organisation, was not the more radical on votes for women. Alan Taylor later recalled, 'My mother, I think, felt embarrassed that she was not a suffragette, and her embarrassment took the form of being very hostile to the suffragettes, whereas my father, who was always tolerant, thought that if women wanted to be suffragettes they were entitled to be.'[19]

For Percy Taylor, Joshua Blackwell provided congenial male company and his daughters offered substitutes for the deceased Miriam. Alan Taylor recalled that his father often told him that he never ceased grieving for Miriam.[20] The Blackwells had three daughters – Elizabeth, Lillias and, several years younger, Eunice. Percy Taylor got on especially well with Lil, who was a shy, very considerate girl. She realised how miserable it was for him to have such impaired hearing and took pains to speak carefully to him. Percy and Connie Taylor also took an interest in Eunice, later in the early 1920s buying her and her husband, Clifford Holliday, a wedding present of silver and Percy taking her to her wedding in the Southport Congregational Chapel.

Though six years older than Alan, Eunice often provided rare young company for him. On some Saturdays Percy Taylor took Alan and Eunice into Southport. The two children always wanted to go to Southport's 1465-yard-long pier, the second longest in Britain. Occasionally they went to the fairground. Never, so Eunice Holliday told me, did they go to the shops or for morning or afternoon tea. For both children the big attraction was the diver, Bert Powsey (known as 'Professor Powsey'). Alan Taylor later recollected,

His most sensational dive, which I witnessed, was the dive when he
tied both his hands to his sides, tied his legs together, then plunged in
and emerged safe and sound with all his ropes loosened. The climax
at the end of the whole show, as I remember, was the bicycle dive, an
expedition which he conducted down a steep board into the sea with
the bicycle alight and blazing around him.[21]

Similarly, Eunice provided company for Alan when Percy Taylor and
Joshua Blackwell went after chapel on a Sunday to the sand-dunes the other
side of the railway line from the Taylors' house on Crosby Road (where
they lived from 1908 until 1913). There they all walked or played on the
dunes, or sometimes paddled in the sea. As his autobiography and Eunice's
later recollections make clear, he played in the sand like any other little
boy. Indeed, Mrs Eunice Holliday, some seventy years later, was amused
when she recalled the males playing cowboys and Indians. 'It struck me as
very funny because they went to church and they sang about peace and not
fighting: and yet Alan was on this side of the hill, and father was on the other
side, and they were hiding behind little hills, saying, "Bang, bang, bang!"'
    The Blackwells' house in Stanley Avenue was less than ten minutes' walk
away from the Taylors', and was next door but one to the small private
junior school to which Alan went. This was owned and run by two sisters,
Annie and Kitty Filmer. After school Alan Taylor often went to the
Blackwells, where he was given a boiled egg for his tea. At the Blackwells
he was very inquisitive, looking into boxes and drawers. He found the bar of
chocolate that Eunice's father used to leave her each day and was allowed
to have half the chocolate, no doubt as part of the process of building him
up from being a delicate child. Eunice later recollected, 'He would have
eaten all my chocolate if mother had let him.' He also loved to read or
have read to him Beatrix Potter's books. Eunice recalled, 'I had got the
books. Father used to read to us. Father sat on his chair, I sat on one side
and Alan sat on the other.' In 1983 Alan Taylor informed her in a letter
that he had walked down Stanley Avenue when making a 1980 television
series on four Lancashire coastal towns and had found 'the school of the
Misses Filmer...now dilapidated. I remember the boiled egg your mother
gave me so often after school and the joy I got from reading your set of
Beatrix Potter.'[22]
    When the Taylors went to the Blackwells' house for political discussions
Eunice kept Alan quiet by playing a board and dice game, 'Prince's Quest'.
She later recalled, 'I soon discovered that Alan had to win, otherwise there
was trouble...So I arranged for him to win and he was happy. But oh I was
so bored with the game. Also my dog had to be shut in the kitchen [as]
Alan was afraid of (or didn't like) dogs.'[23]

He also used to talk with Mrs Blackwell. According to Eunice her
mother was very good with children. 'Mother talked to him as an adult,
she always did with children. She did not talk down to him.' On one
occasion when he was six he got into a long argument with her as to which
language Jesus spoke, with him arguing for one answer and she another.[24]

The significance of the Blackwells – and of Eunice in particular – was
that the young Taylor had very few contacts, let alone friends, other than
the occasional visits of relatives, including cousins of roughly his age, and
his partners in some dancing lessons in Birkdale Town Hall. Later, he even
commented, 'I used to walk to school in the gutter so as not to have to mix
with the other children on the pavement.'[25] This is easy to believe. His
studied aloofness at the Filmers' junior school cannot have endeared him
to his fellow students. He sat separately, as he could already read, and read
on his own while the other children were taught. Having neither brothers
and sisters nor close friends who would ensure he did not become too used
to having his own way, he became very wilful. Eunice Holliday recalled that
though he was 'not a very pugilistic little boy...he would be angry...he
got very cross with people'. When he asked one of his classmates home to
tea the boy knocked over some of his toy soldiers and he gave him a bloody
nose – thus seeing him off for good.[26] He was also a very observant boy,
taking in what he saw and keeping much of his knowledge to himself.
Later he commented of his powerful recollections of his early years, 'being
an only child and detached...you see things more and you watch with
more amusement'.[27] He was very much a solitary and self-contained child.

When the Taylors went on holiday, they took their small, near-closed
social world with them. They went to the Lake District in 1909 and 1913,
the Isle of Man in 1910 and 1912 and Rhos in north Wales in 1911. On
each occasion Percy Taylor paid for several relations to accompany them,
as well as Alan's nurse. In 1912 Percy took Alan's two grandmothers,
Amelia Taylor and Martha Thompson, two of his brothers and Connie's
brother, Harry Thompson. In 1913 Joshua, Polly and Eunice Blackwell
went as well. Then, for a fortnight, the Taylor party took over much of a
hotel at Borrowdale, at the top of Derwentwater, and all but young Alan
and his nurse enjoyed long walks.

The other notable feature of his childhood was that he was a spoilt
child. 'He was spoilt in all ways,' recalled Eunice Holliday, 'except that
certain people would keep him in order,' one being her father. Given the
early death of his sister Miriam and Alan's delicate health, it is not
surprising that he was a much-looked-after little boy. Indeed, as Eunice
Holliday later commented, he was 'more than looked after...they adored
him'. With a few exceptions, including his mother, he usually got what he
wanted from people. In terms of possessions he was given large numbers

of toy soldiers, many visitors bringing him a box of them. These he laid out in part of the house's large attic area, and spent long hours on his own playing with them.

His father doted on him. Percy Taylor's poor hearing kept him from substantial participation in the political debates at the Blackwells' house. However, he could enjoy children's company, especially that of his son. Alan clearly loved and admired his father, though he came to deprecate his generosity with money and his sensitive relationships with women. On these matters he admired more the financially very prudent and patriarchal ways of his grandfather James Taylor, even if he himself did not fully match his patriarchal ways in practice. Eunice Holliday recalled of the father and

The only child.

young son, 'They were so happy together.' As Alan grew older he identified
with many of his father's views. When reviewing *Father Figures*, the autobiography of Kingsley Martin, editor of the *New Statesman* (1931–60), he
quoted with approval Martin's words about his father: 'His causes became
my causes, his revolt mine.' Alan Taylor then declared, 'I had much the
same relationship with my father and I have derived nothing but strength
from his example. Father–son hostility is a great waste of time…it prevents
a dissenter from getting on with the real job which is to kick against
the world.'[28]

He was also spoilt by Annie Clark, who was first employed as a general
maid and then as his nurse. She was initially in her twenties, from
Newcastle upon Tyne and remembered as being careful, responsible and a
very nice person. She met well young Alan's requirements from women:
'With Nanna there was no doubt that I was the dominant male. She adored
me, hugged me, gave me whatever I wanted.'[29] As well as Annie Clark, the
Taylors had a second resident maid, a daily charwoman (whose tasks included
washing the family's clothes), for some time a young woman, who took
Alan for walks and occasionally bathed him, and a gardener.

He did not get his way, at least not as much as he wished, with his
mother. In his autobiography, *A Personal History* (1983), she comes close to
being the villain of the piece. The criticisms included:

> She was the disciplinarian in the household as her own mother had
> been before her. She was the one who made me sit on my pot or eat
> up food I did not like, particularly rice pudding…Once, when my
> mother threatened to spank me, he [his father] stood between her and
> said, 'If you lay a hand on that child I'll never speak to you again.'[30]

Yet, as has already been remarked, there is much to suggest that he was
unfair towards her. It is highly likely that she was both a loving mother and
a person who found it hard to express her emotions. Given the concern
over Alan's delicate health, the insistence on eating his rice pudding seems
sensible enough, and his habit of behaving sufficiently badly at the dinner
table to be sent to finish his meal in the kitchen, with Annie Clark, who
spoilt him, may well have merited some form of retribution. Eunice
Holliday recalled Connie Taylor as 'a nice person' but 'not an affectionate
person, a cold person', unlike her husband, who was 'very affectionate'.
Yet, as well as being extremely anxious over her son's health, she may well
have felt marginalised by her husband and son.

Alan Taylor, into old age, felt cheated that his mother had not shown
him more affection. Shortly, before his seventy-ninth birthday he expressed
this vigorously to Éva, his third wife. She summed up his views in her
diary: 'His mother was always interested in something else. Alan was

always used as a means to an end.'[31] In this he may have had later developments in mind, such as her travels abroad with Henry Sara. But, if this
view were applied to this early period of his life, then there would be an
element of the pot calling the kettle black. He and his father appear often
to have paid little heed to her interests. His mother liked to go frequently
for morning coffee in Thom's Japanese Tea Rooms in Southport, just with
Alan on some weekdays. On Saturdays, when Percy was available, he and
Alan instead 'escaped' to Pleasureland or the pier. She enjoyed golf, but,
after playing it with her some Saturdays, Percy made it clear that he
preferred the attractions of Pleasureland and the pier. His father, apparently,
also used his deafness to avoid doing other things which his wife proposed
and he did not like.[32] Connie Taylor came from a family which greatly
valued culture. Percy Taylor quite probably read more widely than his
wife, but he could not enjoy music.[33] Connie Taylor coped silently on the
whole with her lot, though Eunice Holliday once overheard her confide in
Eunice's mother: 'It is very difficult whispering sweet nothings in the ear
of a deaf person.'

Connie Taylor clearly had a distressing experience of childbearing in
these years. She was 24 when Miriam was born in 1902, 27 when Alan was
born in 1906 and about 34 when she gave birth to a stillborn child in 1913.
These experiences were emotionally shattering and after each childbirth
the Taylors moved house, at first within Birkdale and then, in 1913, away
from the area. In his autobiography Alan Taylor did not reflect on his
mother's misfortunes. He commented, 'I was pulled up by the roots without
warning,' but added, 'I cannot say that I had much in the way of roots to
be pulled up by.'[34]

– 2 –

GROWING

The strongest influences on the youthful Alan Taylor were his home life, with its radical intellectual conversations, Bootham School and his omnivorous reading. His parents' wealth enabled him to become familiar with much of continental Europe before he was 21. By that age he was still closely tied, emotionally and intellectually, to his parents and their views. At school and then at Oxford University he displayed precocious abilities.

He first went abroad for the winter of 1913–14. He and his mother spent several months at Alassio on the Italian Riviera and then Lugano, over the Swiss border. In 1921 he returned to Switzerland with his parents. In 1924 he went with his mother and Henry Sara to Berlin and other parts of Germany, followed by Paris. In the summer of 1925 the three went to Soviet Russia, returning via Riga and Berlin. In addition he went on school trips to Normandy. Hence journeys to continental Europe, often lengthy ones, became for him a norm, just as it was customary for the family to migrate to Borrowdale, Buttermere or Hawkshead in the Lake District or elsewhere for part of the summer. In later life he in turn came to expect to spend part of the summer with his first family on the Isle of Wight. This was a comfortable, gentlemanly style of life, more common in the Edwardian and inter-war years than after 1945. His early stays abroad may well have influenced him choosing later to study on the continent of Europe, and, once in Vienna, eventually adopting a topic involving northern Italy.

After a brief stay with his maternal grandmother in Lytham on his return from Italy in 1914, Alan Taylor lived in Buxton. His family rented a large house, 10 Manchester Road, close to the Crescent and the Pump Room. In his autobiography he commented that it was 'not as big as the house in Birkdale',[1] but it was a large house by most people's standards. He lived happily at home at first, playing with other children, cycling up and

down the surrounding hills and enjoying outings in his paternal grandfather's car. He attended day schools: first a private preparatory school run
by a Buxton woman and her Swiss husband, Monsieur and Madame de la
Motte, and second, from early 1916, Buxton College. After a period of
ordinary, rumbustious schoolboy life there, his mother removed him to a
public school sooner than planned, perhaps because she feared he was
becoming coarse.[2] At any rate, that was one explanation he offered in his
autobiography. His alternative explanation is more convincing: that when
his mother became vehemently opposed to military conscription and she
learnt that he and other younger boys had been shown 'the trenches where
the older boys trained in the OTC' she removed him 'immediately from
the shadow of the OTC'.[3] He would have soon gone to Rugby but, as that
school expected its pupils to join the Officer Training Corps, she withdrew
his name and instead reserved a place for him at the Quaker Bootham
School in York for when he reached its minimum age of 13. In the interim
he was sent to another public school, The Downs at Malvern, owned and
run by Herbert William Jones, a Quaker.

The First World War had a very major impact on the political views
of Connie and Percy Taylor, and so on their son. Percy Taylor was quickly
disillusioned with the war, apparently from reading Bernard Shaw's
Commonsense about the War, which was published on 14 November 1914 as
a 32-page supplement to the *New Statesman*. Shaw disliked Herbert Henry
Asquith, the Liberal Prime Minister, and Sir Edward Grey, the Foreign
Secretary, whom he deemed to be 'a Junker from his topmost hair to the
tips of his toes…[with] a personal taste for mendacity'. In his booklet he
argued that Grey's justification for the war, a 75-year-old treaty, was feeble.
He urged people to demand that the belligerent governments openly state
their war aims and that a just and democratic peace be made to avoid a
future European war. He supported the British war effort as a struggle for
survival with Germany but warned, 'Nations are like bees: they cannot kill
except at the cost of their own lives.' Shaw's arguments disconcerted Percy
Taylor, who commented to his wife, 'Asquith and Grey are honourable
men. I don't believe they would have lied to us.'[4]

Shaw's arguments also appeared to have had an impact later on Alan
Taylor, who discussed Shaw's pamphlet in his *The Trouble Makers* (1957),
observing: 'Shaw enjoyed pricking moral pretensions; he also enjoyed teasing
his fellow Dissenters.' Shaw's formulations seem also to have influenced
his thinking and style. For instance, Shaw's assertion: 'Democracy without
equality is a delusion more dangerous than frank oligarchy and autocracy.
And with Democracy there is no hope of peace.' This seems to presage
such epigrams of Alan Taylor as: 'Without democracy socialism would be
worth nothing, but democracy is worth a great deal even when it is not

socialist.'[5] More generally, Shaw was one of the authors whom Taylor would admit had influenced him. Thus, in a letter to the historian Robert Cole, he wrote, 'You won't find a single book that influenced me except Shaw, in style, and perhaps Cobbett. Once upon a time Samuel Butler influenced me until I discovered how silly he was.'[6]

Shaw's arguments in the autumn of 1914 'for open democratic diplomacy, for full civil rights and a fair livelihood for the soldier and his dependants' were still in support of Britain fighting the war. He hoped that, 'Properly handled, this war can be led to a victory, not only for the Allies over Germany, but for democracy over its worst enemies both at home and abroad.'[7]

However, with the introduction of conscription in two stages in January and May 1916, Connie Taylor became vigorously anti-war and in favour of those who opposed continuing it. In this she was influenced by her much-loved brother, William Henry (Harry) Thompson, being a conscientious objector. Margaret Cole, one of Harry Thompson's circle of socialist friends, wrote of him that he 'was a tall handsome athletic fellow, excelling in all games'. She added, 'He was one of the few men I have known who managed to devote his life to "causes" without ever losing either his sense of humour or his power of enjoying himself.'[8] Funded by Percy Taylor, Harry had trained as a solicitor in an old Preston firm, probably Fazackerleys, where life was still sufficiently leisurely for him to play billiards many afternoons. After qualifying on 1 April 1908, he joined a firm of solicitors in Longton, Staffordshire. He gained his introduction to trade union work through John Ward, secretary of the Navvies' Union and Liberal MP for Stoke-on-Trent. The grounds of Harry's objection to being conscripted was, according to his nephew, 'a belief in individual liberty'. Another opponent of the war in his age group, Molly Hamilton (a Labour MP, 1929–31), later wrote that 'resistance, primarily emotional, to the glorification of war was the main-spring of resistance to the majority view'. Connie Taylor shared such sentiments, as well as Molly Hamilton's other observation,

> That war means the massive, selective slaughter, the killing, maiming, blinding, shell-shocking of men was a fact no one could refuse to see… Against this stark background, the elevated chatter of publicists and parsons went on; against this, the glitter of the 'home front'; against this, the well-nigh universal pretence that those who had to endure things we could not even bear to think about were helped by our behaving as though those things did not exist.

In Connie Taylor's case she walked out of the Buxton Methodist chapel, never to return, when the minister referred to conscientious objectors as shirkers.[9]

When conscription had been introduced Harry Thompson had turned to Connie for support. Years later Alan Taylor could recall his uncle coming over from Longton 'on a two-stroke [motorbike] to see my mother in 1916 and I heard this one phrase, "I'm not going"'. Once called up, he refused military service or alternative service. As an 'absolutist' he was treated badly. He was among those sent to Wakefield Prison for the 'Wakefield experiment' of offering absolutists better conditions in return for less intransigent attitudes to co-operation. Harry Thompson was one of an advisory committee, chaired by Walter Ayles and including Henry Sara, which organised the absolutists in Wakefield gaol and rejected the Home Office's proposals for them. He was released from prison in April 1919.[10] For the rest of the war and 1919 Connie devoted herself to her brother and to the cause of the conscientious objectors. Harry spent lengthy terms in gaol, and his sister took great pains to support him in any way she could. In the summer of 1919 the Taylors gave holidays at their rented holiday house in Hawkshead to a stream of conscientious objectors newly released from prison and selected by Harry Thompson. One of these men became Connie Taylor's frequent companion for the rest of her life: Henry Sara.

Sara was a tall, good-looking man who devoted his life to being a political propagandist. He did various work after leaving school, including being a brewery engineer. He read Robert Blatchford's socialist newspaper *The Clarion*. In 1908 he took up revolutionary syndicalism, becoming a member of the Industrial League, which in 1911 became the British section of the Chicago Industrial Workers of the World (IWW). From late 1913 he assisted Guy Aldred with his hybrid revolutionary Marxian anarchist propaganda, notably with his paper *The Herald of Revolt* (published between December 1910 and May 1914) and its successor, *Spur*, with its sub-heading *Because The Workers Need A Spur* (published between June 1914 and April 1921). Sara became an anti-war hero through his campaigning against the war in north London and throughout the country in 1914 and 1915 and his subsequent suffering as a conscientious objector. He was arrested as early as 28 September 1914 for an anti-war speech in London. After the introduction of conscription for single men in January 1916 Sara returned his call-up papers, declaring that he conscientiously objected to the war on socialist grounds. He was arrested in London on 3 April 1916 and, although he suffered from defective eyesight (a wall eye), he was passed as medically fit for the army. He was beaten and humiliated at the Harrow Road Barracks of the 3rd (Reserve) Battalion London Regiment before being sent to Hurdcott Camp. He was then sentenced to 112 days' imprisonment in Wormword Scrubs. From there he went on to Parkhurst Prison, Isle of Wight. He was returned to the regiment, beaten, sentenced to further imprisonment and returned to Parkhurst. After his case was aired in the House of Commons, later in 1916, he was taken before the Central Tribunal, which accepted he was a conscientious objector. However, as he was an absolutist, refusing alternative work, further courts martial resulted in a two-year prison sentence in Exeter and then Wakefield, where he was offered, but resisted, the temptation of comfortable quarters under the 'Wakefield experiment' of September 1918. After another court martial, in October 1918, he went on hunger strike, and was released (subject to recall) under the 'Cat and Mouse' legislation originally intended for suffragettes, in February 1919.

After his release from prison Sara resumed working with Guy Aldred, promoting the Communist League and its journal *The Communist* by making lengthy propaganda tours round the country. Aldred's communism was anti-parliamentary and he was very critical of Lenin's policies for Britain. His group remained separate from those who formed the Communist Party of Great Britain (CPGB) in January 1921.[11] Henry Sara broke with Aldred, first supporting Sylvia Pankhurst and her Workers' Socialist Federation. After she had left the Communist Party he joined it, in 1922, having been to the Soviet Union in 1921. Reg Groves later gave this portrait of Sara in the 1920s:

> Henry, tall, strong of build, with eloquent, resonant voice, and a commanding platform manner, incisive, informed in debate and discussion, brought much to us [discontented CPGB members] in the way of knowledge of Marxism, socialist theory and labour history… A popular outdoor orator in Finsbury Park and elsewhere before, during and after the war, and a skilful lecturer at socialist and secularist halls all over the country, he had hesitated to join the Communist Party at the time of its foundation, knowing as he did most of its leading personalities from pre-war days. But a visit to Russia…decided him, though the suppression of the Kronstadt uprising caused him some uneasiness…[12]

Sara also did a lot of work for the National Council of Labour Colleges (NCLC, formed in 1921), under the aegis of Len Williams, who was an organiser of the NCLC (and later general secretary of the Labour Party). Alan Taylor later wrote of the NCLC:

> This involved adult evening courses of a more or less Marxist character or, in more grandiloquent terms, 'education as a partisan effort to improve the position of Labour in the present, and to assist in the abolition of wage-slavery'. The Marxism taught by the Labour Colleges was entirely pre-Bolshevik.[13]

The Taylors would have known from the *Manchester Guardian* of Sara's ill-treatment in 1916. His case was taken up by MPs Joseph King (Liberal) and Philip Snowden (Independent Labour Party – ILP) and by Dr John Clifford, the eminent nonconformist leader. For Connie, Sara became a second heroic figure, along with her brother; a contrast to her kindly, worthy but not romantic (in any sense) husband. Alan Taylor liked Sara and was much influenced by him, especially when he was in his teens. Quite possibly he was the strongest intellectual influence on him until Lewis Namier.

Nonetheless, Taylor also appears to have seen Harry Thompson and Henry Sara as competitors for his mother's attention and esteem. Faced with the heroic pair of conscientious objectors, he made much of the unpleasant features of The Downs. He hated the 'rigidity and rules' and felt persecuted because 'we were timed over everything', from the moment they got up in the morning. His uncle kindly humoured him, observing: 'Prison was nothing like as bad as that. You have had a tougher war than I did.' In his autobiography Alan Taylor wrote of his time at The Downs, 'I originally called this chapter Shades of the Prison House. But there were no Shades about The Downs School. It was the Prison House itself, at any rate for me.' This was another instance of his bidding up his experiences to a literary level, in this case drawing from William Wordsworth's 'Ode on Intimations of Immortality'. After such huffing and puffing, he admitted, 'I suppose life at the Downs was not as unrelievedly grim as it seems in retrospect.'[14]

However, for the young Taylor his time at The Downs must have come as a shock: not to be the centre of attention from all but his mother, to lose all the comforts he had taken for granted, to have little or no privacy and to have to make beds, clean shoes and carry out other such tasks for himself. In short, it was what he needed. Not surprisingly, his parents ignored his pleas to be removed.

He enjoyed Bootham School more, at least after his first year. He still had to make his bed, clean his shoes and take cold baths. But he was getting older and he developed interests which he enjoyed all his life. He became fascinated by church architecture, examining and recording details with the enthusiasm that many of his age group had for train-spotting. Over many years he filled 'seven large volumes of archaeological diaries containing detailed observations' on the churches he visited; these he destroyed before the mid-1960s.[15] His fascination was fostered by a retired teacher, Neave Brayshaw, nicknamed 'Puddles', who encouraged his young charges to form their own judgements without guidebooks. Perhaps this approach was later reflected in Taylor's diplomatic history, where he displayed a mastery of the printed documents combined with a strong disposition to accept few views on their subject second-hand. It was also characteristic of the young Taylor that his favourite hobby should have been both intellectual and suitable for one who had a few friends but was nevertheless something of a loner.

Many years later, in 1983, Alan Taylor contributed a piece to Bootham's booklet *150 Years of Natural History*, in which he paid tribute to Brayshaw, observing that he 'gave us a feel for medieval architecture and then left us to carry on for ourselves'. He then commented,

> I compiled diary after diary devoted to village churches. Soon I was ambitious enough to include pages of mouldings and in time I could turn out ground plans with the styles duly hatched or painted. When I ran out of local churches I moved on to the Minster which absorbed my attention for the best part of a year. Best of all were the neighbouring Cistercian abbeys, my ground plans of which nearly got me an appointment as an Inspector of Ancient Monuments some years after I left school.

He added, 'Hardly a day passes when I do not bless the name of Bootham Natural History Society and above all Puddles.'[16] His considerable knowledge of Gothic architecture proved decisive in him securing a scholarship to Oriel College, Oxford.

In many ways his public school years, at The Downs and Bootham, display him adopting the traditional survival strategies of the schoolboy immersed in hostile, alien surroundings away from the cocoon of a well-to-do home. In fiction, such as Thomas Hughes' *Tom Brown's Schooldays* (1857) and Rudyard Kipling's *Stalky and Co* (1899), and in autobiography, there are such recurring themes as the central figure engaging in periods

At Bootham (at centre of back row).

of rebelliousness to secure peer group approval, systems of cribbing to assist weaker boys avoid their masters' retribution, patterns of loyalty of almost a tribal kind to houses and even dormitories, and either enthusiasm for, or avoidance of, sport.

The precociously clever but physically small and slight Alan Taylor could sparkle and attract the limelight as a rebel. At the start of 1923 he was just under five feet five inches tall and weighed nine stone (153 pounds). Moreover, being agin and being able to argue with vigour came naturally to him given his home experiences. At The Downs, according to his autobiography, he was elected to the school's Cabinet and for a while ran it to subvert the masters' powers of punishment. At Bootham, he fitted in better; perhaps The Downs School had been a preparatory experience for Bootham. Here, he just scoffed at and queried some of the Quaker assumptions and as a reeve bent the position's powers to grant himself leave from playing football, instead spending the time exploring York.[17] It is striking that both at The Downs and Bootham he rose to positions of authority with his peers, and at Bootham he seems to have been a poacher turned gamekeeper. He later observed, 'I, having been a rebel, was a stern disciplinarian when I became a reeve.'[18] This has echoes of his later role of rebel, when he was one but from within Oxbridge, and within his college a stickler for upholding its traditions.

He also won some peer group approval through the long-hallowed public schoolboy practice of cribbing. Winston Churchill in *My Early Life* (1930) recounted how at Harrow he wrote English essays for a friend in return for Latin translations. Taylor, in his autobiography, recalled that he 'learnt how to exploit my cleverness, doing the prep of the bigger boys and winning protection in return'.[19]

At Bootham he exhibited leadership among his fellows in the loyalties accruing to houses and even dormitories. He clearly revelled in such competitiveness within the enclosed public school society. He was in Penn House, bedroom 24, in the period before 'bedrooms were based on age groups which changed yearly…so the allegiance to a bedroom throughout one's school life was no longer of any significance'.[20] Indeed, he was 'head of the bedroom' in his last year at Bootham, 1923–24. In 1921 he initiated 'No. 24 Chronicle', a miscellaneous series of jottings, including 'in-jokes' concerning the six to ten members of the dormitory. He was teased over his small size. For instance, one entry included, 'It is rumoured that Tailor's [sic] nurse has been on the way but is coming per return post. The baby of many initials being highly excited told an excellent story about the wilds of Africa.' The chronicle also recounted raids on other dormitories, including one which noted that 'the opposing forces under A.J.P.T. had been put to flight, retreating into their mountain stronghold'.[21]

Though much involved in dormitory boisterousness, Alan Taylor was very much the antithesis of a sporting hero. While at The Downs his doctor, fearing that one of his lungs was near to collapse, recommended that he should spend his time in the open air. In his autobiography Taylor described this as 'a stroke of luck' and indicated it was better still when the doctor gave him a certificate of exemption from playing football. At Bootham, he had to play this team game again – in his eyes 'an agony made worse by the fact that all except the two top elevens had to bicycle over a mile to the playing field'. That is, until he became a reeve and gave himself a dispensation from compulsory football. Cricket was voluntary, so he played tennis instead.[22] Hence his routes to prominence and respect among his fellow pupils had to be intellectual, not sporting.

Part of his intellectual distinctiveness stemmed from his very unorthodox radical home background. There can have been very, very few public schoolboys at that time who came from a wealthy home in which the Bolsheviks were revered and where political opinions were divided between the Left of the Independent Labour Party (ILP) and the Communist Party of Great Britain. The October Revolution in Russia moved his parents from dissatisfaction with the Liberals and support for conscientious objectors to socialism. Alan Taylor wrote in his autobiography, 'While others talked, Lenin had acted: he had ended the war.'[23] Thereafter, when he went home he found plenty of ILP pamphlets to read. With the arrival of Henry Sara into the family circle, from 1919, he gained a Marxist mentor who guided his socialist reading.

The young Taylor wore advanced political opinions like a badge on his clothes. He made no secret of the unorthodox views which were rampant at his home. One of his few female acquaintances of this period recalled seeing Connie Taylor in the following words: 'this famous mother, whom I had heard of because we had heard of her...as a communist...which was something rather exciting to be.' She added that his red mother 'was part of the general impression of advanced views and sophistication generally that Alan gave'.[24] It is notable that the 'Chronicle of Bedroom 24', Penn House, Bootham, early on became the 'Soviet Chronicles', beginning:

> On Friday the Soviet G [government] was established in No. 24, its object being to establish liberty and independence [sic] for shirkers. The other members, who live across the ocean, opposed its opinions and declared war. Hearing of this, Krupp's Arsenal was erected to protect the new PM and his colleagues.

He presented orthodox Marxist views in an attention-seeking but prize-winning school essay, 'Communism'. In this he sternly observed, 'The Communist incentive is not an emotional one – they leave it to social reformers to go into hysterics over slum conditions.' In the course of a heavy-handed explanation of the materialist conception of history he wrote of the diffusion of

...different forms of dominant class ideology through the schools – how many of my hearers have heard of the Materialist Conception of History before – the churches – Blessed are the meek – the universities and, above all, the Press, while the subjection of the proletariat is secured by the legal and military systems, centralised under the state.

He also emphasised, 'Regarding the instruments of bourgeois "democracy" as merely the organs of class domination, the proletariat must therefore build its own institutions moulded to suit its own needs, in order to supplant the plutocratic state.'[25]

He also presented himself as a stern, unbending orthodox Marxist in a letter he wrote to the *Communist*, 3 June 1922, a newspaper which appealed to middle-class intellectuals and which sold around 8000 copies. The 16-year-old Alan Taylor remonstrated with Raymond Postgate, then aged 25, over an essay on 'Literature and Communism' in the *Communist*, 27 May 1922, condemning Postgate for being a bourgeois and failing to understand the 'Materialist Conception of History'. In writing from Bootham the young Taylor apparently saw no irony in observing, 'I have always been afraid that bourgeois culture was too deeply ingrained ever to be eradicated or even completely nullified by doses, however, continuous, of *Plebs* and the *Communist*.'

It is difficult not to suspect that Henry Sara encouraged or put him up to writing the letter. Postgate, who had been a conscientious objector, was a founder member of the CPGB, was on the executive committee of the Plebs League and had been editor of the *Communist* from June 1921 until about 20 May 1922, when he resigned from the editorship and, within two years, from the CPGB, disgusted by communist political tactics of orchestrating opposition to those with whom they disagreed. The biographer of Rajani Palme Dutt, the CPGB's orthodox theoretician, who scrapped the *Communist* in February 1923, observed of the departure of Postgate and others: 'Those who could not accept the demands of ideological purity and party discipline were forced to leave the organisation.'[26] Presumably, the CPGB hardliners enjoyed a schoolboy from Bootham 'getting the line right' in a letter against the recently departed editor. Postgate himself in his reply observed, 'The logical corollary is that I should be expelled from the party.'

In terms of a biography of Alan Taylor the most interesting aspect of this letter and his 'Communism' essay is that it displays his concern to impress his mother and Henry Sara. His attitude towards his mother was very ambivalent, combining love and hate, marked by repeated attempts to win her love by intellectual brilliance. He later wrote to the historian Robert Cole, 'I inherited my cleverness from my mother and disliked her all the same. She was totally self-centred, a sort of aspiring Madame Bovary as so many women are. She treated my father badly, and maybe I have revenged him by taking it out on the women in my life.'[27]

While appearing the Marxist tyro, Taylor also supported his father in his ILP activities. Percy and Connie Taylor moved in early 1919 to 17 Rose Terrace, Ashton-on-Ribble, Preston, very close to where they had been children. James and Amelia Taylor had lived at 25 Victoria Parade since the late 1880s, while William and Martha Thompson had lived at 27 Beech Grove.[28] Number 17 Rose Terrace, an attractive, substantial detached house (now a nursing home), was to be Alan Taylor's home throughout his years at Bootham and Oxford, and, indeed, until 1931. His parents moved later in the 1930s to 8 Mulgrave Avenue, Ashton-on-Ribble, a little more select and close by Ashton Park. Percy Taylor became a stalwart of the Preston branch of the ILP, a predominantly working-class body. He became a member of the gas workers' branch of the General and Municipal Workers' Union, thereby being eligible to be a delegate to the Preston Trades and Labour Council, of which he was a member for the rest of his life. Alan Taylor joined the ILP in 1921, when he was fifteen. In his autobiography he recalled that he had gone each Sunday evening with his parents to the ILP meetings, just as he had earlier gone to chapel with his mother: 'I even addressed a meeting, I cannot remember on what – probably an attack on parliamentary democracy, a theme I then mistakenly favoured.'[29]

17 Rose Terrace, Preston, as it is now (with blue plaque to the right of the door).

Thus there was little difference initially between the arguments he could put within a left-wing ILP branch and his intellectual support for the CPGB.

His parents' involvement in politics led to various national politicians of the Left staying at their house. These included such leading Labour figures as Arthur Henderson and George Lansbury, and also Harry Pollitt of the CPGB. Alan Taylor later commented that while a schoolboy he had heard Henderson speak in Preston, probably at a meeting chaired by his father. He recalled him as being 'a good speaker – very effectively making his points'. He added that, while he was something of the stolid trade unionist, 'that he had been a Methodist preacher came through very clearly'. As for Lansbury, like his father he had great admiration for him, observing: 'He was a very good speaker, putting a lot of heart into what he said…he had a lot of understanding of people. He was also a man with a good sense of humour. As a speaker he was good at lifting his audience.'[30] He also liked Pollitt, not least because he was willing to play solo whist.[31] Perhaps being accustomed at an early age to talk with the Left's leading lights encouraged him later to expect to lead from the top in CND, a celebrity variant on *noblesse oblige*.

His parents were going their own ways in their lives as well as in their socialist politics. Percy Taylor sold his share of the family business in early 1920, at the peak of the post-war boom. After an unsuccessful attempt to develop a wholesale confectionery business, he devoted himself to local Labour politics and lived on his dwindling capital. He diligently attended the Sunday morning meetings of the Preston Trades Council from about 1921. He was elected on to the Board of Guardians (who ran the work-house). He stood unsuccessfully as the Labour candidate for Preston Council for St John's ward in 1925, losing with 1587 votes to the successful Independent, who polled 1641 votes. He also lost in by-elections in Ashton and St Peter's wards. In October 1926 he lost again, this time in Fishwick ward, polling 1158 votes to the successful Conservative candidate's 1312 votes. The Conservative leader, in congratulating the successful candidate, said he would have disliked her seat being contested less 'had Comrade Taylor been a pucka [sic] working man. He added, 'I have no use for these rich intellectual doctrinaires who are sheltering under the Labour flag.' Percy Taylor won a by-election for Park ward, which followed an aldermanic elevation, on 24 November 1926 by 2371 to 1961 votes, and was the first Labour candidate to win that ward. He held it in the 1928 municipal elections by 2140 votes to the Conservative candidate's 2047 votes. He lost the seat in 1931, but returned to Preston Council in 1932 for Fishwick ward, winning by 1627 votes to the Conservative's 1472. He held the seat comfortably in 1935 and 1938, remaining a councillor until his death. The town council was his 'consuming interest'.[32]

Connie Taylor was also involved in politics, supporting Henry Sara in his communist propaganda. Taylor recalled,

> My mother, I think, still hankered to play a great revolutionary role. She made large financial contributions to the Communist Party, as the records of Special Branch probably show. But it was not her own money. It was relayed to her from a Soviet bank in London and she passed it on to the Communist Party, thus, it was hoped, concealing the source...

However, she did finance Sara for a very long time. Also, in 1924, the year that members of the Communist Party were banned by the Labour Party from standing as Labour candidates, she stood for Preston Council and lost as a Labour candidate for the St John's Ward (and was succeeded as candidate in 1925 by her husband).

However, her 'consuming interest' was the Labour colleges movement. Sara worked for the NCLC until 1948, and in the 1920s and 1930s he stayed with the Taylors for months each year while lecturing in Lancashire and Yorkshire. Connie Taylor was secretary of the Preston Labour College. Percy gave lectures on the cotton industry and wrote suitably hardline Marxist analyses of the industry's problems for *Plebs*.[33] Sometimes the teenage Alan Taylor went with his father or Sara, often operating the slide projector for illustrated talks. These experiences gave him the taste for such meetings, hence probably his enjoyment later in speaking to Historical Association meetings. In the 1920s Connie Taylor was also often away from home, sometimes for several weeks, travelling with Sara or one of her old school friends.

Percy Taylor also had his friend Doris Sharples, nicknamed 'Little Dolly'. She was a younger sister of Sydney Sharples, one of the local ILP members. Their father, a hairdresser, died of pneumonia in 1917, leaving a widow, four boys and seven girls. Sydney brought two of his sisters, Doris and her younger sister Hilda, to the ILP children's Christmas party in December 1919, at which Percy Taylor was dressed up as Father Christmas. Doris later recalled,

> My younger sister Hilda had been very ill and Mr Taylor suggested he took her to stay with him and his wife for a week or two until she got stronger.
>   They lived in a big detached house in Ashton...They kept two maids who lived in, so Hilda was well looked after...Hilda stayed with them for about six weeks and certainly looked a lot better physically for her attention.

Doris Sharples had been born on 6 November 1909, so was a few years younger than Miriam would have been. For Percy Taylor she and Hilda were substitutes. She recollected, 'He did with my sister and I [sic] all the things he should have done with his own children. He never stopped talking about little Miriam.' He took them for car rides in the countryside, bringing along 'one of his maids to accompany us'. He took them to Stratford-upon-Avon, where they saw a play, went on the river and visited Anne Hathaway's cottage. When Connie Taylor was abroad, Doris remembered,

> Pa Taylor used to invite my sister and I [sic] to stay at their house for a few weeks during our school summer holidays. He still kept two maids in the house to look after us, and once or twice Alice, the cook, would come with us if we were travelling a long way and had to stay the night in a small hotel.

Percy Taylor also paid for the two girls' education at Moor Park High School for Girls, Preston, enabling them to stay until 14 (two years beyond the minimum age).[34]

For Percy Taylor, the two girls made up not only for the dead daughter but also for the much-loved son away at boarding school. Over the years, 'Little Dolly' (she never grew taller than four feet eleven inches) became his favourite of the sisters. Alan Taylor liked her. He also helped his father conceal from his mother how often they met. Doris later commented of Percy Taylor, 'He was the nicest person I had ever met. I was young and impressionable then. I had lost my own father when I was seven. Percy had lost his own little girl when she was eighteen months old...So he was to me the father I had lost, and I was to him the daughter that he had lost.' She also delivered the judgement: 'He was worth two of Alan. He was a very good man.' In contrast, she observed of Connie Taylor, 'She was something of a dragon. She had been a teacher – but got married to get out of teaching. I should imagine she was an awful teacher as she did not like children.'[35] When Doris married Arthur Nicholson at Preston Registry Office in 1932, it was Percy Taylor who gave her away.[36]

As well as enjoying the company of Doris Sharples, Percy continued to enjoy treating other children, notably his nephews and nieces. They later remembered him as their favourite uncle – 'a delightful person', 'a nice bloke'. He had a strong sense of fun, so much so that they warmly recalled that 'he wasn't like a grown-up at all'. On one occasion he had everybody in laughter when he rolled the housemaid up in a carpet. He also took his nephews and nieces on outings. Two were taken to the Isle of Man, where they went to Douglas. There they went round and round the harbour on open trams, enjoying 'a marvellous packed lunch of cold lamb chops', and even more throwing the bones on the promenade. When their mother was told of her brother-in-law's day out, she laughed, observing 'just like Percy'.[37] By all accounts he appears to have been the archetypal kind uncle.

Alan Taylor made friends at school and university, but made few at home. Having no surviving sisters, his contact with girls was infrequent. At Buxton, when he was nine or ten, he had been friendly with Eileen Mills, the daughter of the landlord of the George Hotel, and he also saw his cousins, Margery and Nancy Taylor. When he was a teenager he seems to have adopted a 'laddish' attitude at Bootham, at Oxford University and in Vienna. This is epitomised by his comment on entering York one afternoon: 'Our belief that the girls at the cocoa works supplemented their wages by immoral means was, I fear, unfounded.'[38] The corollary to this kind of immature macho posturing was an awkwardness with girls of his age.

In York the boys from Bootham met the girls from the Quaker girls' school, The Mount, on Sunday mornings at the Friends' Meeting and on a few special occasions. It is possible that, in his mind, the young Taylor made a brief acquaintanceship with Kathleen Constable into more of a friendship than she felt it to be.[39] However, it is also possible that in later life she downplayed her pleasure in his friendship. He first met her when they were the lead speakers in a joint debate between Bootham and The Mount on the motion 'That the progress of civilisation has not tended to increase the happiness of mankind', held in The Mount in March 1923. He must have been much impressed by her. Later that year, in December, he went to The Mount, when both schools put on open exhibitions of schoolwork, to hear Kathleen Constable give a short talk on Shakespeare's theatre, and sat listening attentively during it. He also sought her out at the Rowntree family's leaving party for pupils of both schools, held in their cocoa works. According to Kathleen Tillotson, this 'was regarded as something of an ordeal as we were supposed to mix up and we weren't used to mixing up'. She recalled she intended sitting just with her brother, but a shy Alan Taylor joined them, 'so there we were, three of us, sitting rather self-consciously and Alan doing almost all the talking'.[40]

Notably shy and awkward with girls of his age, he did develop stronger friendships with a few boys of his age group. In his autobiography he wrote of one, George Clazy, 'Suddenly I fell in love with him. George was very highminded, next door to a prig, and our relations were entirely innocent. His attraction for me was as much intellectual as physical. When I first took up with him he was staggeringly beautiful.'[41] This seems to be the not unusual puppy love of single-sex schools. Writing of the economic historian Eileen Power, Maxine Berg has observed of 'the passionate schoolgirl-like friendships of a single-sex college' that these 'could accommodate and transcend their relationships with the opposite sex and their marriages'.[42] Alan Taylor had brief crushes of this kind at school but, while having a few effusive male friendships which lasted long, his norm was undoubtedly heterosexual relationships. Where men were especially important in his later life they tended to be more father figures: Lewis Namier, A.P. Wadsworth and Beaverbrook.

George Clazy remained Taylor's best friend until well into his Oxford undergraduate days. His early departure from Bootham turned him into a pen pal and a friend to meet up with in vacations. Together they went on walking holidays in Scotland and the Lake District, including during the summers of 1925 and 1926. The two also holidayed in Germany and Austria in the summer of 1928, a year after Taylor had graduated. However, the friendship ended tragically, with a lovelorn Clazy committing suicide over an attractive young woman in mid-1929.[43] But by then Taylor was not emotionally involved, and apparently was not greatly upset by the news of his death.

Another particular friend at Bootham, albeit briefly, was Roger Moore. When George Clazy was not available to join Alan, his mother and Sara on a six-week holiday in Germany and France in summer 1924 he invited Moore, with whom he often discussed books and current affairs. In his autobiography, Taylor commented, 'He was a sweet character but he did not fit in. He was shocked by the incessant political arguments and Marxist talk.'[44] Kathleen Tillotson, who had known Moore longer than Taylor had, having known him at home as well as when he was at Bootham, was surprised at the time that they became friends: 'I wouldn't have thought of him as having very much in common with Alan...I think his particular interest was in mathematics...and he was a quieter type.' By chance, she was also surprised to come across them with Connie Taylor and Henry Sara on the boat back from the Continent in the late summer of 1924. It is notable that Alan Taylor's interest in her remained very high. She later recalled that, after the passengers had transferred from the boat, 'Alan came down the train looking for me, and sat down and talked to me on the journey and talked about what he had seen and had been doing.'[45]

By the later years of his time at Bootham Taylor had made his name in the school. Dennis Constable, two years his junior, later judged him to have been 'quite impressively clever'. His sister, Kathleen, had been immediately impressed by his performance when she debated against him, later recalling that, while she had prepared her speech rather like an essay and half read it, 'his idea was much better, much more lively', using notes and contesting points she had made. That he was the Bootham choice to be its main speaker was indicative of how highly regarded his intellectual and debating skills were, while the other Bootham speaker was a member of the Rowntree family, Geoffrey (who seconded Kathleen Constable). In 1991 she gave the verdict that she 'did then realise that here was somebody very clever, even then one could recognise it; [but] it is difficult to know how much one reads back'.[46]

For one who prided himself on being a rebel, Alan Taylor clearly participated and competed. He had a substantial list of achievements in the Bootham school magazine on his leaving. As well as his exhibition at Oriel, it recorded:

> He was on the Committee of the Natural History Club (1920–24), of which he was Secretary, and also the Committees of The Senior Essay and Debating Societies. He was a distinguished archaeologist, for he won the Old Scholars' Exhibition for Archaeology, and was placed several times in the Inter-Schools Diary competition, winning the first prize once. He was also the winner of the B.B. Letall Essay Prize (1921); and was a reeve during his last year.[47]

He was sufficiently clever to win a scholarship to Oxford, but not the one he first went for. He was intensely competitive and tried to win a scholarship to Balliol. This he did not get. In his autobiography he explains his failure in terms of a radical riposte to what should be done to Oxford under a communist society, and to preference being given to a poorer student who would have been unable to study at Oxford without a scholarship. There seem to me to be two persuasive interpretations of his account other than just to register distaste at the 'blow it up after I have gone down' anecdote.[48] The first is to recognise it as a literary reply to the specific point put to him (what should be done with Oxford in a communist society?). It was an echo of the Eton headmaster's comment, when Henry Salt resigned as a master from the school in order to devote himself to humanitarian causes: 'Socialism! Then blow us up! There's nothing left for it but that.'[49] The second is to observe that a feature of his autobiography and other recollections is that he seems to have been unable to admit to having simply failed; there is usually a striking anecdote of a righteous and radical stand made to suggest that it was his radical views which cost him dearly. Probably these anecdotes were embellished after the event; but, possibly, in some cases, they were true accounts of his actions, but these were a defensive mechanism of one who was insecure and wanted an alibi for a failure. Whatever the case, this suggests that he felt greatly the need to achieve to impress his mother.

However, there is no reason to doubt that his success in winning a scholarship to Oriel College was due to his deep knowledge of Gothic architecture. But it was also buttressed by his broad knowledge stemming from very extensive reading.

While his family and Bootham were very big influences on the young Taylor, the third undoubtedly was his love of books. He was the archetypal young bookworm. He wrote in his autobiography of his early teens, 'Life

did not exist for me except at second hand – no experiences, no one to talk
to. I had day dreams of becoming a revolutionary leader, curiously enough
always dressed in Cromwellian armour.'[50] Writing to Éva Haraszti in 1972
of his efforts to write about his youth in his autobiography he commented,
'When I try to remember it, I can only remember the books I read,
beginning with *Pilgrim's Progress*.'[51]

He read from an early age. He greatly enjoyed such children's classics
as the books by Beatrix Potter, especially *The Tailor of Gloucester* (1902),
Frances Hodgson Burnett's *The Secret Garden* (1911), as well as the adventure
stories of G.A. Henty, with *A Roving Commission* (1899) as his favourite.
Later, he read all the Harrison Ainsworth historical novels, including *The
Tower Of London* (1840), that were in Buxton public library. In contributing
in 1974 to a *Times Literary Supplement* feature on the children's books 'that
made the deepest impression … in childhood' he wrote of *Pilgrim's Progress*
(1678): 'I had it read to me before I could read. When I could, I read it
again and again. I skipped the conversations. One of the greatest books in
the world and the most subversive.'[52] In early October 1979, when staying
with Roy Avery (a former pupil) and his wife, Taylor surprised them, when
the conversation got on to *Pilgrim's Progress*, by quoting a sizeable section
of it from memory.[53] From this and other nonconformist classics he acquired
a habit of mind which on occasion came near to personifying people in
Bunyanesque ways. This was notably so with the titles of book reviews or
essays, such as 'Mr High Mind's Party' or 'Recalling Mr Fearful – for Truth'.
He may well have been encouraged in this by Malcolm Muggeridge
dubbing Ramsay MacDonald 'Mr High Mind' in his *The Thirties* (1940), a
book which much influenced him.

He was also greatly influenced by Samuel Johnson and, especially, by
James Boswell's *Life of Johnson* (1791), which he described as 'my favourite
book'.[54] He liked to quote Macaulay: 'Homer is not more decidedly the
first of heroic poets, Shakespeare is not more decidedly the first of
dramatists, Demosthenes is not more decidedly the first of orators, than
Boswell is the first of biographers. He has no second.' The sharp-tongued
epigrammatic style of Johnson was a forerunner of Taylor's comments, in
sentiment as well as style:

> Though we cannot out-vote them, we will out-argue them.
> Every man has a right to utter what he thinks is truth; and every other
> man has a right to knock him down for it.
> Martyrdom is the test.
> That fellow seems to possess but one idea, and that is a wrong one.

All are not Taylor but Dr Johnson (at least as recorded by Boswell); but all
could be in Taylor's writing.[55] He also drew examples from Johnson, as he

did from Bunyan. For instance, he joined Johnson in enjoying the chapter of Horrebow, *The Natural History of Iceland*, 'Concerning snakes': 'There are no snakes to be met throughout the whole island'. He applied the anecdote to a review of books searching for the roots of European unity.[56]

Alan Taylor drew more from Johnson than style and examples. He tried to emulate him, to be a quick-witted and a great arguer. Boswell wrote, 'Johnson could not brook appearing to be worsted in argument, even when he had taken the wrong side, to shew the force and dexterity of his talents.' Taylor had a similar passion for winning an argument and for 'hitting hard', as he exhibited memorably on television current affairs discussion programmes in the 1950s. He also adopted Johnson's irascible persona from at least his late fifties, dealing tersely with anyone whose views or questions annoyed him. He also was Johnsonian in his pig-headed use of the terms 'Scotch' and 'Scotchmen', much annoying many people in the mid-1960s.[57]

Alan Taylor knew his Boswell and quite a lot more about Dr Johnson. He knew how vivid the distinctions between Whigs and Tories were to Johnson and had reservations about Lewis Namier's rewriting of 1760s British party politics. He may well have warmed towards Johnson's almost postmodern reflections on history, made in the presence of Edward Gibbon: 'We must consider how very little history there is; I mean real authentick history. That certain Kings reigned, and certain battles were fought, we can depend upon as true; but all the colouring, all the philosophy, of history, is conjecture.'[58]

When elderly, Taylor was asked by Michael Parkinson, on his BBC television 'chat show' 'Parkinson', whether he thought historians were born or made. In replying he said that he had been 'obsessed with history as a small boy'. He had enjoyed his father telling him stories. He had asked his father: 'What happened next?' and had been doing this ever since.[59] He was especially encouraged in his history reading at Bootham by Leslie Gilbert, a Manchester University graduate, who arrived as history master in 1920. Frank Thistlethwaite, who was also taught by Gilbert, later recalled him as 'a man with a first-class mind' who 'had a big impact on his best pupils, especially in encouraging them to write well. He stood for "no sloppy paragraphs".'[60] Gilbert, a devout Quaker (and keen cricketer), according to Alan Taylor wished 'to save my soul from Marxism'.[61] In the short run he failed in this, but he spurred him on to read the multiple volumes of the classic historians and also the then current textbooks.

While the young Taylor read a very impressive quantity of great literature, he did read major works of history at Bootham and at Oxford. Indeed, he had read a substantial number of classic historical works even before arriving at Oxford.[62] He built on this foundation while there.

He was well read in such older historians as Edward Gibbon (1737–94), Lord Macaulay (1800–59), George Grote (1794–1871), Bishop Stubbs (1825–1901), S.R. Gardiner (1829–1902), Sir J.R. Seeley (1834–95), Lord Acton (1834–1902) and F.W. Maitland (1850–1906), as well as major figures still writing, such as Sir Frederick Pollock (1845–1937), T.F. Tout (1855–1929), Sir Charles Oman (1860–1946), Sir J.A.R. Marriott (1859–1945), Sir Charles Grant Robertson (1869–1948), H.A.L. Fisher (1865–1940), G.M. Trevelyan (1876–1962) and R.H. Tawney (1880–1962).

He was also remarkably well read in socialist classics and contemporary socialist writing. He was well versed in many of the publications of the Plebs League, which promoted Marxist education through evening classes and local labour colleagues, and its successor the NCLC (established in 1921). Alan Taylor eagerly read the works of Eden and Cedar Paul, observing later that, though not much remembered fifty years on, they had been influential in their day.[63] Eden Paul was a retired doctor, who had practised medicine in Japan, China, Perak, Singapore and Alderney between 1895 and 1912 and had worked for the French Socialist Party 1912–14. He had been the *Times* correspondent with the Northern Japanese Army in the Sino-Japanese War, 1895 and had been the founder and editor of the *Nagasaki Press*, 1897–99. He was a founder member of the CPGB, he and his wife working after the war as translators and authors. He helped popularise Marx's views and he rebutted anti-socialist critics such as W.H. Mallock in pamphlets such as *Karl Marx and Modern Socialism* (Manchester, National Labour Press, n.d., but perhaps 1908–10). Cedar Paul, who described herself as a singer as well, was a member of the ILP, 1912–19, Secretary of the British Section of the Women's Socialist and Labour Organisations, 1917–19, and served on the executive committee of the Plebs League in the mid-1920s. The historian Stuart MacIntyre, in his study of Marxism in Britain 1917–33, commented,

> In the labour colleges…there was considerable resentment against the middle-class intellectuals who came into the Plebs League during and immediately after the war. Two books written by Eden and Cedar Paul, *Creative Revolution* (1920) and *Prolecult* (1921), attracted criticism for their obscure vocabulary – they coined words like 'ergatocracy' to replace the ugly 'dictatorship of the proletariat' – and generally school marmish tone.[64]

Middle-class intellectuals – such as Connie Taylor and her son – were not put off by the Pauls or their tone. He read their *Creative Revolution* and *Prolecult* in mid-1921, substantial political reading for a 15-year-old. He read *Creative Revolution* again a year later. In *Creative Revolution* the Pauls argued, 'Until quite recently, all forward spirits have imagined themselves

to be moving "Towards Democracy".' Now, 'left-wing socialists in all lands
are agreed...that parliament is outworn and that the growing economic
power of the workers must fashion new forms of political expression'. For
them 'revolution is a transcendent creative act, wherein man's will, guided
by accumulating knowledge, asserts its freedom, widening the bounds of
freedom alike for the individual and the race'. For a period Taylor held
similar views to those expressed by the Pauls, which he derived from their
and other Marxist writings, notably William Paul's *Communism and Society*
(1922), as well as works by Marx, Lenin, Trotsky and Kautsky, all read
before he arrived at Oxford.[65] Quite clearly, he undertook the equivalent
of a Plebs League Marxist course on his own, reading also such Plebs
League textbooks as the ones by T. Ashcroft and others, *Outline of Modern
Imperialism* (1922), W. McLaine and W.T. Collyer, *Outline of Economics*
(1922), and J.F. Horrabin (the editor of *Plebs*), *Outline of Economic Geography*
(1924), when they were published. It is far from surprising, given his
family background and his schoolboy espousal of Marxist politics, that he
joined the Communist Party of Great Britain when at Oxford University.

However, while Taylor enjoyed displaying advanced views, thereby
marking himself out as someone a little special, he did not devote a great
deal of attention to politics as an undergraduate. Away from his parents
and Sara, his political stance might well have been summed up by the reply
he claimed to have made to the comment that he had a reputation for
holding strong political views: 'No...extreme views, weakly held.'[66]

In his early months at Oxford he aired Marxist views here and there.
This, predictably, resulted in a stream of drunken Oriel males descending
after pub closing time to redeem him from such views. In his autobiography he noted that this encouraged him to keep such views to himself,
adding: 'In this way I survived unharmed though it took a good deal of the
fun out of life.'

Alan Taylor, writing of the mid-1920s in his *English History 1914–1945*
(1965), wrote,

> The strange one-sex system of education at public schools and uni-
> versities had always run to homosexuality. In Victorian times this,
> though gross, had been sentimental and ostensibly innocent. At the *fin
> de siècle* it had been consciously wicked. Now it was neither innocent
> nor wicked. It was merely, for a brief period, normal. By the end of
> the decade, even public schoolboys were beginning to discover that
> women were an improvement on painted boys.[67]

He aspired to female friendships, though opportunities were very limited
for undergraduates at Oxford then. He left a note for Katharine Constable
soon after she arrived as an undergraduate at Oxford, suggesting they meet

for afternoon tea in a café. She later recalled, 'It was not particularly successful. He was very self-conscious I remember. He must have told me a bit about Oriel where he was.' He did not repeat the invitation, though he did see her at the Labour Club and at a gathering of ex-Bootham and The Mount students at Ruskin College organised by the Quaker warden, Alfred Barratt Brown.[68] In his final year he frequently went to tea on Sundays with the sister of a friend of a friend, Moura Stuart, and her mother. He later recalled her being an intelligent girl. In his autobiography he commented, 'I certainly did not know how to treat women, perhaps I have never learnt. But I dimly appreciated for the first time that I preferred women's company to that of men...'[69]

Like so many others from public schools, the predominant background of Oxford undergraduates, Alan Taylor created his own world within Oxford with a small circle of male friends. It was not a 'hearty' sport and beer-swilling group but one of 'reading men'. In such a circle Taylor had near-Olympic-gold qualifications, the volume and quality of his reading at Bootham being exceptional for his age. He read broadly at Oxford. He could afford to, given the head start he had in reading classic works of history. Moreover, it seems that among 'reading men' of his time it was not the done thing to read only what their tutors set. Taylor's close friend, J.I.M. Stewart, expressed this in a later novel in which the central character comments on undergraduate reading at Oxford, 'Of course you're expected to browse on the fodder in the library enough to scratch up your essay. But I believe your tutor actually hopes you're spending quite a lot of time talking about this and that in a general way.'[70]

Alan Taylor's small coterie began with Norman Cameron, Charles (known as Billy) Gott and John Theodore Yates. In addition he went most weeks to the Oxford Playhouse with Cyril Simey, saw Tom Driberg for communist discussions and, more generally, the members of the Labour Club. Norman Cameron, from Edinburgh, had his rooms in Oriel on the same staircase. In some ways Cameron, who had been educated at Fettes, and Taylor were kindred spirits. Cameron, who was over six feet tall and frail, disliked sport but eagerly read and was notably witty. He was a very able poet and at Oxford was assistant editor of *Oxford Outlook* and one of the best contributors to *Oxford Poetry*, 1926 and 1927. He took Taylor along to gatherings of young Oxford poets, which included Wystan Auden and Stephen Spender. For Taylor he was a breath of fresh air from football- and other sports-obsessed students, with both cultural and womanising aspects to him. He was of Left inclinations, going with him to Preston in the General Strike and helping the strikers. Charles Gott, from a well-to-do family, partly army, was a science student. Taylor later wrote of him that he 'had fewer affectations and perhaps more merits' than the others.[71]

The third, Jack or (as he was known at Oxford) Theodore Yates, represented an aspect of Alan Taylor's character. He was of a well-to-do upper-middle-class family; his father was the vicar of St Michael's, Louth. He aspired to be a gentleman of leisure, a person who developed eccentricities and lived without concern for 'getting on'. In short, the antithesis of the deeply competitive and near-workaholic that was to be A.J.P. Taylor. Taylor later described Yates as having 'elegance and culture without intellect', walking with a silver-headed ebony cane and affecting to be 'a distinguished elderly man'. Innes Stewart referred to him to Taylor as 'your silly friend'. Another of Yates' acquaintances later wrote of him: 'Yates was part of Evelyn Waugh's "Bright Young Things" – a species that had to be protected. From their days in Oxford at the St George Restaurant to the Savage Club they seemed to drift through life without a care in the world.'[72] Theodore Yates and Norman Cameron were Alan Taylor's links to this world. John Betjeman, also of this circle, later recalled of Norman Cameron to Warren Hope: 'He was one of a group which were known...as the "Corpus Aesthetes"...they spilled across the road to Oriel College and thus included Norman Cameron and Jack Yates.'[73]

For Taylor, Yates was the friend par excellence who took him into the world of the Oxford Aesthetes, where Harold Acton was king. He wrote of Yates, 'He stayed in bed until midday, dined every evening at the George and sat up half the night drinking whisky.' He often went with Yates to the George Restaurant, the favourite haunt of the aesthetes, and even 'exchanged a greeting with Harold Acton'. Taylor recalled in 1985 that the George was the place to be, rather than at the Scholar's Table at the centre of Hall in Oriel:

> it was more important to go to the George Restaurant...It went on as a restaurant well until the Second World War, and then after that it gradually faded away...It was the most...specifically social restaurant. Oxford citizens could come in if they wanted to but it tended to be taken up by the better-equipped. I had dinner there at least once a week with the same Oriel friends...Oxford was very nicely equipped...[with] cafés in a way that it isn't now.

Acton himself recalled, 'I believe very much in colour, so when I went up to Oxford after the First World War, everything seemed very drab... One had to revolt against that and bring a little colour into the scene with bright shirts, bright waistcoats and so forth. One could express oneself in beautiful clothes.'

Acton and his circle also took up the latest dancing from the United States, the Black Bottom and the Boogie Woogie after the Charleston, and indulged in this at a bohemian club, The Hypocrites, 'where we had tremendous goings-on'.[74] This was a leisured and very affluent world to which a part of Taylor aspired. He gained a taste of it then, when in the company of Yates or Driberg. He was later to gain a good taste of it by courtesy of Lord Beaverbrook, and a small taste of it when dining with Sir Oswald Mosley.

Although Taylor was an outsider to Acton and the well-to-do aesthetes, he was himself among the better-off undergraduates and had a car to flaunt. While he was not in the league of Viscount Weymouth, who ran a car and had the then huge sum of £600 a year as an undergraduate, and still in a year ran up £2000 in debts, Percy and Connie Taylor ensured that their only child was comfortable while at university. He was given a fishtailed open-top Rover part-way through his first year, on his nineteenth birthday. He was one of the few Oriel undergraduates to have a car. He enjoyed racing it with Theodore Yates, revelling in the speed and noise when accelerating past other drivers with the car's silencer cut off. Others in his circle were markedly less affluent. This was notably the case with his closest Oxford friend, J.I.M. Stewart, whose parents struggled to fund him through university.[75]

Innes Stewart, a shy and bookish Scot from Edinburgh, arrived at Oriel one year after Alan Taylor. Although Taylor thought otherwise, they had much in common. Both were only children, had shown a streak of rebellion at school and were great readers. They both were admirers of the writings of George Bernard Shaw, going to his plays and even, in the summer of 1926, according to Taylor's memoirs, driving out from Stewart's home to Gleneagles to gaze upon Shaw from afar.[76] Also, they were both avid readers of detective stories, a *genre* in which Innes, as 'Michael Innes', was later to excel. Above all, they were both very able, each gaining First-Class Honours degrees.

However, Alan Taylor felt that their scholarly styles were very different, with Taylor deeming Stewart 'precious' and detesting his approach to literature, which he judged to be 'elegant appreciation in the style of Walter Pater or Edmund Gosse'. Nevertheless, they were each other's best friend at Oxford. Taylor later observed of Innes Stewart, 'He is without doubt the nicest man I have ever known. He has charm and kindness that are irresistible. His precocity was...very bad for me, encouraging my tendency to flippancy and lack of concern.'

Stewart recalled of Taylor as an Oxford undergraduate, 'I saw him as being as able as anybody on the horizon.' He added, with perception, that Taylor 'inwardly was as diffident and misdoubting as outwardly he was tough and arrogant'. Stewart drew on his memories of Alan Taylor and others of this group in his later novels.[77]

As well as being a 'reading man' with some aspirations to being an aesthete, Alan Taylor was also active in sport during his first two years at

Oxford. He took up rowing as a break from reading, and enjoyed it. In his second year he was stroke of Oriel's second boat and was joined by Innes Stewart as cox. He left Oriel's boat club after his second year, perhaps because he was disappointed at not making it into the first eight, or regularly into it, or, less likely, because he was working hard for his finals;[78] either way, it was most probably an outcome of Taylor's strong competitive streak.

He did attend and join the university Labour Club, keeping this secret within Oriel. He joined by contacting the current chairholder, A.L. Rowse, and remaining 'a freak member on a special university list', rather than starting an Oriel College group. One appeal of the Labour Club, according to his later reminiscences, was that it was the one place Oriel males met the opposite sex. At the Labour Club meetings he took a hard Left stance, impressing the future Labour MP for Stroud, Ben Parkin. His arguments also led to Ieuan Thomas approaching him to join the Communist Party. This he did. It was a case of putting up or shutting up. Ieuan Glyn Thomas, who was the same age as Alan Taylor, was born in Llanelli and before going to Merton College, Oxford, had worked in Llanelli Mechanics Institute. Taylor, however, avoided vanguard activism; no early morning selling of Communist publications at factory gates for him. He continued to make Marxist speeches at Labour Club meetings, while his friend Tom Driberg took a higher profile both in the university and city, also suffering from the hostile attention of young Tory undergraduates. In his memoirs Alan Taylor memorably wrote of himself as Driberg's rank and file, with just the two of them meeting in Driberg's rooms in Christ Church College, with the curtains drawn and jazz records playing. However, there were more than two members. These at the least included not only Ieuan Thomas, described by Margaret Cole as a 'consumptive undergraduate', who ran the duplicating at the Coles' house during the General Strike and who eventually left Merton after excessive harassment by 'hearties', but also an Australian Rhodes scholar, Percy Reginald Stephenson, Graham Greene and Claud Cockburn.[79] Taylor remained friends with Greene and also Driberg after they left Oxford.

Perhaps encouraged again by Henry Sara, in March 1925 Taylor displayed an ultra-rigid line in another letter denouncing Raymond Postgate. Postgate had pointed in dismay at divisions in the Italian Left, thereby making it easier for Benito Mussolini and his Fascists to control Italy. Taylor's riposte deplored Postgate's 'sneering reference to the Communist International, the greatest class-war organization of the world'. This display of loyalty to the orthodox CPGB party line appeared in the Plebs League's monthly journal, *Plebs*, which appears at this time to have been close to being Taylor's political bible. Postgate a little later argued for *Plebs* to be taken over by the National Council of Labour Colleges, while Eden and Cedar Paul (and presumably Sara) argued against this.[80] The editor of *Plebs*, Frank Horrabin, was a friend of the Taylors and Sara.

His hardline sentiments in *Plebs* were followed by a pilgrimage to the promised land itself, Soviet Russia. Visiting Russia had confirmed Henry Sara in deciding to join the Communist Party of Great Britain in 1921, and in the summer of 1925 he escorted Connie and Alan Taylor to Leningrad, Moscow and Nizhny Novgorod (later Gorky). As Alan Taylor later commented, 'In 1925 Soviet Russia was in the halcyon days of NEP [New Economic Policy, a mixed economy] and almost a free country.' It was like Yugoslavia after the Second World War, 'Communists in power but not much of a Communist economic system.' They met Kirov, Kamenev and Litvinov, heard Zinoviev speak and saw the body of Lenin. Taylor felt Lenin looked attractive, with a 'reddish beard and a quizzical smile'. In his autobiography he delivered the judgement, 'I decided then that he was a really good man, an opinion I have not changed.'[81] Indeed, Alan Taylor's views of the Soviet Union long remained coloured by his visit during the relatively mild communism of the mid-1920s.

His uncle Harry Thompson provided him with an introduction to Douglas (GDH) and Margaret Cole. The Coles had moved to 8 Holywell in September 1925, after his appointment to the new Readership in Economics. As a rigid *Plebs* man, Alan Taylor took a critical view of the Coles' work for the Workers' Educational Association (WEA). Nevertheless, he was a frequent visitor to the Coles, where he met socially other Labour Club members, including Hugh Gaitskell, John Dugdale and John Parker, who all held office under Clement Attlee in the 1945–51 Labour governments.[82] He later recalled, 'Cole did not tell the young men what to think. For most of the time he sat silent, encouraging them to think for themselves.' In time Taylor came to admire Douglas Cole, giving the verdict in 1960 that he 'came as near to complete integrity as any man of his time'.[83]

During the General Strike of 1926 the Coles and the Labour Club co-ordinated support within Oxford University from the Coles' house. This University Strike Committee liaised between the Oxford Council of Action (based on the Oxford Trades and Labour Council) and the Trades Union Congress (TUC) and Labour Party in London, produced local strike bulletins and propaganda leaflets on equipment in the Coles' home and arranged for their distribution in the university and the villages around Oxford.[84] Taylor maintained his hardline Communist Party stance. In his autobiographical writings he claimed to have gone to the Communist Party headquarters at 16 King Street, London, before the General Strike began. This is unlikely, but not impossible given the Communist Party's predictions for some months that there would be a major industrial clash in May 1926. It is more likely that it was on the first day, 4 May. That was the day Jack Yates later recalled, as he accompanied Alan Taylor in his car from Oxford to the *Daily Herald* offices in London, where they met Tom Driberg. As the building was picketed, they could not remove copies for distribution. Instead, Taylor, Driberg and Yates drove to the King Street headquarters of the CPGB nearby, where Taylor and Driberg unsuccessfully sought instructions. He and Jack Yates drove back to Oxford.

Alan Taylor's recollections of his role at the start of the General Strike are particularly interesting, biographically, in two respects. When he drove Tom Driberg to King Street, he recalled, 'an elderly Scottish Communist called Bob Stewart appeared. He said, "There's no one here. I am only the caretaker. Get along home with ye."' This is curious, as Bob Stewart was caretaker secretary of the party. He may even have said only 'caretaker' to get rid of two unwanted Oxford undergraduates. However, it is surprising that Taylor, as the young enthusiast of the Left, either did not know or claimed later not to have known that Stewart was acting secretary of the party after twelve leaders had been gaoled in December 1925. Stewart replaced Albert Inkpin, who, with Harry Pollitt (who stayed at the Taylors' home in Preston) and three others, received twelve months in prison. Stewart may have seemed elderly to the young Taylor, but he was 49. It also had its amusing side, beyond the humour Alan Taylor saw in the situation. Jack Yates, in his recollections of the incident, recorded, 'I waited in the car wearing a rather good tweed cap and smoking a pipe with a silver band on, hoping I looked like a young squire.'[85] Little wonder, faced with the Rover car and the three Oxford undergraduates, Bob Stewart wanted quick riddance of them.

The second interesting feature of this episode is that Driberg persisted, while Taylor did not. In his autobiography Driberg also recalled Stewart as 'old' and 'a veteran of the party' (a reasonable description given Stewart's radical career, but of a party only five years old). However, he commented that after Stewart 'initially showed some scepticism' he 'eventually instructed me to collect a big bundle of workers' bulletins, meet another comrade at one of the northern stations – I think King's Cross – and set off by car to distribute the bulletins in various provincial cities'.[86] Quite clearly, Alan Taylor, who drove Driberg to King Street and had his car available, did not dally. Driberg had to rely on the other 'comrade' for motor transport. His active involvement on behalf of the Communist Party soon resulted in his being arrested and taken to Bow Street station. Perhaps the young Taylor was acute enough to realise that this was highly likely, and he took the first opportunity to distance himself from the likely political martyrdom to follow as an outcome of his Marxist bluster.

After his brief visit to King Street he left the Communist Party behind him, metaphorically as well as physically, even if he still held Marxist ideas. Back in Oxford he returned to Cole and the University Strike Committee. He did not warm to the suggestion he should campaign in the nearby villages.

On 6 May there was a public meeting in St Giles addressed by Frank Horrabin, the friend of the Taylor family, and his current partner, Ellen Wilkinson MP, as well as Douglas Cole. Before this time, or soon after, Alan Taylor departed for Preston, taking with him Norman Cameron and Innes Stewart. Taylor later recalled,

> I said to Norman, 'I am going to Preston' where my father was active in the labour movement and chairman of the strike committee – 'far better to be in an industrial town during a strike'. 'Think I'll come with you,' he said. So we piled into my car and off we went. My father was a bit taken aback by the two of us. My only qualification was the ability to drive a car, which was rather rare then. So for the whole of the strike, I drove a car taking strike leaders around to various meetings and so on. Norman was much more enterprising. He went down to the local Labour Party, met a jobbing printer named Cunningham, and the two of them brought out a strike sheet – Preston Strike News or something it was called.[87]

Innes Stewart stayed one night, attending an emotional public meeting, then, after incurring Norman Cameron's wrath for being patronising, went by train to Edinburgh.

This episode was symbolic, a political turn towards his father, not to his mother and Henry Sara. From his parents' comfortable home Alan Taylor happily drove his car, carrying out errands for the strike committee and proudly showing his TUC card to those manning road blocks in mining and other villages.[88] He firmly took a nonconforming position over the General Strike, but he did his bit at home, where he could help his father and the Preston labour movement and avoid the attentions of the 'hearties' in Oxford. He was not a martyr like I.G. Thomas or David Ayerest (whose failure to gain a permanent post at Oxford was allegedly due to his role in the General Strike in Oxford).

The General Strike had less impact on Percy Taylor's political views than those of his son. He wrote an orthodox Marxist analysis, 'The Plight of the Cotton Industry', for the December 1927 issue of *Plebs*. In it Percy Taylor condemned the conservatism of the cotton trade union leaders at home and deplored their failure to do 'anything to co-operate with their poorer fellow-workers in the colonial countries and to form with them a common united front'. He was notably critical of the Independent Labour

Party and its policy of calling for a government enquiry into the industry, asking: 'Do the ILP want Workers' Control, or are they anxious to teach the cotton masters their business?'[89] While Percy Taylor continued as before, his son soon shook off his links with the Communist Party of Great Britain but held views which were his own mix of socialism, owing much to the different emphases of his father and Sara.

After the General Strike was called off Alan Taylor returned to Oxford and resumed his place in the Labour Club, but now without divided loyalties. He attended a predominantly Labour Club dinner in New College for 'those of us who had served on the right side', and he noticed the new face of Hugh Gaitskell, who had helped. Taylor recalled fifty years later, 'My experiences in the General Strike cured me of communism...I decided that the Communist Party was not for me and quietly lapsed, thus escaping the soul torments that troubled so many intellectuals during the 1930s.'[90]

As he also later observed, 'I still regarded myself as a Marxist.' He appears to have been less rigid in his Marxism after 1926. He also became more critical of the Soviet Union. This criticism was initially of Stalin and Stalinism following the purge of Trotsky in November 1927. He later often commented that 'a party that expelled its greatest member was not for me'. Such sentiments enabled him to retreat without loss of face from his youthful posturing. Also in such concerns, he was in line with the thinking of Henry Sara. Sara was a great admirer of Trotsky, wearing from the early 1920s a badge with a photo of Trotsky on it, and emerged as a leading figure in a Left opposition group within the Communist Party of Great Britain, the Balham Group. In August 1932 two of the leaders, Reg Groves and Harry Wicks, were expelled from the party, as was Sara, after initially being suspended.[91]

Taylor and Driberg remained friends after the General Strike. Driberg worked in the university vacations for the *Sunday Worker*, edited by William Paul. This paper was committed to the National Left Wing Movement, which, among other things, campaigned to reverse the Labour Party's decision to exclude Communist Party members from its constituency parties. Through Driberg Taylor took on reviewing some publications about the General Strike for the *Sunday Worker*, but his review was not published. This was likely to have been because of his very critical view of the role of Communists in Preston and elsewhere in the General Strike. Tom Driberg was one of the friends he invited to his 21st birthday dinner party, which he held at the George Restaurant, the aesthete's haunt, at which Driberg made repeated attempts to seduce a waiter.[92]

In spite of his taste in later life to depict his time at Oxford as being (in current parlance) 'laid back' and near-effortless, Alan Taylor appears to have been diligent and, apart from his political views, conforming. He got on well with the Provost of Oriel, the Reverend Lancelot Phelps, who had developed himself into an Oxford 'character'. Phelps liked the young Taylor. He was one of several undergraduates Phelps invited to lunch and went with for walks. Phelps fascinated the more intellectual undergraduates with his talk of Matthew Arnold and Cardinal Newman. Taylor's moral tutor, Professor W.D. Ross, later Phelps' successor as Provost, was a more intellectual figure, before whom, in his first year, Taylor read essays. That year he won the college's essay prize. He later recalled, 'Ross, the philosopher, was in the curious position, that he had very high standards of Christian morality but a somewhat embarrassed approach towards Christianity because he was not at all deeply convinced about it.'

The Oriel of Taylor's undergraduate years still had some airs of the Victorian era. In 1985, talking with Brian Harrison, he reflected,

> Oxford now is a very different place from what it was when I went up. And it went on changing...I think the Second World War for different reasons changed things a great deal. More, for instance, mixing of men and women. But quite different standards; class distinctions were hard-hit by the Second World War. After all, it was more important to be a first-rate pilot than to be of high rank. Yes, I think Oxford was changed radically by the impact of the Second World War far more than the impact of the First.

He also felt that Oriel in 1924–27 still had a Christian and moral atmosphere. The Fellows, he believed, 'had no devotion to their work as tutors', unlike those of Balliol. In Oriel they merely 'covered the ground'. He said that, if they were interested in anything,

> it was much more *moral* discussions about their situation in Oxford, in the community. They gave an air...of deep thought...[about] what was the position of undergraduates in society...I was puzzled about this, because at the time I was an intense socialist, and I thought if you talked about duty to society, you did this in terms of socialism, not in terms of a rather abstract religion...[93]

Later, Taylor was disappointed that he was not taught more historical skills or historical understanding as an undergraduate. As Innes Stewart later commented, his was 'a profoundly discontented sort of ability'. In his autobiography Taylor complained that 'of the recent history to which I have devoted my life I learnt at Oxford precisely nothing'.[94] Yet it is difficult to believe he gained no benefit. Indeed, one recurring note in his memoirs is that no one inspired or assisted him in a major way, that he was his own self-made historian; he owed nothing, or at most very little, to anyone at Oxford or to A.F. Pribram in Vienna and was mixed as to the impact of Lewis Namier in Manchester on him. If so, at Oxford it was in part his own fault through going to few courses of lectures and making a point of reading mostly non-historical books. In this attitude he was buttressed not only by the attitude of many of his fellow students but also his own home-bred views. He later expressed this sentiment: 'Sustained by Marxist arrogance I ignored such ideas as Oxford had to offer.'[95]

Yet he did learn much about pre-1688 British and European history while at Oxford from Stanley Cohn and G.N. Clark. Cohn, who taught Taylor his special subject on Richard II, gave him a feel for medieval history. Though Cohn apparently came to dislike him and even tried to thwart his return to Oxford in the 1930s, Taylor nevertheless paid tribute to Cohn in his autobiography, observing that 'he had a brilliant mind and an enthusiasm for medieval history' and that 'he taught me a great deal'.[96] In conversation with Brian Harrison, Taylor commented, 'He represented the Balliol view that tutoring has to be very systematic and standards high, and the tutor shows an intense interest [in] the pupil he has.' Indeed, he recalled that Cohn felt he (Cohn) was a Balliol man in exile in Oriel;

> he was constantly quoting what would have been done in a particular situation if he had been at [Balliol]... He was quite young, he had Balliol arrogance... He was very unhappy at Oriel. He detested Ross and he did not get on with the others. He preferred hearties to intellectuals and found lots of hearties in Brasenose College...

In an early draft of his autobiography he also observed that Cohn 'was laboriously trying to turn himself into a character' and resented Provost Phelps for succeeding in becoming an Oxford character 'without effort'.

In contrast, Alan Taylor liked George Norman Clark, but claimed to have learnt little from him. Asked by Brian Harrison in 1985 why Clark had so little impact on him at Oriel, he replied, 'Well, because he greatly disliked tutoring: he found it very tedious, and complained every time I went to have a tutorial with him...how tedious and pointless it was, and not a right form of education.' He added that he 'didn't much like personal contacts...' and especially 'teaching men who got seconds and thirds, and he grumbled about this all the time...He didn't grumble at me, he just grumbled at the waste of time with others.'[97]

When G.N. Clark had sabbatical leave he was also taught by David Ayerest at Christ Church and Francis Urquart at Balliol College. David Ayerest, only two years older than Taylor, was then working on the history of the American revolution. Ayerest was chairman of the Oxford University Labour Club during the General Strike, and it was most probably his influence that moved W.H. Auden to drive a car in London for the TUC. Ayerest was impressed by Taylor as an undergraduate, writing to his mother that he was the only 'first-class man' that he taught but was 'a Communist who suffers from a slightly too rigid fanaticism'.[98]

He was given a very different perspective on nineteenth-century Europe by F.F. Urquart, the son of the pro-Turkish Radical MP David Urquart (later the joint subject of Taylor's second lecture in his Ford series 'The Trouble Makers'). 'Sligger' (apparently a corruption of 'sleek one') Urquart, later Dean of Balliol College, was a very influential European history tutor in his day. Lord Boothby, who was earlier taught by him, gave the explanation for this: 'He genuinely liked the young, he was the kindest man I have known, and he was always out to help.' Urquart liked to take some favoured students of promise to the Swiss Alps, for reading and alpine walking. Boothby later recollected of one such summer reading party that 'the company was excellent, the atmosphere as exalted as the altitude and the fare somewhat too frugal for me'.[99] While Taylor did not warm to him as many others did, he wrote to Bob Cole in 1969, 'The only tutor from whom I benefited was F.F. Urquart of Balliol…' He went with Henry Phelps Brown as a pair to Sligger for two terms when G.N. Clark was on sabbatical leave. Taylor's later recollections were that Sligger

> knew a great deal, he had a lot of experience; he was ready to formulate advanced Conservative views. He held that the Italians would have been better off and would have been governed better if they'd continued under the prestige of the Pope…Sligger was now rather elderly, and I don't think he'd been ever interested in the techniques of history. What he liked was the wide approach.[100]

Urquart stimulated his interest in European history, much as Namier later was to do. Taylor may well have sought to emulate him in one respect. In the summer of 1939 he invited a bright and likeable undergraduate, Robert Kee, to join him and his family in their chalet for alpine walking.

Although he later claimed he avoided nearly all lectures, Taylor did attend lectures on European history by the Rev. J.M. Thompson at Magdalen College. Thompson gave a series of 22 lectures on European history from 1494 to 1789 to first-year students. These lectures were often focused on the big figures of the time and began with attention-grabbing anecdotes. For instance, the beginning of the lecture on Richelieu began:

> The dagger which killed the best of French kings brought the son of his old age, an infant of eight, to the throne…While the young Gustavus was learning languages, and the art of government, Louis XIII spent his youth hawking, cock-fighting and playing cards. He was soon tired of his tutor and said, 'If I give you a bishopric, will you shorten my lessons?'[101]

Taylor benefited from these lectures, both their content and style, when he gave a course of lectures as a new lecturer at Manchester University in 1930.

While Taylor was sustained at Oxford by his coterie of friends, he did mix with older university people. As well as Provost Phelps and G.D.H. Cole, he saw much of G.N. Clark, also a former Bootham pupil. He recalled that 'we became close friends and I was often at his house'.[102] Though Alan Taylor set little value on his Oxford education at the time, he quickly came to value this scholarly world where he was taken seriously. Certainly, he was eager to return in less than a year of leaving – and, again, in 1931, within a year of teaching at another university. Yet, while an undergraduate, the ideas and expectations of his home life still had a strong hold over him, and continued to do so for a further few years.

– 3 –

BREAKING
FREE

Until his marriage in the summer of 1931 Alan Taylor remained
very much entwined in the close-knit world of his family.
It was the major intellectual and emotional backdrop to his
life, even when he was away in Vienna; as it had been at The Downs,
Bootham and Oxford. However, in the years after graduating at Oxford
he was becoming restless with the quirks of both parents, and began to
go his own way. Marriage marked one turning point, his opposition to
appeasement, which required a major intellectual reappraisal on his part,
another.

He had gone to Oxford highly suspicious of its education, himself
filled with Plebs League attitudes. His intention, in line with his mother's
wishes, was to get through university and then to train as a barrister, with
the aim later of dealing with Labour movement cases, many of which
would be brought to him by his uncle Harry Thompson. Hence, he put
down his name at the Inner Temple, and for two years as an undergraduate
travelled to London to eat dinners there, as required. Before his final year
as an Oxford undergraduate this plan was altered to him training as a
solicitor in his uncle's practice, with the prospect of him becoming a
partner when he had qualified. After a leisurely summer in Preston, driving
his car, swimming in the municipal pool and reading, he began as an
articled clerk in London in October 1927.

In this venture, as in all others, Percy and Connie Taylor provided
lavishly for his comfort. He was established in 'an expensive six-room flat
on the edge of Hampstead Heath', with a housekeeper. This also served as
a London base for his mother, who, to his irritation, stayed a month with
him that autumn. He later commented, 'I did not like her company. We
had no common interests and she was obviously only waiting for Henry
Sara's appearance.' Sara, who at this time described himself as a 'lantern

lecturer and propagandist', was living at 15 Briston Grove, Crouch Hill, fairly near Hampstead.[1]

Harry Thompson had set up in London on his own account after the First World War, initially in partnership with James Scott Duckers. He had met Duckers when they had both been in gaol as conscientious objectors. However, he and Duckers differed increasingly on politics. Duckers was a Liberal, who after the war was Asquithian. He went on to be Liberal candidate in one of the most famous inter-war by-elections, the Westminster, Abbey by-election of March 1924. In this the local Liberals effectively ran him as a candidate to spoil Winston Churchill's chances of returning to Parliament (and to the Conservatives) as an Independent. Churchill lost by 43 votes, while Duckers polled 291 votes. Duckers received little or no support from the Liberal leadership, Asquith being ill and Lloyd George, after the result, complaining that Duckers was 'just the type of candidate who tars Liberalism with the Little England brush'. Duckers had also a different, more old-fashioned style about him. He kept in his office a gardenia. Alan Taylor later recalled, 'They were totally incompatible. I can remember Harry complaining of Scott Duckers always having a top hat in the office.'[2]

In contrast, Thompson's political trajectory was to the Left, especially so in the three or four years after the end of the First World War. He was a member of the Central London branch of the Independent Labour Party, one of the branches which seceded to join the Communist Party of Great Britain on its formation in early 1921. He stayed in the CPGB for up to two years. Thereafter, he remained a man of the Left. He delighted in shocking neighbours in Welwyn Garden City in the late 1920s by putting out a red flag on May Day. In August 1921 he had married a very radical woman, Joan Beauchamp, then 31, a former student of Royal Holloway College, London University. Margaret Cole described her as 'a militant left-wing suffragette'. She was also notable as a leading figure in the No-Conscription Fellowship, beginning as an assistant in the political department and going on to edit and publish *The Tribunal* (from 25 October 1917 until 10 April 1919). She was repeatedly prosecuted by the police. With Lydia Smith, she succeeded in continuing to print the paper for twelve months in spite of Scotland Yard attempts to locate the press and close it down. Eventually, in early 1920, she spent eight days in prison. After the No-Conscription Fellowship was wound up she served on the Committee to Oppose Military Training in Schools, very much a cause dear to the heart of her sister-in-law, Connie Taylor. She was a founder member of the British Communist Party and worked for *Labour Research*. She wrote the books *Poems of Revolt* (1924), *Agriculture in Soviet Russia* (1931), *British Imperialism in India* (1935) and *Women Who Work* (1937).[3]

Not long after his marriage, Harry Thompson separated from Duckers, setting up his own independent practice. Many of the staff as well as clients chose to go with him. Thompson built up his practice quickly, specialising in defending trade unionists and left-wing political activists and handling many workmen's compensation cases. In 1921 he took on a very high-profile task, representing George Lansbury and the other Poplar Guardians during the legal actions following their refusal to levy high poor rates in their impoverished area. Thompson acquitted himself well in what proved to be a lengthy struggle, involving a spell in gaol for 30 councillors. Four years later he was involved in another major political legal case. He acted for the Communist Party leaders when twelve of them were arrested in October 1925 for publishing seditious libels and inciting people to commit breaches of the Incitement to Mutiny Act, 1797, and much suspected subversive material (including a strange metal sphere, a lavatory ballcock) was seized at their party's headquarters in King Street, Covent Garden.[4]

By the time Taylor joined his uncle's practice it was well established and thriving. Harry Thompson was ably assisted by Mr Cornish, his managing clerk, and two young women, Miss Crisply and Miss Mowbray (later Mrs Cornish). He also employed another qualified solicitor. Shortly before Taylor arrived this had been Mr Winter, a chess champion, but he had left and been replaced by Peter Stone, who later became music critic of the *Jewish Chronicle*. Alan Taylor did not fit in. He arrived dissatisfied, convinced his uncle was out to trick him. He rejected his uncle's first version of a partnership deed, having got his father, Percy Taylor, to take legal advice as to whether it would bind him for twenty years in the way Percy had been bound to his father's business. He disliked the work from day one. Harry's son Robin observed seventy years later of the work, 'At that time it would be far more routine than now.' He made clear his preference to be judged an Oxford 'reading man' by reading in the office whenever an opportunity arose. There he read, among other books, a set of Charles Dickens he had bought with £10 he was awarded by Oriel for gaining a First.[5]

Alan Taylor did not get on well with his uncle. They were both used to being the centre of attention, and had been spoilt by their parents. They were also both used to getting their way. Thompson, unlike his nephew, was tall and athletic, and had a strong sense of humour. This humour he liked to exercise on his nephew, who did not care to be the butt of his jokes. His son later commented, 'My father was outstanding at putting anyone down and had an extremely strong personality. I would not think anyone got the better of him. I am sure it would not suit Alan to be dominated by such a personality.' Taylor did not care for either the work or for playing second fiddle to his uncle.[6]

However, his uncle did provide him with many valuable left-wing contacts. Some were made in the 1917 Club, of which his uncle and aunt were members. Alan Taylor in his autobiography wrongly commented that it 'had been started by pro-Bolshevik Leftwingers'. In fact its name related to the February, anti-Tsar Russian Revolution, and its membership included radical Liberals. Its zenith was in 1924. One member later wrote that 'after 1924 the general atmosphere was one of benevolent bohemianism'. Taylor's best friend at Oxford, J.I.M. Stewart, gained his first job through Taylor's acquaintanceship with Francis and Vera Meynell of the Nonsuch Press. This contact stemmed from Harry Thompson and quite possibly from the 1917 Club. Francis Meynell was an active member of the club, a former conscientious objector and assistant editor of the *Herald*, then of the *Daily Herald*.[7]

Alan Taylor himself benefited from his contact with Tom Wintringham, whom his uncle Harry had represented in the 1925 Communist Party leaders trial. Wintringham, remembered as 'a supremely modest person', had then been assistant editor of the *Workers' Weekly* and was later to be an early commander of the British Battalion of the International Brigade in Spain.[8] He took pity on Taylor, who complained that the 1917 Club was full of older people, and put him in touch with the local Young Communists. As a result, Taylor briefly went out with a girl possibly called Dora, his first girlfriend, when he was 21 rising 22. Although often brash on the subject of women to his male friends, his practice was more timid. He was characteristically reticent with Dora, recalling she gave him his first kiss and also 'taught me something of how to treat a woman but not much'. A later letter to his friend Charles Gott suggests that there may have been more to this relationship or that there was another. In early July 1928 Alan Taylor wrote of going to Essex to see a girlfriend, a relationship which was not sexual and in which neither expected it to lead to marriage. In the same letter he wrote of a wealthy, charitable couple, named Brown, who helped 'lame ducks (like my woman). He has adopted her child.'[9] In his autobiography Alan Taylor comments that his mother learnt of his friendship with Dora and feared for him 'as the prey of a harpy and was desperate to get me away from London'. If Dora had had an illegitimate child during an earlier relationship, Connie Taylor might well have feared for her inexperienced son. However, with Taylor and his friends then there was much in-joking and indulging in whimsy, so it is difficult to judge what, if anything, this relationship with the woman in Essex amounted to. Yet, if his mother did intervene, then this would help explain why later he married without informing his parents.

Otherwise, Alan Taylor's London social life depended on weekend visits from his Oxford friends, Innes Stewart and Theodore Yates. This included a Monday off, 16 January 1928, when he and Innes went to Thomas Hardy's funeral in Westminster Abbey.[10]

Before Easter 1928 Taylor broke his articles and left London. His father had never been keen for him to be bound to his uncle Harry. His mother grasped that he did not fit in to the practice and, perhaps, as he later claimed, she did not care for him to be going out with a local girl. He himself was keen to return to Oxford, having lost his earlier disdain for the place. The appeal of a return was enhanced as his best friend was still an undergraduate there. As usual, he had his way, with his parents paying.

Shortly before leaving London he made another move which was not linked to the socialist-communist-conscientious objector nexus of his family. He went to see Gerald Barry, the young editor of the *Saturday Review*, a periodical which he aspired to make 'an organ of the most persuasive kind of Conservatism'. For Barry, Taylor built on his reading of books by and about Charles Dickens by writing a review of a new edition of John Forster's classic, *The Life of Dickens* (originally three volumes, 1872 and 1874). This review was confident and opinionated. The young literary critic judged that while Forster's was 'an extraordinarily interesting biography' it was not as great a work as Boswell's great work on Samuel Johnson. 'Boswell shows us a grown man; the picture of Dickens is always (and quite truthfully) that of a precocious child.' He exhibited his own precocity in arguing that before the Idea of Progress men, 'full of the classical tradition, were perpetually chastened by the knowledge that there had been better men than they were', whereas the Victorians 'believed that, automatically, they were better than their fathers'.[11]

Perhaps even before returning to lodgings in Oxford, Taylor busied himself working on a prize essay. The topic for the Gladstone Prize Essay was the foreign policy of the British Parliamentary Radicals in the 1830s and 1840s. He failed to win, but he did return to the topic twenty-eight years later in his Ford Lectures. However, more important for his future career was the advice he received from G.N. Clark when he did return to Oxford. This was that if he wished to become a historian he should learn German. German history was then clearly a major area where there were relatively few qualified people available for academic posts. Clark also offered to write him an introduction to a German historian based in Heidelberg. Taylor was not attracted to this scholar's specialism, British constitutional history. Instead he wrote to Werner Sombart in Berlin, but received no reply.[12] This initiative suggests that he took Clark's suggestion very seriously and took some care to review possible German historians to approach. In Sombart he selected one who bestraddled history and sociology. His *Der Moderne Kapitalismus*, first published in 1902, was issued in a final new edition in 1928. Although Sombart was not of the Left, far from it, the topic of his famous book was very much in line with the young Alan Taylor's *Plebs*-style interests. Sombart was also famous for his *Sozialismus und Soziale Bewegung im 19. Jahrhundert*, 1897 (translated with the title *Socialism and the Social Movement*, 1898) and *Warum gibt es in den Vereinigten Staaten keinen Sozialismus?*, 1906 (translated seventy years later as *Why is There No Socialism in the United States?*) It would have been very interesting if he had been supervised by Sombart on one of these areas. Taylor's actions in seeking a supervisor also undermine his later preferred self-image, of one who languidly drifted rather than one who was eagerly proactive in determining his future.

Nor does it fit with his image of being a dilettante that he secured the advice that in due course determined his career from the Regius Professor of History. He would have needed to seek an interview with Professor H.W.C. Davis, doing so quite probably through G.N. Clark. In his autobiography Taylor protested too much his ignorance: 'I have not the slightest idea who was Regius Professor of History at Oxford when I was an undergraduate. Was it still Sir Charles Firth? Or had Fluffy Davis already succeeded him?' This was part of his later belittlement of Oxford chairs. Davis, Regius Professor 1925–28, in succession to Sir Charles Firth, was a Fellow of Oriel. Alan Taylor's best friend Innes Stewart even includes an anecdote in his autobiography of meeting in college the unassuming, reserved and modest Davis, so it is highly unlikely Taylor did not know of him. The relevance of Davis for Taylor in the early summer of 1928 was that he was knowledgeable about continental Europe and had many good academic contacts. After the First World War Davis had served on the British delegation to the Paris Peace Conference and then at the Department of Overseas Trade. He had also written *The Political Thought of Heinrich von Treitschke* (1914). Davis warmly recommended Professor Alfred Pribram, then aged 69, in Vienna, and suggested a topic on eighteenth-century British diplomacy. Taylor immediately took up his suggestion, arranging an almost immediate meeting in late May in Vienna.[13] All this was possibly within a month of his return to Oxford.

Alan Taylor clearly had his father's backing to go quickly to see Professor Pribram in Vienna. His travel arrangements were of an order unknown to nearly all modern postgraduate students. He left immediately by sleeper and on arrival stayed at the Bristol Hotel, which he deemed to be 'the most luxurious in the city'. He liked the elderly, scholarly Pribram, who was happy that he should initially study a topic following on from his recent prize essay research. This was to be the relationship between the British Parliamentary Radicals and the Viennese Radicals before the 1848 revolutions. Pribram himself was then working on the 'hot topic' of the time, the origins of the First World War. Taylor returned to Oxford, where, in June 1928, he indulged in 'a period of total idleness' – which, no doubt, he felt was his due having exerted himself to set off on a new career, linked to History. It was one of his last opportunities to play the leisured aesthete. Though he liked to present his move to Vienna as a casual matter, it was a career move, even if the outcome was not – and could not – be firmly defined at the outset.[14]

Another agreeable outcome of his change of proposed career was that he had another long summer to enjoy. He spent the first part of it holidaying with his parents. By this time, like many 22-year-olds, he was chafing at their company. In his case his comments on his mother were venomous. At the start of July Percy, Connie and Alan went on a motoring holiday in the West Country, ending with stays in Bude, Princetown and Salisbury. From Dartmoor he wrote to Charles Gott,

> There can be little boyish fun with this bitch about, who is now more than usually intolerable in bad weather. You cannot imagine how loathsome. Bude was rows of lodging houses, inhabited by broken down missionaries on leave, and nothing at all to do. My mother went into tantrums because it rained and my father just couldn't think what to do with her. Yesterday we motored here and she is a little better.

After that the Taylors as usual set up house in the Lake District. In 1928 they stayed at Buttermere, with Henry Sara and others as visitors.[15]

Later in the summer Alan Taylor holidayed with his two best friends, Innes Stewart and George Clazy. Stewart had graduated with First-Class Honours. In his memoirs he commented that they 'decided it would be perfectly reasonable to top off a university education with a kind of Grand Tour, and we set off for Germany and Austria accordingly'. Quite probably Percy Taylor paid much of the three's costs. They travelled to Vienna via Berlin, Dresden and Prague. Taylor disliked both Berlin and, on that visit, Prague. Part of the appeal of Dresden was visiting an attractive young Swiss woman, Charlotte, married to a German actor, whom he had liked when she was working as a governess for John and Sarah Thompson, his uncle and aunt.[16]

He was as comfortably provided for in Vienna by his parents as he had been in Hampstead in 1927–28. His stay was helped by very favourable exchange rates for the pound sterling. He lived the life of the gentleman scholar. He even recreated for part of his stay a small circle of friends, such as he had enjoyed while an Oxford undergraduate. Innes Stewart stayed for six or seven months, while Charles Gott joined him for the first half of 1929. In addition two Bootham friends stayed, George Clazy, briefly in October 1928, and Geoffrey Rowntree, also for the first six months of 1929. In addition, there were other 'like-minded youths coming and going', as

Innes Stewart later recalled. Among these was a wealthy American, Teddy Pratt, who was learning German and researching Metternich's Spanish policy. Taylor enjoyed a long friendship with Pratt and his partner Paul von Saffin.

Alan Taylor and his friends made the most of Viennese music. They arrived during the Franz Schubert (1797–1828) centenary celebrations and went to many of the remaining concerts. He, thereafter, rarely missed a chamber concert, went regularly to the opera and in his second year bought a season ticket for the Vienna Philharmonic Orchestra. Taylor and Stewart also learnt to ride well, the former much enjoying horse jumping. They both also learnt to skate, their first lodgings being behind Vienna's Concert House and close by the open-air skating rink. Stewart later wrote of his time in Vienna that, while he had acquired skills on horseback and on skates there, 'Alan, somewhat contrastingly, had mastered Austrian diplomatic history from Metternich onwards'.[17]

Taylor had not gone to Vienna to study diplomatic history, the area in which he was to gain international renown. He had gone, as he put it later to Éva Haraszti, with the 'idea…to study the relationship between English and Austrian radicals', especially 'the influence which the Anti-Corn Law League had'.[18] He soon found that this was not going to work out, presumably because of a relatively small relationship between English radicals and those of Austria and even smaller available archival material. Whatever the reason, Pribram steered him towards the broader theme of Anglo-Austrian relations, on which there was ample material in the Chancellery, the state archive. As, no doubt Pribram intended, Alan Taylor found a more narrowly defined topic as he worked in the state archives. This was to study an aspect of international relations affecting Austria in 1848, the problem of northern Italy (then still under the control of the Habsburg monarchy).

He had gone to Vienna as much as anything to equip himself to learn German while he continued to study history. He taught himself calligraphy, to write in the older-style German script (German Schrift) in order to be able to read it in archives. He also learnt German, partly by reading history written in German with the aid of a dictionary and partly through paying a local schoolteacher of English to give him individual tuition to improve his German. To improve his spoken German the teacher introduced him to one of her former pupils who was keen to improve her spoken English, Else Sieberg, then nineteen. This provided him with the opportunity of a series of 'dates' with an attractive young woman.

The friendship with Else Sieberg helped him, when 22 to 23, to begin to move away from rather immature 'laddish' approaches to women. There was much posing as young bucks around the town by his circle of friends, especially in their letters to each other. The visit by Charlotte Brun in Dresden had been followed by much giggling over Innes Stewart or George Clazy suggesting that her wooden darning mushroom was her contraceptive. There was persistent denigration of women as 'bitches', and an underlying assumption that they were stupid, sexual playthings for men and interested only in becoming wives. Even of Else Sieberg, an English correspondent in an exporting firm, he 'assumed that she was feather-brained like most Viennese girls' (or so he wrote in his autobiography). How he arrived at this judgement of 'most Viennese girls', when he and his friends were notably unable to enter relationships with them, is a moot point. In his autobiography he added, for good measure, 'I think she would have made me a good wife but she might have been homesick for Vienna.'[19] In some respects, Alan Taylor's relationships with women only reached maturity after he married for the third time.

His first 'serious' girlfriend was Margaret Adams, who was in Vienna studying German and taking piano lessons. Teddy Pratt introduced him to her. She was from a well-to-do Catholic English family based in India. After early years in India she had been sent to England for a convent education. She had rebelled against Catholicism and had radical views. Yet she still had some of the attitudes and assumptions of the expatriate upper middle class accustomed to having servants in India. In Alan Taylor she found a well-heeled rebel who, like her, was keen on music, widely read, and sexually inexperienced. From early on Taylor took a serious view of their relationship. He later recalled, 'I worried about the future, doubtful whether her religious or family background would consort with mine.'[20] In Vienna, they ceased being lonely and fell in love. In spite of serious ruptures in their relationship later, there remained a bond of understanding and sympathy between them for nearly all the rest of their lives.

Although acting the part of the gentleman scholar in Vienna, Taylor did put in many hours of work in the archives. He complained later,

> I had never seen a diplomatic document before and simply plunged in at the deep end without any instruction. I did not know the difference between an official dispatch and a private letter. I had no idea how to weigh the reliability of historical evidence. I did not even know that I must note the number of each document, an ignorance which caused me much unnecessary labour. Nowadays graduate students are taught these things in their first seminars. I operated as though no one had worked in diplomatic archive before.[21]

In this he makes good points but overstates his exceptionalism. There were relatively few doctoral students then, and such archival training was not a norm until at least the 1970s. However, British History degree courses (including Alan Taylor's) did have special subjects in which documents were assessed as to what they could reveal and for reliability. Many postgraduates, at least before the 1970s, acquired good archival practices (such as careful recording of classifications of documents) from studying citations in earlier books and theses in their area of research (or even by common sense).

Taylor later understated Alfred Pribram's assistance to him. In his autobiography he firmly stated at the start of a paragraph, 'Pribram never gave me any guidance after his initial suggestion [to study Anglo-Austrian relations] and it is quite wrong to suppose that I was influenced by his method or historical outlook.' He almost gave the impression that he and Pribram had barely met. Yet when *The Italian Problem in European Diplomacy 1847–1849* (Manchester University Press, 1934) was published his Foreword included, 'From Professor Pribram I first learnt what diplomatic history could be and he taught me the elements of scientific detail.' Moreover, he later wrote of university lectures, 'I had heard of none I admired except Pribram's and these seemed beyond my range,'[22] and he also stated that he had followed Pribram in lecturing without notes. Pribram, the Austrian representative of the Rockefeller Foundation for research fellowships, put him in the direction of securing a fellowship. Above all, it was directly through Pribram that he secured his first academic post at Manchester University. Pribram also invited him to his home occasionally for social gatherings. So Pribram's impact on Alan Taylor as his supervisor was far from insubstantial.

Until at least the early 1950s Taylor readily acknowledged Pribram's influence. Keith Kyle, who studied under Taylor in 1943 and 1947–50, later recalled that he 'was lavish in his expressions of admiration for the work of Alfred Pribram and Lewis Namier', as well as that of Louis Eisenmann.[23] Kyle was then studying the Habsburg monarchy in the context of international relations and he 'was one of those invited from time to time to his house outside of tuition periods' to discuss questions raised in Taylor's Habsburg book.[24]

Not surprisingly, in the late 1930s and 1940s Taylor was seen as a product of Austrian historical scholarship. For instance, when his *The Course of German History* was published in 1945, Sigmund Neumann wrote in a review in the *American Historical Review* that the book was 'a challenging essay, packed with substantial summaries and spiced with brilliant observations, reflecting his scholarly maturity, his lucid mind and his Vienna training under Pribram and the Austrian school of Friedjung and Redlich'.[25]

Pribram reviewed the 1941 version of *The Habsburg Monarchy*. After praising it as 'a clear and concise account', Pribram observed,

Little attention is devoted to foreign policy, and this seems to me a defect of the book. The connection between external and domestic policy is close in all states, but nowhere closer than in the Danubian Monarchy. It can be shown that all important events in its domestic policy from the Vienna Congress till the collapse of the Empire were determined by successes or failures of foreign policy.[26]

This was advice that Alan Taylor took. His rethinking of the subject was aided by discussions of foreign policy issues with his students. In the second edition he wrote of one of two major changes:

it treats Austrian foreign policy with greater detail and relevance. The Habsburg Monarchy, more than most great powers, was an organisation for conducting foreign policy; and its fate was determined quite as much by foreign affairs as by the behaviour of its peoples. The creation of the Austrian Empire was dictated by Napoleon; the establishment of Austria-Hungary by Bismarck; and the Monarchy fell at the end of a great war, which it had helped to bring about. My attempt to write the history of the Habsburg Monarchy without discussing Habsburg foreign policy made much of the original book puzzling; and I hope I have now remedied this defect.[27]

Hence, the early influence of Alfred Pribram is clear.

After Pribram's death, Taylor was cool when reviewing his posthumous work, *Austria-Hungary and Great Britain, 1908–1914* (1951). He welcomed such a new assessment by a distinguished scholar but wrote that it was 'of an almost forbidding dryness'.

His narrative is diplomatic history pure and simple, with no flavour of human interest. It is based almost entirely on the British and Austro-Hungarian documents which were published in the inter-war years, and those who have studied these collections will find here simply an abstract of them. Moreover, the three crises with which it principally deals – the Bosnian affair, the Balkan wars and the outbreak of the world war – have all been themselves the subject of detailed and repeated study.[28]

Taylor was to provide more than a flicker of human interest in his first book, *The Italian Problem in European Diplomacy 1847–1849* (1934). His research in Vienna in 1928–30 provided the kernel of the book. He quoted or cited some 260 documents from the state archives. However, the book depended on further archival work carried out later in Paris and London.

He took an important step towards becoming a professional historian when he went in 1929 to be interviewed for a Rockefeller research fellowship. In those more relaxed times about the conduct of interviews, the interview took place at J.R.M. Butler's club, the United University in London. To secure the fellowship, which was in the social sciences, Taylor needed to make his diplomatic research appear appropriate, so he played up the aspect of British public opinion towards Italy. Perhaps he did not need to try hard, given that Butler's major work was *The Passing of the Great Reform Bill* (1914), itself not notably social science in approach.[29] The award of the Rockefeller research fellowship encouraged him to make greater research efforts in the Austrian archives in 1929–30.[30]

Alan Taylor's first academic job came through A.F. Pribram's strong endorsement of him to Professor E.F. Jacob of Manchester University in spring 1930.[31] Jacob, then 35, was in his first year as Professor of Medieval History at Manchester and was faced with a great need for a Modern History teacher by that autumn. John Neale had resigned from the Chair of Modern History in 1927 and not been replaced, and a young lecturer was leaving in the summer of 1930.[32] Jacob, who was a graduate of Oxford and who had taught at Oxford from 1924 to 1929, was quickly impressed by Taylor's Oxford First-Class Honours and Pribram's advocacy, and invited him to Manchester University to interview him, presumably in a shortlist of one, for the post of assistant lecturer from September 1930. Alan Taylor checked that his other job preference, working for the Inspectorate of Ancient Monuments, was not then available before going to Manchester.

In his account of all this, he protested far too much. He wrote, 'I had hardly heard of Manchester University.' Given his family's connections with Manchester, this would appear disingenuous. The subsequent sentence – 'Certainly it had never occurred to me to go there' – is more to the point. Taylor was still smitten by Oxford chic, and, to use a later generation's terminology, it was not 'Oxford cool' to go to teach in Manchester. He also wrote later that he wished to research in the Paris archives, and so 'I thought I would at any rate go for an interview to Manchester which would conveniently pay my fare from Vienna and back to Paris'. This is curious, given that when he reached Paris he again studied in style, booking into the convenient and highly attractive Hôtel du Quai Voltaire 'solely for the reason that Oscar Wilde used to stay there'.[33] Again, it was not a style of living experienced by many history postgraduates and not suggestive of his need to go to Manchester to get his travel from Vienna to Paris paid for.

Taylor wanted to be in England that spring to be with Margaret Adams, who had left Vienna. She was 25, he was just 24 and they were eager to spend a romantic five days driving in the Thames valley, in a car borrowed from Charles Gott. They consummated their relationship, both shedding at last their virginity. His later talk of experiences with a prostitute seems highly improbable and contradictory to his other recollections. The Manchester interview gave him a good reason to be in England then and, quite possibly, the Manchester post was reluctantly welcome as it removed the uncertainty which inevitably besets anyone on one-year funding and coming to the end of a task.

He worked hard in the Quai d'Orsay's archives in Paris in the early summer of 1930. From that research period and later briefer returns he explored the French part in the Italian disagreements of 1848–49.[34] That the archives were only open in afternoons gave him scope in mornings in the Bois de Boulogne to build on his horse-riding skills acquired in Vienna. He continued to act the gentleman scholar, enjoying his relatively expensive form of exercise as well as Parisian food and evening entertainment. He spent evenings with another English historian, Noel Fieldhouse. Fieldhouse remained a friend and contributed an essay on the radical journalist Noel Buxton to the *Festschrift* which marked Alan Taylor's sixtieth birthday.[35]

After the summer closure of the French archives from Bastille Day, 14 July, Taylor returned home to Preston. After the nearly two years away in Vienna and Paris, he had literally and metaphorically distanced himself from his parents' unusual left-wing world. When he had arrived in Vienna, he had with him a letter of introduction from the British Prime Minister, James Ramsay MacDonald, to Otto Bauer, leader of the Social Democratic Party. This had been secured for him by his uncle Harry Thompson.[36] He duly saw Bauer, but otherwise took no interest in socialist politics in 'Red Vienna'.

He had left home in 1928 unsure of where his future lay, even if clear that it did not lie working in his uncle's legal practice. In going to study in the Austrian archives it would have been clear from the outset that it could lead to an academic career. His lingering hopes of an attractive post in the Ministry of Works looking after historic buildings had ended in the early summer of 1930, when he had been told that there would be no vacancies in the near future. So, when he returned home in July 1930 he had settled his future career, at least in the short term, by his acceptance of the post at Manchester University from that October.

In the period away he had also transformed himself into not only a diplomatic historian but also a specialist in the history of central Europe. While he continued in his chosen role of Oxford gentleman scholar, he combined as always his ample and well-funded leisure pursuits with hard work. He assiduously learnt German, paying for individual lessons, practising the spoken language wherever he could (including with the grooms at the riding stables), and, through Alfred Pribram's good offices, improving his understanding of written German by working with a professional translator, Ian Morrow.

Ian Morrow was a colourful figure, who was 33 in 1929. He had moved
to Vienna from London in 1928, after ill-health while translating Rudolf
Binding's *Aus dem Kriege*, which was published as *A Fatalist At War* (1929).
In Vienna he made the acquaintanceship of A.F. Pribram and translated
(with some assistance from Alan Taylor) Glaise von Horstenau, *The Collapse
of the Austro-Hungarian Empire* (1930). He later reviewed Taylor's *Germany's
First Bid for Colonies* in the *Times Literary Supplement* and translated Pribram's
Austria-Hungary and Great Britain, 1909–1914 (1951). Morrow was also
fluent in French. Taylor last saw him in Paris in the summer of 1930, when
Morrow asked him to be a second in a duel; but Morrow returned to
England before the appointed time.[37]

This Viennese period was highly important to Taylor's subsequent
outlook as a historian. He learnt German, he later recalled, 'with a slight
Austrian accent'. However, he added, 'Now I have entirely lost my good
German and can speak only Viennese.'[38] Working on the Habsburg
monarchy's archives, he had also become accustomed to looking at the
German past from an Austrian perspective. This had been reinforced
by reading and being influenced by major Austrian scholars, including
Heinrich Friedjung and Arthur Redlich. This Austrian perspective affected
his major historical works from *The Habsburg Monarchy* (1941) and *The
Course of German History* (1945) through to *The Origins of the Second World
War* (1961).

He also left Vienna with a lifelong interest in and attachment to
central and eastern Europe. On the way to Vienna he had visited Berlin,
Dresden and Prague. From Vienna he went to Budapest, Bratislava and
Split. To this list can be added a romantic trip that he made with Margaret
Adams in 1930 to Melk Abbey, by the Danube. This was not extensive
touring, but in British universities in the 1930s it was sufficient to reinforce
his credentials as a central European historian.

He had visited his parents during his period in Vienna. He had
returned home for Christmas 1928 and had spent much of the summer of
1929 with them. That summer they had gone on holiday together, with
Henry Sara, to Malvern for the George Bernard Shaw festival. There he
had been delighted to see Shaw with T.E. Lawrence. In 1929–30 he did
not break away from the politics of his parents; he simply gave politics a
rest, and other matters occupied his time.

Away from home he had indulged in much music. Before going to
central Europe he had never been to the opera. He went for the first time
in Dresden in 1928. In Vienna he was already spending much money on
attending concerts before he met Margaret Adams. Music was a passion
they held in common and was to be a major strand in their life together in
Manchester, Oxford and London.

The most obvious omission from accounts by him of his return to Preston is Margaret Adams. Her mother and stepfather spent much of their time in India, and at times so did she. Nonetheless, he did meet them and a wealthy aunt in London, and was impressed by their upper-middle-class wealth and style. He could have brought Margaret home to meet his parents in 1930. Perhaps he feared her response to the unusual relationship of his parents with Henry Sara, or to the argumentative and highly radical political conversations of the household. It is also highly likely that he was happy to pigeon-hole her in another part of his life and to avoid any personal inconvenience arising from his parents and Margaret meeting, at least while she was a girlfriend, not a fiancée. When Margaret did return from India in late 1930 he did not take her home, but they spent time together in Manchester, including going to a Hallé concert.

He spent much of later July, August and September 1930 preparing lectures on European history from 1494 to 1914 for Manchester University. He had studied the period 1494–1878 at school and at Oxford. For the later period he turned to the works of historians such as G.P. Gooch and Sidney Fay and anti-war Liberals such as Bertrand Russell, H.N. Brailsford and Lowes Dickinson. He later wrote that he 'prepared for my future students a Union of Democratic Control version of events in which the Great War was all the fault of the Entente Powers'.

He was not slow in agreeing to speak on history locally. He was a great supporter of the Historical Association, founded in 1906, which acted as the voice for History and which linked academic historians, teachers and those generally interested in the subject. His first lecture to a branch of the Historical Association was in December 1930. That he was the third speaker in a monthly programme running from that October suggests he must have been asked within two months of his return from Paris. Quite possibly the invitation to speak arose from some contact of his father, a town councillor. The Lancashire (Central and North) branch report lists 'December, "Metternich as an Austrian and European Statesman", by Mr A.J.P. Taylor'.[39] The meeting was held in Winckley Square, Preston. It is notable that in his first public lecture he adopted what was to become the highly distinctive set of initials of 'Mr A.J.P. Taylor', the 'A.J.P.' still being widely recognised well over a decade after his death. In 2003, when W.L. Webb was reflecting on the award of the first Booker Prize for literature in 1969, he wrote that they chose 'a good novelist known by his initials, P.H. Newby, a style then thought to be rather unhip, except in the case of Leavis, F.R. and Taylor, A.J.P...'[40]

In his first year as a lecturer at Manchester University, Taylor stayed four nights a week in term time in comfortable lodgings found for him by his mother's sister Kate (whose Swedish husband Gustav was chief electrical engineer of Metropolitan Vickers). At weekends he returned home. He lived well beyond the means of an assistant lecturer, running a car, subscribing to the Hallé and still regularly riding. In the Easter vacation, 1931, he and Margaret went to Vienna, where they revisited their old haunts and became friends with William and Patience McElwee.

The History Department was in a state of flux. Not only had John Neale, the Professor of Modern History, left but so had F.M. Powicke, who had held a chair in the department from 1919 until 1928. Powicke was Regius Professor of Medieval History at Oxford, 1928–47. The department had been built up and dominated by the great medieval historian T.F. Tout, who held the Chair of History from 1890 to 1926 and had introduced special subjects and dissertations into the syllabus. Tout had also played a major role in the university, not least in setting up Manchester University Press, and though he had gone, according to Taylor, 'his shade still dominated the department'. Tout's impact was reinforced by James Tait and A.G. Little. Tait, who taught in the department from 1887 to 1919, ranged over ancient, medieval and Tudor history. Little, who had been Professor of History at University College, Cardiff, from 1898 to 1901, taught part-time as Reader in Palaeography at Manchester from 1902 to 1928. Powicke was to recall, 'A great scholar, A.G. Little, came regularly from Sevenoaks to give instructions to beginners in palaeography and kindred aids to study; he was the first man to do this as a part of training in historical method.' In 1930 both Hugh Hale Bellot, who had been Reader in Modern History, 1927–30, and took a Chair of American History at University College, London, and Mabel Phythian, Assistant Lecturer in Modern History, had left.[41]

In 1930–31, as a new lecturer, Alan Taylor was much influenced by his head of department, Ernest Jacob. Alan Taylor recalled, 'He ran the department as a democracy, a startling innovation for Manchester.'[42] Alan Taylor and Ernest Jacob got on well and respected each other. When, in 1938, Alan Taylor was seeking to leave Manchester for Oxford, Professor Jacob readily testified to the high quality of his lectures.[43]

Alan Taylor's long and vigorous support for the Historical Association may have been influenced by the strong support for it given by Ernest Jacob and others of the Manchester History Department. Jacob served on its national council as a vice-president from 1929 to 1958, was chairman of the Manchester branch from 1936 into the Second World War and was a frequent lecturer at other branches. Professor Powicke had also served on its council when at Manchester and from 1928 was a vice-president. The Historical Association's immediate past president (for 1926–29) was A.G. Little. The president of the Manchester branch was William Pantin, Lecturer in Ecclesiastical History from 1926 to 1933, who also left for

Oxford (as a Fellow and Lecturer in History at Oriel). He had succeeded Powicke, Neale and Hale Bellot as branch president. The major feature of the Manchester branch's programme in 1930–31, held in the university, was a set of four medieval lectures by Jacob, Powicke, Pantin and Dr Bertie Wilkinson, another Lecturer in Medieval History at Manchester. Another meeting was held jointly with the History Department's staff seminar, which had been established in 1921. When Lewis Namier arrived he was rapidly invited to lecture, doing so in his first term on 'Jewish Migration in Modern Times'.[44]

If Alan Taylor did not attend the medieval lectures, it is probable he attended Namier's lecture. He may also have been attracted to Professor Jacob on 'German Sculpture in the late Fifteenth and Early Sixteenth Centuries', a joint meeting with the Ancient Monuments Society, in 1932–33, and A.P. Wadsworth on 'Cotton' in 1934–35. Whether or not he did attend, he clearly would have known of such activities from his colleagues. It would be especially interesting to know if he heard from William Pantin or other colleagues, or personally attended, the meeting held in 1930–31 in the university's seminar room on 'the case for the broadest history lesson, advocated by two representatives whom the British Broadcasting Corporation kindly sent along'. When in 1937–38 the Manchester branch devoted most of its lectures to the theme of foreign affairs, Namier gave the first in the series on 'Diplomacy, Secret and Open' and Taylor gave the second on 'The Foreign Policy of Sir Edward Grey'.[45]

In his early period at Manchester University Taylor was actively involved in his department for four days a week. At first he shared an office with Ted Hughes, with whom he got on with very well. Hughes had studied under George Unwin, who had held Britain's first Chair of Economic History at Manchester from 1910 to 1925. After five years at Queen's University, Belfast, Hughes taught at Manchester from 1927 to 1939, before becoming Professor of History at Durham. While sharing an office with Taylor he was completing *Studies in Administration and Finance, 1558–1825* (1934). Alan Taylor also got on well with another of Unwin's former pupils, the distinguished economic historian Arthur Redford. Taylor was one of the few close friends whom Redford permitted to use his nickname, 'Jimmy'. Like Taylor, Redford was proud of his northern origins, in his case Mancunian. Unlike Taylor, he had been an undergraduate under Tout at Manchester University and he stayed in the university until his retirement. A later description of Redford could have been written of Taylor: 'In early life he seems to have been extremely and warmly disputatious, and although he later mellowed somewhat in this respect, his general outlook tended to be one of cautious pugnacity.' In the early 1930s he published *Economic History of England, 1760–1860* (1931) and *Manchester Merchants and Foreign*

Trade (1934). Alan Taylor also knew T.S. Ashton, then Reader in Currency and Public Finance (and at Manchester University, 1921–44) and another of Unwin's students, who published his *Economic and Social Investigations in Manchester, 1833–1933*, also in 1934.[46] So Alan Taylor began his career in an academic environment where the publication of major books was a norm.

He was kept busy with his large teaching load, which included two courses of 48 lectures. When he asked who had taught this before, he was told, 'Oh, Tout. He said that modern history was not a serious subject and anyone could lecture on it.' Powicke recalled Tout talking in 'an exciting and discursive way…about modern history'. For his first year only Alan Taylor wrote his lectures in full; it was hard and lengthy work, even if he drew them from a few textbooks. He had had immense practice in arguing rigorously at home but not in lecturing. He quickly learned how to be effective in front of a hundred students, and a key part of this was not to rely heavily on notes. The author Anthony Burgess, a first-year English student in 1937–38, recalled in his autobiography, 'A.J.P. Taylor lectured to a hundred or so of us and earned my enmity by scoffing at James Joyce's *Work in Progress*. He wrote on the blackboard ambidextrously. On my first term paper, which was awarded a fail mark, he wrote, "Bright ideas insufficient to conceal a lack of knowledge."' Later, Burgess said that his dislike of Taylor was due to him being then 'too young to respect'. Nevertheless, during his Manchester University years, like his Oxford years, Taylor took an interest in his students and invited a few home for tea. Betty Kemp, later a distinguished historian, was one, Maurice Oldfield, later the head of MI5, another.[47] At the end of his first year he hoped to move on to Oxford. He applied unsuccessfully for a Fellowship and Lectureship at Oriel College, Oxford, vacated by G.N. Clark when he became Chichele Professor of Economic History and Fellow of All Souls in 1931.

In the summer vacation of 1931 Alan Taylor worked in the Public Record Office in central London. He returned to the 1917 Club in Gerrard Street, to find that it was on its last legs and, as one member later commented, 'more than ever resembled a slum tenement'. It had factionalised and was by 1931 seriously divided between the pro-Communist group and the rest. Ironically, the club was collapsing financially as world capitalism was in a slump. Taylor recalled,

I even attended the final meeting when the members, instead of worrying about the financial position, were indignant because one of the waitresses had been dismissed for stealing money from the till. To crown the confusion, J.A. Hobson, the distinguished economist, withdrew in protest against this unbusinesslike performance, only to fall heavily downstairs.[48]

In going to London he was also rejoining Margaret. After more than eighteen months of the most important relationship hitherto in either of their lives, he proposed to her, and they agreed to marry in the Marylebone Registry Office. On their marriage day he arrived with his friend from schooldays, Geoffrey Rowntree, but changed his mind. They left Margaret devastated and went to the 1917 Club. Was this more than doubts about his feelings for Margaret? The question almost asks itself as this unpolitical, young woman from a wealthy background immediately went off on an Intourist excursion to Russia. Was this her response to a continuing concern on his part that she would not fit in to a family committed to the ideals of the Bolshevik Revolution and early Leninist Russia? In his autobiography he noted of his mother that 'She never forgave Margaret for not being a left-wing intellectual'.[49] Perhaps her Russian trip had even been their planned honeymoon holiday. There may have even been an element of him fearing his mother's hostile reaction, given her probable intervention earlier to prevent what she felt to be an unsuitable relationship.

The second remarkable feature of this rejection of Margaret at the registry office was that he did not tell his parents. Nor were they told of the second visit to the Marylebone Registry Office in the Town Hall on Saturday 3 October 1931, when Alan Taylor did go through with the ceremony. As the Taylors' only son, on whom they had always lavished money, it must have come as a severe shock. Weddings were rites of passage for parents as well as the couple concerned. Percy and Connie Taylor may have heard by telephone that their son was married and on his way with his wife to stay with them, or even have only found out on their arrival. Either way, it is not surprising that he received a very frosty reception from them.

He and Margaret left his parents in Preston after two days. He had to be present for the start of his second academic year as a university teacher. His parents, still deeply committed to the Left, were absorbed by the general election, imminent for some days and formally announced by James Ramsay MacDonald, Prime Minister of a National Government, on 7 October. His parents got over him keeping his wedding secret. But it was a dramatic final departure from 'the nest'. Of course, there had been more normal stages of departure: Oxford, working for his uncle in London and, greatest of all, Vienna. Emotionally, he appears to have given up trying – perhaps even wishing – to impress his mother. Quite possibly the summer 1929 holiday at Malvern was a late straw, if not the final straw, for him. Then, she and Henry Sara went to the theatre together, leaving Alan and his father to their own devices, and on one occasion she had a major row with Sara in front of Alan and his father. His relationship with his father was only briefly harmed by the wedding. Indeed, at some point in

1931, probably after his marriage, his father gave him a £2000 insurance policy.[50]

With the new academic year, he found a new father figure to admire in Lewis Namier. According to Alan Taylor and Lewis Namier, Ernest Jacob offered Namier the Chair of Modern History on the strength of G.M. Trevelyan's review of Namier's *England in the Age of the American Revolution*. This may be the case, but Professor Jacob would have known from Professor Tout, or possibly from Professor Neale, or from the press, of Namier's membership with them on the Committee on the Records of Past Members of the House of Commons, set up in April 1929. Namier was a major scholar who was a strong candidate for a chair anywhere.

Namier was striking both in his appearance and in his views. Namier was a big man, six feet tall and broad-shouldered. As G.S. Rousseau observed, 'He was different: spoke differently, looked foreign, possessed exotic charisma, impressed everyone he met.'[51] Taylor was fascinated by Namier, as he was so often with those who had first-hand knowledge of places and periods he wrote about. Namier had grown up in Austrian Galicia, a fringe of the Austro-Hungarian Empire, and had deep insights into many aspects of central European history.

In his later years Alan Taylor was very touchy on his relationship with Namier. He was often emphatic that he was not Namier's pupil, that he was not greatly influenced by Namier.[52] When I was preparing the large bibliography of his writings (published in 1980) he only once made an emphatic point that was intended to influence my biographical introduction to that book. He said most firmly that it would be wrong to suggest he was influenced as an historian by Namier. Yet, while he was not Namier's pupil, Namier's views, especially on European history, did have a big impact on his European history thinking and his writing of history.

Namier captivated him with his talk of the various nationality clashes within the Austria-Hungarian Empire, and of Prague and Vienna in the early 1920s. Namier was very prone to monologues. Taylor was one of those who did not find him a relentless bore, but quite the reverse. Arnold Toynbee, who also was stimulated by his conversation, recalled Namier on his first visit 'trailing clouds of Eastern Europe. These clouds floated into my room behind him, and they quickly filled it as [his] stream of talk flowed on.'[53] For Taylor and others Namier was a unique, living source on the details of recent east European history.

Namier greatly reinforced such anti-German feelings as Taylor had. Taylor had disliked Berlin when he visited it for a few days in 1928 and tended to look at Germany through Viennese spectacles. He avoided Italy because of Mussolini and detested the Nazis. Namier's hatred of Germany was legendary, stretching back to before the First World War. In 1942

Namier accurately commented, 'It did not require either 1914, or 1933, or 1939 to teach me the truth about the Germans. Long before the last war I considered them a deadly menace to Europe and civilisation.'[54] One might be tempted to comment that in the 1930s and 1940s Lewis Namier and Alan Taylor encouraged each other in anti-German attitudes, but Namier in fact needed no encouragement whatsoever.

Although Namier was only 41 when he took up his chair, his background was colourful and fascinating. His world and Taylor's had connected twice before. They had both gained First-Class Honours in History at Oxford, Namier in 1911 and Taylor in 1927. Namier had also been connected with the Lancashire cotton trade. He had worked in Czechoslovakia on behalf of Neil Rawnsley, a Lancashire cotton trader, for three years from August 1921. This commercial work had arisen from him writing for the *Manchester Guardian* and he had combined being its foreign correspondent in Prague and Vienna with his cotton business activities.[55] For Alan Taylor there was not only Namier's youthful experiences of the Austro-Hungarian Empire to hear about, but also his recollections of the Foreign Office during the First World War, his attendance at the 1922 Genoa Conference, his detailed knowledge of the central European financial crises of the early 1920s and his Zionist work with Chaim Weizmann.

Ernest Jacob later wrote, 'With A.J.P. Taylor fresh from Vienna a most powerful combination began to revive modern history in the university.'[56] While Alan Taylor was able to help Namier by telling him about the needs of the modern history programme and how Manchester University operated, he was in a state of near-adulation of his new professor. Within Manchester University he was long remembered as being Namier's devoted, yet very able, acolyte.[57] Namier's presence energised Taylor. His competitive nature ensured his lectures became increasingly better in substance and in delivery after his first year, when he had had full texts derived from the standard textbooks. He aspired to shine beside Namier.

Namier helped him to achieve. This was not only through being an intellectual example and by fascinating him with details and anecdotes of the recent central European past. He discussed with him the nature and significance of his research in diplomatic history. Taylor later testified, 'Talking to him was always an inspiration, bringing out the best in me and giving me confidence.'

Alan Taylor, always politically aware, was familiar with contemporary beliefs in the relevance of diplomatic history. In an article entitled 'A Plan for the Study of Contemporary History', published in *History* in 1929, R.W. Seton Watson had urged that 'a close study of recent history is an essential corollary of the new international peace movement which centres around the League of Nations, and on which the avoidance of fresh upheavals must so largely depend'. While Namier had no time for the League of Nations, he and his protégé, Taylor, had no doubts then about the importance of diplomatic history.[58]

Having completed his archival research in London in the summer of 1931, Taylor spent the next year completing his typescript of what became the book *The Italian Problem in European Diplomacy*. Namier, as well as his friends Teddy Pratt and Innes Stewart, read and discussed his work with him. In the book's Foreword he thanked Namier for giving him 'advice and criticism with unfailing patience and wisdom'. As well as wise advice on the writing of high-quality diplomatic history, Namier's other notable input was in successfully urging Taylor to cut out a flowery opening couple of pages. In his original introduction he had reflected on the current renewed popularity of the Victorian Age, writing, 'It is no longer disgraceful, it is at worst wistfully humorous, to be Victorian; literary amateurism has even gone so far as to find refuge from the ugly realities of post-war England in the innocent faeryland of the Second Empire.'[59] This passage was a little reminiscent of the rather precious style of his review of Forster's *The Life of Dickens*. While his reflections on the Victorian era were excised, the book still contained many such aphorisms which, at their least effective, suggested an attempt to appear wise beyond his years.

Namier also pushed him towards early publication of his research. He had taken on the editing of a series of books for Macmillan entitled 'Studies in Modern History' and was eager to have his bright young colleague's archivally researched book in the series. Offering a place of publication also fitted notions of the holder of a chair providing opportunities for able colleagues. However, Taylor expected a market price for his work. When Macmillan expected him to put the then large sum of £50 to its publication, he had second thoughts. He wrote to Harold Macmillan that he could not afford the £50 as he had bought a house and spent much on improving it. While this was true, and would have placated Namier, the sum involved was relatively trifling for him, his relatively wealthy wife or his ever-indulgent parents. Although on a salary of £300 a year, his income was over three times this amount when including Margaret's private income as well. Whether or not he had liquid assets after buying the house, he would have been able to raise the money easily had he so wished. More likely he was aware that Manchester University Press was likely to publish its academics' quality publications, even if their quality had to be demonstrated by entering them for a PhD. Even if Namier sneered personally at being a candidate for a PhD, within Manchester at the time it would have been deemed good for the History Department for a clever assistant lecturer to go forward for a PhD, followed by publication of the thesis by the university press. For Alan Taylor an academic press, which would welcome lengthy footnotes, may have been more attractive than Macmillan. Moreover, there was considerable prestige in the Manchester University Press's series for a young lecturer in the Manchester History Department, the first volume in its history series having been James Tait's study of medieval Manchester. Taylor's thesis was duly passed by Namier and R.W. Seton Watson, after an oral examination.

By this time the Tout Memorial Publication Fund had agreed to sponsor publication. Having declined to pay Macmillan £50, he now declined to pay Manchester University the eighteen guinea fee required before the PhD was awarded.[60] He enjoyed avoiding this payment, Manchester University having recently chosen not to promote him from assistant lecturer to lecturer (with an accompanying increase of a third in salary to £400 per annum), claiming lack of funds. Taylor, who felt he had performed the work of a senior member of staff, let alone that of a lecturer, was outraged at being given only a further three-year assistant lecturer contract. Always punctilious to collect every penny he felt to be his due, he felt bitterly that Manchester University had cheated him. One can only wonder why Jacob and Namier failed sufficiently to exert themselves to secure him promotion to a lectureship in 1933.

In addition to this, Alan Taylor, though competitive and ambitious, still liked to see himself as a gentleman scholar. From this point of view, 'Mr Taylor' with an Oxford First was, in cricketing terms, a gentleman rather than a player. Moreover, aspiring always to return to Oxford, his Oxford First was sufficient without a provincial university's PhD, an award which could have harmed his chances in most Oxford colleges of that time.[61]

Taylor's book was an impressive first scholarly monograph. Unlike much of his later work it was based on archival research, and the sources he used were meticulously listed in the footnotes. Like most young scholars he quoted too much, above all in the footnotes – something he avoided doing after he left Manchester in 1938. Several footnotes in small print ran for all or most of a page, in contrast to much of his later work, which would have benefited from more referencing.

In his first book he also strove hard to emphasise the relevance of his research and place it in a wider context. He began the book with something of a manifesto on his belief in the deterministic nature of diplomatic history and of the need for historians to analyse the underlying assumptions of diplomacy. He wrote,

At first sight the European diplomatic system appears to proceed in the most haphazard way... But on a closer view, there emerge more and more clearly certain principles, until the petty struggles of day-to-day diplomacy take on the appearance of a battle of Platonic Ideas.

From a study of almost any isolated instance, one might deduce all the
differences in political structure and political outlook among the states
of Europe...the course of national policy is based upon a series of
assumptions, with which statesmen have lived since their earliest years
and which they regard as so axiomatic as hardly to be worth stating. It
is the duty of the historian to clarify these assumptions and to trade
their influence upon the course of every-day policy.[62]

This passage displayed self-confidence beyond his years. There was
the certainty of 'a great arguer' among his Taylor and Thompson relatives
or with Henry Sara. There was a depth of historical thought which was his
own, but which owed something to Pribram and the other Austrian scholars
whose works he had read in Vienna and something more to the stimulus
of discussions with Lewis Namier. Pribram argued that statesmen were
restricted in their actions by the fundamental interests of their countries.
Hence, in his Ford Lectures, published in 1931, he had written of Lord
Grey, British Foreign Secretary 1905–16, 'Certain fundamental and enduring
factors and influences that served to formulate and condition his policy
must be ever present to his mind.'[63] Namier also held a deterministic view,
in his case economic. Linda Colley has written of Namier that, while he
rejected Marxism, 'he retained all his life a tendency towards economic
determinism and an interest in the correlation between political decision-
makers and their social and economic background'.[64] These were not unusual
views, but carried additional weight for Taylor through being held by
his mentors.

Encouraged by Pribram, he had taken up a period, 1848–49, near to
his initial interests in British radicals when he went to Vienna, and in
so doing he avoided the most explicitly polemical area of international
diplomatic history, the origins of the First World War. This was a decision
broadly in favour of the advice he had from Professor H.W.C. Davis at
Oxford, rather than to follow an area that might have been seen as very
politically relevant by his parents and Sara. In his book Taylor made (what
he later dubbed when done by others) 'sales talk' concerning his chosen
period. He argued that it was especially good for grasping the underlying
assumptions of diplomatic history:

The nearer we get to our own day, the more are the general principles
taken for granted: there are few who expound the general course
of policy in a telegram or in a telephone conversation. To get the
assumptions stated we must go back to the days of dispatches, and the
Italian problem of 1848 is almost the last European crisis in which the
telegraph played no part – or practically none. Statesmen still had
time to state their cases.[65]

In arguing that it was the historian's duty to expose such underlying assumptions he was making a democratic point in a period when diplomatic history had a very high profile and was highly political in its impact, as politicians and nations sought to explain what had gone wrong in 1914. Professor Charles Webster of Liverpool University had outraged the British Foreign Office by his memorandum on public access to Foreign Office records:

> Access to the Foreign Office Records is a vital consideration in all attempts to make Foreign Policy depend on the popular will. The History of past Diplomacy is essential to the proper understanding of the present. If British Foreign Policy is really to represent the wishes of the people it can only be successful if the people are adequately instructed; and no text-book or pamphlets will supply the necessary information unless the preliminary work of scientific investigation can be also adequately carried out.[66]

His views had reached a wider audience in an article, 'The Labour Government and Secret Diplomacy' in *The Nation and Athenaeum*, June 1924.

At much that time Alan Taylor's reading had included H.N. Brailsford's, *The War of Steel and Gold* (1914). His reading reinforced the radical and socialist foreign policy discussions he heard and participated in between his parents and Sara. Brailsford's book condemned finance capital for creating European instability and an armaments race through imperial expansion yet offered the prospect of a radical democracy remedying the situation.[67] Taylor later wrote in a reassessment of J.A. Hobson's *Imperialism* (1902) that Brailsford's was

> a more brilliant book than Hobson's, written with a more trenchant pen and with a deeper knowledge of international affairs. Though less remembered now, it had probably a stronger influence on its own generation, and American historians between the wars, in particular, could not have got on without it. Our own thought is still unconsciously shaped by it.[68]

So although Taylor's chosen area was not highly political, nevertheless his case for it had a political dimension. Having argued what he felt was the broad duty of a diplomatic historian, he went on to make his first study something of a skills exercise. He made explicit his close textual reading of sources. For instance, in considering a discussion of Palmerston and the Austrian Minister in London on the subject of the recognition of Austrian control of her Italian provinces, he observed of two sources (one in Vienna, one in London) that what they referred to was 'obviously the same conversation', and added, 'I have therefore ventured to run the two accounts together.' Of another document, written by the Austrian Prime Minister, Pillersdorf, which summarises a conversation with Sir Stratford Canning, the British ambassador in Vienna, Taylor wrote at the end of a very lengthy footnote,

> The whole report of the conversation is probably complete fiction, composed by Pillersdorf much later in order to rebut charges of weakness and incompetence that were made against him. The conversation is dated May 20, when both Stratford Canning and Hummelauer [Austrian Counsellor] had left Vienna (although Pillersdorf says that it was this conversation which put the idea of mediation into his head); there is no report in Canning's dispatches of the conversation, although Pillersdorf says he expressly promised to make one; and Pillersdorf is represented in the conversation as haughty and resolute, Canning as acquiescent and docile, which is not what other impressions of both men would lead us to expect.

The more confident, older Taylor would not feel a need to display his judgements on sources in this way, other than if major issues hinged on them. He also took pains to show that he could locate his study in a wider Austrian context. In this he generalised rather crudely: finding Austrian policy 'conservative, pacific, almost timorous' in 1815–48 and 1871–1906, in contrast with it being 'violent, aggressive, almost bullying' in 1848–66 and 1906–14.[69]

His display of skills included style. In his later criticism of Pribram he called for human interest in diplomatic history. In *The Italian Problem in European Diplomacy* Taylor took care to provide portraits of the main diplomatic figures, often doing so with epigrams. Of Prince Metternich, he wrote:

> Metternich recognised what his successors forgot, that Austria was a despotism based on consent and that her main strength lay in her tradition, not in her army. Indeed, it is not going too far to say that Metternich had adapted the political philosophy of Burke to a country without a parliamentary constitution.

Of Lord Palmerston, he wrote:

> Palmerston's impudence and jaunty air have blinded later historians as well as Metternich to the real merits and the real significance of his political philosophy. We have grown so used to talking of Pam's lectures that we have forgotten what he lectured about; his pride in England was so aggressive that it concealed the cause of his pride. But no man controls the foreign policy of a country for nearly thirty years and lives to see himself a parliamentary dictator – dictator too in a parliament that contained Gladstone, John Russell, Bright, Cobden and Disraeli

– merely because he has a ready wit and a thick skin; Palmerston was
the hero of England because he deserved to be.[70]

The tone and assurance of such writing were greater than that usual for
the first book of a provincial university's assistant lecturer. It was more like
the work of a professor or a Fellow of an Oxbridge college. The book was
very much a major part of his repeated bids to return to Oxford.

While the book displayed his skills and his self-assurance, it also gave
first versions of later themes. He was much gentler with the Habsburg
monarchy and with Metternich than he was in later books and essays.
Metternich is portrayed here as an able conservative who was restricted by
the Habsburg monarchy's system of government from being more effective.
Taylor displayed his taste for great generalisations about nationalities. Here,
it is France, not Germany, which received particular attention for such a
long-term view. He wrote of *realpolitik*,

> The word, curiously enough, is German, but the practice is French.
> For, whereas the Germans have had only one *realpolitiker*, Bismarck, the
> French have never had anything else. The statesmen of all other nations
> appear sometimes to be influenced by sentimental, idealistic, unselfish
> motives – the French, never. Whether the phrases are monarchic or
> republican, conservative or revolutionary, pacific or bellicose, it is
> French interests and French interest alone that are being pursued.[71]

Not surprisingly, when a similar view was later applied to Germany, with
Hitler as one of various leaders following a persistent national policy, it
caused considerable controversy.

He also engaged with the then topical issue of the impact of public
opinion on diplomacy. It was a theme he had taken up in order to give his
successful bid in 1929 for a Rockefeller grant a social science slant. However,
his response was more to do with rebutting the significance of such works
as Kingsley Martin's *The Triumph of Lord Palmerston: A Study of Public
Opinion in England before the Crimean War* (London, Allen & Unwin,
1924). He later wrote of it, 'There is an odd study of public opinion
in … *The Triumph of Lord Palmerston* (1924),' which could be construed as
an odd aspect of the book or an odd book.[72] Alan Taylor delighted in being
precise in his comments and he probably meant the former. There is much
in the book which would have appealed to Taylor; there are aspects of
style, wit and tone which he probably emulated in his own writing. Kingsley
Martin, like Taylor, combined accounts of diplomacy with colourful portraits
of the main figures. Palmerston, for instance, 'was in a peculiar manner a
representative man – "Minister for England"'. Martin frequently delivered
pithy judgements, often with a Nonconformist tinge to them, his father

having been a Congregationalist minister. His Palmerston book contains
many clever witticisms, not unlike those Alan Taylor later wrote, at least
in book reviews or short essays.[73]

Kingsley Martin later recalled, 'I wanted to find out why people are
pleased at the beginning of a war.' He added that 'it used the press not to
establish facts about which other sources are more reliable, but to show how
an illusory picture of the world scene can be painted on the public mind
with the result that quite irrational actions seemed morally imperative'.[74]
In his book Taylor was sceptical about ascertaining public opinion:

> The opinions of the man in the street on foreign affairs (so far as he
> has any) are by their nature unascertainable; what usually passes for
> public opinion is the opinion of a small, politically conscious class –
> leader-writers (themselves on the fringe of diplomacy), members of
> parliament and the less instructed members of the Cabinet. In 1848
> this opinion in England had little interest in the things for which
> Palmerston cared – the European system and the preservation of
> the Balance of Power: it had a sentimental desire to see Italy freed,
> although it was not prepared to contribute, by active intervention,
> towards that freedom.[75]

Nevertheless, at the end of the same paragraph he wrote, 'Public
opinion in short tends to want the glory without the suffering and the
prize without the pain. It is not prepared to translate the threats of
diplomacy into action and yet it is angry when the diplomats do not
threaten.' Indeed, a little earlier in the book he had written that 'in 1848
no Italian politician is of European stature; it is only the people of Italy
who provide a problem for the European powers. And not only the people
of Italy – public opinion in England and France (in Austria to a much less
extent) is an essential element in the Italian problem of 1848.'

So, while being dismissive of those writing of public opinion and
diplomacy, he did recognise some significance for public opinion. He
concluded his remarks,

> Nineteenth-century statesmen use phrases to satisfy public opinion in
> the same way as earlier statesmen had used the phrases that would
> satisfy their Kings. But in both cases the essentials of policy are little
> affected by the phrases. The statesman, unless he is a very poor
> statesman indeed, adheres to the broad principles of national policy
> and it is the interaction of the differing national principles which in
> the long run determines the history of Europe.[76]

His very deterministic approach in his first book contrasts with the 'accident-
prone' interpretations of his later years. As for public opinion, he remained
highly sceptical of its significance.

The book was generally well received. Professor W.A. Phillips, the Lecky Professor of Modern History at the University of Dublin, for instance, warmly praised it in the *Times Literary Review* as

> a valuable contribution to our knowledge of the interplay of influences and forces outside Italy by which the issue of revolution was largely determined. But it is more than this; it…reveals the broad principles which in the end always determine national policies in spite of the haphazard way in which diplomacy seems to function.

There were criticisms. Two reviewers regretted that he had not discussed Russian and Prussian attitudes and one that he had not carried out research on Italy. He was also criticised by J.P.T. Bury in the *Cambridge Review* for not assimilating into his text the substantial material in his footnotes.[77]

Given his ambition to return to Oxford, Denis Brogan's review in the *Oxford Magazine* was especially important for him. This was mostly very favourable:

> References to the Napoleonic empire as 'the worst (because the most extensive) tyranny since the time of Attila' are not encouraging, but once Mr Taylor has unburdened his soul in this fashion, he sets to work to tell his story with great skill and original learning. The result is a really important contribution to our knowledge of the *Risorgimento*, of the doom of Austria and of the methods of Lord Palmerston.[78]

Having published his first book with Manchester University Press, Alan Taylor was now eager to move to a commercial publisher and a larger audience. However, his first opportunities were with the scholarly series edited by his mentor, Lewis Namier, for Macmillan. He suggested that 'Studies in Modern History' should include a translation of Heinrich Friedjung's major work *Der Kampf um die Vorherrschaft in Deutschland* (1897). Namier was very attracted to the idea, and the publication of an abridged version of the two-volume work, based on the 1917–18 edition, was agreed.

Publishing Friedjung had been an idea that was awaiting its time. After Friedjung's death in 1920, A.F. Pribram had acted as his literary executor and was keen for his work to be better known in the English-speaking world. Taylor was a great admirer of the book, observing that it was his model for writing diplomatic history in Vienna. Alan and Margaret Taylor had become friends of Pribram's other English postgraduate, William McElwee, who had studied under Ernest Jacob in Oxford. In the early 1930s McElwee, like Taylor, was a lecturer at a provincial university, in his case Liverpool, aspiring to return to Oxford, and they were young British

academic specialists on Austrian history.[79] The book proposal depended on
them both being willing to undertake a major task of translation. Taylor
later recalled that Bill McElwee had taken the lead in the translating and,
while he had played his part in that, he had written the introduction.
Taylor worked on the book from at least the early summer of 1934,
breaking off for a holiday in Spain. He enjoyed discussing the translation
and his introduction with Namier that autumn and in January 1935, when
he completed his work on the book.[80]

Alan Taylor's introduction to Friedjung's book was a thoughtful assessment of not just Friedjung's work but also his political career as a German
nationalist within the Habsburg Empire. His discussion of nationality issues
had considerable depth and maturity, reflecting his wide reading and much
thinking about Austrian history when in Vienna, as well as the benefit of
later frequent discussions on central European history with Lewis Namier.
As with his study of Italy in 1847–49, he was particularly good at incisive
portraits of major figures. Bismarck appears as a 'titanic figure' and he
refers to 'the personal greatness of Bismarck'. In contrast, the Emperor
Francis Joseph 'did more than any other man to bring the empire to ruin',
using up 'the capital of imperial loyalty which he had inherited from his
reforming ancestors'.

In blaming Francis Joseph, Taylor argued that the fall of the Habsburg
monarchy was not inevitable. He claimed that 'for the Austrian Empire to
survive there had to be an abandonment of nationalism', but with 'the
refusal of the nationalities to compromise or to abate their claims…the
empire foundered'. Attempts by the Emperor to turn it into a struggle
between the international ideologies of socialism and clericalism, red
and black, failed. Taylor argued that just as Friedjung's book had political
relevance in the mid-1890s, with its message that reforming German
nationalists could save the empire, so it had in 1935, with the problem of
Austria and its relationship with Germany unsolved.[81] Hitler's solution, the
Anschluss on 13 March 1938, was later seen by Taylor to have marked the
beginning of the pre-war phase to the Second World War.[82]

There was much in this substantial piece by Taylor to suggest later
to Namier that Taylor could write a history of the Habsburg monarchy.
However, soon the thrusting and ambitious Taylor had another proposal
for Namier's book series. This was to be *Germany's First Bid for Colonies
1884–1885: A Move in Bismarck's European Policy*. That it was again to focus
on three countries' diplomatic moves over a short period would have
worried Lewis Namier less than many other senior historians.

The book marked Alan Taylor's move from substantial overseas archival
research to heavy reliance on printed documents. He had made a last use
of his earlier archival material of 1930–32 in a long and lacklustre chunk of

diplomatic history, 'European Mediation and the Agreement of Villafranca, 1859', published in the *English Historical Review* in January 1936.[83] After that, while he did work on British Foreign Office records, he made much use of a set of *Die grosse Politik der europäischen Kabinette 1871–1914*, 40 volumes in 54 parts (1922–27), which he had bought from a German Jewish refugee in 1933. Although the German diplomatic documents had been presented in the way best to present Germany as innocent of war guilt in 1914, they provided major access to Germany's diplomatic records.[84] In 1933–34 Taylor read the first 22 volumes, along with twelve volumes of French and nine volumes of British documents, in preparation for teaching a special subject on European international relations, 1890–1909, in the 1936–37 academic year.[85]

From his reading of the documents Alan Taylor came to believe that Bismarck was manipulating the issue of German colonies to affect his European diplomacy. He had argued similar points of Palmerston's and Louis Napoleon's use of the Italian issue in 1848–49. However, as he implicitly acknowledged in his autobiography, he pushed his argument too far, not balancing the diplomatic motivation with domestic pressures – something he was to do far more dramatically in his book on the origins of the Second World War in Europe. In his autobiography he wrote,

> Going through the French and German documents I was struck by the way in which Bismarck used German colonial ambition as an instrument in his European policy. Of course there was a genuine push for colonies in Germany even if Bismarck himself was not affected by it. But my point was worth making, the more so that I could take a jab at the fashionable theories of economic imperialism.[86]

The book started out as an article for a learned journal, but outgrew that format. It became a 99-page short book. In order to become a book, Namier required him to write an introduction and an epilogue to provide a context for his detailed study. In sending a revised script to Macmillans Taylor was careful to comment, 'Professor Namier has read this additional material and authorised me to say that he approves of it.' Namier also went through the proofs, suggesting revisions.[87]

As with his first book, but in a much more restrained manner, he fully referenced his sources and also signalled his skills and abilities with the German documents.[88] Also, as with his earlier book, he provided incisive and memorable character sketches of his major diplomatic figures, including Bismarck, his son Herbert and Lord Granville. He ended the book with a characteristic paradoxical touch. He commented of Bismarck,

> But he left an unfortunate example to his successors, who imitated his unscrupulousness without possessing his genius. Short of a run of

Bismarcks, there is perhaps something to be said for government by gentlemen, even when they are such incompetent muddlers as Lord Granville and Lord Derby.

The book is also notable for his dark comments on 'the German mind'. This came as part of his examination of underlying German attitudes to foreign policy. He wrote, 'To the German mind friendship with one power necessarily implies hostility against another, and Germany, to make herself presentable to France, had to provoke a quarrel with England so that Franco-German friendship should have the solid foundation of anglophobia.'[89] Such weight given to 'the German character' was a strong feature of Lewis Namier's outlook, as well as other historians, and Taylor would expand on this theme in his *The Course of German History* (1945). Overall, *Germany's First Bid for Colonies* reads as if it was intended to display his abilities to those appointing in Oxford colleges. As if it were a scholarship essay, he enjoyed displaying his wit. Early on he commented, 'In the first decade of the twentieth century the Germans demanded "a place in the sun"; by this they meant someone else's place in the sun, their own having proved too hot.' This worked well. He tried too hard elsewhere. For instance, he wrote, 'The apparent exception, the aggressive Imperialism of the nineteenth century, was merely part of the diabolism of the Naughty Nineties, with Chamberlain as the Oscar Wilde of politics.'[90]

The overall theme of a diplomatic explanation of imperialism was a clear breakaway from the Leninist views of his home and his youth. It was also a move away from the very radical Liberal views of J.A. Hobson of *Imperialism: A Study* (1902), akin to Taylor's move away from radical Liberal foreign policy and peace politics in 1936.[91]

His study of German demands for colonies was also topical. While he was fortunate in the timing of his book, he saw diplomatic history as highly 'relevant' to the 1930s, and like the Friedjung translation he was eager for it to contribute to the informed debates on current international issues. He was also shrewd enough to know that such a study which privileged diplomatic over economic explanations would do much good in his efforts to return to Oxford.

Germany's First Bid for Colonies received some very warm praise. Ian Morrow, his translator friend in Vienna, was effusive in the *Times Literary Supplement*: 'A brilliant study … [it] fulfils the highest standards of scholarship…His narrative powers and pleasantly ironic style at once arouse his readers' interest and retain it to the close.' Professor W.K. Hancock commented in *International Affairs* that 'Mr Taylor has already won for himself a foremost place among the younger diplomatic historians'. He concluded his review, 'The reader of his volume is probably expected to conclude that something very similar is true today. The book will also suggest that the student of world politics should draw for their rules of interpretation rather less on Marx and rather more on Machiavelli.'

Others were more critical. Gavin Henderson in *History* complained, 'What should have been a most tentative hypothesis is described throughout the book – in the title, the text and even the index – as unassailable fact.' In the *Oxford Magazine* Richard Pares suggested he exaggerated his main hypothesis and reprimanded him for his flippancy. 'Diplomatic historians – even believers in 'pure' diplomacy like Mr Taylor – ought to know that their explanations of history must be barren and will probably be mistaken if they will not attend to the subject-matter of diplomacy. It cannot be dismissed with undergraduate levity.' However, E.L. Woodward, Fellow of All Souls College, Oxford, who was to assist Taylor in his desired return to Oxford, wrote in the *Spectator*: 'A model of the way in which diplomatic history should be written,' but felt that he probably overstated his case and should 'have given a little more space to an estimate of the strength of the colonial movement in Germany'.[92]

Alan Taylor later had doubts about his own interpretation. He aired these in two book reviews. When reviewing the third volume of Eric Eyck's biography of Bismarck in 1947, he commented that Eyck

> ...agrees with my interpretation...that, insofar as the colonial demands had any purpose in foreign policy, their object was to improve relations with France by a trumped-up dispute with England; but he is of course right to insist that they were directed against the German Left even more than against England; and I recant anything of mine which may have obscured this.

Twenty-two years later, he came up with one of the trivial explanations he then delighted in to explain great historical events. He wrote of an essay by H.R. Turner,

> He rejects the attempt which I made years ago to fit this conversion into Bismarck's diplomacy and argues that Bismarck was acting mainly from fear of otherwise being left out. Colonialism was thus part of the change to protective tariffs. There is some evidence in favour of this view. I now incline to believe that the principal explanation lay in Bismarck's bad temper, when the British government failed to do what he wanted. This explanation sounds trivial but there is more evidence for it than any other.

Others were also critical and pointed to alternative explanations for Bismarck's brief colonial phase. Hartmut Pogge von Strandemann emphasised domestic pressures, with the colonial policy being intended to influence the 1884 elections to the Reichstag so as to weaken the Left Liberals and the Social Democrats. Hans-Ulrich Wehler, who dismissed Taylor's book as offering only a 'simplistic theory', also saw Bismarck being influenced primarily by domestic considerations. In his case he emphasised economic depression as spurring Bismarck on to avoid stagnation and subsequent class conflict. Another suggestion has been that Bismarck wished to divide the pro-British Crown Prince and Britain by causing serious friction over colonial policy. While Taylor's argument has very few supporters now, at least if not combined with other explanations, at the time it helped to bring about his return to Oxford.

In the 1930s Alan Taylor began his career as a remarkably prolific book reviewer. His opening with the *Manchester Guardian* came through Namier, who was slow at reviewing and not very keen. Too busy to review quickly a life of Robespierre, Namier suggested to A.S. Wallace, the literary editor, it should be done by Taylor, given that he taught a course on French history 1789–1914 at Manchester University. Taylor soon showed that he wrote incisively with memorable aphorisms and delivered his copy quickly. In his first newspaper review he delivered judgements with confidence. Of Robespierre, he wrote: 'His tragedy was not that of a good man succumbing to the lust for power; it was that he expressed the Revolution without ever dominating it. Robespierre had intelligence, courage and honesty, but he lacked personality...'[93] By early October 1938, when he had moved to Oxford, he had had 73 reviews published in the *Manchester Guardian*.

Taylor was very eager to contribute to the *Manchester Guardian*. He had first met A.P. Wadsworth, the future editor, when out walking with Malcolm Muggeridge in early 1932. Once writing reviews he went out of his way to cultivate people who worked for the newspaper. Several couples, including the Wadsworths and Kemps, were weekend guests at 'Three Gates'. He was also friendly with Paddy Monkhouse, who had joined the *Manchester Guardian* in 1927, and his father, Allan Monkhouse, an author and the literary editor before Wallace. Taylor later wrote with pride, 'I was the only member of the university staff who frequented the office of the *Manchester Guardian* and whose name appeared in its columns every week.'[94]

A.P. Wadsworth was a major influence on Alan Taylor. The son of a master tailor, Wadsworth had left Rochdale Fleece Street School at the age of 14 and worked his way up the newspaper industry. In 1907 he was one of the first students of the Workers' Educational Association, being taught in Rochdale by R.H. Tawney. Wadsworth wrote two notable economic history books, *The Cotton Trade and Industrial Lancashire 1600–1790* (1931), with Julia Mann, and *The Strutts and the Arkwrights 1758–1830* (1958), with R.S. Fitton. Wadsworth liked to draw on the past in his leaders and other contributions.[95] This taste provided the opportunity for Taylor to write feature articles. The first was a discussion of historical parallels with the resignation of Anthony Eden as Foreign Secretary in February 1938, in which Taylor in conclusion observed, 'We are now to see, with some variants, what would have happened if Grey had resigned after the Haldane Mission of 1912 and his place had been taken by one of his more sentimental critics who was determined to get an agreement with Germany at any cost.' A second piece, written six months later, shortly before he left for Oxford, compared the revision of treaties in 1830 (Belgium) and 1938 (Czechoslovakia).[96]

Taylor later wrote, 'Wadsworth became a great friend of mine. I learnt nothing from him and did not share his alleged sound Labour policies.'[97] However, later still, in his autobiography, he paid fairer tribute to Wadsworth (while understating Namier's impact).

> Wadsworth, not Namier, was my teacher at Manchester, so far as I had one. Wadsworth taught me to write taut journalistic prose. He constantly said to me, 'An article in the *Guardian* is no good unless people read it on the way to work.' I followed his instruction, worrying about my style as much as my scholarship. In my opinion the writings of an historian are no good unless readers get the same pleasure from them as they do from a novel.[98]

Married and in an academic job in Manchester in the 1930s, Taylor continued to be driven by his strongly competitive nature, but, as in the past, he partially disguised this by affecting to be a gentleman player. For several years he continued to express strong socialist and anti-war views, which remained broadly in line with those of his parents and Henry Sara. In Manchester he combined this legacy of very radical views with a consciousness of his upper-middle-class roots in the once flourishing Manchester cotton trade. Indeed, in this combination his model continued to be of a generation earlier, his grandfather J.T. Taylor, who displayed strong radicalism as well as a healthy acquisitive urge.

Although he was famously 'agin', often being a rebel against authority, Taylor as a young lecturer was ambitious. In terms of Kingsley Amis' novel of university life, *Lucky Jim* (1955), Alan Taylor was nearer the well-heeled and cultured world of Professor Welch than of the impoverished 'Lucky Jim' Dixon. Indeed, Dylan Thomas' raids on Taylor's home-made beer and his general mockery of his routines and rigidities at home were almost a precursor of 'Lucky Jim' behaviour.

Alan and Margaret Taylor began their married life without financial worries. He recalled, 'Margaret had some income from her mother. I had my salary and the increasing income from my Stock Exchange operations, altogether over £900 a year, almost as much as a professor. I recorded each fragment of income and divided it into two.'[99] She paid for the household expenses; he ran his car, a luxury still beyond many university professors. The young couple had no major domestic chores as they employed a woman to do these on a daily basis.

They often took their place in well-to-do society. It was his birth-right, as a member of one of the wealthy cotton families of the city. He later recalled, 'At one house, that of Godfrey Armitage, where we often went to dinner, I received a card on arrival giving me the name of the lady I was to take into dinner. At the appropriate moment I introduced myself, took her arm and led her in.'[100] Alan Taylor always remained very conscious of his grandfather's activities as a Manchester businessman, even noting that before concerts they ate 'at the very chop house where James Taylor had eaten every afternoon fifty years before'.[101]

Margaret Taylor's musical tastes were fully catered for. As in Vienna, they did not stint expenditure on music. They subscribed to the Hallé concerts which took place on Thursday evenings and went to other musical occasions. He pressed Margaret to keep up her piano lessons for the first year of their marriage. Later she was the founder secretary of the Manchester Chamber Concerts Society.

After living for a few weeks in a furnished flat, they moved to an unfurnished flat at the top of 'The Limes', a large house at 148 Wilmslow Road, Manchester. The young couple made friends with other young tenants in the house. In the flat below were George and Dorothea ('Dolly') Eltenton, a young couple with a newly born baby, Anya. He was a scientist at the Shirley Institute and a very committed communist. Taylor later recalled, with some measure of hubris, 'With my greater experience of the labour movement, I often doubted whether George had much idea of what Communism meant.'[102] This view he had to revise later, given that Eltenton went to work in Leningrad for a while and was involved in Soviet attempts in 1942 to gain information from the Radiation Laboratory at the University of California, Berkeley, which resulted in J. Robert Oppenheimer losing his senior post.[103]

Alan Taylor found livelier and irreverent conversation with the inhabitants of the ground-floor flat, Malcolm and Kitty Muggeridge. They also had a young child, Leonard, then three. They came from similar well-to-do socialist backgrounds as Taylor. While he always respected his father's socialist commitment, Malcolm and Kitty Muggeridge delighted in ridiculing his father, Henry, Labour councillor and briefly a Labour MP, and her aunt, Beatrice Webb. Much later, when Taylor's autobiography was published, Malcolm Muggeridge gently ridiculed the kindly Percy Taylor, recalling meeting him in 1932: 'a stocky, well-built man, ready on request to stand on his head, and often accompanied by a charming young girl called Dolly Sharples.'[104] It is also highly probable that he mocked Alan Taylor as well, along with others, in his novel *Picture Palace* (suppressed 1934, published 1987). The novel is a savage satire of C.P. Scott ('old Savoury') and the *Manchester Guardian*, with much scorn for the League of Nations. Muggeridge ridiculed old Savoury's worthy editorials; the tone is exemplified in an extract from one spoof editorial: 'Effort is necessary, and the shedding of old prejudices, and the continued application of right principles.' He went further in his ridicule, writing: 'The *Evening Gazette* – an extremely profitable enterprise – waxed fat on racing tips and pornography; its fatness enabled the *Courier* to be lean and virtuous.'[105] This scarcely veiled attack on the *Manchester Guardian* and the *Manchester Evening News* provided the main grounds for the *Manchester Guardian* taking legal action, which led to the suppression of the book.[106]

Picture Palace also has a theme of the overwhelming value of human love, as experienced by the characters (Pettygrew and Gertrude) based on Malcolm and Kitty Muggeridge. Alan Taylor is the basis for part, but only a part, of the university lecturer Rattray, who falls in love with Gertrude and whom Pettygrew allows to make love to her. Rattray, like Taylor in 1934, 'lived in a cottage in the country, and took a great interest in his garden, and accumulated a large number of books'. After his moments of passion with Gertrude, Rattray calms himself with *The Decline and Fall of the Roman Empire* by Gibbon, including reading some of it aloud to Gertrude![107] Perhaps Alan Taylor, who found Kitty very attractive, rashly said so to Malcolm Muggeridge, who for all his free love talk was immensely jealous concerning his beautiful wife (as displayed in the novel). There is no reasonable case for seeing the newly married and somewhat gauche Taylor attracting Kitty Muggeridge and them having an affair; but there is a high probability of Malcolm Muggeridge enjoying building on some of Taylor's 'laddish' comments in this way in his novel and also deriving wicked amusement from portraying him as reading Gibbon after making love. Or, perhaps, Taylor remonstrated with Muggeridge over one of his and Kitty's marital tiffs and thereby aroused his satire. Taylor always admired and valued Kitty and was aghast at her husband's apparent willingness to break with her. Looking back, much later, he recalled that 'he often tried to break away until Kitty quelled him with the words, "You'd better stick with me. No one'll love you as I do".'[108] We shall never know if Alan Taylor linked Rattray with himself when he read *Picture Palace*. However, it may be safe to guess that Taylor would have shared Muggeridge's wry amusement at a book which satirises the endless proclamation of liberal values by the *Manchester Guardian* editorials being itself suppressed by the newspaper for being too free in its speech.

Whatever else, Malcolm Muggeridge was no bore. Alan Taylor was stimulated by his cynical wit and amused by his jeers at the idealism of the worthies of the *Manchester Guardian*. He was still in his own Left phase, albeit freelance by this time. He enjoyed striding along with Muggeridge, talking politics and journalism. He sometimes kept Muggeridge company as he went briskly along his favourite local walk, which he called 'the Round', a route 'following the raised bank of a turgid stream that wound its way through a stretch of wasteland for some reason unbuilt on, just behind where we lived'.[109] Taylor, three years younger than Muggeridge, appears to have been more fascinated by Muggeridge than Muggeridge was with the 'whimsical' Taylor (as Muggeridge later referred to him as being at this time). Muggeridge was more stimulated by Ted Scott, the son and successor to C.P. Scott of the *Manchester Guardian* and, later, by the author Hugh Kingsmill. Muggeridge was, perhaps, the last of a run of youngish men whom Alan Taylor adored. Later, reflecting on their long friendship, Alan Taylor wrote, 'I have been a sort of Sancho Panza to Malcolm's Don Quixote for fifty years, and have experienced laughter, gaiety and good fellowship.'[110] From Muggeridge he gained not only intellectual stimulus and entertainment but also a renewed taste for striding out into rugged landscapes (now Derbyshire as well as the Lake District) and, some years later, a lighter style in his writing, drawn partly from Muggeridge's *The Thirties* (1940).

Both he and Margaret missed Malcolm and Kitty Muggeridge when they went to Russia in September 1932. However, like most left-wing people of the time, he was shocked by his friend's exposure of the harsh realities of Stalin's Russia in his reports to the *Manchester Guardian* and took it upon himself to put Muggeridge right. In February 1933 Taylor prefaced a lengthy letter in which, with some arrogance, he wrote, 'I must answer all the mistakes of your letter,' with the declaration: 'You'll realise that I'm not hitting you, because I love you – as man to man – more than anyone else I know, but your ideas: rather like the wrestling match of Birkin and whatever his name was in *Women in Love*, though with no sexual significance.' In the ensuing remonstrance he rejected Muggeridge's past admiration of communism on moral grounds, arguing instead for the tough necessities of class war. In many respects this was the juvenile Taylor again putting Raymond Postgate right.

The Alan Taylor of 1933 was a very long way from the freelance radical of the 1950s and later. His later self would have cringed if he had reread part of his peroration:

Attack the leaders if you like, attack their policy: but have the grace and good sense to recognise that – as in England there is a solid workers' movement which is going forward, despite ups and downs – so in Russia there is a workers' movement which is holding on somehow – on forced rations – until we, the workers of the rest of the world, come to rescue it.

These comments ended with: 'If you can't praise the Workers' State, well for God's sake leave it alone and come away.'

However, this stern revolutionary stalwart stance was undermined by the distinctly Pooterish tone of his concerns about money he had lent them, possibly £90 for furniture in their Moscow flat. He told Muggeridge that he had written to Kitty 'not to bother about the money – as long as you pay me interest once a year'.[111]

After Malcolm had joined Kitty in Switzerland in spring 1933, Taylor wrote again. He urged him to return to England.

I do hope, for our sakes, you will come back to England, so that we may see you, for dear Malcolm and dear Kitty we miss you terribly and think of you every day. If you want somewhere to live in England for a little while you know how glad we should be to have you – however large your family – and you need never go near Manchester. Please do come to England at any rate, so that we may meet.

After this gushing opening, Alan Taylor set about insulting Muggeridge's integrity in a quite remarkable way. After suggesting when they met they should both keep off the subject of Russia, he wrote,

I really would like to say what terrible grief and pain your late articles about Russia cause your friends, but then what's the good? We all have to do pretty unpleasant things to raise money and it's not for me to tell you how you should or shouldn't finance yourself. When my Manchester friends bring up your articles, I just say – I didn't love Malcolm because he was a Bolshevik and I don't hate him now because he's an anti-Bolshevik. So I don't care (oh I care but I mean it makes no difference) what you say about the Workers' state: I shall be glad to see you just as much and I hope you feel the same.

By the time of this second letter to the errant former believer in the Soviet Union, Taylor's concern for finance was getting the better of his affection for the Muggeridges. He ended the letter (immediately before 'love Alan'), 'When you pay me some interest in September, may I suggest that you pay me £10–£20 of the principal as well, according to taste?'[112] Given these letters, one might think that Taylor got off lightly in the portrayal of Rattray in *Picture Palace* (which Malcolm Muggeridge revised in London in early 1934).

In his letter to Muggeridge in February 1933 Taylor had written, 'Margaret and I are thinking of going to live in a cottage at Disley! You'll love it – very high and open: miles away from anywhere.' This cottage was in Higher Disley, then a village separated from the Manchester suburbs stretching through Stockport to Disley. High up the hill above Disley, the cottage was exposed to severe weather each winter but enjoyed memorable views eastward towards Kinder Scout and to the north across the valley, over New Mills. 'Three Gates' was more realistically located for his post at Manchester University than somewhere in the Hawkshead area, where he and Margaret had first sought a place in the country. The building, two old cottages knocked into one, had been partly modernised. It cost the Taylors £525, a high sum then for such a property had it not been for the views.[113] It represented another of Taylor's adopted images. This time it was of a rugged-outdoor variety. In fact, there were more images than one encompassed by his Peak District pursuits. There was a manliness in striding out into the harsh high moorland, long walks which required stamina and strength of character. The most challenging and lengthy of such walks were often seen as for men only: occasions for male bonding and for character development. Yet there was also a strong radical element, drawing on notions of the land being for the people, not plutocrats, and that trespasses at Kinder Scout and elsewhere were assertions of basic democratic rights. Taylor's enthusiasm for the great outdoors had been fostered in the Lake District and by his taste from Bootham for starting the day with a cold bath; but it was also encouraged by the enthusiasm of friends such as the Muggeridges for long tramps in the Derbyshire hills and the recent mass trespasses at Kinder Scout and in the Derwent Valley.[114] He recalled of another such incident,

> Some time in the mid-thirties university students organized a mass trespass. There was a battle between students and gamekeepers and some of the students were sent to prison. They were threatened with expulsion and the Students' Union held a meeting of protest…I was the only staff speaker, by no means for the only time. The meeting was probably unnecessary. Stopford, the vice-chancellor, was a man of great sense and could be relied on to brush aside the threats of expulsion without encouragement from a protest meeting.[115]

They had five happy years living on the edge of the Derbyshire Peak District. Each weekend they went for a whole-day walk, sometimes trespassing at Kinder Scout or Bleaklow Hill. Taylor enjoyed marching his visitors, including Lewis Namier, out across the moors. He took inordinate pride in his gardening skills and he enjoyed preparing home-made beer.

Yet, for all his rosy recollections, there were some drawbacks there, not least affecting Margaret.

'Three Gates' was in an exciting location but it was a cold house, very dependent on its central heating; and it required the installation of electricity when they bought it. It was relatively isolated, not like their usual urban or suburban locations. He was less there than Margaret Taylor, as he went off in term several days a week in his open-top car, with a rug and a hot-water bottle in addition to the car's hood in cold weather. For Margaret it could be lonelier there, though she had Freda Robinson, a local farmer's daughter, do housework on a daily basis.

However, Alan and Margaret Taylor, as an affluent young couple without children, made the most of Manchester's cultural life. They held a subscription to the Hallé orchestra, attended most theatre productions and often went to the cinema. In the mid-1930s Margaret Taylor began to develop a cultural role for herself, having no paid employment. With Philip Godlee, chairman of the Hallé orchestra, she began the Manchester Chamber Concerts Society. In her role as its secretary she secured the best quartets. For the rest of her life she remained very proud of this initiative and that the society continued to exist.[116] When they were not away visiting Percy and Connie Taylor, company came at weekends; the weekend guests were her husband's university and *Manchester Guardian* friends. Then they went for day walks across the moors or, in summer, swam in a high pool in the Dane valley. Even Lewis Namier and Percy Taylor joined in the moorland bathing.

After the Muggeridges, their particular friends were Len Palmer, a philologist, and his Austrian wife Lisl, a botanist. Len Palmer had also studied in Vienna in 1927–30, gaining a PhD in philosophy from Vienna University, and was an Assistant Lecturer, then full Lecturer, in Classics at Manchester University 1931–41, later becoming Professor of Comparative Philology at Oxford University. The two couples were sufficiently close to share a holiday cottage in Colthouse, Hawkshead, in the summer of 1935, the cottage being where Wordsworth stayed when at school.[117]

While music was a major part of both their lives, the Taylors' other cultural interests included poetry. At Oxford, Alan Taylor had gone to poets' parties with his friend Norman Cameron, where he had seen W.H. Auden and Stephen Spender. In the 1930s it was through Cameron that Alan and Margaret Taylor met Robert Graves, Cecil Day-Lewis, Louis MacNeice and Dylan Thomas. Margaret Taylor liked her husband's poetic friend and, on one occasion, took pains to impress on one of Norman Cameron's colleagues at the J. Walter Thompson advertising agency that Cameron was a notably kind and sensitive man even if he appeared blustering and arrogant at first. The Taylors often stayed with Norman and Elfrieda Cameron in their flat in British Grove, Hammersmith. The Camerons frequently spent weekends at 'Three Gates'.[118] 'One day early in 1935,' Taylor later recalled,

> Norman wrote me that a marvellous new poet had appeared, young and very poor; it was everyone's duty to support him; would I have him for a week or two? I agreed. One morning the door bell rang and there stood Dylan Thomas, curly haired and not yet bloated, indeed looking like a Greek god on a small scale.[119]

Alan Taylor could not rival a poetic Greek god in looks, nor Dylan Thomas for boisterous fun when fuelled by alcohol. For his part, Dylan Thomas eagerly turned on his charm for whichever women were present. Margaret Taylor was not immune from the appeal of the avowedly bohemian young poet and enjoyed him reciting his verse to her, but the relationship was platonic.

Alan Taylor at first enjoyed Dylan Thomas' company. They happily read and discussed Rabelais, drinking his home-made beer into the early hours. In true Taylor fashion he set the poet to work to earn his keep, whitewashing the exterior walls of 'Three Gates'. Dylan Thomas wrote verse and enjoyed the views, including towards Kinder Scout. He enjoyed even more being looked after, with Margaret Taylor cooking and fussing around him in the way his mother did in Swansea and with Freda Robinson often there to tidy up after him. His stay lengthened from one or two weeks to nearly a month, from mid-April to mid-May 1935. However, Alan Taylor, who always favoured genteel aesthetes of the Harold Acton and Jack Yates kind, was soon shocked at Dylan Thomas' massive depredation of his stock of beer and by his total disregard for his creed of thrifty and sound personal finance. Moreover, he was disconcerted at his wife's admiration for the young poet. Taylor tried to assert himself, laying down minimum standards of reasonable conduct and a ration on the beer. Dylan Thomas responded as he usually did when thwarted by middle-class sensibilities, by playing on his host's apprehensions and distastes (or, in current parlance, 'winding him up'). He also evaded the alcohol ration by going down the hill towards Disley to 'The Plough Boy', where his ready wit and charm secured him beer from Mr Bloom and other regulars at the pub. When eventually he did decide to leave, he successfully tapped Alan Taylor for £2, ostensibly to replace a lost train ticket. It was but the first Danegeld Taylor would pay to get the poet away from his wife and home. Dylan Thomas nevertheless added the Taylors to his mental list of potential patrons; and, in late 1937, gave their names as likely subscribers for a planned limited edition of a collection of short stories, *The Burning Baby*.[120]

Dylan Thomas apart, 'Three Gates' was also a happy memory for Alan Taylor as it was where his and Margaret's family began. Their first child, Giles Lewis, was born on 12 April 1937. An ovarian cyst probably delayed Margaret's ability to have children, so Giles' safe arrival delighted them as much as Alan's birth had pleased his parents. The proud parents secured what was considered to be the best care money could buy for their first child, employing a Norland nurse (or nanny), who wore the distinctive full-length oatmeal coat, felt hat and white gloves when out. The Norland nurses' training was based on the belief that a child's attitude to learning was formed very early in life.[121] The Taylors followed the childcare precepts of Truby King, with everything for the baby carried out on a carefully timed daily schedule, and also followed what Alan later deemed 'cranky' ideas on diet. When the nanny had her day off, Alan Taylor cared for his

With the Thompsons. Front row, left to right: Harry Thompson, Joan Beauchamp, AJPT; behind: Connie Taylor, with probably John and Sara beside her, and a brother-in-law at the back.

son, much as Percy Taylor had thirty years earlier. His names came from
St Gilgen in Switzerland, where Taylor had spent the summer of 1932,
and Lewis after his senior colleague, Lewis Namier. Not many university
lecturers have named their first child after their professor. He later noted,
'Lewis was rather embarrassed by this.'[122]

Looking back on his life in 1978 Alan Taylor wrote, 'I should say that
I was politically active only between 1933 and 1936 (anti-war) and 1958
and 1962 (CND).'[123] In these years in the 1930s he was anti-war but,
equally notably, he was still militantly socialist of an ILP hue. He spoke for
the Manchester Peace Council and also for the Manchester and Salford
Trades Council.

The anti-war campaigning combined both the Nonconformist elements
in his outlook as well as the views which were a norm at his parents' home.
In Geneva Arthur Henderson, former Foreign Secretary and Labour
Party leader, chaired the meetings of the World Disarmament Conference
from February 1932. The issue of avoiding war was taken up by international communism, with a world Anti-War Congress in late August
1932. Afterwards the British communists, other left-wing groups and
pacifists launched local anti-war councils. In Manchester Taylor spoke at a
touring disarmament exhibition. He struck a hard-Left stance, not simply
condemning the tradition radical target of arms manufacturers but
proclaiming that a socialist government was the only security against war.
Later he recalled that his speech much impressed the young Frank Allaun,
the future left-wing Labour MP for Salford East, who told him: 'The anti-
war movement in Manchester has found its speaker.'[124]

He then played a full role in the Manchester Anti-War Council and,
when it was renamed, the Manchester Peace Council. It was a very broad
front, and he was listed as representing Manchester University. He was at
home as a rogue radical on the body, shocking some of the Nonconformists
by his advanced socialism yet annoying the local communists by often
opposing their proposals. He was one of the Peace Council's most assiduous
speakers, often addressing trade union branches or other groups twice a
week. He denounced the National Government for helping the Nazi
regime to survive and urged that the western European powers should
unite with the Soviet Union against the threat from Germany. Yet, like
Henry Sara, he was hostile to Stalinism within Russia and was suspicious
of the motives of the British Communist Party.

The timing of Taylor's arrival as an anti-war campaigner suggests that
his period as a political activist began with the Manchester Trades Council
and this body provided him with contacts or at least motivation for his other
activities. Why else should Frank Allaun or someone else have invited him
to speak at the disarmament exhibition? While radical intellectuals received

much respect in Manchester, Alan Taylor at 26 or 27 was not in the league of a G.D.H. Cole or Bertrand Russell.[125]

In taking part in the Labour movement through trades council activity Taylor followed in his father's footsteps. Percy Taylor had become a delegate to Preston Trades Council after the First World War. In his autobiography Alan Taylor wrote, 'I suppose I ought to have joined the Manchester Labour Party but I could not face the Didsbury branch which was entirely composed of middle-class intellectuals.'[126] While this may appear not to have been inappropriate for him, going to the trades council enabled him to meet more 'United Front' aspirations – aspirations held by his parents and Henry Sara, the Independent Labour Party, and still shared by him.

Indeed, it is possible that his not joining the Labour Party then owed more to indecision as to the way politics were going as capitalism appeared to be in serious difficulties after the Wall Street Crash, 1929. The Independent Labour Party disaffiliated from the Labour Party in 1932 and campaigned for working-class unity against the challenge of fascism. In 1932–34 Alan Taylor's views appear to have been similar.

The Manchester and Salford Trades Council was one of the biggest in the country.[127] It met in Caxton Hall, Chapel Street, Salford. In the early to mid-1930s there were over 360 delegates. Albert Purcell had reinvigorated the trades council as secretary from 1929. He had returned to play a major role in Manchester labour politics after being a national figure as a Labour MP, 1923–24 and 1925–29, and a member of the TUC's General Council (and its predecessor, the Parliamentary Committee), 1919–27, and the TUC president in 1924. Purcell had also been a founder member of the Communist Party of Great Britain, resigning in 1922 yet remaining committed to most of its policies.[128] He had been particularly prominent in promoting Anglo-Russian relations as chairman of the Anglo-Russian Parliamentary Committee, 1924, and when he was president of the International Federation of Trade Unions, 1924–27; his presidency ended when continental anti-communist trade unionists ousted him, deeming him to be a communist and an agent of Russia. Yet the Communist Party of Great Britain, prodded on by Moscow, denounced him as a former left-winger who was responsible for the failure of the General Strike in 1926.[129] Professor Calhoun has written of Purcell that he was 'a strong, forceful person, blunt and often extreme in expressing his opinions, rather too obviously contemptuous of those who refused to accept them, totally lacking in tact, finesse or diplomacy'. He added that 'Few men could get close to him' and that he was 'the left's most vigorous and irrepressible pulpiteer'.[130] Yet Alan Taylor, at 26, did get near to him and soon was one of the select few Purcell chose to speak at big demonstrations.

It is likely that the Taylor household influence was important in securing him entry and acceptance in the trades council. His father could have told him how to join the General and Municipal Workers' Union. This Alan Taylor did and, within six months of his marriage, he was nominated as a delegate to the Manchester and Salford Trades Council. Once there, it was probably Taylor's ability to speak and the Broad Left outlook displayed in his Peace Council speeches that brought the young academic to Purcell's notice and encouraged Purcell to let him address public meetings on behalf of the trades council. Taylor appears somewhat naïve even in later life, being surprised that the General and Municipal Workers' Union did not mandate him on trades council issues. Had its members been that keen they, not a university lecturer, would have gone to the trades council. He clearly went not for the trade union business, which he recalled as 'discussions of the utmost tedium',[131] but to support Broad Left politics and, if possible, to speak at meetings. He may well have still believed that capitalism might imminently collapse, given the world recession, and wished to share in the triumph of Albert Purcell and the Manchester proletariat.

Alan Taylor was a delegate to Manchester and Salford Trades Council from May 1932 until March 1936. After 1932 (when he attended twice) he was among the most assiduous attenders, missing only, or mostly, the summer meetings when he was away. In summer 1932 he was in Austria and Bavaria, revising his book *The Italian Problem in European Diplomacy* and holidaying. The following summer he spent four months in Hawkshead in the Lake District. Nevertheless, in 1933 he managed to attend nine of twelve monthly meetings.

The non-business parts of the trades council meetings were filled with the international working class solidarity concerns of Purcell and his supporters. In February 1933 Purcell's former colleague, W.P. Coates, secretary of the Anglo-Russian Parliamentary Committee, spoke about the potential benefits to Britain of a successful conclusion of the then current trade negotiations. In March the trades council agreed a statement 'on the Hitlerite victory' in the German elections and the following month they discussed 'the treatment of the workers and their organisation in Germany'. Taylor and the other delegates were given 'Hitlerism' and other pamphlets in June and 'More Anti-Soviet Lies Nailed' at the October meeting.

Working-class unity was the major political cause of Purcell and his supporters. It embraced most political issues, from campaigning on housing and unemployment to international concerns. It was given practical effect on 9 May 1931 at a People's Congress held in the Free Trade Hall, with over 2000 delegates. There was wider support for such unity following Hitler's securing of power in Germany.[132] In Manchester the theme was further developed in 'Working Class Unity in Manchester and Salford', a statement issued by the executive committee at the October 1933 trades council, which affirmed that 'the imperative need today is the creation of a strong Central Body in Manchester and Salford, representative of all sections of the Trade Union and Labour Movement'. The verbose and rather repetitive statement included:

> In this world of crumbling capitalism, tumbling into frightful disorder and chaos, it is the solemn bounden duty of all understanding workers to seize on every opportunity to bring the workers together, to organise them, to bind them in class unity, with the strongest ties of solidarity, and to so weld and fashion their organised forces so as to create a power strong enough to beat back and finally overcome the powers of disruption and reaction, and to meet all the dangers and difficulties now besetting us.

A month later the trades council followed a TUC Statement on War with a call for trades councils to 'be given full opportunity to associate in every effort to plan and to carry out the organisation in the localities to prevent war'.[133]

Taylor was given his chance to speak in the trades council's public campaigns in 1934. He attended eight of the twelve monthly meetings that year, being away in Spain part of that summer. In February 'a German comrade addressed the delegates on the situation in Germany'. On 25 February the trades council held a meeting in the Free Trade Hall which protested against 'the murderous destruction of the democratic constitution...and the suppression of trade union, socialist and co-operative organisations by the armed ruffians of Fascism' and expressed admiration for 'the heroic stand made by the Austrian workers' earlier in the month.

This was the occasion of Alan Taylor's first public speech. He spoke after Vipont Brown of the Society of Friends and before Charles Dukes, the general secretary of the General and Municipal Workers' Union, and Elijah Sandham of the ILP (both of whom were heckled by communists in the audience). Other speakers included Aubrey Herbert, Liberal, and George Brown, Communist. The *Manchester Guardian* reported,

> Mr A.J.P. Taylor said that they met in bitterness not only against the Austrian Fascists but also against our own government, which had done nothing to protest against the horrors which had taken place, and which had recently given permission for the further arming of the Austrian troops against the workers. The first reaction of the workers in this country had been to say, 'Thank god, at any rate they have fought.' It was on that reaction that they in this country must build. The mistake the Austrians made was not in fighting, but in fighting

too late. It was our duty to learn from Austria that we must be prepared, that capitalism knew no mercy to women and children when it had to defend its hold over the workers.

As a speaker from the university he met Purcell's desire for the involvement in trades council campaigns of a broad front of working people. Yet, nevertheless, he would not have been given the opportunity had there been doubts about his Broad Left orthodoxy, even with his recent experience of Vienna. It remained a golden memory for Taylor, who later recalled,

> With my Austrian memories still fresh I spoke from the heart. Even apart from the cause it was a wonderful opportunity: actually to speak from the platform of the Free Trade Hall and that in days before microphones...I had only ten minutes. But my voice carried as well as any accomplished orator. That Sunday afternoon at the Free Trade Hall convinced me that I too could be a public speaker when I found a cause to believe in.[134]

In June Taylor's next opportunity to speak at a big meeting came when the trades council held three meetings condemning the Incitement to Disaffection Bill: at Ashfield in Salford and at Platt Fields and Queen's Park in Manchester. In spite of the challenge of fascism, the National Government's Incitement to Disaffection Bill, introduced in April 1934, was aimed at the communists and specifically at stopping them distributing literature to, or speaking with members of, the armed forces with the aim to cause or encourage disaffection. The Bill (and subsequent Act) appeared to threaten liberties, with people liable for arrest for acts deemed preparatory to committing an offence and provision made for search warrants if there were grounds for suspicion; hence fears were expressed of a return of autocratic 'general warrants'.[135]

Alan Taylor spoke at the Queen's Park meeting after Joe Compton, the former and future Labour MP for Manchester Gorton, and George Brown, Communist. The *Manchester Guardian* reported,

> That the bill revived war-time legislation and DORA [Defence of the Realm Act] was the contention of Mr A.J.P. Taylor of the Manchester Anti-War Council. 'We are on the verge of a new European war, and the National Government is preparing for that war by the increased expenditure on the army, navy and air force. This Disaffection Bill strikes at all of us who are in favour of anti-war propaganda.'[136]

He spoke at a third trades council demonstration on 21 October. Then a procession of two or three thousand people with bands and banners at its head marched from All Saints to Platt Fields. There, three teams of nearly 30 speakers addressed the crowds from three horse-drawn drays, with a resolution condemning fascism and the Incitement to Disaffection Bill being carried unanimously at each. The speakers included the Labour MPs Arthur Greenwood, Aneurin Bevan and William Dobbie (Rotherham), the Communist Party's William Gallagher and George Brown, the Conservative MP for Manchester Rusholme, E.A. Radford (who explained why he supported the Bill), local clergymen and councillors. Taylor spoke on the same dray as was seated Samuel Alexander, the retired former Professor of Philosophy at Manchester University, who was then 74 years old. Of Alexander, he later recalled, 'With his long beard and Jewish appearance he looked like God Almighty and I am sure he could have filled the role. Certainly he was the greatest man I have known.'[137] The *Manchester Guardian* reported, 'Mr A.J.P. Taylor said the bill was a war measure; a deliberate preparation for the next European war. "Are we going to allow ourselves to be slaughtered," he asked, "or are we going to refuse to fight for capitalism and raise instead the standard of Socialist England?"' However, Alan Taylor lacked vocal power for an open-air rally and later commented that the meeting taught him 'never to speak in the open air again'.[138]

In his autobiography he wrote that 'Purcell's patronage' gave him the opportunities of speaking in the Free Trade Hall and at Platt Fields in 1934. In 1935 no further opportunities arose, perhaps because Alan Taylor had no special claim to expertise as for Austria or for historic precedents (the reintroduction of general warrants before the English Civil War) as with the Incitement to Disaffection Bill. Or perhaps he was becoming uneasy about peace campaigning. The trades council held a big demonstration for peace on 28 July 1935, when he was probably away. In October the trades council declared 'its full support for the League of Nations as the Final Court of all International Disputes', condemned Italian intervention in Abyssinia and fully supported sanctions being imposed on Italy. On Christmas Eve 1935 Purcell died suddenly of a heart attack. Taylor saw out his time on the council, attending the first two meetings of 1936 but not returning as a delegate after his union branch's AGM.[139]

Most probably Alan Taylor's departure from the trades council owed more to convenience than to his changing political views or Purcell's death. While he worked in Manchester he would be eligible for membership of the trades council, but moving out of Manchester to Higher Disley in 1933 may have been one bridge too far for one of the Manchester branches of the General and Municipal Workers' Union by 1935–36. Even if the branch had been happy to continue nominating him, by 1936 he may have preferred not to keep up the commitment of city centre evening meetings.

That he was still keen on political activity was shown by his active participation in the Macclesfield Divisional Labour Party and especially its

Disley branch. Having spoken before two mass audiences at trades council demonstrations in 1934, Taylor was very ready to speak to election audiences on behalf of the Labour Party in the 1935 general election. The parliamentary candidate for Macclesfield was only a year older than him. George Darling was a former railway engineer who had gone on to study at Liverpool and Cambridge Universities and at that time worked as a journalist for the co-operative press.[140] The seat was safely Conservative; the Conservative candidate polled 52.5 per cent of the votes cast in 1935, compared to 32.0 and 15.5 per cent for Darling and the Liberal candidate respectively. Not surprisingly, Taylor did not take up an offer to be nominated to be the next prospective parliamentary candidate for Macclesfield; the seat was fought unsuccessfully by a university lecturer in Economics in the 1945 general election.

In mid-December 1935 Alan Taylor was still speaking publicly in line with the trades council's policy. The Hoare–Laval Pact of 8 December rewarded rather than condemned Italian aggression in Abyssinia. He later wrote of the uproar and collapse of the Hoare–Laval agreement, 'The League died with it. The outcry in England against the Hoare–Laval plan was the greatest explosion over foreign affairs for many years, perhaps the greatest since the campaign against the "Bulgarian horrors" in 1876. Like that campaign, it was effective only in negation.'[141]

At the time the pact's impact on the League of Nations' standing was not so clear. On 17 December Taylor was the speaker at a meeting in Manchester, chaired by the philosopher and First World War hero Professor John Stocks and convened by the university's League of Nations Society, Liberal Association, Socialist Society, Anti-War Group and Student Christian Movement. He made the traditional radical case that it was 'a matter of great moment that the reputation of this country as a country prepared to see just treatment for small nations should be maintained'. He then explained the details of the Hoare–Laval Pact as being in the interests of British imperialism. 'It is no accident that the one bit of Italian territory to be surrendered to Abyssinia is Assab; because Assab, a fortified port, would be a great menace to Aden...This government has pursued a policy of buying Italy off in order to pursue its own imperialist aims.' The meeting condemned the Hoare–Laval Pact by 234 votes to two.[142]

Forty years on Taylor commented on the Manchester University meeting, 'What did the other 3000 students think if they thought at all? This is a parable of what public opinion amounts to.' More generally, he observed: 'No amount of public meetings could secure the oil sanctions in the five months after the Hoare–Laval plan. Public opinion, in short, was more effective in preventing a policy than in imposing one.' He also believed that the National Government's 'dishonesty over the Hoare–Laval plan made Labour more reluctant to support rearmament under such leadership'.[143]

Taylor rightly saw Hitler as a greater threat than Mussolini. According to his autobiography it was the imminent threat of a German military reoccupation of the Rhineland that prompted him, in February 1936, to reverse his views and to call for rearmament at a Manchester Peace Council meeting.[144]

While the developing international situation was the main reason for the major change in his views, there were others. These were historical, to do with his research in German diplomatic history and the powerful influence of Lewis Namier's views. He later wrote that, when reading the published German diplomatic documents in 1933–36 before starting to teach his special subject at Manchester University in the autumn of 1936, his views changed: 'I no longer thought that Germany was the innocent victims of Entente diplomacy. I was not even sure that the First World War happened by accident.'[145] Similarly, by the autumn of 1937, when *Germany's First Bid for Colonies* went to the publisher, he was critical of Germany's pre-First World War stance on colonies. He wrote,

> The average Englishman was ashamed of the British Empire and believed (quite wrongly) that it had been acquired in some wicked fashion... This sense of sin placed British governments at a disadvantage in their negotiations with Germany; they were convinced of the justice of the German grievances even before the grievances were expressed. British governments had spent most of the nineteenth century trying to prevent the growth of the British Empire, and still it had grown; German governments had done their utmost to encourage colonial enterprise, and yet their empire was a failure; clearly it was the fault of British governments and they must put it right. Of course they wanted to put it right without annoying the colonial governments or the British public; there they stood, ears anxiously cocked for the next German complaint.[146]

He also criticised the views of the great radical peace writers in the pages of the *Manchester Guardian*. In March 1937 he was critical of Francis Hirst's *Armaments: the Race and the Crisis* (1937), observing, 'He misses no opportunity of approving of German grievances.' He observed, 'Great armaments are abhorrent, but they are not themselves the cause of war; they are the symptoms of international conflicts; and war can be prevented only by removing the causes of conflict, not by denouncing the symptoms.' As for the second edition of the late G. Lowes Dickinson's *The International Anarchy 1906–1914* (1937), he commented in 1938 that the book was 'a curious memorial of a time when well-meaning men thought that peace could be secured by being sympathetic to Germany; that the Concert of Europe could be made real by calling it the League of Nations; and that the League of Nations could then over-awe the law-breaker without the backing of superior force'.[147]

Alan Taylor was also appalled by the arrests and murders of communists, socialists and trade unionists by the Right in Austria and the Nazis in Germany. He came to know several refugee academics who found posts at Manchester University, notably Michael Polanyi, Professor of Physical Chemistry, and Reinhold Baer, a mathematician.[148] He and Margaret also provided work for Henrietta Werner, a 28-year-old social democrat refugee from Vienna. He had met her once in Vienna in 1929, but the stronger connection was with Percy Taylor's friend, Sydney Sharples. She had met Sharples at the 1929 International Meeting of Socialist Youth in Vienna and stayed first with his family on coming to Britain.[149]

Lewis Namier reinforced his anti-Nazi and even anti-German sentiments. Taylor recalled meeting Namier at Disley station shortly after Hitler had ordered the murder of Ernst Röhm and some seventy Nazis and political opponents on 30 June 1934. 'As his train drew into the station, he put his head out of the carriage window, waved his newspaper, and cried joyfully, "The swine are killing each other! The swine are killing each other!"'[150] Namier had responded to Hitler's advent to power by establishing in March 1933 a Manchester Academic Society, which tried to place refugee German academics for at least a year in Manchester and other universities, with their salaries funded by donations. This foundered on insufficient funds and insufficient university places for the refugees to go to after a year. Namier also spoke vigorously on behalf of poorer Jewish refugees from the Nazis.[151]

Alan Taylor in effect helped Namier by taking on committees and teaching that Namier otherwise would have had to do. Namier chose to ignore or misunderstand Manchester University's procedures and Taylor readily rescued him from his own wilful ways. In dumping his work on colleagues, he would expostulate, 'What have the others got to do with their time?'[152] Namier devoted much time in the 1930s to trying to assist Jewish refugees. Taylor's practical response of employing Henrietta Werner, a refugee social democrat, was a statement that he too did his bit to look after his people.

In 1938 his childhood friend Eunice Blackwell wrote to Alan Taylor concerning the plight of an Austrian Jewish refugee. His reply shows his acute awareness of the predicament of central European Jews. He wrote,

I'm afraid I can't be of much help about the young Austrian – I am absolutely snowed under with such requests. His scheme seems to be impracticable: it is not possible for a young man, particularly a foreigner, to earn his keep in a family and work for a degree – an au pair job is full-time work. His only hope is to find an English family who will house him out of charity (we did this with a German refugee at one time) without expecting anything in return: even this is pretty unsatisfactory. Where will his pocket money, train fares etc. come from? Woburn House – the Jewish organisation – might be able to suggest something.

His wisest policy would be to attempt somehow to get to Palestine & that is now v. difficult: but he's just the type they want. Not of course as a professional man, but as a peasant. The Jews in Austria & Germany don't yet realise that they'll be lucky if they get jobs as crossings-sweepers in any free country: they must stop at nothing to get out – the only alternative is suicide. It seems terribly hard to say this, but it's true.[153]

Unsurprisingly, Alan Taylor was also involved in the Left Book Club from 1936. It was founded by the publisher Victor Gollancz, who selected the books with the assistance of the left-wing intellectuals Harold Laski and John Strachey. The first two titles, published in May 1936, were *France Today and the People's Front* by the French communist leader Maurice Thorez and *Out of the Night*, on man's genetic future, by Professor Hermann Muller, Professor of Zoology at the University of Texas but then on leave at the Institute of Genetics in the USSR. Left Book Club discussion groups sprang up quickly. One of the first was organised by Frank Allaun in the Manchester-Salford area, another was formed within the *Manchester Guardian* and one of the others in Manchester met in the Burlington café, close to the university. Taylor often attended and spoke at the Burlington group.[154]

It was not one of his political activities he wished to recall in his autobiography. He came to see the Left Book Club as a Communist Party front, which was a part of international moves for Popular Fronts. When he came to write *English History 1914–1945* (1965), he referred to it as 'an agency of Communist influence' which achieved 'a membership ten times greater than the ILP or the Communist Party had ever secured, solidly based on intellectuals, particularly school teachers throughout the country'. He commented of Labour Party hostility, 'Now the Left Book Club was diverting high-minded school teachers into reading Communist tracts when they ought to have been joining the Labour Party and working for it.'[155] In his autobiography and other autobiographical writings he carefully omitted that he had been an eager high-minded participant, though one who would have taken his own left-wing line.

Taylor had a final phase of political activity in Manchester shortly before he left for Oxford. In Manchester there was widespread outrage at the Anglo-French moves to give Germany Czechoslovakian territory. The Labour Party, the Liberal Party, the Manchester and Salford Trades Council, the Council of Action and the Peace Pledge Union were all involved in a considerable number of protest meetings from 24 September 1938. These included a Council of Action meeting at Lancashire College, Whalley Range, on Saturday afternoon 24 September and a South Manchester Peace Council meeting in Platt Fields the next afternoon. In spite of his changed views, the Manchester Peace Council allowed Taylor to speak at its meetings before the Munich conference. He later recalled,

> Having just come back from France, I was convinced that the French would not fight. However I was also convinced that Hitler was bluffing and would move against Czechoslovakia only if Great Britain and France allowed him to do so... I suppose I addressed half a dozen meetings on the theme of Stand up to Hitler. They were terrible. I tried every argument: national honour, anti-Fascism, Hitler's weakness and the certainty he would climb down. Always came the reply, 'What you are advocating means war. We want peace.'[156]

One of his last actions before leaving Manchester was to write in his national honour mode to Duff Cooper to congratulate him on resigning as First Lord of the Admiralty over the Munich Agreement. 'May I express my appreciations that in this time of national humiliation there has still been found one Englishman not faithless to honour and principle and to the traditions of our once great name? If England is in the future to have a history, your name will be mentioned with respect and admiration.'[157]

This somewhat obsequious tone of his congratulatory letter was a long way from his speeches before Alf Purcell and the trades council or from the political arguing of his home. His letter was also notable for being headed 'Magdalen College' and having after his name 'Fellow and Tutor'; it was a notable first-day missive in his new appointment, and it sufficiently impressed for its illustrious recipient to keep it among his papers.

Taylor had succeeded on his third attempt to return to Oxford. After his 1931 endeavour to go to Oriel, he had been unsuccessful at Corpus Christi College. As was his wont, he later portrayed his failure as due to him paying the penalty for individualistic integrity and wit. His intense competitiveness seems to have made it impossible for him to admit, or possibly to accept, that his talents could be second best. At Corpus Christi he later suggested that his downfall was due to his reputation for political activism. Apparently Sir Richard Livingstone, the president, put it to him: 'I hear you have strong political views,' to which he gave the reply (noted earlier), 'Oh no, President. Extreme views weakly held.'[158] Yet, given his mid-1930s speeches, perhaps this was his best defence.

By 1938 his strong views against appeasement were very acceptable to Livingstone and others. His views on German culpability for the First World War had also moved in a direction more acceptable to most of his academic elders. His application for the Tutorial Fellowship in Modern History at Magdalen was greatly helped by enthusiastic support by E.L. Woodward, who was the Modern History external examiner at Manchester. He wrote to his friend Stephen Lee, the senior history tutor at Magdalen, that Taylor, who had earlier been a pupil of G.N. Clark, 'has developed extremely well under Namier's direction. He has just written a v good little bk on the German colonial hunt.' More formal support, all very positive, was given by his referees Lewis Namier, Ernest Jacob and Humphrey Sumner of Baliol, who had also been a Modern History external examiner at Manchester University. They emphasised not only first-rate ability and that he was the coming man of international history but that he worked hard as a lecturer and took a real interest in his students. Humphrey Sumner predicted, 'He will certainly continue to produce historical work, and it should be not only very individual, but of marked distinction.'[159]

By the mid-1930s Alan Taylor had largely broken away from his parents – physically, intellectually and financially, much as other middle-class children did. His departure was more unusual than many in that he had long sought to impress his parents, and especially his mother, by his intellectual abilities and socialist integrity. He had imbibed deep radical individualism from his grandfather, JT, and Marxism from his parents and Henry Sara. The radical individualism remained, as did vestiges of his own reformulations of socialism. However, by 1936 he had moved on intellectually, responding to the changed international realities. Lewis Namier's encouragement and his own competitiveness had also set him firmly on an academic course, but one which he could press into being compatible with a high public profile.

–4–

WAR AND WIDER
RECOGNITION 1938–48

From 1938 Alan Taylor enjoyed dividing his working life on an Oxford–London axis. He later wrote that 'if I had stayed in Manchester I should never have achieved anything except a few academic books. Without the contacts I made in London, which was easily reached from Oxford, I should never have become either a journalist or a television star.'[1] For the rest of his life his Fellowship, and later his Honorary Fellowship, at Magdalen College was very dear to him.

Magdalen College is the most attractive of Oxford colleges, notable for its architecture and its spacious grounds. It had been one of three colleges considered suitable for the Prince of Wales in 1912 (the others being Christ Church and New College). Albert Mansbridge, a member of the Royal Commission on the Universities of Oxford and Cambridge 1919–22, wrote,

> Magdalen is the richest Oxford College; her total income in 1920 was £92,172, and she had 194 undergraduates and 33 Fellows, in addition to the Head. She paid £13,129 to the teaching staff, and granted £4,057 in scholarships, exhibitions etc. Let it be remembered that the College has an expensive chapel which it should be encouraged to maintain, and that it is generous to the university…yet, in spite of all this, the ordinary observer will find it difficult to understand why Balliol, with a total income of £20,246, should be able to pay £2,261 more than Magdalen in respect of scholarships and exhibitions, and to support a Head and 15 Fellows, in addition to 264 undergraduates…[2]

Like Christ Church, Magdalen had strong ties with Eton; a sixth of its undergraduates came from there alone in 1920. George Stuart Gordon (President of Magdalen College, 1928–42) showed none of a later age's economic-driven eagerness for overseas students when not accepting an

Indian applicant in 1934. He informed a Harrow schoolmaster that 'the College is very English in its atmosphere, and with the best will in the world, seems unable to absorb anything quite so foreign'. Apart from Magdalen's employment of women for assisting its running, it remained a male preserve. Only a sixth of Oxford University's tutorial Fellows in 1937 had not been educated at Oxford, while a fifth had been undergraduates in the colleges that employed them. Taylor, as a white male, from a wealthy family, educated at a public school and Oxford, was clearly no outsider. The less usual feature of his career was eight years teaching at a provincial university, a matter which then did not secure the waiving of a probationary year within Magdalen in the way that a year elsewhere in Oxford University would have done.[3]

When he arrived George Gordon had just begun a three-year term as Vice-Chancellor of Oxford University. During the 1930s Magdalen had been effective in its aim to admit more academically minded applicants and achieve better examination results. By 1938 the number of undergraduates had risen to 221 and the Fellows to 42 (and ten lecturers).[4] According to Taylor, all but the economist Redvers Opie had been undergraduates at Oxford and had been elected Fellows immediately after graduation. Many were unmarried and lived in the college. 'Married fellows,' Brian Harrison has written, 'were treated as honorary bachelors, and felt a strong obligation to dine regularly. They often lived nearby in houses owned by the college - one-third did so in 1946 – so they and their wives were readily drawn into the college family.'[5]

On being offered the Fellowship, Taylor had negotiated what he felt to be suitable accommodation. He wanted a house out in the country, to keep up his lifestyle at Higher Disley. Bruce McFarlane, who was to be his Medieval History colleague, told him he had to live near the college and showed him Holywell Ford. Taylor greatly admired the buildings; he later wrote of it, 'With its William Morris style, it looked medieval.' Attractive and spacious, it was beside the river Cherwell and in a rural location, although just beyond the walks around Magdalen's grounds. Although warned by the college's bursar that the rent was beyond his salary, Alan Taylor insisted on taking it from October 1939. He also appears to have tried unsuccessfully to negotiate a special hours of work arrangement. For on 1 August 1938 an irritated McFarlane wrote to A.L. Rowse, 'He has climbed down about hours and residence, I was rather sorry, as this trouble has made me feel that we should be well rid of him.' He added, 'I don't like him.'[6]

So for his first year Alan and Margaret Taylor, with young Giles and Henrietta Werner, lived in a rented furnished house on the Marston Road in Headington. They tried to be hosts in this cramped accommodation, in the manner of their weekends at 'Three Gates'. Instead, as he later ruefully recollected, 'It became clear to me that we ought to give dinner parties in college instead of inviting people to our home – a form of expense to which I was unaccustomed.' At first Alan and Margaret Taylor avoided the classical music on offer in Oxford, believing it would be well below the standards of the Hallé orchestra. As with the lack of entertaining at home, this stance had a greater impact on her than him. In Manchester she had been the linchpin of the Manchester Chamber Concerts Society. In Oxford there were times when she was the academic equivalent of a golf widow, though the Taylors compensated by holding their own music evenings at home, and in due course she organised lunchtime concerts in Oxford, putting much energy into ensuring that they were successful. In this she was emulating those put on in central London at the National Gallery by Myra Hess. Visiting musicians, including Benjamin Britten, stayed overnight with them at Holywell Ford.[7]

He enjoyed his Fellowship at Magdalen and spent much time there in carrying out his various duties. He took his teaching and administrative tasks seriously and came to love and revere the college's ceremonies and traditions.

Taylor was elected a Fellow in time to participate in the dinner on Restoration Day, 25 October 1938, to mark the 250th anniversary of the restoration of President John Hough and the Fellows. They had been expelled earlier by King James II when he was thwarted in imposing his nominee as college President. Alan Taylor and the zoologist Peter Medawar were the newest Fellows and were among the speakers. Taylor established his radical credentials by comparing the resistance to James II with the failure to resist Hitler at Munich less than four weeks earlier; a message especially barbed given the presence of Geoffrey Dawson, the pro-appeasement editor of the *Times*. Forty years on, Taylor often said, and also wrote in his autobiography, that his remaining ambition was to attend the 300th Restoration dinner. Sadly, although alive in 1988, he was not sufficiently fit to go.

In Magdalen Taylor quickly came to admire Thomas Dewar Weldon (nicknamed 'Harry' after a famous music hall comedian). He later said of Weldon, 'He came back immediately after the first war, and he found a college dominated by very aged religious philosophers…and he fought against them persistently and either pushed them out or pushed them aside.' Weldon and his associates successfully pressed to raise the intellectual requirements of admissions and to improve the quality of teaching. For this Weldon received much hostility from the more conservative Fellows and some Etonians. Medawar wrote that all the Oxford colleges had 'one or two cynical, sardonic, and ostensibly world-weary dons who derived the utmost pleasure from dazzling and as often as not bewildering the young with epigrams and aphorisms'. He added that for anyone engaging with people such as Weldon or Maurice Bowra (Wadham College) it proved 'a formidable experience and admirable corrective against any tendency towards complacency or acquiescent conventionality of thought'.[8]

Alan Taylor's feelings were less warm towards another notable Fellow, the Ulsterman C.S. Lewis, the tutor in English. He did not care for Lewis' far from progressive politics and his earnest evangelical Christianity. He preferred the world-weary cynicism of Weldon to Lewis' circle of male friends, who met in a pub and read their work to each other – the Inklings. Lewis, who had searched for belief before becoming a fully believing Christian, viewed Weldon with distaste; yet, ironically, a conversation with Weldon in which Weldon asserted that the resurrection may well have occurred was one of several events which transformed Lewis' religious life.

Humphrey Carpenter, in writing of the Inklings has commented that Lewis believed 'that the college was ruled to a large extent by the unofficial junto of "progressives" under the leadership of Harry Weldon…Weldon was the perfect enemy for Lewis, militantly atheist, ruthless, subtle, everything that Lewis was not.'[9] Lewis was prone to see organised groups where there was no such formal cohesion among others who took a different view from him. The two men respected each other's abilities and were wary of each other. Medawar later recalled of the war years that Lewis was 'the most formidable member of the governing body – with whom even Harry Weldon was chary of entering into a dispute'.[10]

Alan Taylor also respected Lewis' abilities and they often talked. Nevertheless, he disliked what he felt to be his 'urgent Low Church piety which he preached everywhere except in the college common room'.[11] While Taylor saw the elderly Paul Benecke, tutor in Ancient History and the Senior Fellow, as a caricature and a warning, Lewis saw him as a saintly ascetic, a person worthy of emulation.[12] Taylor was very much more in sympathy with Weldon.

His relations with another notable Fellow, Bruce McFarlane, were more complex. Taylor later recalled that they never had a cross word in 25 years. However, he added, 'We really did not see eye to eye,' and that 'like most homosexuals he was neurotic', an uncharitable generalisation) and of a kind that he made several times; yet surprising, given his lengthy friendships with Teddy Pratt, Tom Driberg and Jack Yates. Until Taylor opposed his bid to be college president in 1942, the two seem to have got on well. Taylor would have warmed both to McFarlane's professed communist politics and to his fervent love of visiting English parish churches. However, they had very different approaches to teaching. Bruce McFarlane and John Morris, Magdalen's law tutor, were adept at getting students involved in detailed work on their subjects. Sir Keith Thomas has commented, 'At its most intense, as in the teaching of Morris…or of his Magdalen colleague K.B. McFarlane, the tutorial could be an experience which could mark the pupil's interests and intellectual habits for life. Young men were sometimes so imprinted by their tutors that they even unconsciously copied their gestures, mannerisms and way of walking and speaking.'[13] Taylor later felt that McFarlane greatly disapproved of his more relaxed approach of wishing to stimulate his students to independent study, leaving him more free for writing.

Alan Taylor's relationship with John Morris was unequivocally good. This was in spite of Morris being critical of some of his radical views. Taylor, for his part, admired Morris' honesty and reliability. He later commented of him that he 'was rigidly honest' and 'he'd never cheat'. Morris would grumble that over some college conflict he would have to support Taylor because he was right, saying, 'I shall have to stand by you this afternoon, Alan.'[14]

Taylor also enjoyed the stimulus of the company of other outstanding scholars. John Austin was one of the most eminent philosophers of the period. Later, Magdalen had a second in its midst as Gilbert Ryle became an Honorary Fellow when he became Waynflete Professor of Metaphysical Philosophy, 1945–68. Both were anti-appeasers, making their position known during the 1938 Oxford by-election. Austin's slogan then – 'A vote for Hogg is a vote for Hitler' – greatly appealed to Taylor. So did Austin's astringent wit and cheerful company. It was later observed of Austin that he 'tended to write and speak of Aristotle as though he was an interesting but slightly exasperating colleague living on the next staircase'. Austin had been to Moscow in 1935 and had returned impressed. Alan Taylor later recalled him as being a very able and likeable man: 'I came to love him though his mind was beyond mine.'[15] Taylor also admired C.T. Onions, the lexicographer, whom he deemed to be the most distinguished Fellow in 1938. In spite of the handicap of a stammer, he was a notable presence in the senior common room, where, according to another Fellow, Jack Bennett, 'his astringent rejoinders to questions on etymology and English usage were much relished'.[16]

Alan Taylor was not overawed by the wit and erudition of his colleagues and made his mark as a witty and opinionated academic. Although out of the college for many meals as a married man, he readily played his part in college affairs, serving on many of its committees. When the college President, George Gordon, died in March 1942, Taylor, then Senior Tutor, played his part in electing a successor. He later wrote, 'The election, though bitterly contested, was not at all like the one depicted by C.P. Snow in *The Masters*. We said harsh things at our meetings and forgot about them afterwards. At any rate I did.'[17] He vigorously supported Sir Henry Tizard, whose cause was championed by Leslie Sutton, the tutor for Chemistry, against his fellow historian, Bruce McFarlane, then Acting President of Magdalen. Tizard won by one vote, becoming the first scientist to be the head of an Oxford college since the seventeenth century. Tizard, a former undergraduate of Magdalen, was attracted by the post but was also eager for a prestigious non-Whitehall post, having been eased out of government circles by Lord Cherwell (formerly Professor F.A. Lindemann), who had Winston Churchill's full support.[18]

Taylor had hopes that Tizard would push further the reforms that Harry Weldon and others had begun. Harold Hartley later wrote that Tizard 'gave much thought to the financial fortunes of the college, incidentally reorganizing the bursary', and 'he gave a clear lead to those who worked closely with him in small committees'. However, Hartley observed that he had been less successful at large meetings, adding, 'Perhaps he had too authoritarian a background to fit easily into the democratic ways of a college.'[19] Taylor, who was one of Tizard's inner circle at Magdalen, echoed some of Hartley's points but was more critical as to his achievements. In his view, Tizard was too keen to avoid rows in the college and, perhaps as much as this, he was disappointed Tizard came and went in four years, returning to Whitehall at the end of 1946 as chairman of the Defence Research Policy Committee and Advisory Council on Scientific Policy after Clement Attlee had replaced Churchill as Prime Minister. Tizard failed to avoid acrimony in the college, and Bruce McFarlane and C.S. Lewis were in the strong minority pleased to see him depart.[20] When C.P. Snow wrote *Science and Government* (Oxford, 1961) Taylor criticised his account of the Tizard–Lindemann feud. He commented, 'I knew Lindemann slightly, and have never met anyone more dislikeable. I knew Tizard intimately when he was President of Magdalen – perhaps better than any non-scientist did. I served him devotedly, and remained friendly with him after he left Oxford.' He acknowledged Tizard's abilities, but went on,

> But he had his weaknesses. He liked to settle things behind the scenes: a quiet committee meeting ending in a recommendation, drafted – I must say incomparably – by himself, and then formally carried at some larger body. Open debate shook him; opposition unnerved him... Tizard was as much a dictator as Lindemann, but he disliked publicity. He wanted to be an anonymous dictator, and dictator off-stage... Tizard was meticulous, cautious, worrying about the inventory of college furniture or about his pension.

When Taylor published his autobiography twenty-two years later, Tizard's abilities seem to have dwindled still further, while his own role in mentoring

Tizard grew; much as he portrayed his role in almost tutoring Namier at Manchester.[21]

Another early acquaintance in Oxford, after his return in 1938, was Richard Crossman. Crossman and Taylor had several things in common. Crossman had been a Fellow of New College, 1930–37, but a second marriage to a colleague's recent wife hastened his departure. He had broadcast on BBC radio on Germany and also on Plato between 1934 and 1936, but was then dropped until late 1939 as he had proved too radical and individualistic for the BBC's hierarchy. Crossman was leader of the small Labour group on the Oxford City Council (1935–40), was an anti-appeaser and taught for the Workers' Educational Association. Alan Taylor met him when Crossman was making a Guy Fawkes Night bonfire for his stepchildren. Crossman then urged him to follow Percy Taylor's example and stand for the local council. Crossman was also a significant contact, in Taylor's eyes, as he was then the newly appointed assistant editor of the *New Statesman and Nation*.[22]

Taylor began work on his book *The Habsburg Monarchy* during the later part of his first year as a Fellow of Magdalen College. It was a book he had been moving towards since his research years, 1928–30, in Vienna. He had discussed aspects of Austrian politics in some depth in his introduction to Friedjung's book. He also spoke on a major theme of his Habsburg book at the Bolton branch of the Historical Association in the autumn of 1937: 'The conflict of nationalities in the Austrian Empire'.[23]

He wrote to Harold Macmillan, 'I have been thinking for some time of writing a history of Austria in the nineteenth century, either from 1815 or 1848; it would draw on the latest German & Austrian works & fill a gap in English history books. It would be one volume & not too learned.' The two most interesting features of his letter and its successors were that he was seeking to make money from his writing and that, unlike his first two heavily footnoted, archive-driven books, this was to be based on secondary sources. Having arrived at Oxford, he no longer felt the immediate need to impress and could begin to address the wider public, whose attention he sought.

When Harold Macmillan offered the standard ten per cent royalty for scholarly books, Taylor bargained. In this he may have been emboldened by knowing that Macmillan had tried to get Namier to write a book on Austria's history; at least, Taylor recalled Namier declining such a proposal. Although there is no other evidence for this, it is not improbable that Macmillan may have spoken to Namier of this – or even that Namier might have claimed this in order to get Alan Taylor moving on the subject and still writing for Macmillan. He was also encouraged by having had another publisher, possibly Duckworth, approach him.[24] Alan Taylor, emulating his revered grandfather, JT, as a northern hard man of business, firmly insisted on better terms than those first offered.

> I don't really think there is any misunderstanding. The book I have in mind is not a work of scholarship, but one from which I should like some money; and the other publishers, whom I mentioned to you in my original letter, had that sort of book in mind. So I am afraid I must definitely withdraw the suggestion I made to you and wait until I can offer you another book later.[25]

In this he was repeating his stance over *The Italian Problem in European Diplomacy*, when eventually he declined Macmillan's offer to publish on terms which involved a financial guarantee from him.

That Harold Macmillan was willing to improve substantially his offer this time owed much to his admiration for Lewis Namier, who he very much saw as Taylor's mentor. That he did was by this time very galling for the 33-year-old Alan Taylor, who felt he had fully arrived in his own right as a Fellow of Magdalen. Macmillan had sent Taylor's initial letter proposing the book to Namier. Macmillan minuted Taylor's letter withdrawing his suggestion: 'No reply is, I think, necessary.' Quite possibly, Namier pressed him to persevere with Taylor, even though Macmillan was realistic about the book's likely restricted market. Anyway, Macmillan went to Magdalen on Saturday 27 May and played bowls and dined with Taylor. The visit, with the offer of better financial terms and the promise of two maps in the book, secured the contract.[26]

Alan Taylor determined to write much of the book during the summer vacation of 1939. With Holywell Ford unavailable until October, he expected to be able to spend a full three months' sojourn on the Continent. With the historian's characteristic inability to predict the future from knowledge of the past, he was confident war was not imminent. He wrote to Malcolm Muggeridge on 1 May, 'Well, the world's on the move: everything is set for doing the dirty on the Poles (what could be more appropriate for they are dirty indeed) & then we can have conscription of everybody (except the rich) all the time.' He felt that the various international players were set in their ways:

> One of the few things one learns from history is that chaps can only behave in a given way – despite their ambitions...
>
> For that reason I don't think we'll have a war. Hitler wants bloodless victories & doesn't know any other way – so he will never start a war. And Bonnet & Chamberlain have bloodless defeats & they know no other way. So more alarms & more gas masks for babies & bigger arms profits & more stern protests by the Trade Unions. It must move

in this pattern until one day the bottom falls out. But what then? Then things will be really interesting.[27]

The bottom fell out of international affairs sooner than he expected. Nonetheless, he made full use of two months' writing time in Savoy in July and August 1939. He was to write, in the mornings, quickly and fairly effectively, relying on his memory and his own vigorous views as to interpretation, having few books with him. It was an approach he repeated in the summer of 1954, holidaying on the Isle of Wight, when he successfully wrote much of his biography of Bismarck. On the way to France, Alan, Margaret and Giles Taylor had spent much of the last fortnight of June with Malcolm and Kitty Muggeridge in their home, Mill House, at Whatlington, near Battle, in Sussex. On 17 July he informed Muggeridge,

> We have found a delightful little house on the Lake of Geneva about fifteen miles from the Swiss border. Unfortunately we have it only until the end of July, when we shall have to go to another house in the mountains, as the lakeside is too full of people. We have had grand weather and Giles has insisted on going into the lake up to his neck. I have written 20,000 words, but I'm afraid I've written it too quickly; it's a bit flaccid, but that's my weakness, I go slapdash at a thing until I get it done and it doesn't work as well with writing as with lecturing.[28]

So by mid-July he had written the first four chapters of *The Habsburg Monarchy 1815–1918*. He continued to make good progress, with more than two-thirds written by late August.[29] He relaxed in the afternoons with Margaret and Giles, spending much time on a beach at Lake Geneva, near Yvoire. He and Margaret also visited the League of Nations headquarters and met Robert Dell, the veteran French correspondent of the *Manchester Guardian*.[30] In August the Taylors and Henrietta Werner moved into the mountains, taking a chalet at Montriod. It was sufficiently large to have guests, and their old friends Teddy Pratt and Paul Saffin and a student of his, Robert Kee, then nearly twenty, stayed with them. Teddy Pratt spent some of his time reading the manuscript of *The Habsburg Monarchy* and suggested amendments.[31]

Their third month in France was hastily abandoned with the imminent outbreak of war in Europe. On 1 September Teddy Pratt and Paul Saffin took refuge in Geneva and the Taylors, Henrietta Werner and Robert Kee set off for Dieppe and Britain, via Autun. Arriving at Dieppe just after Britain's declaration of war, Alan Taylor abandoned his car in order to board an earlier ferry, his car being brought across to Newhaven a week later. Instead of Savoy, the Taylors spent September at Bickmarsh Hall, near Bidford-on-Avon, the home of Margaret's mother and stepfather,

Harold Lancaster.[32] There he probably succeeded in writing a further two chapters of his book.

With the move into Holywell Ford, his teaching and other writing and some dislocations of war, he did little more on his book until summer 1940. In early January he informed Harold Macmillan, 'I have written 80,000 words of my book on Austria and, unless anything untoward happens, I shall finish it within the next six months. It might come out just in time to catch the Habsburg revival.'[33]

He wrote the last two chapters of the book in Oxford either during the latter part of the 1939–40 academic year or at the beginning of the summer vacation. These chapters are livelier and sparkle, in contrast to many of the earlier chapters. It may have helped to be with his books and access to the Bodleian. It certainly helped that he was stimulated by the recollections of Count Michael Karolyi, much as Beaverbrook's reminiscences uplifted him twenty years later when writing *English History 1914–1945*. Karolyi had been the Habsburg Emperor's last Prime Minister from 30 October 1918 and then Provisional President of the Hungarian Republic between 16 November 1918 and 22 March 1919.

Alan Taylor finished the book in late June and much of July 1940. In forwarding his typescript, he recognised the realities of wartime: 'I leave it entirely to your discretion whether to publish it now, or to postpone it to some later time; but it would be a great convenience if it could be set up so that I could correct the galleys in the fairly near future.' He preferred the title 'The Habsburg Monarchy', and to avoid imprecision about the empire's change of name in 1867, after much agonising, gave the book the sub-heading 'A History of the Austrian Empire and Austria-Hungary'. He also pushed hard to get the best maps he could, emphasising Harold Macmillan had agreed to them:

> What I want are two maps: the first geographical – rivers, railways, mountains, coal and iron. The second political – each province marked with its capital shown; perhaps this map could be coloured to show the nationalities. Each map must be on a good scale and should, of course, fold. Perhaps the simplest thing would be to put me in touch with some map-maker, to whom I could explain my needs.

He added as to the map-maker, 'J.F. Horrabin is a personal friend of mine – approach him?' Horrabin's cartography included H.G. Wells, *The Short History of the World*, 1922, and *The Plebs Atlas*, 1926.

Taylor later recalled that he had known that H.G. Wells had paid a lot for Horrabin's cartographical work. So he asked Horrabin if he would be willing to forgo profits and do it out of friendship. He readily agreed to do so. Taylor also commented, 'Horrabin knew all the inside stories of the

Labour Party and was usually a good source. However, he was prone to the knowing remark.' He said that this might mean that some of his stories needed other corroboration. Taylor said that he (AJPT) had known Ellen Wilkinson, 'a fiery, lucid speaker' who preached a message of 'very basic socialism of the "come on to the streets" variety'. He had heard that 'Ellen Wilkinson had committed suicide over Herbert Morrison from several people – but in each case the original source had appeared to be Frank Horrabin'.

Taylor was very fortunate that his book did go quickly into production. He had corrected his first proofs by mid-September 1940. By this time he was no longer firmly for folding maps. He wrote then,

> I am arranging with Mr J.F. Horrabin to draw two maps. I have suggested that they should go on the end papers, and he will shortly be writing to you to ascertain the exact size of the book so that he will know what space he has to work on. If he finds it impossible to fit them in to the end papers then we must have folding maps, but I never regard these as satisfactory.[34]

This fickleness over maps is a small point, but very characteristic. It was important to his image, perhaps to his self-image, that he come across as a northern man of business, with clear views, firmly held. However, on occasions it seems the firmness was more important than the actual view.

He also displayed in his letter another notable characteristic: a determination to show that he was someone who would expect his full financial due and should not be seen as a pushover. He wrote that he wished to prepare the index, adding: 'I do not know whether this is usually included in the author's work, but if it is not, no doubt you will pay me the appropriate fee.' Finally, he wrote, 'I am tempted to suggest that soon after this book is published I might follow it up with a pamphlet in your new series on the Present or Future of Central Europe; but no doubt much will have happened in central Europe (and elsewhere) before then.'

The book was published in February 1941. Although he had returned final proofs in early November, he had optimistically written then, 'It would be a great personal convenience to me if I could have advance copies by Christmas, as I could then give them as Christmas presents; but it is a point of no importance.' When his copies of the book arrived he found them 'attractively produced' but regretted that his previous Macmillan publications were not mentioned on the jacket. Later, in September 1941, when further copies of the book were bound, he was – not surprisingly – disconcerted to find his name incorrectly printed ('A.J.B. Taylor') on the spine.[35]

More serious for the book was that it was published just as war was changing so much in central Europe, as Alan Taylor recognised. Although ending in 1918, the book offered analysis of an alternative power structure to central and south-eastern Europe than German dominance. Was a supranational authority revivable? Was the Habsburg monarchy inevitably doomed before military defeat in the First World War?

The residual influence of Karl Marx on him was apparent in the book. He later recalled that, as an undergraduate, 'I cultivated the revolutions of 1848 after reading Marx's *Eighteenth Brumaire of Louis Napoleon*, the book of his – apart of course from the Communist Manifesto – that I most admired'.[36] In *The Habsburg Monarchy 1815–1918* he discussed Marx's views on Germany in 1848.

> Of all the German revolutionaries of 1848, Marx had been the first to grasp clearly the reluctance of the German liberals to take over responsibility for the running of their country; this reluctance he ascribed to their fear of losing their property, though it was perhaps due even more to the political immaturity of the German middle classes and to the tenacious defence by the dynasties of their inherited position.

He went on to discuss Marx's view that the working class would provide leaders to bring about 'the revolution which the liberals had failed to achieve'. Then, in his account, Taylor gave his approval of Marx's revolutionary credentials:

> For Marx was a Socialist because he was a revolutionary, believing that only revolutionary Socialism could unite the masses. He recognised that a Socialist party must win the confidence of the masses by leading them in the day-to-day struggle over wages and working conditions, but he never lost sight of the ultimate moment when the Socialists would bring existing society to an end and would take over the conduct both of industry and the state.

In Taylor's book there are several instances of him taking a Marxist deterministic view of the working class's historic role. For instance, with universal suffrage in 1907 he found the working class's voting less than satisfactory, observing, 'It might be very foolish of the industrial working class to feel nationalist instead of concentrating their energies against their real enemies, the employers; but not even the working class is free from folly, and the division of the Austrian trade unions and Social Democratic party into national sections showed that their leaders were as little exempt as their followers.'

He also took up what he saw as Marx's insight into the German middle class in 1848, and, curiously, applied it to Britain and France. He wrote,

> To take over responsibility for the running of a great state is a terrifying prospect for anyone other than a hereditary dynasty or a hereditary

governing class which has grown used to the idea: in England nearly three hundred years passed (roughly from the beginning of the reign of Elizabeth to the end of the reign of George III) before the English land-owning and commercial classes would take the plunge, and the French bourgeoisie, after the French Revolution, resorted to all kinds of desperate expedients for avoiding responsibility – empire, revived monarchy, sham monarchy, sham empire – until the failure of all left them with no escape from responsibility under the Third Republic.[37]

Yet, beside his Marxist or sub-Marxist approaches, there was much old-fashioned radical moralising: views which would not have appeared strange to radicals of his grandfather's generation. For instance, there was the view that 'the basic weakness of Metternich's policy – as of all reforming conservatism – was its attempt to achieve reforms without co-operating with the liberal spirit'. His use of 'the invention of tradition' had a similar, dubious moral to it:

> Like the later nationalist leaders, Metternich was not reviving traditions, but inventing them; and in both cases the result was the same – to make a difficult problem insoluble. For men can always reach a compromise with reality; but to make events conform to a tradition which never existed is a task beyond their powers.[38]

Increasingly, individualistic radicalism became more prominent in his outlook, especially when the Cold War was fully under way. Marxist-Independent Labour Party views remained until at least late in his life, but diminished in his written history after this 1941 book. It was notable that when writing to the anti-Marxist Malcolm Muggeridge before the outbreak of war in Europe he emphasised what he owed to the French Revolution. He wrote that 'the ideas of 1789 really do mean something. Yes I believe that: the ideas of '89 were worth while, despite the mess of the revolution, & they're what made us, they're what we've got to offer at the day of judgement.'[39]

In the first version of *The Habsburg Monarchy* Taylor, although sceptical, suggested that the Habsburg monarchy was not necessarily doomed before the First World War. Early on he asserted, 'The Empire could not be saved by any juggling of bureaucratic committees nor by any changes of bureau-cratic personnel, but only by calling in the ruled to the assistance of the rulers.' Later on, he reiterated this possibility: 'A change of system, indeed a change of spirit and a change of heart, and not diplomatic tricks, could alone have saved the Habsburg monarchy...' Yet he ridiculed others who had been 'confident that the Empire could survive if only this or that Utopian idea were realised'.[40]

To a certain extent it was important to his more polemical purposes to suggest that there had been policy options for the Habsburg monarchy. He intended the book to set him up as an authority, or at least a media pundit, on central Europe. Early on in the book he was unequivocal that there were lessons to be learned about the Habsburg Empire,

> as long as history counts for anything: that lord and servant, master and slave, the privileged historic nationalities and the submerged nationalities who have won their way to freedom, can never work together. Magyar and Pole, German and Italian can co-operate; but German and Czech, Italian and Serb, Magyar and Roumanian, Pole and Little Russian cannot.[41]

These were not strange sentiments from the author of *The Course of German History* (1945) but were from the later Alan Taylor, who was emphatic that there were no lessons to be learned from history. In a synopsis or 'blurb' he supplied for Macmillan's spring 1940 book catalogue, he also claimed that the book 'will appeal to all who believe that only through understanding the past we can make a better future'.[42] In seeking lessons from the Habsburg past he was to be in what was, later, very influential company; Henry Kissinger looked back with adulation on Metternich and more generally on European diplomacy 1812–22 in his *A World Restored* (1957 and 1993).[43]

The likely topical interest in his book in 1940 was related not only to an alternative central European power to Germany but also to the history and expectations of the other nationalities. In his synopsis for Macmillan's catalogue he declared the 'key to this century of history is found in the relations of dominant and subject people'. He emphasised, 'The collapse of the dynasty followed on its failure to give the subject peoples political and economic freedom – a lesson still valuable for any new attempt to give stability to central Europe.' Taylor was soon to champion subject people; notably the nations of Czechoslovakia and Yugoslavia, including Yugoslavia's case for Trieste.

Alan Taylor, like Lewis Namier, was greatly influenced by Otto Bauer's *The Social Democrats and the Nationality Question*. He had been less influenced by the man than the book. He wrote to Bob Cole of his meeting with Bauer in 1928, 'I found him superficial and I never saw him again.'[44] Taylor found Bauer's left-wing socialism wanting in the last years of the Habsburg Empire. He wrote,

> Otto Bauer stood on the extreme left of the Socialist party and had never accepted the easy doctrine, put forward by Karl Renner, that the Habsburg Empire was already a state above nationality which the Social Democrats ought to preserve; he saw clearly the fundamental

importance of the cleavage between the historic and non-historic
nationalities and recognised that, as democrats, the Social Democrats
must support the claims of the underprivileged races. But the imperial
advocacy convinced Bauer that Francis Joseph too was on the side of
democracy and the unprivileged races – that he would co-operate with
the Slavs against the Magyars and with the masses against the
employers; and belief in the 'revolution from above' led Bauer even to
urge that Hungary be put under military rule, but with a programme of
universal suffrage and trade union rights for the agricultural labourers.
There can be few conceptions more bizarre than this picture of the
Habsburg army, the army of the Counter Reformation and of anti-
Jacobinism, carrying on its shoulders the banners of democracy and
Socialism...[45]

Undoubtedly, *The Habsburg Monarchy 1815–1918*, with its maps by
Horrabin, its reflections on Marx and its upbraiding of Bauer for lack of
revolutionary zeal, was a book that could be placed in the hands of his
mother and Henry Sara, and, had he not died in February 1940, his father.
Taylor was keen that it should be brought to the notice of people who knew
the Taylor family in Preston and Manchester. He asked Harold Macmillan
to see that 'The copy to the *Lancs. Daily Post* should be accompanied by a
note that I am the son of the late Councillor P.L. Taylor'.[46] His book was
intended to convey a message for its times and, written without footnotes
and extracts from documents, it was intended for a wide public audience.
Taylor carefully underlined that it contributed to current debate in his
Preface, noting of those who read his typescript, 'None of them agrees
with my conclusions: Dr E.J. Pratt believes that the Habsburg Monarchy
both could, and should, have been preserved; Count Karolyi believes in
the possibility of a Danubian Confederation of free and equal peoples; my
wife regards all political communities as folly.'

Yet he also intended the book to be treated seriously by an academic
audience. He dedicated it 'To L.B. Namier, This Token of Gratitude,
Affection, and Esteem'. In his two earlier books he had demonstrated his
skills with diplomatic documents and diplomatic history. With this book
he displayed his ability to write concisely and lucidly about the main issues
and major figures of the final century of Habsburg history, dealing with
high politics, constitutional and nationality issues. He drove his narrative
forward, focusing on the Emperors and the attempts of an almost bewildering array of ministers to secure consent, or at least acquiescence, in
Habsburg rule. Much of this was less than scintillating for the general
reader, especially in the first version of 1941. He had been criticised by
Richard Pares for undergraduate humour in his previous book. In this

book he appears to have deliberately repeated this trait, airing contempt for Italy (who had entered the European war in June 1940), referring to it before 1914 as 'this ridiculous simulacrum of a national state, impressive only to professional diplomats and literary visitors, [which] could have been defeated even by Austria-Hungary' and in 1918 commenting: 'After the armistice had been signed, but before it came into force, the Italians emerged from behind the British and French troops, where they had been hiding, and captured hundreds of thousands of unarmed, unresisting, Austro-Hungarian troops in the great "victory" of Vittorio Veneto – a rare triumph of Italian arms.' He also jeered at the monarchists in the future Yugoslavia, referring to the Serbian King as 'Peter, the successful brigand leader of a group of brigands'.[47]

The book achieved both his main objectives. He did establish himself as an authority on central European history and was sought by BBC radio and the press. The book also added to his academic reputation, both for being a writer of high-quality history and one who was unusually productive for that era.

It was mostly well reviewed. Oscar Jaszi, a leading Radical, a close associate of Count Karolyi and his Minister for the Nationalities in 1918–19, as well as the author of *The Dissolution of the Habsburg Monarchy*, 1929, praised Alan Taylor warmly in a review in the *Journal of Modern History*, saying that he had 'accomplished his task not only skilfully but brilliantly'. He praised his 'highly individualistic style, a quick wit compressing the essence of personality or of a period in a few admirably formed phrases – a quality reminding us of some of the best essayists'. Overall, he felt Taylor was

> successful in penetrating into the real spirit of this strange experiment. Few foreigners have understood the complication of this problem as clear as the author...He belongs to that rare class of historians who are able to supplement the factual evidence with a high grade of psychological insight and artistic imagination...What we read in his book is not dead history but an often thrilling analysis of personalities and mass psychological insights.[48]

Others trying to influence the reshaping of central Europe disagreed with his more polemical message. Justin de Courcey in *Free Europe* observed, 'We can be grateful to him for expounding in considerable detail the elements of the vast problems which faced the Austrian Empire in the nineteenth century, even if we cannot accept his conclusion that there is no place for the Habsburgs any more in Europe.'[49] Henry Wickham Steed, the former editor of the *Times* and author of work on Austria, praised it with reluctance in the *Times Literary Supplement*, sneering that 'It is a work of "book learning"'. Taylor, on a fairly rare occasion that he rose to criticism in reviews, wrote back to confess that, in not writing on the basis of 'first-hand observation', 'I never met the late Prince Metternich, by gross carelessness I did not witness the revolutions of 1848', but that in this general failure he was in the company of Gibbon and Macaulay.[50] In fact he had gone beyond his books, eagerly learning some aspects at second-hand: Polish Galicia from Lewis Namier and some aspects of the final days of the Habsburgs from Count Karolyi, as well as what he picked up in Vienna in 1928–30.

He received academic praise from R.W. Seton-Watson and F.M. Powicke. Seton-Watson praised the book in *English Historical Review* as 'scholarly, well proportioned and realistic', adding: 'Mr Taylor's judgements are acute, balanced and admirably fair, even when he reveals very definite sympathies.' Powicke, then Regius Professor of Modern History at Oxford, wrote in the *Manchester Guardian* that it was 'a very able book. He is not only a master of his subject: he knows how to present it, and he is thorough...It is the work of a good scholar who, without pose or effort, beats the men of words at their own game. He is, in short, a very intelligent man who knows what he is writing about.'[51]

While Alan Taylor's extracurricular activities increasingly were to be focused on London, when he was at first in Oxford the Lancashire connections remained important. The Taylors spent a final Christmas in 1938 at 'Three Gates', before the house was sold for a substantial profit in early 1939.[52] They also visited his parents in Preston, including for Christmas 1939. The *Manchester Guardian* remained his major breakthrough into the media, until he became a regular radio broadcaster for the BBC from the middle of the Second World War.

The death of his father on Monday 26 February 1940 at the age of 65, coming before that of his mother, was a shock for Alan Taylor. He later recalled that, at Christmas, 'My father told me that my mother had not long to live. He was wearing himself out looking after her but did not expect to do so for long.'[53] However, he had a bad chest, suffering bronchitis most winters; and a few weeks after their Christmas visit pneumonia followed bronchitis and killed Percy Taylor. There was a fulsome appreciation of him by a columnist in the *Preston Herald*:

He went his kindly, tolerant way, interested in everything, travelling widely, seeing all there was to be seen. Although deaf, he greatly appreciated good music and all good art, particularly the modern, had a lively appeal for him. Yet with it all, he was a simple man: children instinctively took to him and he would contentedly play with them by the hour, telling them the most wonderful stories, made up as he went along. His pleasure in his son's brilliant academic career was naïve and wholly delightful...At one time and another the house has been the refuge for all manner of persecuted and hunted people, and known as such all over Europe. These will miss him – and all they represent will miss him, the poor and the oppressed have one generous friend and faithful companion the less.[54]

Taylor greatly grieved for his kindly father, recognising his father's unstinting love. This seems to have been contrasted with his mother's failure to give him the warmth and adulation he had sought. He may even have partially blamed her for his father's death, for not taking care to look after him when he was suffering from bronchitis. He certainly became bitter about his mother's preference for Henry Sara over her husband. Later, he was angry and concerned when Margaret appeared to be treating him in the way that his mother had treated his father. However, he remained angry about his mother, whereas in his later years he was hurt and even bewildered about the breakdown of his first marriage but was concerned about Margaret and her health.

It was very apparent that his mother could not stay long on her own in their large house at 8 Mulgrave Avenue, Preston. Alan Taylor wrote in his autobiography,

> I moved her to Oxford and, after trying a nursing home, bought a house where she lived with two nurses. My conscience reproached me that I ought to have had her live with us...I went to see her two or three times a week, and I think she was as content as an almost non-existent person could be. I thought the situation would not last long. In fact my mother lived for another six years. But as a human being she had ceased to exist for me long before.[55]

This was a severe, even savage, view of her last years. Nevertheless, he did visit her, often with his two sons. Giles later remembered them playing cards with her on her bed.[56] She had Henry Sara visit her regularly. Harry Thompson and his children were also frequent visitors. His son, Robin, remembered visiting her in the nursing home in Oxford, where she was bedridden. On another occasion Harry Thompson was outraged to find that she had been badly burned by a hot-water bottle,[57] and insisted that Alan Taylor ensure she received better care. Robin Thompson later recalled, 'Relations between him and my father were I think very icy. My father as one of the youngest in the family was largely brought up by Connie, for whom he had great affection. In latter years I think he did not feel AJP looked after her well enough. I am sure this led to a serious breach.'[58] Connie Taylor died in April 1946, with Henry Sara among the few present at the crematorium.

His connection with the *Manchester Guardian* remained important to him after his move to Oxford. In his first year at Oxford he published twenty book reviews in the *Manchester Guardian* (as well as writing others for academic journals). His style was appropriate for the readership of such a newspaper. Occasionally he displayed flippant, almost schoolboy humour. For instance, he wrote in a review of a biography of Madame de Staël, published soon after his return to Oxford, 'Madam de Staël believed that she was persecuted by Napoleon, but anyone who reads her life or looks at her portrait will feel that in sending her to exile Napoleon was for once behaving in a wholly admirable way.'[59] Perhaps he was seeking applause for laddish humour from the misogynists among the males of the Oxford common rooms. In the 1930s he reviewed 26 popular histories and biographies of the French Revolutionary and Napoleonic era, which remained one of his areas of particular interest.

He also had the opportunity to comment on some of the weightier histories of the time in his reviews of the early part of the war. For instance, in the *Manchester Guardian's* Christmas Book Supplement he praised J.H. Clapham's third volume of his *Economic History of Britain* (1938): 'No greater work of scholarship has been produced in our time;' Winston Churchill's fourth volume of Marlborough; J.L. Hammond's *Gladstone and the Irish Nation* (1938), 'the most important study in recent political history', of which he added, 'It is rare to find original research and fine style so happily wedded;' and E.L. Woodward's Oxford History of England volume, *The Age of Reform, 1815–1870* (1938), 'at once a textbook and a work of original scholarship', which he deemed to be 'enlivened... with many stimulating judgements and illuminating asides'. With these volumes he had selected major works of the period. He was also right to be less enthusiastic about another volume of the Oxford History of England, Basil Williams, *The Whig Supremacy 1714–1760* (1939), which he criticised for taking no notice of Namier's researches and because 'for the most part the account is laudatory and even complacent'. He added, 'All the actors and all the institutions are in their best clothes and on their best behaviour.'[60]

He was also critical of historians favourable to appeasement or the National Government. He commented of the fifth edition of A.J. Grant and Harold Temperley's, *Europe in the Nineteenth and Twentieth Centuries, 1789–1938*, that it was a very valuable textbook but the inter-war years were an apologia for the appeasers.[61] As for Arthur Bryant, he was strongly critical of his *Unfinished Victory* (1940), which he condemned as 'an argument for the peace of appeasement', the review being entitled 'A Nazi Apologist'. When reviewing *English Saga* (1840–1940), he commented sharply on Bryant's rapid change from being a notable defender of the appeasers to becoming the historian of collectivist democracy: a transformation which was brilliantly dissected by the historian Andrew Roberts over fifty years later. Less than two years later he was more favourable to Bryant's *The Years of Endurance 1793-1802* (1941), but observed: 'Tory England defending itself is a theme congenial to his pen...'[62] He was milder about the second edition of G.M. Trevelyan's *British History in the Nineteenth Century and After* (1937), observing that its spirit was still 'urbane, enlightened Whiggism' but, as a National Liberal, Trevelyan was too favourable to Sir Edward Grey and too unsympathetic to David Lloyd George.[63]

The book reviews gave him a public platform to express his views. In August 1938 he gave *Manchester Guardian* readers his view of the value of history. It was a view which he held for the rest of his life, though he often gave alternative views according to the occasion. He wrote,

> The only danger to history today is that historians are sometimes too modest and try to find excuses for their task. It is safer as well as sounder to be confident. Men write history for the same reason that they write poetry, study the properties of numbers, or play football – for the joy of creation; men read history for the same reason that they listen to music or watch cricket – for the joy of appreciation. Once abandon that firm ground, once plead that history has a 'message' or that history has a 'social responsibility' (to produce good Marxists or good Imperialists or good citizens) and there is no logical escape from the censor and the Index, the O.G.P.U. and the Gestapo.[64]

He also commented on contemporary affairs in his reviews. He was critical of Stalin's Russia before departing from Manchester. In August 1938 he denounced a passage in a Left Book Club volume which was critical of Austrian workers' resistance to the Right in Austria, observing that it was 'downright offensive to anyone who knows that many of the same workers escaped to the Socialist paradise and are now suffering in Russian prisons for their Socialist beliefs'. In the period of the Nazi–Soviet Pact (August 1939–June 1941) he remained implacably hostile to Nazi Germany. He saw Soviet Russia as a crucial future ally. In late 1939 he observed, in regard to a book on Stalin by B. Souvarine, 'deliberate villainy plays less a part in world affairs than is sometimes supposed'. However, his own political outlook in the period was best expressed in his comments on John Strachey's *A Faith to Fight for* (1941). While he praised it as 'an impassioned statement of the democratic socialist faith', he commented that Strachey was 'wrong in asserting that it is the only faith worth fighting for or that unless we adopt it we shall lose'. Alan Taylor, who greatly admired Churchill's leadership in 1940, commented that many people were fighting 'not...for a better England but for the England they know'. He also wrote one of his most memorable aphorisms: 'Without democracy socialism would be worth nothing, but democracy is worth a great deal even when it is not socialist.'[65] These were surely sentiments that George Orwell would have endorsed. After February 1941, when his friend Graham Greene became literary editor of the *Spectator*, Alan Taylor also wrote a few reviews for that journal.

Alan and Margaret Taylor enjoyed Holywell Ford from October 1939, in spite of the war. It was large enough for them to be able to entertain at home again. They had one large room, in which they held parties, sometimes with music provided by their very expensive EMG Handmade Gramophone with its large horn (made by the British manufacturer E.M. Ginn), then deemed to be the highest-quality record player available. In term they often held two music parties a week for undergraduates.

His gramophone was the possession which gave him greatest pleasure. He insisted on cutting wooden needles, feeling strongly that steel needles damaged his 78rpm records. He listened with full attention, no reading of books and using the music as background. Sebastian recalled that his favourites included Verdi's Requiem and Wagner's Ring cycle. Margaret Taylor enjoyed spending much time with him listening to his records.

Holywell Ford was also large enough to have weekend guests or longer-staying visitors. Early on in the war Friedjung's daughter Paula Reinkraut, her husband and children stayed, in spite of their strong nationalist opinions. Taylor had needed her support for the translation of her father's book. After the Anschluss, he had written to Harold Macmillan concerning their need to leave Vienna and their wish to go to the USA. In April 1939 all had seemed to be going well and he informed Macmillan, 'You'll be glad to hear that I got a permit for Friedjung's daughter and her family. It only remains for them to comply with the regulations at the other end.'[66]

Holywell Ford in 1998.

However, with the outbreak of war the Reinkrauts needed his financial help to get out of France and into England. He complained to Macmillan at the start of 1940,

> Ultimately she got satisfactory affidavits to make an American visa secure, and I gave them a guarantee to enable them to spend the intervening months in England. They came to England last August, and asked the American consulate in London to have their papers transferred from the consulate in Vienna. Then the war intervened, and the transference seems to be held up, as others, who applied later than they did, are now receiving American visas. You may imagine that it is no fun to be saddled with two adults and two children for an indefinite period, and it occurred to me that you might know someone in the American consulate to whom you could give me an introduction. I could then at any rate discover whether there was any chance of their papers coming through before the end of the war.[67]

Whether or not Harold Macmillan helped, the Reinkrauts secured their papers in early 1940 and Taylor paid their fares to the USA, securing part-repayment later.[68]

Some other guests paid. This was so in June 1941 with Stephen and Natasha Spender. Norman Cameron had been a friend of Spender's since Oxford, where Spender had succeeded him as president of the English Club. Cameron admired Spender's poetry, dubbing him 'the Rupert Brooke of the Depression'.[69] He and Alan Taylor were also impressed by his *Forward from Liberalism*, the main Left Book Club choice for January 1937, in which he asked 'why the liberals failed to achieve exactly that kind of freedom for the whole of society which the free individualist demands for himself, and which would be scarcely distinguishable from the final goal of communism', and discussed his doubts about communism. Spender's membership of the Communist Party was even briefer than Taylor's, Spender being disillusioned quickly by Communist Party behaviour in the Spanish Civil War.[70] Spender was newly married to Natasha Litvin, a concert pianist.

Margaret Taylor had heard her play a solo in a concert held in the Holywell music room earlier and had met her with Stephen Spender during their engagement. Natasha Spender later recalled that when she moved to Oxford during the Blitz, Margaret Taylor 'offered me the use of her piano when my own (in the library of St Mary's church) was needed for choir practice. From that time I used to play nursery tunes for Giles and Sebastian after my own work was done, and Margaret and I became friends.' She played for at least one of Margaret's Town Hall concerts, along with Leon Goosens and Elsie Suddaby. The Spenders fitted in very well with the Taylors' music-focused social life.

Margaret Taylor was at the hub of this, by the early part of the war making a name for herself as 'a sort of middle-class Lady Ottoline Morrell'. She was especially keen on meeting poets and was very pleased when the Spenders introduced Cecil Day-Lewis to her. She also made friends with students at the Slade School, which was evacuated to Oxford in 1940. It was in this mode that Margaret Taylor urged the Spenders to bring back from London 'someone, anyone', but somebody literary for a weekend at Holywell Ford. To the Taylors' surprise they returned with Dylan and Caitlin Thomas, Dylan seeing at least Margaret Taylor as a probable future patron. Stephen Spender had known Dylan Thomas since giving him a favourable review, had subsequently raised a fund to help support him and published some of his poems in *Horizon*.[71] On another occasion during the war the Taylors gave a party at Holywell Ford, with both their cultural lions (Thomas and Spender) and some thirty to forty undergraduates present. Natasha Spender recalled wartime Holywell Ford as 'a very lively household'. As well as the music there were visitors such as Lord Berners, Nevill Coghill and various intelligent undergraduates, with Alan Taylor encouraging discussion of the course of the war and politics. Margaret Taylor also invited the Spenders to give a lunch at Holywell Ford with influential people present who might help secure paper for *Horizon*, in spite of the wartime shortages.[72]

The reappearance of Dylan and Caitlin Thomas put further stress on the Taylors' marriage. Margaret Taylor had become unhappy, at least for some periods of time, after they moved to Oxford. Perhaps dissatisfaction with the way her life was slipping by peaked after the birth of her children: Giles (1937), Sebastian (1940), Amelia (1944) and Sophia (1945). Margaret had been inordinately infatuated with Robert Kee in 1939–40 and on his return from a prisoner-of-war camp in 1945. She became famously devoted to Dylan Thomas, notably in 1947–50. These enthusiasms for others caused Alan Taylor immense emotional distress, not least as he was devoted to his children and greatly believed in a paterfamilias role for the male in a family.

One of the undergraduates who was often invited to Holywell Ford for lunch or parties in the earlier part of the war was Freddy Hurdis-Jones. Alan Taylor liked him as he was cultured and lively, reminding him of his own aesthete undergraduate friends such as Jack Yates and John Betjeman. After leaving Oxford, Hurdis-Jones wrote in 1944–48 an aesthetic novella giving 'glimpses of an imagined Oxford' in 1942, exquisite in the way of Gerald Berners' writing. The central figure dines at the 'Albert', 'the Café Royal of Oxford' where Harold Acton and Evelyn Waugh earlier dined, and leaves for London, where he finds work and death as an extra in a film.[73] In the early part of the war there were few history students at Magdalen, with the overall number of undergraduates down from 120 to under 80. Another student whom Alan Taylor tutored was later recalled by Hurdis-Jones as 'a very serious young man and probably Alan did not deem him good company'.

As for Freddy Hurdis-Jones, he recalled of Alan Taylor, 'He was fun. He enjoyed everything.' At their first tutorial he was asked by Taylor, 'Do you think Katharine Hepburn is beautiful?' After replying 'yes' he asked Taylor why he asked; and he was told that those who said 'yes' were usually homosexual. At this time, when discussing history, Taylor was notably enthusiastic about the Third French Republic. Hurdis-Jones recalled him saying that, in spite of its scandals and corruption, it was the most successful form of government yet experienced; it was the form of government which gave the greatest possible liberty to its citizens. His fervour then for France and its history included great interest in the French Revolution. In 1942 Freddy Hurdis-Jones accompanied Taylor in his 1935 Ford coupé to Winchester, where Taylor gave a lecture on the Peace of Amiens, 1802, probably to that branch of the Historical Association.[74] During his career Alan Taylor often preceded writing a book by undertaking many book reviews and sometimes some lectures as well on the subject. The French Revolution and later French history, on which he wrote many reviews in the late 1930s, was the one notable area where a book did not follow, or at least not until his last series of television lectures.

Unlike Taylor, Freddy Hurdis-Jones greatly enjoyed Dylan Thomas' company, feeling he was 'a very human, a very interesting person'. He commented in 1991, 'I loved Dylan Thomas. He was one of the most amusing persons I've ever met. He was very likeable, even when very drunk. I thought Alan was very unfair to Dylan in his memoirs.' He also recalled, 'Dylan had a beautiful voice. It hummed in a rather tense concentrated way. There was no trace of Welsh accent. His way of speech was rather affected, as if from an evangelical background.' As for Taylor's comment that Dylan Thomas smelt, Freddy Hurdis-Jones observed that, while the poet had not been that keen on washing, he did not smell other than of tobacco as he smoked heavily. Freddy Hurdis-Jones felt that Dylan Thomas was uneasy with Taylor, having had no university education, while, he observed, 'Alan…had very set ideas about behaviour. This inevitably led to friction with Dylan.'[75]

Caitlin Thomas disliked Taylor. She recalled, 'I thought he was horrible: very opinionated and mean.'[76] He disliked her as much. Freddy Hurdis-Jones was also scathing, later commenting: 'She was an impossible woman. Ninety-nine times nastier than Dylan. She was hysterical. She came from a funny background. She had charm of a flamboyant kind. She looked like one of King George IV's mistresses, with flowing hair and a striking profile.' Taylor and Hurdis-Jones were both present at a party held by

John and Phyllis Young in late 1942 at which Caitlin danced around their
living room in a totally unrestrained manner, knocking all the ornaments
off a mantelpiece with her feet. Hurdis-Jones later commented, 'She could
not control herself. She was not insane, but she was not wholly normal.'[77]

When Hurdis-Jones, a scholarship student, ran into financial difficulties
in late 1942, Taylor was notably concerned. His mother lived on an annuity
and with wartime inflation the annuity lost some 40 per cent of its value.
He rejected Taylor's advice to live in a garret and survive on bread and
onions to finish his degree; Hurdis-Jones replied that that did not appeal,
least of all as he had been used to lavish dinner parties and spending much
money. This high living included availing himself on one occasion of an
expensive college service; his college was the last to provide high-quality
meals prepared by the chef and served in an undergraduate's rooms to his
guests. Taylor was annoyed at Hurdis-Jones' unwillingness to stay and rough
it, and after he left at the end of 1942 they did not make contact for nearly
thirty years, and then by chance, meeting in a pub in Camden Town.[78]

He also taught two undergraduates who went on to make major
contributions to writing history, Michael Thompson and Keith Kyle.
F.M.L. Thompson, who had been educated at Bootham and was an undergraduate at Queen's College, went to Taylor for tutorials in autumn 1942.
Taylor saw him in a room with large numbers of books in it. Sometimes
Michael Thompson stayed for lunch, which was prepared by Margaret
Taylor, 'who kept very much in the background'. He remembered eating
salsify, purple goat's-beard, which Taylor had grown. In his own college,
Queen's, there was only one historian, Norman Sykes, who had been
evacuated from another university. Sykes was a specialist in eighteenth-
century ecclesiastical history. Michael Thompson later recalled, 'He put me
off the eighteenth century for many, many years.' In contrast, Alan Taylor,
who taught him nineteenth-century European history, 'switched me on
dramatically'. Taylor was then full of Habsburg history. Michael Thompson
greatly enjoyed this and bought a copy of *The Habsburg Monarchy* (1941).[79]

Alan Taylor also taught Keith Kyle, who was a Magdalen undergraduate
for two terms from the autumn of 1943, returning to complete his degree
in 1947. He recalled Taylor as being 'brisk, shortish, perverse, with a
devilish sense of humour'. His recollections of being taught by him in
Holywell Ford include presenting a paper on the French Third Republic.

> While I read he appeared to be entirely occupied with two pursuits:
> with one hand stroking a large, white cat that sat contentedly on his lap
> and, with the other, worrying with the stem of his pipe the prominent
> wart at the dead-centre of his ample forehead. I ploughed on about
> the absurdity of the French Pretender in missing his chances for the

sake of insisting that the white flag of the House of Capet must replace the revolutionary tricolour. With immense force, Taylor suddenly shivered my timbers with a single word, 'Why?'. I blustered and spluttered with an ineffective response. Alan then launched into a tremendous oration to the effect that a King could only be of use as a constitutional monarch if he were above the political battle, but that this would be impossible if he were to embrace one side of France's great divide. Regardless of the particular merits of the issue, I had learnt never to engage in automatic writing again.[80]

Taylor was assiduous in writing to favoured former students engaged in war service. When Keith Kyle was in the army he wrote him lengthy letters full of college gossip. Kyle later observed, 'I found them at the time tremendously buoyant, amusing and full of the writer's mischievous spirit. They gave an enormously encouraging whiff of the Oxford I was yearning to go back to.'[81]

He also wrote to Robert Kee, who served in the RAF from 1940. After Kee was shot down, he wrote to him in his Stalag Luft. In his autobiography, Alan Taylor commented,

His letters were strange, full of messages to non-existent aunts. After some time a mysterious stranger called, showed me some secret-service card and told me not to be surprised at anything in Robert's letters. The allusions were in fact coded reports by bomber pilots who had been brought down. Keeping the letters going was one of my humble services in the Second World War.[82]

How humble were his services? Was there more to his activities in Whitehall than his memoirs divulged? When I prepared the Introduction to the bibliography published in 1980, I wondered if there were some secret wartime activities which would come out one day. I was told then of rumours in Oxford during the war that he was involved in some intelligence work. It seems he was not. At least, no evidence has come to light. Perhaps he was seen as a security risk given the past links with the Communist Party of his mother, Henry Sara and himself. A.L. Rowse was similarly sidelined. Or perhaps those in authority saw him as likely to be awkward and thought that he would not fit in to a team.

In the early stages of the Second World War he did not press to join the services. Given his upbringing in a household in which his uncle Harry, Sara and other 'absolutist' conscientious objectors were revered, it is not astonishing that he was not a volunteer for active military service. Any such residual pacifist inclinations that he had would have been reinforced by his distrust of Neville Chamberlain and most of the National Government, who were deemed by many on the Left more likely to support an attack on the Soviet Union than to wage a vigorous war against Nazi Germany. In the so-called 'phoney war' period, 1939–40, his early contribution to the war effort was to grow large quantities of vegetables and raise chickens and ducks at Holywell Ford.

For the early part of the war, at least, Oxford was (as Taylor put it in his memoirs) 'a haven of peace'. Initially, it appeared that the New Buildings in Magdalen College would be occupied as offices by the Judicial Committee of the Privy Council. C.S. Lewis and other Fellows emptied their offices, taking their books to the cellars. When this plan was rescinded, the academics recovered their books and their rooms. The government made clear that university teaching would continue and that this work would be an accredited reserved occupation. Nevertheless, eighteen Fellows of Magdalen enlisted for military service. While there were fewer staff and students and a black-out was enforced, otherwise life continued mostly as usual, at least for the early part of the war. Magdalen in particular was fortunate in its stocks of spirits and wine. After the Munich Crisis distillers supplied their regular customers with a percentage of their 1938 levels of purchases; as Magdalen's Steward had restocked heavily earlier in 1938 the college did relatively well. It could remedy a shortfall in port by exchanging whisky for some of New College's ample supply. Later in the war there was greater austerity, which included less than adequate wood fires in Magdalen.[83]

Alan Taylor took on public roles vacated by others going to war service. His lecturing on the war, his enhanced role of writing leaders for the *Manchester Guardian* and his entry into BBC radio programmes were all opportunities arising from others leaving. In the autumn of 1939 he agreed to take an Oxford University adult education class at Princes Risborough. He recalled in his autobiography, 'In Manchester I had never been involved in adult education, regarding it as a capitalist device for misleading the workers.' This recollection passes over the key point that earlier in Preston he had been close to the Marxist National Council of Labour Colleges' education work, at the very least assisting Henry Sara with his presentations on several occasions and, very likely, also accompanying his father. He had also had the experience of giving a few lectures to Historical Association branches, audiences similar to those he addressed in 1940–43 on the development of the war.

He very soon branched out from adult education into other talks. The Oxford University Delegacy for Extra-Mural Studies ran education for the armed forces in its area. Throughout the war Taylor went out three or four times a week to address service personnel in groups ranging from three to 500. 'I was welcomed and approved of by Tory Colonels and Group Captains and after June 1941 by Communist aircraft technicians.' C.S. Lewis, whose war activities paralleled some of Taylor's, visited service personnel for religious education. According to Taylor, Lewis was popular with female audiences while he was popular with male ones. He and Lewis donated their fees to a Magdalen College charitable fund. Alan Taylor clearly greatly enjoyed himself driving around southern England with a generous petrol allowance at a time of strict rationing. Later, he was even allocated a Women's Transport Service driver.[84]

In the period 1939–41 the British Communist Party supported the Soviet Union's line that the war was an 'imperialist war'. Taylor emphatically did not hold this view. He was vigorously anti-Nazi Germany. However, with the Russo-Finnish War he feared that the Chamberlain government would use sympathy for Finland to come to terms and even support Hitler's Germany. In Oxford the University Labour Club followed the Communist Party's line and was disaffiliated by the Labour Party. The minority, which followed the Labour Party's line and which included Anthony Crosland and Roy Jenkins, set up a Democratic Socialist Society. Alan Taylor recalled that they

> wanted some senior figure for their inaugural meeting. [G.D.H.] Cole, the obvious person, as usual could not make up his mind between the rivals and the loyalists turned to me. I was as much against Communists at home as I was on the side of Soviet Russia abroad and so could not well refuse. I hope that in my speech I managed to combine loyalty to the Labour Party with insistence that the war against Hitler was the only war that mattered.[85]

This was a long way from the Taylor of the 1920s. The Second World War greatly reinforced his support for the Labour Party. He was not alone in this.

Alive as always to historical and literary precedents, Taylor was eager to preach an anti-Nazi and anti-German message in the manner of Bolshevik missionaries during and after the October 1917 revolution in Russia. Clearly no communist fellow traveller in 1939–41, he successfully offered his services to the Ministry of Information and was until February 1943 one of the regular speakers used by its southern region, based in Reading. Asked to explain, not preach, he spoke frequently on 'a regular beat' consisting of 'Oxford, Banbury, Aylesbury, Wolverton, Bournemouth, Swanage and other places', including Southampton.

Not surprisingly, his talks on the recent developments of the war, with some speculation about the coming weeks, were very popular. He was fluent and often provocative, getting lively discussions going. He greatly enjoyed speaking to such audiences. Also not surprisingly, there were a few complaints. With his talks to the armed forces the complaints arose from him predicting that Franco would bring Spain into the war on the side of Nazi Germany. With the talks for the Ministry of Information the few complaints were more substantial. One was to do with him observing that, 'with the Mediterranean closed, the loss of Egypt and the Suez Canal would be of little importance'. He said this at a meeting in Oxford and it was taken up in the House of Commons on 24 October 1940 by the local MP, Quintin Hogg, who was well aware of Taylor's political outlook.[86] Another complaint came from communists in 1942, when he outlined the practical obstacles to opening a Second Front in Europe. A third complaint in February 1943 followed a US reverse in Tunis; Taylor's observation that US troops were inexperienced and bound to make mistakes sufficiently annoyed the senior Ministry of Information staff that he was taken off the list of its speakers.[87]

Perhaps it is surprising he was not removed sooner. The Ministry of Information was keen to prepare and to enthuse the British population for a massive war effort and Taylor, while arousing enthusiasm, was too individualistic and unpredictable for safety. C.S. Lewis apparently declined to join the Ministry of Information as he felt it would involve propaganda and lies.[88]

However, Taylor's experiences were far from unusual. He was but one of many lecturers who attracted complaints, not least in the Oxford area; others included the very left-wing MP D.N. Pritt and the vehemently anti-Soviet Sir Paul Dukes, who had served in British Intelligence in Russia in 1918–20. In the Oxford area in January 1940 the commanding officers had sought 'to approve beforehand the subjects of the Lecturers'. A.D. Lindsay, the Master of Balliol, as the vice-chairman of the Central Advisory Council on army education, drew up in May 1941 a memorandum on rules to avoid partisan lectures. As chairman of army education in Oxford he was faced with Taylor's protests after the complaints on his Franco talk. He soothed Taylor, yet wrote to the organisers of the lectures that Taylor should be kept off the subject of Spain.[89]

In mid-1940 the Local Defence Volunteers (soon renamed the Home Guard by Churchill) were set up. Alan Taylor and C.S. Lewis were among the first to join the South Company of the Oxford City Battalion. By this time Taylor strongly supported the government now that it was a genuinely broad coalition under Winston Churchill. The company had been formed by Frank Pakenham, with Maurice Bowra as his number two. Taylor was one of many Oxford Fellows in that company, others including John Austin and Edgar Lobel.[90] A citizen guard, especially one intended to repel invaders, was much favoured on the Left, and Taylor was well aware that he was a likely victim of the Gestapo were Britain to be occupied. However, at the time, as he later recalled, he 'argued from the analogy of the Napoleonic Wars that the threat of invasion was a bluff to cover the real German intention of an attack on Egypt'.

He had met Frank and Elizabeth Pakenham during his first year back at Oxford. He had gone with Bruce McFarlane and Redvers Opie to the

Pink Lunch Club, a weekly discussion group attended by G.D.H. Cole, Richard Crossman, Patrick and Audrey Gordon Walker, Frank and Elizabeth Pakenham, Isaiah Berlin, John Austin, Stuart Hampshire, A.J. Ayer, Roy Harrod and other left-wing Oxford dons.[91] Elizabeth Pakenham first visited the Taylors in their temporary accommodation in Marston Road and later at Holywell Ford. She became friends with Margaret Taylor. They discussed poetry, books and children, both having young and growing families. They pushed prams together in the parks in Oxford. Alan Taylor discussed politics and the war with both Frank and Elizabeth Pakenham.[92]

It was through the Pakenhams that Taylor came to know Lord Berners, one of his friends whom Alan Taylor later commented that he would like to recall from the dead. Elizabeth Pakenham recalled that she and her husband met Berners at 'one of the many wartime discussion groups founded to keep culture afloat'. In turn, Taylor met him at a discussion group Frank Pakenham organised 'to discuss the future of the world'.[93]

Gerald, the 14th Lord Berners, met two needs for Alan Taylor on his return to Oxford. He flattered that part of him which saw himself as an Oxford aesthete. A dozen years before, Taylor, with Theodore Yates or Tom Driberg, had enjoyed dining in the George Restaurant, on the fringes of this society. Taken up by Gerald Berners, the young academic (in his early thirties) now became a welcome member of the 'smartest set' in the restaurant and a frequent guest to Berners' home, Faringdon, outside Oxford. Secondly, Berners offered literary and artistic connections. This was one way Alan Taylor could please his wife, who otherwise tended to languish beyond the male social world of Magdalen College.

Berners was a colourful figure who had been on the bottom rungs of the British diplomatic service in Constantinople and then Italy, 1910–20. After inheriting in 1918 the Berners title and the wealth that went with it, he had been able to develop himself as an eccentric as well as to become an accomplished composer, a writer of witty but slight novels and a modest painter. Berners liked to hold court in the George Restaurant as well as at Faringdon, and Taylor saw much of him at both places. During the war Berners classified donors' blood in Oxford and regularly met the Taylors. Alan Taylor recalled, 'Gerald came to dinner with us every week or took us to The George Restaurant, where he was greeted obsequiously as My Lord, while the Duke of Leeds at a neighbouring table was ignored.' Berners combined wit, culture and a great knowledge of Europe (especially Italy). Like Namier earlier and Beaverbrook later, he offered an irresistible fund of good anecdotes and well-informed conversation.[94] For Margaret Taylor, Berners provided a route into the literary and musical circles she aspired to join. Berners' visitors included many major society and cultural figures. These included the Sitwells, the Mitfords, Clarissa Churchill, Harold

Nicolson, Cecil Beaton, John and Penelope Betjeman, David Cecil, Gertrude Stein, Salvador Dali, Max Beerbohm and Aldous Huxley. Berners claimed that the central figure, Emmeline Pocock, in his *Far from the Madding Crowd* (1941) was based on Clarissa Churchill. He also offered country-house gracious living, with exotic birds and a folly built in 1935 in the grounds. He made visits memorable by the jokes abounding in his home, for instance the blank books with suggestive titles on their spines. For some, such as Edith Sitwell, his humour could be too unrelenting. Margaret Taylor was much taken by Berners, whose compositions included music for ballets, and who gushed with enthusiasm about music. However, Berners, like Dylan Thomas, could not resist mocking her, though this may have been a display of male and upper-crust superiority over a middle-class woman. On one occasion, after Margaret Taylor left Berners in the George, where he had some gold ornamental chickens with him, he followed her down the street shouting: 'Maggie, Maggie! Wait a moment! I do want to show you my cock.'[95]

For Berners, Taylor was agreeable, cultured and witty company. In writing of his schooldays Berners wrote of a friend, 'I longed for the self-confidence of a Marston that would enable me to electrify the company with some sensational remark.' Taylor's comments were witty, sharp and amusing, if not sensational. In turn, Taylor enjoyed and remembered some of Berners' observations. This was so in regard to their similar disbelief in religion, Berners recalling his friend Marston's comment, 'Religion is like measles. When once you've had it and got over it, it's unlikely you'll have it again.' Both Berners and Taylor had needed a survival strategy in schools where sport was king, and both had been notably awkward in their relations with women.[96] Berners' title and wealth aside, they had much in common.

Alan Taylor also greatly valued his friendship with Count Michael Karolyi. They both were radical, and not communists but not vehemently against the Soviet Union. The two men enjoyed each other's company, meeting fifteen to twenty times between 1940 and 1951.[97] Even more so than Beaverbrook, Karolyi had been at the centre of politics in tumultuous times. Like Beaverbrook, he was present to talk about his part in the times about which Taylor was then writing. Taylor also admired him for being a radical. He wrote of him in 1968, 'Karolyi believed that liberty and equality were the only principles which mattered in life. He served them always without hesitation and without regret. Michael Karolyi was a very good man.'[98]

In his autobiography Karolyi commented on their first meeting, 'Did I live up to his expectations? It is not for me to say – all that I know is that we have remained friends from that day on.'[99] Alan Taylor responded to these remarks,

The answer is simple: I loved him. He was not an intellectual but a man of action. He was impatient, restless in thought and deed. Yet, with it all, he was pure gold all through, the noblest man I have ever known. He was guileless, a man to whom idealism came naturally. He had a great sense of fun.[100]

For Michael Karolyi, Taylor was a clever, witty and highly sympathetic Oxford academic. It is highly likely that he misjudged how much influence Taylor would have with British policy-makers, even Labour ones. Nevertheless, Taylor gave him some realistic advice about the pro-Horthy inclinations of the Foreign Office and about Whitehall generally. The British Establishment welcomed the stability of the reactionary regime of Admiral Horthy (1919–45) in Hungary and the fact that it was a bulwark against Soviet Russia, even if until the middle of the Second World War it had warm relations with Nazi Germany. In contrast, the views within the relevant part of the Foreign Office, the Political Warfare Executive, were hostile to Karolyi. One memorandum in September 1941 commented, 'Michael Karolyi is a liability to us. He and his associates have been branded, and in respect to our middle-class audience, successfully branded, as traitors…Moreover, his name smacks too much of the reduction of Hungary to Trianon proportions.' In mid-1942 it was bluntly stated, 'Karolyi…is regarded – perhaps unfairly – as a Kerensky, who paved the way for the excesses of the Bela Kun regime'. They preferred to rely on the views of C.A. Macartney, even though it was explicitly recognised that 'many people regard him as a Hungarian propagandist', as he was 'recognised in Hungary as a friend of the Hungarian people'.

Alan Taylor hoped that the British official attitude to Karolyi would change after the departure of Horthy and the change of government in Britain. In November 1945 Karolyi had an interview with Ernest Bevin, the Foreign Secretary. It was friendly but led nowhere for Karolyi. That the interview occurred was due to Taylor, who later recalled that Karolyi's 'letters, asking for a meeting, never reached the Foreign Secretary and that Ellen Wilkinson finally approached Bevin privately at my prompting'. Taylor's connection with Ellen Wilkinson was probably through their National Council of Labour Colleges work, and possibly more generally through their Manchester connections, she being a former city councillor and a graduate of Manchester University's History Department.[101]

The friendship with Michael Karolyi also began Alan Taylor's connections with the world of émigré groups in Britain, each aspiring to form the future governments of their country. Taylor, writing of the subject nationalities of the pre-First World War Austro-Hungarian Empire, was eager to hear more of the 1918–19 activities of Michael Karolyi and Oscar

Jaszi, and to take up the causes of free Czechoslovakia and Yugoslavia. In this he was consciously following in the footsteps of Lewis Namier, R.W. Seton Watson, Arnold Toynbee and other historians who had played significant roles in the shaping of a new Europe after the First World War.[102]

His desire to establish himself as a nationally recognised authority on central Europe was also boosted by the move of 'Chatham House' (the Royal Institute of International Affairs) to Balliol College, where it reverted to its earlier name, the Political Intelligence Department (PID) of the Foreign Office. Founded by John Buchan as the Intelligence Bureau of the Department of Information, it had been transferred to the Foreign Office in early 1918. Taylor unsuccessfully tried to join PID. He was, however, invited to write a paper on the British government's war aims. He later recalled,

> This was an instructive exercise. I read all the ministerial statements both before the war and after its outbreak, reaching the conclusion, now obvious enough, that the British government had no war aims nor indeed any idea what they were doing. I was in the process of writing a report on these lines when I was abruptly told to cease work: orders had come from on high that war aims were not to be discussed. As the British government were then considering how to get out of the war, this was not surprising.[103]

However, Oxford's nearness to London, its relative safety and the presence of numerous foreign policy experts at PID or in the colleges brought many eminent refugees from continental Europe. As a protégé of Namier and as an academic consulted by Count Karolyi, as well as being in the right place at the right time, he was soon speaking with, and providing advice to, other émigrés. He saw Baron Louis Hatvany, a Hungarian newspaper owner, who had been a member of the last Habsburg Council in 1918 with Count Karolyi and Professor Jaszi. Hatvany entertained him with anecdotes of Hungarian political and literary figures.

These friendships with prominent Hungarians reinforced his standing as a Left-leaning expert on Hungary. In September 1943 he wrote to W.P. Crozier, as editor of the *Manchester Guardian*, offering his services.

> I have recently had occasion to study contemporary Hungarian politics, and I think that I now know as much of the situation in Hungary as anyone in England. Because of the way I got my knowledge I can hardly write an article for publication just at the moment; but I could let you have an intelligent summary for private use, if ever you felt the need for it. At any rate, I am now better equipped to visit central Europe, if ever you – and events – give me the opportunity to go.

This was the first of several occasions he made clear his wish to go somewhere in central or eastern Europe as a special reporter for the *Manchester*

Guardian. He was to go to Czechoslovakia in summer 1946 and to Yugoslavia nearly a year later.

In writing to Crozier he took pains to suggest his ability to make critical judgements, albeit based on his views which had been reinforced by those of Karolyi and other exiles. With Crozier he was wary in being critical of the established expert, Robert Seton-Watson, who had just written for the *Manchester Guardian.* He soon showed less restraint when writing to his younger successor, A.P. Wadsworth. To Crozier, he added:

> I thought the two articles of Seton Watson admirable, as he always is. I am sure that the Trianon frontiers ought to be imposed on Horthy Hungary. At the same time, I think we ought to put the emphasis less on treaty revisions and more on the essential need for a democratic and social revolution in Hungary; and make it clear that a truly democratic Hungary would be able to negotiate adjustments of territory. S.W.'s schemes for Transylvania are attractive, but I believe impracticable.[104]

Crozier was on holiday, so Wadsworth replied. He invited Taylor to write a thousand-word piece on Hungary, covering 'how Hungary came in to the war and why, her attitude during it, the political forces inside, and the things for the allies to watch'. Taylor quickly wrote the piece and again pressed to be employed by the *Manchester Guardian* in a central Europe liberated from Germany.

> I enclose an article on Hungary, publishable I think; and a series of notes for your own information or Crozier's. You will see that some of it is not for publication, though there is really nothing in it which cannot be extracted from the News Digest. I send it to you really as a proof that I should be adequate as your observer in central Europe.
>
> I have finished the work I have been doing for P.W.E and so, after a decent interval, do not need to hide my light under a bushel. If ever there is anything really exciting from Hungary and I can be of use, give me a ring.[105]

While Crozier was still editor, Alan Taylor supplied a leader on Hungary, which was published on 23 March 1944. Entitled 'A Feudal Society', it elaborated the need for a genuine democracy, otherwise the landowning elites would again be allies for Germany. By May, Wadsworth, now the editor, was observing to Taylor that there was then 'no special urgency or even interest in Hungary'.[106]

By the autumn of 1944 Taylor was painfully aware that he was not the only associate of Michael Karolyi who wished to be the *Manchester Guardian's* special reporter in Hungary. He informed Wadsworth,

I had a visit the other day from Karl Polanyi, Misi's brother, formerly an economist in Vienna and now the *Haujude* or *eminence grise* of Karolyi. He, too, has had the bright idea of being sent to Budapest by the *M.G.* but he does not wish to go permanently. I told him my plans and also said that Ignotus had expressed an interest in the project. But I promised to mention his name to you. He would really be half-way between Ignotus and me, a three- or six-month assignment. As an economist, he would probably do things better than I should; and he has had journalistic experience in Vienna. But he would be even more marked than I should be as a Karolyi partisan; if there were a Karolyi regime, he would be wanting to advise it; and if there were not, he would hardly be admitted. However, these are abstract speculations.

All I wanted to do was to throw his hat into the ring. Misi would give you a full, but I think rather critical, picture of him.

Wadsworth responded by observing that he felt Ignotus was more promising than Karl Polanyi.[107] Taylor's opportunities increasingly were in Czechoslovakia and Yugoslavia.

Alan Taylor also became friendly with the leading figures of the Czechoslovak provisional government-in-exile. The Czech government-in-exile moved to England in 1940 and was recognised by the Soviet Union and USA as well as Britain in 1941. Czechoslovakia's future security was intended to be guaranteed also by the Czech-Soviet Treaty of Alliance, July 1941. Herbert Ripka had a house in Oxford and Taylor enjoyed not only his company but also his whisky and cigars. Eduard Benes, President in exile, lived some twenty miles from Oxford, near Aylesbury at Aston Abbotts. Like Karolyi, Benes believed Taylor to have some influence in Whitehall. Benes frequently sent a chauffeur-driven car to Oxford to bring him over to discuss how to build up British support for Czechoslovakia.

Taylor vigorously championed the eastern European successor states to the Habsburg monarchy in the press. For instance, he helped publicise the repudiation of the Munich Agreement of 1938 by the British and Free French in August–September 1942. He was adept at utilising book reviews to propagate his views on international politics. In writing of Tomas Masaryk, Benes' predecessor as Czech President, he was as eulogistic as he was in his history of the Habsburgs. For instance, in April 1940, he asked rhetorically, 'But how can one expect a perfect biography of the greatest man of his age, a man who honoured us by being our contemporary?' In March 1942 he enthusiastically observed, 'Masaryk was the greatest democratic politician of this century; every word of his is precious.' He matched this hyperbole in another review: 'Masaryk was the greatest man whom the Four Years' War brought on the world stage; Lenin, his only equal, had a more limited influence in his lifetime, and all others were pygmies in comparison...the creation of Czechoslovakia was a political performance without parallel.'[108]

Taylor was very sympathetic to the view of Benes and Ripka that the Sudeten Germans should be expelled from Czechoslovakia at the end of the war. He wrote in *Time And Tide* in May 1942,

> To remake Czechoslovakia will demand as much ruthlessness, foresight and energy as the Germans brought to its destruction; it will involve as much suffering, though not by the same people. But unless Czechoslovakia is remade with complete political and economic independence, Germany will have won the war...[109]

He also shared with Benes and Ripka the view that Soviet support for Czechoslovakia was highly desirable. He needed no tutoring in being favourable to the Soviet Union in its external policies. He was more critical of its internal policies, sharing at least some of Henry Sara's criticisms of Stalinism. Hence, for example, his impatience with Walter Duranty's *The Kremlin and the People* (1942). He dismissed the book for failing to penetrate to the Soviet reality and for being too favourable to Stalin.[110]

Taylor had been advocating an Anglo-Russian accord from before the war. In July 1937, for instance, he had deplored suggestions of leaving Russia and Czechoslovakia to fend for themselves in the face of Nazi Germany. Once the war had begun, he argued that Anglo-Russian estrangement was 'the most profound cause of the present war'. As for Poland, whose violation was the direct cause of Britain's entry into the war, he was sympathetic to Russia's views. In a review in 1941 he was critical of 'Great Poland', the Poland of the great estates. He commented of Germany and Russia, 'Poland has two neighbours: one is, and always has been, bent on her destruction; the other is, and often has been, ready to recognise and support ethnic Poland, but will always oppose Polish rule over Lithuanians, Little Russians or White Russians.' In 1942 he argued that at the heart of the Russo-Polish conflict was the Russians' determination 'to free Russian peoples from their Polish lords'.[111]

However, his pro-Soviet views proved too much for Lady Rhondda, owner and editor of *Time and Tide*. She was outraged by his review of Bernard Newman's *The New Europe*, which he dubbed 'a blue-print of a new cloud-cuckoo land'. He complained, 'There is no speculation either about how to undo the economic effects of German conquest or about how to build a more stable economic structure,' and (with reference to the Soviet Union) 'Not a word of loyalty to our allies' and a readiness to 'distribute our allies' territory to all and sundry'. He argued, 'Russian policy has a single object, security, and she regards the frontiers of 1941 as essential to this object.' He added, 'The peoples of Europe can enjoy freedom only under the joint protection of England and Russia; and just as we postulate a group of friendly states in western Europe with similar social and political systems to our own, so does Russia in eastern Europe.'

Not surprisingly, the review provoked outrage beyond the proprietor, including from among the émigrés from Poland and the Baltic states. Taylor had no more compunction about sweeping national sentiments aside than, say, Metternich when arguing for a new international system for stability. One writer, F.B. Czarnomski, complained of 'great disloyalty to Britain's first ally in the war', praised *Time and Tide* for standing for the 'equality of rights between nations, great and small' and stated, 'If this war has demonstrated anything it is that no country in Europe was capable of defending itself single-handed against the German war machine.' Adam Pragier, in another letter in response to Taylor, commented,

> Mr Taylor is fighting for 'Peace with Reality' but he bases his 'reality' on 'power politics pure and simple', on complete indifference to the fate of 200 million people living in small countries in Europe, and on exclusive interest in the security of Germany and Russia without giving even a thought to Great Britain. Indeed, the most faithful and natural allies of Great Britain on the Continent are those small and medium-sized nations which Mr Taylor neglects. If these small countries are strengthened by strong federal structures, the balance of power in Europe will be restored and a basis for British influence on the Continent created.

After four lengthy letters hostile to Taylor's review, Lady Rhondda complimented herself on the 'considerable freedom' she gave reviewers, before observing: 'We are ourselves in accord with almost everything our correspondents have to say with regard to Mr Taylor's review, with which we profoundly disagree.'

Alan Taylor demanded, and received, a right of reply. His response was five-sixths the length of the original review. It was characteristically defiant and combative. He began by expressing his exaggerated feelings of grievance:

> It is almost impossible for a mere Englishman to talk sense about eastern Europe without being subjected to Polish 'terror by correspondence'. This uproar is designed to conceal the fact that the eastern territory of Poland, conquered from Russia in 1921, is mainly inhabited by peoples of Russian stock; the frontier of 1939 was not perfect, but it was much nearer to ethnic justice than the frontier of 1921 and no Polish juggling with statistics can conceal this.

He went on to argue,

> The experiment of excluding Russia from Europe has already been tried, was in fact the principal cause of the present war; and I do not believe British opinion favours its repetition. Only an Anglo-Russian alliance, buttressed on each side by friendly neighbours, can give Europe permanent peace and the nations of Europe national independence; that was the lesson of 1814, let alone of 1941...
>
> Great Powers must possess more power and influence than small Powers, just as big cars go faster than small cars. This may be 'power politics'; to pretend the opposite leads to powerless politics, which has brought on us our present difficulties.

Lady Rhondda followed his letter with an editorial comment on it, nearly as long as Taylor's reply. She began by referring to Britain's entry into the war being expressly to protect the rights of small nations and, in particular, Poland. She commented on Polish concerns, observing it was hardly surprising that they had an 'obsession with the borderlands'. She concluded, 'It is true that big cars go faster than small ones but – according to British rules of the road – they are not on that account given licence to obliterate or even to run into their smaller brethren.' This controversy should have given Taylor a warning as to the likely uproar when he explored the origins of the Second World War in Europe in 1961.

One unremarked feature of this controversy was the personalised nature of Taylor's attack on Newman. On the whole his critics did not reply in kind. He began the book review with sharp criticism of Bernard Newman as a lecturer favoured by the Ministry of Information.

> Mr Newman is a popular lecturer, in fact lecturer No. 1 on international affairs both to the Forces and for the Ministry of Information. His secret is simple: he tells his audience what they know already, spiced with some vague history...and personal anecdotes, collected while touring Europe on a bicycle. The audience is flattered by hearing its own views repeated in polished form; readers of this book will enjoy the same experience.

He was similarly critical of others used by the BBC, a feature of his behaviour in the period when he was struggling for public recognition.

When he appealed to Namier for support, Namier made it clear that he was unwilling to jump into the hole which Alan Taylor had dug for himself. Taylor later recalled, 'Lewis explained he had had enough trouble over the borderlands after the First World War and did not want to be involved again.' Taylor wrote two further reviews for *Time and Tide*, one on international history and the other, six months after the Newman review, on Masaryk, both subjects where his views were not at variance with those of Lady Rhondda. Thereafter, he was dropped as too much of an apologist for the Soviet Union's external policies.

In early 1944 his views on Poland angered eminent diplomatic figures. He wrote to the *Spectator* a letter in which he argued that the Poles should not aim to recover long-lost frontiers nor believe that 'Poland could ever again be a Great Power'. He called for 'the Polish government…to recognise the liberty and national unity of the White Russians and the Ukraine', and more generally to realise that they must choose the friend-ship of either Russia or Germany, their two powerful neighbours. The British ambassador in Moscow telegrammed the Foreign Office to inform it his letter had been published in *Izvestia*. The British ambassador to Poland complained to the Foreign Office, arguing that as Alan Taylor had been employed writing the Hungarian handbook for British troops he should be restricted from engaging in political controversy. However, it was pointed out that he 'was paid on a piece-work basis and did much of the work at Magdalen in his spare time'. So the Foreign Office did not 'therefore think he could properly be regarded as a temporary Civil Servant' nor had had access to secret information.[112]

Alan Taylor's views on the Soviet Union were very acceptable to Karolyi, Benes and Ripka. The Czechs invited him to give a public lecture at the Czechoslovak Institute in London to promote his views on the future of their country. The lecture took place on 29 April 1943, with Jan Masaryk, the Czechoslovak Minister for Foreign Affairs and Deputy Prime Minister, in the chair. In his lecture Taylor outlined themes he had developed in *The Habsburg Monarchy 1815–1918*. He argued that Czechoslovakia's function in European relations was to succeed the Habsburg monarchy as a bulwark against German expansionism, observing: 'The vast German power has threatened for a century to destroy the liberties of Europe…' He also argued that it was to be the meeting place between the Western democracies and Soviet Russia, with the role of being 'the interpreter of the Slav spirit in England and America and the missionaries of democracy among the Slavs'. He deemed Czechoslovakia to combine the best values of both Western and Slav societies; whereas 'Germany has accumulated inside itself all the vices of both West and East'.

The Czechoslovak Institute issued a twenty-page pamphlet based on his lecture, but more important for the dissemination of this view of Czechoslovakia's future was a feature article, entitled 'Czechoslovakia's 25 Years: Her Place in Europe', published six months later in the *Manchester Guardian* to mark the anniversary of the founding of the state at the end of the First World War. Taylor confidently declared that 'the independence of Czechoslovakia was the greatest blow ever dealt to German ambitions and the Czechoslovak achievements during the twenty years of freedom showed that a solution to the German problem had been found'.[113]

Just over a year later, in late May 1944, he wrote a short leader on Benes, at Wadsworth's request. Both he and Wadsworth were eager for him to go to Czechoslovakia on behalf of the *Manchester Guardian*. In early December 1944 Taylor felt that the time was right for Wadsworth to contact Ripka to help facilitate this.

Alan Taylor seems to have an inflated idea of the role of historians in remaking national boundaries, a view which was influenced by the past activities of Namier and Seton-Watson. Wadsworth was more realistic than Taylor on the political limits to altruism in such matters. After Taylor had written a leader on Carpathia, Wadsworth wrote to say it could not then be used. 'Benes and Ripka may have expressed in private their willingness to part with the territory, but is not the official public attitude still against it? They would not thank us if we were to split up and give away their country in advance.' Nevertheless, Wadsworth remained eager for Taylor to go to Czechoslovakia, asking in early February whether he had any news of the Czech leaders' return and if there was a chance of Taylor accompanying them. Wadsworth added, 'If they go through Moscow it might, of course, mean that for some months the country would be as much cut off as are the other "liberated" countries in the Russian zone.'[114] The Czech government-in-exile returned to Czechoslovakia in 1945, but Taylor waited a further year before going.

In early November 1944 Taylor met delegates of the Slovak National Council. He had very little sympathy for Slovak nationalism, the independent Slovakia of 1939–45 being run by close allies of Nazi Germany. A Slovak rising against the Germans, supported by Benes, was suppressed in October. After seeing the Slovak representatives he wrote to A.P. Wadsworth that they had not thought through fully their position.

> They want to be a separate Nation, but at the same time they want Czechoslovakia stronger than before, as they realise that without Bohemia they must be dependent on Germany – or on Hungary. I asked them what they meant by being a separate nation. They said they meant culturally independent: their own press, literature, schools. Separate tariffs or economic planning? No, certainly not. They want a Czechoslovak plan, by which the resources of Bohemia will be used to raise their standards. But suppose the Czechs insist on being a separate nation? That they would not like at all. A separate army? No. But then what is to be the language of command? They were troubled about this and said there would have to be an agreed Czechoslovak tongue for army purposes. Then there is a Czechoslovak nationality? No. And so on.

The non-communists among them were unlikely to be enamoured of Alan Taylor's advice that 'if they wanted security, they must go with Russia',[115] for Stalin had not acted to try to rescue the Slovak resisters the previous month. However, it was realistic, the Red Army defeating the German forces in Slovakia in March 1945.

Taylor's first high-profile support for Yugoslavia came with a lengthy letter praising Rebecca West's, *Black Lamb and Grey Falcon: The Record of a Journey through Yugoslavia in 1937*, published in two volumes in 1942. This was a curious episode, where Taylor helped gratify Lewis Namier's wishes. Henry Wickham Steed had been dismissive of the book. Lady Rhondda wanted her friend's book to be treated better, Rebecca West being a director of *Time and Tide*. Rebecca West had reviewed favourably Taylor's *The Habsburg Monarchy*. Namier urged him to come to her defence, being eager to please Lady Rhondda and also as he was a friend of Rebecca West. Taylor obliged with an assessment which acknowledged inaccuracies in some details but argued that it was not intended as a travel guide or a history, 'her profound purpose' being 'to depict the soul of a people as a novelist draws the character of an individual'. Overall, he drew this moral, 'The existence and compelling reality of national communities is the fundamental, inescapable fact of European politics both past and present.' In his autobiography he reflected, 'I greatly admired the book, now I think too much so...'[116]

The long letter to *Time and Tide* was much appreciated by both Rebecca West and Lady Rhondda. Alan Taylor and Rebecca West became friends for some years, though falling out later. At the time Taylor wrote several times to her trying to convince her that she should back Tito, not General Mihailovic and the Chetniks, who supported the government-in-exile. His tone was very similar to that he had employed on Muggeridge over Stalin's Russia: didactic and very much the over-frank friend. As her biographer Carl Rollyson has commented, his comments on Russia would have outraged her. Taylor wrote, 'The Russians are not democratic now, but there is a chance they may become so; there's not much chance for us.' Worse still, with echoes of Karl Marx, he added, 'The peasant must disappear; that is the lesson of all civilisation. Nasty for him, but it can't be helped. And in the long run, the Russian way of liquidating him is no worse than our way in the eighteenth century, which has made us the civilized people we are.'[117] Given such 'tough thinking', it is not surprising some liberal and democratic socialists of the period, such as George Orwell, could think of him as a potential 'fellow traveller' with the communists.

Given his work on the Habsburg Monarchy and Italy he was naturally especially interested in the border issue of Trieste and its wider area, the Julian Region or Venezia Giulia. In his autobiography he claimed that, while he was not in sympathy with Polish nationalist claims, 'I was warm towards the Yugoslavs and preached their claims to Trieste on behalf of the Royal government long before Tito came along. In fact I taught the Yugoslavs the justification of their claim which they had not earlier grasped themselves.'[118]

The Julian Region, half of which is Istria, was divided fairly evenly between Italians, mostly living in the cities, the coastal towns and coastal rural areas, and Slovenes (living in the rural north) and Croats (living in the rural south). While Venice had served Italy, Trieste had become the major port for the Habsburg lands, being under Habsburg rule from the fourteenth century until 1918 (unlike the Istrian coastal towns, which had been linked to Venice). It was a predominantly Italian city with what was to become Yugoslavia as its immediate hinterland. The Yugoslavs did not need to be schooled in their case for Trieste by Taylor, having made it, and for Rijeka (Fiume), at the Paris Peace Conference in 1919. They had subsequently learnt that, in spite of the Treaty of Rapallo, which made Rijeka an independent city state, force succeeded. For, after an occupation by the Italian ultra-nationalist Gabriele D'Annuncio, most of the city was taken for Italy by Benito Mussolini under the Treaty of Rome, 1924. In the areas of the Julian Region under Fascist rule, leading Slovenian and Croat nationalists were murdered or imprisoned and land was taken over by Italians.

With the Second World War, Yugoslavia was invaded in 1941 and divided between Italy and Germany, with the Yugoslav government-in-exile eventually being based in London. Inside Yugoslavia, the major opponents of occupation were the Chetniks and the Partisans, led by Tito, the secretary of the Communist Party. While the Chetniks' effectiveness as an active military force was limited, the Partisans were effective in sabotage and in selective attacks on the Italian, and later the German, occupying forces. Tito was even more successful in convincing Churchill and the British Foreign office of the power of his forces by the time of the Tehran Conference between Churchill, Roosevelt and Stalin in late 1943. In August 1944 Churchill secured King Peter of Yugoslavia's public support for Tito's leadership of the Yugoslav resistance. By October 1944 the Red Army had cleared Serbia of Germans and Tito had his headquarters in Belgrade.[119]

Hoping to move Yugoslav forces into the Julian Region, Tito wished to secure British goodwill. One important aspect of this was to influence British opinion-makers regarding the Yugoslav case for Trieste. Hence, in late 1944, General Vladko Velebit appeared at Holywell Ford to request that Alan Taylor write a pamphlet stating this case. Taylor wrote in his autobiography,

I was fully in sympathy with these claims though I doubted whether a
pamphlet would help them. I said to Vladko, 'Get to Trieste before
the Allies. That is the only argument that will count.' Vladko, with his
captivating innocence in worldly affairs, insisted that British public
opinion would respond to a fair case.

Vladko Velebit undoubtedly needed no lessons in the value of occupying
a contested city, but the Communists were well aware of the anti-Red
interventions in central and eastern Europe supported by the Western
Allies after the 1918 Armistice and wanted to try to guard against a repeat.
Moreover, the Italian Communists wanted Trieste to be Italian, while the
Slovenian Communists expected it to become part of Yugoslavia, the
matter being deferred by the head of the Comintern in Moscow until after
German defeat. Tito was disinclined to wait, instead launching propaganda for securing Trieste for Yugoslavia. The Italian case for Trieste had
been made effectively by two historians, Benedetto Croce and Gaetano
Salvemini. He wanted a British historian to counter it.[120] Perhaps Taylor,
not Velebit, was more the innocent.

Alan Taylor published his first essay in support of Trieste becoming
part of Yugoslavia in the *New Statesman* in December 1944. This was
entitled 'Trieste or Trst?'. The essay, which was a shorter version of the
pamphlet (published in early 1945), ended with a statement promoting
the Anglo-Soviet alliance: 'Here the Slav world and the world of Western
democracy can overlap and combine. In short, we can be more confident
of the future of the Anglo-Soviet alliance when we have learnt to think of
Trieste as Trst.'[121] This ending was removed from the pamphlet at the
request of the Yugoslav government. Taylor recalled their view: 'It was
not for them…to advise on the relations of the Great Powers.' He also
observed,

> At the time I supposed this to be an exaggerated demonstration of
> Yugoslav independence. Now I know better. The only chance for the
> Yugoslavs was to base their claim on historic and national justice; Soviet
> backing, far from being a help to them, drove the other Great Powers
> into uncompromising opposition. The question of Trieste and of Istria
> was conducted purely as a trial of strength. The Russians backed
> Yugoslavia in order to show that they could protect their satellites; the
> others opposed Yugoslav claims in order to weaken the Communists
> in Italy and in order 'to keep the Russians off the Adriatic'.[122]

His pamphlet was a very lucid and cogent statement of the Yugoslav
case for Trieste. It was well based on the economic and social past of
Trieste and the Julian Region, and it made effective comparisons with
Danzig and other inter-war treaties to argue that decisions comparable to

giving Trieste to Yugoslavia had been made without dire results elsewhere. He was helped with some information by a Yugoslav academic, whom he was to meet again some thirty years later when in Zagreb.[123] At 38 he was self-confident, now established in an Oxford Fellowship and finding he was consulted by central and south-east European politicians. It was an able statement of a case, which has deserved reprinting, even if it argued for one side. It was countered at the time by Gaetano Salvemini in his essay 'Trieste and Trst' in *Free Italy*, April 1945.

Taylor's enthusiasm for Tito was not shared by A.P. Wadsworth. In January 1945 Wadsworth observed, 'I am not sure you are right in saying that Tito is more a British protégé than a Russian. He certainly takes military orders from Russia. I was told the other day by a high military authority just back from those parts that there are a number of Serb bands (besides Mihailovich) which we have never helped nor got into contact with but which have been doing useful work against the Germans.' In April Taylor commented, 'I'm glad that someone has spoken up against Seton-Watson. I'm rather for Tito than for Mike [Mihailovich], but his assertions were too emphatic and without solid foundation. S-W has always been "Yugoslav" and therefore anti-Serb.' To this Wadsworth replied, 'The Yugoslavs are quite beyond me, but I am afraid there is going to be some nasty trouble about Trieste.' He added, in a further letter, that he felt 'the Jugs...are rather a dirty lot. Why can't they clear the *Germans* out of their own country instead of rushing to annex territory? No, I think we have probably made too much of Tito...'[124]

Taylor was genuinely enthusiastic about Yugoslavia and its people. He was also pleased to be establishing a name for himself as an expert on one of several areas where Great Power conflict was occurring, and which before long became a Cold War area of major contention. He hoped to go to Yugoslavia, as well as to Czechoslovakia, as a special reporter for the *Manchester Guardian*. When he confirmed that he wanted Wadsworth to write to Ripka, he added, 'As soon as the Yugoslavs have a proper Foreign Minister I will ask you to write to him too. The Tito people wanted me to go now, but I think I'd better wait until things are more settled.'[125] He was to wait until 1947.

Taylor's broadcasting career began with him commenting on the war. His opportunity largely came because so many people were away at the war. He was already speaking on the war to adult education audiences and on behalf of the Ministry of Information. Oxbridge academics were sufficiently near to the BBC's studios and were attractive to the many Oxbridge graduates working for the BBC. C.S. Lewis also took the opportunity to broadcast during the war, first giving a series of talks on a Christian theme in August 1941.[126]

Alan Taylor began appearing in a fifteen-minute slot on the forces network (the precursor of the BBC Light Programme and later Radio 2), in March 1942. He had approached the BBC at the start of the year to be considered for radio broadcasts. He was invited to make an appointment when he was next in London. This he did for the late morning on 5 February 1942. Perhaps this arrangement fell through, as he was asked to write a lengthy letter giving his views. After reading this letter, Trevor Blewitt wrote back, 'You say so much that I agree with…although, of course, naturally quite a lot with which I disagree.' He invited him to meet Lloyd Williams, the assistant director of his department, and to be auditioned for the series 'The World at War – Your Questions Answered'. Blewitt added encouragingly, 'I am hoping the whole layout of the programme will be changing very shortly, and I think you could help us very much.'[127]

After successfully being auditioned, Taylor joined Edward Montgomery and others in a small team of speakers. He was quickly asked to appear on a programme. However, from the outset, he made it clear that he would only dance to the BBC's tune when it fitted in with his other commitments. He agreed to a first appearance on 17 March providing he was recorded in Oxford. Similarly, he stipulated that a preliminary meeting to discuss his answers with Trevor Blewitt must be held after 1.00 p.m. on Saturday 7 March, though he offered Blewitt accommodation at Holywell Ford that night.

For the programme much consideration was clearly given by the BBC as to what questions were used and the nature of his answers. In his autobiography Taylor wrote,

> In theory the questions came from bomber pilots, soldiers in North Africa and naval ratings in the Atlantic. In fact they were made up by Guy Chapman, later a professor of history at Leeds. I did not attach much importance to this work. Indeed, I took it on mainly so that Nanna, my old nurse in the Isle of Man, could hear my voice. But it taught me radio technique.[128]

While Guy Chapman may well have written some questions when they had too few, the BBC archives are highly suggestive of the questions coming in from various sources and being taken seriously. For instance, Taylor was sent 'a complete set of questions we have received up to date', and was told that those 'ticked in red have already been answered and those with names against them were not considered suitable for the programme and have been sent to other departments'.

Far from him being indifferent to appearing on the radio, the records show him intensely eager to get on the air; though, indeed, he aspired for major, popular programmes such as 'The Brains Trust'. Certainly, he worked hard for his fifteen minutes on air, and did so not just for the sake of his old nanny. His draft script was returned on 12 March with pencilled suggestions on it, plus 'some material on several questions about Germany which you might like to answer all together if you have room'. By 14 March he had rewritten it, making it 'more simple'. On this being received, he was required to rewrite again the introduction, removing much 'guessing', and to introduce 'a breathing space into the script – at present it is tough going for our audience'. In addition, it was cut in length.[129]

He spoke a further six times on 'The World at War – Your Questions Answered', between 31 March and 23 June 1942. After that he was not hired again for that programme. In early September he wrote to Blewitt,

> For some reason of their own the Communists are running a campaign against me in Oxford and are saying, among other things, that as a result of my answer about the *Daily Worker* I have been banned from the BBC. I assume that this is quite untrue, but I should like to be sure. If you find it embarrassing to answer I will write to the Controller, but I thought it too trivial to bother him with.
>
> I hope you are coming to spend a weekend with us before the summer is over. The river is now wonderfully fresh and warm after the rains and there is rich food from the gardern [sic].[130]

In writing a 'Dear Trevor…Yours Alan' letter, with the offer of hospitality akin to those given to major figures of the *Manchester Guardian* when he lived in Manchester, he was clearly striving to re-establish his foothold in the BBC. He was receiving criticism from Communist Party members. But it is more probable that he was dropped because he was alarming some of the great and the good in the area of foreign policy. Trevor Blewitt did, however, encourage him to keep in contact. In December 1942 he invited Taylor to meet him when next in London 'to discuss one or two ideas for programmes'. Any such discussions came to nothing and he did not return to radio broadcasting until October 1944.[131]

If his strong desire to make a name for himself on the radio was thwarted for a couple of years, his hopes of major government work were boosted in May 1943. He was called to London to work for the Political Warfare Executive (PWE). The PWE had been established in 1941 and its work included black propaganda to Germany, including broadcasting lurid accounts of the lifestyles of leading Nazis. It also assessed and acted on other proposals. For instance, in 1941 Winston Churchill eagerly pressed Anthony Eden to get PWE to consider the dropping of large numbers of leaflets on Italy referring to the numbers of Italians who had been sent by Mussolini to die in the Ukraine.[132] Taylor was sworn to secrecy under the Official Secrets Act. He subsequently revealed that he wrote a handbook for troops likely to occupy Hungary and a chapter for one on Germany. Perhaps he did more for the PWE. For four months he had leave from Magdalen College and lived in London as a paying guest of Stephen and Natasha Spender.

Alan Taylor believed he had been selected to write the guide to Hungary because PWE leaned to the Left and he was the established left-wing historian of the Habsburg monarchy. The purpose of the many guides to occupied European countries was, as the Hungarian scholar Attila Pók has commented, not just to provide the troops with information as to the politics and culture of countries liberated from Germany but, through the troops' understanding, to encourage the people 'to look upon the British soldiers replacing the Germans not as new invaders but as liberators'.[133] Taylor prepared the Hungarian guide quickly, being told that British troops were expected to be in Hungary that autumn.

His major input was in the historical and political chapters. He gained the necessary information on the way Hungary's government worked and on its economy from Hungarian refugees. He was helped directly by Michael Karolyi on Hungarian politics. He wrote a lengthy chapter on Hungarian history. As PWE was under the Political Intelligence Department of the Foreign Office the proofs of the guidebook were sent there for approval. Taylor later recalled, 'They returned a little later with my chapters on Hungarian history and politics entirely deleted and a Right-wing version, no doubt by C.A. Macartney, the historian, pasted over them.' Alan Taylor kept his copy for many years but, later, threw it away. This he was to regret, notably after marrying Éva Haraszti.[134] He was delighted when Attila Pók located a copy in the Public Record Office (PRO).

Pók found that Alan Taylor's version of the handbook had indeed been sent to Macartney, a Research Fellow of All Souls College, Oxford, who was then working in the Research Department of the Foreign Office. Macartney damned Taylor for being hostile to Admiral Horthy, his colleagues and to Hungary and complained that not all the data was up to date. Sir Owen O'Malley, Britain's last pre-war ambassador to Hungary, confirmed Macartney's judgement, and echoed the Foreign Office's still prevalent Chamberlainite sentiments: 'In a general way we try to tell the truth but having regard to our friendship with Czechoslovakia and Russia and the rather leftish outlook of the British government [Churchill's coalition government], we have given the booklet a bit of a twist to the left.' This 'twist to the left' would have been imperceptible to the untrained eye, not least in regard to a passage in which the massacre of 5000 civilians was deemed only the result of an irresponsible individual's decision. The PWE successfully pressed that this passage by Macartney be removed.[135]

Taylor had admired Macartney's pre-war work. He had reviewed his *Hungary and Her Successors*, 1937, stating that it was invaluable and its author 'knows more of the problems of the Danube basin in 1937 than any other living man'. However, he was vehemently opposed to Macartney's support for Horthy during the war. In October 1942 he had gratuitously criticised Macartney in his controversial review of *The New Europe* by Bernard Newman for *Time and Tide*. He had written, 'Mr Newman here presents a more popular version of the role so long played by Mr C.A. Macartney: a divine Arbiter acting on behalf of 'world opinion' (meaning England and America), who allots territory here and moves populations there according to the impartial promptings of his inspired wisdom.'[136] In 1943 Macartney in the Foreign Office's Research Department could purge Taylor's anti-Horthy writing. After the war, when Macartney wrote a book on Hungary in the period 1929 to 1945, Alan Taylor was vigorous in condemning the book. He commented, 'It is a political tract despite its display of scholarship; neither more nor less than a defence of the Hungarian collaborators and, implicitly, a denunciation of those who condemned them.' He went on,

> I must not conceal my own interest in this dispute. In the days when Mr Macartney was preaching collaboration with the collaborators, I saw the only hope for Hungary in a new democratic order under the leadership of Michael Karolyi. This, too, was a barren enterprise, as things turned out; but it was at least an honourable one. Michael Karolyi was the noblest man I have known. It turns my stomach to read Mr Macartney's cheap sneers at him – he is even condemned for living at one time in North Oxford – and at the fulsome praise of men who were not fit to clean his boots.

He ended in commenting in favour of the leaders of the Hungarian rising of 1956:

> the book will be used to bolster the Communist legend that the Hungarian revolutionaries were hoping to restore the Horthy system with Western aid. Maybe free Hungary has no future. But those who hope otherwise should advise the Hungarians to remember the legacy of Michael Karolyi and to forget all about Horthy, as indeed most Hungarians have already done.[137]

Having had his historical and political sections of Hungary deleted in autumn 1943, PWE invited Taylor to contribute a chapter on the Weimar Republic to the German handbook for British troops occupying Germany. This he did. Again it did not please. It was rejected at the suggestion of the German historian, F.L. Carsten, a socialist refugee from Nazi Germany. Carsten worked for PWE from 1942. He condemned Taylor's chapter as too one-sided. As a committed member of the German Socialist Party (SPD), Carsten was outraged at Taylor's vigorous condemnation of the Weimar Republic. He would have had reason if he had also felt that Taylor's writing on Germany was strong on opinions, light on primary research.[138] Alan Taylor recalled, 'I had taken the line, perhaps somewhat exaggerated by wartime feelings, that Germany had not been democratic even in Weimar times and that Hitlerism, far from being an aberration, grew out of what had gone before.' His view of German history was also deemed too gloomy in lectures to British officers. The feeling was that there was a need 'to tread a difficult line – so as not to paint the Germans too black for the troops to believe...[but] not to let there be any doubt that the Germans were guilty'. He was replaced by E.J. Passant. Taylor's Weimar chapter and his German lectures were expanded into his book, *The Course of German History* (1945), at the suggestion of Denis Brogan, a fellow historian and a director of the publishing firm Hamish Hamilton. Passant's lectures also became a book, but much later, and it was widely used in schools in the 1960s. Taylor deemed Passant's book to be competent but colourless.[139]

Taylor was dissatisfied with the sales of *The Habsburg Monarchy*. At much the same time A.L. Rowse, with whom he was then still friendly, was unhappy with his publisher for not pushing harder his 1941 book, *The Spirit of English History*. They both moved publisher, Taylor to Hamish Hamilton and Rowse to Macmillan. They both upset their former publishers by presenting them with *faits accomplis*.[140] In the case of Alan Taylor, he was on the rebound from having his PWE chapter rejected and was flattered by the interest of Denis Brogan and Hamish Hamilton in his rejected work being expanded.

He at first intended *The Course of German History* to be a short book, some 50,000 words long. He affected a flippant tone in his first letter to Hamish Hamilton, aware that he only had a survey book to offer. 'I had in mind to write a general summary of German history for the layman, such as ought to appear in the works of the various intelligence departments who are producing handbooks on Germany...In fact a 1066 and all that in German terms.'[141] In this he was making quite clear that what he had in mind was not a research-driven study, and he was also guarding against a further rebuff. While his skin was not as thin as Rowse's, he was notably sensitive to criticisms and rebuffs. Hamish Hamilton was proficient at hooking attractive authors, flattering them, making much of the big names on his list and emphasising his track record in securing large sales for his authors.[142] In this case he soon secured Taylor's agreement to write a full-length book. By mid-May he had written 20,000 words and by mid-September 1944 he had completed it, with just over 105,000 words.[143]

Alan Taylor, perhaps aware that he could be deemed to have treated Macmillan badly, made much of his grievances on sales in a letter which was clearly intended to make a firm breach with Macmillan. Daniel Macmillan, Harold's elder brother and chairman of the firm, can rarely if ever have received such an abrasive letter, which condemned his firm's marketing failure for *The Habsburg Monarchy*, and went on:

> I should be glad…to know if this book is still in print. If so, I should like some explanation why it is not stocked by any bookseller; if not, whether you intend to reprint it within the six months specified in your contract. I might also inform you that I have just completed a history of Germany in the nineteenth century; but in view of the disappointments I have had with the Habsburg Monarchy I have offered it to a publisher who is interested in selling books.[144]

In this Taylor was again following the style of his grandfather, JT, rather than his father. His bluster scarcely disguised the key information in the final sentence. Not surprisingly, his old firm was angry with him.

The Course of German History was intended, as he wrote, to be 'a pièce d'occasion', with a wide readership. It was also a survey of German history addressing what he felt to be the then serious historiographical issues. The German minority issues that Hitler raised with regard to Austria, Czechoslovakia and Poland were critical in understanding the outbreak of war in Europe in 1939, and so linked current affairs and history. In a review published in the journal *International Affairs* in late 1939 Taylor had given the opinion: 'The German penetration into eastern Europe and the conflict of nationalities which this created is one of the most fundamental processes of modern European history and cannot be too often studied.'[145]

In reassessing German history he was emphatically moving away from the radical views of his parents and probably of his grandfather, JT. In so doing he was challenging the Liberal received version of German history, notably expressed by G.P. Gooch. When reviewing Gooch's *Studies in Diplomacy and Statecraft* in 1942, he observed that 'informed opinion in England on these topics has been more influenced by Dr Gooch than by any other writer'. Gooch, as 'a pupil of Acton and a Liberal member of the 1906 Parliament…, was convinced of the civilised character of Germany and this has influenced all his scholarship' and this 'historical outlook… produced the post-war British policy'. He urged, 'The new generation of historians has now the obligation to make a new analysis of the underlying forces in Europe which will be closer to reality and so to prepare a British policy which will suffer from fewer illusions and make fewer mistakes.'[146]

In urging a rethinking of German history Taylor was following others, not taking a lead. The supposed peculiarity of German history, or indeed of Germans, had been reignited as an issue by the advent of Adolf Hitler and the Nazis to power. The 'Prussianism' of First World War propaganda and of fact was reinforced by the outrages of 1933 and after.[147] A.L. Rowse, whose background had some similarities to Taylor's in that he had been a member of the Oxford University Labour Club, had at one time held Marxist views and had been politically active but preferred an academic career, expressed briefly in 1937 views not dissimilar to Taylor's in *The Course of German History* (1945). Rowse began his 'What is Wrong with the Germans': 'There is something wrong with the Germans, something profoundly wrong, the whole of modern European history in the past century is so much evidence.' He wrote of the 'struggle for the German soul', outlining a good side but then claiming there was the other side:

> The forces of barbarism, the denial of reason and culture, the cult of violence and aggressions, the inflamed inferiority complex, the envy, the jealousy, the *schadenfreude*, the megalomania – in all these things Hitler is the very mirror of the German soul, or the dominant elements of it: hence his success…

Rowse went on to explore the history of Germany, notably from Luther, in order to discuss 'their own hideous Teutonism' and the practice of the Germans of 'making their very worst faults and characteristics a national creed and doctrine'.[148]

A more substantial analysis of this kind was Rohan Butler's *The Roots of National Socialism 1783–1933* (1941). Like Rowse, he wrote of a German dual soul. After mentioning the praiseworthy characteristics, he wrote of how

> individual Germans…can suddenly…forget themselves completely and eagerly merge their being in a national whole distinguished for its aggressive ferocity and its ruthless disregard of the accepted principles of conduct in a civilized society. Tentative explanations of this phenomenon have been advanced; it is sometimes held that the Germans have a peculiar psychological kink which periodically produces otherwise inexplicable lapses from normality…

Butler also went back to Luther in his review of the German political and intellectual background. He came to the grim conclusion that the spirit of 'Germanity' entailed that 'law is jungle-law, might is right, fanaticism is virtue, ruthlessness is common sense, fear is master over all, ruling in the name of the ideal'. In his view, the Nazis brought such values and instincts to the surface and extended them.[149]

Such views of Germans and German history were not confined to British historians. Both Rowse and Butler were impressed and influenced by the writings of Professor Edmond Vermeil of the Sorbonne. And so, directly or indirectly, was Taylor. Vermeil's analyses of German history also argued that Nazi doctrine was 'the degeneration and vulgarisation of the intellectual tradition of Germany'. Vermeil was one of three historians whom Butler gave particular acknowledgement, and Rowse greatly praised Vermeil's *Doctrinaires de la Révolution Allemande, 1918–1938* (Paris, 1938), and his 1941 study, published in Britain as *Germany's Three Reichs* (1945). Taylor's book was not intellectual history but it did depict, even nearly caricature, the theme of there being a dark side to the German psyche. When reviewing the English version of Vermeil's 1945 book he deemed it 'A remarkable book, constantly stimulating, but by no means an easy book to read'.[150] While Butler's book was primarily intellectual history, Taylor's was political history.

In his autobiography he observed of *The Course of German History*,

> The book has been a good deal criticized as reflecting the passions of wartime. I do not think this is so. I learned most of my approach from Eckart Kehr, a brilliant and at that time neglected historian, who had developed in detail the evil consequences of the marriage between the Junkers and heavy industry and who died before Hitler came to power.

Kehr had enraged the nationalist German historians by his radical-liberal critiques of the received wisdom of the German recent past. He argued in 1933 that for over a century German historians had rejected liberalism and praised the powerful German state. Taylor drew on Kehr, but he did not follow him so far as to write thematic, more social-orientated history. As for style, he attributed his heavy use of epigrams and paradoxes to Albert Sorel, whose study of Europe and the French Revolution and his collected essays he read during 1944.[151]

However, the biggest influence on Taylor remained Lewis Namier. Alan Taylor had been very hostile to Germany since the occupation of the Ruhr and his attitudes had been reinforced by the near-lifelong anti-German attitudes of his mentor. On many points their comments were similar. For instance, Namier wrote in 1941 that Hitler was not uniquely evil but was 'probably one of the most representative Germans that ever lived'.[152] Taylor repeated such sentiments in criticising Lindley Fraser's *Germany between Two World Wars* (1944): 'Its weakness is its assumption that the Germans had to be argued into supporting Hitler (and therefore can be argued out of supporting him). In reality Hitler did not argue with the German people, but expressed, in somewhat violent form, their outlook and wishes.' While later writers have assumed Taylor believed Germans were incurably brutal, in fact he was sometimes more optimistic. In this instance he concluded, 'It is therefore not enough to demolish Hitler's case; there must be a positive alternative to put in its place.'[153]

About the time Taylor wrote his PWE chapter on the Weimar Republic he began writing on Germany for the *Manchester Guardian*. He wrote two pieces entitled 'German Unity', which were published on 29 and 30 March 1944. The first, with the sub-heading 'The Background of the Reich', started off briskly with, 'What is wrong with Germany is that there is too much of it. There are too many Germans, and Germany is too strong, too well organised, too well equipped with industrial resources.' The two essays in practice were responses to the issue of whether Germany could be returned to its former situation of comprising many independent states. His conclusion was that

> the German States have always been as much artificial, as much manu-factured, as the Reich; they have always been imposed upon Germany from without. It is sometimes proposed to revive them in order to save the victorious Allies the burden of policing Germany, but the moment the Allies cease to police Germany the revived States will collapse. It is more practicable to make Germany's neighbours strong than to make Germany weak.[154]

In July 1944 he wrote on East Prussia, arguing: 'Were Germany deprived of East Prussia it would injure the Junker class very little and the military class...not at all.'[155]

While writing *The Course of German History* Taylor reviewed several books on German history, and in these expressed views in his suppressed PWE essay. He aired his strong socialist views in a review in mid-June 1942: 'German economic control, established by legal means, is now so complete throughout Europe that if private capitalism survives German domination will survive with it.' Generally, his arguments were on the need to restrain forcibly the Germans. He warned in June 1943, 'Socialism will succeed if it offers to Germany, in Lord Vansittart's phrase, "a full larder and empty arsenals"; if, in the name of equality, it either gives Germany full arsenals or empties the arsenals of others, then the German state will have its third, and successful, opportunity.'[156]

He also emphasised his soon to be familiar theme that the 'good Germans' were as guilty as the 'bad Germans'. When reviewing Thomas Mann's *Order of the Day* he praised him as 'the outstanding intellect amongst the German opponents of Nazism', but argued,

> Hitler is the logical, inevitable outcome of the Reich; and the Liberal Nationalists of seventy years ago were his begetters. A Thomas Mann regime in Germany would save the Reich, as the Weimar Republic did; and would produce another Stresemann, the St. John the Baptist of the Nazis. For if they save the Reich they will save the future for the Nazis; the Reich has no meaning except as an instrument of domination.

Similarly, he criticised another author: 'His point of view is German-liberal, and of all observers it is the well-meaning liberals who have understood least.'[157]

In many respects *The Course of German History*, although a slighter work, complemented *The Habsburg Monarchy 1815–1918* (1941). One of the major themes of the book was the importance of the Habsburg monarchy as a power in Germany and south-east Europe, thereby being an obstacle to a Greater Germany based on all German people plus Slavs to the south-east and east. He also built on Otto Bauer's insights into the importance of the non-historic nationalities for understanding Austria-Hungary for also understanding profound underlying forces in Germany. Hence he wrote of the Weimar Republic era, 'Only if Germany made reparation for the First World War; only if Germany remained disarmed; only if the German frontiers were final; only, above all, if the Germans accepted the Slav people as their equals, was there any chance of a stable, peaceful, civilized Germany.'[158]

Like *The Habsburg Monarchy 1815–1918*, his approach was akin to what was later called 'high politics'. He analysed where power lay in the government of the Hohenzollerns, and later the Weimar Republic, as he had done for the Austrian, and then the Austro-Hungarian, monarchy. He offered incisive assessments of the constitutional realities of both regimes as well as impressive, colourful pen portraits of the major players (as he had done earlier in his diplomatic studies). In *The Course of German History* many leading figures came to life but most notable is Bismarck, who becomes something of a hero in his wiliness on behalf of the Junkers and in thwarting the Greater Germany programme. His study of high politics and constitutional history is leavened with a dash of economic history, stemming from his Manchester University days with 'Jimmy' Redford, his admiration for the work of Sir John Clapham and his residual Marxism.

The Course of German History still displays some economic determinism which Alan Taylor had drawn from Marx. This is especially so with his treatment of the middle class. Thus, for instance, Bethmann Hollweg's 'sin was to belong to a class which had failed in its historic task and had become the blind instrument of Power which it could not itself master'.[159] As well as drawing on Marx in his analysis of the German middle class, he also drew on, from towards the other end of the political spectrum, the work of Werner Sombart (whom in 1928 he had hoped to have as his research supervisor). He quoted approvingly Sombart on the Prussian liberals forsaking politics to concentrate on business.[160]

Generally in *The Course of German History* he went out of his way to be critical of Marx and revolutionary politicians. The very blunt wording emphasised his breach with his family's intellectual idols. Writing of 1848 he observed,

But not even the few extreme radicals such as Marx, who called themselves Socialists, had any real concern for the masses or any contact with
them. In their eyes the masses were the cannon fodder of the revolution;
and they had no words too harsh for the masses when they wearied of
filling this role. Nothing could exceed Marx's horror and disgust when
his friend Engels actually took an Irish factory girl as his mistress; and
Marx's attitude was symbolical of the German revolutionaries.

He even went further, suggesting that Marx and Engels' aim was to
secure a German nation state through revolution. He wrote of there being
a 'few extreme radicals' after 1848.

> Next time, they believed, the masses must be drawn in; the cause of
> national union must be adorned with the attractions of Socialism. This
> was the programme of Marx and Engels to which they devoted the rest
> of their life, until their national starting-point was almost forgotten.
> They advocated Socialism so as to cause a revolution; only much later
> did their followers suppose that they had advocated revolution in order
> to accomplish Socialism.

He proudly told Hamish Hamilton in December 1944, 'My book is so full
of cracks both at Marx and the Communists that the Russian generals
should jump at it.'

He followed up this Left equivalent of *lèse-majesté* by denouncing the
Spartacists of 1918–19. Of them he wrote,

> To this revolution [the SPD programme stemming from Marx and
> Engels] everything else was subordinated; but in fact the national aim,
> which they would have had to operate if they had ever gained power,
> was Pan-German – in Rosa Luxemburg's phrase, 'a great united German
> republic', as Marx had demanded in 1848, including... both the Czechs
> of Bohemia and the other Slav peoples of Austrian Empire. Thus the
> Spartacists objected to the programme of Pan-Germanism only that
> it was being achieved by counts and generals and the Hohenzollern
> Emperor instead of by Rosa Luxemburg and Karl Liebknecht.[161]

In contrast, Alan Taylor's German heroes and heroines of 1919 were the
members of the USPD, the large anti-war splinter group from the SPD who
rejected Pan-Germanism. While the comparison is not fully convincing,
one might comment that he was supporting the equivalent of the ILP, as
had been favoured by his father. Clearly, such views as these expressed in
The Course of German History were not those of a Stalinist fellow traveller.

His condemnation of Germans and German history followed on from
his Habsburg work with his championing of the Slav against the 'historic'
nations. In *The Course of German History* he pushed his arguments about

choices between a Greater and a Lesser Germany too hard. Hence, in arguing that the German working class did not want a Lesser Germany, the programme of the German urban workers of early 1918 is argued down; he observed that there was 'among the more obscure points the item of "a speedy peace without annexations" – speed, rather than no annexations, bring the serious consideration'.[162]

While the book looked back to his earlier publications, it also looked forward. His Greater/Lesser Germany dichotomy took him later to appreciations of Bismarck. He was also already debating with himself who was responsible for war in 1914. His verdict in this book was a precursor of his later view: 'In fact to accuse Germany of having consciously planned and provoked the outbreak of war in August 1914 is to credit Germany with more direction than she possessed.'[163] His knowledge of economic history, much of it derived from Sir John Clapham's *The Economic Development of France and Germany 1815-1914*, Cambridge University Press, 1921, led him to emphasise the importance of the railways to Junker landowners and the Prussian state and then to air his famous 'war by timetable' argument. In this book and in his *The Struggle for Mastery in Europe* (1954) Alan Taylor wrote of 1866 and 1870 rather than 1914. He argued that what made the Prussian generals exceptional was that their general staff applied 'business methods to the conduct of an army. As always "war was the national industry of Prussia" and the Prussian staff officers brought to war accuracy, precision, system. The basis of their success was the railway time-table.'[164]

The Course of German History also marked another stage in the development of Alan Taylor's distinctive style. He later deplored the book as one in which he was too clever by half. It is a period piece and its major arguments regarding the German people and their history are no longer acceptable to most historians or readers. Yet his statements of such views are often highly memorable. This is so with the most famous paragraph in the book, on 1848.

1848 was the decisive year of German, and so of European history: it recapitulated Germany's past and anticipated Germany's future. Echoes of other Holy Roman Empire merged into a prelude of the Nazi 'New Order'; the doctrines of Rousseau and the doctrines of Marx, the shade of Luther and the shadow of Hitler, jostled each other in bewildering succession. Never has there been a revolution so inspired by a limitless faith in the power of ideas; never has a revolution so discredited the power of ideas in its result. The success of the revolution discredited conservative ideas; the failure of the revolution discredited liberal ideas. After it, nothing remained but the idea of Force, and this idea stood at the helm of German history from then on. For the first time since

1521, the German people stepped on to the centre of the German stage only to miss their cues once more. German history reached its turning-point and failed to turn. This was the fateful essence of 1848.[165]

This passage is notable for its explicit emphasis on political history, not social – the German stage being clearly for 'high politics'. It also has echoes from Rohan Butler, Edmond Vermeil and G.M. Trevelyan.

In changing publisher, Alan Taylor's tone in communications had not improved. In ensuring his book had maps, he wrote brusquely to Hamish Hamilton, 'I take it that you will provide, at your expense, the maps asked for in my original letter. I have quite forgotten what maps I suggested, but maps are certainly essential and I shall expect you to pay for their being drawn. Would you let me know that this is understood.' He later asked for four maps, which he got; but not as he suggested, 'on the end papers, so as to avoid being torn out'.[166]

When he had completed the proofs and provided an index he pressed Hamilton:

I know that with the thin books that come out nowadays, an up-and-down title on the back is almost inevitable; but as my book will be rather fatter, 230 pages, may I put in a plea for an across title, if at all possible? I should be very grateful if I could see the list of papers and periodicals to which you are sending review copies, so I may be able to make some suggestions. Please warn me in good time when you are going to distribute review copies. So that I may see my friends review it. I will get Rowse to do it in the *Sunday Times* and Namier the *Manchester Guardian* but must have notice.

What is your arrangement about press cuttings? Macmillan used to send them to me automatically. Is this also part of the Hamilton service? I think I deserve it for doing the index.

Not content with these remarks he added a note in ink to his typescript concerning his plea for an across title on his book's spine: 'I loathe up & down titles & am always tempted on that score to slash your books in review – but you publish such good books!'[167] Taylor's book was published with its title on the spine in the way he wished. Rowse and Namier did review his book, though they most probably would have done anyway without any prompting on his part.

A.L. Rowse wrote very favourable reviews of both Rohan Butler's and Alan Taylor's books. He described Taylor's book as 'this useful, trenchant, independent-minded book', and urged that it be prescribed 'as essential reading for all those who are concerned with German affairs' and be translated into German 'so that Germans may learn what their record looks like to (intelligent) people outside'. Given Rowse's later very bitter attitude to Taylor, his comments in 1945 were notably warm:

> He is one of our leading authorities on nineteenth-century foreign history, particularly that of Central Europe, and belongs to a generation of historians not educated in Germany or imbued with German ways of thought. That is the value of his book; he writes with an admirable North-Country forthrightness and gives us an English reading of German history, how the ghastly record of political failure and irresponsibility, the worship of power and conquest ending in crime, strikes an Englishman of scholarship and political sense.[168]

Lewis Namier reviewed *The Course of German History* in the *Times Literary Supplement*, not in the *Manchester Guardian*, as Taylor had expected. Taylor eagerly asked Hamish Hamilton to ensure a copy went immediately to Namier at the Jewish Agency, 77 Great Russell Street, London, as he would soon be going to Manchester.[169] Namier praised Taylor in his lengthy, front-page review, commenting,

> Years of study, usefully recapitulated and tested in lectures and tutorials, have equipped him for the task... a rough realism and independence, blended with a quick and lively spirit, debar him from the abstract and ponderous, systematic and yet vague thinking of the German. Still his combination of ruggedness and impressionable veracity renders him also impatient of the careful labour of perfecting and polishing – he discovers precious stones by the handful and puts them half-cut into circulation... The basic ideas of Mr Taylor's book are sound, but would have profited by further examination and unfolding... the book should prove of high value in the study of the German problem.[170]

Other reviews were also mixed, praising its flair but regretting the more flippant comments. Robert Birley in *International Affairs* complained, 'It is too facile an attempt to discover some continuity in German history which can compare Charlemagne with Hitler,' and warned, 'The economic crises of the late nineteen-twenties are minimised. In the effort to make the Nazis, not in large measure the result of this anarchy, but a normal development quite to be expected, of German history, Mr Taylor nearly succeeds in making them respectable.'

Sigmund Neumann, in a review published in the *American Historical Review* in July 1947, welcomed it as 'a challenging essay, packed with substantial summaries and spiced with brilliant observations'. He went on,

> An answer to a burning query, it is an impatient book, vivid and tempestuous, pointed and pugnacious, concise and over-zealous, severe and sarcastic, ambitious and angry. Grandiose in style it often overshoots

its mark. The profound is mixed with the wisecrack. It has the short-comings of its virtues. It will shock the scholarly reader but it must challenge him too. A returning American scholar reports that it challenges equally German historians, some of whom admit that it will make them rethink their modern national history.[171]

The frequent post-war bouts of rethinking German history did not focus on Taylor's work. Indeed, the presumption that there was a long-running 'German problem' made *The Course of German History* seem dated by the 1960s. Indeed, by the early 1970s it was being depicted as a caricature of anti-German historical views.[172] Taylor's anti-German sentiments reflected widespread British popular attitudes of the 1940s (and beyond), which were not surprising given the press and propaganda of both world wars.[173] Such sentiments were initially widespread among British historians, including not only Butler, Namier and Rowse but also John Wheeler Bennett.

Among German historians the more substantial debates were less to do with the alleged peculiarities of the German character than with the alleged distinctive, even aberrational, path that Germany followed to emerge as a modern industrial state. This view of Germany's path, the *Sonderweg* thesis, put forward by Hans-Ulrich Wehler in his 1973 study of the Kaiserreich 1871–1918, also put great weight on the failure of the German middle classes in 1848 to bring about a democratic revolution. Wehler's explanation was that, while the German economy had modernised, social and political structures had not. While Taylor was often quoted on German history failing to turn at its turning point in 1848, and *The Course of German History* cited as one early example of those attributing much to the alleged oddity of the German character, his work was not substantially involved in the debates.[174]

His theme of continuities in German history had seemed earlier to be reinforced by the work of Fritz Fischer and the controversies it engendered. Fischer's books and articles of 1959–69 argued that the First World War was brought about by Germany's elites seeking hegemony in Europe. He suggested that Germany's annexationist war aims preceded the outbreak of war in 1914 and resembled the later policies of Hitler. Unlike Taylor – certainly in terms of 1939 – Fischer put great weight on internal economic, social and political developments in Germany before 1914, a theme Taylor would have done well to have taken up fully for the period before 1939 for his *The Origins of the Second World War*. Taylor noted, with some exaggeration on his own impact overseas, 'Since the revolution in German historical outlook launched by Fritz Fischer, the younger German historians, I observe, take much my line and even exaggerate it.'[175]

Among other major public debates on the German past were those on Daniel Goldhagen's best-selling book *Hitler's Willing Executioners* (1996).

This in several ways seemed to go back to the arguments of the collective and historic guilt of the German people prevalent in much writing of 1938–45, including by Taylor. Goldhagen argued that the anti-Semitic past of the Germans made Germans generally potential 'willing executioners' for Hitler. His study was roundly condemned for lacking comparative perspectives (the marked anti-Semitism elsewhere), ethnocultural determinism and circular arguments.[176] Hans-Ulrich Wehler observed that the book was a 'reversion to the state of play in 1950 (when the prevailing slogan was "From Luther to Hitler")'.[177]

Like Taylor's book, Goldhagen's book sold very well. But, like Taylor, he was left with the issue of whether or not the 'German character' could change. Wehler noted of Goldhagen that, faced with the post-1945 record of West Germany, he did acknowledge in a footnote that there was no 'timeless German character' and that since 1945 this had changed 'dramatically'. Earlier, Richard Evans had pointed out that Taylor's view of the 'German character' gave him problems when faced with the democratic West German state, with its firm suppression of anti-Semitism.

> It is revealing to note Taylor's attempt to struggle with the implications of his view in his preface to the 1961 edition… ('Maybe the Germans will forget their imperialist dreams so long as they remain prosperous. I have almost reached the point of believing that I shall not live to see a third German war; but events have an awkward trick of running in the wrong direction, just when you least expect it.')[178]

Alan Taylor became uneasy about *The Course of German History* as history (as opposed to a polemic for the times). In December 1970 he wrote to Éva Haraszti, 'My unfavourite, as too clever and showy.' Yet, while he got on well with individual Germans, he still harboured a strong dislike of the older generation of Germans. He wrote to Éva in April 1973 of elderly German tourists in Florence,

> They looked so orderly, civilized, restrained. Yet they must have been in the prime of life under Hitler and most of them must have been Nazis. You think one man is a quiet distinguished scholar; perhaps he was once a German officer, massacring prisoners-of-war in Russia. And that grey-haired lady. She was no doubt a Hitler mädchen and after that a guard in a concentration camp. How could ordinary people have been so surpassingly barbarous? It is beyond my understanding.[179]

Taylor's residual anti-German sentiments, along with his friendship with Lord Beaverbrook, contributed to his later hostility to the European Union; and, later still, to his posthumous emergence as a hero of the British anti-European Right. With German reunification and the strengthening of the

European Union the 'German character' resurfaced as an alleged issue. It was cast in a very bad light at a meeting of historians summoned by Margaret Thatcher in 1990. Later, in 1996, a writer in the *Daily Telegraph*, reflecting on Daniel Goldhagen's book, gave the opinion that 'Germany has not completely civilised itself' and claimed that German leaders 'demand ever-greater European unity in order to protect their nation from the beast within'.[180]

When he was writing *The Course of German History* in 1944–45 Taylor had hopes that it would sell well and attract sufficient attention to strengthen his moves into national prominence via the press and radio. The early sales – over 6000 within six months of publication in July 1945 – exceeded his hopes. He was effusive in a letter to Hamish Hamilton less than two months after publication: 'Pleased with success, I must have the grace to share the success with my publisher: you certainly know how to make books go. Macmillan have not sold 2000 copies of *The Habsburg Monarchy*, a much better book.'[181] Taylor wanted scholarly success, but he also craved more than that. To some extent his attitude was reminiscent of the young Disraeli, who on one occasion wrote bluntly, 'I must publish yet more, before the attention which I require can be obtained.'[182]

Taylor wanted attention both through books which sold in large numbers to the general public, emulating Gibbon, Macaulay and G.M. Trevelyan, and through being an intellectual on the radio and television. The two aspirations could and did reinforce each other. He eagerly told Hamish Hamilton in July 1945, 'Vansittart, Barbara Ward and I are doing a wireless discussion on Alliances on July 20, so I shall be in the public eye at the right moment.'[183]

However, he seems to have been pushing harder to ensure a return to national radio broadcasting. *The Course of German History* widened his apparent expertise as a radio pundit. He had taken pains to make an impact on Austria, Hungary, Czechoslovakia and Yugoslavia. He was always very willing to write or talk on France. In 1944 and 1945, as American and British forces moved through France towards Germany, the futures of these countries were hot topics, and Taylor was insistent that he had much to say on them.

After his early run of BBC radio broadcasts ended in June 1942 he kept up with his BBC contacts while working for the PWE, which was housed on the ground floor of Bush House, the BBC's headquarters. He saw Dennis Brogan, who worked for the French Service. He also saw Heinz Koeppler, a former Senior Demy at Magdalen and an Oxford University Lecturer in History (1937–39) as well as a friend of Richard Crossman, who worked for the German Service.[184] He also fostered good relations with Trevor Blewitt, his earlier major contact in the BBC, who was a German specialist.

Yet, though eager to return to the radio, he was discriminating as to what he did. In September 1943 he declined to broadcast to Austria, observing that propaganda there could have dangerous consequences. He also turned down in February 1944 a request to talk on aspects of the British past which might throw light on the imminent invasion of Europe. He observed, 'If the historic parallels mean anything, they would lead to the conclusion (a) that the British invasions of the continent never succeed; and (b) that we should sit back and wait for the Russians to do the job.' Instead, he offered to give a talk on the fortieth anniversary of the Anglo-French entente, adding: 'It would be red hot.' He also pressed for what he most wished to do: 'I am expecting that you will get me on the brains trust. I should do it much better than most of those whom they employ.'[185]

In repeatedly pressing to appear on 'The Brains Trust' Alan Taylor was bidding for widespread public recognition. 'The Brains Trust', first broadcast on 1 January 1941, was at the height of its popularity during the later part of the war. Asa Briggs has given the verdict that, with ITMA ('It's That Man Again'), it was for BBC radio 'the outstanding popular triumph of the war'. The BBC's Director of Variety saw it as 'serious in intention, light in character' and its aim was to be provocative. Questions of varying kinds were put to three personalities, originally a regular team of C.M. Joad, Julian Huxley and Commander A.B. Campbell. Broadcast on Tuesday nights, it was attracting just under 30 per cent of the listening public each week in early 1945. Audience research suggested it attracted each week many of the upper middle class and a good proportion of the lower middle class.[186] This was very much the 'middle England' type of audience who later flocked to Taylor's Historical Association lectures. Taylor secured his wish, appearing on the programme on 23 January 1945.

He wrote to Trevor Blewitt, eight days before the broadcast, that he might call in on him 'before the Brains Trust lunch (made it at last!)'. He added, 'I do believe you have forgotten me and have fallen for Donald MacCullough's [sic] pin-up girl.' In this remark he was being unpleasantly derogatory of Barbara Ward. Far from being only the chairman of the panel's favourite, she was the most popular member of the Brains Trust panel in the summer of 1945. She was described by Asa Briggs as 'young, attractive, lucid and vigorous' and by Ruth Dudley Edwards as 'an inspirational and radical influence', and also as 'the social conscience' of *The Economist*.[187] After his appearance Taylor sought reassurance, feeling his performance was disappointing. Blewitt replied, 'I don't think you were dreary in the Brains Trust. Nor does Arnot Robertson, who sends you her greetings.'[188] Nevertheless, he appeared only once more on the programme.

However, he was succeeding in establishing himself as a lively commentator on international affairs. In his autobiography he wrote disingenuously of *The Course of German History*, 'The book set me up, perhaps undeservedly, as an Authority on Germany.' Yet he had been swift to press his book on the attention of his main BBC contact. When Blewitt wrote in August 1944 to say that he and Miss Bucknall were now responsible for foreign affairs broadcasts for the Home Talks Department and asked to visit him in Oxford, Taylor responded, 'I am just finishing a short history of Germany, which is as hot as can be – a good thing it doesn't have to pass your censorship.' Before long Blewitt was referring to him as part of his 'German team'.[189]

Taylor's credentials as a commentator on international affairs were also strengthened by his widening sphere at the *Manchester Guardian* from May 1944. Then A.P. Wadsworth, who had just succeeded W.P. Crozier as editor, had written to ask 'if you could conceivably produce an odd Long Leader or so. We are decidedly short at the moment.' Taylor had been unpushy, even uncharacteristically modest in his response: 'Nothing could give me greater pleasure than to write for you, though I can hardly feel I deserve it…I am not an experienced journalist and know it; but I'd do anything for the MG.'[190] He had already written a leader on Hungary for Crozier, and went on to write many on European and international relations topics between mid-1944 and the end of 1945.[191]

His first mainstream radio discussions were on 'The Future of Germany', transmitted as three programmes on 13 and 20 October and 1 December 1944. Taylor chaired the discussions and took part in them, the other three participants being Kingsley Martin, editor of the *New Statesman*, Robert Vansittart, the former Permanent Under-Secretary of State for Foreign Affairs and notable anti-appeaser, and Barbara Ward.[192] Taylor was confident speaking in an area which he had thought much about for both his wartime talks and his book. He pressed hard his view that Germans would have to renounce long-standing territorial claims in eastern Europe. He was unambiguous in his hostility to the majority of Germans. In the final programme he commented,

> Well, I'm frightened of this non-political German. I agree that there are millions of them, millions of Germans who tolerated Nazi rule, Nazi atrocities, who before that tolerated the militarism of the Kaiser, and before that tolerated the conquest of Germany by Prussia and then, when things didn't come off, turned round and said, 'Oh, we've nothing to do with it, we're absolutely non-political…'[193]

Taylor's lack of confidence under his usual self-confident demeanour was shown in his apparent need to build himself up by denigrating his fellow pundits. He wrote to A.P. Wadsworth after the first two programmes were recorded but before they were broadcast,

I had fun making our BBC discussion. Vansittart is quite inarticulate, but charming. Barbara Ward is, for a woman, very clever; and with the sort of charm which a clever woman has. That is she has everything a woman can have except what a woman ought to have. But K. Martin – I always forget, until I see him, how intolerable he is: vain, ignorant dreadful.[194]

Whatever else he was, Alan Taylor was certainly not a forerunner of the 'new males' of the late twentieth century. Women were very much the help-meets of males, in his eyes; though, later, Éva Haraszti had some success in modifying his views in this respect. Ironically, Taylor's comments on Ward were similar to those which Ward had ably contested in *The Economist* a year earlier, then expressed by Harold Nicolson in the House of Commons when rejecting the view that women could become diplomats.[195]

As for Kingsley Martin, Taylor was soon to benefit from his wisdom. Martin, like A.P. Wadsworth, believed in the merits of measured expressions of view in the media. Some academics who engage in public controversy in the press do so from their private addresses. Alan Taylor did not. He liked to emphasise his Fellowship of Magdalen College, which upset some members of Oxford University. He discovered why after his first national radio broadcast, when the first two programmes on Germany led to a lengthy and vigorous correspondence in the *New Statesman* which contested his claims that the Germans were uniquely iniquitous.

He reiterated his view on the central importance of the alleged long-term desire of Germans to support expansionist foreign policy aims. He asked, 'How many German refugees, living securely in this country, are prepared to recognise the full national independence of the east European peoples, and to renounce for ever all prospects of a European system under German leadership?' He responded to an expression of doubt whether any other people would have been more vigorous in resisting Nazis, with a list of dissenters from British foreign policy. He also commented,

> The real opponents of Pan-Germanism were persecuted and murdered under the Weimar Republic, with the acquiescence of German Liberals and Socialists of the day, some of them, in fact, murdered by Free Corps organised by Social Democrats. I am unaware that Noske was expelled, or even censured by, the Social Democratic Party, for his butchery of the Independent Socialist leaders.
>
> It may be a hard doctrine for Liberally minded Germans that, until they struggle for the freedom of others, they cannot themselves be free; but it is a doctrine which they must sooner or later accept.[196]

Far from this robust defence, with its doctrine with Cobdenite or Trotskyist echoes, seeing off his critics, it set off a London-based socialist critic who had had links with the USPD in Germany. C.A. Smith vigorously rebutted his arguments, and asked,

> But why does Mr Taylor so carefully avoid the most obvious facts of all? If the German nation as a whole is rabidly Pan-German, why could Hitler never win a majority in any free election? Why had he to destroy the freedom of speech and press? Why had he to crush out all political parties save his own and destroy the free trade unions? Why have the monster concentration camps been filled with Germans until the reputed total of their victims exceeds 2,000,000?

To add insult to injury, Smith ended by parodying Taylor's rhetorical style of arguing:

> During the shameful period of British history when the German opponents of Nazism received neither help nor encouragement from the Baldwin and Chamberlain governments, did neither Mr Taylor nor I make a single protest comparable in sacrificial cost to that of the humblest German who drew his last tortured breath in Dachau or Oranienburg?[197]

Taylor made a lengthy reply, in which he commented that in the Weimar Republic 'There was an anti-democratic majority at every election after 1919. The Republic was the product solely of the Allied victory and owed nothing to German efforts. Freedom was, and will be, imposed upon the Germans from without.'[198] Smith responded with equal vigour. He condemned Taylor's 'reckless mixture of truths, half-truths and untruths', adding, for good measure, 'If it is a sample of the "history" now taught at Magdalen College, Oxford, there are other people besides the Germans in need of re-education.'[199]

Taylor, like many others who hit hard, was more sensitive to his own *amour-propre* than to others. He was outraged that Kingsley Martin should have published such a letter, which he deemed to be defamatory. He wrote to Martin intimating that he would take legal action if there was not an apology printed in the journal. As Adam Sisman has commented, Kingsley Martin wisely saved him from damaging himself through undue sensitivity. Martin pointed out that, if he forced an apology on the *New Statesman*,

> In the future (if you persist) the attitude I and other editors would have to adopt is that this is a man who hits hard in controversy himself, but takes libel actions if he thinks his opponents unnecessarily offensive. This attitude would make it difficult for us to continue our pleasant personal and business relationship. Perhaps more important, the public would judge that you are a touchy, irrascible sort of person who 'can't take it'.

Taylor quickly backed down, probably telephoning Kingsley Martin soon after receiving his letter. Martin welcomed his change of attitude and commented, 'I am not sure if you realise how "provocative" you in fact are.'[200] He was not alone in this. A.P. Wadsworth had also greatly urged restraint in 'hitting hard' on Alan Taylor. After he had reviewed George Bilainkin's *Maisky* (1944), dismissing it as consisting mostly of press cuttings on the Soviet Union, the aggrieved author sent the *Manchester Guardian* a letter of rebuke. In asking Taylor for 'a very short reply which could go underneath it', he urged, 'But don't be too savage as I think the man is out of a job at the moment.'[201]

The heated correspondence in the *New Statesman* followed the recording but preceded the broadcasting of the third 'What Shall We Do with Germany?' discussion, which focused on 'The Re-education of Germany'. In this Alan Taylor and Lord Vansittart were notably severe on what they saw as 'the German character'. At one point Taylor observed, 'I would say that the German people have forfeited, for a very long time, the right to be a great people, and that in our lifetime they must put up with the fact that they shall not possess any of the things which a great people possesses.' He also made clear his concern for good relations with the Soviet Union. He said that one of the few things that a historian can be confident about

> is an almost mathematical rule, that fifteen years after defeat, a great nation, a great people, seeks revenge, and it doesn't really very much matter whether you treat them kindly or harshly … [For the Germans] the greatest educative force is the overwhelming superiority of the Anglo-Russian combination, and it must be ready in fifteen years' time to 'kick' 'em back into line.

While Taylor worried about a resurgent Germany during the next two to three years, and pressed for the Anglo-Soviet alliance to continue in order to keep Germany in line, others feared Soviet expansionism. In the radio debate on the future of Germany Kingsley Martin had predicted that Germany would 'be occupied by Americans … for some time, by British for some time, and by the Russians probably for even longer'.[202]

Taylor, like most other people of the time, saw Britain as still a Great Power and relatively free to determine her own policies. Indeed, later, with the Campaign for Nuclear Disarmament he would argue on the presumption that in some way Britain was, or could be, a great moral leader. In April 1946, when discussing 'What is a Great Power?' on the radio with his old friend Frank Horrabin and Major Hugh Fraser, MBE, the Conservative MP for Stone, Taylor claimed that the more Britain 'exercised our responsibilities [outside Britain], the more the whole world benefits'. As for what made a Great Power, he argued,

There is a great tendency for people to talk as though you can estimate greatness simply by looking at economic resources. In fact, surely, a great deal depends on national will. For instance, the shift of power between France and Germany in the nineteenth century was not due entirely to the fact that Germany had superior economic resources; it was also due to a failure of will on the part of France. Germany's greatest industrial development and increase of population came after France had been defeated in 1870.

In this discussion Taylor clearly saw Britain as the Great Power which would act altruistically in the world, believing both the USA and Soviet Russia to be isolationist. He asked, 'Don't you think that by a wise use of our present resources and by a wise foreign policy you could remain a Great Power on our present basis?' He had in mind Britain still operating a policy based on the balance of power, with Britain weighing in with Russia. He commented, 'Surely it's worth paying a high price not to become the 49th state in the Union?'

He rebuffed Horrabin's suggestion that it would be more realistic for Britain to remain a major influence by being 'part of a Western European Federation or Association', with the view that western Europe was not 'near enough to us in spirit'. On being pressed, he observed

> The countries of Western Europe aren't by any means at the same level of economic development, still less of political outlook. Most of these countries...have strong clerical parties, as in France or Italy or Belgium, where it is the strongest party. In fact, they haven't reached our stage of social democracy – if every country in Western Europe had the same or better sensible social democratic government that we have, then it might come together. I might stomach working with Communists, but with Clericals – oh no!

So his long-held opposition to the EEC at this time was linked to his belief that Britain could still be a Great Power and should maintain an alliance with Russia in line with Britain's traditional balance of power policies. In this radio debate in 1946 Hugh Fraser pointed out that the Labour Party leadership and the British public would not prefer it to an alliance with the USA, that it could lead to civil war in Europe and conflict with Australasia, Canada and South Africa.[203] Alan Taylor stuck stubbornly to his Anglo-Soviet alliance propositions until long after most people felt them to be unrealistic.

By the end of 1945 A.P. Wadsworth's and Alan Taylor's views on the Soviet Union had diverged so far that Taylor was no longer employed as a leader writer. Soon after the end of the war in Europe Wadsworth was joking about Taylor's views. In August he wrote, 'I think your political morals are scandalous, and the sooner you get near to an atomic bomb the better.' A month later the tone was still jocular, but clearly there was a very marked difference in their views, when Wadsworth wrote again.

> Well, well! You aren't so bad after all and show signs of returning sanity. You will be recanting your ingenious tour de force on Trieste yet. Poor Tito. I am sorry you have withdrawn your favour from him. His gang really are pretty bad and the more one hears of the whole boiling [lot] the less respect one has for them.

He concluded his lengthy letter by replying to Alan Taylor's complaint that he was over-fond of using 'iron curtain', a term first used by a German minister. 'Isn't it an "iron curtain"? You try to get behind it, my lad, and you'll see.' Wadsworth wrote, when commenting in October 1945 to Alan Taylor on Bertrand Russell, that he published 'your examples of brilliance and irresponsibility' and would do the same for the philosopher.[204] Taylor responded somewhat bitterly in December 1945,

> Russell is over 70 & can plan a future war against Russia without planning to be involved in it: but I am not yet 40 & am on the point of having 4 children. Don't blame me if I can't join in your anti-Bolshevik crusade which is making a third world war certain. Or perhaps, like Paul Winterton, you think we should take the passing advantage of the atomic bomb & knock the Russians off their perches now.
>
> I'll write a more serious letter soon.[205]

Taylor and Wadsworth remained friends even though their views were diverging over the Soviet Union. Wadsworth encouraged Taylor to write centenary and similar essays for the *Manchester Guardian* as well as continuing to review for the newspaper. He also remained willing to encourage him to visit central and eastern Europe and to provide the *Manchester Guardian* with his assessments on his return.

A fortnight before going to Czechoslovakia in June–July 1946 Taylor wrote to Wadsworth,

> All I know of my programme is that I am to lecture in Prague, Brno and Bratislava on some innocuous subject which will justify the British Council's paying my fare (when there I shall be the guest of the Czechs…). My only plans are to see the Communists, whom I don't know at all; to talk about their educational plans and difficulties; and to discuss their economic plans, especially in regard to foreign trade. If there's anything in particular you'd like me to ask about or anywhere you'd like me to go, drop me a line. I'll have it in mind to write something when I come back; but I'm a dim academic and not a journalist.

I'd very much like to go to Budapest to see the Karolyis, but I doubt whether this will be possible.[206]

He enjoyed his three-week visit. He saw President Benes in his palace in the Hradcany area and Hubert Ripka, including at a garden party in the American Embassy. Benes attributed Prague's emergence largely unscathed from the Second World War to his acceptance of the Munich proposals in 1938, a point Taylor reiterated in his *The Origins of the Second World War* (1961). He also enjoyed visiting Bratislava to investigate the political situation in Slovakia. He met Michael Karolyi for dinner there, Karolyi breaking his journey between Budapest and Prague to see him.[207]

Taylor returned to Oxford on 12 July 1946. The next day he wrote to Wadsworth,

> How many articles, if any, can you stomach on Czechoslovakia? I saw most of the politicians from the Prime Minister down, heard him deliver the declaration of the new government and also had three hours with Benes. I've also been in the country and to Bratisľava, where I saw the Slovak political leaders; but I doubt whether the Slovak problem is worth an article to itself. I suggest two: one on the political situation after the elections, and one on the international position of Czechoslovakia. I could manage more if you have space...I am rather worn out but had a most enjoyable and also useful trip.[208]

Wadsworth asked for three, including one on Slovakia. On receiving them he commented, 'They are good but fierce.' He asked for them to be shortened. The first essay dealt with the political situation in Czechoslovakia. Taylor argued that the current situation depended internally on the Communists remaining democratic and 'on the resolution with which the non-communist parties defend their liberal morality and philosophy without slipping into a defence of capitalism'. The second article discussed Slovakia. The third dealt with foreign policy and trade, in which he argued that the Czechs were anti-German and as firmly linked to Russia as the British dominions were to Britain. Wadsworth insisted on removing the final paragraph in Taylor's original text for the third, observing, 'It is a new one to me that if we try to act in our own self-interest – a free world market – we shall help the Communists. I don't think we can let you say this.'[209]

Taylor returned to Prague the following year, on his way back from Yugoslavia. He and Margaret stayed with Hubert Ripka. Ripka was confident that Czechoslovakia would move towards the West. When Alan Taylor saw President Benes, he made it that clear he felt, if forced to choose between East and West, his country would go with Russia. Taylor thereafter was convinced that the February 1948 crisis in Czechoslovakia began not as a Communist coup but as an anti-Communist move which failed because of Benes' opposition.[210]

Alan Taylor's friction with Wadsworth over his pro-Russian views in international relations was matched in his relations with those commissioning speakers at the BBC. He had no friend, no Wadsworth, there at the top. He also wrangled endlessly over the scale of his payments. Yet he could be relied upon to be opinionated and very argumentative. Trevor Blewitt acknowledged this when arranging a discussion on alliances between Lord Vansittart, Barbara Ward and Taylor. He wrote to Taylor, 'One of the difficulties is…going to be to get real disagreement. Perhaps Vansittart's points will stimulate you to be your usual and endearing aggressive self.' When the recorded programme was delayed and was due to be broadcast live Taylor was suitably abrasive in his response.

> I shall certainly want to revise what I said, e.g., if England is going to be a capitalist democracy with its PM saying that socialism involves the Gestapo, obviously England & Russia can't work together & a written alliance won't make them.
>
> May I ask why my name appears fourth in the list of speakers although in alphabetical order it should be second? Is it that I am regarded as the least important?[211]

In the programme broadcast on 20 July 1945 he did differ from the other participants in speaking up for the Anglo-Soviet alliance and not being in favour of a western European grouping. He commented, 'The Anglo-Russian alliance is to last for twenty years. At the end of that time it may not be necessary; that doesn't make it any the less essential now.' Vansittart was critical of Alan Taylor's argument that Russia sought only to be left alone, observing that Russia had a positive policy 'which tends to the creation of an extensive sphere of influence'.[212] At the time Taylor felt that Vansittart was not a sufficiently vigorous arguer but, later, he remembered above all 'his almost irresistible charm' although adding that 'it must be confessed that he was not suited to be Permanent Under-Secretary for Foreign Affairs'.[213]

Alan Taylor's first row at the BBC came over Trieste, not the role of Russia as such. He aroused much criticism for speaking on a radio programme on the subject of Trieste although he was a notable protagonist for one side of the dispute. Many years later John West in the *Daily Telegraph* referred to him as the 'only distinguished outside supporter' of the Yugoslav case.[214] After the 'World Affairs' programme on 24 September 1945 Dr Massey, Reader in German at Bedford College, London University, telephoned in a complaint. This was passed on to the producer: 'She said that Taylor's book made it clear that he was a biased person on this subject and that even if this script was objective it was wrong for the BBC to allow a person with his reputation on this subject to speak on it.'

There was also government pressure put on the BBC. The same evening that Dr Massey complained, so did Mr Grubb of the Ministry of Information, who 'indicated that he did not wish to interfere in the BBC's domestic affairs but asked whether such scripts were shown to the Foreign Office'. The Controller of Talks, R.D. Rendall, informed him they were not. Rendall added, 'It appears that some concern has been expressed in some other government office that a man with such well-known views on the Yugoslav question should be speaking on this subject at a time when it was about to be decided upon.' He concluded that 'it is – as we have already agreed in discussion – obviously important that we should not allow Taylor to use the occasion to press his own viewpoint in regard to Yugoslavia'.[215]

Mr Grubb's queries paved the way for a complaint from Victor Cunard on behalf of the Political Intelligence Department in cooperation with the Foreign Office. With shades of George Orwell's Big Brother, Cunard apparently told G.R. Barnes that 'Taylor at a dinner party the night before [the broadcast of 24 September] had expressed himself unwisely as regards the use he might make of his broadcasting to favour the Yugoslav case. He had agreed also to write certain pamphlets for the Yugoslav government.' The last sentence, presumably, was a muddled understanding of the fact that he had written a pamphlet already. Cunard agreed that in his talk Taylor had not gone in for propaganda. Nevertheless, Barnes promised to seek assurances from him.

Taylor saw Rendall and George Barnes on 30 October, when he reassured them that he had told the producer of his pamphlet on Trieste. Rendall wrote,

> He regarded himself primarily as an academic, and though he was a member of the Labour Party he thought it unlikely he would take a public part in politics or undertake other activities likely to embarrass us. He would have preferred that his Trieste pamphlet, which expressed entirely his own views, and was not touched by the Yugoslav government, should have been published independently, but it was only in this way that he was able to get paper.
>
> Barnes and I were impressed by his candour and good sense, and his appreciation of our problems in this field.

Taylor's candour had its limits. His draft pamphlet most probably was not vetted by the Yugoslav government but he was helped by a Yugoslav scholar, albeit only a little. He also had no qualms in 1947 in accepting a holiday for two from the Yugoslav government 'as a reward for the aid I had given them' (as he put it in his autobiography).[216]

After this episode it seems that scripts of his broadcasts went to the Foreign Office before publication in *The Listener* or elsewhere. His later scripts have the usual producer's editorial marking but sometimes especially controversial comments were deleted, possibly by a reader for the Foreign Office. For instance, in the script of 'What Is a Great Power?' (April 1946) the part-sentence 'a sham state like Trans-Jordan – have a concealed British dependant' has reference to the highly sensitive Jordan heavily deleted.[217]

While the BBC officials greatly liked Alan Taylor's abilities to argue a case strongly, they were increasingly anxious about his pro-Soviet views on foreign policy. In February 1946 Taylor wrote to Trevor Blewitt asking to speak on Soviet affairs. He was frank about his views when he outlined what he had in mind to say:

> General argument would end: Bolshies too want peace and prosperity, not to conquer the world; they are hesitating whether to get it by spheres of influence or by co-operation. Therefore, we have to go on trying to co-operate. There wouldn't be anything I have not said before; but it would be in a more systematic form. The explanation of the internal conflicts of opinion in the Communist Party, or at least in the governing circles, would be new for England. It would not be pro-Bolshevik except in the sense that I am always pro-Russia, i.e., I have no sympathy with anti-Russian hysteria and think that we should judge Soviet affairs with the same cordial, but friendly, detachment with which we judge American affairs.

Blewitt wrote to his superior, 'I do not wish to press the Russian topic,' and he also commented, 'Middle East *is* a good topic, but again Russia would come in.'[218]

Taylor spoke on 'Russia Today' on 27 February 1946, one of eight appearances he made on 'World Affairs: A Weekly Survey' on the BBC's Home Service. After the war there was still sufficient public interest in international affairs for such a series and for edited versions of the programmes to be published in the BBC's journal, *The Listener*.

He continued to urge working with the Soviet Union in other broadcasts in this series. For instance, in 'The Middle East' on 20 March 1946 he argued that the Second World War had shown that the Suez Canal was not the 'lifeline of the British Empire' as 'the Mediterranean route was closed to us for the best part of three years'. He commented that in the Middle East 'there was money to be made, railway concessions and oil concessions to be gained; but these, I believe were secondary; in fact, as for instance with the oil concessions, were often made to strengthen our political position'. By this he meant that the local government and the local population were dependent on the country operating the concessions. He said that Britain really wished to see that no one else took over the area. In the case of Russia, Britain could either fight, as in the Crimean War, 1854–56, or share. 'The modern form of sharing is not partition,' he suggested, 'but to put the responsibility on to the United Nations.' He said this should be done not only with Constantinople and the Straits but also with Suez and the Middle East generally.[219]

After a further talk in the series, Blewitt decided to drop Alan Taylor from the series. He wrote an internal memorandum of justification, in which he wrote,

> Not so much because he is a cause of anxiety every time we put him on, but because I think his admirable qualities (courage, intellectual brilliance, if not profundity, ability to avoid the claptrap of the age, whether from Right or Left, vigour) are vitiated by a certain cynicism which is out of place in an objective and ultimately educational series for the ordinary listener!
>
> The cynicism has been kept in check in the past, but possibly because Taylor has not been granted his request for a higher fee, or because in any case he feels broadcasting is not worthwhile, or even because he has been irritated by the inevitable whittling down of pieces involved in getting a script on the air, he does seem to have let his cynicism 'rip' – and it is apparent in his tone of voice at the microphone quite as much as in the 'tone' of his script.[220]

The scripts were notable for radical views and for debating-society-style arguing. For instance, in his talk on the Middle East, when he called for the UN to be given responsibility for the Suez Canal and the Middle East generally and not just for the Straits, he enjoyed saying, 'This is the foundation of present British policy, as Mr Attlee and Mr Bevin have said.' While this may have been seen as mischievous at the time, the case for a relatively weakened Britain placing the Suez Canal under the United Nations' control might well have been one which in 1956 Sir Anthony Eden, with hindsight, might have wished had been acted on in the late 1940s.

Taylor's views were raised in the House of Commons in December 1946 over the second of a series of four broadcasts entitled 'The Roots of British Foreign Policy'. In the preliminary discussions for the series Taylor had written to Trevor Blewitt,

> it seems to me rather idiotic to talk about the past of British foreign policy when all the previous assumptions have been destroyed. The only thing I have thought of that we learn from history is that the English people have always talked a lot of nonsense about the Muscovite period, but I don't think I can make four talks out of the roots of Russophobia.[221]

In the first programme Alan Taylor called for fresh thinking and a willingness not to be stifled by the old orthodoxies when reflecting on British foreign policy. He argued that the Second World War had dramatically changed the context of foreign policy, with the British navy no longer supreme and the balance of power gone on the mainland of Europe, leaving Russia as the only Great Power there. In the second programme he dealt with Anglo-US relations. He deplored Britain's pose of being the equal to the US, while timidly agreeing to all that the US required. He commented, 'They are only concerned to use this island (like Japan on the other side of the world) as an aircraft carrier from which to discharge atomic bombs.' He was also scathing on the US attempts to restore pre-war conditions, observing that 'it does not occur to them that if you restore the circumstances that existed before Hitler you restore the circumstances that created Hitler'.[222]

This broadcast outraged Henry Strauss, the Conservative MP who represented the Combined Universities. Strauss was a barrister who had resigned from junior office in Churchill's government in February 1945 over the treatment of Poland by Churchill, Roosevelt and Stalin at the Yalta conference. After he had read out extracts of Taylor's broadcast in the House of Commons on 11 December, Herbert Morrison, the Lord Privy Seal, gave his verdict that 'the broadcast was anti-British, anti-American and not particularly competent. And that is all I can say about it.'[223]

Taylor was also condemned by Robert Ensor, who followed two further lectures by Taylor in the series on 'The Roots of British Foreign Policy'. He objected to what he deemed to be 'shallow half-truths' and to 'his jaunty cocksure manner' in Taylor's four lectures. He complained vigorously to Harman Grizewood, the Director of Radio Talks, demanding a right of reply. As with the earlier vigorous correspondence with C.A. Smith in the *New Statesman*, Alan Taylor revealed a thin skin, complaining to Grizewood, 'I daresay it did not occur to you or to others ... looking after the programme that I had feelings to be hurt; but I have. I made these talks at the request of the BBC and was encouraged by you and others to make them lively.' He was told in effect that this was part of the price of engaging in current affairs broadcasting. The BBC officials were also well aware of how eager he was to be regularly on the radio and his desire to broaden into giving frequent talks on history. Taylor responded by telling Grizewood that Ensor's remarks were a 'useful precedent for me'; but this was a handwritten postscript on a letter setting out arrangements for Grizewood to spend the weekend at Holywell Ford and to dine at High Table in Magdalen College. Quite possibly he enjoyed the notoriety arising from being criticised by a leading politician. He apparently sought out the Foreign Office view of his criticisms, and was disappointed to be told that the officials were not concerned about, but were dismissive of, his views.[224]

Taylor's disengagement with the cause of the Anglo-Soviet alliance
began with his long-awaited trip to Yugoslavia as the guest of the Yugoslav
government. This took place in April 1947. He wrote to A.P. Wadsworth
in March,

> This sounds rather a wild undertaking but I thought I had better get
> there before Tito is pushed over by the dollar. I expect you have had
> enough about the Slavs from Price for a long time, but I'll try to look
> into some things which he passed over, e.g. university life and tourist
> possibilities. I've said I'm going to see churches and scenery, not
> Communist bosses, but I doubt whether I have been taken seriously.
> If there's anything in particular you'd like me to look into, let me
> know. I shall visit Prague on the way.[225]

Alan Taylor had been reading about medieval Serb architecture and went
eager to view the orthodox monasteries. His former contact over Trieste,
Velebit, who was now the Deputy Foreign Minister, organised a tour of
Macedonia, with accommodation provided through the local Communist
Parties. He and Margaret stayed at Studenitsa, Pristina, Gracinitsa, Skopje,
Zagreb and elsewhere. Later, he wrote of the monasteries,

> The architecture was interesting but what really counted were the
> frescoes which displayed the richness of the renaissance a couple of
> centuries before it developed in Italy. This great art was quite unknown
> in England, so much so that when on my return I tried to promote an
> exhibition of Yugoslav art in London, I was rebuffed by the Director
> of the Arts Council who said it had no artistic value. The Yugoslav
> churches revived my zest for medieval architecture which I had neglected
> for years past.[226]

Perhaps his focus on medieval buildings signified a lessening of his
wartime fervour for national causes. He was greatly impressed by Yugoslavia
and its brand of communism. He was indiscreet in saying so when in
Zagreb. Soon after he returned to England A.P. Wadsworth wrote asking,
'What on earth have you been up to to displease Moscow so much?' He
quoted a BBC Monitoring Report on Moscow broadcasts which included
an item on a visit by a 'Professor Taylor' to Yugoslavia, 'the substance of
the matter being that the Professor had allegedly disseminated anti-Soviet
doctrines in the manner of "Goebbels and Churchill", but that the
"justifiably indignant" people of Yugoslavia were well able to distinguish
him as "an agent of foreign imperialism"'. However, soon afterwards
Wadsworth and Taylor were delighted that the BBC monitored favourable
Yugoslav comments on his two essays in the *Manchester Guardian* on
his trip.[227]

These essays were entitled 'Impressions of Yugoslavia'. In the first, on 'A Regime of Youth', he wrote warmly of the energy and enthusiasm in the country. Finding many of the leaders to be former teachers, he observed, 'The effect is as though the Left Book Club suddenly took over both the central and local government of this country.' In the second, on 'Economics and Politics', he discussed Yugoslav plans for economic development and urged the West to be generous with economic assistance.[228]

The Soviet and the Yugoslav responses to his trip made him acceptable again to the BBC hierarchy as a broadcaster on Yugoslavia. He enthused, 'Yugoslavia is an exciting country, exciting in its great past, and excited now about what it is going to do in the future.' He also observed, 'The constant criticism by western countries of Communist rule in Yugoslavia has had the result of turning the communists into the champions of national independence. In fact the more foreigners abuse the dictatorship, the longer it's likely to last.' His views went out on successive days to BBC listeners in Africa, the Pacific, North America and elsewhere.[229]

Margaret Taylor went with her husband to Yugoslavia. It may have been an attempt by both of them to save their marriage. The war years had put strains on it, though such stresses were probably magnified later with hindsight. During the war they continued to share pleasure not only in their growing family but also in music and in entertaining at Holywell Ford. With his growing ambitions regarding broadcasting from London, in 1944 they rented a top-floor room from their Oxford friend Jane Douglas. This was at 33 Percy Street, off Tottenham Court Road and near Goodge Street tube station, and not far from the British Museum. They had many good times in London while occupying that room. He later remembered, 'We had an active social life and often went to the theatre or cinema.' She later recalled how in the later part of the war they had both helped run the lunchtime concerts held at the National Gallery. These hugely popular daily concerts were organised from 1939 by Myra Hess, a distinguished orchestral and chamber concert pianist whom Margaret had first met in Manchester. Alan Taylor often handled the money, Margaret having warm memories of him cycling back to their room with heavy bags of half-crowns on his handlebars.[230] As late as 10 July 1945 he was eagerly inviting Malcolm Muggeridge to join them for lunch in Percy Street and commenting, 'Did I tell you we have a delightful daughter? Margaret is expecting in October: she says I must tell you she has belatedly caught up Kitty.'[231]

Matrimonial problems became serious firstly when Margaret was eager to see Robert Kee again and secondly, and more substantially, a few months later when Dylan Thomas re-entered her life. Taylor was devastated when her enthusiasm for Robert Kee was again excessive, and hurt when she gave over their Percy Street room to him. But Kee, fourteen years younger, was happily going out with women of his age, notably Janetta Woolley, whom he married in 1948. The hurt for Alan Taylor was compounded by his feelings that Margaret did not hide her preference for the younger man to their acquaintances in Oxford. His considerable fears of being treated like his father were made tangible.

However, as he acknowledged in his autobiography, their post-war life in Oxford was dismal for her. Her wartime concerts had ended and she was excluded from Oxford's musical society. The émigrés had gone, Lord Berners rarely visited Oxford, and her husband was involved in teaching and much else in Magdalen College and restlessly ambitious to make a national reputation in broadcasting and the press as well as as a historian.[232] The reappearance of Dylan and Caitlin Thomas brought her the excitement again of literary gatherings and much uninhibited partying.[233] For a woman of 41 the Thomases represented fun and an opportunity not to play second fiddle to a disapproving husband who was very clear as to what he wanted but not sensitive to her social needs. Moreover, he was notably undemonstrative emotionally, and, as he later acknowledged, his insistence

In his garden.

on separate beds did not help their closeness. In contrast, Dylan and Caitlin's emotional feelings were unbridled and very often on public display.[234]

Alan Taylor's autobiography notably muddled the dates of his anguish over the third phase of his encounters with Dylan Thomas. They reappeared in late 1945, not 1946. He suggests Caitlin suggested that Margaret was in love with Dylan on the eve of their trip to Yugoslavia in spring 1947. While this suggestion of her being in love may have been news to him, for his wife was still eagerly promoting Robert Kee with BBC producers through Dylan Thomas' contacts in July 1946, it can hardly have been this late that he first feared she was obsessed with Thomas.

Dylan and Caitlin Thomas, with their six-year-old son and two-year-old daughter, appeared at Holywell Ford not long before Christmas 1945, having nowhere to live and Dylan with a broken arm. At first they stayed in Holywell Ford with the Taylors. For a year from mid-March 1946 they lived in its large one-room summer house beside the river Cherwell, while the daughter stayed in the main house.[235] Margaret Taylor, no longer organising lunchtime concerts in Oxford, now eagerly tried to organise the Thomas family's lives. It cost her her savings, the valuable paintings from the walls of her home, a caravan for Dylan to work in and eventually her marriage; but her enthusiasms for Kee and Thomas were symptoms of some deeper dissatisfaction. She seems to have felt belittled by the drive of her overachieving husband. She could not only talk of poetry with Dylan Thomas and his circle but get him to read her verse. On one occasion, probably in early 1946, he wrote a very thoughtful and probably very kind assessment of thirteen of her poems. This included explicit encouragement to continue her writing.[236]

Alan and Margaret Taylor's departure for Yugoslavia also marked the end of the Thomases' sojourn at Holywell Ford and its summer house. The Taylors went to Yugoslavia in early April and the Thomases, with Caitlin's sister Brigit Marnier and her son, departed for Rapallo on 8 April 1947. The financial impetus for the move to Italy came from a Society of Authors grant to Dylan Thomas of £150. On top of this Margaret Taylor and others provided substantial supplementary funds. Caitlin Thomas later recalled Margaret Taylor spending £300, which she had received after her mother's death in 1941, to rent for them the Villa Beccaro at Scandicci, close to Florence.[237] If so, paying the rent in Britain could have got round exchange control restrictions on directly funding the Thomases in Italy. The Thomases stayed there from 12 May until 20 July, before moving on to Elba for three weeks.

With the Thomases leaving for several months Margaret Taylor was eager to accompany her husband to Yugoslavia. They were together again on holiday. The focus was on sightseeing. Perhaps his insistence on a tour of monastic architecture was somewhat dry compared with the lively pub humour of Dylan Thomas and his entourage. He recalled, 'Time and again, after a day at some splendid monastery, Margaret spent the evening railing at me for bringing her to this ghastly country...when she wanted to be in Italy with Dylan and Caitlin.' On their return, another attempt by Margaret Taylor to make her own mark failed, when the BBC turned down her script on Nazor, Yugoslavia.[238]

Soon after the Taylors' return, Margaret set about meeting Dylan Thomas' request of mid-April to find his family a house not too distant from Oxford. By late May she had selected a dilapidated old farmhouse, grandly named 'The Manor House', at South Leigh, near Witney.[239] Alan Taylor, who desperately wanted the Thomases away from Holywell Ford and his family, as well as an end to Dylan Thomas' pub talk of Margaret, agreed to finance the £2000 required on the proviso that Margaret gave the Thomases no more money and that they paid rent. Margaret Taylor made the purchase of the house, arranged the repair work, provided much furniture and a gypsy caravan for Dylan to work in and rented the house to the Thomases at £1 per week. They soon did not pay the rent and, after a period of not giving way to Dylan's begging for money, she did provide them with more money, outraging her husband; he later wrote of this, 'Breaking one's word over money went against my deepest principle – the sanctity of contract.' She also went frequently to South Leigh, acting as unpaid home help, leaving an outraged Alan Taylor with their children. On one occasion he cycled out to South Leigh and had a vigorous row with her.

Alan and Margaret Taylor went to Brittany for what turned out to be a last holiday together as a married couple in August 1948. He liked Belle Île but for him it was spoilt by his wife voicing her regrets that she was not with the Thomases. When the Thomases wanted to leave South Leigh and return to west Wales, Margaret arranged it. In 1949 she bought 'The Boat House' in Laugharne, a house which Dylan and Caitlin Thomas had admired when they lived in that town in 1938–40. This she again rented to the Thomases from May 1949, though again the rent was later unpaid. The house was leased and improved with the money from the sale of the South Leigh property and a further £2000 from Margaret Taylor (two-thirds of her capital). Alan Taylor acquiesced, but, as he later recalled, he wrote to Dylan Thomas stating that 'he was destroying our marriage and that he should lay off if only for the sake of the children'. The response was predictable: a postcard with 'FUCK OFF' on it.[240] Margaret Taylor remained involved with the Thomases until and beyond Dylan's death in 1953, seriously straining her own finances. Alan and Margaret Taylor separated in 1950 when he left Oxford to spend a year's study leave in London.

It was a very sad end to a marriage, not least because of their deep affection for their children. They had come together when in a foreign city, Vienna. They were from similar well-to-do backgrounds, were somewhat pampered only children, shared a love of music and were neither sufficiently good-looking to be sure of many admirers of the opposite sex. In Manchester they had had the company of lively young people of their age and had frequent weekend parties out at Higher Disley, and Margaret had carved out a musical role for herself. This had weakened at Oxford, her musical entrepreneurship had ended with the war and the lively parties or pub evenings for Margaret Taylor were increasingly linked to Dylan and Caitlin Thomas, not her husband. While she hero-worshipped the leech-like poet, it is improbable that her passion for him was requited.[241] Alan Taylor gained great satisfaction from his children but, to use a current word, he got his 'buzzes' from radio and later television appearances, as well as from academic acclaim.

– 5 –

FAME AND
ACADEMIC ESTEEM

By the 1950s Alan Taylor had become a household name, an early radio and television personality. As a result he became accustomed to strangers greeting him in the streets, something he rather liked. Yet he also achieved considerable recognition as a major academic historian, even if one of Oxford University's glittering prizes which he sought proved to be beyond his reach.

With the end of the Second World War he adjusted to teaching larger numbers of students again. Former students, whose studies had been broken by war service, and older ones whose entry had been delayed mingled with those fresh from school. These post-war undergraduates included future historians such as John Grigg, Keith Kyle, K.D. Haley, Alfred Gollin and Karl Leyser and the future politicians John Biggs Davison and William Rodgers. K.D. Haley, who attended his lectures immediately after the end of the war, recalled that he still lectured with the help of some record cards then. Haley was much impressed by the lectures, liking the way Taylor avoided them being chunks of history and how he dealt in a non-chronological way with themes such as Prime Ministers and Foreign Secretaries. John Grigg, who was at New College, came into contact with him after he had been one of those who set up the Sydney Smith Society. When Taylor spoke at the society, John Grigg sat next to him. He recalled, 'Unlike many dons he was not full of himself. He was a good conversationalist – witty, but he also listened.'

Alfred Gollin, who had served in the US army 1943–46, recalled in 1977 the impact of Taylor's writing on him:

> When I first went up to New College, my tutor, Alan Bullock, was not especially pleased with my essays. He then assigned me a question on the Austro-Hungarians and a book he asked me to read for it was

Taylor's *The Habsburg Monarchy*. At first I could not make head or tail of the book but I suddenly saw what Taylor was doing and re-read the whole thing. My essay, based on Taylor's book, was the first that Bullock ever approved of. Bullock said, 'You have arrived, laddie.' I did not then know Taylor but, after that I looked out for everything he wrote... As a young American I found the Oxford system rather strange and quite different. After this incident I began to see what was required of me there.[1]

Alan Taylor was very involved in college politics before Tizard retired in 1946. In October 1945 he wrote to Trevor Blewitt, asking not to broadcast on 14 November 'owing to the outbreak of controversy in the College', as he did not wish to miss a committee then.[2] Squabbling in the college helped to speed Tizard on his way. Whereas Taylor had worked closely with Tizard and had helped get him elected, he did not support his successor Professor Thomas Boase, the Director of the Courtauld Institute, and they disliked each other. For a while Taylor tried to play a part in Oxford University's Faculty Board for History, but he was blocked by the medieval historians. Instead, he, with Alan Bullock and other modern historians, formed the Recent History Group, which was intended to popularise the study and teaching of history beyond 1914.[3] In pursuit of this aim they secured the publication by Oxford University Press of *A Select List of Books on European History 1815–1914* for the Group in 1948, which they revised in 1957. They also did what they could to promote the study of recent history, mentioning contemporary history as often as possible.[4]

Taylor also continued to promote the claims to greater recognition of Lewis Namier. Indeed, his zeal was at times embarrassingly excessive. In December 1939 he had written a survey of history and politics books of that year for the *Manchester Guardian*'s Christmas Book Supplement. Of Namier's collection of essays *In the Margin of History* (1940) he enthused, 'No reader of these hard gems of wisdom will ever ask again what is the use of history – or of historians.' He twice reviewed Namier's next collection of essays, *Conflicts* (1942). In *Time and Tide* he was eulogistic in his praises of Namier's style and clarity but criticised Namier for being 'inclined to overlook the merely economic'. In the *Manchester Guardian* he suggested that the essays 'should be compulsory reading for every student of history and of international affairs'.[5]

His *Manchester Guardian* review was toned down by W.P. Crozier. He wrote to Taylor observing that he also admired Namier but that his piece was 'rather too much of a personal tribute to go with the general severity of "review" columns'. He therefore cut out two pieces, including a 'Namierism' which he felt was 'an amusing aphorism which passes well in conversation but hardly stands the test of cold print'. A contrite Alan Taylor replied, 'I found it very difficult to write and I am sure that the cuts you have made improve it, so that it now says all I wanted to say more clearly.'[6]

After the war there were more substantial works by Namier for Taylor to praise. He deemed his *1848: The Revolution of the Intellectuals* (1946) to be 'a contribution to nineteenth-century European history of the first importance'. He was even more enthusiastic about Namier's *Diplomatic Prelude 1938–1939* (1948), a work which did influence his thinking about the origins of the Second World War in Europe. In his review for the *Manchester Guardian* he wrote, 'A show piece of the historian's art... Meticulous scholarship and deep insight go together, and a sentence often says as much as many pages by another writer.'[7]

He spent much energy in 1947 unsuccessfully lobbying for Namier to succeed F.M. Powicke as Regius Professor of History. He gained the support of Harold Laski, who had been involved with Namier in high-level discussions on Palestine in 1930–31. However, as the post was filled on the recommendation of the Prime Minister and Clement Attlee loathed Laski, this was maladroit. More problematic was the widespread dislike in Oxford of Namier. Taylor later observed of Namier's opponents, 'They resented his outspoken criticism of other historians... They did not want a Jew. They thought Namier a bore. In short he was socially unacceptable.' Taylor was successful in securing for Namier the invitation to give the first Waynflete Lectures at Magdalen College. Namier characteristically wrote the first and then extemporised the later ones, losing his audience other than Taylor and Alan Bullock. These lectures on 'The German Problem in 1848', like his later Ford Lectures, were never published.[8]

Taylor also promoted Namier on the radio. Well before the publication of *Diplomatic Prelude* in January 1948, he suggested to George Barnes that he should review it along with others. He wrote,

> Wheeler-Bennett on Munich and Namier on *Diplomatic Prelude* would be first rate excuses for a talk on the origins of the recent war; and, as I have reviewed most of the French memoirs and other books on this theme either for the [*Times*] *Literary Supplement* or the *Manchester Guardian*, I could cover a wide field.

Anna Kallin, who had earlier worked with Trevor Blewitt on 'World Affairs', invited him to review Namier's book on its own, observing, 'I am sure Professor Namier would give you his proofs.'[9] These were secured ahead of Alan Taylor's radio review.

The review went out as a twenty-minute broadcast on the Third Programme at 6.20p.m. on 13 January 1948. With the title 'An Exercise in Contemporary History' Taylor was promoting his modern corner at

Oxford. He said that most historians saw contemporary history as only journalism, and much of it was only that. However, he observed, 'The first aim of the journalist is to interest, of the historian it is to instruct – of course the good journalist and the good historian try to do both.' He went on to praise Namier, claiming that younger historians under 45 recognised the greatness of Namier. 'Namier has been too forthright in his judgements, too ruthless in his scholarship and too disturbing in his discoveries to be welcome to the established.'

Taylor then gave some early thoughts on the origins of the Second World War, the theme of the book he would publish in 1961. He expressed admiration for Namier's revisionism, which he said ignored the legends of the six-month period before the outbreak of war in Europe in September 1939. He then highlighted themes that he would develop in his own book. He said that 'you can find in Namier the more humdrum truth, discreditable no doubt to both sides in the negotiations – not discreditable from wickedness or sinister intention, discreditable from short-sightedness, vanity and ignorance'. In this Neville Chamberlain was not alone. 'Certainly, Hitler aimed at German domination of Europe, but he too went about this in the most blundering way and, as Namier shows, was quite taken aback at the end when he found that, against all expectations, Britain and France were really going to war.' He concluded,

> If there is a moral, it seems to me to be this: those who really know what they want, get it – not necessarily of course in the way that they want, but they get it somehow. But those who hesitate between different objectives and seek only some compromise which will postpone difficulties, get nothing – not even the postponement they long for. In 1939 none of the Great Powers – not even Germany – was directed by a ruler who knew what he wanted; and the plans of all, in the event, miscarried.[10]

Namier had written his book relying heavily on the evidence given at the Nuremberg trials of 22 major defendants conducted between November 1945 and October 1946, the early British and other official publications and the early published memoirs of prominent participants in the events of 1939.[11] Alan Taylor followed him in using such printed sources, reviewing numerous French memoirs in particular.

He reviewed Georges Bonnet's memoirs in the *Manchester Guardian* in November 1946 and successfully pressed a not very enthusiastic Wadsworth to let him review General Gamelin's memoirs in March 1947 and February 1948 and Paul Reynaud's in August 1947. He also wrote on Bonnet and Gamelin for the French journal *Critique*, a connection which had come about through his friendship with its founder, Georges Bataille, who wanted articles about books rather than just reviews. From Bonnet's memoirs Alan Taylor cynically drew the conclusion that the diplomat had not been capable of Machiavellian plotting to destroy Czechoslovakia or to organise a coalition against the Soviet Union. Overall, he believed, 'Twenty years of taking phrases for reality produced their inevitable result, and the statesmen of every country behaved meanly, feebly.'[12] In short, blunders explained more than scheming.

Taylor eagerly continued to review memoirs of the Second World War. He often reviewed the same book twice – or even three times, counting both French and English versions. Between 1948 and the end of 1952 he wrote on books by Pierre Laval, Paul Baudouin, General Weygand, Yves Bouthillier, Jacques Saustelle and Robert Coulondre in a range of British and French newspapers and journals. He also reviewed books by or about such German figures as Hjalmer Schacht, Ernst von Weizsäcker, Paul Schmidt, Hans Speidel and Franz von Papen. In addition he reviewed the memoirs of Cordell Hull and Admiral William D. Leahy, two Americans. Such reviewing provided him with a background to future writing about inter-war international relations and in some cases made him rethink the history of the late 1930s, though his writing was by no means all marked by revisionism. He continued to reiterate his views as to the wickedness of most Germans. For instance, in one of his three reviews of von Weizsäcker's memoirs, he commented that, if the various recent German memoirs were to be believed, then Hitler was an even greater genius than hitherto believed, as every German opposed him. He displayed similar cynicism in writing about the memoirs of Paul Reynaud, the French Prime Minister in 1940, commenting that he 'wages against his critics a more successful war than he waged against the Germans'.[13]

John Wheeler-Bennett's history of Munich did give him an opportunity to reflect again on that crisis. In a review of it in May 1948 he observed, 'If after 1936 there ever was a chance of stopping Hitler without war Munich was the moment; but perhaps there was no such moment.' He also expressed the view that the failure to bring Russia 'back into the system of European order' was 'the ineffaceable sin, before their own people and before posterity, of the men of Munich'.[14] As in his 1945–47 view of an Anglo-Soviet alliance, Taylor was thinking in balance of power terms for European relations.

His views on the origins of the Second World War were also shaped from April 1947 by the publication of the British and, later, the French and Italian documents on foreign policy. These volumes provided him with much of his highly valued source material, just as in the 1930s and after he had drawn much of his knowledge of international relations before 1914 from *Die Grosse Politik der Europäischen Kabinette, 1871–1914*

(1922–26). Several of his major reviews of diplomatic documents were published in the *Times Literary Supplement*. His reviewing for the *TLS*, as for the *Manchester Guardian*, came through Namier's patronage as a result of his unwillingness to write many reviews quickly.

In his review of the first volume published of the *Documents on British Foreign Policy* Alan Taylor made a powerful critique of past official collections of diplomatic documents. He observed of *Die Grosse Politik* that it 'was as good as a military victory for Germany, for it was a decisive weapon in shaking the moral foundations of Versailles'. It succeeded by re-ordering the documents into themes, thereby hiding the links between actions, which revealed them as aggressive. He criticised the British editors for following the German model, for excluding private letters and minutes (which would help explain why actions were taken), not revealing who saw the documents and for not following G.P. Gooch and Harold Temperley in their volumes on the period before 1914 in insisting that there was a statement in the volumes as to their editorial independence.[15]

Such criticisms were very much to the point, but outraged Llewellyn Woodward, who secured a public apology over the slur on editorial independence. More than that, he was able to breach the *Times Literary Supplement*'s policy of safeguarding the anonymity of its reviewers, and thereafter was no longer a patron of Taylor but a virulent enemy. There may have been an element of pique in the review, as Woodward believed, Taylor chastising Woodward for editing the British documents with Rohan Butler, eleven years younger than Taylor and more of an Oxford 'insider'. Be this as it may, this review of the first volume of British inter-war documents provided Taylor with the front page of the *TLS* on which to display his critical judgement on the editing of diplomatic documents and his radical sentiments in asserting that those carrying out such editing 'must regard themselves as watchdogs of the public, not as employees of the Foreign Office'. Perhaps he himself was happy enough for others in the field to work out quickly who the author was, so Woodward's task of discovering the reviewer was an easy one. Taylor recalled in 1978, 'The review, provoked by Stanley Morison, caused a terrible row and blew Morison out of the editor's chair.' This, however, was not the case, Morison retiring happily. Taylor's linking his piece with the timing of Morison's retirement was to have an unduly high estimation of the review's impact outside academia. However, Alan Taylor was not alone in being so critical of the editing of the documents. Professor Herbert Butterfield, a fellow dissenter, was vehemently critical of such 'official history', campaigning briefly against such state employment of historians as a threat to independent history concerned only with historical truth. In a letter, he informed Taylor, 'I am as an historian against all governments, or rather I believe that something oblique is going on behind all governments, giving them a seamy side.'[16]

Taylor's many later reviews of volumes of British and German diplomatic, however, contributed to his rethinking of the diplomatic history of the inter-war years. It is notable that some of his most controversial points in his *The Origins of the Second World War* were first aired in several of these reviews. For instance, in December 1949 he first dismissed as of little importance the Hossbach memorandum on Hitler's conference in the Chancellery on 5 November 1937, at which he discussed possible war scenarios with his leading military advisers. He wrote then of Hitler and the Hossbach memorandum, 'This is evidence that he was a violent and unscrupulous man; it is not evidence that he had any concrete projects, and his prophecy of events bears no relation to what actually happened. For instance Hitler talks of war in the period 1943–45 though he does not say against whom...' More generally, of the Hossbach memorandum and the other published German documents, he observed that the volume

> does not provide the evidence that there was a German, or even a Nazi conspiracy against peace, if by conspiracy is meant a coherent objective plan. It provides the evidence that the Germans, and especially the German governing class, allowed a criminal lunatic to establish himself in supreme power; and that they were abetted by those in England and France who, from feebleness or fear of communism, treated the lunatic as a sane man.[17]

While he later dropped referring to Hitler as a lunatic, he continued to depict Hitler as an opportunist. In April 1950 he wrote of 1938 in another review of published German documents, 'Still Hitler did not settle his course even at the end of May. British appeasement, not Czech resistance, made him decide to provoke a crisis before the autumn. Until the Runciman mission even Hitler could not believe that the British would carry their surrender so far...' He went on to develop his oft-stated theme that Hitler was an unusual German politician only in the extremity of his views.

> He differed from the generals and diplomats in method, not aim; indeed, since he was incapable of systematic thought, he had no aim except to take advantage of the moment. The old-stylers were infinitely more dangerous to the rest of Europe, once they were more skilful in method and clear as to their intentions. They meant to establish Germany as the dominant power of Europe; and they would have done it except for Hitler's pursuit of theatrical violence. We should therefore be very grateful that Hitler broke loose in 1938.[18]

Alan Taylor was in a very fertile period of writing in the late 1940s and early 1950s. While writing reviews and generally reflecting on inter-war diplomatic history, he was engaged on writing his major work on European diplomatic history 1848–1918 and doing some work on two other books, the new version of *The Habsburg Monarchy* (1948) and a collection of essays entitled *From Napoleon to Stalin* (1950).

Why did he rewrite *The Habsburg Monarchy*? It was partly money, the desire to have it still bring in income for several more years; not least as he had been annoyed at the low sales of the first version. However, while he was eagerly concerned about the financial details, even pointing out to Hamish Hamilton that had he stayed with Macmillan a reprinting of the book would have pushed his royalties up to 20 per cent, this was secondary to his major concern to keep the book in print. It was his major work in what he then felt to be his prime area of expertise among historians at Oxford and in the eyes of his patrons in the press and radio.

After Hamish Hamilton had been notably lukewarm about taking over the book, Taylor took a copy of the 1941 edition to give personally to the publisher when he visited his firm's offices at the start of 1946. Hamilton was out, but appears to have seen him the next week. Then he secured Taylor's help in trying to secure for his firm either a book by Lewis Namier on 1848 or his autobiography. On 19 January Taylor reported to Hamilton his lack of success as a go-between. 'No luck with Namier's reminiscences. I'll talk to him again about his book on 1848 when it is more advanced.'[19] When Hamilton agreed to take up *The Habsburg Monarchy* later that month, he wrote back that he had raised the matter of a new edition early, while Macmillan still had stocks and well before he was bound by his contract to give them six months' notice of changing publisher once it was out of print. He did so 'simply to know whether I should have to undertake a thorough revision or rewriting, which would have taken me the best part of a year'. He clearly still hoped to reprint the 1941 version, observing: 'I suppose photographic reproduction will allow me to alter a word (truly not more) here and there?' He concluded, 'I don't mind how small the edition is. I think the book even as it stands, is a good one; and I want it to be available in the future to the discerning few who wish to read it.'[20]

By the autumn of 1946 he was changing his mind. He wrote to Hamilton,

> But, looking at *The Habsburg Monarchy* again, I do not think I should like it to appear in its present form. I daresay it has some good stuff in it, but I should like to make it much better. In fact I should like to rewrite it from start to finish: this would make a livelier book and a rather longer one … You'll curse me for these hesitations and changes of plans, but I really think I must rewrite it. I could do it while on holiday next summer and let you have the manuscript in the autumn.

If this is impossible, then I think that the best thing is to let the book
die unless the demand for it becomes overwhelming...

Of course this is idiotic, too. I ought to be getting on with The
Struggle for Mastery in Europe; but the flood of undergraduates puts
me off serious work. 60,000 words are done – but I want to do
200,000.[21]

On 3 November he wrote further on the matter.

I think I must rewrite it. Namier, who was here the other day, agreed
very strongly on this and agreed to give me his detailed suggestions...as
soon as he has got his pressing commitments out of the way – that is,
next summer. In this way I should produce a book of more than
100,000 words instead of the present 85,000, and it really will be a
new book. Besides I have a name now which can be exploited, and I
have every confidence in your ability to exploit it. I shall be able to
deliver it to you in twelve months from now, which I have no doubt
suits you.

He recognised that he could not expect an advance but readily agreed to
Hamilton's offer of 15 per cent on the first 2500 and 20 per cent thereafter.[22]

Taylor rewrote most of The Habsburg Monarchy during the university
summer vacation of 1947. By the time he went to France in mid-August
he had written 50,000 words. He delivered the book, at 120,000 words, in
late November. To his horror, given his very strong belief in the sanctity
of contracts, in view of rising production costs the publisher required the
initial royalty to drop to 12.5 per cent for the first 3000 copies, though a
higher selling price would earn him the same amount as had been agreed
verbally a year earlier. He commented of his agreement, 'I do so as a fit
penalty for my own carelessness, and shall take good care not to get
into this position again.' However, writing to Roger Machell of Hamish
Hamilton, he observed, 'I don't really care what I am paid so long as the
Habsburg Monarchy comes out.' To make matters worse, Hamish Hamilton
suffered a fire at his offices and Taylor ended up proof-reading his book
once more and making the index again. He tried, unsuccessfully, to gain
insurance money for his work on the replacement index.[23]

This was a bad incident for Alan Taylor. He had been very impressed
by Hamish Hamilton and he had loosened up briefly in terms of money.
It was a big sign of trust on his part to write to Hamilton, 'Don't bother
to prepare a contract. I'll write and ask you for one when I get down to the
work of rewriting.'[24] The firm's later insistence on worse terms than he had
been led to expect made him again convinced that in money matters
everybody was out to strike a hard bargain at his expense. So he reverted

to behaving in the way he believed his grandfather JT had behaved. He wrangled over the other terms of the contract and, with some relish, told Hamish Hamilton, that 'when it comes to settling a contract, I expect you to look after your interests and I do my best to look after mine. If you don't like this attitude, you must keep clear of writers who are born in the North of England.'[25]

The negotiations over the revised version of *The Habsburg Monarchy* were also revealing as to his academic relationship with Lewis Namier. Clearly, Hamish Hamilton saw Taylor as Namier's protégé, and one with influence over the elder scholar. Taylor did help Hamilton secure some Namier books for his list, albeit lesser ones. It may be that Hamilton would have been even more resistant to taking on a revised version of a book of which he felt Macmillan had already had the cream of the sales had Taylor not been connected to Namier. It is equally notable that, eight years after leaving Namier's department in Manchester University, he was still seeking Namier's advice and was apparently much influenced by it. This is surprising in a well-established scholar of over forty years of age.

Amidst the wrangling over his contract Taylor observed, when revising a clause which would have let his book go out of print when sales dipped, 'You can't expect a work of history to sell on a large scale every year, but you can expect it to sell something every year for at least twenty years; and I write my books with the thought of the steady sale in mind.'[26] This was more than an argument of the moment. He sought to write books which would reach a wide audience.

One of the most notable features of the second version was that it was much improved in style. In this he was emulating Namier as well as the great historians of the past, such as Gibbon and Macaulay. A good illustration of this is the opening lines of the second chapter. In the 1941 book he wrote, 'There has never been an Austrian people, only the peoples over whom the House of Austria ruled. Austrian meant an inhabitant of the Empire, or, more positively, one who was loyal to the dynasty...'

In the 1948 version of the book he employed an anecdote he had used before in other writing to open the chapter. 'Francis I, told of an Austrian patriot, answered impatiently: 'But is he a patriot for me?' The Emperor was needlessly meticulous. Austria was an Imperial organisation, not a country; and to be Austrian was to be free of national feeling, not to possess a nationality.'

He also acted on A.F. Pribram's criticism of the 1941 book by giving some attention to foreign policy. He purged his earlier text of what he deemed to be 'the liberal illusion' that the Habsburg monarchy could have survived if some of its leading figures had acted more wisely.[27] His views here had been changed by the developments of the war and immediate post-war years, and also by his own visits to Czechoslovakia and Yugoslavia.

The book was not only bigger but covered 1809–1918, with an epilogue on the inter-war years. The reviewers generally welcomed its broader scope but felt he was more opinionated. Wickham Steed in the *Times Literary Supplement* praised it for being 'fuller and more detailed' but felt it was less readable than the 1941 version. He complained, 'It is not easy to resist the impression that in rewriting his book Mr Taylor has indulged a dogmatic temper at the expense of a well-considered appraisal of men and things.' Wickham Steed had changed his views from his pre-1914 study of the Habsburg monarchy, which had been sympathetic to it and foresaw no major crisis, to his *The Doom of the Habsburgs* (1937), which saw its decline as inevitable. C.A. Macartney in *History* paid tribute to Taylor's 'acute perception, ability to find a way through tangles, and a great skill in making short *précis* of long sources' before condemning him for 'cock-sureness and a complete intolerance of those whom he disapproves, whether living or dead. Everybody has to be scored off, and with very few exceptions, almost everyone who figures in his pages is a villain, an impostor or, more frequently still, a fool.'[28] In contrast to Wickham Steed, Macartney had remained sympathetic to the Habsburg monarchy and did not see its end as inevitable. While it irritated these established figures of an older generation, the book proved to be one of Alan Taylor's most successful and most admired, and has stayed in print for over fifty years.

Yet, in many ways *The Habsburg Monarchy* (1948) is the twin of *The Course of German History* (1945). Both gave very blunt and firm views, based on a deterministic view of history. In one the Germans were the bullies of Europe, the misdeeds of 1939–45 being only an extreme episode in a long history of illiberal policies. In the other the Habsburgs were also a bad lot, albeit of a less competent kind. For Alan Taylor, Gladstone had got their measure when, in the 1880 general election campaign, he had bluntly (and undiplomatically) observed, 'There is not an instance – there is not a spot on the whole map where you can lay your finger and say: "There Austria did good"'. Taylor followed earlier specialists in modern Habsburg history – such as Oscar Jaszi and Joseph Redlich – in seeing the Habsburg monarchy's downfall as inevitable. He was also one of several historians who depicted Francis Joseph as a colourless, worthy bureaucrat.[29] Where many historians offer cautious assessments, Taylor in these two books offered clear and vigorous judgements, and these helped to attract a large readership.

His emphatic view of the inevitability of the decline of the Habsburgs did not remain the largely unchallenged orthodox view for long after the 1948 version was published. In comparison with the virulent nationalism, fascism and then communism of central Europe after 1920, the Habsburg Empire seemed attractive to some historians, some of whom even saw it as a benevolent supranational power. It was not just Cold War susceptibilities which led to serious questioning of whether the Habsburg monarchy's demise was inevitable. Greater attention was given by other scholars, such as Alan Sked, to the internal economic, social, intellectual and political history of the empire. Sked, whose doctorate was supervised by Taylor, took the view that after the crisis of 1848 the Habsburg monarchy 'in many ways *rose* rather than *declined* before 1914. It can even be argued that there was no domestic or even foreign threat to its integrity until 1918.' In seeing the Habsburg monarchy not in decline in 1914, Sked compared its situation with Russia, where recent historical interpretations have doubted it was on the verge of collapse then, and Germany, where nobody has seriously seen the régime in danger before the First World War.[30] Such comparative reflections are well worthwhile, but nationalism was more advanced in the Habsburg lands than in much (but not all) of the Russian Empire, and the Habsburg Empire's future was in greater jeopardy in 1914 than the other two empires.

From Napoleon to Stalin (1950) was another instance of Alan Taylor following in Lewis Namier's footsteps. Namier had published four collections of his essays between 1931 and 1947; these reflected not only his research into the eighteenth century but also his standing as a major commentator on contemporary history and contemporary affairs. Taylor was very ready to take up the opportunity to publish such a mix of essays when interest in his views was aroused by his *Manchester Guardian* and BBC radio work.

He wrote eagerly to Hamish Hamilton in 1946,

> I have been approached by Allen and Unwin with a suggestion to publish my broadcast talks and occasional articles. This seems to me a crazy idea from the publisher's point of view, since the book will be nothing more than stale Manchester Guardian leaders, independent essays of 1000 to 2000 words. However, if they are mad enough to want to do it, I don't see why I should refuse them. But first I want to be sure that you do not object. It never entered my head for a moment that anyone would ever want to read again the day-to-day stuff that I have written. It's not bad and it's not especially ephemeral: I mean most of it hasn't gone out of date, but the subjects are naturally dictated by current events, and every essay is short. French North Africa; Trieste; Russian Foreign Policy; President Benes; the Middle East. You know the sort of thing. Altogether it comes to about 50,000 words. The longest are a short history of the war (8000 words) which I did for the

BBC European Service last summer; Trieste, 7500 words; and an article on National Independence and the 'Austrian' idea which I wrote for the Political Quarterly. The others are all short essay-leaders and fifteen minute talks. If you have the slightest interest in this hotch-potch on European themes, I'll turn Allen and Unwin down; otherwise I'll go ahead and see what money I can make out of them, though I can't help thinking they'll repent of their suggestion when they see the stuff before them. I've told them already that my next serious book is pledged, so you don't need to feel that there's an obligation on you. As I say I think they are mad to suggest such a book; and I should think you mad if you showed much interest in it.[31]

For all the depreciation of the approach, he was clearly very keen to have such a book appear, whether published by Allen & Unwin or Hamish Hamilton.

However, A.P. Wadsworth was unwilling to give him permission to reprint his leaders. He wrote stating that he thought 'a number of years ought to expire before authorship is revealed'. He had recently enforced this principle with regard to a collection of leaders on France, a high proportion of which had been written by J.L. Hammond. These were published anonymously, but with an introduction by Denis Brogan. Hammond suffered a heart attack on 23 June 1944, returning two months later. Alan Taylor helped to cover for him.[32] Taylor later recalled that 'reviewers of the collection tried to guess who had written what'. He was very amused by these reviewers 'praising Hammond for the style and impact of pieces which he (AJPT) had in fact written'. Some thirty years later he could clearly remember only one piece – 'Quatorze Juillet' (1944). In this he reflected on the Rights of Man and on Anglo-French friendship, 'a matter of life and death, both material and spiritual', for Britain.[33] This was less ephemeral than most of his leaders, which would not have made good pieces for a book of essays. He tried unsuccessfully to interest Hamilton in his BBC broadcasts on British foreign policy, but they were neither sufficiently attractive nor substantial in length.[34]

Even without such pieces *From Napoleon to Stalin* was his least sparkling set of essays. Fifteen essays dealt with European history from Napoleon to the early twentieth century while fourteen were headed 'Contemporary', dealing with 1938–48 and based mostly on reviews of memoirs. He took the opportunity to include among these one piece, 'The Austrian Illusion', which clearly meant a lot to him. Austria was then still occupied by America, Britain, France and Russia. In the essay he argued that Austria could not be a state independent of Germany, 'an effective barrier against German nationalism'. He bluntly claimed, 'The fragment of German territory called Austria has no roots in history, no support in the feeling of its people, no record even of resistance to Nazi rule.' He had offered it to Wadsworth in March 1947 'just to complicate the proceedings of the Moscow conference [the Council of Foreign Ministers], but I'm not sure that it is on your present line'. In May he informed Wadsworth he had nothing to offer 'except an attack on Austria which is still maturing'. In September he finally sent the essay which he felt would 'explode the Austrian myth', observing that 'you can give it the title, A Recantation'. Wadsworth declined it, observing: 'A brilliant tour de force, but I don't think it would do any good for us to publish it. It would create such a stink in Austria, and so depress the poor things without doing any good to anybody.' This was one of several occasions when Taylor's determination to demonstrate what he saw as his fearless views could be deemed by others to be irresponsible: in this case, given the circumstances before Allied occupation of Austria ended in 1955.

In preparing the book of essays the major difficulty was to secure a satisfactory title. Alan Taylor first presented Hamish Hamilton with a list of essays, amounting to 6200 words, under the title 'Echoes' in March 1949. He sent a first batch of essays to Roger Machell on 24 May as Hamish Hamilton wanted the printer to begin setting up the book. He promised Machell a shorter second part of 'Contemporary Echoes'. A few days later he wrote again, observing:

> I have to translate some of the later essays back from the French and shall not tackle it until the Vacation. I think I can promise the rest of the copy by the middle of July. It can go direct into page proof: I am not of Namier's habits!
>
> I will certainly think of the title. I suppose a subtitle – essays historical and political would do. Europe yesterday and to-day [sic] is a tolerable, though not an accurate, description. I should also welcome any criticism of the arrangement or presentation when you have the complete table of contents. At present it is strictly chronological and looks rather forbiddingly academic.[35]

When he forwarded the rest of the essays for the book to Roger Machell he commented,

> As to title, if you don't like Echoes (which I admit doesn't sell a book) would EUROPEAN THEMES do or is this too like Brogan? Or EUROPE YESTERDAY AND TO-DAY, if no one has had it before. Actually there are two English and one American essay, but these are not far off Europe. A sub-title, Historical and Political Essays, might help it out. If we change the title, I think I had better rewrite the preface...[36]

These suggested titles were none too alluring so he came up with *From Napoleon to Stalin*. Hamish Hamilton was enthusiastic but urged 'in the sub-title I prefer "Studies" to "Essays", as the booksellers (and presumably public) shy off anything with the word "essay" in it'. He added, 'Also it's a good idea to invent an underlying theme in your introduction for the benefit of the reviewer.' To this Taylor responded, 'As to the subtitle, I do not much like Studies. How would "Comments on European History" or "Comments on History and Politics" do? It has a rather less hackneyed ring and co[n]veys something of the character of the pieces.'[37]

His Introduction offered an attempt to argue there was a cohesiveness to the collection. It was also a statement of his objection to Stalin's Russia. He wrote,

> What I offer are echoes from the past, called forth by a centennial occasion or by the publication of some book of memoirs. All the same there is an underlying theme. It is the theme which has run through European history since the French Revolution – the search for stability in an unstable world. The great revolution destroyed tradition as the basis for society; ever since men have been seeking for something to take its place.

After reflecting on Napoleon he observed,

> Stalin, at the end of the period, shows the same contrast – the revolutionary who has become the man of authority, or, in less personal terms, the revolution which has itself become a tradition and a dogma. For Marxism has carried to an extreme the rationalism of the French Revolution; yet (as the personal experience of the final essay shows) will no longer tolerate the free play of intellect.[38]

The final essay was Taylor's account of the Wroclaw Congress of Intellectuals held in the College of Technology, by the Oder, in August 1948, at which he dramatically and emphatically made clear his opposition to Stalinist oppression. His action there caused George Orwell to cross his name off his draft list of fellow travellers that he supplied to Celia Kirwan and the Information Research Department (in effect, to the British Security Services). Orwell, when crossing out Taylor's name, wrote: 'Took anti-CP line at Wroclaw Conference.' It also led, perhaps assisted by his comments just quoted on Stalin in the Introduction, to his *From Napoleon to Stalin* being a 1950 selection of the Right Book Club, run as a rival to the Left Book Club by Foyle's Bookshop of Charing Cross Road, London, from 1938.

Alan Taylor had been part of the British group attending a conference which the Communists intended would deliver an international condemnation of the USA. Four months earlier, Malcolm Muggeridge had his revenge for Taylor lecturing him in 1933 on his attitude to the Soviet Union by accusing him of being a fellow traveller. According to Muggeridge, 'He was slightly disconcerted, I fancy, but said that he quite recognised the impracticability of the position of the socialist who believes in working with the Communists, but that he prefers this position, even so, to working with Anti-Communists.'[39] By this time Taylor's belief in the possibility of non-Communists working with Communists had been shaken by events in Czechoslovakia, notably the probable murder of Jan Masaryk, the Foreign Minister, in March, and the resignation of Edward Benes as President on 7 June 1948. At Wroclaw, he made an emphatic break with Communists. Indeed, he clearly revelled in leading defiance to the blatant Communist manipulation of the conference. In his autobiography he recalled, 'I had experience of standing up to Communists in pre-war days and now used much the same technique.' According to George Weidenfeld, who was next to him in the conference hall, he sat through the anti-American speeches of the leading Russian delegates, Alexander Fadayev and Ilya Ehrenburg, 'with hunched shoulders and grim face'. He gave a vigorous speech on tolerance and freedom of thought. He made there points he had often made in the press and on the radio in Britain:

> In America, and now in England too, more and more people say that there is nothing to choose between the Soviet Union and Nazi Germany, that both want to conquer the world. Many intellectuals, in America as well as in England, have fought against this view. And now, when we come here, what do we find? The same views in reverse. The same bogeys; here it is called American Fascism, over there it is called Russian Bolshevism. We intellectuals, instead of inflating these bogeys, should be trying to bring peoples on both sides to their senses.

Kingsley Martin's report of his speech ended, 'These remarks were made with a stern ferocity which no Communist delegate could have bettered... He looked at the rostrum like a British bull terrier challenged to fight by a Russian wolf.' After his speech was translated 'a sepulchral silence fell on the assembly' broken only by 'some desultory clapping and some muted booing'. When he returned to his seat he muttered, 'Now I understand what Martin Luther must have felt at the Diet of Worms.'[40]

His Wroclaw speech crystallised in dramatic fashion views he had already been expressing. The previous month, in a BBC radio broadcast on totalitarianism, he had commented, 'The more men talk about democracy, the less they respect it in practice' and declared, 'I care for liberty above all other causes.'[41] After the Wroclaw Congress, when he found himself a hero in the West, he stated in a letter to the *Times*, 'In demanding freedom of thought the intellectual ... is making his greatest contribution to the cause of peace.'[42]

His media friends warmly welcomed his stance at Wroclaw, realising he had fully burnt his boats in the eyes of communists. Malcolm Muggeridge praised him in a *Daily Telegraph* leader, noting in his diary that this was partly so it 'might ruin him in regard to his left-wing friends and associates'. He also congratulated himself on Taylor's speech: 'Made me feel glad that I had given him such a talking to last time we met.' A.P. Wadsworth, perhaps intending to reinforce his rift with communist intellectuals, informed Taylor that the Russian writer Ilya Ehrenburg, who had been present at Wroclaw, had spoken of him in a broadcast in Polish transmitted from Moscow as 'an elegant professor of history from Oxford... with a big flower in his button-hole he behaved like an actor'. Two years later Alan Taylor had the opportunity at a lunch with the staff of the *New Statesman* to pay Ehrenburg back, having a blazing row with him. By this time thoroughly anti-communist, he wrote to Wadsworth, 'These Bolshie emissaries really are poisonous – almost enough to turn me from being a fellow-traveller!' Wadsworth also rightly guessed that, after Wroclaw, for a while the Yugoslav authorities would tread carefully in inviting him there, lest it enrage Moscow.[43] Wroclaw did, however, make him more acceptable to those running BBC radio.

Wroclaw also made him an acceptable choice to be the twin editor with George Orwell of a two-volume collection of political pamphlets put together by Reginald Reynolds. In his introduction he warned,

> The most monstrous tyranny is on the march, and not only in countries which have never known freedom... For a hundred and fifty years authority... has been on the defensive... Communism is the first serious counter-offensive by the forces of authority and tyranny. Instead of apologising it claims that oppression is actually better...
>
> But Communism is not solely a movement of power; it is much more a disease of the mind, a perversion of the liberal world. Though you cannot argue people out of Communism, you can shake their faith in it by the general atmosphere of argument which it is still possible to breathe in the western world.

In later life Taylor regretted having written the introduction to this book, presumably because of the Cold War sentiments he expressed. His essay contains his first use of 'the Establishment', but contrary to widespread opinion he did not coin the expression. It was used before the Second World War with a connotation derived from the Established Church.[44]

Later, his Wroclaw views also made him an attractive choice to introduce *The Communist Manifesto* (1848). It was a characteristically irreverent essay, in which he observed, '*The Communist Manifesto* must be counted as a holy book in the same class as the Bible or the Koran. Nearly every sentence is a sacred text, quoted or acted on by devotees.' In the bibliography he further argued, 'Works on Marxism are divided, as a works on all great religions, into those by believers and non-believers.' Curiously, his royalties from this edition became one of his most steady sources of income. He also wrote for Penguin an introduction to John Reed's *Ten Days that Shook the World* in 1964, but its publication was delayed for thirteen years until the copyright veto exercised by the Communist Party of Great Britain had lapsed.

While Wroclaw made clear his commitment to democracy and hostility to Russian Cold War propaganda, nevertheless he remained critical of US Cold War propaganda. In October 1953 he wrote of *Encounter*, a journal then edited by Stephen Spender and Irving Kristol, and later revealed to have been CIA-funded, 'It is difficult to resist the suspicion that the practical impulse which brought them [the contributors] together was anti-communism.'

Alan Taylor enjoyed the notoriety and the adulation arising from Wroclaw but he was also keen to emphasise that he had not forsaken his radical views. This he did in the introduction to *From Napoleon to Stalin*. After referring to Herbert Morrison's condemnation of some of his post-war radio talks he wrote that 'they seemed too dated to reprint'. He then stated,

> All the same I should not like it to be thought that I was ashamed of the opinions which I then expressed. I still think that the alienation of the Soviet Union after the second German war was in part the fault of the Western Powers. First we were sentimental in Russia's favour; then we were sentimental against her. I would have preferred hard, though fair, bargaining, a preference founded, I think, on past experience. At any rate I thought there was a use for a historian who would discuss Russian and Communist aims with the same detach-ment as he would discuss anything else. The BBC thought otherwise; they wanted those who would expound 'the British way of life'. I hope never to be numbered in this band of secular missionaries.

The book received the kind of review from Elizabeth Wiskemann in the *Spectator* that Taylor and his publisher must have feared. She pointed out that the book did not live up to its title and that the essays had not been revised. However, she observed, 'All this is very disappointing because Mr Taylor very often is brilliant and very often states unpopular facts which it would be of major importance that the British public, or a larger section of it, should grasp.' Other reviewers praised his brilliant style and perceptive-ness, though hinted he was sometimes close to being glib. After praising the volume for 'intermittent flashes of insight lighting up a whole period rather than for any systematic presentation', E.H. Carr in the *Times Literary*

Supplement commented, 'While it would probably be fair to sum up the volume...as an obituary of Liberalism, Mr Taylor's own roots are in the liberal tradition. His inherent tendency is to believe that God is on the side of the small battalions...'[45]

After the publication of *From Napoleon to Stalin* Alan Taylor tried to evade committing his next book to Hamish Hamilton. Hamilton complained, writing that 'it will be a bitter disappointment after our success with your two most recent books, you are contemplating a change of publisher'.[46] Taylor's embarrassment was due to his very understandable desire to publish his major study of diplomatic history in a major new series of the Oxford University Press. Hamish Hamilton had to make do with another collection of essays, *Rumours of Wars* (1952). The mix was similar to *From Napoleon to Stalin* but there were weightier pieces from *English Historical Review*, *History Today* and *The Listener*. The publisher's blurb on the dust jacket stated, 'Though Mr Taylor is by profession a diplomatic historian, he excels in personal portraits.' It added,

> Those who enjoyed Mr Taylor's previous collection will rejoice again in his wit and daring, his bluntness and – perhaps – his *gaminerie*. They will be more surprised to meet the Taylor who is a serious scholar, cautious and painstaking, but still concerned to write well. He is that special English type, a hard-headed radical: no respecter of persons, a Utopian without illusions.[47]

The reception of this collection of essays was warmer than for *From Napoleon to Stalin*. What is especially notable is the considerable respect expressed for his work, and this before the publication of *The Struggle for Mastery in Europe*. Martin Wight, then Reader in International Relations at London University, commented in the *Spectator* that the essays were 'peppered with half-truths and overstatements' but that was 'the price of assiduous journalism'. However, he stated, 'With the exception of Sir Charles Webster, he is our most distinguished international historian, the one who offers the most creative interpretation of the balance of power and of tensions and limitations of diplomacy.' He also brought out a major feature of his writing: 'Mr Taylor is distinguished from so many professional historians by possessing not only a trenchant style but also a historiographical personality. This is the reason why he is so readable and worth reading.' The distinguished American historian Sidney B. Fay commented in *American Historical Review*, 'Mr Taylor is a master of brilliant paradox, startling juxtapositions, and dogmatic brevity.' In the *New Statesman* Asa Briggs, while taking exception to Alan Taylor's essay 'Crimea: The War that Would not Boil' ('the morals he draws from the story are really the preconceptions with which he begins'), gave the overall verdict: 'This is a brilliant book; almost every sentence crackles and there is often a whiff of fire and brimstone in the air.'[48]

E.H. Carr in the *Times Literary Supplement* praised five of the more substantial essays as 'solid contributions to historical thinking' and the others as 'short, sparkling pieces' for the general reader. Of these short essays, Carr wrote,

> Generally...Mr Taylor shows a flawless mastery of the art of fitting subject to style and scope. Like every good journalist he knows that an effective article is built up, at the cost of much over-simplification, round one or two outstanding points; and he makes his points so competently and sharply that the critical reader will be conscious that he has been made to think the issues over again. This is a book which deserves the overworked epithet 'stimulating'.

Carr deemed him to be 'a historian of high quality – one of the outstanding British historians today', but nevertheless felt that there was 'a certain lack of depth' in his writings.[49]

This assessment was characteristically generous on the part of Carr, given Alan Taylor's recent reviews of his work. For a short period Taylor displayed his new fervour for anti-communism in criticising Carr's work. He was unequivocal on Carr's *Studies in Revolution* in June 1950, writing, 'There is no moral condemnation of communism; and no suggestion that the failure of communism may be due to the moral revolt of mankind, not to the blunders in tactics.' He went further, moralising, 'To write about evil with detachment is to be on the side of evil.' Later in 1950 he was critical of the first volume of Carr's monumental *A History of Soviet Russia*, which was on the Bolshevik Revolution, complaining that he had 'written a history with the events left out'. More woundingly, he argued that Carr's criterion of historical judgement was success and as the Bolsheviks succeeded in achieving power he was uncritical of them. He returned to this theme when criticising Carr's *The New Society* in 1951, observing, 'Like Hegel, he tries to discover where history is going, in order to go with it; like Bismarck, he wants the governing classes to save themselves by leading the revolution and so keeping it within bounds.'[50]

The notion that E.H. Carr's history was notable for explaining and celebrating the successful was not confined to Taylor. Carr took particular exception to Isaiah Berlin's criticisms. He wrote to Berlin in 1962, 'I am still puzzled by this winner-and-loser business. When I write my History of Cricket, I shall give space to Sir Jack Hobbs' 200 centuries. And you will call me a worshipper of big scores, and say that I have consigned to the rubbish heap the nice young man who muffed that catch and lost his place in the team. This seems peculiarly English.'[51] Carr simply did not see the point of studying those who unsuccessfully opposed policies. As Richard Evans has observed, 'Carr's formative intellectual years were not spent in the ivory tower of academia but in the practical world of the diplomatic service and the Foreign Office, where nothing was of direct interest unless it made a contribution to the formulation of policy.'[52] Taylor, characteristically, stood this approach on its head, and gave his Ford Lectures at Oxford University on the opponents of official policy, dissenters and, at the time, losers; he dubbed them 'The Trouble Makers'. Perhaps it was significant that, later, Carr gave the title *From Napoleon to Stalin* (1980) to a collection of his essays.

Yet Alan Taylor did find much to admire in Carr's work. Indeed, in his contributions to the *Manchester Guardian*'s critics' choices of books of the year in 1937 he selected Carr's *Michael Bakunin*, and in a review deemed it to be one of 'the great biographies in our language' and 'a masterpiece of scholarship and wit'; and in 1939 he picked Carr's *The Twenty Years' Crisis*, of which he commented that it was 'the most important book on world politics published this year, learned, witty and free from hollow phrases, but I cannot follow Carr in believing that the problem of peaceful territorial change is the most urgent we must solve'. Taylor reverted to high praise for Carr when reviewing his second and later volumes of his *A History of Soviet Russia*. While still critical of Carr's treatment of ideas, he wrote, 'But regarded in detachment as a study of the development in Bolshevik economic policy, this is a work of the highest excellence.' He also delivered a verdict more cautious than in the past: 'For, detestable as is their political tyranny, the Bolsheviks found out how to make Socialism work.' However, he qualified this verdict by stating that it was a solution for an industrial but not an agrarian society.[53]

Carr, reconciled to criticism from Isaiah Berlin and others, was critical of Taylor whether Taylor was praising or condemning his work. Although Taylor greeted his third volume with the comment 'No more important work of contemporary history has been written in our time', Carr, when writing disparagingly of the book's reviewers, included the observation: 'A.J.P. Taylor at his most irresponsible, but at bottom the Manchester Liberal who, if driven to it, will swallow Carlyle in preference to Marx.'[54]

The third book Alan Taylor was working on in the post-war years was *The Struggle for Mastery in Europe*. He had begun work in 1941 on European diplomatic history from 1878 to 1918 after completing the first version of *The Habsburg Monarchy*. He had written some 60,000 words on 1878–1902, the part commented on by Llewellyn Woodward, before he stopped work on it in 1944 in order to write *The Course of German History*. He readily agreed to write a book for a longer time-span for Oxford University Press for a series initiated by Alan Bullock, his colleague in promoting modern history.

Bullock had discussed the need for a European equivalent of the Oxford History of England with Arthur Norrington and Dan Davin of Oxford University Press's editorial staff in April 1947. Bullock wanted a series of twelve books, with the divisions 'by times not by countries and the treatment would be economic and social as well as political and diplomatic'. He praised R.C.K. Ensor's *England 1870–1914* as a model. At a further meeting in November Taylor was suggested in regard to a volume on Germany. When it was objected that he was difficult, 'Bullock agreed he was difficult but thought him a better historian than his books so far show him'. By January 1948 Taylor was listed as the potential author for 'Europe 1848–1914' with the comment: 'A.J.P. Taylor: he is essentially a diplomatic historian and better on general than regional history. But he would need firm handling.' Six months later they had cooled on the idea of Taylor, preferring Llewellyn Woodward, but when he was unenthusiastic they made a firm approach to Taylor. Nearly a year later, in May 1949, the matter had progressed so far as Taylor informing Dan Davin, 'I am unwilling to sign a contract until I see a little more how the series is going to shape; as soon as it is clear that others will commit themselves, I am ready to do the same, but not till then.' He also specified his requirement of 'a number of maps and charts' and offered the provisional title of 'The Relations of the Great European Powers 1848–1914'.[55]

Alan Taylor, feeling he had been bested, if not cheated, in his past business deals with Macmillan and Hamish Hamilton, girded himself up in the manner of his grandfather, JT, to do business with OUP. His behaviour was almost comic; not surprisingly, he gave major offence to the gentlemanly entrepreneurs of OUP. In a letter to Dan Davin listing changes he desired made to the contract, he concluded,

> I know the Press prides itself on driving a harder bargain than any other publisher; and I have agreed to your general terms. All the more reason to meet me over the details.
>
> With any other publisher I should assume, without statement, that I am to receive galleys. With you perhaps it had better be put on record.

Davin, in commenting on this to Bill Deakin, Bullock's co-editor of the projected series, wrote of the 'harder bargain' part: 'Words fail me for this gratuitous offensiveness,' and deplored 'the atmosphere of suspicion which the whole of Taylor's letter breathes'.[56] Thereafter there was much grumbling about how troublesome Taylor could be, but he proved to be the first author in the series to be published by many years. Indeed, in October 1953 Davin suggested that Taylor be considered for the 1789–1848 volume, observing, 'Ever since we got him committed he has shown himself an admirably efficient author and both editors agree that he would do this

volume as well as he has done the one we are now printing.' After he had
been approached by Alan Bullock, Davin wryly reported, 'AJP says that he
is prepared to write all the volumes in the series provided that it is called
Taylor's History of Modern Europe edited by Bullock and Deakin.'[57]

Alan Taylor had several reasons for not writing such a major volume
on European diplomacy 1789–1848. First, there was a lack of commitment
to the series from other scholars, with not even the editors writing a
volume. Second, as Dan Davin noted in early 1955, 'He now has his Ford
lectures to interest him.' Third, his interests were moving more to the late
nineteenth and the twentieth centuries than back to the late eighteenth
and early nineteenth centuries. Fourthly, he had reason to be irritated by
the way OUP went out of its way to humour the embittered Sir Llewellyn
Woodward when he insisted on an acknowledgement for reading part of
the draft book during the Second World War be removed, even though
Woodward had read the first chapters that he had written. Woodward,
who had learned in the United States of the acknowledgement from Max
Beloff, bluntly expressed the reason for his grievance when complaining to
the Secretary of the Press: 'The offensive personal remarks which he made
with regard to the editing of the British Documents.' In the ensuing
wrangle between two stubborn men, Taylor came out of it better than
Woodward.[58] Yet, for all this, it was a pity he did not take on either this
or the 1914–45 volume. It is highly likely another such volume would
have done his reputation more good than *The Origins of the Second World
War* (1961).

Taylor's *The Struggle for Mastery in Europe* (1954) made, or at the very
least confirmed, his reputation as a major historian. It immediately became
the major book on European diplomacy 1848–1918 and long held the
field; even now, though it reads as a work of another era of diplomatic
history, it is still in print and on the reading lists of many universities'
courses. Yet in many ways it was dated even when Taylor delivered the
manuscript to Oxford University Press in July 1953. Taylor appears to have
realised this within a couple of years of its publication. In an essay entitled
'The Rise and Fall of "Pure" Diplomatic History', published in the *Times
Literary Supplement*, he wrote of the inter-war propaganda battles over
who was responsible for the First World War and observed, 'We were
asking the wrong questions, using the wrong method. We must turn from
the Foreign Offices to the more profound forces which shape the destinies
of men.'[59]

In his own major work he did little of these things. It was old-fashioned
'pure' diplomatic history taken to its finest limits. Soon after he had first
embarked on writing on the 1878–1918 period, he had been airing the view
that European diplomacy in the nineteenth century could be a subject for

someone to establish a significant reputation. He wrote, 'It is strange that...
the story of the Struggle for Mastery of Europe has never been attempted...
It would be a superb opportunity for an English historian, if one could be
found with real standards of scholarship and understanding.'[60] Like Macaulay,
his major work was a detailed, chronological narrative. Like Macaulay,
he took pains in his portraits of the leading figures, in his case Louis
Napoleon, Bismarck, Cavour and Disraeli. Where Macaulay had provided
a memorable third chapter on the social history of England in 1485,
Taylor put his economic history into eight pages of his introduction. This,
no doubt, was not what Alan Bullock had intended when he hoped his
series would integrate economic history in the coverage of its various topics.
Taylor also enhanced what could have been a dry narrative with aphorisms
as well as with his pen portraits, presenting worldly wisdom as if he was a
latter-day Sam Johnson. To give two examples: on Austrian policy in 1859
in relation to their Crimean War mistakes, 'Men always learn from their
mistakes how to make new ones;' and, on France and Tunis in 1881,
'Imperialism, in fact, was a means of enjoying the sensation of greatness
without the trouble and expense which this usually involved.'[61]

Alan Taylor later wrote to his future third wife, Éva Haraszti, '*The
Struggle for Mastery* is very scholarly, very learned, with a very good bibliography, but boring to the last degree.' A little later, when writing his
autobiography, he was more favourably inclined, commenting that it was
not only scholarly but 'entertaining as well, or so I thought when I read it
a few weeks ago'. He also observed that it

> is, I think, very good at what it claims to be: a work of detailed diplo-
> matic history. Certainly there is little about the 'profound forces' that
> were then becoming fashionable, though they came in more than
> might be thought. I agree that public opinion, economic factors and
> perhaps military calculations counted for more as the nineteenth century
> wore on. Nevertheless diplomacy...still had an autonomy which it
> lost after the First World War.[62]

In his introduction he also stated that it was 'the last age when Europe was
the centre of the world', a view which he overlooked a few years later when
he wrote an equally Eurocentric study of diplomacy leading up to war over
Poland in September 1939. As for 'the struggle for mastery', this was clearly
a struggle by Germany and so followed on from his theme in *The Course
of German History* (1945).

In taking on the Oxford University Press commission he needed to go
back in time before 1878, his original starting point. Initially, it had been
envisaged that the first diplomatic volume would cover 1789 to 1849. Alan
Taylor was emphatic on when he should begin, writing to Dan Davin, 'I must

be able to deal with 1848, on which I have written a book already.' The 1848–78 part of the book was written mostly in 1949–51. He later recalled,

> I lived entirely in the diplomatic world between the revolutions of 1848 and the Congress of Berlin, going steadily through the volumes of Austrian, French, Italian and Prussian documents that had been or were being published. Most of this was new ground to me in a detailed way. I found it fascinating and I think it is the best part of the book.[63]

He also entered territory new to him when he discussed the diplomacy of the First World War.

One of the oddest features of the book was that he carried out little or no new archival research. Some years earlier, when reviewing William Langer's two-volume diplomatic study *The Diplomacy of Imperialism 1890–1902* (1935), he had praised it as 'an exhaustive and painstaking account' yet felt it had limitations, most of which stemmed from the author only using printed sources.[64] In his autobiography he gave a strange reason for his own abstinence from archival research: 'I did not go near the Record Office: archival material from one country only would have made the book unbalanced and there was plenty of information from printed sources.' While there is some validity in this, nevertheless he could have made skilful use of British archival information to add to the quality of his work. Given that he spent a year's sabbatical leave in London working on the book, it would have been easy to have allocated time to working in the Public Record Office, then located in Chancery Lane. Although he claimed to spend no time then in the Public Record Office, at the time he made the occasional comment about going there. So it is likely he did at least check some information there. The prime reason for avoiding much archival research was to get the large book written quickly. Perhaps a lesser reason was that by this time he was enjoying being an intellectual 'personality' in London, appearing on radio and television, writing for newspapers and journals, seeing friends and acquaintances in his club, The Athenaeum, and researching in printed sources in the London Library.

Nevertheless, that *The Struggle for Mastery in Europe* should be an academic success was very important to him. He was well aware that his substantial involvement in the media made many other academics question his commitment to scholarship. He later observed that the book did him much good in academic circles and that 'thereafter no one dismissed me as a playboy'. It ensured his election to the British Academy in 1956 and several years later, in 1961, brought him an invitation to give a lecture at the Sorbonne.[65]

The Struggle for Mastery in Europe was well received by those reviewing it. Asa Briggs praised it in the *New Statesman*,

Sometimes we need to rest and think three times about his brilliant epigrams; sometimes we pine for a closer study of the economic and social background... On more than one occasion we feel the necessity for applying microscopes as well as binoculars for the detailed scrutiny of particular problems and judgements. But whatever we do will be influenced by what he has done, for he has re-opened the nineteenth century rather than closed it down.

C.W. Crawley in *History* commented,

In working out this theme, not in itself novel, Mr Taylor is original in keeping his eye relentlessly on the ball of power... and in dismissing all else as irrelevant to his purpose, and consequently in his caustic judgements upon almost every actor on the stage... this is a work of a serious, acute and extremely well read writer, who stimulates more than he annoys and redeems his acidity by his zest.

E.H. Carr was more ambivalent in the *Times Literary Supplement*. He readily recognised that the book was an eminent example of 'diplomatic history in the strictest sense' and praised it for having 'an infinity of patient detail... an outstanding book'. However, Carr regretted that Taylor did not follow Lenin's stages of imperialism, and so focus on the European Powers' division of the world and the subsequent redivision of the world through warfare. Also, as a Marxist, Carr perceived Taylor as reverting to the outlook of late Victorian and Edwardian liberalism, observing,

Mr Taylor is so eager not to be taken for a Hegelian or a Marxist – or... for a Spengler or Toynbee – and to disclaim belief in determining causes or scientifically demonstrable trends, that he sometimes comes perilously close to the old Liberal view... propounded by Augustine Birrell... or by H.A.L. Fisher, who held that there is no pattern in history at all, but merely an accidental concatenation of unrelated events.

This was indeed the way that Alan Taylor's explanations of the past were going. Carr called on the errant former Marxist to repent, writing,

If Mr Taylor would shed his distaste for ideas, recognise that history would not be worth writing or reading if it had no meaning and cease to give so many hostages to the assumption that the important explanations in history are to be found in the conscious purposes and foresights of the *dramatis personae*, he would stand in the front rank of living historians.[66]

While E.H. Carr enjoyed Taylor's company, he remained convinced that his history lacked seriousness and depth. When Carr gave his Trevelyan lectures in 1961 on 'What Is History?', discussing major interpretative issues of history, Taylor was one of many targets. Indeed, given his deliberately

simplified and provocative radio and newspaper pieces, he was something
of a sitting duck. Thus, he observed,

> The great man theory of history…has gone out of fashion in recent
> years, though it still occasionally rears its ungainly head. The editor
> [A.L. Rowse] of a series of popular text-books started after the Second
> World War invited his authors 'to open up a significant historical theme
> by way of a biography of a great man'; and Mr A.J.P. Taylor told us
> in one of his minor essays that 'the history of modern Europe can be
> written in terms of three titans: Napoleon, Bismarck and Lenin', though
> in his more serious writings he has undertaken no such rash project.[67]

The quotation came from Taylor's essay marking the fiftieth anniversary
of Bismarck's death, originally published in the *Manchester Guardian*. It had
been the penultimate sentence in the piece, with the surprise for a radical
readership of his final sentence: 'Of these three men of superlative genius,
Bismarck probably did least harm.'[68]

Like many of Alan Taylor's striking and controversial statements, he
made it more than once. In July 1950 he discussed 'How History Should
Be Written' on the radio with Harold Nicolson. Afterwards he observed,
'I much enjoyed Nicolson. Despite our agreements, our *tone* was different
enough. What an old teddy bear.' He was accurate in this: they did mostly
agree; but the programme did draw Taylor out on the subject of history.
On the subject of 'great men' in history, he said,

> The history of our century would have been very different without
> Lenin…I would say Napoleon, Bismarck, Lenin are the three who
> pulled our modern history almost out of step as it were, but I'd also
> agree on the whole that the whole pattern of society, its economic
> developments, its religious outlook, its judgement on morals, on the
> things that are worthwhile and so on, these are the things which must
> shape history and the great problem for the historian is how to bring
> this down to earth; how to relate the vague social and moral and
> intellectual forces to the actual practical facts; to show that this is the
> way in which history is made.

Asked by Nicolson if he believed in the spirit of the age, he replied,

> Yes, I think it's something the historian has…to allow for, and its one of
> the great problems. The really great artists who have been historians
> are those who have been able to make one feel…that there is some-
> thing called the climate of the age. But I would say on the other hand
> that it's extremely important for the historian to remember when he
> talks about the climate of the age…that there is no such thing, that
> there are a number of individuals who shade in together but who are

different as individuals. That is why I'm always very hesitant to accept the sort of historian who can see in everything a planned working out of a system, and who can take…a single class and say this is what the working class feels; or who can talk about a single civilisation.

He agreed with Nicolson that Arnold Toynbee's *Study of History* was an attractive book but said that he found 'the pattern much clearer and more defined than I could accept'. He also agreed with Nicolson that it was inevitable that like Macaulay, historians would have their sympathies and antipathies. On this he added, 'I always regard with the greatest distrust the historian who claims to be detached…above any feeling for human behaviour, and calls himself impartial, that in fact it seems to me that impartiality is the most dangerous form of taking sides because it has the air of misleading superiority.' Indeed, when discussing Herbert Butterfield's plea for 'technical history' in a book review, he said he rebelled at Butterfield's view: 'We must judge men according to their standards, not according to ours.' He asked,

> Is it enough to say: 'The Inquisition tortured and burnt thousands of heretics; Hitler sent millions of Jews to the gas-chamber. They did a fine job according to their light'? Pursue this argument to its logical conclusion and the only wicked Nazis were the ones who tried occasionally to spare a political opponent or a Jew.

Alan Taylor, in the programme with Nicolson, as on many other occasions, emphasised that his purpose was to write so that general readers would enjoy his books. He bluntly stated that his books should have a note at the front saying: 'Most of my judgements are in fact a great deal more dogmatic than they ought to be. You'll understand that I'm prepared to modify them if challenged but I've got to present a verdict to the general reader.'[69]

He liked to present himself in the national press and journals as a historian writing for ordinary people. For instance, in reviewing a book on French popular songs of 1789, he wrote, 'My taste in history is old fashioned and orthodox. I like narrative based on documents: no guesses, no psychological jargon, no attempt to turn history into anthropology.'[70]

A month after his radio encounter with Harold Nicolson on writing history, he wrote an essay 'History in England' for the *Times Literary Supplement*. In contrast to Carr's later verdict, he praised A.L. Rowse's series, observing that with it 'the attempt is made to relate a single figure to a wider historical theme – even though it must be added that the attempt is more praiseworthy than the achievement. The great figures remain great figures, suspended above events rather than absorbed in them.' In contrast, he was critical of G.M. Trevelyan's *English Social History*, complaining,

He regards social history as 'history with the politics left out'. This is a curious doctrine, a last gesture of defiance on behalf of the political historians of the past. For it implies, on the one hand, that politics is not a social activity and, on the other, that – while it is political to make speeches or to pay taxes or even to fight wars – there is no political significance in the way men till the fields, mine coal, write verses, or build houses. In other words, social history is no more than entertaining gossip about the past, without pattern or purpose.

After praising the work of Lewis Namier, J.E. Neale, Sir John Clapham, R.H. Tawney and others, he reflected on the dangers of class labels.

Implicit in them all is the doctrine: 'Tell me a man's class and I will tell you how he behaves.' This doctrine is essential if the history of Russia, of Germany, or of France is to be brought within a reasonable compass. Nevertheless, the historian has to bear in mind that these class descriptions – like the national labels that he must also use – are stereotypes; they are the historian's shorthand which may be safely used in order to save space, but not in order to save thought.

He concluded his survey by making a passionate plea for better style in the writing of history:

What used to be called 'vulgarization' is now equally the duty of the professional scholar. Tired metaphors and flabby sentences should be as unforgivable in a historian as a faulty reference or an inaccurate quotation; and it would be no bad thing if academic promotion were open only to those who could hold listeners or win readers. For, although history may claim to be a branch of science or of politics or of sociology, it is primarily communication, a form of literature... The historian has to combine truth and literary grace; he fails as a historian if he is lacking in either.[71]

Taylor did respond to E.H. Carr's *What Is History?* In a review in the *Observer* in 1961 he made it very clear that he admired Carr as a historian and much in his lectures on history, but commented, 'I cannot understand how knowledge of the past provides us with morality, let alone with knowledge of the future.' He stated, reaching almost postmodern minimalist claims for the subject,

My view of history is more modest than Carr's. The task of the historian is to explain the past; neither to justify nor to condemn it. Study of history enables us to understand the past; no more and no less. Perhaps even this is too high a claim. In most European languages 'history' and 'story' are the same word. So history deserves Carr's condemnation as 'literature' after all: 'a collection of stories and legends about the past without meaning or significance'.

Eleven years earlier, in the radio discussion with Harold Nicolson, he had expressed clearly his view of history as one of the humanities:

> I'm sure that history is the one way in which you can experience at second hand all kinds of variations of human behaviour; and, after all, the greatest problem in life is to understand how other people behave, and this is what history enables us to do: to see people in all kinds of situations, in all kinds of walks of life and … it makes the reader, and to a certain extent … the historian too, somebody with a fuller, much wider life than he could possibly have merely by his own private experience.[72]

By the early 1950s Taylor was much more London-orientated, not least in order to be more readily available for radio and television work. He and Margaret had enjoyed the London cultural life which had come with the central London room in 1944–45. In the late 1940s Alan Taylor made efforts to promote his wife's desire to secure recognition in her own right and not just in his reflected light or that of Dylan Thomas. In May and December 1947 he pressed Hamish Hamilton to meet her, on the second occasion stating: 'She has teamed up with a very gifted children's artist called Verney and could now show you a specimen page (letter P) in which countless things beginning with P are happening to P-people.' After Hamish Hamilton's office fire he asked on Margaret's behalf 'whether English Fairy Story is preserved'. Earlier, he also tried to promote her with the BBC.[73] Margaret's hoped-for careers as a children's author or radio script writer did not take off. Their marriage steadily collapsed.

Alan Taylor had become aware of Eve Crosland when she was a 23-year-old student attending one of his lectures in 1944. She visited him at Holywell Ford to consult him when she was considering studying for a PhD. As she knew some Russian, he recommended she research an aspect of Russian history. Instead, after impressing A.P. Wadsworth with an economic history essay, she became a journalist, working for the *Manchester Guardian* in London from 1947 to 1950.[74] After the demoralisation of finding that his wife preferred Robert Kee and Dylan Thomas to himself, Taylor was uplifted and reinvigorated by finding that he was attractive to a forceful and beautiful woman fourteen years younger than himself. Eleven weeks after raising his wife's children's books with Hamish Hamilton, he wrote to Roger Machell asking for one copy of *The Habsburg Monarchy* to have its dedication changed from Namier to 'To Eve'.[75]

Apparently, the first approach after his postgraduate advice came after an interval of a couple of years, from Eve Crosland. She wrote to him concerning her new employment. He telephoned her and took her to lunch at the 'Gourmet' in Soho, a top-class restaurant. When she had visited him at Holywell Ford she had seemed prim and severe. Now she seemed a woman of the world, wearing make-up and smoking. They cuddled in the taxi back to the *Manchester Guardian*'s London office. Soon afterwards they spent a day at Kew Gardens, followed by evenings dining out or at the opera. This broke up for a while, with him jealous that she had other male friends. He soon wanted to see her again and they resumed going out together in evenings. They also sometimes met in Brighton. It seems that, after feeling humiliated by the widespread knowledge of his troubles with Margaret, he enjoyed introducing, or referring to Eve, to those he respected and liked, notably A.P. Wadsworth, Kingsley Martin, Malcolm Muggeridge, Bill Ash of the BBC and Robert Kee (in whose Brighton house they often met). After tea with Eve in late 1949, Malcolm Muggeridge noted in his diary: 'Pretty dumb, but better looking than before' (i.e. than Margaret).[76] On her intelligence, he was very mistaken. Margaret Taylor learned of her husband's relationship with Eve in early 1948. As she was eager to be with Dylan and Caitlin Thomas, she suggested that he invite Eve to Holywell Ford. From this point on his relationship with Eve was a serious one, although there was a break in it. They went to France over Easter 1948, visiting Avignon, Apt and Paris. From October 1948, when Eve had a flat in Kensington, he stayed with her on his trips to London to broadcast for the BBC or to carry out historical research. He had been jealous in Paris when his friend Christian Megret proved attractive to her, but he had more reason in autumn 1948 when Eve had an affair with a Canadian journalist whom she compared to the film star Cary Grant. This relationship did not last long.[77]

In the summer of 1949, after his unsuccessful holiday on Belle Île with Margaret and his children, he went to Venice and then Yugoslavia with Eve. When he and Margaret split up at the start of his sabbatical year in London, he kept on Holywell Ford. He and Eve married on 23 May 1951 at Kensington Registry Office, witnessed by his media friends Robert Boothby and Philip Zec, editor of the *Sunday Pictorial*. He chose the honeymoon locations, Alassio in Italy and Étretat in Normandy – places, significantly, that he had enjoyed earlier, one with his mother and the other with Margaret and their children.[78]

He later complained that he never understood how Eve's mind worked and, similarly, she never understood him. In his case he made little effort, or, if he did, his understanding was extremely limited. He was outraged that Eve did not find his and Margaret's children fascinating and adorable. He was surprised that she wanted children of her own, even suggesting that he had enough already. Fearful of being treated again like his mother had treated his father, he aspired to be more like his grandfather, JT, who expected his wife to run the house while he pursued his career. From May 1951 his prime commitment should have been to Eve, yet he readily fell in with Margaret's suggestion that he should spend weekends with her and their children. He had envisaged Holywell Ford as the home for his children in the summer holidays when they were away from their boarding schools, presumably with Eve as a benevolent housekeeper. This was a truly extra-ordinary way to begin a second marriage. When it proved unworkable, he was clear that the culprit was Eve, who was unreasonable. This was a notable lack of empathy in a man who was generally good-hearted and considerate, as well as being a witty and entertaining companion.

Initially, the newly married Eve went to Holywell Ford and reopened it as their home. As it was a large house they took in lodgers, partly for financial reasons but partly to give her company while he was away in London. Having resigned from her *Manchester Guardian* job, she now wrote as a freelance journalist, writing pieces for the *Times Educational Supplement*, *The School Master*, *The Sphere* and *Truth*, and also for the *Oxford Mail*. As Sebastian was at school in Oxford, at the Magdalen College School, he regularly called on Wednesday afternoons to see his father. Giles later recalled of his and his brother's visits, 'She found it hard to get on with us, and we found it hard to get on with her.'[79] However, with Eve unhappy to host extended summer visits by Taylor's first family, he looked elsewhere to spend lengthy summer holidays, and also time at Easter and Christmas, with his children. He visited the Isle of Wight in 1952 and was enthusiastic. Margaret and their son Sebastian found Plevna House in South Street, Yarmouth.[80] This Margaret Taylor bought as a summer home for her family, an arrangement which further undercut his second marriage. It was hardly surprising that it was a major source of friction between him and Eve. In 1953, for instance, he was in Plevna House from at least early August to well into September and he returned on 18 December for the Christmas vacation. He added to this insensitivity to Eve's feelings by reflecting on marriage in one of the *Daily Herald* columns he wrote while he was there. The issue of 5 September 1953 had his column headed 'Why not a seven year marriage?', and in it he suggested all marriages should be dissolved automatically after seven years, as most people marry by chance and do not really know the other person. He returned to this theme on 5 December, shortly before his next stay at Plevna House.

By 1953 it was apparent that there was little point in having Holywell Ford as their home. He relinquished his lease on the property in July 1953 and he lived in his college when in Oxford. His life was more focused on the London media than before, while, as a Londoner, there was little merit for Eve in being based in Oxford. In 1954 they moved to Fordington Road,

Muswell Hill. Eve often accompanied him on his lecture tours and they were closer together than they had been in the later period in Oxford. To her delight they had two children: Crispin in December 1955 and Daniel in 1957. Again, very curiously, Alan Taylor kept his second family secret from Margaret Taylor for several years, though their elder son Giles learned of this. The arrival of the second family gave him much pleasure and also ensured that he had to think more of the interests of Eve as they raised their two sons. Also, as the children of his first marriage grew older, although he treasured their company more and more as friends, inevitably they increasingly led their own lives. He did go to Normandy with the older children of his first family and to the Vosges with Giles, but in the early to mid-1960s he went on European holidays with Eve. In 1962 they went to Italy, following Samuel Butler's route in his 1881 book *Alps and Sanctuaries of Piedmont and the Canton Ticino*, and visited Sacro Monte. The following Easter they went to Rome, where he gave a lecture, and then stayed with Lord Beaverbrook at Cap d'Ail on the French Riviera. There were other European holidays together.

Later, in 1991, when she was upset, feeling that the good years of her marriage were being undervalued, Eve Crosland made very rare comments on her private life in an interview for the *Independent on Sunday*. She said, 'All I know is that we preferred being in each other's company, we were good companions; we were *fine* sexually...' She observed, 'There was always a bundle of problems caused by Margaret, but somehow we were able to overcome those until just before our final split.' Their marriage effectively ended in 1968. John Grigg, who was working in the Beaverbrook Library in central London on the day the break occurred, recalled that Alan Taylor, as he left, 'dropped over my shoulder, without any comment, a folded-up little note. It was just like the ones schoolboys pass. It read, "I'm leaving Eve tonight. I hope you and Patsy will give her some company." That was all.' He added, 'He was an extraordinary man in some ways.' For Eve at least, their marriage ended in bitterness. Nevertheless, she never remarried, and in the 1991 interview commented, 'He was the only man I've had deep feelings for, despite all his hang-ups,' and insisted, 'I had his best years in terms of his age and health and work.'[81]

By the early 1950s Alan Taylor was very much a leading radio and television personality. Initially, this was due to his vigour as an arguer on current affairs; later it came from the impact he had as a giver of televised history lectures. In a period of only one television channel, Taylor was one of the early stars. For many he became 'the History Man', the popular face of History, just as Sir Mortimer Wheeler was that of Archaeology, Lord Kenneth Clark of Art, Bertrand Russell of Philosophy and F.R. Leavis of English Literary Criticism.[82]

His breakthrough into being a regular panel member of a major current affairs discussion programme was assisted by his vigorous anti-communist outlook. Earlier, in the late 1940s, with Communist control, or threatened takeovers, in parts of central and south-eastern Europe, he was likely to be a political embarrassment. In frustration he wrote to Peter Laslett, then head of Home Talks for BBC radio, in February 1948,

If your enterprise was at all enterprising, you'd put me on to talk on the Czech crisis, when it blows up or over – as it should in the next few days. I've expected it ever since the autumn and probably know more about it than anyone else you are likely to get.

But then you are not very successful in putting me on the air.[83]

By this time he had already annoyed many people by his vigorous criticism of the United States. In particular, he ruffled many feathers with a review of James Byrnes' memoirs. Asked by Laslett to review them he responded by correcting the proposed title of the talk, 'James Byrnes, Roosevelt's Last Secretary of State', bluntly telling Laslett: 'This won't do and you must change it,' as he was appointed by President Truman, and suggesting instead, 'America and Russia Face to Face: Mr Byrnes' Record of Eighteen Months of Peacemaking'. His robust criticism of Byrnes greatly upset Lord Vansittart, who complained to the BBC,

I was really nauseated. He was extremely offensive both in manner and matter, and also in many instances calculated to mislead the public at this grave moment.

I should be most reluctant to let this offence pass without comment. As therefore I have 67 words to spare at the end of my broadcast, I would like to add the following: 'You will see that all this is very different from the account given by Mr A.J.P. Taylor on the Third Programme on December 27. That, however, was not an analysis but an assault. I always think it was a pity that those who have no experience whatever of either politics or diplomacy should be quite so offensive to those who have.'

Vansittart added that, if such a reply to another broadcaster was not acceptable, then 'I shall have to demolish him on another occasion'. The BBC soothed Vansittart with the idea of a series entitled 'Second Opinion'.[84] After Taylor's review of Namier's *Diplomatic Prelude* in mid-January 1948, which was arranged before his broadcast on Byrnes, he was kept off the Home Service radio for nine months. He did continue broadcasting on the overseas services.

However, after his sturdy anti-communist speech at Wroclaw, he was soon given a second appearance on the Brains Trust. Chaired by Gilbert Harding, and with Kingsley Martin, Collin Brooks, and Wilson Harris,

MP, the programme was recorded on 28 October 1948 and broadcast three days later. Taylor and Kingsley Martin were the radicals, balanced by a journalist and editors of conservative outlook.

Taylor was well aware of his enhanced position for broadcasting in his new role as a noted anti-communist. On 19 October 1949 he suggested to Anna Kallin that

> a good piece would be made of *The God that Failed* by six ex-Communists, including Silone, which Crossman has edited. It would suit the BBC line of anti-Communism.
>
> I'd have liked to deliver a blast against Isaiah Berlin's propaganda for America: but I realised it would be hopeless even to suggest it.
>
> Everyone seems to have been in Trieste; I alone in the Yugoslav zone.

The attraction of broadcasting on the book for Taylor was not only in its subject matter, personal accounts of leading intellectuals' revolts from communism, but also that it involved people he knew well, in Stephen Spender and the author of its introduction, Richard Crossman. Three days later he wrote again to Anna Kallin, pressing the case for the book, this time observing, 'It would make a good theme, though it would deepen the anti-Communist stamp on me.' Nearly three weeks after he first suggested the topic, she told him H.S. Deighton had got in before him.[85] Perhaps this was a diplomatic way of declining his offer after the Byrnes review or if they had concerns about him puffing up a book by his own publisher. However, he did record a review of the book for the European English Service on 25 January 1950.

There had been much talk at the BBC of using Taylor in a general current affairs or, more specifically, international relations discussion programme on the radio. After the February 1950 general election the BBC set up a current affairs discussion programme on television based on a team of speakers. In retrospect, in 1953, George Barnes deemed the aim of this programme, entitled 'In the News', to have been 'to stimulate discussion... rather than to elucidate and inform'. To ensure lively discussion the team consisted of unconventional political mavericks of the political Left and Right. The initial programme on 26 May 1950 had Michael Foot, MP, a left-wing Labour MP, in discussion with Robert Boothby, a very able backbench Conservative MP, and W.J. Brown, an independent MP and a dissident former white-collar trade union leader.[86]

Alan Taylor, who kept up well with the people he knew at the BBC, almost certainly would have been aware that plans were being made for such a programme on television. He wrote to Mary Adams, the Head of Television Talks, who had been one of the first four television producers,

I wondered whether you ever had an opening for a lively talker on current affairs in television. As you know, I can do very nicely in impromptu discussion; and if you are ever thinking of this sort of thing, I'd be grateful if you'd think of me. I realise it is a new trade, but I'm not too old to learn it.

Grace Wyndham Goldie, then one of her television talks producers, wrote back to say that, when in December she had been asked to organise 'some illustrated debates rather than discussions' on current affairs for spring 1949, 'I had you very much in mind as a possible speaker if you could be persuaded into television'.[87]

Taylor had not met Michael Foot before he took part in 'In the News' on 25 August 1950.[88] Foot was editor of the socialist weekly *Tribune*. Alan Taylor had been on discussion programmes before with both Robert Boothby and W.J. Brown. A broadcast discussion with Brown on 11 October 1948 in the 'London Forum' series on the theme of whether democracy was capable of voluntarily rising to face its crises was deemed to be 'brilliant' by Peter Laslett, with him eagerly looking forward to a second discussion with Brown on 17 November.[89] That Taylor was judged to have performed very well with Brown and Boothby helped ensure that he was added to the 'In the News' team.

While Taylor recognised that television was 'a new trade', 'In the News' did not. Cecil McGivern, who had been appointed Head of Television Programmes in 1947, was keen to see current affairs on television develop differently from radio. However, 'In the News', originally under the direction of Norman Collins, the Controller of Television, was essentially a televised radio discussion programme, its visual impact depending much on the emotions of the participants.[90] Boothby, Brown, Foot and Taylor held each other in mutual respect but were inclined to be very argumentative and even angry in discussion. Maurice Richardson, the *Observer*'s television critic, commented on one programme that the 'team seemed to be not only on the verge of, but actually, losing their tempers with each other over the desirability or otherwise of the House of Lords. Boothby boomed, Foot fumed, Taylor trephined, with apparent real malice…Anyway it was first-class television.'

At this time Randolph Churchill wrote of Taylor, 'He has only to see a television camera in order to lose resemblance to a human being. He then becomes an angry mountebank and buffoon.' To this Taylor replied, 'Am I cantankerous? I don't think so. Assertive, yes, and ready to hit back if anyone attacks me. But without malice or bad temper.'[91] Others at that time saw him as aggressive in discussion. Yet this was what the BBC wanted for good television. Other older regulars were too gentlemanly, such as Harold Nicolson, or too quiet and formal, such as Lord Vansittart.

'In the News' attracted a large audience, roughly half of those who had television sets. It was one of the rare programmes which became a subject of popular discussion for many viewers at work. It was helped by being on in the period of only one television channel in Britain and by the increasing numbers of people possessing televisions; between 1947 and 1950 the number of combined radio and television licences in the UK rose from 15,000 to 344,000, before jumping to 4,504,000 in 1955. Regular exposure in a successful television programme made Boothby, Brown, Foot and Taylor national celebrities. Dingle Foot, who sometimes also appeared on the programme, later commented of his brother Michael, 'He was the first political leader who owed his advancement to television.'[92]

However, the success of 'In the News' proved its undoing. The leadership of the Conservative and Labour parties did not like the maverick backbenchers, Boothby and Foot, gaining massive public attention and saying what they pleased on the issues of the day on what for a period became the most prominent media forum of political discussion. By early 1951 George Barnes was under political pressure to ensure that on occasion representatives of 'the main core of opinion' in the two parties appeared on the programme. The pressure increased after Aneurin Bevan resigned from the Labour government in April 1951, given that Michael Foot was a prominent supporter of Bevan. By the end of 1951 Barnes was consulting the Conservative Chief Whip and Conservative Central Office as to which Conservative MPs might appear on 'In the News'. Others in the BBC felt that Barnes was too concerned to avoid upsetting politicians. Grace Wyndham Goldie once saw Barnes white with anger. He had been away and, on returning, found that somebody had arranged for J.B. Priestley to go on the radio. This anger was due to Priestley's wartime broadcasts having enraged Winston Churchill.[93]

Alan Taylor greatly enjoyed the cut and thrust of 'In the News'. From earliest days he had enjoyed arguing about politics. He also craved the acclaim that public prominence could bring. Harriet Lane, writing of the comedian Victoria Wood and some people's desire to be on television, commented, 'I'm on television, therefore I am. As Victoria grew up pretty much starved of attention, it was always top of her wish list...'[94] A comparison can be made with Alan Taylor, who had had male attention from his father, but had felt bitter about the lack of adulation given to him by his mother. With his regular appearances on 'In the News' being undermined by the determination of the Conservative and Labour parties to secure orthodox (or safe) MPs on the programme, Taylor looked to secure regular appearances on some discussion programme without party politicians.

He pressed Barnes in May 1952 to meet to discuss his concerns and his ideas. He wrote saying that he wanted to see him

> partly to work off some grouses, partly to air some ideas. Despite my seeming irresponsibility, I worry a great deal about the use of television…I know how anxious you are to develop the medium, and I'd like to be useful. I have no axe to grind except of course for the enormous enjoyment I get from sometimes succeeding and some- times no doubt making a mess of this exciting medium.[95]

George Barnes had lunch with him in the Athenaeum in June 1952, and they discussed the possibility of an alternative discussion programme for television. They discussed the matter further that September. The following month Taylor floated such a programme 'which won't talk about politics or at any rate talk about them on party-lines', and suggested that the regular team should include his friends John Betjeman and Malcolm Muggeridge.

Barnes wanted only one such programme which was on a radio format. He responded to Taylor's concerns about discussion becoming mere party slogans by commenting: 'Do not worry. If "In the News" becomes as dull as a party debate we shall have to take it off but I do not myself share your misgivings about this tendency.' He then went on, showing clearly he knew his Taylor, 'If we were to replace it we might certainly consider four irresponsible people on non-political subjects but the trouble is that all subjects become political in the hands of the irresponsible and I have never heard you talk for more than five minutes without making a political judgement.' He suggested that such a programme should best be 'an occasional ingredient of the party pudding', but first he wished to see how much of its audience 'In the News' could retain 'with the present dilution of the original four'.[96]

Having had his idea for an alternative programme rebuffed at least for the present by Barnes, Taylor returned to 'In the News' with a heightened feeling of dissatisfaction. The very next time he appeared, on 14 November 1952, he threw something like a tantrum when, first, he was accused of being part of a leftish organisation, which was especially galling to him as he was the only non-MP on that programme, and, secondly, when the others all spoke on party lines on a housing issue. Taylor turned his back on the other participants, ignoring an attempt by James Callaghan, then Labour front bench spokesman on transport, to bring him back into the discussion. For the last five minutes of the programme he was 'the sulky don', staring moodily at the camera.[97]

John Irwin, the freelance producer of 'In the News', was emphatic: 'Whatever the ramifications this incident may have, it was TELEVISION.' He also commented,

It seemed to me that he had not been rude to the viewers and as the other members of the panel were in a position to comment on his attitude there was no need for me to exclude him from the screen. To have done so might have given the viewers a false impression that he had left the table. From a purely technical point of view, Taylor's expression of vehement emotion was more vivid than the other speakers so I showed it from time to time.

The BBC was 'inundated with press calls' and received 254 letters from viewers after the programme. To the press Irwin observed, 'This is the kind of dramatic incident which can occur only in a GENUINE unscripted and unrehearsed controversial programme.' He also responded to questions as to whether Alan Taylor would no longer appear on the programme by saying, 'This was an expression of opinion. I don't see how the question of penalising him arises, though of course I don't know what the BBC's attitude will be.' Taylor himself told the press, '"In the News" should not be used for "party politics".'[98]

George Barnes was affronted by Taylor kicking over the traces after two private discussions with him. Moreover, Taylor had taken to being critical in public of the BBC's management. In a piece entitled 'Stuffed Shirts at the BBC' in the *Sunday Pictorial* in July 1951, he had argued that the BBC's claim to be discharging a great social function was impertinent and that it would be better if the programmes aimed to be fun rather than to do the public good. A few days after his 'In the News' protest, he spoke of the shortcomings of 'In the News' and also disparagingly of the BBC, deeming it to be obstructive of technical change as an 'evil monopoly'. As a result Barnes had no difficulty in carrying a BBC board of management meeting on 1 December in support of his recommendation regarding 'In the News' that Taylor 'should be rested from it during the next quarter or longer and that he should be so informed after his next appearance', which was on 12 December. Even before the board had agreed, complicated changes were made to the rota of the next twelve weeks to replace him:

1...Michael Foot should take his place in 1, 5, 11, a left-wing inde-pendent or ex-MP to be placed in 2, 9, 12 (suggestions to follow);
2...balance to be adjusted by a substitution of Law for Hudson in 4 or a Tory MP for Hailsham in 2 or 9, or a Labour Lord for a Labour MP.[99]

Alan Taylor's 'sacking' led to Barnes being defensive. He wrote to Taylor on 15 December explaining why he was being 'rested', yet offering a meeting early in 1953. He reassured Barbara Wootton that he was out only for three months. 'There is no ban on his appearance in Television and no reason why he should not return to "In the News".' After also providing a summary of his views on the development of the programme he ended, 'I hope this explanation will convince you as it certainly will not a more wilful don.'[100]

Taylor remained resentful. He wrote a notably rude letter to Barnes in late February 1953.

> On December 15 last you wrote and suggested to me a meeting with Edgar [Lustgarten], Cecil [McGivern] and yourself 'early in the new Year'. A day or two later the press were told that discussions with me were already in progress.
>
> It is now Lent. The new Year is over. The meeting has turned out to be a mirage, dangled before me and others to avoid a fuss. Such gestures of conciliation may be necessary for success in public life. I prefer straight dealing.

Nevertheless, he was invited to appear in the hundredth 'In the News' in April 1953; but, having been told it would include the old regular team, he declined when he found Michael Foot had been omitted. The long-promised meeting was held in late April, with a discussion over lunch of subjects which were topical but not party political, with divorce and Marxism among those mentioned.[101] Not surprisingly, Barnes did no more.

Alan Taylor soon took another public swipe at the BBC in a newspaper column. He wrote in support of Gilbert Harding, one of the stars on the panel of 'What's My Line?'. Harding, who could be irascible, rude and arrogant as well as charming, was under attack for being offensive on the television. In his *Daily Herald* column, under the heading 'Let's be rude!', Taylor called for more plain speaking. He stated, 'I have faith in democracy. People will find out what is best for them without having to rely on the good taste of the BBC.'[102]

He was very eager to take up other opportunities to participate in television discussion programmes. This was displayed in July 1953 in his response to a telegram offering him an appearance on a new programme. He replied, 'I am in the dark about the programme...But I can be in London on July 23 and 24; and shall be available for anything you have in mind.' This was a trial run of a different format for a discussion programme. The *Radio Times* introduced 'Private Opinion' with the sentence, 'A visit to the London home of Peter Smithers MP and Mrs Smithers, where Mary Grieve, Marghanita Laski, John Newsom and A.J.P. Taylor are talking about a controversial subject.' The participants dined between 7.30 and 9.00p.m., when the discussion was transmitted live. Andrew Miller Jones, who presented the programme, wrote afterwards to Taylor,

> For my own part I thought the experiment well worth doing, but any future programmes on the same lines will obviously benefit from the

lessons we learnt last time. There was undoubtedly too much over-talk, and some means of unobtrusive discipline of the speakers will have to be devised.

Although Grace Wyndham Goldie liked the trial programme, it was not turned into a long-running series.[103]

As a result of his public criticisms of 'In the News' he did not return to the programme until 30 October 1953, nearly a year after his protest in front of the camera. He even publicised his return in his *Daily Herald* column, under the heading 'TV forgives me!'. Nevertheless, he was very happy to continue to disparage the BBC, commenting in a December publication that it was a bastion of respectability and that it was 'highly tolerant of whatever does not matter'.[104] In his first appearance after his long period off he vigorously denounced colonialism in Malaya and Kenya, at the time of communist insurgency in one and the nationalist Mau Mau violence in the other.

Barnes, whose knighthood had recently been conferred in the Lime Grove television studios, was appalled. He complained to Taylor that after the programme

> we had some very moving letters from people who had in the same week lost relations in Malaya, referring to your statement of oppression of the natives and black men (why black?) by rubber planters and tin miners. I can understand such statements being made in the heat of debate but your statement, however keenly you may feel about our action in Malaya, is surely irresponsible in view of the involvement of some of your audience in a personal matter of life and death. Again, on Kenya, remarks like 'the white man has stolen the African's land in Kenya' can cause great sorrow as well as bitterness at the present time, however expressive of a point of view about colonisation which you no doubt sincerely hold.
>
> Please ponder this and do not either (a) invoke Milton and accuse me of stifling free speech, or (b) think that I would lightly criticise your style.[105]

He sent this letter to him via Edgar Lustgarten, to ensure that he had it before the second of his return appearances, on 27 November.

Whether because of his comments on colonialism or otherwise, he was 'rested' for a further five months from 'In the News'. He appeared on 'Any Questions?' in March 1954 and made his final three appearances on 'In the News' in April, May and December 1954. Thereafter, he did not appear on BBC television again until August 1960.

While his tussles over 'In the News' may well appear pig-headed to many, to him he was making a stand on his principles. He was right to see the regular team on 'In the News' being popular. According to Asa Briggs, his departure from the programme reduced the index of viewers' appreciation by five points.[106] Nonetheless, Barnes was in charge and had a case for introducing on the programme people new to the television audiences, such as Jo Grimond, Enoch Powell, Margaret Thatcher and Tony Benn. The rights, if any, of popular panellists was an interesting question. He seems to have had a view which came near to workers' control or, perhaps more probably, that BBC employees should service the wishes of the well-known, cultured upper middle class – VIPs' rule. An alternative would be in some way to let market forces select. This was in essence the appeal of commercial television to him.

Like many people who are highly sensitive to minor slights to them, he appears not to have been sensitive to the impact of his letters on Barnes. Indeed, there is a certain naïvety, given his brusque letters and public criticisms, in writing to Barnes in July 1953, 'Did you notice the account of 'It's a Problem' in the June 28 issue of *The New Yorker*? If it is as good as the TV critic made out, it must be an impressive programme, and just the sort of thing I had in mind when I talked to you last. I suppose it is red hot.'[107]

For Alan Taylor, his principled stand, as he saw it, cost him. It not only kept him off 'In the News', which he deemed to be the most enjoyable experience of his life, but it also lost him income at a time when he was maintaining two wives and four children.

Alan Taylor's relationship with BBC radio was also very mixed. He was also 'rested' on domestic radio as an international relations speaker after Herbert Morrison had denounced his 'Roots of British Foreign Policy' talks in December 1946. He tried to move into other areas. After the opening of the BBC Radio's Third Programme in September 1946 Alan Taylor wrote to George Barnes, 'I am anxious to escape from the controversies of political commentary into the more serious tasks of history and I think I have some suggestions that might appeal to you.'[108] He followed this up by marking what he deemed to be outstanding lectures on the Oxford University list of lectures for 1946–47, including Asa Briggs on Bright, J. Stevens Watson on Disraeli and Robert Ensor on Gladstone. He suggested a series of talks on Prime Ministers and also one of historians on past historians. He made clear his willingness to lecture on Prime Ministers, adding the patronising proviso: 'But I can't run in harness with the youngsters, Briggs and Bullock, unless I have one of the seniors to keep me company. I hope you'll forgive this measure of reinsurance in the academic world.' He hoped to secure as the senior speaker one of a list including Herbert Butterfield, Robert Ensor and Lewis Namier. As for historians, he wrote, 'I'd like to talk on Sorel (Albert, not Georges), but shd. probably

find myself doomed to Treitschke. I'd also offer Friedjung, the Austrian.'
He was invited to act as general editor of a series on Prime Ministers.[109]
He soon found it was hard to find willing speakers, let alone senior figures;
Namier was too busy, Butterfield only willing to speak on a historian and
A.L. Rowse pulled out of discussing Sir Robert Peel.

Alan Taylor gave the first and last lectures in the Prime Minister
series, on Lord John Russell and Lord Salisbury. Both lectures have stood
repeated republication, yet – as Kathy Burk has rightly observed of the
first – 'the talk aroused disproportionate anger and disgust in the BBC'.[110]
This was at least partly due to Barnes' anger at any broadcaster who upset
the politically powerful, and Alan Taylor had notably done this three
months earlier (and after his part in the Prime Minister series was beyond
recall). Barnes' disapproval, however, also reflected his very real interest in
broadcasting. He wrote to Taylor detailing his substantial views, observing
that his two talks

> contributed nothing, in my opinion, to the very difficult question of
> how to treat history over the radio ... these talks did not make me alter
> my opinion that a lecture, however skilfully potted, will never obtain
> the interest of the critical listener in history. A lecturer in a university
> or with a WEA class can stimulate the interest of his audience by
> paradox or any other device, knowing that its members will form their
> opinions not only from what he says but from reading the books set
> for the course or the examination. The radio audience is different. It
> is made up of people with widely differing knowledge who listen for
> widely differing purposes. A provocative talk about Pitt *may* send the
> listener to check his impression with Rosebery or Holland Rose but it
> is more likely, if he is ignorant, to foster a prejudice. History is surely
> not a matter of snap judgements and if radio listening is to contribute
> anything to the critical evaluation of historical events there is a lot of
> hard thinking to be done about the method first of all.

Taylor felt this was too negative a view of presenting history on the
radio. He defended his two talks, pointing to the praise in *The Listener* and
the *New Statesman*, and observing,

> I had hoped ... that my talk would succeed in starting people off
> thinking about the subject, and my aim ... was to stimulate by new
> thought not merely by provocation. As you say, a fool can be provo-
> cative; and I try not to be a fool. My effort on Salisbury was meant as
> a serious attempt to understand Victorian Conservatism at its moment
> of transition; and for that matter Russell was meant to be a study of the
> transition from Whiggism to Liberalism. I assumed that I must aim at

the same level as, say, Huis Clos or Les Noces; and I don't honestly see what other assumption one can make when writing for the Third Programme.

He was also able to point out that his original plan had been for an introductory programme which asked a series of questions and a final talk which would assess the extent to which they had been answered. This, as he pointed out, had been firmly rejected.[111]

Three years later he unsuccessfully tried to get the BBC to take up a talk on whether we learn too much from history. He wrote,

It is provoked partly by my beginning to write a survey of international relations since 1848, partly by reading The Discourses of Machiavelli, which set out to discover the universal rules of politics from Livy. But can they be found?

... But all I'd be prepared to say of history [is] that it tells you about the past. From this there may be analogies useful or even amusing; not, however, real guides. Probably horizontal patterns are more important than perpendicular ones. I mean that Hitler had more in common with Churchill or Roosevelt than he had with Bismarck or Metternich.[112]

After the Prime Minister talks his main opportunities on BBC domestic radio were book reviews. Here, after the Wroclaw Congress, he aired his now highly critical reflections on communism. In his broadcast on The Stalin–Tito Correspondence in January 1949 he was characteristically irreverent to most points of view and yet very perceptive on Stalin's response to Tito. He commented

Communism is a creed held by millions of people all over the world; in fact it is the only living religion which can command fanaticism on a mass scale. A man is not won over to Communism by argument: he is converted, 'saved', and from that moment his mind is closed to reason. He is ready to do whatever authority prescribes...

Communism is a great secular religion; it aspires to be a universal church and offers to everyone the choice only of conversion or extermination – just like Islam or the Roman Church in its days of supreme power.

He argued that communism would be weakened by 'the revolt from within', much as the Roman Catholic Church was by Luther: 'The only appeal from dogmatic authority is to the judgement of the individual.' He concluded that the best such comparison with Tito, however, was Henry VIII: 'Henry VIII, too, was strictly orthodox in point of doctrine, indeed Defender of the Faith; only he wanted to be his own Pope.'

Taylor concluded, 'The best outcome for the eastern European countries would be communist states independent of Moscow and checking Moscow as Tito does. More, the best thing for us and for the rest of the world in general is that we should be America's Tito.'[113] He was not far from the views of Henry Sara in this call for a policy of 'neither Moscow nor Washington'.

Later in 1949 he gave a talk which was in effect the partner of his thinking on Tito and Stalin. This was a review of the biography of Benjamin Constant by Harold Nicolson, in which he gave brief reflections on democracy and liberalism and so the key to his own political views. He commented,

> Of course there's a close relationship between Whiggism and lib-
> eralism...But there was also a difference...The Whigs, from Locke
> to Burke, thought that government ought to be restrained; Constant
> thought that government...ought to be criticised. Goethe, who with
> all his genius was very much a man of order, regarded criticism as
> a mark of the devil and makes Mephistopheles say: 'I am the spirit
> who always denies.' A hundred years later, when the liberal idea
> was victorious, Victor Hugo was content to make the principle of
> Mephistopheles his own. When asked his politics, he replied: 'I'm
> against, je suis contre.' Bakunin carried this outlook to its logical con-
> clusion. When he was asked what he would do if the utopian society
> he dreamed of was established, he answered: 'I should at once begin
> to pull down everything I had made.'

He concluded, 'What Constant's career suggests above all is that the liberal intellectual must have no loyalties except to the spirit of free enquiry.'

In turning away from most of his former hard Left beliefs, Alan Taylor turned towards the radicalism of his grandfather JT's era. At this time he had not fully adopted his 'trust the people' populist mantle. Indeed, in this broadcast he praised 'liberal' as an attitude of mind and appealed to middle-class values, observing,

> We often talk about our democratic system, as though that were the
> essential thing...Democracy, if it means anything, means the rule of
> the majority, of the poor, of the masses; and that's not a system likely
> to produce the qualities we prize. Unchecked democracy wouldn't
> have much respect for the rights of minorities, wouldn't care about
> freedom of thought or expression, wouldn't trouble to do things
> according to fixed rules, according to law...No, it's liberalism which
> sums up the virtues of tolerance and criticism and discussion which
> are what we value.[114]

Alan Taylor continued to broadcast book reviews on the BBC's Third Programme during the 1950s. He also appeared occasionally on 'Any Questions?'. He was successful in suggesting in July 1951 that he give a centenary talk to be entitled 'The Man of December' on Napoleon III's coup d'état of 2 December 1851. 'No one has yet done Louis Napoleon properly – not that I am likely to.' He was invited to give 'a dazzler about the Napoleon III coup d'état on December 2'.[115] There were no rumbles on high after this talk. In March 1952 he offered a talk on John Bright to mark the tercentenary of the Society of Friends, observing: 'I am, with G.N. Clark, the only historian of Quaker training (and Clark is ashamed of it) and a school-fellow of Bright; so for once I'm qualified.' This was declined as programmes marking the tercentenary were under way, and it was claimed that 'the Quakers do not seem to love [Bright] as much as they do some other Friends'. However, his next historical talk which was not a book review, broadcast on 31 March 1954, was 'John Bright and the Crimean War', a shortened version of a public lecture he gave in Manchester.[116]

While television and domestic radio made Taylor a household name, the bulk of his broadcasts were overseas. The appeal for him was in a large part the opportunity to comment on and debate with others current international issues and also to take part in quiz programmes, not being sufficiently in demand for a regular place on television successes such as 'The Brains Trust' or 'What's My Line?'. It was also in the steady and substantial addition to his income, as, in the early 1950s, he was funding or helping to fund two wives, four children and accommodation in Oxford, London and the Isle of Wight.

From 1945 he frequently spoke on international relations on overseas broadcasts. After a dip in the number of his appearances in 1946 and 1947 (to three and seven) he appeared much more often from 1950 onwards (that year 25 times). This volume of appearances was assisted by one of his able former students, Keith Kyle, becoming producer for a series of talks on the North American Service from the autumn of 1951 until the summer of 1953. Taylor broadcast 40 editions of 'London commentary', four-minute fifteen-second pieces on current issues, in the ensuing thirteen months, and a further 40 by autumn 1955. These alone brought him in over £750. Keith Kyle recalled,

I initially commissioned one talk but I ran into difficulties with him, not the BBC. He would only be interested if he got a guarantee that he would appear once a week. I knew that to obtain this I would need to refer the request upward and, knowing his controversial reputation... I though this unwise. Moreover, I realised that I was taking a bit of a risk in having him on at all on my responsibility.

I therefore told him that I didn't have the authority to do what he asked but I would give him a private assurance that, provided there were no rows, I would in practice have him on regularly. I also briefed him against one-sided advocacy. On the day of his first broadcast he arrived with very little time to spare and with no script. This was not encouraging. However, he asked for a pad, took out his pen and wrote with his neat handwriting and with no hesitation or alteration an admirable script of exactly the right duration. It was scrupulously balanced. My only comment was that in a couple of places the listener required some transition, however brief, between two brilliant ideas. With a quick movement of his pen he supplied what I asked.[117]

John Grist also worked for BBC External Services in 1951–53, dealing with the North American broadcasts. Taylor's draft scripts came to him, and he passed them on for approval. It seems the weightier pieces were vetted in Whitehall. Sometimes they returned with comments on them. Then Grist saw Taylor before the broadcast and they went through these comments. He recalled that Taylor used to explain clearly why what he had written was alright, before amending the script and giving it on air.[118] Taylor used to say he was willing to take things out of scripts but would not be told what to put into them.

He enjoyed the opportunity to participate frequently in discussion programmes. He appeared on 'London Forum' twenty times between 1948 and 1958. The programme varied from discussions on major international issues to lighter general interest topics. The former kind included 'Is the German Menace Over?' (in which Taylor promptly said it was not, July 1948) and 'Is Russian Policy based on Communism or Imperialism?' (September 1950). In April 1952 he discussed 'The Foreign Policy of the Soviet Union' with W.J. Brown. Later, he discussed such general topics as 'Why Do We Travel?' (August 1953), 'Does Civilisation Depend upon the Middle Classes?' (August 1955), 'Red Brick Universities' (May 1956) and 'Wine and Food Snobbery' (December 1956). He also appeared on three of the 'Question Time' programmes broadcast on the Far Eastern Service. In these he argued with leading politicians, such as Hugh Gaitskell, Lady Astor and Lord Hailsham, and media figures, such as Kingsley Martin, W.J. Brown and Dr Jacob Bronowski. However, most of his 180 overseas broadcasts in the decade 1945–54, the peak years, were on his own with him giving his comments on the international events of the time. In one, in 1953, he was able to return to the issue of Trieste, pointing out that the West had used it to boost the Italian anti-Communists but then found Tito in revolt from Moscow. He concluded, 'It could be settled quickly if Italy and Yugoslavia were on good terms. But they'll never be on good terms until it is settled.'[119]

Alan Taylor's television fame also brought him lucrative opportunities in the national press. Philip Zec, the editor of the *Sunday Pictorial*, hired him to write a regular column (which appeared once or twice a month). This was at first captioned 'A million people see and hear this man on Friday nights'. He wrote much on international affairs, mostly urging moderation in responding to the Soviet Union. He argued in February 1951 that 'the world balance, far from moving in Russia's favour, is moving against her'. After the defection to Moscow of two British Foreign Office officials, Guy Burgess and Donald Maclean, he argued that greater harm would be done than anything they revealed by launching witch-hunts as these would 'catch the people whom the communists most hate: the people of independent judgement who try to make up their own minds, without fear of communists or of anyone else'. He followed this up by a piece headed 'I back America', in which he praised the Marshall Plan and other aspects of the United States' policies, condemned its race relations and concluded that the country revered freedom and that it had 'stuck to the principles of the Declaration of Independence'. This and later reflections on the US for the *Daily Herald* belie later critics' claims that he was entirely anti-American. In another piece, reflecting on a century of change from 1851 to 1951, he deemed the most exciting feature of 1951 to be the fact that in China, India and Africa 'they are shaking themselves free from slavery to nature and from slavery to their white exploiters'. His *Sunday Pictorial* pieces mostly dealt with weighty issues, rather than populist causes, though he did rejoice in the dwindling support for organised religion (to the outrage of some readers) and condemned the British licensing laws. When, after thirteen months, Hugh Cudlipp replaced Philip Zec as editor, he did not take any more articles by Taylor during the rest of his contract.[120]

Nearly a year later Taylor resumed his career as a newspaper columnist by writing a weekly column for the *Daily Herald*, the Labour movement's newspaper. While the *Sunday Pictorial* had a circulation of 5,170,000 in 1951, the *Daily Herald*'s was then at 2,071,000. Taylor's *Daily Herald* pieces were generally lighter and more populist in tone. A lot appeared to be controversial for the sake of it, not least the suggestion that the House of Commons be selected at random from the population, encouragement for smokers to ignore health warnings, and various comments on women which at the time would have been regarded as sexist (such as, in 'Marriage is a soft option', stating that women get married in order to get 'a man who will keep them in idleness for the rest of their lives'). Yet he also called for complete equality for women, including equal pay.

However, among the 164 *Daily Herald* columns he did express liberal and sometimes radical views. He repeatedly condemned colour prejudice, including hostility to West Indian immigrants to Britain and to mixed marriages, and colonialism. He condemned the wasting of resources, such as electricity, and called for more cycling and less use of cars, especially for short distances and in cities. He called for the abolition of privilege in education, with public schools abolished and the buildings used for adult education, and the closing down of Oxford and Cambridge, on the grounds that they 'are the most effective way ever invented of taming the rebellious and discontented'. He also discussed nationalism in Scotland and Wales as well as in Europe, and declared, 'National freedom is as important as economic freedom or the freedom of individuals.'[121]

He continued to warn against Germany and to condemn communism. In January 1953, at the time of the trial in France of those accused of the Second World War massacre at Oradour, he wrote that the Germans had not changed since Hitler's time: 'Our country is within sight of committing a great international crime. That crime would be the rearmament of Germany.' He added, for good measure, 'The massacre of Oradour will happen again if Germany is rearmed.' The following year he warned that Germany as an independent power would be on the side of neither Russia nor the West: 'She'll be on the side of Germany.' However, by May 1956 he had to admit that the German problem had gone, though, he added, at least while Germany was divided. While Taylor was at the fore in expressing such sentiments, he was far from being alone. Aneurin Bevan and several of his supporters, including then Harold Wilson, issued a Tribune pamphlet *It Need Not Happen: The Alternative to German Rearmament* in about 1954, and as late as 1963 Harold Wilson wrote in the *Sunday Express* an article entitled 'Danger!…the German finger is reaching for the H-bomb trigger'.[122]

Alan Taylor also made clear his opposition to the Soviet Union in the early to mid-1950s. In an article in *Picture Post* at the start of 1953 he commented, 'Korea showed a real war could be as much a stalemate as a cold one…The cold war is here to stay.' He argued, 'Democracy will only win if it believes in the superiority of its ideas for all men, whether White, Black, Brown or Yellow,' and concluded, 'We must hold on until Communism destroys itself.' The following year he informed his *Daily Herald* readers that 'co-existence' between communism and the West was a sham: 'Communism and freedom can't live together, sooner or later one will destroy the other.' After Stalin's death in 1953 he wrote that he was disgusted by 'the sight of Stalin's creatures in Russia turning against him and loading all their crimes on his dead body', and added that the conduct of the Communist leadership in the satellite countries was even worse. He was unamused by those in Britain who saw Nikolai Bulganin and Nikita Khrushchev, who succeeded Stalin, as jokes. He commented, 'They are two men of sinister power who have fought their way to the top by the most unscrupulous means and now control the fiercest dictatorship in existence.' After Khrushchev denounced Stalin's crimes, Taylor jeered at the apparent surprise expressed by Communist leaders round the world at Khrushchev's speech. After a visit to the Moscow Circus in May 1956, when it was in London, he predicted that 'one day soon 200 million gay Russians will clear the poker-faced Communists out and have the circus all day long'. His anti-communist credentials by this time were sufficiently robust for him to be invited to write a three-part account of 'The Birth of Red Russia' for the 'patriotic' weekly *John Bull* in April 1956.[123]

While condemning Soviet Communism, he took pains to contrast US and UK democracy very favourably with it. After deploring the activities of Senator McCarthy in the United States, he said that, nevertheless, 'the United States remains a country where there is trial by jury and more freedom of expression of every sort of opinion than anywhere else in the world – including England'. He also praised democracy in Britain. He stated that, for all its antiquated procedures and other faults, 'the House of Commons is the greatest institution in the world…It represents freedom.' In contrast, he wanted the House of Lords abolished: 'If the Second Chamber agrees with the first, it is unnecessary. If it disagrees, it is undesirable.' As for monarchy, he observed, 'A constitutional King is better than the politburo.'[124]

In his newspaper articles, as on the radio and television, he portrayed himself as a disillusioned democratic socialist. He often preached an idealistic socialism which was a long way from his own lifestyle. His advocacy of the abolition of Oxford and Cambridge and equal pay for all are examples, as was his condemnation of the craving for publicity, which he deemed a major bad feature of the time! He looked back to utopian socialism which had more to do with William Morris, or possibly the early days of the Independent Labour Party, than the Labour Party. In 1954, in regretting the loss of what he believed to be the early idealism of the Labour Party, he observed, 'In my opinion, socialism is a way of life, not a programme of social reform. It has to do with men's motives, not with rewards.' On his 48th birthday he commented in his *Daily Herald* column on his loss of faith in seeing a socialist Britain during his lifetime and on his disillusionment with Soviet Russia. Occasionally, he would speak up for international socialism, arguing that it was the 'way of giving the world peace, security and prosperity' and, in particular, of avoiding nuclear war.[125] Such comments were the reason why his former friend, A.L. Rowse, referred to him as a Trotskyist.

Looking back on his *Daily Herald* pieces in 1980, he was critical of them. He commented, 'I am rather ashamed of all those terrible *Daily Herald* articles I wrote. The trouble was that they were rush jobs. I only had a couple of hours in a newspaper office in which to write them.' He commented that his contract had been terminated 'because he was too irreverent and not sufficiently party-line for the trade union establishment which controlled the paper'. An alternative explanation would be that he had simply run out of steam after several years, the pieces not being as fresh and lively as they had been earlier. For a period, between writing for the *Daily Herald* and the *Sunday Express*, he later recalled that 'he considered writing for any paper that asked him'; and so he wrote on 'The Rising Generation' for *Reynolds News* in late 1956 and on 'Our Destiny' for the *Sunday Graphic*, and on the need for real choice between parties in British politics for the *News Chronicle* in late 1957.[126]

While he was delighted with his ability to earn money as a journalist for the popular press, holding a National Union of Journalists' membership, his first love remained writing for the *Manchester Guardian*. As well as writing leaders, Taylor had enjoyed writing short feature articles for the *Manchester Guardian*. Increasingly these became commemorative historical essays. He had written on 'The Entente Cordiale' on its fortieth anniversary in 1944 but his big opportunity came with the centenary of the 1848 revolutions. On 17 October 1947 he asked,

> Have you any thoughts on the revolutions of 1848? I think they ought to be celebrated – I suppose the best dates would be February 24 for the French revolution; and March 13 for the revolutions in central Europe. But both Germany and Italy deserve separate treatment. Would you like a couple of articles (or more)? Or alternatively a leader at the appropriate moment – both article and leader if that isn't too greedy?

A.P. Wadsworth readily agreed that there should be several articles, observing 'altogether a harvest for historians'.[127] Taylor provided '1848: Year of Revolution' for the issue of 1 January 1948, the French revolution and 'Vienna and Berlin' on the dates suggested, with a fourth – 'The Slav Congress 1848: Central Europe and the Habsburgs' – in June and a fifth, 'Francis Joseph: The Last Age of the Habsburgs', in December. In addition, he also commemorated the fiftieth anniversary of Bismarck's death and of the Fashoda incident in August and September. Moreover, the *Manchester Guardian* published fifteen of his book reviews that year. It was indeed a profitable, not least as these essays were reprinted many times in his books of essays, as well as a prestigious connection.

He continued to write historical essays during the rest of Wadsworth's editorship. He wrote one piece a year in the next three years, marking the fiftieth anniversaries of the outbreak of the Boer War and the death of Queen Victoria, and the death of Thomas Masaryk. In 1953 he wrote on Lord Salisbury on the fiftieth anniversary of his death, and the following year to commemorate the centenary of the Crimean War. In the last months of Wadsworth's editorship, in 1956, he marked the centenary of James Keir Hardie's birth and the 150 years since Charles James Fox's death. On Wadsworth's retirement on 31 October Taylor paid tribute to him as 'a great editor…His Radical spirit has never faltered even when he has stood alone.'[128]

With Wadsworth's death four days later, he lost not only a father figure but his main patron at the *Manchester Guardian*. They had differed over the Soviet Union at the end of the war and that had brought Taylor's leader writing to an end. 'Wadsworth was already fighting the Cold War,' he later recollected. 'I was against this attitude.'[129] This did not harm their friendship, which partly rested on their shared radical view of British and European history.

After Wadsworth's death his contacts with the *Manchester Guardian* faded out. He wrote three more commemorative pieces in his area of expertise, marking the fiftieth anniversaries of the Anglo-Russian entente in 1957 and the Agadir Crisis in 1961 and the twentieth anniversary of Munich in 1958, as well as on Oliver Cromwell 300 years after his death. Otherwise, his only other *Manchester Guardian* article in this period was a piece in 1958 discussing the current lack of sharp controversy in British politics. His reviewing for this newspaper dropped off after 1959, ending with one review a year in 1963 and 1964. He recalled later that in his early *Sunday Express* contracts he had ensured that he was allowed to keep writing for the *Guardian*, but as that newspaper no longer asked him to write much he let that clause in his contract lapse.[130]

His large output of book reviews was unaffected by the fizzling out of his relationship with the *Guardian*. He was reviewing very regularly for the *Observer* and the *New Statesman*. So much so that Arthur Crook, who was assistant editor then editor of the *Times Literary Supplement* between 1951 and 1974, found that Taylor could only do a few of the books he had wanted him to do because of his contract with the *Observer*. Taylor reviewed for the *TLS* between 1946 and 1965 and then again from 1971 to 1976. With the *Observer* he was a successor of George Orwell, and joined Harold Nicolson, writing reviews from 1953 until ill-health incapacitated him in 1984; and, along with the *New Statesman* (to which he was also contracted) and, less frequently, *The New York Review of Books* from 1964, this was where a large public read his views on major historical books of the day.[131]

Alan Taylor used his media fame, which made him 'the History Man' to much of the general public, to help promote history. He was one of a galaxy of historians who supported the journal *History Today* from its launch in January 1951. G.M. Trevelyan, the most popular of historians then, wrote a message for the first issue which included, 'History, today, has a very large popular audience, eager for serious, scholarly exposition of the past, provided it is so written that he who is not a professional may read it.' Taylor very much saw this as an important role he could play. He went out of his way to commend the new journal. He also wrote for it, providing 'Crimea: The War that Would not Boil' for its second issue and 'Lord Palmerston' for its seventh, and later writing reviews of books on the League of Nations and Napoleon in April and May 1952.[132]

From the 1950s he was seen by the media as the man who was notably good at presenting history to the general public. Thus, for instance, a BBC producer wrote in a memorandum concerning a centenary talk on the Treaty of Paris 1856, 'Any excuse for a talk by Alan Taylor on an historical topic is worth taking.' He also came to see himself as the Great Communicator of history, eager to transmit major findings by others. This was very much so in the case of Fritz Tobias' work on the Reichstag fire, first published in *Der Spiegel*. When he wished to give a BBC radio broadcast on the subject, he was bluntly told, 'The story seems to me to be too slight and it seems an awful waste of your talents on a talk which, in the end, only repeats the detective work of someone else, and allows you only a few comments.' Nevertheless, he wrote on the subject for *History Today*, spoke on it on the BBC television programme 'Tonight' on 18 November 1963 and wrote a brief introduction to the English edition of Tobias' book.

As well as backing *History Today*, Alan Taylor was also strongly supportive of the Historical Association. While he had spoken for it before the Second World War, after it he became one of its most popular lecturers. He usually offered Historical Association branches commemorative topics or the subjects related to his current writing. In the 1950s he gave 'The Origins of the First World War' several times, including at Southampton in early 1953, Oxford in autumn 1955 and Lincolnshire in 1956–57. He spoke on 'Sarajevo' to the Worcester branch in autumn 1957, to fit a series on 'Conspiracies', and gave it again in Coventry a year later. At Bristol in early 1957 he spoke on 'Queen Victoria', a person he had written on for the *Manchester Guardian* fifty years after her death. He appears to have had two special lectures geared to Historical Association audiences: 'Do Men Think?', presumably not a proto-feminist piece, given at Ealing in autumn 1955, the Isle of Wight in April 1956 and Bolton in early 1958; and 'Taking the Mind out of History', at Bournemouth and Hertfordshire, both in early 1957. His lecture at Bolton drew the branch's largest ever audience, over 200 people attending. Afterwards, he and Sebastian went to the headmaster of Bolton Grammar School's home, where he held forth to a circle of admirers. As a major attraction, some Historical Association branches proclaimed his coming more than a year in advance, the Burnley branch, for example, noting in its 1957–58 report that 'a big event is scheduled for the 11 December 1959, when Mr A.J.P. Taylor is to visit us'. In the case of the North Devon branch they noted more than a year before that, in August 1957, Alan Taylor would be lecturing 'sponsored jointly by the branch and the Devon Festival of the Arts'.[133]

He enjoyed lecturing to these enthusiastic, largely middle-class audiences. The Historical Association branches were made up of people similar to his wartime audiences and a substantial part of his radio and television audiences. Like many other bodies in the 1950s, several Historical Association branches ran their own Brains Trust evenings; they also went eagerly on trips to churches and cathedrals, much as Taylor did. In 1956, at its fiftieth anniversary, Taylor warmly praised the Historical Association in his column in the *Daily Herald*.[134]

With his increased fame from his radio and television appearances and his writing for the popular press, Taylor also enjoyed giving notably confident and polished performances when lecturing at Oxford. The wider acclaim outside the university world boosted his self-esteem within the university, while his university lectures gave him a regular opportunity to practise his craft. The two fed each other. Beneath his supremely confident exterior there always was shyness and a need for reassurance.

In the late 1940s and early 1950s he gave international history lectures which, in published form, became *The Struggle for Mastery in Europe*. Alastair Parker, in 1993, recalled these as superb lectures. He said Alan Taylor was a consummate showman. He entered Schools at five past nine and strode vigorously into the lecture room. Reaching the front, he put the lectern aside with a great flourish. He then gave his lecture with no notes. At 9.55, with exaggerated moves, he pulled out a watch, ended his lecture and strode out. Parker said he was mightily impressed, and when he went to Manchester University in 1952 he too marched into a lecture theatre and gave improvised lectures with no notes. However, some years after he returned to Oxford, he heard Taylor lecture twice on Beaverbrook within two months. He was amazed to find that he heard the same lecture each time, even down to the 'spontaneous asides', his characteristic 'I was going to say x, but I shall say y' observations. He spoke of this to some of his colleagues at Magdalen, who told him that Alan Taylor took great pains with his lectures, memorising and practising them before delivering them. Alastair Parker concluded, 'Thus Alan's lectures were a great theatrical performance; like those of the great comedians, apparently spontaneous but in reality carefully prepared.'[135]

Bill Rodgers, an undergraduate at Magdalen between January 1949 and mid-1951, recalled of Taylor's highly popular lectures,

I admired his ability to recapture with a provocative anecdote the attention of his audience when it appeared to wander. His eye would roam over his listeners to detect anything less than rapt attention. Then his voice would rasp and squeak as it changed gear, and we would become his captives again.[136]

Another student of that period, David Perkin, also remembered his showmanship as a lecturer, adding to Alastair Parker's recollections that he used to sit on a table at the front of the hall, twiddling his bow tie and just talking to his audience. According to him, Taylor was much respected by many students for his enthusiasm for history, his steady stream of publications and his very considerable reputation as a hard worker.[137]

His impact appears to have been less in supervising undergraduates. While he assiduously carried out his duties, he preferred students to opt for work in his own research areas. If they chose another area, he would agree, saying with good grace: 'OK, if you really want to do it.' He was sometimes terse with the less able or lazy. Generally, though, undergraduates found him impressive and liked him.[138]

However, many of his fellow academics were far less impressive. Many distinguished historians were wooden before television cameras. Some were also poor performers on radio; in contrast, as an Australian broadcaster emphatically told Henry Loyn, Taylor was 'the ideal [for] putting history across on the radio – he had all the necessary virtues'.[139] Those who deplored academics doubling as television performers, those who aspired to television fame but never had the opportunity, and those whose lacklustre performances terminated their encounter with television were all likely to be critical of Taylor. Moreover, his revelling in his media acclaim angered or irritated many.

There were also doubts about his political stances. Bill Rodgers observed, when recalling that he and Taylor differed over Russia's responsibility for the Cold War, that 'it was difficult to know what he really cared about and whether his expressed views were serious or contrived'. Francesca Wilson, who had recently written on the former Habsburg lands, visited Catherine Karolyi at Holwell Ford in August 1949. She wrote that, while she admired *The Course of German History*, 'I hate the flippancy with which he talks of politics and the unscrupulous way he veers about and suits his sail to the wind'. She added that an Oxford friend of hers said that if Britain had been occupied 'he would have been the first to become a Nazi'. Of this she wrote, 'This may be too severe – but he does not inspire confidence.'[140] His switch from warm supporter of Soviet Russia to anti-communist had not enhanced his reputation for political consistency and raised suspicions of delayed opportunism. However, the lack of genuineness that Francesca

Wilson detected in both Alan and Margaret Taylor in August 1949 may well have been at least partly due to their efforts to disguise their impending marital breakdown.

Alan Taylor's friendship with A.L. Rowse collapsed in these years. Rowse was notably thin-skinned and a fallout was probably inevitable, not least as Taylor received increasing public adulation. It probably occurred over his book reviews, which for Rowse, like Namier, needed to be adulatory. Taylor had reviewed Rowse's *The Spirit of English History* in 1943, hitting the right tone: 'Fascinatingly readable, a triumph of restraint and artistry...If it errs it is in not attempting to modify traditional views according to the evidence of more recent historians.'

However, ten years later Rowse was irate when Taylor was dismissive of a history of France that Rowse had translated and had completed. Rowse's biographer, Richard Ollard, noted of Lucien Romier that he was 'so far removed from Rowse's own understanding of the recent past that he some-times found it necessary to rewrite his author'. Taylor complained that Romier provided a history of the French monarchy not the French people, and observed that Romier's 'historical law', which attributed great authority to monarchs who sided with the people against the nobility, was the author's own invention. He concluded by commenting on Rowse's part in the book,

> Mr Rowse was delighted to discover a French historian who shared his enthusiasm for the values of the Elizabethan age. He has translated Romier's book admirably. He was, however, ill-advised to carry on the story from 1789 to the present day, partly from Romier's draft, partly on the basis of his own prejudices and whims. It is difficult to decide whether Romier's monarchical cynicism or Mr Rowse's blustering denunciations of everybody are more out of place. The reader would have a better idea where he was if he had been told that Romier ended as a Minister in Pétain's Government at Vichy.[141]

An enraged Rowse wrote an immediate and vitriolic letter to A.P. Wadsworth as editor of the *Manchester Guardian*. Wadsworth wrote to Taylor saying he had had 'a very abusive letter' from him and that his 'less libellous sentences' stated that only three chapters were by him (Rowse), which 'merely completed the book from 1885 to 1944'. Wadsworth added that he would print this part of his letter but he would 'certainly leave out the accompanying abuse'. Alan Taylor replied,

> What a silly goose he is. I said exactly what it says in his letter. Of the section after 1789 part is by Romier and the rest by Rowse. Ought I to have specified the number of pages? I am baffled by his complaint, since I merely repeated what it says on the dust-cover. But if you want something more lively:

'There is no indication in the text where Romier leaves off and Mr
Rowse begins – except that the judgements become more eccentric.'
    I'd prefer you to print the whole letter. In which case append:
    'Every friend of Mr Rowse will appreciate this latest effusion of
his pen.'[142]

Not surprisingly, Alan Taylor's waspish replies, on this and other
occasions, were frequently not appreciated by the recipients. On this
occasion he ignored two of Rowse's main complaints, namely that he
(Taylor) had stated that the new section was based partly on Romier and
partly on Rowse's 'prejudices' and that Romier's typescript had gone to
1885 from 1789, though this was not clear from Rowse's editing.
    Alan Taylor was rather too prone to the sharp retort. In his auto-
biography he confessed he had even been too keen to score off his wife,
Margaret. He also was prone to make witty or derogatory remarks of others
which, if they got back, would hurt or, with people such as Rowse and
Namier, lead to the storing up of resentment. For instance, with regard to
Rowse, he responded in 1944 to a request for a radio broadcast on the
historic parallels to the forthcoming D-Day landings: 'The man you want
is Rowse: he would give you a fine turn about Agincourt, the Armada and
what not, without much relation to the facts. As a historian he has no
reputation to lose – I have.'[143] This was very unfair. Alan Taylor did himself
no favours in making such denigratory remarks and it is likely that some
of these got back to the people concerned.
    Also, as A.L. Rowse moved further away from his earlier socialism, he
became angered that Taylor had not repented his earlier radicalism. He
deplored his early Cold War sympathies for the Soviet Union and detected,
probably rightly, some Trotskyist notions amidst his highly individualistic
political views. Added to this was resentment that Taylor, and not he, was
in great demand on television and radio; a success he ascribed to a willingness to say almost anything, not to ability or charisma.
    In Rowse's case it is also possible that he did not care for Taylor's odd
lifestyle after breaking up with Margaret. His friendship with the Taylors
in the 1940s had owed much to her literary gatherings. Rowse, himself a
poet, had much enjoyed sparkling amidst poets and other writers. He
would have been pleased to be named in Stanley Parker's interview with
Taylor in June 1943. That piece recorded,

We went into the garden. A.L. Rowse was there, his conversation for
sheer hard glittering brilliance, putting to shame the sequins on the
sunlit waters. Mrs Graham Greene, with her two children. W.R.
Rogers, the Irish poet whose 'Awake' has been like a spiritual call to
arms. While in the distance, Chang Lee, 'The Silent Traveller', whose

discovery of the English counties has been as exciting for us as for himself, poked among the flowers and preserved his customary silence.[144]

Whatever the mix of reasons, Rowse came to detest Taylor. He was frankly jealous that Taylor, not he, had been invited to give the Ford Lectures. He was outraged by his *The Origins of the Second World War* (1961) and later wrote, 'That book ended any friendship with him.' His dislike was expressed privately in his diaries and increasingly frequently in his various publications. In his *Oxford in the History of the Nation* (1975) he got in a jibe at Alan Taylor and Beaverbrook, writing of John Wyclif that 'he became notorious as a reformer and the catspaw of the political interests of John of Gaunt (who manipulated him as a newspaper magnate might manipulate a notorious don in our day)'. After Taylor's death he was especially scathing in an obituary in the *Evening Standard* (London) and in a chapter of his book *Historians I Have Known* (1995), in which he praised certain 'remarkable gifts' but argued that he suffered from 'psychological instability'.[145]

Another often vigorous critic of Alan Taylor was Max Beloff, who had followed in Taylor's footsteps in that he had lectured at Manchester University before moving to Oxford University in 1947. Beloff's views are indicative of how the conservative Oxford establishment viewed Taylor. In 1952 and 1954 he wrote very hostile reviews of books by Taylor for *Time and Tide*. 'Peter Pan: Historian', a review of *Rumours of Wars* (1952), began by sneering at him as 'the d'Artagnan of the screen' for his 'In the News' performances, then observed that 'Mr Taylor's audience would get a rude shock from at least parts of this volume where Mr Taylor shows himself possessed of all the academic virtues, including dullness, a quality he is so severe on in others', and ended by suggesting that he was something of an impetuous youth aged only seven. In between, Beloff, with whom Namier had fallen out over a caustic review, jeered at some length at Taylor for writing of Sir Lewis Namier 'in the tones in which one might imagine a devout young nun referring to the Holy Father at Rome'.[146]

Beloff was equally vigorous in *Time and Tide* on *The Struggle for Mastery in Europe* (1954). In this he made much of Taylor's acknowledgement to Llewellyn Woodward for reading early draft chapters. This included observing that, had Woodward read it, then

> so judicious an historian might have persuaded him to avoid pressing an occasional paradox too far and to resist making unworthy gibes at nations which do not figure high on his list of preferences. And so sensitive a writer might have persuaded him not to overwork his clichés; by the time Mr Taylor's characters have finished putting diplomatic problems 'on ice', he begins to sound like a refrigerator salesman. Mr

Taylor has every quality of a major historian except a sense of the
dignity of his subject.

Beloff here, presumably, did not feel he was like a young nun looking to
the Holy Father in his praise of Woodward; but others, as Kathy Burk has
commented, might well have felt, along with Tony Crosland, that he was
'Alan's great enemy'.[147]

Nevertheless, there was no major breach between them. Max Beloff
contributed to the *Festschrift* that Martin Gilbert edited at the time of Alan
Taylor's sixtieth birthday. In the early 1970s Beloff was one of the authorities
Taylor turned to when seeking advisers for Nelson's *The Dictionary of World
History* (1973), in his role as advisory editor.[148]

Nevertheless, there remained more than just a coolness on Taylor's
part. He may have forgiven but he had not forgotten. When G.N. Clark
was reading his bibliography for *English History 1914–1945* (1965), he
commented to Taylor, 'I suppose you omit Max Beloff's books intentionally.
I know Namier thought very poorly of them.'[149] Beloff's work did not
make the 38 pages of bibliography, an unduly harsh omission. Later,
on 7 February 1979, Beloff gave a paper on the problems of writing
contemporary history to Taylor's research seminar at the Institute of
Historical Research. Alan Taylor was clearly not enamoured with Beloff's
theme that Britain had gone downhill in recent years, saying at the end
of the paper that he felt most historians did not accept that there had
been a consensus in British society which had recently broken down.
Later, his private view was more caustic: 'I thought Max Beloff's paper
was very poor. He had not thought out the problems of writing contemporary history, not even many of the basic ones.' More generally, he
commented, 'One of the good things about Lewis Namier was that he
detested Beloff – and Namier could be very unpleasant to people when he
wanted to be.'[150]

Although Beloff attempted to savage *The Struggle for Mastery in Europe*,
generally it was regarded as a major achievement. A.L. Rowse, even at his
most critical, paid tribute to Alan Taylor's dedication to writing history.
After his study of European relations 1848–1918, Taylor wrote a final
substantial book on central European history, a biography of Otto von
Bismarck. He had become increasingly interested in Bismarck during his
earlier work on Germany and Austria. He commented in 1979, 'Whilst
reviewing Eyck's volumes I very nearly wrote my own book on Bismarck.'
He added that he had taken great care with those reviews.[151]

In assessing Eric Eyck's major biography Taylor appears to have been
putting down a marker for another by himself, much as he had done when
pressing the need for a book similar to what became *The Struggle for*

Mastery in Europe. At the beginning of his 1943 review of Eyck's first volume he observed,

> To write a life of Bismarck within reasonable compass would be one of the greatest historical achievements; but perhaps it is impossible. The material is overwhelming; and to make matters worse, Bismarck himself has left, in speeches, conversations or his reminiscences, versions of all the principal events usually deliberately misleading.

He was critical of Eyck's assumption that Bismarck had always intended to create a united Germany. He commented, 'Bismarck always claimed as most deliberate the events least welcome to him.' He offered his own explanation to Bismarck's career:

> The psychological key to Bismarck is his parentage; he was the Junker son of a non-Junker mother, always aspiring to become a full member of the class from which his intellectual capacity as well as his birth barred him. His non-Junker brain told him the old order was doomed; his Junker prejudices determined him to preserve it. He went with the current of events in order to achieve the exact reverse of this current; and in some ways he achieved it.[152]

He praised the second volume by Eyck, observing that it superseded all previous biographies. However, while it provided a 'painstaking review of incidents', he felt it failed 'similarly to review the general underlying themes'. He also observed, 'The book could have been written by a moderate German liberal in the eighteen-eighties,' and 'It stands nearer to the Life and Letters of one just dead than to the review of a historian.' In reflecting on the middle period of Bismarck's life, Taylor used his current political arguments to inform his understanding of the past: 'German power in Europe was ended when Russia and England were reconciled, first in 1907 and then in 1941. That Anglo-Russian co-operation would be the ruin of great Germany was clear to Bismarck, but is still not clear to Mr Eyck.'

Taylor was strong in his praise of the third volume, especially its treatment of domestic policy, observing that it was 'better than its predecessors in proportion, in subject-matter and in interpretation'. He acknowledged that Eyck was right in his treatment of colonial policy, that it was 'directed against the German Left even more than against England; and I recant anything of mine which may have obscured this'. More generally, he reflected,

> Bismarck had much more in common with Hitler than their background or physical appearance would lead one to suppose. The record of Bismarck's dealings with his political opponents is exceedingly

distasteful; and even worse is the record of his dealings with his colleagues.

...The more I reflect on this record of Bismarck's life, the more convinced I am that it – and therefore German history – cannot be comprehended without as full a grasp of Russia's place in Europe as western historians have shown for that of England and France.

Quite clearly, Alan Taylor believed that he would be bringing his insights as an international relations specialist to an understanding of Bismarck. Even more clearly, at this time his opinion of Bismarck's political behaviour was very low. Indeed, when writing a review of a biography of Karl Marx in early 1948, he wrote, 'Marx would rank as the most unattractive character in nineteenth-century history were it not for Bismarck, who had the same repellent qualities even more intensely.' Ironically, given his later praise, he even commented,

> Mr Eyck has no sympathy for the things which Bismarck attempted after 1871 – the domestic defeat of German liberalism and the main-tenance of Russo-German solidarity. Therefore, he writes with a detachment and clarity born of dislike – the best mood for a historian, and especially for a biographer.[153]

However, he was to feel no such dislike by the time he had finished his first biography, *Bismarck*, and notably felt the opposite when he came to his second, *Beaverbrook*.

He was dissatisfied with other people's short biographies. He reviewed his friend Ian Morrow's biography, praising it as a 'fine narrative, vividly written' but observing that it was 'the Bismarck of legend. Bismarck as he would appear to a decent conservative nationalist of about 1910.' Later, after referring to another short biography, he commented to A.P. Wadsworth, 'Of course I ought really to write a life of Bismarck myself, but the effort to make money on the side to keep four children going distracts me from serious work.'[154] He did, however, write for Wadsworth for July 1948 his piece 'Bismarck: Fifty Years after. The Man of German Destiny', which followed on from his views in *The Course of German History* (1945).

The change in his views came as he wrote the biography. He had the financial motive after the American publisher Alfred Knopf approached him to write on Bismarck and, after negotiations, he agreed, with Hamish Hamilton publishing it in the UK. Apparently, A.L. Rowse also approached him to write such a short biography in his 'Men and their Times' series (which was to include Bruce McFarlane, Veronica Wedgwood and Christopher Hill).[155] He had the time once he had seen off the manuscript of *The Struggle for Mastery in Europe* in May 1953. He launched into reading printed material for *Bismarck* that summer, while at Plevna House, Yarmouth, on the Isle of Wight. Even then he was looking for other major possibilities, that August informing Wadsworth: 'I'm trying to persuade the family to let me finish Lady Gwendolen Cecil's *Life* [of Lord Salisbury], but their prejudice may be too strong.' He then wrote what was in effect an outline of his book as a substantial essay on Bismarck for the 1954 edition of the *Encyclopedia Britannica*. In the summer of 1954 he wrote all but two chapters of *Bismarck*, again while with Margaret and their children at Yarmouth.[156]

He greatly enjoyed writing *Bismarck*, more so than most of his other books. He wrote of this when reviewing a book by Michael Foot; after commenting that Foot had been 'suddenly captivated by events and swept into unexpected waters', he confessed,

> Historians often have this experience, and very exciting it is, though frightening if you are not used to it. The facts get up, hit the historian on the head, and make him go where he did not intend to go at all. I remember well my embarrassment at discovering that I was presenting Bismarck as a moderate, pacific statesman and an attractive character.[157]

His biography was based, like much of his later diplomatic history, on careful reading of the substantial printed sources. In the German edition he frankly admitted that he had never seen an original document in Bismarck's handwriting, nor had he visited his former estates at Varzin or Friedrichsruh.[158]

Perhaps most surprising, given his later hostility to many other authors taking such approaches, was his emphasis, early on, on psychological explanations. He wrote of Bismarck's mother and her children, 'She drove them on; she never showed them affection.' As for Otto,

> He wanted love from her, not ideas; and he was resentful she did not share his admiration for his father. It is a psychological commonplace for a son to feel affection for his mother and to wish his father out of the way. The results are more interesting and more profound when a son, who takes after the mother, dislikes her character and standards of value. He will seek to turn himself into the father with whom he has little in common, and he may well end up neurotic or a genius. Bismarck was both. He was the clever sophisticated son of a clever, sophisticated mother, masquerading all his life as his heavy, earthy father.

He was a man who 'found happiness only in his family'.[159]

The reason for at least part of Alan Taylor's excitement is clear. He could identify Wilhelmine Bismarck with Connie Taylor. The passage reads very much like a description of his mother and his bitterness at her attitude to his father, though Percy Taylor was hardly a 'heavy, earthy father', even if he had his feet more on the ground than his wife or son. This psychological interpretation was the feature of Taylor's *Bismarck* taken up when a book of readings on the statesman was produced in the highly successful D.C. Heath series 'Problems in European Civilization'. Theodore Hamerow introduced the selection by commenting, 'Taylor writes with such urbanity and assurance that like St Paul he almost persuades us.' Yet in turning to psychological explanations he was not alone. Otto Pflanze, while writing his impressive three-volume work *Bismarck and the Development of Germany*, increasingly felt 'that Bismarck's personal life – particularly his physical and psychological condition – was more intimately connected with his political behaviour than has been supposed'; that is, other than by Alan Taylor's short biography.[160]

Alan Taylor's *Bismarck* appeared in the years when German and other scholars were seeking to explain what had gone wrong to produce the rule of Hitler and the Nazis in Germany. To the question of 'whether the seeds of later evil were not already present in the Bismarck Reich', asked by Friedrich Meinecke in 1946, Alan Taylor had already given an answer which, like Namier, implicated the people of 1848 and went back to Luther.[161] His biography placed great emphasis on Bismarck's personal role in the events of 1862–90, depicting him as a wise, yet crafty, conservative, yet stressed, as he had done in the Eyck reviews, that he did not plan the unification of Germany. In this his approach and phraseology were ominously like his later treatment of Hitler and the coming of war in Europe in 1939, down to his use of 'certainly' when his lack of archival research might well have made him more cautious. For instance, he wrote, 'Certainly there is not a scrap of evidence that he worked deliberately for a war with France, still less that he timed it precisely for the summer of 1870.'

In *Bismarck* he also made one of his increasingly frequent pronouncements on the role of the individual in history. His view at this time was:

The future is a land of which there are no maps; and historians err when they describe even the most purposeful statesman as though he were marching down a broad high-road with his objective already in sight. More flexible historians admit that a statesman often has alternative courses before him; yet even they depict him as one choosing his route at a crossroads. Certainly the development of history has its own logical laws. But these laws resemble rather those by which flood-water flows into hitherto unseen channels and forces itself to an unpredictable sea. The death of Frederick VII opened the flood-gates;

and Bismarck proved himself master of the storm, a daring pilot in extremities.[162]

The biography was well received by the reviewers. Michael Howard, in the *New Statesman*, observed,

> Mr Taylor carries out his revaluation in the clear, epigrammatic prose which makes all his work as stimulating as champagne – and which makes one wonder, sometimes, whether it was all really as simple as that. His mind is a convex mirror in which events appear brilliantly coloured, brilliantly distinct, and sometimes a little distorted. He has many of the virtues of Macaulay, and one or two of his faults. The pattern is too sharply etched; the epigrams are too neat; the judgements are too final: but how refreshing it is to read a historian who is not afraid of patterns, epigrams and judgements!

Gordon Craig, the distinguished American historian of Germany, praised it as a readable and balanced account of Bismarck's career, 'a fascinating portrait of one of the most complicated personalities in an age which was filled with gifted and original minds', and for having a final chapter 'on the corrosive effects of the Bismarckian tradition in Germany's intellectual development'. It was also praised in the *Times Literary Supplement* by G.P. Gooch, who had long written with distinction on Bismarck, for 'compressing the most earth-shaking career between Napoleon and Hitler' into a short biography 'with conspicuous success'.[163]

Within the United Kingdom, the book has remained popular. It has been repeatedly reprinted for over fifty years. It has become one of a group of relatively short, well-written biographies of major figures of political history which have held their popular appeal. These include Duff Cooper's *Talleyrand* (1932) and Lord David Cecil's volumes on Melbourne (1939 and 1954). Harold Nicolson, another writer of fine prose, welcomed Alan Taylor's *Bismarck*, commenting that the book 'sheds light into obscure corners, sets up fresh ideas crossing and recrossing in the passages of the brain, combines scholarship with enthusiasm, and possesses such rare charm that the temperature of our interest rises to zest'. However, having debated with Taylor several times on the radio and aware of his irreverence, he observed that his 'thought and method are those of a scholar and whose feeling is that of an adolescent'.[164]

Its place has been less secure in the British academic market, though it has remained on many university reading lists. For one thing, there has been a massive amount of research and a stream of major publications on this period of German history since 1955, not least in Germany. In the English language, there has been a major three-volume work on Bismarck by Otto Pflanze as well as many short biographical studies, including *Bismarck and Modern Germany* (1965) by the distinguished diplomatic historian William Norton Medlicott and *Bismarck* (2003) by Edgar Feuchtwanger. In a widely read book which reviews writing on Bismarck, Bruce Waller was especially critical of Alan Taylor's argument that Bismarck had no long-term plans. He argued that there is need for 'an explanation which will allow for a considerable amount of planning and foresight, but also for flexibility, irrationality and downright opportunism as well'.[165] Others argued for more attention to the working-class and middle-class pressures which affected the policies of Bismarck and other leading German figures.

In 1955 *Bismarck* was an impressive follow-up to his major diplomatic work of the previous year. Alan Taylor had made his mark in scholarship as well as in the media. The following year was his fiftieth and the ensuing decade would see greater recognition but also serious controversy which jeopardised his academic reputation.

-6-

HIGHS AND
LOWS

Alan Taylor was at the height of his career during his fifties. In his early fifties he was notably successful in his major endeavours and he was a major figure on television and radio and in the press. To all this he added his campaigning role as a peripatetic speaker against nuclear weapons. However, with the publication of *The Origins of the Second World War* (1961) he suffered a major setback. While the book was a commercial success and a major public talking point, it called into question his judgement. To some extent he redeemed himself in his late fifties with his short *The First World War* (1963) and his substantial volume in the Oxford History of England, *England 1914–1945* (1965).

After the academic recognition that *The Struggle for Mastery in Europe* brought, he was invited in November 1954 to give the Ford Lectures in English History at Oxford University. In his autobiography he attributes the suggestion of his topic, those who dissented from official foreign policy, to Alan Bullock. No doubt this is true, and when the lectures were published as a book he dedicated it to Bullock. But Bullock's suggestion came from much contact with Taylor in that period. Part of the theme of the lectures had been his area of research for his 1928 attempt at an Oxford prize essay. Some of his dissenters were figures Taylor had spoken warmly of in the past, such as John Bright. The whole theme was the antithesis of the study of foreign policy as practised by Llewellyn Woodward and of the treatment of the successful by E.H. Carr. While Taylor admired Carr's work, his dismissal of the unsuccessful as unimportant rankled with Alan Taylor. He was still expressing outrage at Carr's attitude to history's winners and losers at his seminar on 7 February 1979. He observed, 'I once asked E.H. Carr why there was not more on Trotsky in his history of Soviet Russia. Carr gave me a look of complete amazement and said, "But he was on the losing side."'

So Taylor himself appears to have been interested for a long time in the subject. Indeed, there is even correspondence in the *Manchester Guardian*'s files which suggests that Taylor had suggested to Alan Bullock that Bullock take up the subject. He wrote to A.P. Wadsworth in May 1953, 'Alan Bullock is thinking of writing a book on England and Europe since 1898; and I suggested to him that he ought to study radical opinion before 1914. He might make this into an essay for a volume that we are getting up for Namier.' Wadsworth was enthusiastic, feeling it was 'a very good idea', but regretted that his newspaper had not kept a record of who wrote its various leaders.[1] Soon after receiving the invitation to give the Ford Lectures he wrote excitedly to Wadsworth, 'It really is the most exciting thing that ever happened in my life. And yet, if I were asked to choose whether to be Ford's Lecturer or to return with the old team to IN THE NEWS, I'd hesitate. That no doubt is why some people wouldn't have me as a professor.'[2]

Taylor soon approached BBC radio to see if he could combine his academic and his media roles with his Ford Lectures. Anna Kallin expressed interest in March 1955. He soon prepared a synopsis for her. From the start she said that it would be more effective if the lectures were not recorded in the university and urged that a shorter version should be recorded in a studio, observing that this was better 'as you may have noticed in the case of Isaiah Berlin'. They discussed the lectures further during 1955. That November he thanked her, writing: 'Your comments have given me many useful hints, not only for the broadcasts but for the lectures themselves!' In due course shortened versions of each of the six lectures were broadcast twice under the title 'The Other Foreign Policy' on BBC Radio's Third Programme and he secured 270 guineas (£283.50), then a large sum.[3]

He recorded the first two lectures at the BBC's studios on 16 December 1955, the third and fourth on 13 March and the final two on 21 March 1956. In his Preface to the book of the lectures he wrote, 'I gave the Ford Lectures before the University, and then a little shortened in the third programme of the BBC, with no written aid except the quotations.' In this he was being at least a little misleading in two ways. First, he appears to have been protecting his image of giving the lectures spontaneously, armed only with quotations, in the university, whereas he had rehearsed the first two, albeit in shortened version, for radio weeks ahead. Of course, they were broadcast after he had delivered the lectures in Oxford (between mid-January and late February 1956). Secondly, although he had provided the BBC with outlines long before, he was determined to cultivate the notion he gave them without a script, even urging this to be stated in the BBC's description of the programmes. Anna Kallin firmly refused to collude in this, writing to him,

The Ford Lectures are a great success. They do sound unscripted, and I enjoyed listening again to the first two, but we never say – unless it is a discussion – that broadcasts are unscripted.

I am sending you your old scripts, under separate cover.[4]

Nevertheless, Alan Taylor had reason to be nervous before each lecture. It was a major university occasion. But, in addition, there were many in the audience who would be delighted to see 'the TV Don' come unstuck. He eased his nerves by spending the time before each of the lectures with his son Sebastian, a debt he acknowledged in his Preface to the book of the lectures published in June 1957. He had an anxious half-hour before the lecture. Sebastian later recalled, 'I had never seen him lose his confidence before, as he did before the first lecture. He had invited all his friends along, including Michael Foot and Bob Boothby. Bill Brown did not come.'[5] Brown came with John Irwin, his television producer friend, to a later one.

Alan Taylor came to deem *The Trouble Makers*, the book of the Ford Lectures, 'my favourite brainchild'.[6] Why was this? In large part it was because he identified with many of the protagonists. They were his people and through his background he could empathise with the concerns and attitudes of these political dissenters. When it came to the twentieth century, the Thompsons and Taylors, albeit at a much minor level, were as striking examples as the Russells and Trevelyans. In a way he gave an account of his intellectual forebears, and even brought in his own speech at Ardwick in Manchester in 1935 in which he opposed applying sanctions to Italy. It may also have been that he thoroughly enjoyed a change in the sources for his research. He moved away from diplomatic documents in archives and the memoirs of diplomats, Foreign Ministers and Prime Ministers to the collected speeches of Fox, Cobden, Bright, Gladstone, Kossuth (in England), Hansard, the back-issues of the *Daily News* and the *Manchester Guardian* (which he read in the Athenaeum) and a few Oxford and London theses in the Bodleian and Senate House Library. Moreover, a strong feature of his work, from his first book onwards, had been the depiction of people of the past. In his Ford Lectures he could discuss a motley collection of unusual figures ranging from William Gladstone to David Urquart, many of whom – as he put it – were merely 'noises off' the stage in studies of official foreign policy.[7]

In defining his trouble makers in his first lecture he overstated the extent of their dissent. He said,

A man can disagree with a particular line of British foreign policy, while accepting its general assumptions. The Dissenter repudiates its aims, its methods, its principles. What is more, he claims to know better and to promote higher causes; he asserts a superiority, moral or intellectual.[8]

While many of his figures did this, others, such as John Bright and Ramsay MacDonald, were more critics. Many did, however, exhibit a firm belief that they knew better. He was soon to do so as a leading apostle of the cause of nuclear disarmament.

In presenting his theme, Taylor naturally made claims for its importance. In so doing he made the far from novel point that when people wrote of British foreign policy they often really meant 'the few members of the Foreign Office who happened to concern themselves with this question'. He went further, building on his criticisms of the official, edited documents on British foreign policy, to state,

> These lectures are a gesture of repentance for having written recently a substantial volume of what I may venture to call 'respectable' diplomatic history. This time I shall emulate that slightly improper series of guidebooks to capital cities called 'What isn't in Baedeker', and discuss aspects of British foreign policy that are left out of the official perorations. For the one continuous thing in British policy is not that it has been universally accepted but that there has always been disagreement, controversy about it.

In a much-quoted passage, which is from where Hamish Hamilton selected the title of the book of the lectures, he went out of his way to state defiantly his fundamental outlook:

> Conformity may give you a quiet life; it may even bring you to a University Chair. But all change in history, all advance, comes from the nonconformists. If there had been no trouble-makers, no Dissenters, we should still be living in caves. As to being 'rootless intellectuals', the Dissenters have been deeply English in blood and temperament – often more so than their respectable critics.

He went on to criticise the outlook or writings of various historians he deemed 'conservative', not sparing Namier (who might have been offended by the above passage), Hugh Trevor-Roper, Richard Pares and Keith Feiling.[9]

Once past his display of *gaminerie* in the first lecture, the lectures were erudite and, taken as a whole, opened up a fresh theme. Yet, later, there was still much to annoy some of an academic audience. There was also much of his characteristic wit and sparkle in them. Take, for instance, his discussion of the classes in the context of Cobden and Bright. He wrote of the entrepreneurs,

> Sociologists have very curious ideas about the classes whom they claim to analyse, particularly curious ideas about capitalists. I wonder if they know any. Marx, for instance, drew a picture of the capitalist, ruthless,

cold, always obeying the dictates of economic law. But Engels, the one capitalist he knew, wasn't a bit like that … The capitalist does not grow rich by being orderly, rational, modest; he does it by flair, by backing a hunch. Keynes said, 'All business is a bet'; and the successful business man is the unstable eccentric in an otherwise humdrum community. Was Hudson sane? Was Rhodes? Was Northcliffe? Cobdenism may have represented the economic interests of the Lancashire cotton-trade considered in the abstract. But the mill-owners and merchants did not consider their interests in the abstract. Though mill-owners and merchants, they were also outstanding men in a Romantic age – heavily whiskered, living in the gothic fantasies of Victoria Park, grandiloquent of phrase, patrons of Chopin and Liszt, readers of Tennyson, gambling in cotton futures.

He was thinking of his grandfather's generation and its predecessors and had moved a long way from the views of his mother and Henry Sara.

Alan Taylor, in talking of the working class, was moving towards his romanticised view of ordinary English people. They – or rather his view of them – became the heroes of his later writing, not least in the con-clusion of his *English History 1914–1945* (1965). In *The Trouble Makers* he followed his reflections on the capitalists with his 'The People's Alan' view of the working class.

> The working man in politics was more rational and less emotional than the capitalist, once he had got beyond the first instinctive revulsion of Chartism. The worker is by nature less imaginative, more level-headed than the capitalist. That is what prevents his becoming one. He is content with small gains. Trade Union officials think about petty cash; the employer speculates in millions. You can see the difference in their representative institutions. There is no scheme too wild, no rumour too absurd, to be without repercussions on the Stock Exchange. The public house is the home of common sense.[10]

Of course, in this he was engaging in turning received opinions upside down and stretching a point beyond its breaking point. Yet it also reveals his populist belief in 'the people' and their preferences, as also then exhibited in his columns in the popular press. It may also suggest that the clientele of his favoured pubs, such as 'The Plough Boy' at Higher Disley, was very different from those of some inner city pubs, which were not notable for reflection and common sense.

He still felt he was an outsider at Oxford. There is much in his first lecture to suggest that, as in the past, he was preparing himself for disap-pointment; again, he was providing himself with the alibi that if he lost out it would be because he would not compromise his beliefs. It was as if he could not accept simple failure. It had to be the plucky northern nonconformist being downed by the forces of southern orthodoxy and privilege. And yet the underlying message in the lectures was that the colourful dissenters of the past were parts – and innovative parts – of the British past. He was making the case that his history complemented and freshened the Oxford historical scene.

Needless to say, others did not see it that way. Bruce McFarlane for instance, having missed the fourth lecture, wrote to a friend,

> So far he has provided high-class entertainment without either new light or new knowledge. Why he likes 'dissent' becomes clear; it never had to do with anything practical; opposition foreign policy, not of the front bench but of the wildest back benchers, is the only kind he feels any sympathy with; it was always against, never for anything; Alan is revealing himself as fundamentally a nihilist; and yet he thinks the liberals of 1848 absurd because they achieved nothing![11]

Taylor ruffled more feathers at Oxford by rejecting the publishing proposal that Oxford University Press offered him. He felt that £1 1 shilling (£1.05p) was too high a selling price, especially as that involved a reduction in the usual level of royalty. Instead he successfully secured publication with Hamish Hamilton, with a selling price for the book of 18 shillings (90p) and the normal royalty. However, when it did not sell as well as the publisher expected, they reprinted it reluctantly – and at £1 1 shilling – in 1964.[12]

The reviews were also critical. C.M. Woodhouse in the *Times Literary Supplement* felt that the lectures were unworthy of the prestigious occasion. He noted that they ranged 'from Charles James Fox to the almost unidentifiable specimens of the late 1930s, of whom perhaps Mr Taylor himself is to be counted as the only known survivor'. He observed that Alan Taylor was

> very nearly an ideal general reader's historian. He tells them exactly what they want to know, briefly, wittily and often wickedly…It was at first an amusing trick to invent that *enfant terrible* (which may perhaps be anglicised as an intellectual teddy-boy) to serve as the serious historian's *alter ego*; but the trick can well become an obsession, and the obsession can become involuntary and irreversible.

Christopher Sykes, whose review in *Time and Tide* was more favourable, also commented that 'Mr Taylor has evidently much of the chronic dissenter in his own temperament'. The American historian William Neumann made similar comments.

> As the 'Peck's Bad Boy' of British historians Taylor is ever ready to stick a deflating pin in his more pompous colleagues or to tip over the

tribal gods of his profession…conventions of sobriety and cautious generalization are cast aside as Taylor, in the tradition of dissent, strikes out at the 'Establishment' of his profession. The result is a volume which will infuriate or delight the reader, according to his tastes. The reviewer recommends its brilliant half-truths and suggestive paradoxes.

The book was also reviewed by two pillars of the Left. The former Prime Minister and Labour Party leader Clement Attlee was cool towards this Bevanite. While he praised his 'lively style' he felt that 'he tends to over-stress the importance of the intellectuals as is natural in an academic writer'. Almost certainly unbeknown to Attlee, Taylor had been even cooler about his autobiography in 1954, sending it back to the *TLS* with the note: 'I can think of fewer books drearier than the memoirs of Lord Attlee and am therefore unable to review this.' Kingsley Martin, like Woodhouse, felt that, while the content – 'delivered brilliantly, staccato without notes' – made for good lectures, 'they retain their epigrammatic, rather inconsequential, quality in book form'. More generally, he observed that A.J.P. Taylor 'is this generation's Bernard Shaw, at once its unrelenting preacher and its irrepressable debater. Every subject has its moral and every moral its refutation. No one, including himself, is allowed to get away with anything. From every opinion there is dissent; from every dissent there is another Dissenter.'[13]

The invitation to give the Ford Lectures was not his only mark of recognition. To his delight he was elected, along with E.H. Carr, to the then 150-strong British Academy in 1956. The history section's membership had been heavily skewed to medieval historians. Carr and Taylor were elected after G.N. Clark and Charles Webster had successfully pressed for more modern historians. They were both favourable to Taylor, as was V.H. Galbraith, then Regius Professor of Modern History at Oxford, and Lewis Namier. Alan Taylor already saw a campaigning role for the historians of the British Academy: to challenge Whitehall's invented tradition of the secrecy of Cabinet minutes (and other government papers). In his first Ford Lecture he observed,

Things have come to a pretty pass when we cannot consult Gladstone's 'cabinet papers', really private jottings, without the permission of the Cabinet Office – an organization only created many years after his death. The absurd part of it is that these sacred documents, like most secret records, contain nothing startling, though much of interest to the historian; the secrecy is imposed solely to bolster the self-importance of the civil servants who insist on it. There is no limit to my curiosity as a historian. I regard every official as my enemy; and it puzzles me that other historians do not feel the same. What is the British Academy good for if it does not resist this ridiculous ban?[14]

He was one of several historians who over the years argued for a more open policy for British public records.

He became devoted to the British Academy. Although in many ways a solitary scholar, he had a taste for clubs and other select circles. He enjoyed belonging to the Athenaeum and he took much pleasure in being involved in the activities of the British Academy, meeting his third wife through one overseas visit. Similarly, he enjoyed his four evenings a week in Magdalen College.

While 1956 saw a high for him in his election to the British Academy, the following year saw probably the greatest low of his career. This was his failure to succeed V.H. Galbraith to the Regius Chair of Modern History in 1957. He remained bitterly disappointed about this for the rest of his life, a disappointment which, in spite of major efforts on his part, he failed to disguise. In his autobiography he even made the absurd claim that he was 'hardly aware there was such a thing as the Regius Chair', only 22 pages after writing of the previous vacancy in 1947: 'I lobbied hard for Lewis Namier.'[15] Ten years later, while Namier was not the key person in thwarting his attaining this major recognition, he felt betrayed. After 25 years of friendship and, in his case, near-adulation, Lewis Namier had not given him unquestioning support when it mattered most.

Shortly before Sir Anthony Eden's resignation as Prime Minister he had asked the Vice-Chancellor of Oxford to suggest a successor to Galbraith for the Regius Chair. Alic Smith sounded out Alan Bullock and forwarded Alan Taylor's name. However, Smith immediately became ill and was succeeded as Vice-Chancellor by J.C. Masterman, the Provost of Worcester College. Earlier, Masterman had successfully opposed consideration of Taylor for the Chair of Modern History, tenable at Worcester, and he now did much to block him securing the Regius Chair. He greatly disliked Taylor for his media activities, his politics and, perhaps, for the quality of some of his prolific historical output. Masterman favoured Hugh Trevor-Roper for the post, while other Oxford historians favoured Taylor. Harold Macmillan, who had succeeded Eden, wished to nominate Namier, a historian he had earlier greatly admired in his capacity as a publisher. On finding that Namier was too old, he sought Namier's advice. Namier recommended Lucy Sutherland, a distinguished historian of the eighteenth century and former pupil of Namier's. On her declining, as she was unwilling to give up her post as Principal of Lady Margaret Hall, Namier turned to Taylor.[16]

Alan Taylor recorded his recollection of their telephone conversation in his autobiography. In essence, Namier told him he was the best person for the Regius Chair but insisted that he give up his television and press activities. His version of his response included, 'If you think I am the historian best qualified to occupy the Chair it is your duty to recommend me. What I do in my spare time is no concern of yours, or anyone else.' This seems likely to have been in the conversation. But Taylor gave different accounts on different occasions. Another recurring recollection of the conversation was Namier saying that Taylor did not have the necessary social graces for the post, whereas Hugh Trevor-Roper was very well connected and could mix well in society.[17] This has much credibility. It was a view that Masterman expressed and he would have lobbied discreetly for his protégé. It may also have been something Namier would have said, given that it was a reason expressed when he was passed over for the same position earlier, and Taylor could well have been the frank friend to inform Namier of this. Whatever was said, Taylor never spoke to Namier again and rebuffed two attempts at reconciliation made by Namier – one even when Namier was dying.

His total rejection of Namier – 'Namier was dead so far as I was concerned' – is perhaps the saddest aspect of this episode of thwarted ambition. Taylor's long admiration of Namier had been rounded off when Richard Pares and he edited a *Festschrift* for Namier, which was published by Macmillan in April 1956. Taylor contributed to it a detailed account of 'The War Aims of the Allies in the First World War', a substantial spin-off from *The Struggle for Mastery in Europe*. He also masterminded the presentation of the book, ensuring that the terminally ill Pares could attend and taking Lewis and Julia Namier to a celebratory dinner in Magdalen to end the day. The volume had been enthusiastically received by A.P. Wadsworth, who had 'read every word' and 'enjoyed it enormously'.[18] The Namier–Taylor axis appeared to be in as good shape as ever.

However, it seems that Taylor's criticisms of Namier's work rankled. He later told with amusement Namier's reactions to his review of one of Namier's later sets of essays in which he suggested that there was little of Namier's customary sparkle in the book. Namier, on reading the review, had commented, 'Poor old Taylor has gone downhill somewhat. There's not much of his customary discernment in the review. I'm afraid he's rather past it.' While such an incident possibly suggests good-humoured acceptance of differing views, there was too much critical comment on several occasions for Namier. In a *Times Literary Supplement* feature on 'Thoughts and Second Thoughts upon some Outstanding Books of the Half-Century' Alan Taylor had written on *The Structure of Politics at the Accession of George III* and had included the criticism that Namier's big flaw was to ignore principles. 'A political structure without principles does not even work; it runs inevitably to ossification.'[19]

Taylor also criticised Namier in his Ford Lectures. In his first lecture he observed that men 'persist in having ideas and ideals, despite the exhortations of Mr Trevor-Roper and Professor Pares and Sir Lewis Namier'. It is unlikely that Namier would have been amused by one of his digressions on the frequent later tacit acceptance of dissenters' views:

> Look at that noble monument of detached Tory scholarship, *The Structure of Politics at the Accession of George III*. Its central doctrine is that jobbery not ideas, places not principles, were the motive force of politics. I used to puzzle where I had heard this before. Then I realized. It is a more scholarly presentation of what Cobbett called THE THING. And how he was condemned for it!

Namier is likely to have been even less amused at Alan Taylor's scoffing at the project to which he dedicated the last part of his life. At the start of his second lecture, after commenting on those who gave great importance to the composition of the House of Commons, he observed,

> The same outlook underlies the *History of Parliament*, on which some of my most admired colleagues are working. When I heard of the project, I couldn't help reflecting that a History of Parliament existed already, at least for more modern times. We call it *Hansard* ... the history of parliament is to be found in what members heard or said, in what they felt, not in what they were.

For the very prickly Namier, what may have been even worse was that Taylor mocked the work of one of his former students and his most devoted collaborator, John Brooke. In a review headed 'The School of Namier' he recognised Brooke's *The Chatham Administration 1766–1768* as 'first-rate scholarship of its kind' but was very critical of this approach to political history. For good measure, he observed of its author that he 'does not merely use the Namier method: he writes in the Namier style, and even makes the Namier jokes'.[20] Hugh Trevor-Roper, for one, felt that this was decisive. He wrote to an American scholar that Taylor's criticisms were fully justified but 'the master requires absolute obedience; and this gesture of independence was fatal'.[21]

However, Namier would not have seen it like that. Namier had achieved what he desired: high social acceptance. He was being consulted by, and acting for, the Prime Minister. Most likely he was being lobbied by the type of Oxford inner-circle people whom he admired but who had snubbed him in the past. Yet he telephoned Alan Taylor and was willing to back him if he acted in the manner he and such people as Masterman felt appropriate for a Regius Professor. After knowing Taylor for 25 years, though, he seems not to have fully understood Taylor's own prickly independence and his love of writing for the media (let alone any financial need for the additional income to support his lifestyle).

While cutting Namier out of his life, Alan Taylor nevertheless continued to express respect for what he considered to be the best of Namier's scholarship. Within six months of the appointment of Trevor-Roper to the Regius Chair, he reviewed the second edition of *The Structure of Politics at the Accession of George III*, commenting that it was 'irresistible for its meticulous learning, magical for its literary charm'. However, he shrewdly observed that the Namierites 'have never analysed a great popular constituency such as Westminster where real political feeling was likely to show itself', but went on, 'It is hard to resist the feeling that Sir Lewis not merely wished to find an absence of principle in the eighteenth century, but welcomed this as a lesson for the present day.' The following year he also welcomed *Vanished Supremacies*, a collection of the best of Namier's essays.[22]

His failure to secure the Regius Chair in 1957 was not a sign that he was isolated and held in little regard. Far from it. As Kathy Burk has commented, 'All the evidence shows most baldly…that a small group of men – or even one with an acquiescent group of supporters – could go against the intellectual consensus and impose a candidate of their own choice;' albeit one of high quality. Taylor was favoured for the Regius Chair by several leading Oxford historians. Hugh Trevor-Roper soon afterwards wrote in a private letter, 'I must admit that I really think A.J.P. Taylor's qualifications were the highest,' but added that, if Taylor was deemed not acceptable, 'then who am I to spurn this unexpected crown?'.[23]

There is also a mistaken notion that thereafter Taylor was hostile to Hugh Trevor-Roper. He always insisted otherwise, and in this deserves believing. His bitterness was at failing to achieve this position when he felt that given the field of available candidates it was his due. In his autobiography he memorably put it: 'Hugh Trevor-Roper wrote to me that if Lucy Sutherland had become Regius Professor he would have been indignant, but that if I had done so he would have said the better man had won. I replied that I agreed with him.' He also added, 'But as he has enjoyed the Chair and is an incomparable essayist, I do not grudge it to him.'

That autumn Alan Taylor indicated clearly this view of Trevor-Roper in a review of his *Historical Essays* (1957). He wrote, 'Professor Trevor-Roper writes like an angel…Each piece has a zest and perfection of a Mozart symphony.' On one of the notable essays, he wrote that the decline of the gentry is '*an* explanation, but not *the* explanation of the Great Rebellion', and he shrewdly observed: 'I jib when it comes to jettisoning religion' as an explanation. He also aired a fairly widespread view that the book would enable Trevor-Roper 'to conceal for some time the fact that he has not yet produced a sustained book of mature historical scholarship'.[24]

He had been very enthusiastic about much of Trevor-Roper's past work. He had reviewed the French and English editions of *The Last Days of Hitler* (1945) and in 1954 had chosen the book for a 'Personal Preference Appreciations' feature in the *Times Literary Supplement*. He had greeted its second edition with the commendation: 'This is an incomparable book, by far the best book written on any aspect of the second German war; a book sound in its scholarship, brilliant in its presentation, a delight for historian and layman alike. No words of praise are too strong for it.' More generally, he had earlier categorised him as one of the great historians of his time. He asked in 1953,

> What is it that such individual authors as, say, Sir Lewis Namier, E.H. Carr and Hugh Trevor-Roper have in common? Great scholarship, of course; but also literary mastery and clear personal conviction. A work of history, like any other book that is any good, must bear its author's stamp. The reader should feel that no one else could have written this particular book in this particular way.

He also strongly recommended him to Hamish Hamilton when, in 1956, the publisher was seeking a biographer of Cromwell. He wrote, 'Hugh Trevor-Roper is the ideal man to do a life of Cromwell. It would have a fabulous sale.'[25] So Taylor was an admirer of Trevor-Roper's work, and remained so in spite of their differences over his *The Origins of the Second World War*.

He would have been less than human had he not felt that he, unlike Trevor-Roper, did produce big books in his area of specialism. He usually spoke highly of Trevor-Roper and his work. One rare occasion when he was more waspish began with a discussion of Trevor-Roper's introduction to Macaulay's essays. He observed that much of it had appeared in other essays. 'Trevor-Roper has made some of his stuff work very hard indeed.' To the suggestion that Trevor-Roper had gone up an historical cul-de-sac with his book on Sir Edmund Backhouse, he warmly agreed, saying: 'The book tells us nothing about China in that period, nor even answers such questions as how did Backhouse acquire the valuable documents (not the forged ones) which he later gave to the Bodleian.' He regretted the lack of a big work on the seventeenth century, observing dryly, 'Some say that Trevor-Roper has a thousand typescript pages on Cromwell somewhere. I wonder where. Maybe at some railway station, waiting to take a journey.'[26]

Later, he was fairly sympathetic to Hugh Trevor-Roper's plight over the Hitler diaries. He said he would not have been sufficiently confident to judge if the handwriting was a forgery. He felt that Trevor-Roper had come to grief because of his love of publicity. 'Trevor-Roper really should have had an expert opinion on the paper and other such points...[but] he could not resist being the first to pronounce on them. Trevor-Roper probably felt that there would be much less prestige involved if he was not the first to do so. But he forgot that the opposite would be the case if he was wrong.'[27]

Nevertheless, generally in later years there was much warmth in their relations with each other. For instance, in November 1981 he wrote a glowing tribute to Hugh Trevor-Roper when reviewing a *Festschrift* in his honour in the *London Review of Books*. In particular he praised his 'elegance of style and simplicity of utterance' and his skills as an essayist, one with

> no rival, at any rate since the death of Lewis Namier. When I read one of Trevor-Roper's essays tears of envy stand in my eyes. It is not only that his essays are models of English prose. Each has a clear theme which is gradually brought into shape. At the end, we feel there is at least one inevitable characteristic in history: the conclusion of the argument to which Trevor-Roper has been leading us from the beginning.

Taylor also pointed to the similarities in view between them, both rating 'accident as a more potent force in history than any laws, Divine or Marxist'. Implicitly he also suggested their shared literary skills. They were very much of the same species of historians. Trevor-Roper wrote effusively, thanking him for this '*very* generous' review, saying: 'I greatly appreciate such a dewdrop.' He added, 'I am told, by severe spirits, that one should never acknowledge reviews, lest…etc. etc. But to hell with severe spirits! When I am pleased, I purr; and I am very pleased.' When Taylor was seriously hurt by a car in Soho in early 1984 he wrote sending his best wishes for a speedy recovery, commenting, 'I hope you will have no complications and that your incomparable pen can still be wielded with its usual force and pungency. I shall look out for evidence of its activity.'[28]

Disappointed at not securing the Regius Chair, Taylor took some consolation in busying himself in the affairs of his college. He had been upset when a maverick colleague had opposed the renewal of his Fellowship on the grounds of his recent divorce when it came up in 1952. In 1958 he became Vice-President of Magdalen College for two years, thereby becoming the person in charge of the college's celebrations to mark the 500th anniversary of its founding in 1458. He delighted in the role of Vice-President and in the various celebrations. On most matters the arch-dissenter proved punctilious in observing the college's formalities and traditions. He did support some minor changes. His own recollection was,

> The only reform I championed throughout my long association with Magdalen was the admission of women – honourable enough but not very original. Otherwise I took things as they came and must accept some responsibility for the deplorable Waynflete Building which was put up during my tenure of office.

He was more notable for keeping meetings to the point and therefore brief, and, more generally, for efficient administration. As a result of his endeavours he was approached as a potential head of college by people at Worcester and Pembroke, but he preferred his roles as historian and commentator in the media.[29]

He supervised many very able postgraduate students. Many of these went on to be major scholars later. These included Paul Addison, Kathleen Burk, Martin Ceadel, Chris Cook, Norman Davies, Roger Louis, Alan Sked and Charles Townshend. He did not suffer gladly those who expected spoon-feeding, either in regard to selecting a viable topic or in evaluating archival material. He expected research students to get on with their research and come to him with finished work. Before 1961 he was notably protective of his time, which was in short supply given his role in his college, his media and also his CND activities. Nevertheless, to those who got on with their research he was very stimulating. Roger Louis got on particularly well with him, after a false start. He had asked Alan Taylor about carrying out research on Ruanda-Urundi, suggesting Taylor would not know of it. Taylor launched enthusiastically into what he knew of the east African area of Uganda and Tanganyika, coming to an abrupt halt as he realised his mistake, but nevertheless took on being his supervisor. His enthusiasm was infectious. He was especially delighted to discuss the Vienna archives with his former undergraduate Ken Holborn, and even more so when Alan Sked undertook a doctorate on the later history of the Habsburg monarchy.

Paul Addison, who began his research in October 1964, wrote in 1990 that Taylor then had been 'first-class'. He read his draft chapters quickly and returned them with 'crisp and helpful criticisms'. At their fortnightly meetings in term he was 'an inspiring teacher' as well as being a charming and kindly person:

> It was like being spirited away in a time-machine. To say that he brought the past to life would be true but quite inadequate. What he conveyed was the sense that the past was an unexplored country in which the traveller was always on the brink of fresh discoveries... Taylor sketched out many research agendas, but he never told me which to choose or what to think about it.

However, he did air one doubt: 'If there is a case against Taylor, it is that although he inspired research and debate, he perpetuated an Oxford fixation with old-fashioned diplomatic and political history.'

To this, it can be added that, like many of his generation, he was notably unaware of women in history, let alone wider gender issues. For someone who delighted in pen portraits of major figures he found very few women to secure his interest. Other than Queen Victoria, he wrote most memorably of Marie Stopes in his essay 'The Baldwin Years' and subsequently in *English History 1914–1945* (1965). In 1979 he even wrote to Patricia Jalland, whose research had moved from the pre-1914 Irish crisis to aspects of women's history, 'I wonder what women you have in mind. It is a curious thing that even enlightened historians such as myself still regard any political theme associated with women as funny.' He was also very sceptical about the value of oral history, having found when writing the biography of Beaverbrook that people's anecdotes had been 'remembered from other people's books, not actually experienced themselves, though they thought they had'. He was equally scathing about memoirs written after the event. He concluded a letter on the subject to Brian Harrison, 'If statesmen could be persuaded to record their acts and motives the same evening, there would be some use in it. Similarly diaries, when not rewritten, are useful. But old men drooling about their youth – No.'[30]

By the 1950s and early 1960s he was highly confident in his undergraduate lecturing and tutoring. His considerable lecturing ability was reinforced by his high profile in the media. Looking back on his lecturing technique in 1985 he said that he always tried to get a subject clear in his own mind – all the problems sorted out. Then he could go into the lecture theatre and give a lucid lecture with no notes. When Eva, his third wife, observed that he had good nerves, he thought and then tentatively agreed, observing that it was not really a matter of nerves but of being clear in your views on a subject before beginning.[31]

In the late 1950s and early 1960s, as in the previous decade, he impressed those attending his undergraduate lectures. Geoffrey Matthews, who was an undergraduate 1956–59, recalled that then Taylor was the star of the Modern History School and that by his time some 400 students attended his lectures in the Exams Hall. He particularly recalled very lucid lectures on the Russian Revolution. At that time he thought only Isaiah Berlin and Edgar Wind, the Professor of Fine Art, could rival him for popularity. However, Colin Bonwick, an undergraduate in 1955–58, recalled that even Alan Taylor lost numbers as the term went on when he gave lectures at an unpopular time (late on Friday afternoons) and in an out-of-the-way venue (an obscure hall in Magdalen College, the wrong end of the High Street for most students). He recalled Taylor's opening 'Ladies and gentlemen' being reduced to 'Lady and gentleman'. Robert Houlton, who went to his lectures in the early 1960s, was warned by his tutor that they were very clever stuff but not really the type of thing that students want; but much the same was said about A.J. Ayer's lectures. He recalled that in the lectures Taylor seemed to be conducting a tutorial with himself, discussing all the various points of view on the topic. He said that the lectures were very stimulating, making him want to go straight to the library at the end of them and read more about the topic. This appears to have been a common experience among his audience. Patrick Jackson, for instance, a decade earlier left them 'feeling as if I was walking on air'.[32]

His choice of giving lectures at unpopular times was mostly to do with his preference for free afternoons to walk or, when he had Holywell Ford, to work in the garden. He tried to arrange lectures for 09.00, tutorials between 11.00 and 13.00 and, if needed, between 17.00 and 19.00. This also gave him some quality time in the late afternoon with Sebastian when he was a student at Magdalen College School. On one occasion in the early 1950s one of his colleagues saw them together in the Parks in Oxford. 'Speaking loudly and gesticulating he heard Taylor declaim to the child, "Never trust the House of Habsburg."' Later when it began to rain he told his son, 'You had better put on your mack.' When Sebastian replied: 'Shan't' he responded, 'We appear to have reached an impasse.'[33]

Alan Taylor also favourably impressed his special subject students. Colin Bonwick, for one, learned much from sessions when they worked through documents, as well as from other tutorials by him. He deemed him an excellent tutor, lively in ideas and concerned for his students. Colin Matthew, the distinguished Gladstone scholar, also benefited markedly from his special subject in 1962–63, observing that 'It was the focus of later work'. Ann Wagstaff recalled of his other tutoring, 'When we read our seminar papers we knew if AJP was interested in what we had written because he interrupted all the time. Silence was not a good sign.' She added, 'The main lesson I learnt…was the importance of the first sentence in an essay or book. He told us that if you could capture the interest of the reader with a really interesting and unusual first sentence, then the reader would want to read the rest of the piece.'[34]

Taylor, through his television lectures, capitalised on the latent interest in history that huge numbers of people already had. It is significant that his opportunities to give televised history lectures came after he was an established television figure. They began on independent television, not on the BBC. Indeed, when he suggested to the BBC that it might televise his 'Politics in the First World War', his Raleigh Lecture for the British Academy, they politely but firmly turned him down; not surprising, given his recent many hostile comments regarding the BBC.[35]

He had been one of the few figures on the Left who had been an advocate of independent television. He was influenced by his clashes with BBC officials and he was sympathetic to Norman Collins, who resigned in October 1950 as the BBC's Controller of Television when George Barnes had been appointed above him. The Conservative Party actively promoted commercial television, with the Churchill government bringing in a White

Paper on the subject in 1952. Taylor, along with Malcolm Muggeridge, Rex Harrison and some other personalities of the day, supported the Popular Television Association, which had been set up to campaign for commercial television. As the historian of independent television has observed, the campaign 'was actively assisted both officially and unofficially by the Conservative Central Office'. In the *New Statesman* in 1952 Taylor accused Labour of being Puritan and against entertainment. He remonstrated: 'In my opinion it is possible to be a Socialist and still to believe in freedom. And freedom means letting people have what they want, not what I think is good for them – not even what you do.' When commercial television arrived, the *New Statesman* published a cartoon of Taylor as 'the Don in the Window', providing a little academic respectability to the commercial venture.[36]

Alan Taylor was very much one of independent television's assets for displaying some commitment to informative programmes, along with lectures by Dr Jacob Bronowski on science and Sir Kenneth Clark on the visual arts. Ahead of Taylor's first lecture, John Irwin, his producer, promoted him by describing one of his Oxford lectures, which he had attended unannounced. 'I've seen nothing like it. That audience was hypnotised by Taylor's dynamic personality, his passionate sincerity, his wit, his command of words, his brilliant sense of timing, and his complete mastery of the subject – without a single note.'[37]

His first series was 'The Russian Revolution', comprising three half-hour lectures. They were broadcast at 18.00 hours, when many British families were watching television while eating an evening meal, on consecutive Mondays – 12, 19 and 26 August 1957. They were shorter versions of lectures he was giving at Oxford. These were soon followed by eleven half-hour and two twenty-minute lectures entitled 'When Europe was the Centre of the World', broadcast again on Mondays but at 18.30 (and 18.40 in the case of the two shorter lectures). These ran from 'The Fall of the Bastille' on 23 September 1957 to 'The End of the Story: 1914' on 10 March 1958. There are audience figures of 750,000 for the second series. The two series were judged to be a great success. Norman Swallow, another producer, attributed the success to Taylor's ability to make anything interesting – 'If he chose to talk about a blade of grass he could keep his audience spellbound' – and to the public's interest in history.[38]

Taylor was predictably bullish about these lectures. Before the first series, he commented: 'It's not only me on trial but the whole idea of lecturing on TV,' but he felt confident that 'the British public has an appetite for things which are intellectually interesting and stimulating to the mind'. He predicted, 'I expect we shall have a tremendous university of the air in no time.' He did not resist denouncing the BBC. 'If I had ever persuaded the BBC to televise history lectures, I know what would have followed: endless debate about whether I had chosen the right subjects, and insistence that every word should be approved beforehand. Some "controller" would have claimed to have known more about history than I do and would have been for ever correcting my facts when he was not condemning my ideas.' Elsewhere, he added for good measure, 'If these lectures had been screened elsewhere it would have been because some high-up considered they were "good for the viewer, and he must stick it out even if it is way above his head".' He argued that with commercial television the viewers would decide if there were to be more lectures.[39]

There were further series of lectures, however. His 'British Prime Ministers' series of six half-hour lectures were broadcast at 22.35 on Monday nights between 25 July and 19 September 1960. These were also recorded on gramophone records, later published in *British Prime Ministers and Other Essays* (1999) and, very curiously, 'discovered' by the BBC, as if lost, with extracts broadcast in 2001 alongside comments by Professor Peter Clarke (in spite of the book being then readily available in a Penguin paperback).[40]

By the early 1960s Alan Taylor was very ready to lecture on BBC television. In May 1961 he made a point of letting John Irwin know that after agreeing to a BBC series he had turned down an Associated Television offer.[41] Earlier, in 1958, he fell out with ATV. He commented that he was no longer lecturing on independent television: 'Val Parnell was so angered by my advocating Pay as You View for the new Channel that he struck me off.'[42] He gave two of his better series of television lectures on the BBC in 1962 and 1963. These were also broadcast late in the evening. 'The Twenties' was broadcast at 22.40 or later on Saturday nights in February and March 1962.

In the aftermath of the rows over *The Origins of the Second World War* (1961) the prospect of him lecturing on this theme without clear internal BBC editorial control appears to have created near-panic in some quarters. Leonard Miall, the Assistant Controller, Current Affairs and Talks, Television, declared himself 'considerably disturbed about the Alan Taylor Lectures proposal' and asked, 'Am I expected to deal with the policy problems which will inevitably result from someone as positive in his own opinions as Taylor, about a period as politically tendentious as that between the Wars?' Miall had earlier been outraged by Alan Taylor's highly critical comments about BBC Controllers in the *TV Times* in February 1958, when he gave television lectures on independent television. So much so that Miall had written, 'I suggest it is time to consider whether it is right to continue to offer him broadcasting opportunities in Sound.' Miall was placated but there were still attempts to secure full scripts of the talks in advance and concern as to the choice of topic, with it having to be pointed out that Taylor's lectures were sparkling partly as they were unscripted and that 'The Twenties' had been the BBC's own choice. The BBC hierarchy was also soothed by finding that each programme would cost less than £150 as they required no make-up, wardrobe, property or scenery requirements; though Alan Taylor haggled his fee up from 100 (£105) to 125 (£131.25) guineas a lecture.[43]

'The Twenties' dealt with major themes that he was covering in his *English History 1914–1945*, and for that reason he felt they were too ragged to make a book and he did not reprint them. The first five were substantial surveys, but with the sixth on 'The Great Depression' he bit off more than he could chew. His assessment of the 1929–31 Labour government's handling of the economic crisis and the subsequent decision to abandon the gold standard was ripped apart by the economic journalist Paul Einzig in an essay in the *Festschrift* Martin Gilbert edited to mark Alan Taylor's sixtieth birthday. Alan Taylor acknowledged his errors when receiving the book, commenting that Einzig's essay was 'the most slashing attack I have ever read on an historian's accuracy, and the maddening thing is that most, though not all of it is justified'.[44]

His series 'Men of the 1860s' was broadcast after 22.15 on Mondays during June and July 1963. There was confusion over the title of the lectures, the *Radio Times* heralding it as 'Men of 1862' and *The Listener* publishing the lectures under the heading 'Men of the 1860s'. It seems that the BBC was not happy with the title. His freelance producer, John Irwin, reported that Taylor was quite willing to drop 'Men of 1862' and suggested 'The Coming of Bismarck' (his preference) or 'Bismarck and His Contemporaries', the series being linked to the centenary of his becoming Prime Minister of Prussia on 22 September 1862. He quoted Taylor as saying, 'I shall describe the leading figures in Europe and then take Bismarck last, indicating what difference he made to them. The men would be Napoleon III; Francis Joseph; Palmerston; Alexander II; Marx; and Bismarck. It will put things much better this way.' Until near the first recording date in late August 1962, the series was going to be 'Bismarck and His Contemporaries'; but very late in the day Alan Taylor or the BBC must have had wise second thoughts about such a link. As the last lecture was only recorded on 10 December 1962, the centenary year was missed, making the title 'Men of 1862' seem odd in mid-1963.

The BBC had been tardy in confirming a second series. They had sounded out the availability of Sir Mortimer Wheeler, but to no avail. Taylor succeeded in securing a decision by threatening to return to ATV, and this time he did secure the 150 guineas (£157.50) a lecture that he had sought for the previous series. There was some unease about the simple format. John Irwin was asked to talk with Alan Taylor about having an audience in the studio, but Taylor refused to do so. Irwin reported him as saying, 'Over twenty years I have developed a technique for myself for delivering lectures for an audience of people. During the 30 or 40 lectures I have done to the television camera, I have developed a quite different technique which involves a different tempo and rhythm. I would find an audience distracting and confusing.' However, Irwin did see the BBC's Design Department 'to provide an interesting and appropriate set for him to speak in, and so escape the severity of the black drapes used last time'.[45]

Alan Taylor's 'Men of 1862' were figures he had portrayed in his various books. In the case of the Emperor Francis Joseph his portrait had developed beyond his earlier books on the Habsburg monarchy. He derived part of his depiction of the Emperor 'who moved by clockwork' from such studies as Hermann Broch's *Hofmannsthal und seine Zeit* (1955), in which he was portrayed as 'the abstract monarch'. The Bismarck of this lecture series was a familiar one to his readers: 'With all his faults, I feel he was an attractive and fascinating character. But he had the common German characteristic – he always blamed other people.'[46]

Perhaps because he had published other essays on several of these figures, he did not push too hard to reprint them. He again commented to his publisher, 'You will probably think, as I do, that they are too ragged to make into a book.' He already had *The First World War* (1963) about to appear and was soon to have out a further collection of essays 'mostly on twentieth-century themes', *Politics in Wartime* (1964). When it was suggested he include 'Men of the 1860s' in this volume of essays, he declined on the grounds that they were unsuitable. He also tried to interest the US publisher McGraw-Hill in the 'Men of the 1860s' and other nineteenth-century essays. He broke off these talks when there was an opportunity to publish a larger collection of essays in the United States selected from his three British collections. This volume, *From Napoleon to Lenin: Historical Essays*, was published as a Harper Torchback in 1966, with the suggestion that it would test the market and if it did well two further selections would follow.[47] It was to be the only such volume.

Before the series on the 'Men of the 1860s' was broadcast, he was floating the idea of a series on the outbreak of the First World War for 1964. More than that, he proposed a five-year contract. 'You would agree to take a series of lectures each year; and I would agree not to give television lectures for anyone else – though I could make occasional contributions to other types of programme.' Donald Baverstock, the Chief of Programmes, considered the suggestion but felt that there was no advantage to the BBC in it. He saw no reason to hold him exclusively and was against 'agreeing at this moment that his contribution...should take any specific form such as lectures'. So he was told that they preferred an ad hoc arrangement to any such agreement.

Three months later Taylor came up with three proposals for lecture series. The first was 'The Thirties', dealing with economic recovery, the Spanish Civil War, the Abyssinian crisis, the abdication of Edward VIII, Munich and the outbreak of war. His second was 'Political Battles', from the 1832 Reform Act to the House of Lords crisis of 1910. The third was 'Power without Responsibility', dealing with 'men who had Prime Minister calibre but never gained the office, from Charles James Fox to Aneurin Bevan'. His intermediary with the BBC was again John Irwin. Taylor had earlier informed the BBC when requesting Irwin as his producer, 'While he does not actually own me, he and I are something like a package; and I should be happy with him in the control box.'[48] However, by this time there was insufficient enthusiasm at the BBC for even one series of televised lectures by him.

Taylor was fortunate that Val Parnell was no longer in charge at ATV. His last two television series for a decade were made for independent television, with audiences again at the recordings. In 1964 he gave the second series he had suggested to the BBC, the title 'Political Battles' being replaced with 'Big Rows'. He gave six lectures on big political issues and the general elections linked to them. These ran from the 1832 Reform Act, the Bulgarian Horrors, 1876, the Home Rule Controversy, 1886, the Boer War, the House of Lords crisis, 1910, to 'The Man Who Won the War' (Lloyd George), 1918. These were broadcast at 22.30 on Monday evenings in November and December. His last series of television lectures for a decade were on the Second World War and the start of the Cold War. These went out even later, well after 23.00, on Mondays between June and September 1966. At the core of these lectures were six on Germany, Britain, Italy, Russia, Japan and the US, in which he commented on the war starting at different times for different countries and having different characteristics for each of them.[49]

The most notable features of Taylor's television lectures were his lack of visual aids or notes and his ability usually to fit his lectures exactly to the time available. In his first series the producer put shots of the audience in; but, as this was felt to be a distraction, it was soon dropped. He held audiences spellbound by his narrative skill and his charisma. One reviewer of a later series wrote, 'The background is black, the clothes are neutral, the body is still, the visual display consists only of his attention-demanding right eye balanced by his gesticulating left hand, sometimes signalling the shovelling of parenthesis and sometimes pointing the peda-gogical finger.' A larger part of the success of his television lectures derived from the clear pleasure he gained from talking about his subject.

Part-way through each lecture a glint came into his eyes and he spoke with joy and enthusiasm on his subject; the people and events appeared to really matter to him, and his fascination with his topic was transmitted to the viewer. In 1957 his lecture series were live because they had to be. Twenty years later he lectured in the same manner, with each lecture recorded in one take.[50]

As with his Oxford lectures, he thought out very clearly what he wished to say. He ran it through his mind at home and sometimes in the courtesy car which took him to the television studio. He often also had three alternative conclusions of different length, which he could use according to the time available when he reached the end of his main points. There were times, even when he was at the peak of his powers, when he mis-judged his timing. In the case of Louis Napoleon, the first of his 'Men of the 1860s', he abbreviated what would have been two sentences into: 'In 1873 Napoleon became an exile in England, hoped to come back, was operated upon so that he could sit upon a horse again, died under the surgeon's knife,' before ending calmly with the final sentence, 'At his funeral, the only Frenchman to be with him was a trade unionist.' He appears to have mistimed his second lecture, on Francis Joseph, even more, with the conclusion being very muddled.[51] But this was unusual.

By the later years of Taylor's life his style of television lecturing was viewed as a near-legendary feat. Yet, like 'In the News', it was old-fashioned from the outset. It is doubtful whether many others could have kept audiences' interests for so long over a series of lectures. Other leading historians such as Herbert Butterfield and Hugh Trevor-Roper tried, but they did not scintillate. Taylor was not only a performer – theatrical even in very small movements – but he was also a natural storyteller. Simon Schama, one of his most successful successors, has written, 'Beyond the monk-written memorials and monuments, there remained…a strong unofficial tradition of performative history…So whether he knew it or not, and I strongly suspect he did, A.J.P. Taylor, the grand-daddy of all television historians, was reviving that tradition…' Although presenting history on television in a way which would be foolish today for others to try to emulate, Taylor has often been the starting point for those who reflect on how to present history via television. Sir Ian Kershaw, himself responsible for the highly successful series 'The Nazis: A Warning from History', has observed: 'The stars of a much more elaborate (and expensive) present-day television history, the Schamas, Starkeys and Fergusons, follow in Taylor's footsteps and have inherited the mantle of those who believed long ago that the historian's job was to use their skills and knowledge to bring big and important themes to the attention of a mass audience.'[52]

Alan Taylor's televised lectures did much to popularise history. They had an impact on a whole generation of schoolchildren, with many later historians being greatly impressed by the programmes. Many of those who were in the audience at the Wood Green Empire studio, the Hackney Empire studio or other venues have vivid recollections of his abilities. Francis Taunton had been among one of the audiences for his 1957 independent television lectures. He recalled that, although that night there had been only a dozen people present, once Alan Taylor got in front to record his lecture he 'expanded like a pigeon or turtle dove', no longer the apparently meek and slight figure of before. He said Taylor then had been superb, whereas when he heard him again over twenty years later the elderly Taylor was, not surprisingly, less impressive. Peter Waymark, who was present for two of the second series in September 1957, recalled the dramatic start of his Bastille lecture:

> The 'studio' went dark, but for a pool of light into which Taylor stepped...a very small figure, who took his spot in front of the camera, put his hands together, looked at the ground and then up, and started, 'Ladies and gentlemen' (it seemed to me a very formal way of greeting his audience, even in 1957).

Of the ensuing lecture, he recalled 'how much fresher his version was compared with the school textbooks'.[53]

Taylor and his 'old team' friends also found that independent television's delight at securing them was of limited duration. 'Free Speech', with Taylor, Foot, Boothby and Brown, ran from the first Sunday that independent television broadcast (25 September 1955) until 1959. He wrote to Kenneth Adam of the BBC,

> There's many a true word spoken in jest. You said the BBC would take Free Speech. Well, someone has just virtually killed Free Speech by cutting down my appearance's [sic] and Michael's to almost nothing. If you wanted a discussion programme not tied to party, its [sic] on offer, or rather I am.
>
> Quite apart from this, if you ever thought of using me for discussions or lectures, I am totally uncommitted. I daresay I sometimes cause trouble. But I also give value for money.[54]

This was not to be. The 'In the News'/'Free Speech' format had out-lived its time. Alan Taylor's career as a *regular* political commentator declined, but he increasingly was in demand as a TV or radio personality for a range of discussion programmes. He maintained his friendships with the old team, especially Bob Boothby and Michael Foot. In 1984, in a long and warm letter, Boothby recalled that 'for twenty years when we were addressing audiences amounting to millions together, I was the one who stimulated you most'.[55]

Alan Taylor's political stance became even more unorthodox in the later 1950s. He had campaigned for Labour in the 1945 general election putting much effort in to helping Elizabeth Pakenham in Cheltenham, Frank Pakenham in Oxford and Aidan Crawley in North Buckinghamshire. Elizabeth Pakenham later recalled that she and Alan Taylor went to speak for Crawley one day and he was held up.

> Alan was holding the fort. It was no bother at all for him to make a much longer speech … He was going to make a twenty minute speech and instead of that he made a forty minute speech. When Aidan arrived I thought Alan would sit down immediately. Instead of that he gave us another ten minutes. [This] was my first real insight into how much he enjoyed speaking and politics – and when he got into his theme he jolly well finished it.

At this time she remembered him as being politically 'red hot'. In 1951 he was seen by the Bevanite MPs as a pre-eminent 'friend' outside the parliamentary organisation who might campaign in their marginal constituencies. In the 1955 general election he spoke in the Banbury constituency for N.F. Stogdon.[56]

Alan Taylor had almost endless opportunities of public speaking when he became very active in pressure group politics in the late 1950s with the Campaign for Nuclear Disarmament. The key elements in his taking it up were that he had long deplored nuclear weapons, that he was full of radical alternative foreign policies after his Ford Lectures and, given his high public profile on 'In the News' and then 'Free Speech', he was eager to take his arguing abilities out on tour in promoting what he felt to be the politics of morality.

He had been one of several intellectuals who had been discussing the morality of using the atomic bomb since 1945. In September of that year he had taken part in a radio discussion on the subject, with Professor J.D. Bernal and two Members of Parliament. He had argued then that 'you can't frighten people into an international order with the atomic bomb' and had advocated the creation of 'some sort of international centre for research and not to have secrecy'. He used the issue, as he did most issues at the time, to urge co-operation with Russia. He observed,

> I would tell the Russians about it without any strings being tied to it. I would do so for two very good reasons. First, because they will find out very soon in any case; you gain nothing by secrecy. Secondly, we know the Russians are already working on the other problem of

supplying atomic energy to peace-time use, and they might easily have something to swap for it for us.

During the early 1950s he frequently expressed his concern about nuclear weapons. In the *Daily Herald* in April 1954 he called on Britain to unilaterally renounce them: 'Even if this makes it certain that London or all England will be destroyed, we will not plan to blow up a million people in Moscow or Warsaw.' The issue, he stated, was 'a question of morals'.[57]

Like most of his dissenting heroes in *The Trouble Makers*, his alternative to official foreign policy was different but not an outright rejection of the dominant assumptions of the day. In the case of CND, in feeling that others would take notice and follow a British lead on such a moral issue he was still believing that Britain was at the centre of world affairs, much as Sir Anthony Eden did in the Suez Crisis of 1956. For Taylor, a moral gesture by Britain would impress and have a policy impact on other states.

Throughout his CND campaigning he explicitly linked its strategic aims and methods with those of the Anti-Corn Law League over 110 years before. He believed that the League's orators, notably Richard Cobden, had argued the Corn Law out of existence. He also believed that William Wilberforce and his supporters had similarly won the argument against the slave trade. So, he determined similarly to argue the case against nuclear weapons and to get the British people to press their leaders to renounce them. He later commented, 'My ambition was to be the Cobden of the movement...He was the great arguer – and his aim was to educate the top people.' At the time he wrote in the *New Statesman* that CND 'must never forget that ultimately we have to convert the Labour Party, just as the Anti-Corn Law League converted Sir Robert Peel'. Above all, as he put it in his pamphlet, *The Great Deterrent Myth* (which is dated 3 April 1958), 'There can be no harm in trying morality for a change.'

In being so mindful of the great moral campaigns of the past, he was in danger of being antiquarian in his approach and unreceptive to contemporary alternatives. He complained that the young did not flock to sit to be lectured at by the good and the great. He commented,

> Sooner or later we shall have to win the younger generation back to morality...This country of ours fought two world wars mainly for high principle; and the only lesson drawn from this by the young is that might is right. It now seems unbearably priggish to say that the country which went to war for the sake of Belgium and Poland must not, in any circumstances, drop the H-bomb. But it is true.[58]

In fact, the younger generation was much involved. Giles Taylor, his son, and Euan Duff, the son of Peggy Duff, the dynamic first secretary of

CND, were founders of the Youth Campaign for CND. The Aldermaston marches and more dramatic forms of direct action, organised later by Bertrand Russell and the Committee of One Hundred, did appeal to many young people. Giles Taylor recalled that his father did not think much of the Aldermaston marches, only joining one on its last day; but he did like addressing the huge crowds in Hyde Park at the end of the marches or on other occasions. As his eldest son put it, 'He wasn't keen on direct action. What he was keen on was arguing and making a case.'[59] Also the young people likely to be attracted to CND were likely to be alienated by its early lack of democratic procedures.

Alan was one of the most effective and most energetic of the early CND speakers. He joined CND's executive in April 1958, a few months after CND was formed by Kingsley Martin, J.B. Priestley, Jacquetta Hawkes, Professor Patrick Blackett and others in late 1957. He was one of the star speakers at CND's inaugural public meeting at Central Hall, Westminster, on 17 February. Five thousand people were present there and in three overflow meetings, with possibly a further thousand people turned away. The speakers rotated between meetings. Michael Foot was heckled in the main hall by members of the League of Empire Loyalists.[60] Hearing of this made Alan Taylor even more pugnacious than usual and he gave a notably powerful speech. He later recalled,

> I appeared last, after Michael Foot and Ben Levy. I was last not only because I was not the biggest name, but because many of the speakers had to go off before the meeting ended to see their newspapers off the press. I started pugnaciously, expecting a rough-house from Empire Loyalists. I started off by describing the effect of nuclear bombs on human beings. I demanded, 'Stand up whoever will press the button.' Nobody stood up. So I had nobody to pull apart. I said that those who were against the use of nuclear weapons should wreck the meetings of Ministers, just as the suffragettes had done. We should chant 'Murderers' at them. Having finished, I went home to bed.

However, as he added, a large number of 'middle-class people rushed out and occupied Downing Street – and the police used dogs on them'.[61]

Not all present were favourably impressed by his rhetoric. His former student, Bill Rodgers, was appalled and viewed this and his subsequent CND activities as 'dangerous self-indulgence'. He, like many of Hugh Gaitskell's supporters, 'moved from agnosticism to a firm position – in favour of multilateral not unilateral disarmament'.[62] Those who later wondered why public honours did not flow Alan Taylor's way overlooked the hostility his TV and CND activities and his maverick radical views had aroused in the Gaitskellite wing of the Labour Party, and later on the

Social Democratic Party (SDP) and Labour Right. Roy Jenkins was notably frosty on the subject of Alan Taylor. When pressed, he commented, 'He was prone to bite the hand that fed him.' Interestingly, at the time of Alan Taylor's eightieth birthday, Raymond Carr, commenting on Oxford's failure to give him a Chair, declared: 'You were never defeated by the Tories. It was the SDP types who kept you out.'[63]

After the heady success of the Central Hall meeting, the CND leadership organised large numbers of public meetings across the country. In spite of his heavy commitments as Vice-President of Magdalen College, teaching, writing for the press and appearing on TV and radio, and to two families, he was probably its most regular speaker. For instance, in the early summer of 1958 he spoke at Sandown, Isle of Wight (23 April), Guildford (5 May), St Pancras, London (11 May), Birmingham (12 May), Sheffield (16 May), Cheltenham (19 May), Manchester (21 May), Southampton (30 May), Bristol (2 June), Portsmouth (6 June), Leicester (9 June), Salisbury (26 June) and Brighton (9 July). He had audiences of two or three hundred at the smaller venues and two or three thousand in the big cities.[64]

He gained particular pleasure from his meeting in the Town Hall in Birmingham. 'My best evening came at Birmingham Town Hall where I spoke precisely a hundred years after Bright delivered there his great speech on British foreign policy – "a gigantic system of out-relief for the British aristocracy".' He was also moved to tears by his Bootham history teacher, Leslie Gilbert, now very elderly, being present and coming up to speak to him. Taylor recalled, 'After he had retired he had become religious and had moved to Birmingham... after the meeting, he said, "You do not believe in God. Yet the spirit of God spoke through you tonight."'[65]

Often in the early speaking campaigns several speakers went to each meeting. A later age might have called it the CND Road Show. Taylor recalled, 'Quite often these meetings had [Canon John] Collins in the chair and J.B. Priestley and me as speakers; we were the touring team.' Priestley, however, preferred to speak in southern England, near his home. Taylor thoroughly enjoyed his CND engagements. He later commented, 'I was never nervous before those meetings. The CND case was so powerful it nearly argued itself.' Often Sebastian accompanied his father on his travels, sometimes combining trips for Historical Association lectures with CND talks. They went together to Halifax, staying with Edward and Dorothy Thompson, who organised the CND meeting. Sometimes Eve accompanied him. Ray Challinor, a one-time member of the Committee of 100, recalled her being a very attractive woman but said that she seemed hostile to the proceedings of the meeting. Held in the North Staffordshire Hotel, Stoke-on-Trent, in 1959 or 1960, it was North Staffs CND's most successful ever meeting, with Taylor the outstanding speaker; 'He was in the Radical maverick tradition.'[66]

Alan Taylor was enthusiastic when the CND leadership was mostly an unchallenged elite of celebrities. He was unhappy, as was Canon Collins, with pressure for more confrontational direct action and the demands for a democratic organisational structure. When Collins died in 1982 Taylor wrote, 'I look back with delight and pride to the time when he and I toured the country on behalf of CND. He was…a marvellous leader, tactful and firm at the same time. I have worked more happily with John than with any other leader I have followed.'[67]

The other figure of these years of whom he expressed great admiration was a much more controversial one: Lord Beaverbrook. It was very much a two-way friendship, hingeing at least initially on their knowledge and interest in past British politics. Beaverbrook liked to relive his past, buying collections of manuscripts, commissioning authors and then writing himself accounts of politics during and after the First World War. Many of his former friends were dead or in poor physical shape. Alan Taylor was intellectually lively, a historian with a public reputation and fascinated by the press. For Taylor, Beaverbrook was living history, much as Michael Karolyi had been. He appealed to the aesthete side of him; as with Lord Berners, when he was with Beaverbrook he was an insider among the influential set of people. He also filled the gap left by the death of A.P. Wadsworth and was a boost to his morale when disappointed over the Regius Chair and subjected to much acrimony over *The Origins of the Second World War* (1961). Moreover, he found Beaverbrook to be fun: an irreverent maverick but of the political Right.

In this he joined such diverse people as Michael Foot, Tom Driberg and Alfred Gollin. Michael Foot commented of Beaverbrook that 'the thing that was most notable about him was his gaiety. He could make life gayer altogether than almost anybody I've ever met.' Gollin observed of Beaverbrook, 'He was a charismatic figure. I knew he was using me – but I did not mind.' Taylor similarly confessed,

> Of course Max bribed me as he did everyone else he knew and liked but always with a little personal touch that made his bribes acceptable. For instance he knew I liked claret and not the champagne he showered on others. So there was always a bottle of claret on the sideboard at Cherkley when I went to dinner and a case of claret, not champagne at Christmas.

However, Beaverbrook was wise enough to know that Taylor would be hooked more by history than burgundy or cigars, and hence early on (28 July 1958) tried to invite him to dine with Winston Churchill. It also helped that Eve Taylor liked Beaverbrook and was delighted when the press lord invited them to dine or stay with him at Cherkley, his Surrey home, or Cap d'Ail, in the south of France. Beaverbrook did not like Eve, while Margaret Taylor disliked Beaverbrook.[68]

Taylor's connection with Beaverbrook came about through Beaverbrook's interest in history. His career as a politician long over, Beaverbrook wanted to write accounts of the high politics of his own time. Who better to turn to than Taylor, a historian with a high profile in the media? Beaverbrook first wrote to Taylor on 2 March 1955, having read *The Struggle for Mastery in Europe*, which he referred to as 'this splendid book'. He asked Taylor for his source as to Lloyd George playing with the idea of being 'the Man who made Peace' during the course of the First World War. On another issue, whether the Conservative leaders consented to Grey's plan to concede Constantinople to the Russians, he tantalisingly wrote: 'I think I can produce evidence' to show the reverse. Taylor provided his justification for his comments, while observing: 'I should be very interested to see the evidence on the other side.' He also responded to Beaverbrook's praise with flattery of his own: 'It is agreeable to please historians; but even nicer to satisfy those who have made history.'[69]

This contact with Beaverbrook may have made Taylor more favourable to him when he reviewed his friend Tom Driberg's biography *Beaverbrook* in the *Observer* in early 1956. He commented, 'What Lord Beaverbrook demands from life is excitement... When life fails to provide excitement, his newspapers do it instead... He ranks with C.P. Scott, not with Northcliffe: a crusader, not a Press Lord.' This would have done him no harm with Beaverbrook.

That autumn he reviewed Beaverbrook's *Men and Power, 1917–1918*, the sequel to his *Politicians and the War*. He wrote, 'The present book is equally exciting and equally entertaining. It is less systematic. Instead of ordered narrative, it leaps from one crisis to the next.' He also commented, 'he may sometimes exaggerate the part that he has played in events. No one can exaggerate his gifts in chronicling them.' Of this Michael Foot, who was present when Beaverbrook read the review, remarked to Taylor on the radio, 'It was one of the most thrilling days in his life. Your review changed the whole of his outlook about the writing of books, and it also changed the attitude of other people about his writing of books.'[70]

A year later, in October 1957, Taylor began his long career as a columnist for the *Sunday Express*, with a characteristic piece warning against German reunification. In his autobiography he wrote, 'It is often said that I got on to the *Sunday Express* thanks to Lord Beaverbrook's patronage. This is a myth... I settled into the *Sunday Express* before I ever met

Beaverbrook.'[71] While it is true that he had not met Beaverbrook at that stage, he had corresponded with him. Moreover, Beaverbrook was very well informed about columnists in other newspapers, so he would have been aware of Taylor's earlier contracts, and he was likely to have seen him on television, and he knew Michael Foot and Tom Driberg. It seems highly improbable that John Junor on his own initiative signed up Taylor without Beaverbrook's active involvement.

While Alan Taylor is unconvincing on this point, it is also difficult to believe that he lasted twenty-five years without journalistic ability. Beaverbrook himself did not suffer underperformers gladly and Taylor survived in this role until his health was deteriorating in the early 1980s. His *Sunday Express* columns were widely popular with readers. In the Beaverbrook Papers there is a memorandum on Taylor which included Hannen Swaffler's comments in *World Press News*, January 1961: 'As for the most consistently "best writer", I would have named A J P Taylor and done so with all the greater pleasure because I used to sneer at the naivety of some of his statements. Since then he has learned his job and become prolific and forthright.' Beaverbrook also expressed his appreciation of his pieces, not least when he was not providing his column. On one occasion he wittily observed, 'We miss you in the Sunday Express. An article by the ex-Archbishop of Canterbury was very weak. I think he is trying to follow in the footsteps of the gentle Jesus. I shall send him the story of the money changers in the temple.'[72]

However, for all this, Taylor's special appeal to Beaverbrook was in his capacity as a major historian. Beaverbrook was very anxious as to the worth of his historical writings. On 31 May 1962 he wrote to Taylor to say that, if his book 'And great was the fall thereof' (on Lloyd George in 1921–22) was 'not up to the standard' of his First World War political histories, 'I will not bring it out'; but he wished for him to give 'an opinion for or against publication'. Taylor gave his verdict on 12 June. Apart from wishing some repetitions removed he was emphatically favourable:

> I have just read your galleys with great excitement. I have no doubt at all that the book should be published. It is full of revelations; it is an important bit of your political autobiography; and it is extremely entertaining. It is not like your other books – or rather something of both, with something of its own added.

Beaverbrook replied, 'Your letter is a most exciting message.'[73]

Beaverbrook's *The Decline and Fall of Lloyd George* was published in 1963. Taylor reviewed it warmly in the *New Statesman*. He wrote that like Beaverbrook's other history books 'it is a unique combination of political history and personal recollection. There is the same sparkling style, an equally rich stock of anecdotes, and the same endearing frankness of Lord Beaverbrook about himself.' Taylor also praised his press lord friend in the pages of the *Sunday Express*, in a sketch to mark his birthday in May 1962 and in an 85th birthday tribute two years later.

After Beaverbrook died in June 1964 Taylor continued to uphold his memory. He edited Beaverbrook's short account, *The Abdication of King Edward VIII* (1966), and for *History Today* his essay 'Two War Leaders: Lloyd George and Churchill'. He also wrote a centenary tribute for the *Daily Express* in 1979, as well as becoming honorary director of the library established as a memorial and writing his biography. Beaverbrook managed to praise Alan Taylor from beyond the grave, providing a short but fulsome piece for the *Festschrift* that Martin Gilbert edited to mark Taylor's sixtieth birthday; a tribute so unexpected to Beaverbrook's widow in its indication that the peer was aware of his impending death that she was convinced for a while it was a fabrication, even threatening to sue Gilbert. Over twenty years after Beaverbrook's death Taylor wrote in his 'London Diary' for the *New Statesman* that if he could recall three people from the dead they would be Max Beaverbrook, Gerald Berners and Michael Karolyi: 'What the three had in common was an enormous sense of fun.'[74]

Alan Taylor was greatly criticised both for his friendship with Beaverbrook and for accepting a contract from the Express Group of newspapers. His *Sunday Express* column gave him a further opportunity to express his quirky views, often a mix of individualistic radicalism and tabloid populism. He had regular bees in his bonnet: the dangers of Germany, the case for releasing Rudolf Hess (Hitler's deputy leader) from Spandau prison, the iniquities of the BBC, the threat of nuclear annihilation, the coming of decimal coinage and zip codes on mail in 1971 and all aspects of the Common Market (or EEC).

His sillier side was well displayed in a series of pieces championing motorists' rights to be unfettered by the state, followed quickly by others critical of private motorists. These read oddly at the time, and even more so in retrospect; especially for those who know he was a notably reckless driver, revelling in speed and, like so many others of the time, driving after drinking alcohol. When upper speed limits were proposed, he repeatedly called for minimum ones to clear the roads of people who drove slowly. He condemned 'a general speed limit on the roads' as it would not reduce the numbers killed or injured. While condemning drunken drivers he argued that the breathalyser campaign smacked of a moral campaign against driving and suggested that the commercial lorry was a greater danger to road safety. A little later, he went further on the breathalyser, declaring 'British citizens will cease to be treated as human beings and will become slaves of the machine.' However, once breathalysers were in use, he argued that 'banning even the single drink is the only way of getting rid of the drunken driver', and, later, reverted to his much earlier arguments in condemning the private car and motorways.[75]

In his autobiography Taylor suggested that writing for the *Sunday Express* did not change his own political agenda. He wrote, 'To my surprise I found myself writing radical articles – not of course socialist ones and certainly not any against the Empire. But there was plenty of common ground between Junor and me.' However, such limitations encouraged his existing hostility to the Common Market, his latent English nationalism and a growing scepticism about changes in society.[76] These tendencies were present in his long-running 'London Diary' contributions to the *New Statesman*, but naturally were not so marked in a Left-looking magazine.

His hostility to the Common Market was to make him posthumously a hero of the xenophobic Right. It was very much a cause he shared with Beaverbrook. In 1961 and 1962 he warned *Sunday Express* readers that Macmillan's government was trying to steer Britain into Europe. In 1962 he called on Robert Menzies, the Australian Prime Minister, to 'speak for Britain' and not to endorse Britain's entry. Later in the year he wrote in *Encounter* that 'the Europe now offered to me is not my Europe', regretting the exclusion of eastern Europe, and adding, 'If any people have put themselves outside by their behaviour, it is the Germans.' In speaking up for the Commonwealth he commented that the 'Europe of the Common Market is a colour-bar community in economics, if not in politics'. In the *Sunday Express* his comments were more strident, promising the proponents of the Common Market a strong fight and, later, using language reminiscent of the Right's on Rhodesia, urging that 'we should stand on our own feet and turn back to our own kith and kin in the Commonwealth'.[77]

His attitude to the Common Market owed much to his warm feelings for the former Austro-Hungarian lands and other parts of eastern Europe. It also owed much to his feelings of being a northern variety of the English bulldog – independent, dissenting and proud. He had his English heroes, such as Tom Paine and William Cobbett. His reflections on *The Trouble Makers* made him proud to be the Little Englander equivalent of Sir Arthur Bryant, with England, or Britain, the centre of his world. Britain was unduly at the centre of his account of diplomacy in *The Origins of the Second World War* (1961) and *English History 1914–1945* (1965), very much, and very proudly, focused on England. In his role in CND he saw a moral role for Britain through rose-tinted glasses. While he protested in his autobiography: 'Not that my opposition to nuclear weapons was emotional,' he conceded that 'emotion was bound to come in', and part of that stemmed from a dated belief in the major impact that moral actions by his country could have in the post-Second World War world.[78]

The Origins of the Second World War, more than anything else, established his name as a historian with a major international reputation, but, for a few years, it also damaged his career. When it was put to him in 1978 that he had worked out many of his ideas in the book reviews of the previous fifteen years, he readily agreed. He commented that as Vice-President of Magdalen he did not have the time to go to the archives, so he had worked up the book on the basis of the published documents which he had been reviewing for many years. He wrote much of the book on summer mornings in Yarmouth Mill.[79] Part of the book also followed on from the final lecture in *The Trouble Makers*, with its discussion of those who campaigned against 'the war-guilt lie' and 'Dissenting faith in appeasement'. George Malcolm Thomson, in reviewing *The Trouble Makers*, unknowingly highlighted an aspect of *The Origins of the Second World War* when he wrote that 'the main impression it leaves is that of men, muddled in motives, blinded by prejudices and stumbling towards disaster. For the trouble-makers...stand exposed as the men who helped to bring the war in 1939.'[80] Hitler, presumably, was not the sole culprit from this viewpoint.

Above all, though, *The Origins of the Second World War* was very much a sequel to *The Struggle for Mastery in Europe*. By 1960 Alan Taylor's style had matured, and *The Origins* has some of his finest prose. He tried to liven up this diplomatic history by argument as well as by his stylistic skills. He followed a by then old-fashioned pedagogic style, more usually used by him in essay writing; this was taking a stance and then arguing through the case for this position, exercising his debating skills and wit to see what new light such arguments threw on an old question. He alerted readers to this approach through the occasional asides. This was notably – even notoriously – so when he argued that Hitler did not have deep-laid plans but proceeded one step at a time: 'Human blunders...usually do more to shape history than human wickedness. At any rate this is a rival dogma which is worth developing, if only as an academic exercise.'

He also slipped into self-parody near the end of the book when he wrote that 'it seems that Hitler became involved in war through launching on 29 August a diplomatic manoeuvre which should have been launched on 28 August'. As with his interpretation of the outbreak of the First World War, he paid especial attention to the short-term and accidental occurrences which led to the outbreak of war in Europe. He observed, 'The Second World war, too, had profound causes; but it also grew out of specific events, and these events are worth detailed examination.' The events were mainly diplomatic, thereby taking him to his favoured sources and away from ideological, economic and social issues.

However, in his intensive revisionism at the micro level, he lost sight of parts of the picture he was making at the macro level. He wrote to his publisher shortly before finalising his manuscript, 'I'm pleased with it. But I think it will annoy the old boys who thought they had settled everything about the Second World War years ago.'[81] However, he certainly did not foresee that he would be accused of being an apologist for Hitler. One of Hugh Trevor-Roper's more telling criticisms at the time was the question: 'Was Hitler really just a more violent Mr Micawber sitting in Berlin...?'

Trevor-Roper was sufficiently incensed to write a lengthy attack on the book in *Encounter*, in which he explained 'why I think Mr Taylor's book utterly erroneous'. He argued that in it 'he selects, suppresses and arranges evidence on no principle other than the needs of his thesis; and that thesis, that Hitler was a traditional statesman, of limited aims, merely responding to a given situation, rests on no evidence at all, ignores essential evidence, and is, in my opinion demonstrably false'. He went on to suggest that his 'defence of Hitler's foreign policy will not only do harm by supporting neo-Nazi mythology; it will also do harm, perhaps irreparable harm, to Mr Taylor's reputation as a serious historian'. To this very serious criticism, Taylor responded equally abrasively, suggesting that Trevor-Roper's quotations from his book were inaccurate and 'might also do harm to his reputation as a serious historian, if he had one'. Trevor-Roper's less than convincing reply was that his summaries were drawn from several passages.

Trevor-Roper was by no means alone in condemning Alan Taylor's arguments. Alan Fox complained in *Socialist Commentary*, 'Besides seeking to level down Hitler's guilt, he seeks to level up that of the Allied powers... The proposition that all are guilty does not involve the proposition that all are *equally* guilty.' He deemed Alan Taylor's view to be 'at once perverse and...irresponsible'.[82] A.L. Rowse complained similarly.

Although Alan Taylor chided Namier for not taking into account the importance of political ideas in Britain in the eighteenth century, he was similarly guilty when it came to Hitler and the Second World War. He was far too blinkered in his dependence on published documents and memoirs. As Kathy Burk has commented, 'Given his belief that statesmen did not plan but reacted to external events, writings such as *Mein Kampf* were largely irrelevant.' Whether he had never read *any* of *Mein Kampf* before the publication of the first edition of *The Origins* is another matter. This is becoming hard fact in several publications. Professor Burk uses his own lists of books he had read, and *Mein Kampf* (in German) appearing only in his list in 1962, along with him apparently being unaware of a shortened British edition, as 'evidence which may be taken as conclusive'.[83] However, he appears to have only listed books read cover to cover, so, while it is quite possible that he had never read it, as she argues, it is also possible and even likely that he had read parts on one or more occasions. Either way, her basic point is good: he paid inadequate attention to it. Norman Goda, in a recent reassessment, has argued, 'The failure to read *Mein Kampf* undermines *Origins*' foundations,' and he suggested that the book 'is best left with the other books we allow to remain unread in the stacks'.[84]

It may be that his treatment of Hitler, as of Bismarck and the Kaiser, stemmed partly from left-overs of the Marxism of his youth, as well as his repeatedly expressed anti-German sentiments (e.g. 'With Hitler guilty every other German could claim innocence'). He showed Hitler and the others as responding to the forces of their time. This was his answer at this time to the historiographical issue of the weight that should be assigned to individuals' actions in history. Of course, conversely, it also fitted his view that most big events in history come about by accident, not design. So either way the individual was not the determiner of history.

Whatever else, *The Origins* showed the inadequacies and the dangers of what he called 'pure diplomatic history', or at least of excessively heavy reliance on diplomatic archives. As Tim Mason has shown, the separation of foreign from domestic policy was especially untenable for the Nazi state, not least given the internal pressures to gain resources by conquest.[85] Later, Taylor himself gave lectures in which he pointed to a range of economic, military and political areas that he wished he had considered carefully.

The BBC was eager to have Alan Taylor's controversial book discussed on the radio and television. The plans for radio were discussed at a Third Programme meeting on 8 June. A suggested discussion involving A.L. Rowse was rejected as it was believed that 'it is too late now to do anything which would not repeat the correspondence in T.L.S. and Trevor-Roper's coming article in "Encounter"'. Instead they took up the idea of a producer, Norman MacDonald, of 'asking a "good" German (and he has an eye on one of them) to comment on Taylor's book from the German point of view'.[86] They then 'urgently pursued von Cornides' to do this. Isaac Deutscher was reported as supporting this as he thought it 'important that someone should blast the book if only because the two Sunday papers gave it the kind of review one would have given to Macauley [sic] or Ranke'. He warned that a discussion involving Alan Taylor 'would become a circus'. However, for the BBC producers this was an attractive possibility, with one enthusiastically writing: 'Give HELL to A.J.P.?!'

However, soon Norman MacDonald reported that on reading Alan Taylor's book he had found

> that the press criticism seriously misrepresented it. Taylor does not suggest that Hitler was not expansionist or did not have a list of targets. Instead he claims that Hitler had no master-plan or time-table for reaching these targets, but could not resist exploiting the opportunities presented by the hesitations of the democracies.

In other words, Taylor's thesis is less controversial than it has been made out to be, and does not lend itself to a discussion on whether he was right to whitewash Hitler because, in fact, he did not do so.

As a consequence, Macdonald suggested: 'As it might be difficult to find an outright opponent of Taylor's real thesis, it might be better to have a conversation in which more than one speaker probed Taylor about his attitude with differing emphasis, but without as much conflict of opinion as appeared likely at first.' This proved less attractive than the hoped-for 'circus'. In the end Taylor discussed his book as guest of the week on 'Woman's Hour', during which he answered some notably unchallenging questions, and later the Home Service broadcast his television discussion with Hugh Trevor-Roper.[87]

Given the acerbity of their written exchanges, the television discussion of the book between Alan Taylor and Hugh Trevor-Roper was eagerly anticipated. In the event the programme, on Sunday 9 July, was an anticlimax. Taylor was on his best academic behaviour, or at least near it. Trevor-Roper appeared ill at ease, looking somewhat anxiously at his university colleague, rather like a mouse at a cat about to spring. He wrong-footed himself by referring to 'Taylor', while Taylor spoke to him as 'Hugh', thereby seeming to put a younger colleague, or even pupil, right on the subject under discussion. Many viewers felt that Taylor came out of it better and very few, if any, can have felt that his book was ripped apart. Beaverbrook loyally informed him: 'You wiped the floor with the young man, who is a Regius Professor,' and added that Robert Kee, who chaired the programme, had saved Trevor-Roper from worse.[88] But this was overstating his performance.

There was a lot wrong with the book, and his abilities to argue on television did not make them go away. While he wisely trimmed on some points in his 'Second Thoughts' (put at the front of the second edition) and in later lectures and publications, the book's impact was due to its being a major revisionist challenge to orthodox views. As has already been discussed, it built on some of Namier's insights, and Namier's trusted collaborator John Brooke believed Namier would have approved of the book. Yet it went much further in revisionism than Namier. Perhaps above all, it came out at the right time: sixteen years after the end of the Second World War, when the events leading up to it could be assessed in better perspective and when the wartime leaders were retired or coming near to the ends of their careers. As the first vigorously revisionist work on its subject by a major historian it inevitably attracted much attention later. What is especially unusual about it as a revisionist book has been the scale and persistence of such attention.

To a certain extent the early critics were as Eurocentric as Taylor himself. Professor William Carr commented in 1985, 'It is a natural temptation for Europeans to assume that the Second World War, which has left permanent scars on the continent and completely upset the old balance of power, was essentially "Hitler's war",' and to see the war in the Far East as a 'sideshow of secondary importance'. He added of Taylor's book that, 'although his book did not overturn the wisdom of the mandarins on the origins of the Second World War, it did most assuredly encourage a more critical evaluation of the assumptions made by Sir Alan Bullock, Lord Dacre and Sir Lewis Namier in the second half of the 1940s'.[89]

While it is unlikely that there is any scholar who is not critical of many aspects of Taylor's book, equally most recognise that it did a major service in challenging a whole range of received opinions. Reference to just a few subsequent books illustrates this. Richard Overy, writing in 1987, commented, 'The significance of Taylor's argument was that it forced people to see that British and French policy before 1939 was governed primarily by *raisons d'état*, and only secondarily by moral considerations.' Richard Bosworth's 1993 assessment of the book included, 'It blew apart the cosy interpretations of the Second World War as Hitler's war or as the perennial product of appeased totalitarianism. It suggested that the endless reciting of the "lessons of the 1930s" was no longer enough.' Andrew Crozier, in 1997, commenting on Fritz Fischer's work as well as Taylor's, observed, 'Taylor...may be said to have been the pioneer of the theory of the continuity of German history from 1871 to 1945, now an accepted element in the literature on the subject of modern German history.'[90] While these comments are of interest in themselves, the point here is that scholars still feel his 1961 book is worthy of evaluation and debate, even if most scholars might well first turn to studies of the subject by such historians as R.J. Overy (with A. Wheatcroft), R.A.C. Parker and D.C. Watt.

Indeed, the book and the subsequent historiography, much of which reacted against his views, became a topic studied at undergraduate and graduate level at a large number of British and American universities and colleges. In Britain, in 1971, Esmonde Robertson published *The Origins of the Second World War*, a substantial and not Eurocentric collection, the title of which had Alan Taylor angered as he wrongly felt it infringed his copyright. Roger Louis, in 1972 in the USA, published a collection of the main contributions to the early debate on Taylor's book. In his introduction to this book in a series entitled 'Major Issues In History', Louis commented that its value lay not only in 'identifying the crucial issues' but also in raising 'questions concerning the responsibility of critics as well as historians (including the important problem of how criticism should and should not be written)'. Fourteen years later Gordon Martel edited a set of original essays reviewing 'The A.J.P. Taylor debate after twenty-five years' (its subtitle), observing that Taylor's book 'has still not lost its power to provoke'. A further thirteen years on, after six printings and thousands of copies sold, a second edition with the subtitle 'A.J.P. Taylor and the Historians' was published which included several major new essays.[91] There have been many other collections of essays on the origins of the Second World War, and these have included consideration of Alan Taylor's work. In addition, this interest in *The Origins of the Second World War* was a major reason for three major journals devoting whole issues to his works: *The Journal of Modern History*, March 1977; *Contemporary European History*, March 1994; and *The International History Review*, March 2001.

However, for some years *The Origins of the Second World War* damaged Alan Taylor's academic career. It helped ease him out of full-time teaching at Oxford University, in the sense that in 1963 there was not a strong enough inclination there either to promote him to a Readership or a Personal Chair or to make some special arrangement. That year he came to the end of a fixed-period Special Lectureship which involved less teaching and more time for research. The Special Lectureships were for five years, renewable once. He had had the full ten years, with his college funding the resulting loss of part of his teaching time. He was unwilling to return to the heavier teaching commitments of an ordinary Lectureship. He released to the press the bare facts of his situation, which implied that he had lost his job due to *The Origins of the Second World War*. So his regular university lecturing career ended then, though he remained a Fellow, then an Honorary Fellow, of Magdalen College until his death. He also later lectured at University College, London, the North London Polytechnic and Bristol University. He also preferred not to secure a Chair elsewhere, either in Britain or the United States. Instead, he used the additional time for writing history and for his heavy media commitments.

It would not be true to say that he was held in little or no esteem in Oxford. Over the years he had gained much respect from his lecturing skills and his output of scholarly books. Moreover, he had been diligent in Magdalen and, more widely, had become something of an Oxford 'character'. He was respected, even revered, by many among the generations of scholars below his own age group, including highly able undergraduates. Later, some of these would be major figures in their profession, such as Martin Gilbert, Keith Robbins and Norman Stone. Norman Stone later observed in the *Sunday Times*, 4 January 1998, that Alan Taylor's history 'will be read as long as historians are read'. Alistair Parker in 1993 said that he had been in contact with three outstandingly clever historians during his career: Alan Taylor, Hugh Trevor-Roper and John Habakkuk. While there was much goodwill towards him, Taylor nevertheless clearly felt – as he put it – 'slighted by my profession', and the end of his ordinary lecturing was another 'down' in his life.

The row over *The Origins of the Second World War* did him little or no harm with the general public, who bought more of his books and flocked to his lectures. *The Origins* sold 10,000 copies in Britain alone within a year and continued to sell well. In the United States it even sold 23,000 copies between 1985 and the end of the century.[92] He continued to be very generous with his time for the Historical Association. Giles Taylor later recalled that when he stopped speaking for CND or giving university lectures 'the one thing he was always prepared to do was to speak for the H.A.'. In the 1960s he also agreed to be president of the Isle of Wight branch for two periods, 1960–64 and 1965–68. Before *The Origins* was published he was attracting unusually large audiences. The Bath branch noted of early autumn 1960, 'Our meeting in the Guildhall was filled for our opening meeting when Mr A.J.P. Taylor spoke on "Two World Wars"!' Among his topics in the three years before the book was published were 'Alliance against Hitler; (London S-W, autumn 1958), 'Munich' (Warwickshire, May 1959), 'The Abyssinian Affair' (Leeds, autumn 1959) as well as 'The Origins of the Second World War' (North Staffordshire, autumn 1960) and 'British Foreign Policy between the Wars' (Chester, autumn 1960). As well as talks linked to his forthcoming book he also lectured on his then stock of topics for Historical Association lectures, such as 'Sarajevo' (Coventry, 1958–59), 'The Rise and Fall of Lloyd George' (Chichester, 1959–60), 'Ramsay MacDonald' (Salisbury, early autumn 1960) and 'The Unification of Italy' (Nuneaton, late 1960).

After the publication of *The Origins* and the subsequent rows over it, from 1962 he spoke often to even bigger audiences and gave even more lectures per year to Historical Association branches. Again, many were linked to this book. When he was speaking at a meeting held in a university, he came with two versions in his head, one for an academic audience, the other if he found a large 'general interest' audience awaiting him. He spoke on 'The Peace Treaties of 1919' (Winchester, 1962–63), 'Adolf Hitler' (Cheltenham and Gloucester, autumn 1962; and Finchley, 1963–64), 'The Abyssinian Crisis of 1935' (Sheffield, December 1962), 'The Causes of the Second World War' (to an audience of 240 at a day school, Plymouth 1963–64; and also at Hampstead, October 1965) and 'Appeasement' (Leicester 1965–66). As well as these, other topics he spoke on included 'The Labour Party in the First World War' (Doncaster, 1962–63), 'The Balkan Wars of 1912–13' (Medway Towns, early 1963), 'Churchill, Stalin and Roosevelt' (Cornwall, October 1964), 'Joseph Chamberlain' (Worcester, autumn 1965) and 'Stalin' (Street and Glastonbury, autumn 1965). Again, the attendances at his lectures were exceptional. At Plymouth, 240 attended the day school he addressed and it was deemed to be 'the highlight of the year'. At the Medway Towns branch there was concern at poor attendances but some 200 people appeared for his lecture; and there was a similar experience at Street and Glastonbury.[93]

It would be less than a full picture of Alan Taylor as a historian to omit mention of his dedication to lecturing to Historical Association branches. He clearly enjoyed performing before such audiences, often made up of professional people, history teachers and sixth-formers. He also enjoyed going around Britain speaking to many of the people who bought his books and who were part of his television and radio audiences. An additional pleasure in it for him was that, up to 1961, he often took Sebastian with him when he drove to meetings. Later, he went on his own by train, travelling by economy fares and, in most instances, with genuine reluctance, accepting reimbursements from the branches for these relatively small amounts.

His journeys around Britain to give such lectures also gave him the opportunities to visit friends. When he was invited to speak at the newly formed Grimsby branch he accepted with alacrity, stating that he would come after speaking to the Sheffield and Doncaster branches and would lecture on 'The End of the First World War'. He followed this up by writing that he would be 'spending the night...with an old friend at Louth, and he will bring me over to the meeting', and asking: 'If you are proposing to give me a meal, could he be invited also?'[94] In the event, he and Jack Yates were well looked after. The branch secretary later recalled that before the lecture they were given dinner by Lord Yarborough and after the lecture the Vicar of Grimsby, Canon Gervaise Markham, opened a bottle of 1914 brandy.[95]

Alan Taylor enjoyed staying with Yates in his old, elegant and large house in Westgate. Its tasteful furnishings included William Morris curtains. Jack Yates had never left behind him the style and affectations of the aesthetes ('the Georgeoisie') who had adorned the George in Oxford in their student days. He had turned himself into a major 'character' in Louth, even being elected as an independent to the county council for one term. He owned a bookshop, though he ran it for pleasure and kept little or no control over its stock or finances. He was a distinguished and active member of the Louth Naturalists' Antiquarian and Literary Society, a founder of the Louth branch of the Civic Trust and a supporter of the Council for the Preservation of Rural England. He shared these interests with John Betjeman, another university friend and with whom he had worked for the British Council in 1945–46. Betjeman persuaded him to be joint author of the Shell Guide to Lincolnshire, where Yates' colourful style is displayed with such entries as that under Louth: 'The Town Hall, whose front looks like an annexe to the Vatican but whose back is more like a slaughterhouse...'

In his later years Yates was 'a tall, silver-haired, very dapper man, who was always beautifully dressed'. He 'held himself erect. He had poise and dignity. He was a very cultivated and polished man.' He stood out in Louth for his style and his Rolls-Royce.[96] He also stood out, in a period when homosexual relations were illegal, as an almost certain homosexual. On one occasion, as a governor of Louth Grammar School, he secured Alan Taylor to present the school prizes. At the end of his speech Taylor wickedly baited Yates, saying: 'I'll now tell you what Jack Yates and I got up to at Oxford.' A look of panic came over Yates' face and, in a rather high-pitched, effeminate voice, he cried out: 'I'll close the meeting, I'll close the meeting,' and did so, stopping Taylor from saying any more. By the time of his death he had spent his inheritance and told an acquaintance that he was broke.[97]

Alan Taylor visited Yates after a second visit to the Grimsby branch on 2 October 1970. He drove from a previous Historical Association engagement in Doncaster, stayed overnight in the Kingsway Hotel, Grimsby, and the next day went on to Louth. When Taylor was invited to the Grimsby branch of the Historical Association for a third time in 1977, he replied, 'I shall be glad to come to Grimsby on 7 October even though I shall no longer have the added attraction of visiting my old friend Jack Yates at Louth.' Yates had died in 1971. In 1977 Taylor drove up with Éva and spoke on 'The Bulgarian Horrors'.[98]

After *Bismarck* Taylor toyed with the idea of writing another biography. However, he was not attracted to his publisher's suggestions of writing a biography of another German, Adam von Trott or Kaiser Wilhelm II, nor Prince Metternich, Charles James Fox or Charles Dilke. Hamish Hamilton did publish his Ford Lectures and he also asked for two further collections of essays in this period. The first was *Englishman and Others* (1956). This suffered a notable production mishap at the printers, Western's. The manuscript was mislaid for over a month. Alan Taylor spent much time reconstituting the book and asked for £50 compensation. The delay enabled him to add two further essays, one on Ranke and the other on the Second International.[99]

In his Preface to this set of essays he wrote, 'I am not a philosophic historian. I have no system, no moral interpretation. I write to clear my mind, to discover how things happened and how men behaved. If the result is shocking or provocative, this is not from intent, but solely because I try to judge from the evidence without being influenced by the judgements of others.' Philip Toynbee, in his review for the *Observer*, responded: 'If it had been true that Mr Taylor eschews moral interpretations he would

surely have been a much duller historian than he is…The fact is that Mr
Taylor is a man of strong and pugnacious moral feeling who is never so
happy as when he is attacking cruelty, pomposity and dishonesty.' Ralph
Partridge in the *New Statesman* observed, 'When not posing in a Preface
Mr Taylor is quite ready to admit his own cantankerous individualism.' He
praised the essays for displaying 'his wit, his power of reaching simple
conclusions from complicated facts, his downright common sense and his
delight in exposing stupidity and error' but was critical that 'a historian
with such an acute mind should be content to roam the jungles of history
like a rogue elephant, bowling over all comers with slashing generalisations'. E.H. Carr was less than enthusiastic about the essays in the *Times
Literary Supplement* but commented that Taylor's 'best work, when he gives
himself the time and trouble to think, matches that of any other living
historian in penetration and originality'.[100]

After *The Origins* Alan Taylor was again working on a major book for
the Oxford University Press. Hamish Hamilton took *The First World War*
but then had to be content with the fourth collection of essays, *Politics
in Wartime*. This title was Alan Taylor's own suggestion, replacing his
publisher's 'The Human Element'. Roger Machell rightly felt that the last
essays on Mussolini and George VI were slight, but they could not use TV
pieces on George V and Mussolini. Alan Taylor also resisted the suggestion
of adding his 'Men of the 1860s' to the book.[101]

Geoffrey Barraclough welcomed the collection in the *Observer*. He wrote
that Lloyd George appeared as the hero of the volume and remarked,
'Perhaps it is natural that the great "rogue" of English political life should
appeal to the great "rogue" of English history.' F.H. Hinsley, in the *New
York Review of Books*, commented that while Taylor was the most prominent
and most controversial of living historians, 'it is not the universal opinion
that he is among the most distinguished'. Twelve years earlier Hinsley had
been outraged at Taylor's review in the *Times Literary Supplement* of his
Hitler's Strategy and had written to the editor to complain of its 'strident
and hysterical' tone, its distortions, its theatrical phrases and his 'three
sneers for my academic status'. In discussing Taylor's collection of essays,
he was more restrained than he felt Taylor had been, though commenting:

> It is difficult to believe that he could slip into so limited and distorted
> an account of the Sarajevo crisis were it not the case that his mind is
> fundamentally one that is absorbed in the what and how of history and
> uninterested in the why. If his weakness as a historian is that he
> neglects 'the profound causes' – and this is his phrase – he will not
> correct it by jumping from his extreme of concentrating entirely on
> the detailed reconstruction of historical episodes to that other.[102]

However, there were two of his more important essays in the collection. 'Politics in the First World War' was his Raleigh Lecture, given at the British Academy on 4 February 1959. Alfred Gollin commented in 1977,

> I believe that pound for pound Taylor's Raleigh Lecture…is a contribution of vital consequence. Although it is a brief composition I believe it opens up the entire subject in a way that has not been done by anyone else…I think Taylor has produced, in this lecture, the most brilliant insights. They help to explain what was previously inexplicable.

'Lloyd George: Rise and Fall', his Leslie Stephen Lecture, given in the Senate House, Cambridge University, on 21 April 1961, was a major, early contribution to the scholarly reassessment of this major politician. Kenneth O. Morgan, who also played an eminent role in this, has paid tribute to 'the stimulating effect he had on Lloyd George studies and the decline of the Liberal Party which around 1970 occupied centre stage in modern historical debates'.[103] While there were some trivial pieces in this and his three earlier volumes of essays, there were many short commemorative essays, often for the *Manchester Guardian*, which were much enjoyed. The distinguished historian Donald Read recalled in his autobiography cutting out of the newspaper his '1848' and other pieces and pasting them into an exercise book.[104] The best of Alan Taylor's essays sold well when repackaged in the paperbacks *Europe: Grandeur and Decline* (1967) and *Essays in English History* (1976).

Alan Taylor also found the time to write an incisive, shrewd and witty brief history of the First World War. He had already written this section of his Oxford History of England when he took up this proposal for an attractive illustrated book by George Rainbird, whose firm specialised in preparing such books and selling the 'package' to a publisher. Having no experience in negotiating terms for such a project, he sought professional advice for the first time, turning to the eminent literary agent David Higham. Though Taylor had intended the relationship to be for this one book, it proved to be valuable for the rest of his life.[105] Hamish Hamilton produced an attractive book in time for both the Christmas 1963 market and the fiftieth anniversary of the outbreak of the war. However, Beaverbrook rightly pointed out to him, 'But the reproduction of the pictures should have been better. If you had handed it over to the Oldbourne Press it would have been a much better job and [done in] colour.'[106] The book has remained in print for over forty years.

The book had its hero, *The Unknown Soldier*. In the Preface he perceptively wrote that in trying 'to explain what the war was about' he was concerned 'particularly to resolve the paradox that men were passionately engaged in the war and hated it at the same time'. Contrary to his own precepts he offered the moral: 'Maybe, if we can understand it better, we can come nearer to being what men of that time were not, masters of our destiny.' He also offered another moral, one which increasingly intruded into his historical writing: 'The deterrent on which they relied failed to deter; the statesmen became the prisoners of their own weapons. The great armies, accumulated to provide security and preserve the peace, carried the nations to war by their own weight.'[107]

The book was generally praised as a short and incisive account of the First World War. In the *Spectator* it was reviewed by Alan Clark, the author of *The Donkeys* (1961), an account of the British army on the Western Front which was notably disrespectful of the Higher Command. He warmly welcomed it as 'a masterful omnibus of generalities, every one of which, taken individually, will stand critical dissection'. In the *Times Literary Supplement* Cyril Falls was critical of some military details but, overall, praised his illuminating judgements.[108]

It was a book of its time. And the time was disrespectful of authority. Looking back, Taylor's book appears to be one of several memorable depictions of the First World War of the period. Others include John Terraine's impressive BBC television documentary 'The Great War'. Another was Joan Littlewood's flamboyant production 'Oh! What a Lovely War', described at the time as a 'potted history of the First World War in song, headlines, dance, photographs and occasional brilliant satire'. It was praised by theatre critics for capturing 'the war's spirit of jollity behind the tragedy' but was denounced by leading military historians as a 'travesty' of history.[109] First performed on 19 March 1963 the play preceded Taylor's book, but for a while the two boosted each other.

Taylor knew Joan Littlewood, who was a friend of Tom Driberg and was enthusiastic for CND. She staged a big CND rally in the Albert Hall. She recalled, 'I'd circulated all the London theatres, and put the word about. Everybody was keen to come along and liven up the meeting. A.J.P. Taylor got a marchpast of Scottish pipers.' When his book came out he asked Hamish Hamilton to send copies to her as well as to Michael Howard, the military historian, and Beaverbrook. He wrote in his autobiography,

> I dedicated the book to Joan Littlewood, then at the height of her powers as the producer of that profound entertainment, *Oh! What A Lovely War*. Shortly afterwards when I visited the show for, I think the fourth time, I found all the cast reading *The First World War*... They were delighted that a serious scholar – well, more or less serious – confirmed the version of the war they were putting on stage.

He chose the play as the suitably irreverent subject of his valedictory lecture at Oxford University, with Joan Littlewood and her daughter Shelagh

Delaney, the playwright, attending. He also repeated the lecture to 'a record meeting' of the Bedfordshire branch of the Historical Association.[110]

When Len Deighton bought the film rights of 'Oh! What A Lovely War' and wanted an adviser, Joan Littlewood recommended Taylor. He joined Deighton in Brighton when the film was being made. Neither thought much of the film, but, as Taylor put it, 'We became close friends as we have remained.'[111] Deighton was thinking of diversifying from writing fiction to non-fiction. According to Deighton, 'It was A.J.P. Taylor who suggested initially that I should write a history book.' Taylor wrote the introduction to Deighton's book on the Battle of Britain, praising his detailed account and in particular his 'brilliant analysis [which] makes clear the technical problems of aircraft design in the inter-war years'. When Deighton revised his book he commented on Rainbird's packaging to Taylor, comments which applied equally to *The First World War*. 'The trouble with such projects is the inevitable errors that come from so many people working together. The advantage is the use of pictures that only good researchers can find [and] only good artists and diagram designers can produce.' In the case of the revised edition of *Fighter* they both disliked the printing of text on coloured paper.[112] Len Deighton, as the author of best-selling Cold War spy novels, was naturally intrigued by Taylor's former pupil and friend Sir Maurice Oldfield, head of MI6 at the time he and Taylor were discussing Second World War intelligence issues in their correspondence. He asked in July 1978, 'If you think your friendship with Maurice Oldfield would not be prejudiced by having me along at the same time, I would be very interested to meet him.' Later, Len Deighton observed of Taylor, 'I enjoyed the generous way he allowed me to argue with him. We both enjoyed being devil's advocate and it was usually a race to see who would assume the most untenable position.'[113]

During the late 1950s and early 1960s Taylor was reading for, and then writing, his second large Oxford University Press book, *English History 1914–1945* (1965). Professor Roger Louis later commented, 'Having been his student during the *Origins* controversy, I rejoiced to see his historical reputation redeemed when *English History* was published.' G.N. Clark had sounded Alan Taylor out about writing the successor volume to R.C.K. Ensor's 1870–1914 volume in early 1957 when, after ten years, Ensor finally withdrew from writing the successor volume on the grounds of ill-health. Clark had consistently been a good friend and patron and had been favourably impressed with the speed with which *The Struggle for Mastery in Europe* had been delivered.

However, when Clark put Taylor's name forward to the delegates of Oxford University Press (the governing body), there was considerable resistance. Professor Austin Lane Poole, the President of St John's College and the author of the volume on the period 1087–1216, had earlier unsuccessfully opposed Taylor being invited to write for the Modern European series, and now he opposed him writing for the British series, fearing it would be 'partisan' (i.e. radical) in its viewpoint. At the meeting of the delegates he expressed concern that Taylor was more an international relations specialist (a valid argument) and that he was writing another book for the European series. George Clark's reassurances that Taylor was not writing for the other series, and that as editor he would ensure that Taylor did not introduce his political views into the book, were sufficient to gain him the contract for the book.[114]

Alan Taylor made an immediate start to preparing to write the book. He took to reviewing large numbers of books on this period of British history. He also wrote to Beaverbrook on 20 May 1957, asking Beaverbrook for his sources for his account of Lloyd George's visit to the Admiralty to insist on convoys on 30 April 1917 in his *Men and Power*. While he got no satisfactory answer to this, Beaverbrook having made it up, Beaverbrook did allow him to see various important documents in his possession. More than this, Beaverbrook dazzled and inspired him with his recollections of the politicians and politics of the period of his Oxford history. In early 1962, when he found himself stuck at the point of writing about 1931, Beaverbrook further stimulated him with anecdotes and recollections. Alan Taylor later testified, 'Beaverbrook did me the greatest service in my life,' adding: 'That night Max saved my intellectual life.'[115]

Given his other commitments, he made relatively quick progress with *English History*. In April 1958, when telling Hamish Hamilton that if he could 'think of something like Bismarck' he would do it, he commented, 'I have a long-term commitment to write a volume in the Oxford History of England on the period 1914–45. But when?' He was kept to his major task by George Clark, who encouraged him to keep writing, read drafts and stood by him during the storm over *The Origins of the Second World War*. Towards the end of 1961 he could report to Clark,

> I'm now halfway. I've got Baldwin out and Labour in for the second time; and I see my way clear through the crisis of 1931. I haven't started to think about the thirties. I haven't even started to read – a terrifying task – about the Second World War. However, I am now beginning to think that one day there'll be a book.
>
> It will be criticised, I think, for being too political. This is partly because it is. It's also because I have dealt with education, local government and even sex (very good!) within the political framework. Maybe I'll have to interrupt the narrative somewhere after all. But I shall resist it if I can.[116]

By August 1962 he had reached 1933 but was concerned about the period from 1936. He confessed to Clark, 'I am worried about 1936–39, because at the present there seems nothing in my mind except foreign policy and rearmament.' At this time he also made it clear he would end in 1945, there having been some talk of the book going to 1951 or 1952. In February 1964 he told Clark,

> Now you inspire me to get on with World War II. I see my way to the end of 1941. Then somehow British history comes to an end – eclipsed by the new great powers. And one feels what's the point of going on? But then what was the point of World War II? I remember feeling very strongly at the time that it had one and now I can't see what it was. Or nearly so.

At the end of June he had only revisions to make to his text. He worried about the wording of what was to be a famous final paragraph, commenting to Clark: 'I'm not happy about the final page. I want to say that I like the English people very much and have a poor opinion of those who claim to guide them. I'll get it right in the end.'[117]

Alan Taylor spent the summer of 1964 revising the text and writing the bibliography. That he had completed it only four years after seeing off the manuscript of *The Origins of the Second World War* owed a lot to the ending of his lectureship at Oxford and also much to Clark's encouragement. When the book was published he wrote to Clark,

> I should have written long ago to say once more how much my *English History* owes to you. Between us we made a respectable and responsible book which has silenced most of the critics…I feel guilty over some things: antibiotics and preventative medicine for instance, and I ought to have done more work on popular taste. But it is a hard subject.[118]

It remained a hard subject for him. Indeed, in populist mode, he wrote disingenuously in his autobiography, 'But what conceivable significance had such writers as James Joyce or Virginia Woolf for the majority of English people? These were coterie interests, irrelevant to history in any serious sense.' He took this rather silly view even further in his next book, *From Sarajevo to Potsdam* (1966), requested by Geoffrey Barraclough for his series 'The History of European Civilisation'. In this he brazenly evaded concentrating on culture, declaring that 'European civilisation is whatever most Europeans, as citizens, were doing'. He continued, 'In the period covered by this book, they were either making war or encountering economic problems. Therefore war and economics make up their civilization.'[119] Even so, there was more politics than economics.

In *English History 1914–1945* Alan Taylor also displayed his growing tendency to be a champion of English nationalism, albeit with a nineteenth-century radical streak to it. In May 1961 he confided in Clark, 'Now I am obsessed with England (a limitation which I take literally: to hell with Scotland, Northern Ireland and still more the Empire!!).' In another letter to him he wrote, 'We shall have trouble with the Scotch (Scots? Scottish?) who claim that England ceased to exist in 1707. I shall speak for England in the preface.' This he did, seemingly modelling himself more on Dr Samuel Johnson than radical English nationalists. His insistence on 'Scotch' not surprisingly offended many people. He was still defending his usage ten years later. This odd English nationalism, combined with his anti-EEC views, led to him beginning to become a hero to some on the political Right. Yet, overwhelmingly, the book – and his political views – were radical.

The Oxford University Press had high hopes of big sales. So, when considering how to promote it, they decided on 'an arresting jacket... different from the series jacket' as this would boost the size of orders from W.H. Smith and other such firms. This was frankly seen, as Dan Davin, the secretary of the Oxford University Press put it, to be 'cashing in on Taylor's reputation, or notoriety'. A colourful jacket was prepared. It had a bright blue background with five photographs across it: Lloyd George and Churchill in 1917; stretcher-bearers in the mud at Passchendaele in 1917; Hitler saluting; Roosevelt, Stalin and Churchill in 1945; and the D-Day landings, 1944. Taylor was outraged by it. He complained,

> I have acquired, I think undeservedly, the reputation of being a jour-nalistic, unscholarly writer. This jacket will confirm the reputation. People will think the book is another piece of provocation by an elderly *enfant terrible*...I have put years of labour into this book, partly with the intention of showing that I was a serious scholar. This jacket will ruin all my efforts.

This had the desired effect, the colourful jacket being scrapped and replaced with one in the series' austere style.[120] The jacket did not prevent the book selling extremely well, in hardback and paperback. Within ten years it had sold 54,484 copies, bringing its author over £10,000 in the first year. In his autobiography Taylor proudly noted that it was the only one in the series to become 'a best-selling paperback in Penguin'.[121]

Like *The Origins of the Second World War* the initial reviews were good, but, unlike the earlier book, its reception continued to be favourable. *English History 1914–1945* was praised as a tour de force by both Noel Annan and Alan Bullock. Annan dubbed its author 'a Populist. Taylor believes that the people are not just equal with their rulers, but are better than them.' Annan suggested that Taylor had achieved one of his early ambitions:

'It...deserves, like Macaulay's history, to supersede for a few days the last fashionable novel on the table of young ladies.' Charles Loch Mowat, author himself of an impressive history of inter-war Britain, observed of the early pages that they 'contain some of his most far-fetched and unsupported observations, as though he must emulate Gibbon not only in pungency but in naughtiness'. Overall, though, Mowat deemed it a great success: 'Here is the history of a generation, comprehensive and comprehensible, well proportioned, seldom rushed, and never flagging in interest.'

The various reviews, emphasised, as did F.H. Hinsley in the *Times Literary Supplement*, that it was 'the most readable book of its size that we have been given for many a day'. He went on to observe that it is 'a book in which his undoubted talents as a technical craftsman of wide learning are at last happily yoked, not only with his accustomed brilliance as a stylist, but also with the balance and the sensibility of a mature historical mind'. Henry Pelling, who might have been seen as the more obvious author of this volume in the Oxford series, gave the verdict that reading the book was 'a very rewarding experience. The narrative, which is exceedingly skilfully woven, never fails to keep up its pace from the first page to the last.' However, he regretted 'Mr Taylor's unwillingness to allow for the strength of social and political forces outside Westminster' and listed many factual errors.[122]

English History 1914–1945 was influential with the next generation of historians, even though, as Taylor noted, he completed it at 'precisely the date when all the official records of the period were still closed under the fifty-year rule'. Paul Addison, whom he deemed one of his very ablest postgraduates, wrote an impressive account of the politics of the Second World War, *The Road to 1945* (1975), with the benefit of access to the public records. Even nearly 35 years on Robert McKay, author of two books on Britain in the Second World War, found Taylor stimulating, observing: 'His real use to me was in raising questions about the war experience that I could investigate elsewhere – that and giving me the opportunity to chuckle, rare enough when reading a history book.' Alan Taylor's book was selected by Professor David Cannadine as his choice in a newspaper series 'I Wish I'd Written...'. He recalled that, after reading much of it, 'I had decided that I wanted to become an historian myself'. For him it was 'the most compelling and exciting history I had read'. Looking back after 33 years he was critical that it was often 'wrong-headedly opinionated', weak on economic, social and cultural history, and subsequently proved wrong on some points, yet he felt that 'it is also a dazzling display of the historian's narrative art, it coruscates with wit and fire, life and warmth, it is a paean of praise to the English people, and it concludes with one of the most memorable paragraphs ever written. It is Taylor's history of Taylor's times.'[123]

– 7 –

MELLOW ELDER STATESMAN

After 1965 Alan Taylor seemed to many people to have mellowed. The storm over *The Origins of the Second World War* had lessened and *English History 1914–1945* was received mostly with warm acclaim. He was no longer competing within Oxford, and this may have lessened his old acerbity towards some of his peers. To a wider public he was increasingly 'the History Man' and, more generally, he continued to be much in demand as a media personality. In 1966, at 60, he had achieved many of his ambitions and was resigned to not attaining others. All the same, he remained something of an ageing *enfant terrible*, appearing to take great delight in disconcerting people by forcibly expressing unconventional opinions, especially on TV or in the popular press.

After the publication of the career-enhancing Oxford histories and his various diplomatic studies, Taylor now pleased himself. He devoted most time to working on his biography of Beaverbrook, but also responded to attractive offers from publishers for survey books. As well as expecting that he would enjoy writing about his famous friend, he also knew that a big biography of Beaverbrook, based on his huge collection of private papers, would attract major newspaper, radio and television attention when it was published. It was also a book on which he could work at what was for him a leisurely pace. Moreover, it provided him with that rare opportunity for a historian: sole access to an important archive.

Initially, in 1965, Taylor had to go to Beaverbrook's large Victorian house, Cherkley Court, near Leatherhead, Surrey. Beaverbrook had allowed several selected authors to work on his collections of twentieth-century political papers. These had included Robert Blake on Bonar Law as well as Frank Owen and John Grigg on Lloyd George. Beaverbrook had also provided selected papers from his collection to Alfred Gollin, who had seen them in the *Express* offices when he was working on J.L. Garvin and Lord Milner, and also to Arthur Marder, when he was writing on British naval history.[1] Taylor, who had not been accustomed to travelling far for his sources since the early 1930s, was taken aback that each visit involved spending three hours driving to Cherkley and back. He later recalled, 'I went two or three days a week and peered at random into the boxes, convinced that I should make no progress.'[2] Cherkley was an inconvenient place for scholars to go to use Beaverbrook's massive collections of politicians' papers and Lady Beaverbrook had no wish for Cherkley to be turned into a record office. With Beaverbrook's family keen for a biography, and for it to be written reasonably soon, the answer was to move the archives wholesale to the *Express* buildings. Beaverbrook's son, Sir Max Aitken, secured Taylor's agreement to be the custodian of his collection of papers. Getting Taylor fully committed to writing the biography may well have been a major part of the motivation for setting up the library, with a general memorial to Beaverbrook being a secondary but substantial aim.

Alan Taylor was happy to be honorary director of the library. He wisely wanted independence, to set his own terms of work and to be free to maintain his high earnings from the media and from lucrative contracts for historical writing.

The *Express* Group's architects made a very good job of converting a floor of an unattractive building at 33 St Bridge Street, just off Fleet Street. Researchers went up inauspicious stairs, not unlike those for a big building's emergency back exit, with at one point a view of huge rolls of newsprint paper, and as they went they often heard the clattering noise of printing machinery. From a bleak landing, readers entered a lush academic oasis, where near the entrance a large portrait of Beaverbrook by W.R. Sickert acted as a screen. Beyond were two rows of glass-topped display cabinets, carefully chosen photographs and cartoons or documents from the collections. To the left of the displays was an office for the secretary, and at the end offices for Taylor and the archivist. Along the walls were framed Low cartoons. So the Beaverbrook Foundation provided Taylor with his own, very modern, air-conditioned archive, with the Beaverbrook and other collections housed in box files in stacks on rollers, and a small staff to assist him.[3] These were near-ideal conditions in which to write his biography. The Beaverbrook Library opened to researchers on 25 May 1967, three years to the day after Beaverbrook's eighty-fifth and last birthday. At the official opening there was a large gathering of Beaverbrook's friends and associates, including Stanley Morison in a wheelchair.

Writing *Beaverbrook* was central to his first four and a half years in charge of the Beaverbrook Library. In August 1970 he wrote to Éva Haraszti,

I have gone through all the relevant Beaverbrook files right up to the end of his life. Now I must settle down and write the chapters on his last twenty years. You know how it feels when a stage of one's work is passed – glad it is over and yet missing it. I can't imagine coming down here every day and not pulling boxes from the shelves. And what will become of me when I have finished even writing the Life?

When, on 4 October 1971, the book had been proof-read and was complete except the index, he commented to Éva, 'I fear I have lost interest in this Library now that *Beaverbrook* is finished. I am restless and discontented...' To John Gordon of the *Sunday Express* he commented that he felt 'quite bereft'.[4]

In his role as honorary director of a major archive he was assisted by a staff of three. Rosemary Brooks, who was 47, had been one of Beaverbrook's secretaries at Cherkley from 1953. She had carried out research for Beaverbrook, helping Sheila Lambert, Beaverbrook's archivist, who had catalogued the Bonar Law and Lloyd George Papers, and after Beaverbrook's death she had been in charge of the archives. Brooks was an apparently self-assured woman, whose knowledge of early twentieth-century British political history helped her answer broad queries from readers. She was devoted to the memories of Beaverbrook and her father, William Collin Brooks (1893–1959), the journalist, writer and broadcaster. Brooks, a close associate of Lord Rothermere, was editor of the *Sunday Dispatch*, 1935–37. He was probably best known through his appearances on 'The Brains Trust' and 'Any Questions?' after the Second World War. She often spoke of him and his diaries, a selection of which have subsequently been published.[5] After the library closed for the day she sometimes joined a few regular researchers in a nearby pub towards Blackfriars Bridge, where she drank Bells whisky with relish. She also enjoyed telling young readers at the Beaverbrook Library anecdotes her father had told her. For instance, to those interested in Austen Chamberlain, she recounted with gusto Balfour's reply to her father's query as to why Austen Chamberlain never became Prime Minister: 'Because he was a bore.' Sadly, she was rather frail, suffering badly from asthma.

Bill Igoe, who was older than Rosemary Brooks, brought the documents to readers. He was an amiable Scotsman with marked nervous mannerisms, who had worked as a journalist for the *Express* newspapers and was in semi-retirement in this post. He took a real interest in readers and their research, especially American academics, of whom he seemed to be in awe. He had encouraged Michael Sheldon to be the biographer of Graham Greene. He was a great admirer of Taylor, perhaps as much for his media role as his historical fame.

Veronica Horne (later Benjamin) was the Beaverbrook Library's secretary. She had previously worked in the *Express*'s typing pool. She was a young and attractive woman, attractive in character as well as in looks. She was very helpful and considerate, especially to impoverished postgraduate students, for whom she took great pains to save money by manoeuvring as much material on to as few sheets of xerox as was possible. She was quietly efficient, very helpful to Alan Taylor in a self-effacing way.

With these three in their posts, Taylor found that the archive could run effectively without much input from himself. He could concentrate on the Beaverbrook Papers or engage in other business. He walked to the Beaverbrook Library from his home near Regents Park, arriving at 9.30 a.m. and usually staying until 5.30 p.m. It was a very convenient base for his newspaper, radio and television activities, as well as for meetings with his literary agent, London publishers or overseas scholars visiting the United Kingdom. He also enjoyed spending his lunch hours exploring the Fleet Street and City areas and their churches.

Nonetheless, the Beaverbrook Library for him was much more than an ideal place to write *Beaverbrook* and a base for many of his other interests. It enabled him to be a part of the international research community working on twentieth-century British political history. It was very much a two-way relationship. He stimulated and encouraged many of the researchers visiting the Beaverbrook Library, his self-appointed role in this being akin to a research professor in a major university. At the same time he himself was recharged by contact with many of the major scholars working on the period of Beaverbrook's political career. He also learned much of the findings of those working through the newly released Public Record Office material for 1916–36, available when the 50 year closure of public records was reduced to 30 years by Harold Wilson's Labour government.

On most days the Beaverbrook Library had two or three readers. At peak periods, such as university vacations, the ordinary capacity of six seats was filled, with eight places occasionally in use to meet the need of overseas scholars. It was an extremely pleasant, air-conditioned, huge room in which to read documents, providing a high-quality environment, rather than a less comfortable one but with numerous spaces for researchers. Younger scholars working there would find themselves working beside such figures from the worlds of politics, journalism and publishing as Richard Law (son of the former Prime Minister Andrew Bonar Law, whose papers were there), Sir Dingle Foot (Liberal and later Labour MP and Solicitor General, 1964–67), John Grigg (working on his multi-volume biography of Lloyd George), American scholars, such as Stephen Koss (prolific author on twentieth-century history) and Bentley B. Gilbert (also working on a multi-volume biography of Lloyd George), and already well-established

British academics such as Charles Loch Mowat, Henry Pelling, Maurice Cowling and Kenneth O. Morgan. Alan Taylor frequently went round the readers, enquiring with interest what topic they were working on and, where he could, often offering advice as to relevant holdings in the Beaverbrook Library. The most striking feature of this was that he gave the newest postgraduate as much attention as the most distinguished visitor.

He also made the facilities available at the Beaverbrook Library known to supervisors of PhD students, especially those at London University, and gave advice to those postgraduates who sought it. One example is my own experiences at Birkbeck College. In early November 1968, agonising over the choice of topic for a PhD thesis, I was sent to the Beaverbrook Library to investigate its holdings. After thinking of possible topics linked to Lloyd George, I returned on 29 November with an appointment to see Alan Taylor to discuss with him whether any of my ideas would make a good research topic. I was ushered into his office at the end of the Beaverbrook Library and he gave my ideas his full attention for half an hour. Afterwards I noted, 'We discussed Lloyd George and the Empire – he agreed it was a non-starter; and he took to my suggestion of "Lloyd George and Labour" and made some very useful observations. He seemed to be a very kind man, and in no way tried to rush me out.' I left walking on air, feeling that there was nothing in the world more interesting that the topic I was about to research. A fortnight later, when working in the Beaverbrook Library, he came up to me and asked if I was happy with my work and, after I had replied: 'Yes,' said that he felt that my research topic was a good one.

As well as providing such individual help and encouragement, Taylor ran an excellent research seminar at the Beaverbrook Library. Before its first meeting he and his colleagues were very apprehensive as to whether readers would return to the library after it had closed at 4.00 p.m. for a series of seminars at 5.30 p.m. In the weeks before, all four of them took pains to press each visitor to the library to come to the first seminar on 12 December 1968. In the event, it was well attended and a success. At it Michael Dockrill gave a paper, 'Lloyd George, Grey and Foreign Policy'. A week later, Taylor's own seminar, on 'Lord Beaverbrook as Historian', was packed, as had been expected well in advance. These two seminar papers, along with two given after Christmas by Geoffrey Alderman and Paul Addison, laid the foundations for a successful series of seminars held in university vacations between then and 1975 (with a gap in early 1971).

Taylor turned to one of his postgraduates, Chris Cook, to help him organise it. Cook later described it as something of a quid pro quo arrangement, with Taylor helping him with the LSE's locating political archives project. The seminar gained a reputation as the best in London on twentieth-century British history. Taylor was delighted that this was stated in the introduction to a second *Festschrift*, marking his seventieth birthday, entitled *Crisis and Controversy: Essays in Honour of A.J.P. Taylor* (edited by Alan Sked and Chris Cook, London, Macmillan, 1976). However, in expressing such pleasure he recognised that 'there were some very boring papers at them – especially on foreign policy'. He returned to this theme later when he commented that he 'had enjoyed the Beaverbrook Library seminars, but they had tailed off towards the end'.

The Beaverbrook Library seminars were initially linked to Taylor's idea of editing a book of some essays written by researchers at the Beaverbrook Library. On 14 October 1968 he had written to Roger Machell of Hamish Hamilton to enquire if he would be interested in publishing such a volume. He commented,

> I have had something like 150 researchers here during the last eighteen months and should like to see something of their researches. Between a dozen and twenty of them are willing to contribute an article (I suppose 10,000 words) to a Lloyd George volume. The subjects would range over Lloyd George's 1909 Budget, Lloyd George and Ireland, Lloyd George and housing and Lloyd George and Hitler. The articles would be, I rather fear, rather academic, though some of them would be very interesting. All the writers, of course, would be young, and most of them unknown.[6]

The book went ahead.

In bringing *Lloyd George: Twelve Essays* (1971) to print, Alan Taylor displayed both his altruism in securing such a publication for mostly young scholars and offering them good advice, and his proneness to great irritability, even tantrums, if things inconvenienced him.[7] He was anything but thorough in checking the proofs of his own books or correcting errors in later editions. In editing these Beaverbrook Library essays he did not think to warn those publishing for the first time that they should not change their copy-edited texts in proof or it would entail costs. Older hands such as Kenneth Morgan made very few changes. However, when the proofs were returned Taylor found that several of his authors had made substantial changes. He wrote to Roger Machell, 'I am afraid that there are a great many corrections. This is no doubt my fault for failing to give precise enough instructions to novices. However, I shall make them pay for it. Could you, therefore, roughly allocate the cost of corrections among the individual contributors, and I will collect from them.' He concluded the letter, 'Never, never again will I edit a volume of other people's essays.'[8]

He had also been greatly irritated by the demands of his American publishers, Athenaeum, who had demanded proofs or typed copies before Hamish Hamilton had set up the British edition. He wrote to David Higham in March 1978 that to meet the demands would swallow most of his share of the royalties from the US edition. He added that, if the American publisher continued to complain, 'you may tell them that their complaint will be met and you should add that under no circumstances will any future book of mine be offered to them'. Later in the month Alan Taylor paid £20 4 shillings (£20.20p) to have the essays copied, then learned that the American publisher preferred to have a photo offset of the London edition. He wrote in wrath to David Higham, recounting this and adding: 'There have been far too many mistakes of this kind in our recent dealings, and this is to give notice that I do not propose to call on your services as agent in any future dealings.'[9] He soon cooled down. Or perhaps he was never that hot. This is quite possible, given his keen concerns where money was involved to get what he felt to be his due; in which case the letter was intended to secure a refund of his copying costs. Whatever the case, good relations were very soon restored with David Higham and he did publish with Athenaeum again.

The Beaverbrook Library seminars became a major forum not only for the contributors to the *Lloyd George* essays but for those researching twentieth-century British history generally. They brought together different generations of British scholars as well as visiting American, Australian and continental European academics. With Taylor in the chair and often a distinguished audience, they were challenging opportunities for younger academics and useful opportunities to try out ideas and report new findings for the more established.

In his autobiography Alan Taylor wrote deprecatingly of his own role in the seminars: 'I was merely required to keep more or less awake during the reading of the piece and then make a few light-hearted remarks afterwards.'[10] Indeed he made quite a pose of being asleep during most papers, resting his head on his shoulder rather like an owl. This greatly disconcerted a few speakers, notably some of those from overseas. In fact, he did listen to the papers, as was usually shown implicitly by his comments after the speakers ended. His remarks were rarely light-hearted – at least, not in the sense flippant. One of the few exceptions was after a very good, scholarly, but not over-lively, paper entitled 'The Struggle over the Ministry of Health, 1914–1919' by Frank Honigsbaum on 24 July 1969. I noted at the time,

> At one point to someone wondering why so few doctors had been in charge of the Ministry of Health, Taylor made the obvious answer that there have been few doctors of ministerial calibre in the Commons. Then [he] commented, only in the legal offices are professional men always in charge. Yet…they know no more, indeed even less, than other people do of the law. If they did, then cases wouldn't drag on so long

and they have to spend so much time looking up past cases, or paying other lawyers to look up old cases. Of course Taylor was joking…

But he did not often indulge at his seminars in populist comments of the kind he delighted in writing in his newspaper columns in the mass circulation press.

The main criticism made then and later was that he did not engage with the points made by the speakers at the seminars, leaving such engagement to occur in the general discussion. His contributions usually were intellectually lively, pithy and highly revisionist reappraisals of the topics under discussion. In this he stimulated discussion, encouraging those present to think afresh about the topics. He was also witty. For instance, after a paper given on 1 July 1971 by Dr Roy Douglas, a notable historian of the Liberal Party, he impishly observed, 'Whilst the Liberal Party declined, the leading figures did nothing to stop it, even helped it. Moreover, they saw to it that the whole process was well documented!'

For all his encouragement of others, Taylor's main task at the Beaverbrook Library was the biography of Beaverbrook. Given that he devoted several years to the project, when he was still at the height of his powers, the outcome was disappointing. Earlier, Beaverbrook, through his financial power and the advice of his libel lawyers, had brought Tom Driberg to heel when he had written a too frank and very critical biography. This, in spite of Beaverbrook having urged Driberg, after reading the first few chapters, '*Now* you'll have to attack me much more fiercely!'[11] Nevertheless, Driberg, who owed Beaverbrook much, not least helping him when he was prosecuted unsuccessfully over an alleged homosexual offence in 1935, had bitten hard the hand that had fed him (as Kingsley Martin observed at the time).[12] With Beaverbrook dead, Alan Taylor had the opportunity for a frank, critical but not unfair biography. His biography had many merits, but it did not live up to the fiercely irreverent and revisionist expectations arising from Taylor's career. His Beaverbrook turned out to be something of a 'troublemaker', perhaps justifying in Taylor's eyes his friendship with the press baron.

Although Driberg's biography was 'mutilated by Beaverbrook's lawyers' (as Driberg put it[13]), it nevertheless remained highly critical of its subject. It depicted Beaverbrook as a Jekyll and Hyde figure, prone to misuse power and relentlessly pursuing vendettas, notably against Lord Mountbatten and Sir Anthony Eden. The book also presented him as a crude materialist, lacking in principle, and derided his major political idea of imperial economic unity as 'an infantile notion not worthy of consideration'. In it Driberg was also critical of that part of Beaverbrook's character which led him to torment friends. Then 'a devil seems to enter into him…[and] he will take delight in contradicting whatever they say, in chaffing them cruelly, in exposing them to the ridicule of the company'.[14] Beaverbrook exercised this cruel streak on employees who dared not answer back. This side of him was vividly portrayed by his secretary of 1961–64, Colin Vines, in his *A Little Nut-brown Man*.[15]

Alan Taylor did not follow his friend Driberg in analysing the less pleasant sides of Beaverbrook's career and personality. Indeed, he was unduly indulgent towards his failings. It is symptomatic that he wrote of Vine and his book,

> He lived in a state of perpetual bewilderment with his employer, a state which Beaverbrook rejoiced to enhance. This strange conflict has produced, in my opinion, the best portrayal of Beaverbrook in his latter days. Here was a great humorist at work. Thanks to Beaverbrook, the book rivals *The Diary of a Nobody* as the funniest in the English language.[16]

Taylor's *Beaverbrook* has other failings. It does not explain how he became rich so young, a matter dealt with more fully by others, including Anne Chisholm and Michael Davie in their biography.[17] While he pointed to some of Beaverbrook's distortions of history (or 'balances') in his narrative, he did not condemn them as he would have done if committed by any other writer of history. He also avoided in dealing in any depth with Beaverbrook's private life. Taylor, although working through the huge Beaverbrook archive, only went further to the Asquith Papers in the Bodleian, Oxford, and, through Martin Gilbert, to the Churchill Papers; a drawback for such a major biography. This also may have encouraged him not to cite his primary references in foot- or endnotes. However, Taylor was explicit as to his attitude towards the subject of his biography, publishing at the end of his Introduction: 'I loved Max Beaverbrook when he was alive. Now that I have learnt to know him better from his records I love him even more.'[18]

Putting such comments into *Beaverbrook* was on a par with his devil-may-care comments regarding the Regius Chair in *The Trouble Makers*. If the book was deemed to be a failure, then he had an explanation: he cared too much for its subject. Possible failure loomed for several reasons: it was a biography of a man known to many of the likely newspaper and journal reviewers, no Bismarck safely beyond living memory; he had avoided labouring on publicly available archives, so it was possible that he might have missed material known to academics; after the success of *English History 1914–1945*, he was less confident of success in biography; and he was aware that he had repeatedly given Beaverbrook the benefit of any doubt and much more. He was very quick to emphasise that he was a historian rather than a biographer.[19] Yet, as with the Regius Chair, his dismissive comments rang hollow. He did care very much about his biography of Beaverbrook and was very anxious about its reception.

He had had his doubts at the outset. He had written to William Thomas on 6 October 1967, 'The Beaverbrook project is a wild affair: some rich bits of information mixed with great tedium. Perhaps it was a mistake to involve myself in a political life because of personal friendship.' When the book was completed, he observed to another friend, 'The publishers expect a great success. I am not so sure.'[20] When the book was published he was full of forebodings and contradictory feelings. He confided these to Éva Haraszti, the person he least wanted to see him publicly ridiculed.

> I have been rather gloomy... I have anxieties about the appearance of *Beaverbrook*... It is far too big and everyone says so... Don't worry for myself. What people say about me does not interest me much. Besides, I know the merits and the defects of the book better than anyone else does. But I worry what they will say about Beaverbrook. I fear I have been too honest about him. Even those who have read the book ask: Was he worth it? What did he do in life – as though that mattered. People are surprised that I, a supposedly serious historian, should have spent five years on writing the life of a rather unimportant man. I try to explain that I did so out of curiosity – his own motive – just to find out about him. Of course I did it also because I loved him, but that memory fades too. Now I often remember the times when I found him exasperating and wondered why I ever wasted my time in his company. Our worlds were miles away from each other, a thing that I appreciated and which I am sure he did not. It never occurred to him that there could be any worlds but his. However, it will all be over soon. The book will come out. The reviewers will misunderstand it as they always do, and I hope people will buy it. I told the *Observer* that I was the only person qualified to review it, but this was not an idea that appealed to them.[21]

This was a case of Alan Taylor's usual self-doubt, though buttressed in this case with the realism that the biography was liable to be attacked. However, this was never likely to be for an excess of honesty about its subject. It was also very characteristic of him to fall into self-pity and to come close to suggesting that Beaverbrook was in some way responsible for his being in a situation where he would be open to justified criticism. He was also in fantasy land, suggesting, even if in half-jest, that he should review his own book in the *Observer*.

When it was published it received a mixed reception. Ronald Blythe wrote in the *New York Review of Books* that it was

> a full, affectionate, brilliantly written and highly readable case for him. Though the book is intended to be a monument it is not an entirely

polite one. Much of it is a kind of secular hagiography in which the virtues of the subject constantly come up against the reader's resistance; but it holds one's attention throughout by its expert marshalling of a vast amount of material.[22]

Kenneth O. Morgan, in *History*, praised Taylor's ability to 'recapture the zest and fascination' of Beaverbrook and highlighted its greatest strength: 'The supreme value of Mr Taylor's book for historians lies in the important evidence from the Beaverbrook archives for British politics in the two world wars. Here, like his subject, Mr Taylor attains full stature.'[23]

However, those in politics or working in the media who had known Beaverbrook were disappointed that Taylor had not been more critical. Tom Driberg wrote a lengthy review of it, mostly favourable. However, after approvingly discussing Taylor's demolition of four myths Beaverbrook propagated about himself, he noted,

> This biography does not pretend to be objective. As such phrases as 'romantic story' and 'admirable embellishments' suggest, Alan Taylor is prepared to make excuses for his hero's waywardness. For he un-ashamedly declares that Beaverbrook *is* his hero: he loved and loves him with true devotion and, like any other lover, will make allowances for the loved one. It is the more to his credit that he has not suppressed some things which might be thought to show Beaverbrook in a less than favourable light.

Nevertheless, he concluded that the book was 'a massive achievement' and very entertaining to read. 'His is a much richer and, obviously more comprehensive book than mine – though, so contradictory was the character that he portrays, he still leaves in some perplexity those of us who are neither so adoring as he nor so hostile as, say, the aristocrats of the Establishment whose arrogance Beaverbrook resented.'[24]

However, the early major savaging of Alan Taylor over *Beaverbrook* came from Richard Crossman on 7 January 1973 in a Sunday evening BBC1 television programme, 'Crosstalk'. Taylor had been a first reserve for Crossman's first series (along with John Freeman, Hugh Greene and Roy Jenkins) but, after Isaiah Berlin declined the invitation to appear in the series, he took part in the first discussion.[25] The theme of this first programme was very close to Crossman's heart, 'that political history is largely fiction'. Crossman was very dissatisfied with historians' depiction of British politics as he had experienced it in Cabinet and in the House of Commons. At the start of the programme Crossman paid a tribute to Taylor saying that if there was a historian 'who when I read him I feel that he does manage to get himself into it and understand what politicians do' then it was

Taylor. Later in the programme Taylor effectively criticised Crossman's repeated suggestions that only politicians could understand and write about high politics, observing that one did not need to be a member of the royal family to write about monarchs of the past nor a farmer to write about agricultural history. He caustically commented that 'it's a great mistake to think – and this is the vanity of politics that you're showing – that in order to understand politics you must have been very high up in it'.

However, after some general talk Crossman homed in on *Beaverbrook*. A BBC transcript of this part of the discussion began with Crossman saying of the book:

> 'When I read your biography it utterly destroyed my belief in Beaverbrook the historian, because you showed that the man lied.'
> 'No, No. That's not so. That's not so.'
> 'No, no? You think he just romanced, do you?'
> 'I think he sometimes rounded out a fully accurate story with a touch of romance, or, as he would call it, drama.'

Crossman went on to discuss one of Beaverbrook's fabrications and ended by saying: 'But a man who does that, Alan, he's not really a historian, is he?' Taylor replied that he was, as 'The historian attaches great importance to great events, to the significant things' and praised Beaverbrook's portrayal of Lloyd George and Asquith, though he conceded that he built up Bonar Law.

Crossman then attacked him for saying that he loved Beaverbrook and believed he had no faults.

> 'You're like him on Bonar Law. You make him your hero, therefore he can't ever be at fault.'
> 'Can't be wrong. Can't be wrong.'
> 'But then how can you claim to be an objective historian writing a biography of a man you claim can't be wrong?'
> 'Well no, I didn't say that, I said he could do no wrong in my eyes. That's quite a different thing. I don't call romancing, adding a romantic touch to history, doing wrong so far as he was concerned. And you yourself say that anything that you discover to Beaverbrook's discredit you find in my book. There's nothing I've suppressed, there's nothing I've done wrong.'

After more probing of Taylor's approach to writing *Beaverbrook*, Crossman concluded the discussion of it by observing: 'I now see why you love Beaverbrook being a romancer, because you yourself are a romancer.'[26]

Overall, it was a powerful demolition job. Alan Taylor had made himself a sitting target by his comments about his own relationship with Beaverbrook. Crossman knew well from Taylor's 'In the News' and 'Free

Speech' days that he would argue his case vigorously, rather than quickly
retreating. So it was. Taylor soon found that he was in a deep hole but kept
digging. The 'Can't be wrong. Can't be wrong' was another example of his
lifelong tendency to repeat his views, defiantly, once he had struck an
attitude. On this occasion he himself saw it was untenable and silly, and,
with Crossman pulling no punches, he had to reposition himself fast. The
experience was all the more of a shock for him as he had escaped such a
vigorous, hostile cross-examination when he had appeared on television
with Hugh Trevor-Roper to discuss his *The Origins of the Second World
War*. Moreover, with *Beaverbrook*, he had earlier enjoyed an amiable discussion with Michael Foot on Radio 4 on 13 June 1972, which had in no
way presaged the robust approach of the 'Crosstalk' programme.

Taylor had been caught by surprise. The night before the programme
he had written to Éva saying that he thought the 'most political history is
fiction' theme was 'merely silly'. His concern was to explain to Crossman
and the television audience that 'History is a version of events. The fact
that there are other versions does not make any one of them wrong. It is
just like taking different views about a human being.' Nearly a fortnight
after the programme he admitted to Éva: 'I had a bad time,' and that he
was surprised by Crossman taking up *Beaverbrook*. He went on,

> I ought to have hit back and didn't. Instead Crossman talked practically
> all the time. There was no meeting of minds. He was a politician pure
> and simple. I refused to accept his standards and could not develop my
> own… If the other man won't co-operate one must take the offensive
> however much you don't want to. So I was miserable and feared that
> I had lost my television gifts.

In his next letter he added, 'The *Listener* version of my Crossman ordeal
was nothing like as bad as the original. It cut out a great deal of what he
said and did its best for me.'

The problem, however, was not that he chose not to hit back but that
Crossman had caught him out on indefensible ground. He was out-
Taylored, in the sense that he was at the receiving end of the fierce arguing
on television in which he had delighted in in the past. In fact the *Listener*
account did not miss out much which was damaging to him. Crossman did
push him harder on his argument that there could be historical truth in a
fictitious account.

> 'But how can a work be true, historically true, and the fiction…how
> can that be true?'.
> 'Well, they're two different types of truth in regard to the past.
> One is truth about events, what happened. Now here the historian is
> obviously superior…'

'You are saying that the historian…recreates the past and imagines what it's like. Now if he imagines what it's like, then you told me you can't write a single page of imaginative fiction. This puzzles me because what you are really saying is, you take the events of the past. You study the books, but of course you imagine it, Alan. You imagine it and you say, I think I understand Palmerston. Now look, there is more in common between you and a novelist.'[27]

Crossman also rightly corrected him when he claimed that the writer of some late Victorian diaries was writing without 'any view to future effect'.[28]

Alan Taylor was shaken by receiving such treatment but viewer response suggests that many of the programme's audience were highly critical of Crossman. One viewer, when praising the programme, made the good point: 'You producing a written quotation of what AJPT had once said suggested less than a spontaneous discussion, as if you had led up to the question with a desire to corner him.' Another complained, 'We were very annoyed that you constantly interrupted Mr Taylor. You hardly let him follow his thread of thoughts, and even when you asked him a question you interrupted and answered yourself. Shall we in the next so-called dialogues only hear Cross(man) talk?' Several others complained similarly and Crossman in replies admitted that he regretted he had interrupted so frequently and he would try to rectify the fault in future programmes.[29]

In 1979, five years after the death of Richard Crossman, Taylor was one of a panel of six who discussed Crossman on a BBC2 'Reputations' programme. In it he deemed him to be 'the most unreliable witness about politics or persons or what has happened that I have ever known, because Dick Crossman had a personality which, as it were, sought to dominate events and to eat them up'.[30] This was his honest general judgement, but it also stemmed from his experience of Crossman's domineering performance on 'Crosstalk'.

While the Crossman encounter was the most public criticism he received, his *Beaverbrook* book also received some equally vigorous, perceptive academic criticism. The most effective critiques were in articles by Peter Fraser and John Stubbs, who both subjected Beaverbrook's First World War histories to the type of scrutiny Alan Taylor should have given them, the title of Fraser's being the blunt 'Lord Beaverbrook's Fabrications in *Politicians and the War 1914–1916*'.[31]

Why did he expose himself to such criticism? Was it that Beaverbrook met his need for an older father figure to admire? Was he grateful that Beaverbrook had not failed to back him when he needed it – a truly foul-weather friend? Was it one of the many attitudes he liked to adopt, and then to defend, terrier-like? Or was it some curious 'keeping the faith' with his deceased friend?

Whatever the explanation, he later took a dismissive approach to *Beaverbrook*. In a conversation in April 1975 his criticisms were that 'it was much too long and not on a mainstream subject'. In a letter to Éva Haraszti on 21 February 1976 he observed, 'Now in retrospect it seems a waste of time: he really was not worth a book on that scale, and it only sold 4000 copies.' However, in a conversation in February 1979, when it was put to him that he undervalued the book, he replied, 'I do like it. I think there is much richness in it.'

While completing *Beaverbrook*, Alan Taylor quarried the Beaverbrook archives. The Lloyd George collections included the diaries and letters of Frances Stevenson, Lloyd George's long-time mistress and later second wife. He enjoyed meeting the elderly Lady Lloyd George when arranging for the publication of these records. He commented,

> Behind the reserve I saw occasional flashes of the Frances who had charmed Lloyd George and other men also. She was immediately alert when a man came into the room and always made me feel that as a hostess she was paying me special attention, simply because she enjoyed entertaining someone of the male sex.[32]

He completed preparing her diaries for publication by mid-July 1970. As for her letters, these were published after her death in 1972.

Taylor's third archival project was to publish the private interviews conducted by W.P. Crozier when he was editor of the *Manchester Guardian*, from 1932 to 1944. These had come to the Beaverbrook Library from Crozier's younger daughter, Mrs Mary McManus, a friend of Taylor. These had particular appeal to him. He was always fascinated by the national press and by major journalists, especially those of the *Manchester Guardian*. He was inordinately proud that he could thrive in this world, a workaday world which was a contrast with Oxford colleges. He was especially interested in Crozier as he had been editor for a lengthy part of the time he had written for the *Manchester Guardian*. Moreover, Crozier's interest, like his own, had been foreign policy.[33]

Taylor next turned to a safer task than *Beaverbrook*. He took up the request from George Rainbird to prepare an illustrated history of the Second World War, which would in effect be a companion volume to his much-admired and also commercially very successful *The First World War*. He himself was proud of them. When he read the draft introduction to a bibliography of his works he commented, 'I am sorry that you did not mention either of my illustrated books on the two world wars, which I think good books and characteristic of my historical method. The one on the second war is virtually the only one that truly combines both areas of conflict.'

In his autobiography he described writing *The Second World War* as 'a fascinating assignment'. As well as his combining the European and Far Eastern wars, he highlighted that he had emphasised that the *world* war broke out 'in December 1941, not in September 1939. Of course Americans have always known this.' He went on to observe, 'I had a second subversive idea and thought of calling the war, The War of the British Succession. This, though it became true in the later stages of the war, harked back to my old mistake, common enough among historians, of making my country the centre of the war and I wisely left it alone.'[34] He felt it was better than his First World War book and was more detached than *The Origins of the Second World War*, other than the final sentence: 'Despite all the killing and destruction that accompanied it, the Second World War was a good war.'

It was a very accomplished book, in many ways a fitting final substantial book in his career. It gave succinctly and in vivid style his mature reflections on the course of the war. As he observed in the Preface, he had thought through many of the issues as they had happened, in his war commentaries given during the war and at its end. Being influenced by his recollections had its dangers, as he realised.[35] He agonised at length as to what unifying theme or argument to adopt for the book. He wrote to Éva Haraszti on 30 October 1972,

> I don't know what impression I want to make. Do I want to show that the war was a terribly muddled affair, as all wars are, or do I want to say that after all it was that unique thing – a just war that was worth fighting despite all the suffering it caused? What will future historians say? Will they understand, as we do, that Fascism had to be destroyed? Or will they lump the Second World War into the same class of European follies as the Napoleonic Wars or the First World War? I don't know what to think.[36]

The book was well received and has sold well. Yet there has not been the enthusiasm for it that there was for *The First World War*. He himself put his finger on part of the explanation for this. He confided in Éva that it lacked 'the speed and zest that my book on the First World War had'.[37] *The First World War* had been daring and irreverent, very much moving with the times – indeed, near the front of the pack. *The Second World War* was not lively and provocative in the same way, and his concluding sentence with its claim that it was 'a good war' seemed an old-fashioned rather than a daring judgement. It also was less sound in its coverage and assessments of some of the warfare away from Europe and north Africa.

Alan Taylor also took up several lucrative publishing suggestions that came his way. Aged 61 in 1967, he was anxious about his continuing earning power, given his advancing age and the expenses he incurred from two families. The most intellectually substantial of these publications was his piece on 'Churchill: The Statesman', written for the American firm Dial Press, for its 1969 set of five essays, *Churchill Revised*, published in Britain as *Churchill: Four Faces and the Man* (Allen Lane, 1969). Taylor had written much and thought hard about Churchill's career. It is one of his best essays, lean and full of well-considered judgements. Although he could not resist in the final paragraph echoing, or perhaps coming near to parodying, his sentiments in *English History 1914–1945*, with: 'The British people raised him up, and he failed them. The British ruling classes did their best to keep him down, and he preserved them.' Churchill as a subject also brought out of him one of his best centenary pieces, 'Daddy, What Was

Promoting his books.

Winston Churchill?', published a hundred years after Churchill's birth in the *New York Times Magazine*, 28 April 1976.[38]

He also agreed to give his name to several very commercial history publishing ventures. Weekly journal publications were going through a phase of popularity: major themes covered in 80 or 120 weekly journals. In 1968–70 he acted as editor-in-chief, with J.M. Roberts as general editor, of a 2688-page *History of the Twentieth Century*, published by Purnell, to which he contributed eleven essays. Parts of this were recycled in two widely sold books *History of World War I* and *History of World War II*, which credited him again as editor-in-chief and both of which included two of his essays from the *History of the Twentieth Century*. He also was on the editorial board of another Purnell weekly part venture, a 3598-page amplification of Sir Winston Churchill's *The History of the English-Speaking Peoples*, published between 1969 and 1971, to which he contributed two essays. He also contributed two essays to *The History of the British Empire*, published in 1973–75, by Time-Life International in co-operation with the BBC. Such publications benefited by trading on his name, while the heavy advertising and wide availability of such publications further enhanced his already high public profile.

He participated in two commercial tapes made by probably the leading educational producer of the day, Sussex Tapes, in 1971. At the time such tapes were deemed to be innovative teaching aids, providing a seminar-style discussion of differing views for sixth-formers. Taylor discussed 'Bismarck and Unification' and then 'Bismarck in Power' with his old friend Geoffrey Barraclough, then the Chichele Professor of History at Oxford University. On another tape he discussed 'The Appeasers' and 'Hitler and World War II' with Christopher Thorne. Eight years later he talked about the tapes.

> He said that on Bismarck he felt Geoffrey Barraclough knew very little and was guessing. Alan Taylor felt the urge repeatedly to say to Barraclough's assertions about Bismarck, 'Bismarck might have done this or that – but in fact he didn't!' He said that with regard to the origins of the Second World War tape Christopher Thorne clearly felt that I [AJPT] knew nothing. Alan Taylor observed, 'I thought otherwise. It was clear that Thorne took it for granted that Adolf Hitler repeatedly chewed the carpet – just as Neville Chamberlain thought he did.'[39]

While it is doubtful that Thorne thought this of Hitler, Taylor rightly sensed that he was already appearing old-fashioned, even a decade after his *The Origins of the Second World War*, among those specialists who had carried out major archival research. Nevertheless, to school audiences Taylor remained the major historian on the subject, and by participating in such tapes he again was reaching a wide audience.

Taylor also accepted lucrative foreign commissions. Like Eric
Hobsbawm, his work was much in demand in Italy. Several of his books
had been translated into Italian: *The Course of German History* (Laterza,
1963, reprinted by Longanesi, 1971), *The Struggle for Mastery in Europe
1848–1918* (Laterza, 1961), *The Origins of the Second World War* (Laterza,
1961, with the new edition with 'Foreword: Second Thoughts' in 1965),
The First World War (Valechi, 1967, with additional material on Italy's role)
and *English History 1914–1945* (Laterza, 1968). He gave a lecture on the
origins of the Second World War in the University of Rome in 1964 and
a talk on Italian radio on 'Neville Chamberlain and the Surrender of the
Democracies' in 1966, both of which were published in Italy. He also
wrote for *Storia Illustria* a thirtieth-anniversary essay on 'The Illusion of
Yalta'. He contributed a 15,000-word survey of British and Irish history
and a shorter piece on Churchill to a 1977 European encyclopedia, edited
by Aldo Garzanti. The appeal for him of such pieces as the encyclopedia
entries was that they earned substantial sums for writing which he could
carry out quickly and with no research, an important matter for a man
with two families.

However, such earnings were overshadowed by his work for the
national press. This he greatly enjoyed, and had been a major motivation
in his choice of living in the London–Oxford area. His book reviewing was
prodigious. Between the start of 1967 and the end of 1975 he wrote 294
reviews, more than two every three weeks. He continued to write articles
on current affairs for the *Sunday Express*, *New Statesman* and occasionally for
foreign newspapers, writing 67 pieces, which were published in 1967–75.

In the *Sunday Express* he could enjoy writing provocative, populist and
libertarian pieces. He was no longer the white knight of socialism, the
champion arguer of the left-wing case. No more the doughty socialist of the
'In the News' and 'Free Speech' years. As with many other people moving
from the Left, he justified his changed political position by blaming Labour
in office for not being socialist enough. After the defeat of the Wilson
government in the 1970 general election he complained in the *New York
Review of Books*: 'Labour men do not believe in Socialism,' and regretted a
lack of real radical leaders: 'In this century we have only had Lloyd George
and Aneurin Bevan, and I am not sure about Bevan.'

Before the 1970 general election his most persistent and consistent line
had been against the European Economic Community. He had condemned
it ten times between 1967 and the June 1970 election. He often sounded
Colonel Blimpish in his reiterated urgings that 'we should stand on our
own feet and turn back to our kith and kin in the Commonwealth'.[40]

He also aired his threadbare and increasingly less impressive 'Beware
the Hun'-style warnings. In the midst of the June 1968 events in France,

he claimed that national character was re-establishing itself in France, with the street barricades, and Germany, with its Grand Coalition government. He cautioned, 'what spells Order for the Germans spells Danger for everyone else,' and urged, 'We too should be true to our tradition. That tradition is one of national independence and Splendid Isolation.' When Harold Wilson supported the West German government over Berlin he dubbed it a blunder, reiterating his long-standing view: 'A divided Germany means peace. A united Germany means war.'[41]

In the *New Statesman* he took up a more radical critique of the Wilson government. While he praised the Capital Gains Tax, he condemned support for America in Vietnam and the Immigration Bill. On the latter he observed, 'CARD (Campaign Against Racial Discrimination) should be by now a bigger movement than CND at its biggest. It isn't. We have all turned cowards.' It was over this issue that he broke for some years from the Labour Party, not renewing his membership. In his autobiography he expressed his disgust at the restriction of immigration from the Commonwealth in these words: 'I could not swallow a party that conformed to colour hostility and betrayed our own people overseas into the bargain.'[42] Thus he opposed not only racism but also the turning from the Commonwealth to the EEC.

Quite clearly, hostility to the EEC also played a substantial part in his opposition to Harold Wilson's government in 1970. He wrote, for the last issue of the *Sunday Express* before polling, an article entitled 'Why I Won't Be Voting Labour This Time'. In it he stated, 'There are some moral principles more important to me than economics. I am against racial discrimination. I am against privilege. I am for the sovereign independence of this country and for the unity of the Commonwealth. Labour does not help me on any of these.' However, the defeat of Harold Wilson and the entry of Ted Heath into 10 Downing Street led even more surely to Britain's entry into the EEC.

For one opposed to Britain supporting the USA in Vietnam, even minimally as Harold Wilson did, it was curious that he praised President Richard Nixon. Was this because Nixon in 1958, when US Vice-President, had visited Magdalen College and been looked after by Taylor, then Vice-President of the College? Or was it because he admired his *realpolitik*? Support for Nixon was more in tune with his liking of Bismarck than his dislike of Metternich or his admiration for his 'Trouble Makers' in British foreign policy. He praised Nixon's diplomacy with China, and observed that Nixon was a man 'who always had the gift, as he showed in the [Alger] Hiss affair, of seeing the simple truth where others saw only complications. And he has always been ready to learn from experience.'[43] During the Watergate scandal, he acted the foul-weather friend. In July 1973 he wrote in the *Sunday Express*, 'The US have a damned good President or had until recently...Nixon has done things that were beyond the much praised John Kennedy and certainly beyond the late Lyndon B. Johnson. Nixon has ended the Cold War.'[44]

Yet, for anyone interested in what made Taylor tick, the most interesting feature of his journalism was the very lengthy stream of libertarian, populist pieces. He appeared as the friend of the overseas holidaymaker, denouncing on one occasion the currency restrictions of £50 per person then in force, and on another calling for no customs checks on returning holidaymakers (regardless, presumably, of the opportunities for those smuggling drugs and other items). He was against interfering with the smoker, being sceptical of the link between cigarettes and cancer. Having earlier been the friend of the motorist, he was now stridently anti-car, wanting private motor cars banned.[45] He also railed at Establishment targets: calling for the abolition of the diplomatic service and condemning pay rises for ministers and MPs, the salaries and other benefits of the chairmen of nationalised industries, civil servants receiving honours and the bureaucrats of the BBC.[46] For him, it was not so much what he was saying but that he was there, at a national forum, as a great arguer. This had been the most admired skill of his adolescence. Also, he was very committed to proving himself an effective newspaper columnist. In this the key person to be impressed was himself. It was a major matter of self-esteem.

He was equally proud of his television performances. In the Beaverbrook Library years (1967–75) he was at his peak as an established 'television personality' and, very important as such, he was at hand in central London. Producers knew that he was good value: consistently entertaining, displaying lively and often unorthodox views, very much a 'character'. He appeared on 'talk shows' – those hosted by Simon Dee ('Dee Time') and Michael Parkinson. Simon Dee, the former disc jockey, was less cerebral than Parkinson and always managed to look surprised at Alan Taylor's historical knowledge. Once, having asked Taylor who his favourite historical figure was and received the reply 'John Bright', Dee looked amazed and asked him who John Bright was.

Taylor was not averse to taking an impish delight in playing on BBC media figures' ignorance of history. In December 1975, shortly after he had reviewed Eric Hobsbawm's *The Age of Capital*, he commented that he thought *Captain Swing* was Hobsbawm's best book. He went on,

> Once the BBC approached me about a series they were doing about the historical figures people most admired. When asked who I most admired, I replied, 'Captain Swing.' They went away – and I didn't hear from them again about it.

As well as appearing on talk shows, Taylor frequently appeared on television discussing recent books, his own and others, in 'Read All About It' and 'The Book Programme'. He also appeared as an historical commentator on current affairs. He appeared on 'Nationwide', 'Newsday' and other programmes discussing such matters as British Standard Time, the possibility of Britain joining the EEC and the Conservative leadership contest of 1975, as well as Lord Beaverbrook, Lloyd George, the Duke of Windsor and Rudolf Hess.

While he was keen to earn much from his writings and his television and radio appearances, Taylor remained very willing to promote history in 'Middle England' through lecturing to branches of the Historical Association. In the Society of Authors' journal in 1969 he observed of fees for lecturing: 'I have operated a minimum of £50 and expenses for some years,' and added, 'Authors are not dispensers of charity just because they are fools enough to write books.' However, he added that free lectures were justified for promotional exercises and 'lecturing to a specialist audience of fellow enthusiasts' such as the Historical Association.[47]

Taylor continued to be the Historical Association lecturer who attracted the largest audiences – by far. His work for this body was recognised nationally by his being made an honorary vice-president, though, in spite of being nominated by numerous people, he was not awarded its Medlicott Medal for services to history. Alan Taylor frequently marked anniversaries in his lectures. In autumn 1967 he lectured on the Bolshevik Revolution, 1917, at Bristol, Rugby and Tunbridge Wells. The report of his meeting at Bristol in October 1967 recorded that it 'was attended by over 400 people; those who could not be fitted into the main hall had the lecture relayed to them in an overflow room by closed-circuit television, thanks to the assistance of the Department of Education of Bristol University'. In November, when he gave the lecture to the Tunbridge Wells branch, 'Nearly five hundred people packed the Skinners' School Hall'. The secretary of the Rugby branch after his visit observed that his 'stimulating lecture…convinced the large audience that there had hardly been a revolution at all!'. That October he also lectured on 'Ramsay MacDonald' to a crowded audience.[48]

The following year he attracted one of his biggest audiences to a branch lecture. In October 1968 he spoke at Keele University on 'The Peace Settlement after the First World War' to an audience of some 600 persons congregated in three different lecture theatres. From that year on he most frequently lectured on thirtieth anniversary topics connected with the Second World War. In October 1968 he lectured to an audience of some 250 people at Taunton on 'The Munich Settlement'. The following October he spoke on 'British Foreign Policy before the Second World War' in

Edinburgh, followed by 'Neville Chamberlain and the Origins of the Second World War' at Walsall and 'The Outbreak of the Second World War' at the Windsor and Eton branch, and he contributed to a series of lectures on 'Britain and the Second World War' at Birmingham. Over the next three years he spoke to large audiences on 'Finest Hour', 'The Origins of the Second World War: Some Revisions' and 'The Second Front in the Second World War' at Grimsby, London North, Luton, Southampton, Wolverhampton, Durham and Sunderland, Gateshead, Teesside and to the Historical Association's annual vacation school in July–August 1975.

By this time Alan Taylor's visits to Historical Association branches were becoming like royal progressions. In 1969 he toured Scottish branches, lecturing on 'The Winning of Irish Freedom', as a variant on the Second World War, to the Glasgow and St Andrews branches. In November 1972 he toured the North-East, speaking on Second World War themes. The Durham and Sunderland branches held 'a well-attended joint meeting'. The North East Counties meeting was held at Newcastle University, the secretary reporting: 'For A.J.P. Taylor's lecture the branch met in the Curtis Auditorium of the School of Physics and a reception was held later in the Physics Penthouse. This meeting, which was attended by some 300 people, proved extremely successful…He also spoke to a packed house at Teesside Polytechnic.'[49]

Taylor was also repeatedly supportive of Historical Association school lecture programmes. He went several years to Birmingham. In 1967, 1969 and 1971 he contributed to series on 'Revolutions in the Twentieth Century', 'Britain and the Second World War' and 'Europe and the Wider World 1890–1914'. The third of these lectures, given on 18 October 1971, returned to an old and favourite theme, being entitled 'The Austro-Hungarian Ruling Elite'. He was also very supportive of his own branch of the Historical Association, Central London. Joan Lewin, the very long-serving branch secretary, later recalled,

> On the first occasion he arrived close to the time he was due to speak, he said, 'Sorry I'm a bit late – the tube was rather slow.' Then he looked rather vague and asked, 'What am I supposed to talk about?' Lewin said that her blood ran cold at this and expressed her anxiety to him. 'He responded, "I think that will be OK" and then he gave a cracking lecture.'[50]

Thereafter, he gave many lectures on behalf of the Central London branch, both to ordinary meetings and to sixth-form conferences. Joan Lewin recollected, 'I used to ask him as often as I felt I could, and he never said "No". Twice he came at very short notice when speakers fell out.'[51] In 1981, on the second of these occasions, she very much hoped that Taylor would cover the advertised topic, which was on the impact of Russia under Alexander I and his successors on Europe, both for her own benefit and as she knew many sixth-formers were coming. She hesitantly telephoned him and explained the specialist nature of the talk to be given in two days' time. She recalled, 'After a brief hesitation he said, "I think I could manage something on that." He turned up and gave an excellent lecture.'

Joan Lewin, like many other branch officers in the Historical Association, found him undemanding and easy to entertain, but eager to leave soon after his session ended. Reflecting on his visits, she observed,

> He came and just gave his talk...Afterwards he answered questions. He always gave the impression he was really interested in the questions – and took pains to answer them. When he was lecturing he had a pleasant affectation. He would pause at a date, as though he had forgotten it. After the pause, he would say, 'What was the date?' Another short pause, and: 'Ah, yes – 1862.' Then he would continue. This he often did twice in a lecture. It broke the flow and kept the audience's interest.[52]

The Beaverbrook Library years were good years for him. The adulation came easily on television and radio and before his Historical Association audiences. His books sold very well, to academic as well as more 'popular' readers, via book clubs as well as bookshops. His family life was important to him, as it had been in his youth. However, these years marked the end of his second marriage, with Eve, in 1967.

He continued to go on walks with his sons. In the 1950s and afterwards he had some half a dozen favourite walks, several across the Downs. These were in addition to summer walks on the Isle of Wight. He frequently walked there for an hour and a half in afternoons. Sometimes he would go for longer: walking two hours in the morning, eating a light packed lunch, then walking for a further hour and a half. It was going on the Pennine Way in the early summer of 1968, with Sebastian and, for part of the route, Giles, which aroused his enthusiasm for long-distance walks. On that occasion Mary Taylor (Sebastian's wife) and Sophia went as well, partly to drive the car. This was a role Janet Taylor (Giles' wife) and Amelia played on other occasions. In 1969 Len Deighton had joined the walking party for the last, northern part of the Pennine Way. In 1971 and 1972 he walked Offa's Dyke with Crispin, joined by Giles and Daniel. After these long walks he returned to the Lake District, often accompanied by Crispin. He also went with his sons and grandchildren to Italy, especially Venice, Ravenna and Rome.

Another major love remained music. From the Beaverbrook Library he enjoyed exploring the City on foot and attending the concerts of the City

Music Society on Tuesdays. He was genuinely delighted and honoured when Ivan Sutton wrote to him in 1975 inviting him to succeed Sir Arthur Bliss as the society's president. He was wisely cautious two years later when he turned down an invitation from Yehudi Menuhin to write on Schubert's chamber music, saying he could only say that he liked it.[53]

Alan Taylor returned to Margaret, his first wife, moving into her home in Camden Town. This was possible because they had maintained a family presence, at least on vacations, and also because of their underlying long-term affection for each other. For both it marked a return to familiar companionship, but it was not a resumption of the marital relationship of the 1930s and 1940s. It had the practical benefit of avoiding him having to contribute to two homes for them (as well as to Eve's accommodation). For both, in their sixties, it was a cautious move with the approach of old age. For him, it took him closer to his first family and enabled him to play the paterfamilias role which was important to him. Yet, like many people highly sensitive to slights by others, he could be markedly insensitive to the feelings of others. In this instance, quite apart from Eve, he was none too thoughtful of Margaret. Not unnaturally, for her his return seemed to entail some degree of commitment to her. However, she was to be disabused of this expectation within a few years.

A few months after he had returned to sharing a house with Margaret, Alan Taylor fell in love again. Or, perhaps, it is more true to say that earlier emotions were re-aroused. A forbidden love affair, so one all the more tantalising, was reignited. In the early spring of 1969 Éva Haraszti spent a month in London on a British Academy scholarship to carry out research on British appeasement in the 1930s. She listed in advance his name as an authority she wished to consult. He met her in the readers' rest room in the then main PRO building in Chancery Lane on a Saturday. She later recalled, 'Alan looked so young and fresh and seemed excited. I was excited too. He had hardly recognised me as my hair was different – fair. I felt ill at ease. We quickly made plans for the coming month.'[54]

Much of the month, when Éva was not working in archives, was spent together. At 63 Alan Taylor was young again, showing an attractive younger woman the places that meant much to him and which she wished to see. They visited Oxford, going to his rooms in Magdalen College and the river by Holywell Ford, and then went on to Blenheim Palace and Sir Winston Churchill's grave at nearby Bladon. He even spent extravagantly, taking her to dine in the Connaught, as well as to other more modestly priced restaurants. His hopes of making love were dashed by news from Budapest that Éva's husband had been taken to hospital with a perforated ulcer. Mutually enjoyable friendship and flirtation remained such and no more, and this was as well for their relationship. As a result there was less sense of recrimination when Vilmos Hudecz died after an operation in September 1969, aged only 44.

In Éva's months of grief and coming to terms with the loss of her husband, Taylor was sensitive and sufficiently mature to make himself a sympathetic, albeit distant, presence in whom she could confide. Éva recalled that, when she wrote to him, she received a speedy reply. 'I had never before had such entertaining and kind letters in my life. I could write about everything to him. I could ask about my problems, of which there was always plenty. I could discuss anything with him, from the upbringing of my teenage sons to the Rhineland Crisis of 1936.'[55] Continuing epistolary contact added more affection to the romantic feelings arising from their intermittent encounters. A year after Vilmos Hudecz's death Taylor secured Éva an invitation to the Ranke Gesellschaft conference in Königswinter on the subject of the diplomatic history of the 1930s. The conference provided another opportunity for them to be together and to behave like young romantics. For him it was exciting to be in love with an attractive younger woman and to know that she found him personally and sexually attractive.

Between 1969 and their marriage in September 1976, his love affairs with Éva added spice to his already complex life, without blowing apart his arrangements for seeing both his families. He corresponded regularly with a secret love, an attractive, intellectual Hungarian woman, seventeen years younger than him. It was a secret correspondence, her letters being sent to him at the Beaverbrook Library. To this there was the added sweet anticipation of periodic assignments in continental European countries, often places much loved by him.

This was very much so of Salzburg and Venice. At Salzburg in October 1971 their relationship moved from young romantics to lovers. Taylor had spent an enjoyable week there during the music festival of August 1932, one year into his marriage with Margaret Taylor, and again with her and a friend in 1936. With Éva, in 1971, they were too late for the Salzburg Festival but, he later recalled, this was 'perhaps the most magical episode of our life together', as they enjoyed each other's company, explored Salzburg, attended a chamber concert and visited St Gilgen and St Wolfgang.[56]

A year later, in September 1972, they spent a fortnight together in Venice, staying in the Hotel Dinesen. Although Taylor had only come to love Venice late in life, in 1963 on a second visit, it became very much one of his special places. There he could enjoy large numbers of churches, the narrow streets and canals as well as music. They both enjoyed Venice but, as Éva later put it, 'I would not say it was the happiest time in our life.'

I went to Venice with the idea that during our stay we should get married and begin our life together. Alan, I think, came to Venice to have a holiday with me, enjoy my company, make love, make things easier and more interesting for me and show me everything that he liked there.[57]

Éva was not interested in periodic flings but, lonely after the death of Vilmos, she wanted lasting love and commitment. An attractive, intelligent, very feminine woman, she – like most people – was driven by conflicting hopes. She was deeply devoted to her two sons, Ferencz and István, and wanted to be near them, yet she was attracted by the possibilities of international recognition as a historian and felt that her career was in the doldrums. She was attracted by Britain. She later recalled, 'I felt that apart from my own homeland it was the only country in which I could ever imagine living for any length of time.' She was attracted by English scholars, and was sufficiently self-aware and self-questioning to wonder if Alan Taylor early on represented an idealised type. After meeting a pleasant English academic in May 1970, she noted in her diary, 'He is a very pleasant, intelligent man, and I felt that what I liked in Alan was not his own personality but the pleasant, understanding, intelligent manner which certain English intellectuals have.' Yet she came to love Alan Taylor as a person, a reassuring older man, who was generally very kind and considerate, yet one who was still an impressive lover.[58]

In the autumn of 1973 Alan Taylor joined Éva three times during a three-month period when she was researching in Paris. During his visits she moved out of her hostel into a hotel, 'where we stayed as man and wife'. Together they explored the city, visiting places with historic associations and ones which held particular memories from past visits for him as well as the major sights. They also argued about Hitler and his policies in the mid-1930s, Éva believing Hitler had more pre-determined purpose in his aggressive policies than Taylor did. Éva later wrote,

Even in Paris Alan told me a great deal about his work and his family but somehow I did not quite take it in that he had his own separate life. Why should he not? After all, I had my life. But for Alan his family life and his relationship with me were two separate strands, whereas in my case, everyone who was close to me knew what he meant in my life.[59]

After Paris they met five further times before agreeing to marry: at Ljublana in the spring of 1974, Budapest and Tapolca in Hungary that autumn, Split in spring 1975, Köszeg in Hungary in September 1975, and finally in London and the Lake District in spring 1976. In Hungary he visited places which mattered to Éva. This was especially the case of Tapolca, a spa town in eastern Hungary. Her family had had small properties there and she later recalled that the place 'represented happiness, physical exercise, sunshine, water, flirtation, dances, a great deal of lying in the grass and reading'.[60]

In marrying Éva Haraszti, Taylor made a bid for happiness in his declining years. He took a big chance, perhaps an unusual one for a person of his age. Yet in so doing he disregarded the feelings of others. She was taking an even bigger risk with her future, involving leaving her own country and being distant geographically from her children. She joined him in London on 11 April 1978. She later recalled, '...I was going to leave my home, my sons and my work...It was like I was going to be executed. But the fateful day came...When I woke up and saw all the luggage, I felt I must be mad.'[61] While Taylor did tell her about his two families, that he was sharing a house with Margaret, and that he intended keeping seeing her and his children, he did not make clear just how close (as friends) he was to Margaret.

As for Margaret, the seriousness of his relationship with Éva Haraszti came as a shock. He was as secretive as his father had been when seeing Little Dolly. While Éva's letters to him had gone to the Beaverbrook Library, he had never phoned her from there or his home. He had phoned while he was on his travels. Even when Margaret knew of Éva's existence, he continued as before in their shared home in St Mark's Crescent. He still frankly and fully discussed the other aspects of his life with Margaret, much as he had done 40 years before. To visitors to the house, they seemed a fond elderly couple, mindful of each other's comforts and firmly fixed in regular domestic routines. In spite of all their vicissitudes she regarded him very much as her husband, and he was happy to be regarded as the patriarch of a large family, with seniority held by Margaret and their children. There were shades about his attitude of his admired, male-chauvinist grandfather, James Taylor.

The Beaverbrook Library gave him an agreeable focus for his working life until the mid-1970s. There were changes there. Rosemary Brooks died during a bad asthma attack on 18 August 1971. Taylor commented to Éva, 'I depended on her very much and she was kind to me during my many troubles. Now I feel very lost.'[62] She had been an older, authoritative figure in the library, had much knowledge of Beaverbrook and his papers, and had greatly helped him as a proof-reader.

Her successor was a trained archivist, Katherine Bligh. She was a young and dynamic person who was emphatically not in awe of 'Mr Taylor'. She was soon knowledgeable about the collections and was generally efficient and very likeable. Taylor admired her professionalism and also her strong commitment, which she shared with her husband, to London Labour politics. Like Taylor, she was (and is) a sturdy, radical Nonconformist. Taylor took a kindly, even grandfatherly, interest in her career. In his autobiography he commented that she 'put the collection on its feet'.[63]

In early March 1973 Veronica Horne left the Beaverbrook Library for an attractive job with the publishers Thames & Hudson. Her replacement was Della Hilton, from Melbourne, Australia. Older than Katherine Bligh and more interested in literature and the media, she admired Taylor as a historian, journalist and television personality as well as liking him as a person. She had substantial interests beyond her job. She was fascinated by Christopher Marlowe, writing most of *Who Was Kit Marlowe?* (Weidenfeld & Nicolson, 1977) in the period when she was at the Beaverbrook Library. Taylor encouraged her, giving her advice on style. She went on to write several other books, including more on Marlowe. She was also involved in organising folk festivals and was active in local Liberal politics.

Della Hilton, an older and less reticent personality than Veronica Horne, was more proactive in helping Taylor with his work. Both she and Veronica Horne looked for ways to be helpful as he wanted only a very little typing done for him. He did his own typing, only asking Hilton to type for him when he had made very considerable changes to his typescripts.[64] She handled publishers and television producers and researchers with much diplomacy, on his behalf. She and Katherine Bligh read proofs for him and turned his television lectures into publishable scripts. Hilton also tidied up matters for him, moved urgent post from the Beaverbrook Library and St Mark's Crescent to him in Oxford, the Isle of Wight or elsewhere, and generally helped smooth his path through his working life.

Taylor's equilibrium was undermined by the closure of the Beaverbrook Library. He had presumed that the wealth of the Aitken family and of the Express Group would secure its future. By March 1973 he was doubting that the library would outlive Beaverbrook's son, Sir Max Aitken. In October Sir Max Aitken told him that the library would be closing. The Express Group needed extra office space after the installation of larger printing machinery in the building.[65] Taylor wrote to his cousin, Karin Wood, that December, 'I am very well though I have had a catastrophic blow. The Beaverbrook Foundation has decided that it cannot maintain the Library any longer. Very soon I shall be turned out and the papers dispersed. I shan't lose much money but I shall lose a great interest and also a fine centre for my work.'[66]

The closure demoralised him for a while. His depression was deepened by his growing anxieties about the likely response from his two families to his relationship with Éva Haraszti. At first, Sir Max Aitken had spoken of keeping the library open until 1976, and so he wrote to Éva that 'while the Library keeps going I'll try to finish my autobiography. Then…I will write a short history of Great Britain from 1901 to 1975.' Soon afterwards Aitken told him that the library would have to close in April 1975. He indulged in self-pity to Éva, writing:

> The killing of the Beaverbrook Library on top of my money worries and general political apprehensions has been almost too much for me. I had counted so much on the Library. After the setbacks I've had in life – not being made a professor, not even being kept on properly at Oxford – I thought: now I really have arrived. Sentimentally, it was good to be doing something for my old friend's memory. Now I feel I have been made a fool of.[67]

He had reason to be upset, but, aged nearly 69, at least he had not been displaced before retirement age. He was also becoming a little muddled on some aspects of the job, most notably the misplacing of some volumes of the Bruce Lockhart diaries (which later turned up); this may suggest some early effects of Parkinson's disease. The main Beaverbrook Library collections went to the House of Lords Records Office, accompanied by Katharine Bligh (who took up a civil service post there from 1 October 1975 until her retirement as the archivist in March 2003). He was especially pleased that the documents were in safe keeping and that Katharine Bligh had continued in archival employment.

Della Hilton and Veronica Horne organised a party (or wake) to mark the closing of the Beaverbrook Library. This was carried out with Margaret Taylor's support. It was held at 13 St Mark's Crescent, from 6.30 p.m. to 8.30 p.m., on 17 April 1975. A considerable number of the regular researchers in the library attended, including Andrew Boyle, John Grigg, Peter Clarke, Patricia Jalland, Chris Cook, Roy Douglas and Michael Dockrill.

Alan Taylor was in genial and talkative mood. One topic he was full of when in conversation with a group of people was the 150 applicants for a Fellowship at Magdalen College. Talking to me, he spoke of, and was happy to discuss, his 'favourite book', *The Trouble Makers*. When I spoke of Michael Howard's review of his *The Second World War*, in which Howard described Taylor as the last of the nineteenth-century historians, he said that there was much truth in the point, that he organised historical material to present an interesting story. However, he also said that he was much more detached in his historical approach than someone such as Macaulay. Macaulay described eighteenth-century parliaments as though they were the same as the Reformed Parliament he knew well. Of course there were similarities, but he [Macaulay] did not have a strong sense of the difference of the past.

He was nearly as happy to talk about literature as history. After he asked me what I was doing in Dorset,

I said I had been reading for pleasure and dipping into William Barnes. He wrinkled up his nose at Barnes and said that he had been outshone by Thomas Hardy. I said that my favourite novel was *Jude the Obscure*. He said he was a great admirer of *The Mayor of Casterbridge* and thought it was one of the greatest novels of all time. He said it was an immensely impressive novel, one really felt that Henchard was helpless before events and that he was inevitably being pushed to destruction. I said that I thought *Tess* was great, but had too many misfortunes stemming from chance, such as the letter to Angel Clare going under the carpet...He agreed with me about Tess, and said that a few years later Jude would have been alright with the Workers' Education Association!

AJP then moved on to Somerset Maugham's *Cakes and Ale*. He said that, despite a disclaimer in later editions, the second figure was Hugh Walpole. He said that Walpole read the book and, after a while, it dawned on him that it was about him. AJP said, 'Just imagine, that you were being vilified in a book, and would be remembered as such as long as English literature is being read!'[68]

The rallying to him of Margaret Taylor when he was distraught over the closure of the Beaverbrook Library was one of several occasions when Éva Haraszti came close to breaking with him. When he told Éva of Margaret's role in the organisation of the party marking its end, Éva was astonished. She later wrote,

> Their relationship was so close that if Alan was upset by something, Margaret always came to his side. I had understood things differently. Alan had always described Margaret in slightly hostile tones and had told me that he was careful not to create a common social circle while he lived there. I felt so bad that I nearly fainted and told Alan that I did not want to see him again.

There were other occasions in the following months when Éva had very serious doubts about the relationship. On this occasion in April 1975 he was very shaken by her determination to end their meetings. Éva wrote,

> Alan telephoned, Alan waited for me, Alan pleaded with me to meet him again. He asked me to come with him to have tea with Margaret in St Mark's Crescent. I agreed. Rather anxiously he met me in Regent's Park and around four o'clock we went to their joint home.

This was not encouraging for Éva either. She felt, in effect, that the house was dowdy and shabby, that Margaret was 'a mixture of snobbery, nursemaidishness and amateur painter' and that Alan Taylor's lot was to be pitied.[69] It can hardly have been a good experience for Margaret Taylor, who clearly put on a brave face.

A year or so later he seemed more relaxed about the closure of the Beaverbrook Library. This was a major topic of conversation over afternoon tea in December 1976.

> Mrs Taylor said that it was a great shock to AJPT that the Beaverbrook Library had been closed down...it was a pity he had not got together an advisory panel of big names such as Alan Bullock, then it would have been harder to close it down. Alan Taylor agreed. She then said it had been done in a disgraceful manner – just an off-the-cuff note. She said that the whole story of the Beaverbrook Library would make a good topic for a book.
>
> He said that the library had been planned and executed by Sir Thomas Blackburn – young Aitken would never have got anything under way. However, when Blackburn had a heart attack he (AJPT) saw that the library's prospects went downhill. However, he did feel that the papers were getting better care and attention in the House of Lords. He disagreed with Mrs Taylor, who felt Beaverbrook would have done better. He talked of Beaverbrook's provisions at Cherkley, how Beaverbrook had felt that the papers could be kept and looked after by Rosemary Brooks alone – scholars should go down to Cherkley by appointment and she would handle everything. He recalled how he went down there and had to specify in advance the topic and letters he wanted to see – and at the end of a day's trip he saw merely a dozen letters.[70]

In March 1976, at the age of 70, he reached the retirement age as a Fellow at Magdalen College. He had to vacate his rooms, and he sold off most of the books he kept in Oxford. He was made an Honorary Fellow of both Magdalen and of Oriel, but his most tangible links with Oxford were at an end. His seventieth birthday was also marked by a celebratory lunch at the London School of Economics, organised by Chris Cook and Alan Sked, as well by a second *Festschrift* edited by them. Éva Haraszti, who was in Britain while on a three-month research trip, attended, as did Michael Foot, Tom Driberg, Robert Blake and Kathleen Tillotson. A photograph of Alan Taylor with Michael Foot was published in the *Times* the next day.

A phase of his life came to an end with the closure of the Beaverbrook Library, or at least in the period within two or three years afterwards. He and Della Hilton remained briefly in the Beaverbrook Library offices after the archives were removed, before going to other Express Group offices. That they were downgraded and marginal to the Express Group was emphasised by their being moved from place to place, three moves in a short period. After the former Beaverbrook Library suite, they went to the main *Express* building on Fleet Street and then to the *Evening Standard* building, close to Holborn Viaduct. Della Hilton's employment finished and the office was wound up on 3 November 1978. Taylor's Beaverbrook Library phase only continued in that he handled queries concerning the papers owned by the First Beaverbrook Foundation and received a small payment for this service. After Beaverbrook's grandson succeeded to the title, he personally signed the cheques, giving Taylor a chill down his spine when the first arrived.[71] Alan Taylor continued to share 13 St Mark's Crescent with Margaret Taylor after his marriage to Éva, only moving out in early 1978. With the arrival of Éva his life entered a final active phase. He made efforts to reinvigorate his career as well as enjoying life anew in Éva's company.

–8–

INDIAN SUMMER AND LONG WINTER

The arrival of Éva at Twisden Road in April 1978 rejuvenated Alan Taylor. He was acutely aware that she had great expectations of an intellectual social life in London, with part of it centred around him. His love for her, his wish to try to go some way towards meeting her expectations and his need to earn extra money all encouraged him to attend more social gatherings, to travel more and to take up additional media opportunities.

In the early 1970s he had almost literally worried himself sick over his double life, split between his return to the old domesticity and his 'secret love' overseas. This was a severe tension between two of his selves: the achieving, home-based one and his desire to be a bit-of-a-devil, sports-car racing man about town. Éva later perceptively commented, 'For all his outward frivolity and light-heartedness, he was at heart a worrier, always looking on the dark side of things and a pessimist about how things would turn out.'[1]

When he had gone to Budapest at the start of September 1976 to marry Éva, he had picked up a virus while swimming. His tongue had swollen and he had had a temperature. When he returned to England he remained unwell for some time. Living in the same house as his first wife, while newly married to someone else, was a strain and quite probably delayed his full recovery.

Before Éva came to London Taylor sometimes seemed to be in danger of becoming a social recluse, other than seeing his family. Although he had reminisced about Tom Driberg after his death in his *New Statesman* 'London Diary' (20 August 1976), and, pressed by Anthony Howard, had mentioned Driberg's commemoration service in his 'London Diary' in December, he refused to attend the service. This surprised many, given the frequency with which he referred to Driberg as his oldest friend and one who had attended his 21st and 70th birthday parties. However, when writing to Bob Cole in 1975 he commented, 'Tom Driberg and I were not close after Oxford,' and recalled only having lunch with him in 1942 and meeting to clear comments about Driberg in his biography of Beaverbrook. He also refused to attend three functions at the German Embassy to which he had been invited, and refused to send his apologies. One close associate at the time of the Driberg commemoration service commented in exasperation that 'he was getting very stubborn and cantankerous, perhaps something one has to expect with elderly folk who have always had their way'.[2]

In recent years he had been excessively anxious about money, fearing that inflation would reduce him to penury. He feared above all following some of his Taylor ancestors, who had fallen from relative comfort to straitened circumstances, if not to rags. He fussed over his finances endlessly and he even predicted doom and gloom for wealthy Magdalen College, Oxford. During the 1974 mining dispute he had written,

> Will there be a miners' strike? If so, will all my investments go to nothing? I had counted on them as security and even comfort for my old age when I could not earn any more. What will happen to my pension? Will it be worthless too? Previously I could always write more books or speculate on the Stock Exchange. Now publishers are not keen on books and there is no opening for speculation – at least I can see none.[3]

He had hitherto worried about generating the money for two families to live in comfort.

With the prospect of Éva coming he needed to find more money. In late 1976 he had found a house in Twisden Road, London NW5, that he felt was suitable for them. However, for this he needed a £2000 deposit. As he did not have sufficient ready cash, he turned to projects which would bring in quick money or pressed for higher payments for media work. He took on writing well-paid pieces for Italian and Spanish encyclopaedias and the introduction or text to two volumes of old photographs, *The Last of Old Europe: A Grand Tour with A.J.P. Taylor* (1976) and *The Russian War 1941–1945*, edited by Daniela Mrázková and Vladimir Remes (1978). The two photograph books are attractive productions, but he had no part in the selection of the photographs. The introduction to *The Last of Old Europe* was good. In the case of *The Russian War 1941–1945* he was pleased to ensure an English-language version of a book first published in Czechoslovakia in 1975. He took the opportunity to comment in the text that the Cold War was 'the greatest disaster in our lifetime', and 'If this book does something to dispel Western suspicions of the Soviet Union it will have achieved its purpose and I shall have achieved my humbler purpose in writing this introduction.'[4]

Similarly, he took pains to maximise his income from television appearances. He was in danger of pricing himself off the screen by demanding higher fees. He appeared on BBC television's programme 'Tonight' on 29 March 1976, when he was interviewed about the candidates for the Labour Party leadership. He required £100 (then a high figure) for his appearance and, instead of arguing with the contracts department, argued with the producer. This succeeded in discouraging the 'Tonight' team from going to him for further appearances.[5] Nevertheless, other producers turned to him. In June 1976, nearly forty years after King Edward VIII's abdication, Alan Taylor spoke of it on 'Nationwide'. He remained an attractive 'television personality' to secure for chat shows and other programmes as he could be relied on to provide intelligent yet provocative and lively comment.

Friction over fees did not prevent the producer, Eddie Mirzoeff, from securing Taylor's return to giving televised history lectures. He did well out of 'The War Lords', the first of his later series. He was paid three times for them: first for the television performances, second for their publication in the BBC's journal *The Listener*, and finally when they appeared in a heavily illustrated book. This was published in hardback by Hamish Hamilton, a book club edition, and a popular Penguin paperback in Britain (and by Atheneum in New York). Payment for the lectures was £250–£300 per lecture. For the book, Kathy Burk estimates that it brought in £13,500 between 1977 and 1994. His return was attractive to the BBC. For the BBC, as Adam Sisman has commented, the unadorned lectures were cheap television.[6] 'The War Lords' also filled difficult scheduling slots, being broadcast at, or after, 10.50 p.m. on five Wednesday nights and one Monday night.

'The War Lords' were the leaders of the major belligerents of the Second World War. This was the most substantial of his later TV lecture series. Alan Taylor was well read on all but the Japanese leaders. He had written often on Churchill and frequently on Hitler and Mussolini. Roosevelt was as near as he got to having an American hero. Asked in May 1983 if Roosevelt might be a possible subject for him to write a biography, he responded that 'when Roosevelt had been alive he had had great admiration for him. He was a great improvement on any other US President, though he recognised that he was very erratic, very unreliable and very unscrupulous.' On the same occasion, when asked for his view of Stalin, he replied, 'As Clarendon commented on Cromwell, "a great bad man". This is true also of Stalin."[7] At the time that 'The War Lords' series was recorded he said he was 'particularly pleased' with the one on Stalin.[8] His lecture on Stalin is a typical Taylor piece. It does depict Stalin as a savage person who liquidated huge numbers of people, but his account does not dwell on the immense human suffering in the Soviet Union brought about by Stalin. Yet it does depict the complexity of Stalin's character and his mix of insight into the war and blundering. It is more a piece of quality historical journalism than a weighty academic reassessment. His choice of 'great men' again, as so often in his past, was suggestive of by now old-fashioned approach to the Second World War.

His urgent need for money also led him to write lesser pieces than he might have done. Or, perhaps, he was already struggling to write substantial sustained pieces. He had been attracted by a proposal made in February 1974 by Thames and Hudson for a history of Britain 1901–1975, intended to be very different from his substantial *England 1914–1945* in the Oxford History of England. In June 1976 he commented that he 'might be doing a popular version of his English History book but this time on *British* history'.[9]

By early December 1976 it was apparent that he was never going to write the book for Thames and Hudson. 'He showed no signs of getting down to it. He had half-heartedly written and rewritten one chapter – and that was all.'[10] With his intellectual energies diminishing, he preferred media-linked historical writing. He did make one further attempt at an overview of British history, on the century from 1879 to 1979, though this was a brief survey for a reference book. Again, after several drafts, he left it unfinished.[11]

Although he no longer had the intellectual energy to write a substantial, research-based new book, he did take up a publisher's suggestion of commissioning a bibliography of his works. John Spiers, founder of the Harvester Press, had earlier begun research on Charles Masterman's role in New Liberalism and had studied in the Beaverbrook Library. He was keen to publish reference books as well as monographs, and so approached Alan Taylor. The timing of Taylor's response seems significant in considering his endeavours to impress his third wife of his scholarly stature in the UK. Alan and Éva Taylor married in Budapest on 15 September 1976 and he flew back to London the next day. On 17 September his secretary sounded out a possible author for the bibliography, which was clearly a large undertaking. From the outset Taylor made clear that he would co-operate with the author and that he was pleased to have his past writings tracked down and listed.[12] The lesser pieces written by him had only been kept for the period before the Second World War, when Margaret Taylor had cut them out and stuck them in a scrap book.

The resulting bibliography underlined a point which had been made earlier by its author to Hamish Hamilton that there were ample essays by Alan Taylor worth republishing in a fresh collection rather than simply recycling the same pieces yet again, as had happened with *Europe: Grandeur and Decline* (1967) and *Essays in English History* (1976), where all but five essays had been in earlier collections. Éva Taylor vigorously backed this view. When he read copies of a long list of potential essays for a new collection, he commented, 'They make my blood run cold...I was delighted to see the piece on [G.D.H.] Cole, less to see the Men of 1862 which may overlap with other pieces. We shall see.'[13]

The final selection of essays for a new collection was a task Alan and Éva Taylor enjoyed doing together. Éva later wrote,

> We went through these essays and articles, adding to them some new reviews, and slowly a good collection was prepared. We discussed each article and it pleased me that Alan and I seemed to be building a close intellectual relationship together like, for instance, the Webbs had done.[14]

When discussing the collection, he commented on one occasion that there were not enough pieces on writers. When he was referred to a piece on George Bernard Shaw, he said that he thought it was 'a good piece, worthy of inclusion', but he 'now wondered about his last line – that Shaw had nothing to say'. He also talked about his essays on historians.

> He said of Lewis Namier that maybe he was ahead of his time in the 1960s but now his...[views on the] eighteenth century...seemed dated. He spoke warmly of Pieter Geyl. He remembered walking down Whitehall one evening and bumping into Geyl, who was wearing a dinner jacket. Geyl sombrely said to Alan Taylor, 'I have committed a great sin,' Alan Taylor said his mind quickly ran through all the things that the old boy might have done. However, the 'great sin' was an anti-climax. Geyl said, 'I have been to a dinner in honour of Toynbee' (an old friend of Geyl's). 'It was a sin against scholarly integrity to go.'
>
> Alan Taylor also recalled Geyl's attitude to his [AJPT's] *The Origins of the Second World War*. Geyl: 'It is a wicked book.' AJPT: 'Yes – but it is true.' Geyl: 'That is so – but it was very wicked to write it.' Alan Taylor added to this story, 'Geyl suffered so much under the Germans.'

As for his amusing but severe review, 'Bottom of the Class', of Harold Wilson, *A Prime Minister on Prime Ministers* (1977), he laughed and said, 'Perhaps I should put it in the section on great statesmen as a joke.'[15] Pieces on George Bernard Shaw (with the prefatory comment 'Even if he had nothing to say, he said it incomparably well') and Pieter Geyl, but not Wilson on Prime Ministers, did make it into the resulting collection, *Politicians, Socialism and Historians* (1980), dedicated to Éva.[16]

Éva was in Britain for his 1978 and 1985 television lecture series. Taylor was quick to grasp her expectations of his being a major intellectual figure in Britain but he was breathtakingly blind to her reasonable expectations of his commitment to her. It is true that they had specified early on the special provision of time that they needed for their own earlier families. Nevertheless, she was pushed to the limit by his continuing holidaying with Margaret and his children on the Isle of Wight in 1978 and the major role Margaret still played in his life at other times. Éva was sufficiently determined not to be taken for granted that on several occasions she confronted him with his selfish and unfair behaviour. Faced with her threatened departure and the collapse of a third marriage, on one occasion he literally went on his knees and begged her to stay. She later published a frank and moving account of both the good and the bad times, *Remembering Alan* (1995). In the second edition (2002) she included the comments of his son, Daniel, on the notable occasion in 1978 when she vigorously expressed her feelings after Alan's 1978 Isle of Wight visit. He wrote,

> I shall never forget your suggesting to Alan that he may wish to discuss his feelings with myself, and then leaving us together. Alan was totally unwilling or unable to share his thoughts and feelings, and looked on me with a blank expression. He similarly never shared any feelings in the aftermath of heated arguments with my mother. He was either incredibly thick-skinned, or completely out of touch with his 'inner world' or unable to express it.

While, as Daniel Taylor also suggested, he may not have wished to discuss matters with his son from another marriage, the probability is more that he was simply still unable to open up and discuss inconvenient emotional issues. Éva forced him to confront this failing, especially in 1978–80.

The major part of his personal problems arose from his unrealistic (at least by the mid-twentieth century) expectation of the roles women should play towards men. He continued to look back to JT's day, when his grandfather treated his grandmother as a domestic chattel. He could not cope with his mother being a 'new woman' of the late Victorian and Edwardian kind, epitomised perhaps by Edith Nisbet and Rebecca West. He might well have come to terms with Connie Taylor's independent ways if she had accompanied them by boosting further his already healthy ego, but he experienced anger and frustration instead. Margaret had been the mother and homemaker, deeply interested in music but not an intellectual rival; but she had wanted fun and even glamour in her life, and such gaiety came with Dylan Thomas and in a different way with Robert Kee. Eve had been a younger, attractive and more intellectual woman, again with a love for music; but she was not the docile housewife, and she gave vent to her reasonable frustration at his treatment by having rows over Margaret and by nagging him. With Éva, they were both older, both had families and she was much nearer his intellectual equal and had expectations of a lively intellectual and cultural companionship as a feature of their marriage. She had not left Hungary for a part-time relationship, especially not one where her husband sometimes confided more in the partner of a marriage which had broken down a quarter of a century earlier than with her. While put under stress by his highly unusual relationship with his first wife, Éva had her own career as a major historian. During her years with Taylor in London she carried out major research in the Public Record Office and wrote five books and ten articles in learned journals, the books including major topics of inter-war international relations and a study of Louis Kossuth as a journalist during his years in England. However, even these achievements were overshadowed by her marriage to Taylor. Anne Chisholm, in a substantial interview with Éva entitled 'The History Woman' in the *Observer*, 5 June 1983, reported: '"A man so famous," she said, wistfully. "I had to stop speaking about myself; nobody was interested in me."'

Éva not only succeeded in making him face up to and discuss emotional issues but also played the major part in making him think again about women's roles in families and society. He expressed notably changed views in a *Sunday Times* 'Man to Man' interview, published on 10 April 1983, with Stephen Pile held at the Taylors' home in Twisden Road. He declared, 'A man today should fit in with whatever women need. Women have fitted in for centuries. Now it is men's turn.' Having some time earlier observed that 'Greenham Common is a feminist plot' (the anti-nuclear weapons peace camp), he backtracked in the interview, saying, 'I called Greenham Common a feminist plot, but then I like plotters.' Pile noted that his eyes twinkled as he said this. Alan Taylor always did approve of dissenting men. Late in the day dissenting women entered his pantheon.

Alan Taylor enjoyed a final phase of television lecturing from 'The War Lords' until May 1984, with 'How Wars End'. The 'War Lords' lectures were followed with 'How Wars Begin' in July–August 1977 and 'Revolution' in July 1978, also for the BBC. These were not profound assessments but they did give him the opportunity to reflect on several favourite themes. In the 1930s and 1940s his reading and reviewing had seemed to point towards a book on the French Revolution and Napoleonic era (1789–1815). He had also been greatly interested in Chartism and the Paris Commune of 1871. These featured in these lectures. However, by this time his skill in delivering well-timed lectures without notes and without visual aids was overshadowing critical interest in the content of the lectures. The military historian John Terraine wrote of the book *How Wars Begin* (1979) that his provocative remarks were sometimes valuable but sometimes liable to cause other historians 'rage and anguish'. He added, 'On the television screen, A.J.P. Taylor has a quite extraordinary skill at

gripping an audience with unscripted historical discourse. Unfortunately...
what may pass for profundity on the screen has a way of looking rather less
so in the cold light of print.'[17]

However, the Taylor of 1976–78 was not as fluent and incisive as the
Taylor of, say, 1963, and lectures given without visual aids by this time
were looking determinedly dated in approach. In his autobiography Taylor
wrote of the 1976–78 lectures,

> In my usual way I assumed my success would go on for ever. Then as
> usual I was dropped as abruptly as I had been invited. Maybe the higher
> powers had not liked the theme of my last series. I imagined I had now
> found a really good subject, one rarely attempted: How Wars End.
> The BBC controller merely asked, 'Surely this is the same as *How
> Wars Begin?*' and struck me off the list.

This was a characteristic, apparently self-depreciatory piece, rather in the
spirit of H.G. Wells' fictional characters Mr Lewisham and Mr Kipps, who
do not determine their own fate but are a little bewildered as life buffets
them. He might have reflected on the quality of content of the lectures and
on the format for television, the kinds of issues he had thought seriously
about for radio some thirty-five years earlier. Also, as earlier, he appears to
have felt that he almost had a right to further series. At the time he seems
to have recognised that the problem was not the theme but the format. He
wrote in January 1979, 'The BBC television controller has said lectures
are not suitable for television so I have no further opening at present.'[18]

Nevertheless, a little later his 'How Wars End' idea was taken up by the
new Channel 4 television. Channel 4 began broadcasting on 2 November
1982. In April–May 1985 it took up Taylor just as independent television
had done thirty years earlier in September 1955. Channel 4 had also
earlier taken up E.P. Thompson after he had been offered and accepted
the task of giving the 1981 Richard Dimbleby Lecture for the BBC, only
to have the offer withdrawn.[19] By 1985 Alan Taylor's delivery was affected
by the onset of Parkinson's disease. He himself commented that July that
he did not think much of the series but added that at least it had increased
interest in his other books. When a viewer commented that he had enjoyed
the Napoleon-era lectures as it was a long time since he had read about
the period, he laughed and responded that it was a long time since he had
done much on it. He added that the link in the series was the problems
that the peacemakers had on each occasion with Poland.[20] Channel 4 were
sufficiently pleased by the series to have wanted another series, but this
was prevented by his deteriorating health.

Although the lecture series did not rise in quality, in his last active
phase Taylor did display a gift for introducing urban history on television,

something which had been displayed occasionally before, notably on Manchester. This suggested that he might have joined the company of his friend John Betjeman and a few others with a talent for providing perceptive and individualistic television guided tours of British towns, had he had opportunities earlier. Indeed, Betjeman had praised his 'Fabric of an Age' programme on Manchester as 'a faultless production'. Travelling to British towns to make such programmes was very much something Alan and Éva could do together. Indeed, the main thread of the four 'Edge of Britain' programmes was autobiographical: the programmes were about what the towns meant to him, about his recollections of each place. As with his autobiography, the programmes were marked by striking, yet sometimes quirky, anecdotes.

The original intention had been to make a Liverpool companion to Taylor's very successful television programme 'Fabric of an Age: On the Rise of Manchester', shown on BBC2 on 16 September 1976. Later, it had been proposed to make a bigger series on Lancashire. In July 1979 he wrote, 'In mid August I go north for a fortnight to make six television programmes on the coastal resorts of the north west.'[21] The series was postponed for ten months, until June 1980, and by then consisted of four programmes made for Granada TV. In the early stages of production he was uneasy as to the quality of the programmes and, probably unreasonably, the degree of control exercised by David Kemp, the producer, and Murray Grigor, the director. In fact it was due to David Kemp that the programmes were made. He had approached Taylor regarding Liverpool. When it turned out that Kemp was the son of Manchester friends of the 1930s, Taylor became eager to co-operate.

Alan Taylor's initial unease may have been generated by a bad experience when making a television programme in April 1980. Then he had begun making a programme to mark the one hundred and fiftieth anniversary of the Liverpool and Manchester Railway, but after a week of filming he was replaced. Éva Taylor later recalled that Alan and the producer had not got on well. She said of the producer, 'He expected us to be larger-than-life characters. He was very disappointed to find that we were a pair of elderly, fairly normal people.' She felt the producer became increasingly critical and scrapped Alan's part in the programme.[22]

Fortunately, the 'Edge of Britain' went smoothly. Taylor had proposed Southport, not Liverpool, to Kemp. He readily agreed to other places on that coast, but he urged unsuccessfully that the series should be called 'The Edge of England', not 'Edge of Britain'. For the four programmes that were made in June–July 1980 he visited Southport, Blackpool, Morecambe and Preston. He thoroughly enjoyed being the centre of attention, taking a film crew around his old haunts and reminiscing; best of all, he could do it in comfort with Éva. He eagerly sought Thom's

Japanese Tea Rooms, Lord Street, where his mother had met her friends, and Funland, where Professor (Bert) Powsey carried out escapologist feats at the end of the pier. Both had gone, but he greatly enjoyed recounting his tales. Éva noted in her diary, 'Alan says Southport does not mean anything to him. But I think it does.'[23] The trip to Southport and Preston brought him happiness. He wrote in his autobiography that the five weeks making these programmes were among the most enjoyable of his life.[24]

Yet, the return to old places in old age also brought sadness. Time had removed family and friends and changed many of the places and, perhaps above all, declining old age was confronted with memories of rising youthful optimism. Éva noted the depression which accompanied his recollection of his past. In Southport she wrote, 'As we walked along Lord Street Alan's profile was moving. Never in my life have I seen such a beautiful sad profile. I told him. He said he utterly detested the whole of life. He said I was the only good thing left to him.'

As for Preston, he passed it over in his autobiographical account of making the programmes. Éva recorded,

> I shall never forget Alan walking along Preston canal, unhappy and elderly, as he explained what a wonderful canal route it had been in his early days and reflected that its present decline mirrored his own. Then he walked sadly along the canal and at the saddest moment he danced. That was very funny and very sad. It was left out of the TV film…[25]

Yet again he was expressing his feelings in literary allusions, this time as the aged Lancastrian equivalent of Zorba the Greek.[26] While the philosophic Cretan peasant did his dance in spite of life's heavy adversities, until the onset of Parkinson's disease Taylor's setbacks in life had been relatively minor and mostly self-inflicted.

Alan Taylor's voice and his presence still commanded attention and interest. The mixture of a little history with much reminiscing worked surprisingly well. There was some pathos, some triumph, attending the small, elderly man, accompanied by his new wife, sitting in the Tower Ball Room, Blackpool, with the mighty Wurlitzer playing, or together elsewhere in the programmes. Peter Davalle, the *Times* critic, commented of Taylor after the showing on television of a one-hour edited repeat of the programmes, 'He makes a matter-of-fact guide; quietly affectionate about the old things and not a bit sentimental, as Betjeman would probably have been.'[27] Unfortunately, there was no sequel. He was unwilling to tackle London, York, the Lake District or Vienna. Quite possibly ten years earlier, had he been asked and had Éva been with him, he would have taken on the English places he knew.

In his later years there were other invitations to appear on television that he readily accepted. The previous year he had been very happy to be one of the 'media personalities' to comment on his choice of film to see again in a BBC2 series 'My Kind of Movie'. In this series interest in old, often-shown classic films was enhanced by having a well-known figure explain their choice in a five-minute interview before the showing of the film. Alan Taylor much enjoyed films, and had a taste for high-quality European productions and also British- and American-made films set in central or eastern Europe. At 10.50 p.m. on 31 January 1979 he was interviewed by Sue MacGregor on *The Mask of Demetrios*, a 1944 film notable for its moody atmosphere. He commented that the film, based on Eric Ambler's book *A Coffin for Demetrios*, was unusual in that it was less grand than many mystery films. Asked if the blackmailer played by Sydney Greenstreet was sinister, he replied, 'Yes, but benevolently sinister, very endearing in his way.' As for Peter Lorre, who plays a nervous Dutch mystery writer who tries to piece together what happened to an unpleasant international criminal, Taylor observed that his 'performance was not as good as when he is a baddie'. He was also enthusiastic about the realism in the novels of Eric Ambler. He commented that he was 'a first-rate thriller writer because his writings have so much more of everyday life. These are things that you think really could happen.' Later, Sue MacGregor recalled him as being 'courteous and charming'. Of his choice she commented, 'I'm not sure that *The Mask of Demetrios* would have been his all-time favourite movie, as participants had to choose from films that were available to BBC2 – but it was a film he certainly admired...He was certainly "good value" on a series which was essentially a little filler...'[28]

In his last active years Taylor also remained an attractive guest on 'talk shows' and current affairs programmes. At the time of the 'Crosstalk' programme one viewer had written to Richard Crossman to complain that Crossman had confined his conversation to *Beaverbrook* when Taylor's views on the issues of the day were fascinating.[29] Taylor retained a considerable personal presence, with an ability to speak directly, controversially and pithily, until Parkinson's disease was well advanced. Sometimes the discussions were quite weighty, as on the Parkinson programme on 25 February 1981, when he was a guest along with Kim Novak, Rose Murphy and Julian Pettifer. Then a substantial part of the discussion focused on his approach to writing history. When Taylor tried to suggest he was something of a dilettante (a pose he had adopted on occasion over the years since his undergraduate years), Michael Parkinson firmly responded, 'Come off it, you work all the time.' Taylor agreed, saying that his trouble was that he loved history and it was as necessary for him as eating and drinking. Asked if he felt history was important, he replied that great history could be like great opera or literature: it told you about humanity. He added that although one tried to write history rationally, 'it is a very emotional subject'.

When the discussion became more specific he was asked if he felt that the issue of conservation was important in history. He replied that he was an old fashioned historian who chose to write narrative, political history, and it was not a theme important to him as a historian; but as a human being he was very upset at the way England's buildings had been destroyed during his lifetime. It harmed the country, for the richness of its historical background gave it its rich character. Asked if he intended to continue to write history, Alan Taylor replied, 'I propose to continue to eat and drink and I expect I shall continue to read history and to write, and maybe to appear on television.' To the last point, Michael Parkinson responded warmly, 'Of course you will, you are a natural.'[30]

Alan Taylor could still secure public attention, and he very much craved the limelight. He continued to cause a stir with his support for Irish nationalism. He condemned the British military presence in Ireland on Irish (RTE) radio in 1976. After this, he was interviewed at some length in the Irish Republican newspaper *An Phoblacht*, in which he reiterated his belief in a British withdrawal. He also warned that the Protestant majority in the North was strong enough to retain control there and advised that if 'the IRA or anyone else want British influence to be used in order to bring pressure on the Protestants the best way to do it is to remain pacific and co-operate with the British and not try and throw them out'. In his 'London Diary' for the *New Statesman* in February 1978 he again advocated the withdrawal of British troops from Northern Ireland, either immediately or by a set date in the near future.[31] Appearing on 'Question Time' on BBC1 television in early March 1983 he condemned the British government's role in Ireland. Speaking privately on 9 March 1983, he was swift to refer to his remark on the police during the programme. 'My comments appear to have caused something of a sensation. People have kept coming up to me in the street to say how much they appreciated my comment of having no views on the police.' When Josie Howie, a historian of Ireland (who, sadly, was to die young), argued against his views on Ireland he responded by saying that the bloodshed in Northern Ireland had become worse since the troops had gone in.[32]

In March 1981 Alan Taylor himself was the subject of a discussion programme, 'A.J.P. Taylor: History Man', with Ludovic Kennedy, Asa Briggs and Robert Skidelsky asking him about his approach to history. Ludovic Kennedy displayed little grasp of Taylor's work while Asa Briggs and Robert Skidelsky were perceptive in probing his views. Skidelsky asked whether style determined the type of history that he wrote. Taylor replied that this was true of everyone. He went on to say that the nature of his books was determined by more than just style. They reflected 'the sort of mind I have and I am sharp and clear and rather impatient with long-winded explanations'. He said that, as in life, jokes were a good thing, epigrams were hard to use, and 'whenever I do work up to a climax that epigram is not just springing from the sentence before, but is a development of everything that has happened until then'.

Asked by Ludovic Kennedy whether his historical equivalent of the gardener's 'green fingers' had ever let him down, Taylor replied: 'Yes.' He added that his intuition was usually right, and cited his view on the Reichstag fire (where he had guessed that the Nazis made good use of an action taken not by them). Asa Briggs asked if he had intuition about whole countries or groups. He replied that intuition was alright about individuals but on groups it was more likely to be mere prejudice. He added, 'The older I become, the more I dislike generalisations about national characters.' He said these were usually due to lazy thinking and were frequently very dangerous and misleading. However, generalisations about class were different as class was itself a pattern of behaviour. Yet, even so, he said that 'class...is very dangerous'. People do not see themselves, say, as one of the masses.

Robert Skidelsky put it to Alan Taylor that he did not believe in lessons from history. He replied that 'lessons are something which the individual historian draws from history, but he is not entitled to say "history tells us this", for it is the historian who tells it to us'. He went on to say that people did not expect to learn lessons from a biography, though reading about Henry VIII might provide some about marital behaviour. He concluded, 'We read biography because of the fascination of human nature. We read history because of the fascination of a different type of human nature.'[33]

There were other television projects which did not come off. One unusual idea, aired in 1982, was for Taylor to read Beatrix Potter. He had admired her work from his youth. Reviewing Margaret Lane's *The Magic Years of Beatrix Potter* (London, Warne, 1978) he had been so enthusiastic about Beatrix Potter's *The Tailor of Gloucester* (London, Warne, 1903) as to write: 'I rank it with the masterpieces of Balzac.'[34] Reflecting on the merits of Lancashire, he observed, 'Most of the land round Hawkshead is now owned by the National Trust, thanks to the profits from Peter Rabbit and Jeremy Fisher. I suppose they were Lancastrians also.'[35] Although he was keen to read Beatrix Potter, copyright problems prevented such television programmes being made, to his regret.[36] After his death, at his memorial service in Magdalen College Chapel in April 1991, one of the readings was from *The Tailor of Gloucester*. He would have appreciated that.

His position as an eminent British intellectual was also underlined for Éva by his activities in the academic community and by the size of the audiences that turned out for his public lectures, mostly given on behalf of the Historical Association. Alan Taylor's research seminars at the Institute of Historical Research, running from 1977 until 1985, provided him with an opportunity to introduce Éva to many of the leading researchers of modern British history. After the closure of the Beaverbrook Library Roy Douglas and others sought ways to continue the successful seminars and, above all, Taylor's involvement in them. The need was for a new central location. A good solution was proposed in June 1977 by John Ramsden. This was to hold twentieth-century British history seminars in the Institute of Historical Research, Senate House (the heart of London University, next to the British Museum), with Alan Taylor as a co-chair with John Ramsden and Martin Ceadel. In 1980, when Martin Ceadel left London University for Oxford, Kathleen Burk succeeded him as a co-chair.[37] These seminars were held in the early evening on Wednesdays in university terms, and began some six months before Éva arrived in England.

As at the Beaverbrook Library seminars, Taylor followed papers with his own reflections on the topic rather than providing a critical commentary on the paper. For younger and more nervous researchers this was often felt to be a blessing. They had the benefit of his views on their subject and received direct critical questions and comments from those present. His comments were received with interest and were certainly a major attraction for many attending the seminars.

The first of the Institute of Historical Research seminars was held on 12 October 1977, with Brian Bond giving a paper on Sir Basil Liddell Hart, the military historian and philosopher of war.[38] After the paper Taylor began the discussion by raising the question of just how far Britain was committed to the continent in the inter-war period. He said that many of the statesmen of the period just pointed to the Locarno agreements of 1925 – but he felt that Locarno was an empty promise. During the Rhineland crisis the French wanted to squeeze Britain out of the Locarno commitment, basically because the French wanted to get out of it themselves.

Taylor argued that there was no real continental commitment until 1939. Then the British were anxious about the French and the commitment given was intended to stiffen their resolve. In the course of time, in 1940, the French pulled out and Britain's commitment came to an end with Dunkirk. This ending of the commitment, he declared, was the salvation of this country. He said that it explained why we had a big victory in 1945 and why we could last until then. We came through the Second World War with so few casualties relative to the First World War because there was no continental commitment.

He further said that a major feature of Liddell Hart's views was that war should be limited and civilised. He said that this was part of the reason why he advocated tank warfare. It appeared more civilised: it was conducted with elite groups and it did not involve mass casualties. Liddell Hart, he commented, felt strongly that the deadlock of the First World War should not be allowed to happen again.

After Easter 1978 Éva Taylor usually accompanied her husband to the seminars.[39] She was first present for Peter Clarke's paper on Keynes.[40] In his response to it Taylor talked of Keynes' influence on the Left. He said that G.D.H. Cole never understood what Keynes was writing about. Evan Durbin explained Keynes' views to Hugh Gaitskell, who was impressed. Gaitskell and Durbin moved away from Cole.

Alan Taylor also spoke more generally of the Left.

> Malcolm Muggeridge said he shared the views of the ILP, though it was clear to me that he had no idea what they were. Before Muggeridge went to Russia I warned him that he would be disappointed. If you go to Russia and it doesn't come up to your expectations, I told him, don't take it out on the Russians. Sadly he has done. He should have known better, as he knew India and other places outside of Europe.

He talked about the attraction of Stalinism to the intellectual Left of the 1930s. He said that everybody had been surprised by the first Five-Year Plan as it had been so exceptional. He said that Stalinism was also an emotional response and this was a feature of anti-Nazism. He said that the problem of the 1930s for the Left was, how does an enlightened Left gain power and then apply it? In contrast to the British Left, in Russia Stalin had the opportunity to use power. The Left was aware of the salt mines and other horrors in Stalinist Russia, but they felt that Russian help was essential to defeat Hitler.

On 24 May Alan Taylor gave a talk on CND to a large audience at the Twentieth Century British History seminar. He gave an interesting personal view of the early history of CND, much of which has been recounted earlier. His answers to some of the questions were especially interesting as his points in these replies were more novel. John Grigg asked him if the early CND leaders had considered running candidates for Parliament. Alan Taylor replied that Lord Beaverbrook had done this in his empire campaigns and Beaverbrook had urged this course on him (AJPT). 'I was keen on this course,' he said, 'but the EC [Executive Committee] had a very solid Labour Party majority.' He went on to say that non-party candidates stood no chance of success and CND did not have wide enough support to be successful. However, he did feel that CND had created the politically conscious generation of the 1960s. While CND was predominantly a middle-class movement, it did appeal to the young, and the young did not divide politically along class lines to the same extent as older people.

I asked Alan Taylor to what extent Michael Foot was effective in getting up support for CND. He replied that *Tribune* claimed to be in the lead but really the problem was Nye Bevan. Michael Foot hoped that if CND got bigger then Nye Bevan might swing back to his left-wing supporters on this issue.

Martin Ceadel asked if he thought that, had the Labour Party been led by a man of the Left, there would have been less Labour Party grass-roots support for CND, it being an outlet for Labour Party discontent. Alan Taylor replied,

> The Labour leadership of the 1930s' advocacy of disarmament nearly ruined the Party. They had thought it was a winning ticket then, but they carried it on too long. In the 1950s the Labour Party leadership as a whole was wary of doing that again. Another point: the Labour Party leadership was responsible for the nuclear bomb. To have come out vehemently against it, they would have denounced themselves.

Martin Ceadel also asked him if the CND leadership wanted the money saved on nuclear weapons to be spent on conventional weapons. He replied, 'Collins was a pacifist. Priestley and I were in favour of conventional weapons. I would pay any price for the abolition of nuclear weapons.'

John Campbell asked him if he had had different speeches for different audiences. He replied that he did vary his talks to some degree, but it was still the same theme. If he felt his audience was intense or very moral he spoke accordingly; if he felt they wanted the use of nuclear weapons ridiculed then he ridiculed their use.

On 18 October 1978 John Grigg gave a seminar paper on whether or not Lloyd George was honest.[41] He said that on one occasion Lord Beaverbrook had told him that it was because Lloyd George was known to be unscrupulous about money that Lloyd George had lost the trust of the general public. John Grigg's paper was a vigorous defence of Lloyd George. Taylor said that he was inclined to agree, observing of Lloyd George's alleged financial dishonesty: 'I think there is very little in this.' Taylor argued that the main harm in Lloyd George's Patagonia speculations as a backbencher was that he involved small investors, while in the case of the Marconi shares he was the small man brought in. He also felt that Lloyd George's sale of honours had been inflated, as many honours had been to do with the war and many were for the Conservatives, who had been long out of office. Taylor then spoke about Lloyd George's principles. He said that Lloyd George did have a consistent outlook but he went a roundabout way to achieve things. 'I've come round to the view,' he said, 'that Lloyd

George was for the Empire much earlier than is usually thought. He was more concerned for this than for the Balance of Power; like me, he did not have a great regard for that.'

Alan Taylor went on to say that the Black and Tans were an irredeemable stain on Lloyd George's reputation, just as Ireland is on Oliver Cromwell's. He said Lloyd George partly atoned for it with the 1921 Irish settlement, which was the only possible solution at the time. The use of the Black and Tans showed the vicious streak in him. He had no principles over Ireland. Unlike Gladstone, he said, Lloyd George did not see Ireland as a righteous cause, and as a result he was willing to use any tactics to secure his end.

Later, in the discussion, he was challenged over his comments on the Black and Tans. He replied,

> Maybe I am high minded on this, but a Prime Minister who instigates a campaign of murder leaves a stain on his record. Lloyd George was lured into this policy by the incompetence of his people in Ireland. Lloyd George did more harm to his standing among the high minded over the Black and Tans than over his treatment of conscientious objectors. His comment on the latter that he would make their path a hard one did him immense harm with his traditional supporters, even if much good with the Tory backbenchers.

A particularly memorable seminar of the 1978–79 series was on George Bernard Shaw, with a paper given by Michael Holroyd on 29 November 1978. It set Alan Taylor off comparing biography and history, and then Shaw and H.G. Wells. He began by arguing that Holroyd had an over-inflated view of historians.

> You do greatly overstate the claims of historians. If I was asked to distinguish between the two tasks, I would say that the biographer actually deals with something which has existed, something that you could touch – someone else. There would have been a time when you literally could have grasped the subject of your biography, shaken him by the hand. The record left is indisputably his record. There are very few people who forge letters about themselves. Biography is connected with real life – someone's parents, someone's upbringing and such like.
>
> History is pure fiction. We have various conceptions we use. These we use as a shorthand to handle vast problems. Namier despaired of the problems and said that the biographical approach was the only way to approach the past. Hence he set off preparing a potted biography of every Member of Parliament as his way to a history of Parliament. I said to Lewis Namier, 'There *is* already a history of Parliament, it is called Hansard.'

Our historical concepts are imaginary. Nations are imaginary. The population of one nation does not act with one accord. Classes are imaginary. All these are dogmatic terms. I have never met anyone who says, 'I am one of the masses.' When I sit on Brighton beach like everyone else there, I don't think I am one of the masses. Some people have fantasies that all the upper class or the proletariat think this or that. You do find the odd middle class idealist who says that they are one of the proletariat, but they are…nothing of the kind. All such terms are the fantasy of the historian.

Historians can give some kind of a picture of society. They try to describe some tendency in society. Even such detailed work as using parish registers for family reconstitution are of this kind. Such methods are just clearing the canvas for literary work. History is essentially imaginative work. It is useful shorthand to describe seventeenth century man as anyone living between 1601 and 1700. But such a description would mean very little to the different people alive in that time span and who would be shocked to find themselves all bracketed together.

With biography there is little fantasy, though it can be difficult to catch some personal aspects of the subject. The biographer is a down-to-earth man who is dealing with a solid subject, some actual person.

Taylor then warmed to the subjects of Shaw and Wells, figures he often liked to discuss in print or verbally.

The study of Shaw is no problem. Shaw was an acute, aesthetic man. I was wrong to write that he had nothing to say [Michael Holroyd had quoted AJPT on this] – but he said it at great length. Bernard Shaw was one of the greatest writers of simple English. He was one of only a few who have been in the same class as Cobbett.

I could claim to be the last Shavian. The educated did not send their children to particular schools to escape Shaw's views [something Michael Holroyd had suggested]. I was made to read him at school. I saw some of his plays when they were first performed. A piece I once wrote provoked a correspondence with him.

Shaw never had the moral or educational influence that H.G. Wells had. Wells' *Outline of History* had an enormous influence on the young of the time. His approach to social problems and to religion also had great influence. I was a contemporary witness of this. People formed Open Societies when Wells preached the Open Society. Shaw never had this impact. No woman champion of emancipation was inspired by Shaw's plays as they were by *Ann Veronica*. Wells was not only a propagandist, and this may have spoiled his novels, but he was also a successful propagandist. Shaw was also a propagandist, but he was not successful. Shaw was a man of simple ideas. However, I do agree with his idea of socialism: 'Equal incomes plus abolition of property equals socialism.'

A year later, on 21 November 1979, Éva Taylor gave a well-received paper entitled 'British reflections on the decisive year of post-war Hungary 1948', based on her research in British Foreign Office papers. Alan Taylor gave a prologue to her paper, speaking of his post-1945 Wroclaw Congress. More generally, he observed that 1948, more than 1945, was the climacteric year of the Cold War; though, he added, 'perhaps it was not fully with us until the Korean War'. After the paper he commented that all the British Foreign Office officials had been in favour of Horthy. 'It was as if the German section of the Foreign Office had been in favour of Hohenzollern return. Perhaps if a Habsburg Prince, Prince Otto, had been available, then they would have been keen on him.'

While the Institute of Historical Research seminars were the most agreeable academic link of his last active phase, they were not the only academic link. He was invited to give papers and lectures at other major venues. The academic debates over the origins of the Second World War still continued, even if they had long left behind Alan Taylor's 1961 book. Alan Taylor gave a lecture on the subject to well over 100 people in the Old Library, All Souls, Oxford, on 17 May 1979. By this time most of the tensions between him and some Oxford academics had gone. He no longer felt impelled to compete and to excel with his peers. His generation was gone or going, with their various major achievements in the past. Much of the younger generation at Oxford either admired him or felt no hostility to him. It was notable that no one came to this paper to 'down him'. It was a valedictory occasion, not an invitation to academic combat. His old friend and colleague, Pat (A.F.) Thompson, simply introduced him and the lecture by saying it was 'Further thoughts on *that* book'.

Taylor spoke without notes, arguing a need for further research on some topics connected with the origins of the Second World War. He said that much of his book was by then inadequate. 'Much of it depended on guesswork, as it was written before much archival material was available.' He went on to say that most of his guesses had been proved to be not far from right. 'There is one wrong guess. I tried to give significance to the Hossbach Protocol. It was not a protocol, it was a forgery. I guessed that it was to do with the exclusion of Schact from government, and this guess was wrong.' He went on to say, 'If historians did not make guesses, practically no history would be written... except The Pipe Rolls.' He said that writing at the start of the 1960s, he exaggerated the significance of Europe in world affairs and also the importance of foreign policy and diplomacy as determining factors. He added that if he were writing in 1979 he would lessen the passages of moral emphasis in the book. He also felt that there needed to be greater emphasis on economic factors, including British interests in Yugoslavia, Romania and Poland, on military policy and on the secret information available.

He returned to this theme in his lecture '1939 Revisited', given as the 1981 Annual Lecture at the German Historical Institute, London. In this lecture he was more defensive, more critical of those who had criticised his book. The lecture did not engage with the considerable research on the origins of the Second World War published in the intervening years between the publication of Taylor's book and the lecture. In the lecture he argued that the greatest flaw was undue emphasis on British policy towards Germany, as British policy was unable to focus only on that. 'Indeed,' he observed, 'if you judge British policy from the defence papers instead of Foreign Office papers (and to do either exclusively is a mistake) the Far East and the Japanese question were for the British a greater obsession and anxiety than Germany.' He also felt he should have examined public opinion more carefully, and also considered carefully when the conflicts of the time deserved the title of 'world war'.[42]

If he disappointed many academics with such reappraisals, he remained highly popular with that part of the British public interested in history. He continued to attract very large audiences to Historical Association lectures in his last phase, up to the association's seventy-fifth anniversary in 1981. He still enjoyed travelling to different parts of Britain and being received and listened to with adulation. His charismatic style of lecturing, much depending on the power of his presence, his sense of timing and his lucid, even simple, narrative approaches, continued to be extremely attractive to Historical Association audiences, which included many retired professional people, teachers and sixth-formers. If he was feeling down, performing before such an appreciative audience would usually lift him.

He enjoyed going to speak to Historical Association branches outside London with Éva. It was very much something they did together, it was very much 'quality time' together. These trips came to matter for Éva and she was hurt when he went to one without her, calling in for tea with Margaret before taking a train from Euston station.[43] For him, as he commented in his autobiography, these lectures 'gave me the opportunity to show Éva places from St Andrews to Chichester that we should not have visited otherwise'.[44] He often liked to arrange a small tour of three or four branches in an area. One such tour was of Scottish branches, which he made with Éva in late October 1978, lasting nearly a week. They began in Stirling, where he gave an excellent lecture to an audience of some 400–500 people in the McRobert Art Centre of the university.[45] They were next taken some ten miles north to visit Dunblane and its cathedral by Alan Taylor's cousin. He was delighted to go and visit that city, as his great grandfather had come from there, moving south as a pedlar and setting up a general store in Heywood, Lancashire. After Dunblane they went on to St Andrews, where he lectured on Lloyd George to an audience of some 150–200 people. They were looked after by Professor Norman Gash, whose work Alan Taylor respected.[46] They went on to St Andrews, where Paul Addison escorted them around the university and town. In the evening Taylor lectured on 'the Bulgarian Horrors' of 1876. Their final venue was the Glasgow branch of the Historical Association. In the afternoon they enjoyed the National Gallery, Éva particularly enjoying the collection of French Impressionist paintings. In the evening he lectured on the Soviet image in Britain to an audience of some 400 people.[47]

When Alan Taylor went with Éva to speak to the Chichester branch of the Historical Association on 9 March 1981 he was delighted to be taken to an old church earlier in the day. John Fines later recalled that when Alan Taylor arrived he was 'in a rather "down", even grumpy mood'. Knowing his love of old churches, Fines took them to St Wilfred's church at Church Norton, off the road to Selsey. This is the site of a very old church, at the place where Wilfred had converted the Saxons. The existing church, surrounded by Norman-period defensive banks, is attractively located by the sea. Once in the church, Fines recollected,

> he was as delighted as a small boy shown an interesting stamp collection. He loved the church, and poked here and there in it, discovering things with great pleasure. When he found in the guide book that some remnants from it had been taken to Selsey, he … declared … 'You must get your car and we must go at once'.

And they did.[48]

That evening he gave a lecture on writing history to a large audience. This was a topic which John Fines knew would appeal to him. This was one of his last reflections on history as a subject, and as such is of interest. In it he reiterated several characteristic views. By this time it would have seemed somewhat dated. Yet, the impact of his talks depended greatly on the delivery: his sense of timing, his charismatic epigrammatic sentences. He delivered his talk without any text, as usual, but Éva Taylor's notes of his talk survive, and these give a good impression of his broad approach.

He began by saying that most historians would answer the question 'What contribution do they make to society?' with the simple truth: history satisfies the elementary human need to know what happened in the past. When a child asks: 'What did you do in the past?' that is the beginning of history. The prime object is to explain what happened in the past, what happened next. He then contrasted such a view with that of the French Annales School, Ferdinand Braudel and others, who he said disapproved of such an approach and searched for fundamental facts.

Alan Taylor went on to observe that every historian reflects his own time. The subject of history is men, not individual men. Historians are concerned with men in society. History begins when men began to read and write, when men were keeping records, roughly 4,000 years ago. History is a record of time. For the historian, events happen in order of time. In history everything changes. There is nothing permanent in human history. History will go on like this, unless civilisation ends. Only a tiny percentage of the records survive. Therefore, history can never teach a lesson. Historians provide a lesson. There is no such thing as a verdict of history. If there are twelve historians, there are likely to be twelve verdicts.

There was a tendency to ascribe to each society in the past specific phenomena: to write of the Middle Ages, for example. We think about patterns. The historians of the nineteenth century invented nationalities. In modern times we know that there are always exceptions. In modern England there are some 50 million people. To write a history about them inevitably involves generalisation. Historians do what they can. Are they reducing it to manageable proportions? Or is their account imaginary? Sexes are not imaginary. Religions are there. History is an art, not a science, which man made himself. History is not an oracle. History is about the varied aspects of human character. History is shaped by the most elusive but fascinating thing: mankind.

Among the questions at the end he was asked, 'What have you learnt from history?' To this he answered, 'Scepticism.' Asked to comment on the future, he replied, 'I never foretell the future.'[49]

As well as travelling around the country together, he enjoyed taking Éva to a variety of social gatherings. They went to the Longfords' fiftieth wedding celebration on 3 November 1981, where he made a humorous speech. Lord Longford noted in his diary, 'Alan boasted that he and I had both "made it" – "it" being fifty years of marriage. He admitted that in his case there had been marriage, divorce, re-marriage, divorce, re-marriage – the rest of the recital was drowned in laughter.'[50]

These years, the late 1970s and early 1980s, were, naturally enough, years when some of his activities wound down. He had successfully enquired about becoming a Special Lecturer at University College, London (UCL), in September 1964. He lectured and ran a weekly discussion class from 1965 to 1978. His lectures were very well attended and did not disappoint. Those in the autumn of 1968 were precursors of his short book *War by Timetable* (1969).[51] In these he argued that all the plans, 'even that of the Germans, were designed to win a war if one happened, not to bring it about'. They all depended on speed, because once put into operation they were difficult to halt because of the complexities of moving armies by rail. He concluded, 'When cut down to essentials, the sole cause for the outbreak of war in 1914 was the Schlieffen plan – product of the belief in speed and the offensive.' He also made the customary warning of his later years: 'The deterrent failed to deter…There is a contemporary moral here for those who like to find one.' He concluded his final public lecture, the Romanes Lecture which he gave in the Sheldonian Theatre in Oxford in March 1982, with much the same moral: 'We have lived under nuclear terror for forty years and are still here. The danger increases every day. Without the abolition of nuclear weapons the fate of mankind is certain.'[52]

After a drive for economies at UCL ended his work there, he took on a similar role at the Polytechnic of North London (later the University of North London). The staff there included such modern specialists as Chris Cook, Roland Quinault, David Carlton and Alan O'Day, and was headed by Robert Skidelsky. Skidelsky had first met Taylor some three years earlier, when he had got him to give two lectures in Bologna at the graduate school of the John Hopkins University. He also accepted an invitation to become the Benjamin Meaker Visiting Professor at Bristol University, a post he held for two years, 1976–78. He was sounded out by John Gross, whom he informed, 'I am attracted by the idea of acquiring a chair after all these years without one.' He was very clearly pleased to become a professor in such a way, without administrative burdens or relocating away from London. The invitation was initiated by Professor John Vincent, an outstanding historian of Victorian Britain. Taylor had not known him before. However, after these short-term positions his teaching days were over. His Romanes Lecture in March 1982 also marked the end of his public lecturing. After it he noted: 'Suddenly I have grown old,' and added, 'I have finished with long journeys or going out late at night in order to deliver stale thoughts on stale subjects.' A couple of years later, at a seminar at the Institute of Historical Research, Alan Taylor responded to John Grigg's saying that he felt he (Taylor) would disagree with his assessment of Lloyd George's 1916 'Knockout Blow' speech by saying, 'My disagreeing days are over. I shall now just sit quietly and listen.' And that was precisely what he did.[53] Bristol awarded him an honorary doctorate in 1978, as did New Brunswick in 1961, York in 1970, Warwick in 1981 and Manchester in 1982.

He ended his membership of the British Academy in a major public row in August 1980. This followed the revelation in Andrew Boyle's *The Climate of Treason* (1979) that Sir Anthony Blunt, an eminent art historian, had earlier spied on behalf of the Soviet Union. After Blunt had been stripped of his knighthood and had resigned other Fellowships before being expelled, the Council of the British Academy put forward a recommendation to its annual meeting on 3 July that he should be expelled.

Alan Taylor initially had suspected there would be a cover-up favourable to Blunt. In a conversation on 24 October 1979 he said that Boyle's book contained little that was new. He went on, 'However, it is scandalous that Anthony Blunt, the Queen's adviser, should be let off yet an ordinary university lecturer and Fuchs, a German immigrant, should be sent down for long spells. It is yet another sign of how the Establishment looks after its own. There are different rules for everyone else.' A month later, on 21 November, he commented that 'the Press had indulged in a disgraceful hunt of the man. He had never given anything worthwhile away – and anyway during the Second World War Russia was our ally.' Before the British Academy's annual meeting Alan Taylor told the *Times* that he was against Blunt being subjected to 'a witch-hunt' and would resign if Blunt was driven out. At the annual meeting there was a discussion which ended with a large majority agreeing to move to the next item on the agenda. His Oxford colleague, Marjorie Reeves, recalled him leaving by one door, loudly stating he would resign if Blunt was driven out, while Robert Blake went out the other door, protesting that he would resign if Blunt was allowed to remain. According to Taylor, Blake was so angry with him (AJPT) he would not speak to him for eighteen months. Taylor, presumably on the

Receiving an honorary doctorate at Warwick University from Lord Scarman, 1981.

basis of his stance before the meeting, wrote eight days later, 'I have ... just defeated an attempt to expel Blunt from the British Academy.'[54]

However, there was sufficient pressure on Blunt for him to resign. When this became known, on 19 August 1980, Alan Taylor resigned. He had written to Éva on 24 November the previous year, commenting of Blunt: 'I wonder whether he will resign from the British Academy. It would give me an excuse for resigning from it also.' This probably had much to do with establishing his anti-Establishment and rebel credentials with her. Being a Fellow had meant a lot to him. A few years later he even quietly enquired if he could become a Fellow again, only to be told that he had passed the upper age limit for election. Nevertheless, when he died, his long and active service to the British Academy was mentioned in commissioning his obituary for its *Proceedings*.[55]

Margaret Taylor's health declined markedly from 1977. Alan Taylor visited her in hospital in June 1977 and later. He attended her funeral in July 1980. Her death took away the major cause of the stress in his relationship with Éva which had seriously endangered their marriage. It also encouraged him to publish his autobiography, *A Personal History*. As well as omitting references to Eve, his second wife, legal advice resulted in many references to people still alive being cut out. One notable example was his comments on Lord Boothby in regard to 'In the News', which began with: 'he had the added distinction of being for twenty years the lover of Lady Dorothy Macmillan, the wife of the future Prime Minister.' This became widely known only after Taylor's death with Robert Rhodes James' biography of Boothby.[56]

The autobiography, begun in 1972 for Éva, was revised over the years. At one time there was an account of his life in the late 1970s and early 1980s, which included the Institute of Historical Research seminars and the publication of the bibliography of his writings. Part of the problem was the increasing severity of the effects of Parkinson's disease. Not surprisingly it brought on periods of self-pity and even bitterness about his past life. Some of this went into the autobiography. Also, like many elderly people, his memory of the more distant past was more vivid than recent times.

The book was generally well received, although the frequent bitter complaints were noted. John Gross in the *New York Review of Books* commented, 'Some of the boasting is merely harmless, perhaps endearing, vanity; some of it takes the form of an unseemly crowing over vanquished rivals and forgotten competitors. And, in retracing his career, Mr Taylor never seems happier than when recalling slights, setbacks and university feuds.' Anthony Quinton, the President of Trinity College, Oxford, observed, 'For quite a long time now ... A.J.P. Taylor has prevailed over all others by reason of general tenacity and staying-power, in hanging on to the position of chief Rude Boy in the British intellectual scene,' and commented that other challengers such as the playwright John Osborne and Malcolm Muggeridge had 'spluttered away after a glittering moment or two'. Muggeridge himself commented, 'It is…Alan's ultimate candour which makes his autobiography, and his historical writing generally, worthwhile; the wings of fantasy carry him away, and then, suddenly, he plummets down to earth again.' Stephen Ross was notably favourable, remarking, 'Charitably disposed to others, Taylor is frequently very hard on himself. That is his prerogative and, as his friends will recognise, his habit.' He also commented that 'there can be no denying the dynamism and sheer excitement he has brought to history'.[57] His autobiography proved popular and was widely read, especially in paperback.

By the time of the publication, in May 1983, Parkinson's disease was increasingly having a severe impact on him. Later in the year he wrote that it 'cripples me one day and leaves me alone the next. I do not see a happy future ahead of me but I struggle on.' This increasing volatility due to illness was displayed most sadly at a private dinner party hosted by Robert Kee and Sir Nicholas Henderson to mark the publication of the book. When Michael Foot praised Taylor for being renowned for speaking the truth, Henderson praised other attributes but said, 'I don't think truth is what he's particularly concerned with.' Taylor, who sometimes dwelt on the search for truth being at the essence of his life as a historian, was outraged and demanded to go home immediately and thereafter broke off all relations with the unfortunate Henderson. As Adam Sisman has observed, the comment 'could have easily been laughed off or ignored'; indeed, a younger, healthier Taylor would have responded with a witticism at Henderson's expense.[58]

Alan Taylor's health seemed to decline rapidly after he was knocked down by a car when he was on his own in Soho on 6 January 1984. One of his routines in later life was to go every second week to buy coffee from a shop in Old Compton Street. Although his pelvis was not broken, the incident shook him and his system substantially. A month later he was still experiencing pain in his leg near his injured pelvis. Soon afterwards he was ill with septicaemia, and from then on he was more prone to other illnesses. He did derive consolation later that it was fortunate it had happened after the recording of his last series of television lectures. 'What a disaster it would have been if it had happened part way through them.' In May he reported, 'I have less pain but am fairly helpless. Venice is out for this year…My wife Eva thinks we might come in September but I only like it in April…'[59]

In his later years he gained much pleasure from the company of his children and grandchildren and also those of Éva. He would go on Sunday afternoon walks with Daniel and Crispin. He also enjoyed going to the Lake District and walking until the early 1980s. Earlier, in about 1975, his last major walk had been with Crispin from Buttermere to the top of Pillar, a walk deemed 'not for the elderly'. He took two groups of grandchildren, aged between about eight and fifteen, to Venice. Predictably, they enjoyed eating spaghetti and playing in an amusement arcade. He returned 'absolutely furious that they were not in the least interested in the glories of Venice'. Generally, however, he gained much joy from his two families. He himself still greatly enjoyed Venice, his favourite place in Italy, and in mid-1985 he was still hoping for further visits there and to Florence.[60]

He also enjoyed getting to know Éva's family in Budapest and in London. He took pains to show her sons round London and Oxford, with all the sightseeing being undertaken on foot. He delighted in showing the small churches, especially those not well known. He took Ferencz twice to the Tuesday lunchtime concerts which meant so much to him. In Oxford he proudly guided Ferencz round Magdalen College, delighting in pointing out the unusual, such as scissors hanging on the Common Room wall for clipping nails.

While he was generous in large matters, he was famous for his parsimony with regard to food. Éva later recalled one occasion when she was very embarrassed at the small amounts of meat that he cut for their visitors. She said, 'In Hungary we try to offer our guests a lot.' Alan Taylor responded by offering more, but the guests only got one small slice each. He then offered more, but by this time all were too embarrassed to ask for a third helping. Éva's younger son, Pisti, on hearing this, added, 'Yes, very few slices of meat – and cut so thin you could almost see through them!' Éva also commented that as her second husband grew older he became increasingly anxious as to the level of his income when he was no longer so well known.

In London, Alan Taylor also supported Éva's efforts in promoting Anglo-Hungarian relations. Ferencz later commented that he had been very supportive of young Hungarian historians visiting Britain. He not only saw them and talked about their proposed research but also wrote letters of support to gain access to archives or for grant applications. Alan Taylor was delighted to go to the Hungarian Embassy to be made formally a member of the Hungarian Academy.[61] He had been honoured similarly by the American and the Yugoslav equivalents the previous year.

On first going to visit Éva and her family in Budapest he had been able to speak only a few words in Hungarian. He had been proud to say: 'Nem, nem soha!' ('No, no never!'), a post-First World War phrase he had learnt from Michael Karolyi. As a result of his lack of Hungarian he had to adjust to the unusual experience for him of not being the centre of attention. He communicated by body language quite well. He helped by washing dishes. When visitors came who spoke some English he enjoyed the conversation but, after a while, he was happy for the conversation to revert to Hungarian.

He greatly enjoyed Hungarian cooking, especially soups (which are prepared in a different way from how they are in England).

He had been vehemently against the Horthy régime. He was very ready to see at least some of those behind the 1956 Hungarian rising as being reactionary. At the time he had been highly critical of the post-Stalin Stalinists but he had not said much about Hungary. In June 1983 he held forth in an interview with an Irish journalist:

> The Hungarian Rising of 1956 was a rising by all the most reactionary forces against the socialism taking place and if victorious would have led to a full restitution of the power of the Roman Catholic Church and a restoration of the great landowners. So I think in every way what happened to Hungary in 1956 was fortunate.

Ferencz, who discussed the matter with his stepfather in some depth, recalled his views as being more complex:

> I felt he had a good understanding of 1956 in Hungary. He saw it as having two aspects, one commendable and one reactionary. He saw 1956 in Hungary as a movement against Stalinism, a movement which had both a Leftist and a reform side. But he also saw it as a move against the socialist system – with a reactionary aim of bringing back the big landlords and returning their lands to them.[62]

As late as mid-1984 Alan Taylor was still in demand with the media. For instance, in July the *Guardian* and *Observer* were wanting him to review books, the *Mail on Sunday* wanted him to write on a current issue, an Italian television crew filmed him on Rommel, and BBC radio wanted him to take part in a programme on the seventieth anniversary of the assassination at Sarajevo. Talking of this, he laughed, saying that he had found out that they expected him to travel to Sarajevo to record it. He said his reply was that they could do it perfectly well in the studio, as he was not prepared to go out to Sarajevo. However, already he was finding that he could not carry out reviews, and requests for these soon tailed off. Earlier in the year he had been pleased to bring out a collection of his diary pieces for *The Listener* and the *London Review of Books*, entitled *An Old Man's Diary*, and to find that it sold better than he had anticipated. With his writing days over there was a void in his life and he felt miserable.[63]

In July 1985, talking of a forthcoming television programme on old age, he told the television people there was nothing to say except that one's powers steadily fade as one gets old. The only thing to add, he commented, was that 'one wants a comfortable chair at the table'. Shortly before his eightieth birthday he wrote a poignant piece, 'When You Have Life Don't Waste It', in which he found many grounds for living. It also had a certain dry humour. 'There are worse things than being eighty. Some people tell me that being eighty-one is one of them. I am curious to verify this.'[64]

One of his last substantial public appearances was on 25 March 1986, at his eightieth birthday party. The idea for the dinner came from Robert Skidelsky, and it was organised at 'The Gay Hussar' restaurant in Soho by Michael Foot. Foot was one of the speakers. He said,

> Alan Taylor has introduced us to the great historians – Macaulay and others. Alan himself is among them. In a hundred years' time – that is if Alan's gloomy predictions about The Bomb have not come true – then the people of this country will be reading Alan Taylor's books just as people now still read Macaulay.

Robert Skidelsky, in his short speech, described seeing Alan and Éva Taylor about final arrangements. He said he presumed he would not like publicity. 'At this,' he continued, 'Alan's eyes widened and he said, "It's the news desks that you want. Ring them on Monday. Don't do it too soon or they won't be interested."' This had all present, including Alan Taylor, laughing.

A few days later he commented, 'I had absolutely no idea there were to be speeches. I thought it was just going to be a meal. I was very surprised when people got up and made speeches. I had not prepared anything to say.' On the night he certainly looked surprised when, after Raymond Carr, the third speaker, had finished, he was expected to respond. He spoke slowly and deliberately.

> This talk of me as another Macaulay, it is all a great deal of nonsense. I am a perfectly steady and precise historian. Sometimes I have written good books. But Macaulay stands above us all. We have brought together more scholarly material than him. But we do not have his gifts. There is much more literary value in his work than ours.
>
> Putting history books together is very hard work. One has got to tell the story, get events in the right order, explain them and, it is very important, to be precise.
>
> I have written many successful books. I am not ashamed of any. Looking back at one or two of the early books now gives me the creeps. If you develop as a historian and come to write books successfully, this is the price you pay.
>
> I am told that Trevor-Roper writes good books. [Much laughter at this.] I've only seen one. This was the one on the death of Hitler. After that he went off the boil. [More laughter.]
>
> When I look at my best books now, I wonder who wrote them.

He then talked to some of those present, before leaving. He was lucid but seemed very tired.[65]

His decline was rapid after his eightieth birthday. In late 1986 he went to the *Observer*'s party, where a photo was taken of him between Stephen Spender and Terence Kilmartin. By this time he was tiring quickly and was increasingly prone to be morose.[66] Éva was struggling to look after him at their home. Eventually, in early November 1987, she was forced to place him under professional care at Moss Lodge, Nether Street, West Finchley.

Éva took great care to ensure that in his room he was surrounded by familiar possessions. As well as a bed, there were several easy chairs and, in frames on the wall, a colourful, fairly recent cartoon of him and the Manchester University certificate of the honorary doctorate given him on 12 May 1982. There was a record player, which he still enjoyed. There were a few books, notably leather-bound presentation volumes of his *A Personal History* and *An Old Man's Diary*, and also *Wainwright on the Pennine Way*. He also had the current *Times Literary Supplement*. In the nursing home he had his down days as well as some much better. When I visited him on 16 November he was in a down spell, often muddled or agitated, but with periods of his old incisiveness and charm. He was still interested in the news on television, going off on time to see the early evening broadcast. In one of his lucid spells he was enthusiastic about the photos in the Wainwright volume. We spoke of places I knew – Hebden Bridge and Hardcastle Crags, Malham Tarn, Harworth and Hadrian's Wall. He was especially warm about the Top Withens ruins and the Harworth parsonage. He commented with pleasure that the book included some fine Yorkshire places.

In the early part of 1988 Alan Taylor had a better spell for some months. Katherine Bligh, who visited him then, recalled that she had quite a good conversation with him. Kenneth Morgan later recalled of a visit he made with his wife in 1988 that, 'after he had tried in vain to inscribe a copy of the *Origins* for my children, I felt bereaved'. As Taylor's stay in the nursing home drifted into years, not months, Éva was pleased that Michael (M.R.D.) Foot, a former pupil of Alan's of fifty years earlier, was visiting him each Wednesday afternoon in order to give her free time to shop. He later recalled that the last words Taylor said to him were, 'The Emperor said he would promote him but he never did.' When I wondered if this referred to Francis Joseph, Michael Foot sensibly replied: 'Quite possibly,' but added it could have been Kaiser Wilhelm II, Louis Napoleon or another.[67]

In early August 1990 Éva was very pleased to find that her husband was more lucid again. The specialist had been saying that he could live to ninety. During that summer he had been outside a lot and eating well, and she felt that his stubbornness and strength of will would keep him going. So she was very surprised by his death on 7 September 1990. He was cremated at Golders Green Crematorium on 17 September, with members of his family and also two of his former pupils and long-term friends, Robert Kee and Pat (A.F.) Thompson, giving addresses. The service began with a welcome by Giles Taylor and, among readings of his favourite literature, Amelia Taylor read E.V. Knox's poem 'The Everlasting Percy' and Sophia Taylor read Shelley's 'The Mask of Castlereagh'. Éva was not alone in finding the service 'very moving'.

His commemoration service at Magdalen College was held on 13 April 1991, a beautiful, warm day, with daffodils and other spring flowers out in profusion by the river. The chapel was crowded. Pat Thompson spoke again, followed by Michael Foot, Alan Sked, Robert Skidelsky and Arthur Adams, the former Dean of Divinity. Cynthia Kee read an extract from Beatrix Potter's *The Tailor of Gloucester* and Rosa Howard, one of his grandchildren, read Tennyson's poem 'Break, Break, Break', which mourns his friend Arthur Hallam. The carefully chosen music included pieces by Schubert and Lord Berners, with Richard Ingrams playing an organ solo. The service was followed by a buffet reception in the President's Lodge.

His death had been reported prominently on British television and radio news. The obituaries were warm not only on his abilities as a historian but also as a communicator. In the *Financial Times* it was predicted that he would be 'remembered not only as one of the … greatest writers of twentieth-century history but also for his unmatched ability to communicate easily with the public through the press and television'. In similar but more disparaging vein he was appraised in the *Daily Telegraph's* obituary as 'a penetrating scholar and an exhilarating writer; he was also a lifelong radical, an unremitting self-publicist, and something of a hack'. That in the *Times* (written by James Joll, revised by Martin Gilbert) commented, 'He was often accused of being simplistic in his basic assumptions, cavalier in matters of detail, and perverse in interpretation. But his critics rarely denied the range of his erudition, the pungent clarity of his presentation, or the creative possibilities of his more outrageous hypotheses.' In the *Independent* Robert Skidelsky included more of a personal assessment than most others, observing, 'He was a shy man who found personal gestures difficult.' He also noted of his later years that he was small and slightly stooped:

> His most prominent features were hooded eyes, encased in thick-lensed glasses, and a mobile mouth which often assumed a mischievous grin. He always wore a bow-tie. He was the most amiable of companions. He loved jokes and gossip, others' as well as his own. He had a wonderful speaking voice, but did not dominate conversations, often responding to some tendentious remark with a quizzical raising of the eyebrows as if to say, 'Do you really believe that?'

Skidelsky deemed his worse fault to be vanity, adding 'as a historian he sometimes sacrificed truth to showmanship, being a prisoner, as well as a master, of style'.[68]

A few years later, when more of his essays and two good biographies (by Adam Sisman and Kathleen Burk) were published, there were some very critical comments. To the surprise of many of those who had known him, these were often not about the shortcomings of his writings but more about the man himself (his behaviour to his wives, his admiration for Beaverbrook or his excesses in his columns in the popular press) or his failure to denounce the Soviet Union at all times. Indeed, his media performances were very open to criticism. He had some messages – notably the need for continued Anglo–Soviet co-operation at the end of the Second World War, the nuclear peril, beware of Germans, beware of the European Union – but much of the time he was very much a free-wheeling critic, making his mark as a 'great arguer', just as his friend Muggeridge did before his Christian phase. Taylor sought public recognition (in both senses) and his TV and popular-press activities were major means to satiating this craving.

In contrast, his friends and acquaintances knew him as a very kindly and genial man, a fascinating conversationalist who listened as well as spoke and was generally excellent company. For them his strengths greatly overshadowed his faults. Some of his books seemed better targets for critics than the man. Many of his publications were markedly dated by then, yet publishers remained eager repeatedly to reissue *The Course of German History* and *Bismarck* and keep others, such as *The Habsburg Monarchy* and *The Origins of the Second World War*, in print. Many academics continued to find value in *The Struggle for Mastery in Europe* (even if more recent work had much to say on areas that he did not cover) and *English History 1914–1945*, which remains probably the liveliest book of its kind on the period, even if dated in many ways. The general public still enjoyed reading these books, some of the shorter ones, notably *The First World War*, and the best of his essays. A year before the centenary of his birth there were still eight of his books available in British bookshops.[69] Particularly striking was the way that articles and editorials in the quality press still often began with quotations from his work. For many, 'A.J.P. Taylor' remained to history what 'Stirling Moss' was to motor racing, long after their finest hours.

In several major respects his type of history was appearing dated before his death. Diplomatic history was no longer centre stage, as it had been in the inter-war and early Cold War years. Professor Mark Mazower has put this well.

Once upon a time there was a respectable subject called diplomatic history which explained the origins of international crises and world wars. It tortured generations of undergraduates with concepts like the balance of power and the Eastern Question until, despite the best endeavours of brilliant showmen like A.J.P. Taylor, the whole approach was mortally wounded in the 1960s. New historiographical trends questioned the validity of an approach to the world's affairs that assumed all that mattered was what happened in the various embassies and foreign ministries of the Great Powers.[70]

Some of his dominant themes seemed especially, or more, dated. To generations born after the Second World War his 'Teutonophobe' writing reads very oddly. The coming down of the Berlin Wall in 1989 and the collapse of the Soviet Union ended the era of Cold War politics against which he had reacted in much of his writing. While his great fear, the atomic bomb, could still end the world, by the start of the twenty-first century the main danger of its use had changed from superpowers to terrorist organisations. Hence many of the fixed points in his outlook had crumbled by his death or soon afterwards.

The major irony is that the great Radical historian 'emerges very clearly', as Arthur Marwick has put it, 'as, in the non-party sense of course, a Tory historian'. In his rejection or ostensible rejection, of Marxism or other 'profound forces' explanations in favour of interpretations dwelling on the accidental, his approach found favour with many historians of a Conservative hue, as did his irreverent questioning of all received opinions.[71]

In his emphasis on the contingent, on the possibilities in alternative 'discourses', he occasionally appeared almost a proto-postmodernist. Nevertheless, his was an old style of history, and he was often pugnaciously proud of it. For instance, writing to Bob Cole of *English History 1914–1945* (1965), he commented that he agreed with critics who judged it to be 'technically old fashioned, straight political narrative as written fifty years ago with none of the social insights people want today,' and added, 'In method there's not much difference between my books and those, say, of the late Sir John Marriott, though he was a Conservative M.P. and I'm not.'[72]

As a major writer of history that appeals to a wide public, Taylor, among twentieth-century modern historians, ranks with G.M. Trevelyan and above Arthur Bryant. Among major academic historians his standing is less clear some thirty and more years after his last substantial book. Sir Lewis Namier, his mentor, had a bigger impact in his prime specialism, reopening eighteenth-century British history. Eric Hobsbawm and E.P. Thompson have had major and wide impacts, going beyond Europe and the USA to South America and elsewhere. Asa Briggs has been as productive and perhaps even more wide-ranging than Taylor. Of his other contemporaries, E.H. Carr has left a major, if much-contested, legacy in Russian history.

If one considers those coming to the fore after Taylor's departure from Oxford, the list would be large indeed.

Alan Taylor has left no school of Taylorites. He wrote much which has been admired, notably his two Oxford histories, and his flawed study of the origins of the Second World War in Europe reopened the subject and, over forty years later, the debate continues. His habit of mind – insistently questioning and highly irreverent of received opinions – has been influential. Much of his work remains enjoyable to read, from substantial works such as *England 1914–1945* to the better short essays in the many volumes which collect them together. Historians whose writing lasts have had notable flaws as well as great qualities, and Taylor fits this pattern.

Like the great historians of the past his major work was very distinctive, stamped with his own style and personality. Max Beloff, whose attitude towards him mellowed in later years, commented that reading his lesser essays was 'a pleasurable experience, largely because of Taylor's gift for muscular English prose – a far cry from the sociological jargon that entraps so many of his successors'. From the other end of the political spectrum Michael Foot wrote, 'The language is very much part of the man; the staccato style bullies the reader into submission, as if he were perpetually having a pistol stuck in his ribs. And these qualities of simplicity and directness, he [AJPT] implies, are the necessary talents for a historian.' Furthermore, he commented,

> What Macaulay and Carlyle and Taylor all have in common, and the reason why they are great narrative historians, is that they are ready to risk making judgements in every paragraph, almost every sentence. They write with simple, reckless passion, like pamphleteers. It is not an easy style to acquire … Study those Taylor epigrams and paragraphs more carefully, and one can see how elaborate their interlocking architecture may be; how he devised for himself a style which could be turned to every purpose and would never lose its appeal. The reader's attention is never lost for a single second.[73]

From the perspective of the centenary of his birth, it seems highly probable that his very distinctive historical voice will continue to command the attention of large numbers of readers for many more years.

Notes on the Text

Introduction

1   For details of his life there are, as well as Alan Taylor's autobiography, *A Personal History* (London, Hamish Hamilton, 1983), enjoyable and very good biographies by Adam Sisman: *A.J.P. Taylor*, London, Sinclair-Stevenson, 1994, and Kathleen Burk, *Troublemaker: The Life and History of A.J.P. Taylor*, New Haven and London, Yale University Press, 2000. For other accounts of his life see C.J. Wrigley, 'Introduction' to *A.J.P. Taylor: A Complete Bibliography and Guide to His Historical Other Writings*, Brighton, Harvester Press, 1980, *idem*, 'Alan John Percivale Taylor 1906–1990', *Proceedings of the British Academy*, 82 (1993), pp. 493–524, *idem*, 'A.J.P. Taylor: A Nonconforming Radical Historian of Europe', *Contemporary European History*, 3, 1, March 1994, pp. 73–86, Robert Cole, *A.J.P. Taylor: The Traitor within the Gates*, London, Macmillan, 1993, and A.F. Thompson, 'Taylor, Alan John Percivale (1906–1990)', in C.S. Nicholls (ed.), *The Dictionary of National Biography, 1986–1990*, Oxford, Oxford University Press, 1996, pp. 445–46.

2   K.O. Morgan, *Callaghan: A Life*, Oxford, Oxford University Press, 1997, p. 108. E.P. Thompson came second in the *Times*' poll. B.D. Palmer, *E.P. Thompson: Objections and Oppositions*, London, Verso, 1994, p. 132.

3   D.C. Watt, 'Some Aspects of A.J.P. Taylor's Work as Diplomatic Historian', *Journal of Modern History*, 49, 1 (March 1977), pp. 19–33.

4   Avner Offer's comments to CJW, 5 April 1997. *Huddersfield Daily Examiner*, 7 July 1970, p. 6. David Cannadine ended his review of Adam Sisman's biography with a paragraph in AJPT's style; reprinted in D. Cannadine, *History In Our Time*, New Haven and London, Yale University Press, 1998, pp. 279–87.

5   On 'Northernness' see the essays by Stuart Rawnsley and others in N. Kirk (ed.), *Northern Identities: Historical Interpretations of 'The North' and 'Northernness'*, Aldershot, Ashgate, 2000.

Chapter 1

1   In his lecture 'The Year 1906', given on 25 November 1981 to mark the Historical Association's seventy-fifth anniversary and published in D. Read (ed.), *Edwardian England*, London, Croom Helm, 1982, pp. 1–13.

2   *A Personal History*, pp. 2–5. James Taylor had entered the trade at a very good time. The volume of exported cotton pieces rose markedly. Giving the volume of exports of cotton pieces in 1869 an index number of 100, the level had risen to 119 in 1871, 126 in 1874, 178 in 1890 (when Percy joined his father) and 182 in 1898 (when Percy became in effect senior partner). Calculated from textile statistics in B.R. Mitchell, *British Historical Statistics*, Cambridge, Cambridge University Press, 1988, p. 356. I am also very grateful to Professor Douglas Farnie for providing me with details of the firm. D.A. Farnie to CJW, 25 June 1998, 23 February and 24 November 1999.

3   Muriel Povey, his niece. Transcript of a Thompson/Taylor dinner party, November 1973 (hereafter cited as Thompson transcript, 1973), p.26.

4   Thompson dinner party transcript, 1973, p.19. For Birkdale and Southport when the Taylors moved there, see *Southport: A Handbook of the Town and Surrounding District Prepared for the Meeting of the British Association at Southport, 1903*, Southport, Fortune and Chant, 1903, especially J.J. Weaver and A.V. Sheeler, 'Southport as a Health Resort', pp.26–34.

5   According to Alan Taylor (and Harry Thompson), John Thompson's radical pamphlets were answered by a local vicar named Pritt, the grandfather of the ultra-Left Labour MP D.N. Pritt. Thompson transcript, 1973, pp.23–24. See also H.W. Clemesha, *A History of Preston in Amounderness*, Manchester, Manchester University Press, 1912, p.252.

6   'Thompson family: A note by Bridget Thompson', October 1985 (an addendum to the transcript), p.137.

7   Thompson transcript, 1973, pp.24–25.

8   'Thompson family: A note by Bridget Thompson', October 1985, p.138.

9   *A Personal History*, pp.2–3.

10   AJPT to Brian Thompson, 16 April 1986.

11   Thompson transcript, 1973, pp.24, 26 and 44–45.

12   This was the case with some passages which were cut out of the published version of *A Personal History*.

13   Thompson transcript, 1973, pp.14–16 and 87–88.

14   Interview with Mrs Eunice Holiday (1899–1993) in Kettering, 12 June 1991. The other quotations attributed to Mrs Holliday come from the same interview unless otherwise stated.

15   *A Personal History*, p.6.

16   *A Personal History*, p.7.

17   J. Lowerson, *Sport and the English Middle Classes 1870–1914*, Manchester, Manchester University Press, 1993, chapters 5 and 7. He gives a contemporary estimate of 40,000 female golfers in 1912. On Lancashire, see Rev. E.E. Dorling, 'Golf', in 'Sports, Ancient and Modern', in W. Farrer and J. Brownbill (eds.), *The Victoria History of the County of Lancaster*, London, Constable, 1908, pp.495–99.

18   Interview with Mrs Eunice Holliday, 12 June 1991.

19   In the first lecture in a Granada Television series, 'Edge of Britain: A Lancashire Journey', which was entitled 'A Southport Childhood', broadcast on 18 September 1980. Printed in the *Spectator*, 20 September 1980, it was reprinted in A.J.P. Taylor, *From Napoleon to the Second International*, London, Hamish Hamilton, 1993, pp.402–7.

20   *A Personal History*, p.7.

21   'A Southport Childhood', p.407.

22   AJPT to Eunice Holliday, 23 February 1983.

23   Notes made by Mrs Eunice Holliday in early 1991.

24   Notes made by Eunice Holliday, early 1991, and interview with her, 12 June 1991.

25   *A Personal History*, p.16, and 'A Southport Childhood', p.405.

26   Interview, 'Atticus' column, *Sunday Times*, 14 November 1976, p.32, and *A Personal History*, p.10.

27   Thompson transcript, 1973, p.39.

28   'The Road to Great Turnstile', *New Statesman*, 71, 1818, 14 January 1966, p.54. Kingsley Martin (1897–1969), *Father Figures*, London, Hutchinson, 1966.

29   *A Personal History*, p.9. Interview with Mrs Eunice Holliday, 12 June 1991.
30   *A Personal History*, p.8.
31   Éva Haraszti-Taylor, *A Life with Alan: The Diary of A.J.P. Taylor's Wife, Éva, from 1978 to 1985*, London, Hamish Hamilton, 1987, p.217 (entry for 23 March 1985).
32   *A Personal History*, pp.11–12.
33   Alan Taylor deemed the Thompsons to be 'a cultivated lot'. There is a possibly apocryphal family story of Connie's brother John coming home late from work and, on being told the family had just finished Beethoven's Fifth Symphony, saying: 'Thank God I've missed the other four.' Thompson transcript, 1973, p.30.
34   *A Personal History*, p.17.

Chapter 2

1   *A Personal History*, p.21.
2   *A Personal History*, p.27. J. Scott Duckers, *Handed Over*, London, Daniel, 1916.
3   *A Personal History*, pp.27–30.
4   Michael Holroyd, *Bernard Shaw*, Vol. 2, *1898–1918*, London, Chatto & Windus, 1989, pp.349–53. *A Personal History*, p.27.
5   A.J.P. Taylor, *The Trouble Makers*, London, Hamish Hamilton, 1957, pp.137–38. Holroyd, *Shaw*, p.352. In a review of John Strachey, *A Faith to Fight for*, *Manchester Guardian*, 7 March 1941.
6   A.J.P.T. to Robert Cole, 2 July 1973.
7   Bernard Shaw to the *Daily Citizen*, published 26 November 1914; reprinted in D.H. Laurence and J. Rambeau, *Bernard Shaw: Agitations, Letters to the Press 1875–1950*, New York, Frederick Ungar, 1985, pp.160–63.
8   Margaret Cole, *Growing up into Revolution* (London, Longmans, 1949), p.67. Alan Taylor observed of his uncle Harry (1886–1947) that he was 'one of the most attractive men who ever lived'. Thompson transcripts, 1973, pp.27 and 41.
9   *A Personal History*, pp.28–29. Mary Agnes Hamilton, *Remembering My Good Friends*, London, Johnathan Cape, 1944, p.71.
10   Thompson transcript, 1973, p.51. J.W. Graham, *Conscription and Conscience*, London, Allen & Unwin, 1922, pp.300–7. John Saville and Bob Whitfield, 'Ayles, Walter Henry (1879–1953)', in Joyce Bellamy and John Saville (eds.), *Dictionary of Labour Biography*, Vol. 5, London, Macmillan, 1979, pp.10–13. John Saville, 'Thompson, William Henry (1885–1947)', in Joyce Bellamy and John Saville (eds.), *Dictionary of Labour Biography*, Vol. 10, London, Macmillan, 2000, pp.206–8. Henry William Thomas Sara (1886–1953) was a major figure in Taylor's life.
11   John Taylor Caldwell, *Come Dungeons Dark*, Barr, Luath Press, 1988, pp.109–93. Guy Aldred, *Letters to the Editor*, Glasgow, Strickland Press, 1940, pp.15–18 (including letters on Sara's arrest, 1916). Guy Aldred (1886–1963) was an anarcho-communist activist. Royden Harrison, Gillian Woolven and Robert Duncan, *The Warwick Guide to British Labour Periodicals 1790–1970*, Hassocks, Harvester Press, 1977, pp.207 and 523. John Quail, *The Slow Burning Fuse*, London, Paladin, 1978, pp.83 and 291–92. *The Tribunal*, 6, 20 April 1916, pp.2 and 17, 13 July 1916, p.3. Henry Pelling, *America and the British Left*, London, A. & C. Black, 1956, pp.92–105. Sam Bornsein and Al Richardson, *Against the Stream*, London, Socialist Platform, 1986, pp.64–66. Mark Shipway, *Anti-Parliamentary Communism* (1988), on Aldred, the *Spur* and Sylvia Pankhurst.

The best account now of Sara is John McIlroy, 'Sara, Henry Thomas William (1886–1953)', in K. Gildart, D. Howell and N. Kirk (eds.), *Dictionary of Labour Biography*, Vol. 11, London, Macmillan, 2003, pp. 238–50. I am grateful to Professor McIlroy for letting me read it before it was published. On the 'Wakefield experiment', see Walter H. Ayles, 'The Absolutists', in Central Board for Conscientious Objectors, *Troublesome People* (1919), pp. 41–43.

12   Reg Groves, *The Balham Group*, London, Pluto Press, 1974, pp. 19–20.

13   *A Personal History*, p. 55. Thompson transcript, pp. 31–32. See also Stuart MacIntyre, *A Proletarian Science: Marxism in Britain 1917–1933*, Cambridge, Cambridge University Press, 1980, pp. 78–81; J.P.M. Millar, *The Labour College Movement*, London, National Council of Labour Colleges, 1979, p. 181; and W.W. Craik, *Central Labour College 1909–29*, London, Lawrence & Wishart, 1964, p. 184.

14   *A Personal History*, pp. 28 and 35. Thompson transcript, 1973, p. 52. I am grateful to Adam Sisman for pointing out to me the relevant lines in Wordsworth's poetry; Adam Sisman to CJW, 18 December 2003. Alan Taylor may also have known 'Stuart Wood' (pseudonym), *Shades of the Prison House: A Personal Memoir*, London, Williams and Norgate, 1932, in which the author recalled his numerous spells in prison, 1901–26. C.J. Wrigley, 'A.J.P. Taylor: Five Faces and the Man', in Attila Pók (ed.), *The Fabric of Modern Europe: Essays in Honour of Éva Haraszti Taylor*, Nottingham, Astra Press, 1999, pp. 225–38 (at p. 234).

15   AJPT to Robert Cole, 29 January 1973.

16   A.J.P. Taylor, 'Myself and the Natural History Society', in *150 Years of Natural History*, Bootham School, York, 1983, p. 93.

17   *A Personal History*, pp. 40, 48 and 62. His height and weight are recorded in his 1923 diary. A.J.P. Taylor Papers, Harry Ransom Humanities Research Center (HRRC), University of Texas, Austin, Texas.

18   AJPT to Clifford J. Smith, Keeper of Bootham School archives, 7 August 1982; Bootham School archive.

19   Winston S. Churchill, *My Early Life*, London, Thornton Butterworth, 1930 (Fontana paperback edition, 1959), pp. 24–25. *A Personal History*, p. 45.

20   Clifford Smith to AJPT, 22 July 1982, concerning the ten volumes of the 'Chronicle of Bedroom 24', covering 1921–39, found hidden under a floorboard in 1972. Sisman, *A.J.P. Taylor*, pp. 36–47.

21   From the first of the ten exercise books of the 'Chronicle of Bedroom 24', Penn House. I doubt if Alan Taylor alone wrote all the entries. At the end of the spring term 1921 he was listed: 'Nicknames baby, AJPT, description petite and tres gros [sic].'

22   *A Personal History*, p. 46.

23   *A Personal History*, p. 36.

24   Interview with Kathleen Tillotson, Gower Street, London, 6 September 1991. She was recalling summer 1924.

25   'Communism'; Bootham School archives.

26   *Communist*, 27 May and 3 June 1922. C. Wrigley, 'Alan John Percivale Taylor', p. 497. James Klugmann, *History of the Communist Party of Great Britain*, Vol. 1, *Formation and Early Years 1919–1924*, London, Lawrence & Wishart, 1968, pp. 213–16. Raymond William Postgate (1896–1971) was a journalist, social historian and founder of the *Good Food Guide*. John and Mary Postgate, *A Stomach For Dissent: The Life of Raymond Postgate*, Keele, Keele University Press, 1994, pp. 114 and 120. John Callaghan, *Rajani Palme Dutt: A Study in Stalinism*, London, Lawrence & Wishart, 1993, p. 52.

27   AJPT to Robert Cole, 11 May 1973.

28 P. Barrett, *Directory of Preston 1889*, Preston, Barrett, 1889. (Also later Preston directories.) Beech Grove, Rose Terrace and Victoria Parade are three parallel streets.

29 *A Personal History*, p. 54. He probably gained his anti-parliamentary views from Eden and Cedar Paul, or, possibly, Henry Sara.

30 AJPT in conversation with CJW, 30 July 1984.

31 *A Personal History*, p. 56.

32 I am grateful to Professor Sam Davies for details of Preston municipal main elections and to Jeff Staniforth for the by-elections. Davies to CJW, 14 September 1999. J. Staniforth to CJW, 3 January 2005. *Preston Herald*, September–November 1926.

33 *A Personal History*, pp. 55–57. McIlroy, 'Sara', p. 243. I am grateful to Professor Douglas Farnie for sending me information on Percy Taylor in the cotton industry. D.A. Farnie to CJW, 1 April 1997.

34 Doris Fell to CJW, 17 December 1990 and 3 December 1991.

35 Interview with Doris Fell (by telephone), 6 December 1991. After her marriage, she lived on the outskirts of Sheffield, later moving to Gravesend, and then Whitstable, Kent (where, as a widow, she married her second husband).

36 Alan Taylor kept in contact with Sydney Sharples (1900–68) until the latter's death, with Sydney sometimes staying with the Taylors. Interview with Doris Fell (by telephone), 22 November 1991.

37 Thompson transcript, 1973, pp. 33–36 and 50.

38 *A Personal History*, pp. 24 and 46.

39 A.J.P. Taylor, *Letters to Éva, 1969–1983* (ed. Éva Haraszti-Taylor), London, Century, 1991, pp. 57, 75, 121 and 154. Letters of 10 January and 15 May 1972, 16 March and 19 November 1973. Kathleen Tillotson (née Constable) told the present author in September 1991 that Alan Taylor had attributed to her his own sentiments, and even imaginings, of their past friendship. Kathleen Mary Tillotson (1906–2002) was Professor of English, Bedford College, London University, 1958–71, and general editor of the *Letters of Charles Dickens*, 1978–95.

40 Interview with Kathleen Tillotson, Gower Street, London, 6 September 1991. See also Sisman, *A.J.P. Taylor*, pp. 46–50.

41 *A Personal History*, pp. 60–61.

42 Maxine Berg, *A Woman in History: Eileen Power, 1889–1940*, Cambridge, Cambridge University Press, 1996, pp. 38–39.

43 *A Personal History*, pp. 61, 76, 82, 89 and 93.

44 *A Personal History*, p. 64.

45 Tillotson interview, 6 September 1991.

46 Tillotson interview, 6 September 1991.

47 Bootham school magazine, 1924, p. 67.

48 *A Personal History*, p. 62. Sisman, *A.J.P. Taylor*, p. 48 and his chapter 4 heading.

49 Henry Salt, *Seventy Years among Savages*, London, Allen & Unwin, 1921; quoted in Fiona MacCarthy, *William Morris*, London, Faber & Faber, 1994, p. 473.

50 *A Personal History*, pp. 16 and 58.

51 Taylor, *Letters to Éva*, p. 88. Letter of 7 August 1972.

52 'I Remember, I Remember', *Times Literary Supplement*, 3796, 6 December 1974, p. 1370.

53 Roy Avery in discussion with CJW, Bristol, 11 March 2000.

54 *A Personal History*, p. 60

55 Wrigley, 'Five Faces and the Man', pp. 225–38 (at p. 233–34). James Boswell, *Life of Johnson* (1791), Oxford, Oxford University Press, 1980 (ed. R.W. Chapman, introduction Pat Rogers), pp. v, 903 and 1073.

56   'Snakes in Iceland', review of books by René Albercht-Carrié and John Lukacs,
        New York Review of Books, 4, 4 March 1965, pp. 8 and 10. Boswell, *Life*, p. 938.
57   Boswell, *Life*, pp. 607, 1150 and 1234.
58   Ibid., p. 628.
59   'Parkinson', 22.50–23.50 hours, 25 February 1981.
60   Frank Thistlethwaite in conversation with CJW, 9 July 1998. Frank
        Thistlethwaite (1915–2002) was a Fellow of St John's College, Cambridge,
        1945–61, and Vice-Chancellor of the University of East Anglia, 1961–80.
        Gilbert graduated with First Class Honours in 1913, when Ellen Wilkinson
        also graduated (with a 2i).
61   *A Personal History*, p. 59.
62   His lists of his reading for 1921–27 are in his papers at the HRRC, University
        of Texas, Austin, Texas.
63   To the author (CJW) in 1976 when the author was preparing *A.J.P. Taylor: A
        Complete Bibliography*, 1980.
64   *The Labour Who's Who 1927* (London, Labour Publishing, 1927), p. 165.
        MacIntyre, *A Proletarian Science*, pp. 99–100.
65   Eden and Cedar Paul, *Creative Revolution: A Study of Communist Ergatocracy*,
        London, Allen & Unwin, 1920, pp. 12, 42 and 217. The book, which was
        dedicated to Lenin, was reissued in a Plebs edition in March 1921, with an
        enthusiastic Foreword stating that it was 'a book for revolutionists', setting out
        'the new psychology' and 'its application to the tactics of the class struggle'. He
        also read in 1922 N. Bukharin and E. Preobrazhensky, *The ABC of Communism*,
        translated by Eden and Cedar Paul (London, Communist Party of Great
        Britain, 1922).
66   At least, his recollection of a failed interview for a Fellowship at Corpus Christi
        College, Oxford. *A Personal History*, p. 132.
67   A.J.P. Taylor, *English History 1914–1945*, Oxford, Clarendon Press, 1965, p. 260.
68   Interview with Kathleen Tillotson, London, 6 September 1991.
69   *A Personal History*, p. 83. Brian Harrison interview with AJPT, 24 July 1985.
70   J.I.M. Stewart, *Mungo's Dream*, London, Gollancz, 1973, p. 128.
71   Norman Cameron (1905–53) became a highly respected poet. He worked in
        advertising for J. Walter Thompson, where his successes included the notion of
        'night starvation' for Horlicks advertisements. Warren Hope, *Norman Cameron:
        His Life, Work and Letters*, London, Greenwich Exchange, 2000, pp. 17, 27–40
        and 80. Gott became a gentleman former in Devon. He died not long after
        Alan Taylor. *A Personal History*, p. 74, J.I.M. Stewart, *Myself and Michael Innes*,
        London, Gollancz, 1987, pp. 59–60.
72   David Cuppleditch to CJW, 25 September 2002. Yates was born 21 April 1905,
        died in 1971.
73   Hope, *Norman Cameron*, p. 28.
74   *A Personal History*, pp. 74–75. Harrison interview, 24 July 1985. Edward
        Whitley, 'Sir Harold Acton', in *The Graduates*, London, Hamish Hamilton,
        1986, pp. 3–4.
75   Whitley, 'The Marquess of Bath', in *The Graduates*, p. 13. *A Personal History*,
        p. 78. J.I.M. Stewart in A. Thwaite (ed.), *My Oxford*, London, Robson, 1977,
        pp. 75–88.
76   *A Personal History*, p. 82. If his memory was correct, it was presumably July
        1926, before the Shaws went for a lengthy stay in Italy. Stewart, *Myself and
        Michael Innes*, pp. 28–36.
77   *A Personal History*, pp. 78–79. Stewart, *Myself and Michael Innes*, pp. 66–67. As
        for Stewart's novels, the character of Mungo in *Mungo's Dream* (1973), for

instance, draws on Alan Taylor and, no doubt, others. Mungo is a first-generation Oxford student, who gets there by a clever essay, was not stretched at school so became a rebel, at Oxford is a reading man but delights in driving too fast, loses his accent, is awkward with women of his age, in his writing is prone to show off and is teased 'Scribble, scribble, scribble' (pp. 2, 15, 23, 70, 89, 122–23, 147, 152–55, 166 and 209).

78   *A Personal History*, pp. 69, 79 and 82. Adam Sisman points out that the Oriel Boat Club records show no sign of him being in the first eight; *A.J.P. Taylor*, p. 59.

79   Thomas Edward Neil Driberg (1905–76) was a journalist and an independent MP (1942–44) and Labour MP (1945–55 and 1959–70). He wrote that his main task for the CPGB was 'to liaise between the city party and the few members in the university'. Tom Driberg, *Ruling Passions*, London, Cape, 1977, pp. 57 and 75. Francis Wheen, *Tom Driberg: His Life and Indiscretions*, London, Chatto & Windus, 1990, pp. 36–57. Cole, *Growing Up*, p. 124. *A Personal History*, p. 73. N.J. West, *The Quest for Graham Greene*, London, Weidenfeld & Nicolson, 1997, pp. 32–35. On Stephenson, see A.J.P. Taylor to John Parker, 28 February 1973; quoted in Robert S. Sephton, *Oxford and the General Strike*, Oxford, Sephton, 1993, p. 31. Percy Reginald Stephenson (1901–65) was an Australian communist and Rhodes scholar at Queen's College from 1924. Lord Birkenhead, Secretary of State for India, tried to have him expelled from Oxford for distributing anti-imperialist leaflets to Indian students.

80   *Plebs*, March 1925, p. 124; quoted in Sisman, *A.J.P. Taylor*, p. 60. Millar, *Labour College Movement*, pp. 8, 86–88 and 90.

81   *A Personal History*, pp. 76–78.

82   Cole, *Growing Up*, pp. 113–14. Margaret Cole, *The Life of G.D.H. Cole*, London, Macmillan, 1971, pp. 138–46. Hugh Gaitskell, 'At Oxford in the Twenties', in A. Briggs and J. Saville (eds.), *Essays in Labour History*, London, Macmillan, 1960, pp. 6–19. Maurice Bowra, 'Oxford in the 1920s', in W.T. Rodgers (ed.), *Hugh Gaitskell*, London, Thames & Hudson, pp. 19–30.

83   A.J.P. Taylor, 'A Bolshevik Soul in a Fabian Muzzle', a review of Margaret Cole's biography (see previous note), in *New Statesman*, 82, 1 October 1971, pp. 441–42; reprinted in his *Politicians, Socialism and Historians*, London, Hamish Hamilton, 1980, pp. 167–71.

84   Cole, *Growing Up*, pp. 122–25. Cole, *G.D.H. Cole*, pp. 154–56. Sephton, *Oxford and the General Strike*, pp. 1–61.

85   *A Personal History*, p. 80. A.J.P. Taylor, 'Class War: 1926', *New Statesman*, 91, 30 April 1976, pp. 572–3; reprinted in his *Politicians, Socialism*, pp. 193–97. Kathy Burk managed to track down some of Jack Yates' recollections; quoted in Burk, *Troublemaker*, p. 54.

86   Driberg, *Ruling Passions*, pp. 71–72. Bob Stewart, *Breaking the Fetters*, London, Lawrence & Wishart, 1967, pp. 165–71.

87   Hope, *Norman Cameron*, p. 32.

88   *A Personal History*, pp. 80–81.

89   *Plebs: The Organ of the Labour Colleges*, December 1927.

90   Taylor, 'Class War', p. 573. On Gaitskell, A.J.P. Taylor, 'His Life was Shaped the Day he Walked down Cowley Road', *Sunday Express*, 25 September 1960, p. 8.

91   Groves, *Balham Group*, pp. 10, 49, 52, 57 and 67–69. McIlroy, 'Sara', p. 244.

92   Driberg, *Ruling Passions*, p. 74. James Klugmann, *History of the Communist Party of Great Britain*, Vol. 2, *The General Strike 1925–1926*, London, Lawrence & Wishart, 1969, pp. 257–62 and 349–50. L.J. Macfarlane, *The British Communist Party*, London, MacGibbon & Kee, 1966, pp. 143–49, 189–92 and 227–29.

AJPT in conversation with CJW in 1976, regarding his early publications. *A Personal History*, pp. 82–83.

93 Brian Harrison interview, 24 July 1985. Lancelot Ridley Phelps (1853–1936) was Provost of Oriel College, 1914–29. He was an Oxford City councillor and alderman and was chairman of the Oxford Board of Guardians and later the Oxford Public Assistance Committee. William David Ross (1877–1971) was a Fellow and Tutor of Oriel College, 1902–29, Deputy White's Professor of Moral Philosophy 1923–28, Provost of Oriel College, 1929–47 and Vice-Chancellor, 1941–44. He received a knighthood in 1938.

94 *A Personal History*, p. 70. Brian Harrison interview, 24 July 1985.

95 *A Personal History*, p. 84. Stewart, *Myself and Michael Innes*, p. 67.

96 *A Personal History*, pp. 70–71 and 132. Stewart, *Myself and Michael Innes*, p. 36–39.

97 Brian Harrison interview, 24 July 1985.

98 Sephton, *Oxford in the General Strike*, pp. 54 and 66. Ayerest to his mother, 24 October 1926; quoted in Sisman, *A.J.P. Taylor*, p. 66. David Ayerest (1904–1992) left Oxford to work on the *Manchester Guardian*. He taught in schools, became a headmaster, was a member of H.M. Inspectorate of Schools, then wrote books about the *Guardian* and *Observer*.

99 Lord Boothby in A. Thwaite (ed.), *My Oxford*, pp. 19–34 (at p. 28). Robert Boothby, *I Fight to Live*, London, Gollancz, 1947, p. 22. C.M. Bowra, *Memories 1898–1939*, London, Weidenfeld & Nicolson, 1966, pp. 119–20. Francis Fortescue Urquart (1868–1934) was the first Roman Catholic academic at Oxford since the Reformation.

100 AJPT to Robert Cole, 28 February 1969. Brian Harrison interview, 24 July 1985.

101 James Matthew Thompson (1878–1954) was a Fellow of Magdalen College, 1904–38, being succeeded by Alan Taylor. His winter term lectures, given 1921–24, were published as *Lectures on Foreign History 1491–1789*, Oxford, Blackwell, 1925 (quotation from p. 171).

102 *A Personal History*, p. 70.

Chapter 3

1 *A Personal History*, p. 85. *Labour Who's Who 1927*, p. 191.

2 Thompson transcript, 1973, pp. 54–55. Chris Cook, 'By-elections of the First Labour Government', in Chris Cook and John Ramsden (eds.), *By-Elections in British Politics*, London, Macmillan, 1973, pp. 56–58 and 61–62.

3 Cole, *Growing Up*, p. 67. Lydia Smith and Joan Beauchamp, 'Ave Atque Vale', *The Tribunal*, 153, 10 April 1919, p. 2. 'Rex v. Beauchamp', *The Tribunal*, 182, 8 January 1920, p. 12. See also D. Boulton, *Objection Overruled*, London, McGibbon & Kee, 1967, pp. 267–73 and 291; Jo Vellacott, *Bertrand Russell and the Pacifists in the First World War*, Brighton, Harvester, 1980, pp. 225–26 and 235–36; T.C. Kennedy, *The Hound of Conscience*, Fayetteville, University of Arkansas Press, 1981, pp. 243–51; *Labour's Who's Who 1927*, p. 217; and John Saville, 'Beauchamp, Joan (1890–1964)' in Bellamy and Saville (eds.), *Dictionary of Labour Biography*, Vol. 10, pp. 19–22.

4 Noreen Branson, *Popularism 1919–1925*, London, Lawrence & Wishart, 1979, pp. 37–38, 49, 68, 90, 93–94, 97–98, 100 and 179. W.H. Thompson, 'Poplar and the Auditor', Labour Research Department, *Monthly Circular*, May 1925. Klugmann, *Communist Party of Great Britain*, Vol. 2, pp. 67–69.

5   Thompson transcript, 1973, pp.57–59. *A Personal History*, p.86. Robin
        Thompson to CJW, 21 February 1999.
6   Margaret Cole, *Growing Up*, p.67. Robin Thompson to CJW, 21 February 1999.
7   *A Personal History*, p.86. John Saville, 'The 1917 Club', in Bellamy and Saville
        (eds.), *Dictionary of Labour Biography*, Vol. 5, pp.100–2. Stewart, *Myself and
        Michael Innes*, p.71. Douglas Goldring, 'The 1917 Club', in *Odd Man Out*,
        London, Chapman & Hall, 1935, pp.267–75. Francis Meynell, *My Lives*,
        London, Bodley Head, 1971, p.236. Sir Francis Meynell (1891–1975) was a
        publisher, book designer and poet.
8   Donald Renton's recollections in Ian MacDougall (ed.), *Voices from the Spanish
        Civil War*, Edinburgh, Polygon, 1986, pp.21–30 (at p.22). *A Personal History*,
        p.86. Thomas Henry Wintringham (1898–1949) was a Marxist, political
        activist and author.
9   AJPT to Charles Gott, 9 July 1929.
10   *A Personal History*, pp.86–87. A.J.P. Taylor, *An Old Man's Diary*, London,
        Hamish Hamilton, 1984, pp.114–15. Sisman, *A.J.P. Taylor*, p.71. Stewart,
        Myself and Michael Innes, pp.48–49.
11   On Barry (1898–1968) see Sir William Haley, 'Sir Gerald Reid Barry', in E.T.
        Williams and C.S. Nicholls (eds.), *The Dictionary of National Biography,
        1961–1970*, Oxford, Oxford University Press, 1981, pp.75–76. *Saturday
        Review*, 145, 16 June 1928, p.774; Wrigley, *Taylor Bibliography*, p.249. Taylor
        almost certainly wrote the review when back at Oxford.
12   *A Personal History*, p.88.
13   *A Personal History*, pp.72 and 88. Stewart, *Myself and Michael Innes*, p.42. J.R.H.
        Weaver, 'Henry William Carless Davis', in J.R.H. Weaver (ed.), *Dictionary of
        National Biography 1922–30*, Oxford, Oxford University Press, 1933. F.M.
        Powicke, 'H.W.C. Davis', in his *Modern Historians and the Study of History*,
        London, Odhams, 1955, pp.118–26, reprinted from the *English Historical
        Review*, 63 (1928). Davis (1874–1928) died on 28 June. Sir Charles Firth
        (1857–1936) was Regius Professor, 1904–25. Alfred Pribram (1859–1941).
14   *A Personal History*, pp.88–89.
15   AJPT to Charles Gott, 9 July 1929.
16   Stewart, *Myself and Michael Innes*, p.67. *A Personal History*, p.89. Thompson
        family transcript 1973, pp.89–92. Apparently, Charlotte Brun was sacked by
        Sarah Thompson and stayed for a while with Sarah's sister Kate. Two of Sarah's
        daughters later visited Charlotte in Dresden.
17   *A Personal History*, pp.90–92. Geoffrey Rowntree (of the cocoa family) went on
        to become a schoolmaster. Another friend, Peter Mann, an artist, may later
        have worked in the City of London. Stewart, *Myself and Michael Innes*, p.67.
18   AJPT to Éva Haraszti, 6 November 1970 and 5 May 1969, printed in Taylor,
        Letters to Éva, pp.21 and 1.
19   For much of the details of his time in Vienna one is dependent on *A Personal
        History*, pp.90–99. The wooden mushroom anecdote is in Thompson transcript
        1973, pp.90–91, and *A Personal History*, p.89.
20   *A Personal History*, pp.96–97.
21   Ibid., p.91.
22   Ibid., pp.90 and 99.
23   Keith Kyle, 'Letters to the Editor', *Times Literary Supplement*, 19 October
        2000, p.17.
24   Keith Kyle to CJW, 10 October 2003.
25   *American Historical Review*, 52, 4, July 1947, pp.730–33. Wrigley, *Taylor
        Bibliography*, p.75.

26   The review is undated and its publication place unidentified, but it was stuck in a scrapbook by Margaret Taylor. The scrapbook is now in the A.J.P. Taylor Papers, HRRC, University of Texas, Austin, Texas. I read its contents in Alan Taylor's home in 1977. Wrigley, *Taylor Bibliography*, p. 69.

27   A.J.P. Taylor, 'Preface', *The Habsburg Monarchy 1809–1918*, London, Hamish Hamilton, 1948, p. 9.

28   *Manchester Guardian*, 25 September 1951, p. 4.

29   The son of a Master of Trinity College, Cambridge, James Ramsay Montagu Butler (1889–1975) was Regius Professor of Modern History, University of Cambridge, 1947–54. *A Personal History*, p. 91.

30   By his second year in Vienna it was less Oxford in exile; there were not so many of his former fellow undergraduates with him. Also, he claims that his first book's research was carried out in 1929–30 in the Preface (though this was wise to show fruits for the Rockefeller money). A.J.P. Taylor, *The Italian Problem in European Diplomacy 1847–1849*, Manchester, Manchester University Press, 1934, p. vii.

31   Ernest Fraser Jacob (1894–1971) was Professor of Medieval History, University of Manchester, 1929–44, and Chichele Professor of Medieval History, Oxford, 1950–61.

32   Sir John Ernest Neale (1890–1975) was Professor of Modern History at Manchester University, 1925–27, then Astor Professor of English History at University College, London, 1927–56.

33   *A Personal History*, pp. 97–98.

34   Taylor, *Italian Problem*, p. vii.

35   'Noel Buxton and A.J.P. Taylor's *The Trouble Makers*', in Martin Gilbert (ed.), *A Century of Conflict 1850–1950: Essays for A.J.P. Taylor*, London, Hamish Hamilton, 1966, pp. 173–212.

36   *A Personal History*, p. 92. Otto Bauer (1881–1938).

37   Ibid, p. 94. Ian Fitzherbert Despard Morrow (born 1896) also wrote *Bismarck* (1943).

38   Ibid., p. 92.

39   'Report from Branches', *Twenty-Fifth Annual Report of the Historical Association, July 1, 1930 to June 30, 1931* (1931), p. 39.

40   'Letters', *Guardian*, 18 October 2003, p. 25.

41   F.M. Powicke, 'University of Manchester, 1851–1951', in *History Today*, 1, 5, May 1951, pp. 48–55, and 'The Manchester History School', in his *Modern Historians and the Study of History*, London, Odhams, 1955, pp. 19–95. John Kenyon, *The History Men*, London, Weidenfeld & Nicolson, 1983, pp. 182–83. Burk, *Troublemaker*, p. 430. Sir Frederick Maurice Powicke (1879–1963). Thomas Frederick Tout (1855–1929).

42   *A Personal History*, pp. 102–3.

43   In a letter to Bruce McFarlane, 8 May 1938; quoted in Burk, *Troublemaker*, p. 115.

44   'Reports from Branches', *Twenty-Fifth Annual Report of the Historical Association*, p. 43. William Abel Pantin (1902–73) published documents relating to the English black monks, 1215–1540, during the early 1930s.

45   'Report from Branches', *Twenty-Sixth Annual Report of the Historical Association, July 1, 1931 to June 30*, 1932 (1932), p. 43. Ibid., *Twenty-Seventh Annual Report…* (1933), p. 40. Ibid., *Twenty-Ninth Annual Report…* (1935), p. 39. Ibid., *Thirty-Second Annual Report…* (1938), p. 40.

46   The son of Edward Hughes (1899–1965) was MEP for Durham 1984–99 and for North-East region since then. Another of the former pupils of George Unwin (1870–1925), Conrad Gill (1883–1968), the author of *The Rise of the*

Irish Linen Industry, 1925, had briefly taught at Manchester and had become Professor of History at Hull in 1928. Redford (1896–1961) was Professor of Economic History, 1945–61. W.H. Chaloner, 'Memoir of Arthur Redford' in Arthur Redford, *Labour Migration in England, 1800–1850*, 2nd edition (ed. and revised by W.H. Chaloner), Manchester, Manchester University Press, 1964, pp. xv-xvii.

47 For the Tout comment see 'London diary', *New Statesman*, 92, 2386, 10 December 1976, p. 836. Burk, *Troublemaker*, p. 113. Powicke, 'Manchester University', p. 55. Anthony Burgess, *Little Wilson and Big God*, London, Heinemann, 1987, p. 171. Roger Lewis, *Anthony Burgess*, London, Faber & Faber, 2002, p. 96. John Burgess Wilson (1917–93) wrote under the name Anthony Burgess.

48 Goldring, *Odd Man Out*, p. 275. *A Personal History*, p. 106. John Saville, 'The 1917 Club', pp. 100–2.

49 *A Personal History*, pp. 106–7.

50 *A Personal History*, pp. 65, 94 and 53.

51 Sir Lewis Bernstein Namier (1888–1960). G.S. Rousseau, 'Namier on Namier' (review essay), *Studies in Burke and His Time*, 13, 1, Fall 1971, pp. 2016–41 (at p. 2019).

52 A point well made by Linda Colley in her excellent *Namier* (London, Weidenfeld & Nicolson, 1989), pp. 99–100.

53 'Sir Lewis Namier', in Arnold J. Toynbee, *Acquaintances* (Oxford, Oxford University Press, 1967), pp. 62–85 (at p. 62).

54 In a letter to Kingsley Martin. Norman Rose, *Lewis Namier and Zionism*, Oxford, Oxford University Press, 1980, p. 137. For similar sentiments in September 1914, see ibid., p. 12.

55 Julia Namier, *Lewis Namier: A Biography* (Oxford, Oxford University Press, 1971), pp. 167–75. Some of Namier's newspaper essays of the early 1920s were reprinted in his *Skyscrapers and Other Essays* (London, Macmillan, 1931).

56 Ibid., p. 223.

57 At least, so he was in the oral tradition aired to me by older members of the department when I first went there as an external examiner in 1989. I was also shown his former office. It is highly probable that it was next to Namier's, with an interconnecting door between them.

58 *A Personal History*, p. 112. Seton-Watson quoted in C. Parker, *The English Historical Tradition since 1850*, Edinburgh, John Donald, 1990, p. 112.

59 Kathy Burk located the typescript thesis and in her biography prints the passages omitted. Burk, *Troublemaker*, pp. 93–95. *The Saturday Review*, 145, 16 June 1928, p. 774. The Second Empire reference is to F.A. Simpson's two volumes on Napoleon III. (I am grateful to Professor Farnie on this point.)

60 Burk, *Troublemaker*, pp. 91–93. AJPT to 'Dear Sir', 1 March and 10 May 1933 and to Harold Macmillan, 17 May 1933; Macmillan Archives. I differ from Kathy Burk in doubting the £50 was a problem and seeing Manchester University Press as rescuing him from difficulty.

61 On the gentleman scholar as one of his 'faces', see Wrigley, 'Five Faces and the Man', pp. 225–38. On declining to collect the PhD, see *A Personal History*, p. 122; Sisman, *A.J.P. Taylor*, p. 96; and Burk, *Troublemaker*, p. 92.

62 *The Italian Problem in European Diplomacy*, p. 1. Quoted in Wrigley, 'Introduction' to Bibliography, p. 11; Burk, *Troublemaker*, pp. 96–97; and elsewhere.

63 A.F. Pribram, *England and the International Policy of the European Great Powers, 1971–1914*, London, Clarendon Press, 1931, p. xi. Robert Cole discusses Pribram's influence on his writing in *The Traitor within the Gates*, pp. 9–12.

64 Colley, *Namier*, p.25.

65 Taylor, *The Italian Problem*, p.2.

66 Quoted in Keith Wilson's excellent 'Introduction: Governments, Historians and "Historical Engineering"' in Keith Wilson (ed.), *Forging the Collective Memory: Government and International Historians through Two World Wars*, Oxford, Berghahn, 1996, pp.1–28 (p.16).

67 Alan Taylor's lists of books read for 1924; HRRC, University of Texas, Austin. His other books read in 1924 included O.H. Norman, *A Searchlight on the European War*. For a shrewd discussion of Brailsford's book, see F.M. Leventhal, *The Last Dissenter: H.N. Brailsford and His World*, Oxford, Oxford University Press, 1985, pp.107–13.

68 'J.A. Hobson's Imperialism', *New Statesman and Nation*, 49, 1255, 26 March 1955, pp.441–42.

69 For these examples of his displays of his skills, see *The Italian Problem*, pp.213, 99 and 4 respectively.

70 Taylor, *The Italian Problem*, pp.17 and 31.

71 Ibid., pp.6–7.

72 A.J.P. Taylor, *The Struggle for Mastery in Europe 1848–1918*, Oxford, Oxford University Press, 1954, p.595–96.

73 Martin, *The Triumph of Lord Palmerston*, 2nd edition (London, Hutchinson, 1963), p.55. Martin wrote of Lord Stratford, 'the home government...would have preferred more obedience and less high-mindedness', and on Jeremy Bentham's era, 'there were only two kinds of journalist – the jackal of the politicians in power and the literary man on holiday'. Ibid., pp.99 and 81.

74 Martin, *Father Figures*, pp.131–32.

75 Taylor, *The Italian Problem*, p.8. Perhaps he was taking a dig at Kingsley Martin in his list of what passes for public opinion. Basil Kingsley Martin (1897–1969) was an Assistant Lecturer in Politics at the London School of Economics (1924–27), a leader writer for the *Manchester Guardian* (1927–30) and editor of *New Statesman* (1930–60).

76 Ibid., pp.7–8.

77 *Times Literary Supplement*, 1720, 17 January 1935, p.27. Walter Alison Phillips (1864–1950) was Lecky Professor in Dublin, 1914–39, and Hon. Fellow of Merton College, Oxford, 1938–50. For summaries of five reviews see Wrigley, *Taylor Bibliography*, pp.63–64.

78 *Oxford Magazine*, 53, 17, 2 May 1935, p.553.

79 McElwee spoke on 'The Fall of the Habsburgs' to the Liverpool branch of the Historical Association in the academic year 1932–33. *Twenty-Seventh Annual Report of the Historical Association* (1933), p.38. He disliked Liverpool University and became Senior History Master at Stowe, the public school.

80 'Translators' Note', in Heinrich Friedjung, *The Struggle for Supremacy in Germany 1859–66*, London, Macmillan, 1935, p.vi. CJW conversation with AJPT, 20 December 1976, when I was preparing the Taylor bibliography. He also spoke very warmly of Bill McElwee then, as he did in *A Personal History*, pp.105–6. There are eleven letters relating to the later stages of the book in the Macmillan archives (13 December 1934–11 May 1935). See also Burk, *Troublemaker*, pp.137–38.

81 'Introduction' to Friedjung, *Struggle*, pp.x, xxiv-v, and xxii respectively for the quotations. The book was reprinted in the United States in 1966 by Russell & Russell, and the introduction reprinted in A.J.P. Taylor, *Struggles for Supremacy: Diplomatic Essays by A.J.P. Taylor*, ed. C.J. Wrigley, Aldershot, Ashgate, 2000, pp.51–67.

82   A.J.P. Taylor, *The Origins of the Second World War*, London, Hamish Hamilton, 1963 edition, p.182.

83   Reprinted in A.J.P. Taylor, *Struggles for Supremacy*, pp.23–50.

84   On the many drawbacks of these documents, see the excellent essays in Wilson (ed.), *Forging the Collective Memory*.

85   Kathy Burk rightly points out that his list of books read suggests that he had read 22, not all the volumes, by 1934 (as he recalled in his autobiography); Burk, *Troublemaker*, pp.139–40.

86   *A Personal History*, p.123.

87   AJPT to 'Dear Sir', 19 November 1937 and 13 January 1938; Macmillan Archives.

88   For instance, he highlights the odd order of two dispatches of 24 and 25 May 1884. A.J.P. Taylor, *Germany's First Bid for Colonies 1884–1885: A Move in Bismarck's European Policy*, London, Macmillan, 1938, p.27, footnote 4.

89   Ibid., pp.99 and 7 respectively.

90   Ibid., 7 and 14 respectively.

91   On Hobson and his analysis of imperialism, see P.J. Cain, *Hobson and Imperialism: Radicalism, New Liberalism and Finance 1887–1938*, Oxford, Oxford University Press, 2002. AJPT's peace campaigning is discussed later in this chapter.

92   Extracts from six reviews in Wrigley, *Taylor Bibliography*, pp.66–67. *Times Literary Supplement*, 19 March 1938, p.178. *International Affairs*, 17, 4, July–August 1938, p.558. *History*, 23, 91, December 1938, pp.276–77. *Oxford Magazine*, 56, 20, 19 May 1938, pp.652–53. *Spectator*, 26 March 1938, pp.537–38. Mary Townshend in the *American Historical Review*, 44, 4, July 1939, pp.899–901, also felt he pushed his thesis too far. Sir William Keith Hancock (1898–1988) held chairs in Adelaide, Birmingham, Oxford, London and Canberra from 1924.

93   Review of Reginald Ward, *Maximillian Robespierre in the Manchester Guardian*, 21 November 1934. Wrigley, 'Introduction' to *Bibliography*, pp.10–11 (based on conversation with AJPT on 28 September 1976). AJPT to Bob Cole, 2 July 1973. Arthur Wallace had begun with the *Manchester Guardian* in 1909 and ended in 1941. Hartmut Pogge von Strandmann, 'Germany's Colonial Expansion under Bismarck', *Past and Present*, 42, February 1969, pp.140–59. Hans-Ulrich Wehler, 'Bismarck's Imperialism, 1862–1890', in J.J. Sheehan (ed.), *Imperial Germany*, New York, New Viewpoints, 1976, pp.180–222.

94   *A Personal History*, p.128. He appeared frequently, in news stories as well as having reviews and articles published, but not literally weekly. Alfred Powell Wadsworth (1891–1956) was editor of the *Manchester Guardian* 1944–56.

95   David Ayerest, *The Manchester Guardian: Biography of a Newspaper*, London, Jonathan Cape, 1971, pp.415–16 and 614–17.

96   'The Case of Mr Eden: An Historical View' and 'The Revision of Treaties: 1830 and 1938', *Manchester Guardian*, 23 February and 23 September 1938.

97   AJPT to Bob Cole, 2 July 1973.

98   *A Personal History*, p.124. This wish for his history to be as popular as the latest novel, following Lord Macaulay, was expressed in the *Manchester Guardian*, 4 December 1936. Wrigley, *Taylor Bibliography*, pp.1 and 255.

99   *A Personal History*, pp.107–8.

100   Ibid, p.128. Armitage was a cotton magnate.

101   Ibid., p.108.

102   Ibid., pp.108–9. Anya Eltenton, born 3 January 1933, became a ballerina at the Royal Ballet, Covent Garden, 1958–65, and after marriage became Lady Sainsbury of Preston Candover.

103 For a summary of the Oppenheimer incident, see Burk, *Troublemaker*, p.120.

104 His review, 'Extreme Views Weakly Held', *Sunday Times*, 29 May 1983; quoted in Sisman, p.92.

105 Malcolm Muggeridge, *Picture Palace*, London, Weidenfeld & Nicolson, 1987, pp.60, 84 and 97.

106 Richard Ingrams provided an excellent introduction to the book in 1987; ibid., pp.vii-xiii. For Muggeridge in these years see Richard Ingrams, *Muggeridge*, London, Harper Collins, 1995, Gregory Wolfe, *Malcolm Muggeridge: A Biography* London, Hodder & Stoughton, 1995, and Ian Hunter, *Malcolm Muggeridge: A Life*, London, Collins, 1980.

107 Muggeridge, *Picture Palace*, pp.204–5, 71 and 70.

108 A.J.P. Taylor, 'Malcolm Muggeridge: Woeful Countenance' (review of Muggeridge's diaries), *Observer*, 29 March 1981 and reprinted in A.J.P. Taylor, *British Prime Ministers and Other Essays* (ed. Chris Wrigley), London, Allen Lane, 1999, pp.349–52.

109 Malcolm Muggeridge, *Chronicles of Wasted Time: The Green Stick*, London, Collins, 1972, p.181.

110 'Malcolm Muggeridge: Woeful Countenance', p.350.

111 AJPT to Malcolm Muggeridge, 13 February 1933; Malcolm Muggeridge Papers, Wheaton College, Illinois. Most of this long letter is published in Sisman, *A.J.P. Taylor*, pp.101–3, and a part in Burk, *Troublemaker*, pp.122–23. For the Moscow background, see John Bright-Holmes (ed.), *Like It Was: The Diaries of Malcolm Muggeridge*, London, Collins, 1981, pp.13–74.

112 AJPT to Malcolm Muggeridge, 16 June 1933; Muggeridge Papers.

113 *A Personal History*, pp.117–18. Burk, *Troublemaker*, p.124.

114 On 24 April and 18 September 1932. Howard Hill, *Freedom to Roam: The Struggle for Access to Britain's Moors and Mountains*, Ashbourne, Landmark Publishing, 1980. Harvey Taylor, *A Claim on the Countryside: A History of the British Outdoor Movement*, Edinburgh, Edinburgh University Press, 1997, pp.259–60. Melanie Tebbutt, 'In Search of the "Wild" Outdoors: Northern Moors and Manly Identity, c.1880s–1920s' (Economic History conference, 4 April 2004). Alan Taylor was friendly with one of the leading trespassers on Kinder Scout.

115 *A Personal History*, p.120.

116 Conversation with Margaret Taylor, 20 December 1976.

117 *A Personal History*, pp.119–21. Leonard Robert Palmer (1906–84) was Professor of Comparative Philology at Oxford University, 1952–71.

118 Hope, *Norman Cameron*, pp.68, 71 and 112. *A Personal History*, pp.74 and 129.

119 Ibid, pp.129–30.

120 Margaret Taylor's recollections are reported in Constantine Fitzgibbon, *The Life of Dylan Thomas*, London, Dent, 1965, p.166. Alan Taylor's are in *A Personal History*, pp.129–31. See also Andrew Lycett, *Dylan Thomas: A New Life*, London, Weidenfeld & Nicolson, 2003, pp.114 and 157.

121 Norland College was founded in 1892 by Emily Ward, with its educational views drawn from Friedrich Froebel. Later, Princess Anne, the Duchess of York and Sir Mick Jagger were to hire Norland nannies. John Ezard in the *Guardian*, 4 April 2002, p.8.

122 *A Personal History*, p.131.

123 AJPT to CJW, 3 October 1978.

124 *A Personal History*, p.124. For the background, see Martin Ceadel, *Pacifism in Britain 1914–1945: The Defining of a Faith* (Oxford, Oxford University Press, 1980), pp.87–168. Frank Allaun (1913–2002) was Labour MP for Salford East, 1955–83.

125   Leftish intellectuals often featured in the Manchester press, and not only the *Manchester Guardian*. For example, in the *Manchester Guardian's* sister publication the *Manchester Evening News* there were essays by G.D.H. Cole on 20 June 1934 and by Bertrand Russell on 9 October 1936.

126   *A Personal History*, p. 115.

127   For its history, see Edmund and Ruth Frow, *To Make That Future Now! A History of the Manchester and Salford Trades Council*, Manchester, Morten, 1976.

128   His closeness to the CPGB is apparent from Klugmann, *History of the Communist Party of Great Britain*, Vol. 1. His role as chairman of the Strike Organisation Committee during the General Strike led him to be denounced with vigour by the Trotskyist Left and others. For example, Brian Pearce and Michael Woodhouse, *A History of Communism in Britain*, London, Bookmarks, 1969, p. 155. For Purcell's career, see Ralph Hayburn, David Martin and John Saville, 'Purcell, Albert Arthur (1872–1935)', in Joyce Bellamy and John Saville (eds.), *Dictionary of Labour Biography*, Vol. 1 (London, Macmillan, 1972), pp. 275–79.

129   Daniel F. Calhoun, *The United Front: The TUC and the Russians 1923–1928*, Cambridge, Cambridge University Press, 1976, especially pp. 371–75.

130   Ibid., pp. 38 and 46.

131   *A Personal History*, p. 115.

132   Nigel Copsey, *Anti-Fascism in Britain* (London, Macmillan, 2000), p. 15.

133   Manchester and Salford Trades Council, *Annual Report and Directory 1932–33* (1933) and *1933–34* (1934). The quotations are from the *1933–34* report, pp. 9–10.

134   Manchester and Salford Trades Council, *Annual Report and Directory 1934–35* (1935). *Manchester Guardian*, 26 February 1934. Kathy Burk is mistaken in placing his first public meeting in June; Burk, p. 130. *A Personal History*, p. 116.

135   On this Bill see Gerald D. Anderson, *Fascists, Communists and the National Government: Civil Liberties in Britain 1931–1937*, Columbia, University of Missouri Press, 1983, pp. 63–98.

136   *Manchester Guardian*, 25 June 1934. Speakers at the other locations included the chairman and secretary of Manchester Labour Party, Annie Loughlin of the TUC and Mick Jenkins of the Tailors' and Garment Makers' Union. Ashfield, a large house with a sports field beside it, housed the West Salford Labour Club and Institute.

137   *A Personal History*, p. 102.

138   *Manchester Guardian*, 22 October 1934. Burk, *Troublemaker*, pp. 131. *A Personal History*, p. 116.

139   Manchester and Salford Trades Council, *Annual Report and Directory 1935–36* (1936) and 1936–37 (1937).

140   George Darling (1905–85) was later Co-op and Labour MP for Sheffield Hillsborough, 1950–74, and Minister of State at the Board of Trade, 1964–68. Alan Taylor's speeches were not reported in the local press.

141   A.J.P. Taylor, *English History 1914–1945*, Oxford, Oxford University Press, 1965, p. 385.

142   *Manchester Guardian*, 18 December 1935. Wrigley, *Taylor Bibliography*, pp. 13–14. John Leofric Stocks (1882–1937) was Fellow and Tutor at St John's College, Oxford, 1906–24, before succeeding Samuel Alexander as Professor of Philosophy at Manchester University. He was Labour candidate for Oxford in 1935 and Vice-Chancellor of Liverpool University, 1936–37.

143   Review of Daniel Waley, *British Public Opinion and the Abyssinian War 1935–6*, in *English Historical Review*, 92, 362, January 1977, pp. 229–30.

144   *A Personal History*, pp. 127–28. See also his essay 'Accident Prone, or What Happened Next', *Journal of Modern History*, 49, 1, March 1977, pp. 7–8.

145   Taylor, 'Accident Prone', p. 8.
146   Taylor, *Germany's First Bid for Colonies*, p. 14. Sisman, *A.J.P. Taylor*, p. 118.
147   *Manchester Guardian*, 12 September 1937. *International Affairs*, 17, 6, November–December 1937. Wrigley, *Taylor Bibliography*, pp. 256–57 and 267–68. Francis Wrigley Hirst (1873–1953) was editor of *The Economist* 1907–16, and author and an opponent of war, from the time of the Boer War onwards. He supported the Munich agreement. Goldsworthy Lowes Dickinson (1862–1932) was a Fellow of Kings College, Cambridge, historian and philosopher and League of Nations Union advocate.
148   *A Personal History*, p. 119. Michael Polanyi (1891–1976), a Hungarian, worked in Berlin before leaving in protest at anti-Jewish legislation in 1933. As well as his scientific writing, he published books on free market economics and became Professor of Social Studies at Manchester University, 1948–58.
149   Kathy Burk interviewed her in June 1991. Burk, *Troublemaker*, pp. 88 and 134–36.
150   A.J.P. Taylor (ed.), *Off the Record: Political Interviews, 1933–1943, W.P. Crozier*, London, Hutchinson, 1973, p. 45. Quoted in Rose, *Lewis Namier and Zionism*, p. 61.
151   Ibid., pp. 63–64 and 73. More generally, see Marion Berghahn, *Continental Britons: German-Jewish Refugees from Nazi Germany*, London, Macmillan, 1984.
152   Norman Rose's interview with AJPT, 20 September 1976; quoted in Rose, *Lewis Namier and Zionism*, p. 59.
153   AJPT to E.M. Blackwell, 24 April 1938.
154   John Lewis, *The Left Book Club: An Historical Record*, London, Gollancz, 1970. Sisman, *A.J.P. Taylor*, p. 113. For contrasting assessments of the Left Book Club, see Betty Reid, 'The Left Book Club in the Thirties', in J. Clark, M. Heinemann, D. Margolies and C. Snee (eds.), *Culture and Crisis in Britain in the Thirties*, London, Lawrence & Wishart, 1979, pp. 193–207 and Julian Symons, *The Thirties: A Dream Revolved*, London, Cresset Press, 1960; second edition, 1975, pp. 92–100.
155   A.J.P. Taylor, *English History 1914–1945*, pp. 396–97.
156   *Manchester Guardian*, 24 September 1938. *A Personal History*, p. 134. He also recalled the hostility he faced at these meetings in his 'Accident Prone', p. 8 and in *1939 Revisited*, London, German Historical Institute, 1981, p. 1.
157   AJPT to Duff Cooper, 1 October 1938; copy forwarded to AJPT by Martin Gilbert, 2 May 1962. Quoted in Sisman, *A.J.P. Taylor*, p. 121.
158   Taylor, 'Accident Prone', p. 8. Sir Richard Winn Livingstone (1880–1960) was President of Corpus Christi College, 1933–50, and Vice-Chancellor of Oxford University, 1944–47.
159   Brian Harrison, 'Politics', in Brian Harrison (ed.), *The History of the University of Oxford*, Vol. 8, *The Twentieth Century*, Oxford, Oxford University Press, 1994, p. 406. For Lee's letters and the references, see Burk, *Troublemaker*, pp. 144–46. Benedict Humphrey Sumner (1893–1951), who specialised in Russian history, was later Warden of All Souls, 1945–51.

Chapter 4

1   *A Personal History*, p. 132.
2   Albert Mansbridge, *The Older Universities of England*, London, Longmans, Green and Co., 1923, p. 209.
3   Brian Harrison, 'College Life, 1918–1939' in Harrison (ed.), *The History of the University of Oxford*, Vol. 8, pp. 85, 95 and 97. *A Personal History*, pp. 137–38.

4   Burk, *Troublemaker*, p. 434.

5   *A Personal History*, p. 137. Harrison, 'College Life', p. 86.

6   Richard Ollard, *A Man of Contradictions: A Life of A.L. Rowse*, London, Allen Lane, 1999, p. 78.

7   *A Personal History*, p. 137. Lady Spender to CJW, 14 September 2004. Margaret Taylor conversation with CJW, 20 December 1976.

8   Thomas Dewar Weldon (1896–1958) was a Fellow of Magdalen College, 1923–58, and Vice-President, 1937. Peter Medawar, *Memoir of a Thinking Radish*, Oxford, Oxford University Press, 1986, pp. 47–48. Harrison, 'College Life', p. 84. Brian Harrison interview with AJPT, 24 July 1985.

9   Clive Staples Lewis (1898–1963), known as Jack Lewis, was a Fellow of Magdalen College, 1925–54, then Professor of Medieval and Renaissance Literature at Cambridge University, 1954–63. His books include *The Allegory of Love*, 1936, *The Screwtape Letters*, 1942, and *The Lion, the Witch and the Wardrobe*, 1950. Humphrey Carpenter, *The Inklings*, London, Allen & Unwin, 1978; Harper Collins paperback, 1997, p. 162. George Sayer, *Jack: A Life of C.S. Lewis*, London, Hodder & Stoughton, 2nd edition, 1997, p. 222.

10   Medawar, *Memoir*, p. 88. Carpenter, *Inklings*, p. 18.

11   *A Personal History*, p. 139. When I eagerly asked AJPT in 1976 whether he had known J.R.R. Tolkien and what he thought of C.S. Lewis, I received a terse, frosty and dismissive response.

12   Paul Victor Mendelssohn Benecke had become a Fellow of Magdalen in 1891. Sayer, *Jack*, p. 188.

13   Keith Thomas, 'College Life, 1945–70', in Harrison (ed.), *The History of the University of Oxford*, Vol. 8, p. 197. Keith Kyle, 'The Devil's Horn and the Half-Hung Man: A Memoir of A.J.P. Taylor and K.B. McFarlane', *Oxford*, 52, 2, November 2000, pp. 23–25.

14   John Humphrey Carlile Morris (1910–84) was a Fellow of Magdalen College from 1936 and University Reader in Conflict Laws from 1951, whose favourite relaxation was yachting. Brian Harrison interview with AJPT, 24 July 1985.

15   John Langshaw Austin (1911–60) was a Fellow of Magdalen College, 1935–52, and White's Professor of Moral Philosophy and Fellow of Corpus Christi, 1952–60. José Harris, 'The Arts and Social Sciences, 1939–70', in Harrison (ed.), *The History of the University of Oxford*, Vol. 8, p. 233. Gilbert Ryle (1900–76) was Student [a Fellow] and tutor of Christ Church from 1925. E.R. Dodd, *Missing Persons*, Oxford, Oxford University Press, 1977, p. 131. M. Ignatieff, *Isaiah Berlin: A Life*, London, Chatto & Windus, 1998, p. 70.

16   Charles Talbut Onions (1873–1965) was a Fellow of Magdalen, 1923–65. He was responsible for the revised *Shorter Oxford Dictionary* in 1933 and the *Oxford Dictionary of Etymology*, 1966. J.A.W. Bennett, 'Onions, Charles Talbut, 1873–1965', in Williams and Nicholls (eds.), *The Dictionary of National Biography, 1961–1970*, pp. 809–11. Jack Arthur Walter Bennett (1911–81) was an Anglo-Saxon and medieval scholar who was a Fellow of Magdalen, 1947–64, and succeeded C.S. Lewis to the Chair of Medieval and Renaissance Literature at Cambridge University.

17   *A Personal History*, p. 161. He was also dismissive of *The Masters* when reviewing C.P. Snow's *The Corridors of Power*; *New Statesman*, 68, 1756, 6 November 1964, p. 698.

18   Sir Henry Thomas Tizard (1885–1959) was Rector of Imperial College of Science and Technology, 1929–42. For one account of his feud with Lindemann see the Earl of Birkenhead, *The Prof in Two Words*, London, Collins, 1961, pp. 39–40,

180–96 and 250–55; and, more generally, Ronald W. Clark, *Tizard*, London, Methuen, 1965.

19 Harold Hartley, 'Tizard, Sir Henry Thomas', in E.T. Williams (ed.), *Dictionary of National Biography, 1951–1960*, Oxford, Oxford University Press, 1971. Brigadier-General Sir Harold Brewer Hartley (1878–1972), tutor and later Research Fellow at Balliol College, was an adviser to the Ministry of Fuel and Power, 1939–47.

20 Clark, *Tizard*, pp.383–85. Sisman, *A.J.P. Taylor*, p.161. Burk, *Troublemaker*, p.196.

21 'Lindemann and Tizard: More Luck than Judgement?', in the *Observer*, 9 April 1961, p.21; reprinted in A.J.P. Taylor, *Politicians, Socialism and Historians*, London, Hamish Hamilton, 1980, pp.230–35. Taylor's more favourable comments on Lindemann were printed on the back of the book jacket of Birkenhead's 1961 biography of Lindemann. *A Personal History*, pp.161–63 and 111 and 122 (on aiding Namier).

22 Anthony Howard, *Crossman: The Pursuit of Power*, London, Cape, 1990, pp.58–77. Tam Dalyell, *Dick Crossman: A Portrait*, London, Weidenfeld & Nicolson, 1989, pp.28–35. *A Personal History*, p.143. Richard Howard Stafford Crossman (1907–74) was later MP for Coventry East (1945–74), a member of the Cabinet (1964–70) and editor of the *New Statesman* (1970–72).

23 Historical Association, *Thirty-Second Annual Report…* (1938), p.28.

24 AJPT to Harold Macmillan, 17 April, 8 and 10 May and 2 June 1939, and Harold Macmillan to AJPT, 2 and 9 May and 1 June 1939; Macmillan Archives. Sisman, *A.J.P. Taylor*, pp.124–25 and 418.

25 AJPT to Harold Macmillan, 10 May 1939; Macmillan Archives. Burk, *Troublemaker*, p.228.

26 L.B. Namier to Harold Macmillan, 20 April and 9 June 1939; Macmillan Archives. Sisman, *A.J.P. Taylor*, p.125. The terms were improved from 10 per cent royalty to 15 per cent (rising to 20 per cent) and a £75 advance.

27 AJPT to Malcolm Muggeridge, 1 May 1939; Muggeridge Papers. Partly quoted Sisman, *A.J.P. Taylor*, pp.128–29.

28 AJPT to Malcolm Muggeridge, 17 July 1939; Muggeridge Papers.

29 A.J.P. Taylor, *The Habsburg Monarchy 1815–1918*, London, Macmillan, 1941, p.viii. It seems highly likely that he wrote the last two or three chapters (1897–1918) after October 1939, and probably in the first half of 1940, even if he had sketched them out at Montriod.

30 AJPT to Malcolm Muggeridge, 17 July 1939; Muggeridge Papers. Robert Dell was then 74. He had been pro-Boer in 1899 and had worked for the *Manchester Guardian* in Paris, until expelled in May 1918, and then again from 1929. He was a friend of Count Karolyi.

31 Taylor, *The Habsburg Monarchy 1815–1918*, p.ix.

32 *A Personal History*, p.146.

34 AJPT to 'Dear Sir' (at Macmillans), 26 July and 18 September 1939; Macmillan Archives. AJPT discussion with CJW, 1 April 1986. On the early death of Ellen Wilkinson (1891–1947), see Betty D. Vernon, *Ellen Wilkinson*, London, Croom Helm, 1982, pp.233–35. James Francis Horrabin (1884–1962) was a journalist and artist. He was Labour MP for Peterborough, 1929–31, and chairman of the Fabian Colonial Bureau, 1945–47. He was also editor of *The Plebs* (1914–17 and 1918–32) and illustrated H.G. Wells' *The Outline of History*.

35 AJPT to 'Dear Sir', 2 November 1940 and 18 September 1941, and to Harold Macmillan, 19 February 1941; Macmillan Archives.

36 A.J.P. Taylor, 'Accident Prone', p.4.

37   A.J.P. Taylor, *The Habsburg Monarchy 1815–1918*, pp.220, 254 and 148–49 respectively. See also the second edition, pp.191 and 150.
38   Ibid., pp.49 and 41 respectively.
39   This was in the context of his visit to Morocco at Easter 1939. AJPT to Malcolm Muggeridge, 1 May 1939; Muggeridge Papers.
40   A.J.P. Taylor, *The Habsburg Monarchy 1815–1919*, pp.50, 275 and 271 respectively.
41   Ibid., pp.26–27.
42   AJPT to Harold Macmillan, 18 December 1940; Macmillan Archives. This is printed in full in Burk, *Troublemaker*, pp.228–29.
43   He reviewed it when published in 1957, 'Hesitation Waltz', *Times Literary Supplement*, 28787, 26 April 1957, and when it was issued again in 1993, 'Kissinger Fireworks', in the *Observer*, 11 November 1993; the later review was reprinted as 'A World Restored 1812–22', in Taylor, *Struggles for Supremacy*, pp.17–19. Neither time was Taylor impressed, feeling the book was notable for a surfeit of epigrams.
44   AJPT to Bob Cole, 26 July 1976; quoted in Cole, *The Traitor within the Gates*, p.51.
45   A.J.P. Taylor, *The Habsburg Monarchy 1815–1918*, p.253.
46   AJPT to Harold Macmillan, 23 February 1941; Macmillan Archives. He had asked for a similar note to be sent to that newspaper with a review copy of his *Germany's Bid for Colonies* (on 11 February 1938).
47   A.J.P. Taylor, *The Habsburg Monarchy 1815–1918*, pp.259, 268 and 299–300.
48   *Journal of Modern History*, 14, 4 December 1942, pp.538–40. For extracts from eight reviews, see Wrigley, *Taylor Bibliography*, pp.68–70. Alan Taylor sent Macmillan the reviews in the *Journal of Modern History* and *American Historical Review*, noting that Professor Jaszi had been 'Hungarian Minister of Nationalities in 1918–1919'; Macmillan Archives.
49   *Free Europe*, 3, 37, 4 April 1941, p.227.
50   'Dynasty in Fetters: Why the Habsburg Monarchy Fell', *Times Literary Supplement*, 2038, 22 February 1941, p.88.
51   *English Historical Review*, 587, 227, July 1942, pp.389–92. *Manchester Guardian*, 28 March 1941, p.6.
52   The Taylors paid £525 in 1933, made various improvements and sold it for £825. Burk, *Troublemaker*, p.432.
53   *A Personal History*, p.149.
54   J.F.B., 'Argus round the Town', *Preston Herald*, 1 March 1940, p.2.
55   *A Personal History*, p.149.
56   Interview with Giles Taylor, 24 September 1999.
57   Sisman, *A.J.P. Taylor*, p.130.
58   Robin Thompson to CJW, 21 February 1999.
59   'Madame de Staël'. Review of Margaret Goldsmith, *Madame de Staël* (1938) in *Manchester Guardian*, 28 October 1938, p.7.
60   'History and Biography: A Survey of the Year's Books', *Manchester Guardian*, 2 December 1938, *Gift Books Supplement*, p.xvii. 'Hanoverian England', *Manchester Guardian*, 11 August 1939, p.5. On his reviews of this period, see Wrigley, *Taylor Bibliography*, pp.262–87.
61   'Contemporary History', *Manchester Guardian*, 31 January 1939, p.7. 'Grant and Temperley' was still the textbook in grammar school sixth forms at least until the late 1960s, probably later.
62   'A Nazi Apologist', 'Tory Socialism' and 'Historic Parallel', *Manchester Guardian*, 9 February, p.3, 27 December 1940, p.8, and 18 November 1942, p.3. Andrew

Roberts, 'Patriotism: The Last Refuge of Sir Arthur Bryant', in his *Eminent Churchillians*, London, Weidenfeld & Nicolson, 1994, pp.287–322.

63   Review in *Manchester Guardian*, 15 February 1938, p.7.

64   'The Historian'. Review of C.H. Williams, *The Modern Historian*, in *Manchester Guardian*, 5 August 1938, p.5. Wrigley, *Taylor Bibliography*, p.265.

65   'History and Politics: A Survey of the Year's Books', *Manchester Guardian*, 1 December 1939, *Gift Books Supplement*, p.vii. 'Feeling about the War', *Manchester Guardian*, 7 March 1941, p.7.

66   Interview with Sebastian Taylor, 27 June 2000. AJPT to Harold Macmillan, 17 April 1939.

67   AJPT to Harold Macmillan, 5 January 1940.

68   *A Personal History*, pp.148–49.

69   Hope, *Norman Cameron*, pp.80 and 135.

70   Stephen Spender, *Forward from Liberalism*, London, Gollancz, 1937, p.9, his essay, pp.231–72, in Richard Crossman (ed.), *The God that Failed: Six Studies in Communism*, and his *World within World*, London, Hamish Hamilton, 1951, pp.71 and 279.

71   John Sutherland, *Stephen Spender: The Authorized Biography*, London, Viking, 2004, p.281. Lycett, *Dylan Thomas: A New Life*, p.227. Caitlin Thomas with George Tremlett, *Caitlin: Life with Dylan Thomas*, New York, Henry Holt, 1987, p.98. Lady Spender to CJW, 14 September 2004. Leon Jean Goosens, CBE (1897–1988), was a very distinguished solo oboist. Cecil Day-Lewis (1904–72), who was Poet Laureate 1968–72, worked for the Ministry of Information, 1941–46. Nevill Henry Kendal Aylmer Coghill (1899–1980) was a Fellow of Exeter College, 1925–57, and Merton Professor of English Literature, 1957–66, Oxford University.

72   Interview with Freddy Hurdis-Jones by CJW and Éva Haraszti-Taylor, London, 22 May 1991. The day after this party Dylan wrote in Freddy's copy of a book of his poems and also drew a picture of Freddy and some other guests at the party. This was later sold at auction for some £400.

73   Joris Hudson (F. Hurdis-Jones), *Love Costs Sixpence More: A Fantasy*, London, Trine Books, 1967, with a preface by John Symonds and drawings by Philippe Julian. The central figure, Robin Mount (the name probably drawn from Hamilton Brown), seems to be very loosely based on its author. The author inscribed CJW's copy 'these glimpses of an imagined Oxford'. Freddy Hurdis-Jones left Oxford for London at the end of 1942, working as an actor with Peter Hall. He worked on 'A Sentimental Journey' and an early fighter film. From 1946 he lived on the continent of Europe, in Paris, Venice and Malta, working mostly as a linguist. He saw Dylan Thomas several times in London.

74   Interview with Freddy Hurdis-Jones, 22 May 1991.

75   Ibid.

76   Thomas and Tremlett, *Caitlin*, p.98.

77   Interview with Freddy Hurdis-Jones, 22 May 1991. Sisman, *A.J.P. Taylor*, pp.143–44. John Zachary Young (1907–97) was a Fellow of Magdalen College, 1929–45, and Professor of Anatomy, University College, London, 1945–74.

78   Interview with Freddy Hurdis-Jones, 22 May 1991.

79   Conversation with F.M.L. Thompson, Institute of Historical Research, London, 6 May 1998. Francis Michael Longstreth Thompson (1925–) was Professor of Modern History, Bedford College, London University, 1968–77, and Director of the Institute of Historical Research, 1977–90. He also went to Bootham School. He was Ford's Lecturer, Oxford University, in 1994.

80   Keith Kyle, 'The Devil's Horn', p.24. Keith Kyle (1926–) worked for the BBC and later was Visiting Professor at the University of Coleraine. His publications include *Suez* (1991) and *The Politics of the Independence of Kenya* (1999).

81   Keith Kyle to CJW, 2 January 1991.

82   *A Personal History*, p.164.

83   *A Personal History*, pp.147 and 154. Sayer, *Jack*, p.267. Sisman, *A.J.P. Taylor*, pp.136–37. Interview with Freddy Hurdis-Jones, 22 May 1991. J.R.R. Tolkien to Christopher Tolkien, 30 January 1945; H. Carpenter (with C. Tolkien) (ed.), *Letters of J.R.R. Tolkien*, London, Allen & Unwin, 1981, p.95.

84   *A Personal History*, p.152.

85   Ibid., p.151.

86   Ibid., pp.159–60. For Hogg's complaints, see Burk, *Troublemaker*, pp.175–6.

87   *A Personal History*, p.165.

88   Sayer, *Jack*, p.267.

89   S.P. MacKenzie, *Politics and Military Morale: Current Affairs and Citizenship Education in the British Army 1914–50*, Oxford, Oxford University Press, 1992, pp.57–173. *A Personal History*, p.152. Alexander Dunlop Lindsay, 1st Baron Lindsay of Birker (1879–1952), a philosopher, was Master of Balliol College 1924–49, Vice-Chancellor of Oxford University, 1935–38, and from 1949 the first Principal of the University of Keele. He was a major early figure in Oxford's Labour Party and Fabian Society and stood as the anti-Munich candidate in the 1939 Oxford parliamentary by-election.

90   Lord Longford, *Avowed Intent*, London, Little, Brown, 1994, pp.92–93. Francis Aungier Pakenham (1905–2001), Lord Longford, was Student in Politics at Christ Church, Oxford, 1934–46 and 1952–64, and a Labour minister 1964–66. Sir Cecil Maurice Bowra (1898–1971) served on the Western Front, 1917–18, was a Fellow, 1922–38, then Warden of Wadham College, Oxford, 1938–70, and Vice-Chancellor of Oxford University, 1951–54. Edgar Lobel (1888–1982) was a papyrologist. *A Personal History*, p.154.

91   Burk, *Troublemaker*, p.155. Elizabeth Durban, *New Jerusalems*, London, Routledge & Kegan Paul, 1985, p.98. Ignatieff, *Isaiah Berlin*, p.70. Ben Rogers, *A.J. Ayer*, London, Chatto & Windus, 1999, p.134.

92   Interview with Lady Elizabeth Longford (Elizabeth Pakenham), 13 November 1991.

93   Elizabeth Longford, *The Pebbled Shore*, London, Weidenfeld & Nicolson, 1986, p.212. *A Personal History*, p.155.

94   On Lord Berners (1883–1950), see Mark Amory, *Lord Berners: The Last Eccentric*, London, Chatto & Windus, 1998; John Betjeman, 'Lord Berners' in L.G. Wickham Legg and E.T. Williams (eds.), *The Dictionary of National Biography, 1941–1950*, Oxford University Press, 1959; A.L. Rowse, *Friends And Contemporaries*, London, Methuen, 1989. *A Personal History*, p.155.

95   Amory, *Lord Berners*, p.187. Edith Sitwell to Hilda Doolittle [1944] in Richard Greene (ed.), *The Selected Letters of Edith Sitwell*, London, Virago, 1997, p.265.

96   Lord Berners, *A Distant Prospect*, London, Constable, 1945, pp.23, 48, 61, 96 and 98.

97   Éva Haraszti's estimate of the number of their meetings, in her essay, 'Michael Karolyi: A Friend', in Chris Wrigley (ed.), *Warfare, Diplomacy and Politics*, London, Hamish Hamilton, 1986, pp.231–47 (at p.232).

98   A.J.P. Taylor, 'Michael Karolyi in Exile', *The New Hungarian Quarterly*, 9, 31, Autumn 1968, pp.18–22.

99   Michael Karolyi, *Memoirs of Michael Karolyi: Faith without Illusion*, London, Jonathan Cape, 1956, p.295.

100 A.J.P. Taylor, 'Introduction', ibid. pp.7–11 (at p.10).
101 Ibid., p.10. 'Plan of Propaganda for Hungary', 29 September 1941, 'Propaganda Policy to Hungary', 22 May 1942, R.H. Bruce Lockhart to Rex Leeper, 16 April 1940, Richard Law minute, 30 July 1942; National Archives, FO989/217. Vernon, *Ellen Wilkinson*, pp.28–29, 57–58 and 65–68. Both Ellen Wilkinson and Alan Taylor wrote for *Time and Tide*.
102 On this see Hugh and Christopher Seton-Watson, *The Making of a New Europe: R.W. Seton-Watson and the Last Years of Austria-Hungary*, London, Methuen, 1981, especially, pp.335–84.
103 *A Personal History*, p.153.
104 AJPT to Crozier, 3 September [1944]; Manchester Guardian Papers, B/T18/8. A sentence and a half of the first paragraph is quoted in Burk, *Troublemaker*, p.236 (but which wrongly has as recipient Wadsworth, his successor as editor).
105 A.P. Wadsworth to AJPT, 9 September 1943. AJPT to 'AP', 13 September [1943]; ibid., B/T19/10 and 11.
106 A.P. Wadsworth to AJPT, 23 May 1944; ibid., B/T19/18.
107 AJPT to 'AP', 5 October [1944]. Wadsworth to 'Alan', 9 October 1944; ibid., B/T19/29 and 30. A week earlier he had forwarded to Wadsworth an article by Ignotus. Paul Ignotus, later Hungarian press attaché in London, was tried by the Communist régime and sentenced to ten years' imprisonment after his return to Hungary.
108 For the eulogy in *The Habsburg Monarchy* (1941), see p.264. Review of Paul Selver, *Masaryk*, in *Manchester Guardian*, 29 April 1940, p.7, and reviews of R.W. Seton-Watson, *Masaryk in England*, in *Manchester Guardian*, 3 March 1943, and *Time and Tide*, 24, 11, 13 March 1943, p.216. He also reviewed a book on Masaryk in the *Spectator*, 29 August 1941, p.212. Tomas Masaryk (1850–1937), a Professor at Prague University, 1882–1914, was first President of Czechoslovakia, 1918–35.
109 Review of S. Grant Duff, *A German Protectorate: The Czechs under Nazi Rule*, in *Time and Tide*, 23, 18, 2 May 1942, p.372.
110 'On Duranty', *Time and Tide*, 23, 23, 6 June 1942, p.470.
111 Reviews of Philip Gibbs, *Ordeal in England*, in *Manchester Guardian*, 2 July 1937, p.7, W.F. Reddaway et al. (eds.), *The Cambridge History of Poland 1697–1935* in the *Spectator*, 5911, 10 October 1941, p.360, and Oscar Halecki, *The History of Poland*, in *Manchester Guardian*, 28 August 1942, p.3. Wrigley, *Taylor Bibliography*, pp.16–17.
112 The second Viscountess Rhondda (1883–1958) wrote a biography of her father, D.A. Thomas, *Viscount Rhondda* (1921), who was Lloyd George's first Food Controller, founded *Time and Tide* in 1920, spent a quarter of a million pounds on it over 38 years, editing it from 1926. Initially her weekly political review was notably left-wing and feminist; later she came to oppose socialism at home and communism abroad. Review of Newman in *Time and Tide*, 23, 44, 31 October 1942, p.873; with letters of complaint and a hostile editorial in 23, 45, 7 November 1942, p.887–88; and A.J.P. Taylor's reply and a further editorial in 23, 46, 14 November 1942, p.907. *A Personal History*, p.167. See also Wrigley, *Taylor Bibliography*, pp.17 and 286, and Burk, *Troublemaker*, pp.238–39. Bernard Newman (1897–1968) was a lecturer with the British Expeditionary Force, 1940, and the Ministry of Information, 1940–45. He published a very large number of books under his name and under the pseudonym Don Betteridge. Many were on spies or on travel (including accounts of his cycling abroad). Letter to the *Spectator*, 28 January 1944 (in response to D.W. Brogan). Sir A. Clark Kerr telegram, 1 February 1944. Sir Owen O'Malley to Frank

Roberts, 29 January 1944. Frank Roberts to O'Malley, 18 February 1944. National Archives, FO 370/39388/C1486/8/55; 34561/C2232/8/55 and 39389.

113   A.J.P. Taylor, *Czechoslovakia's Place in a Free Europe*, London, Czechoslovakia Institute in London, 1943, pp. 9, 14 and 20. Wrigley, *Taylor Bibliography*, p. 133. *Manchester Guardian*, 27 October 1943, p. 4.

114   A.P. Wadsworth to AJPT, 8 November 1944; Wadsworth Papers, *Manchester Guardian* Archives, B/T 19/33.

115   AJPT to A.P. Wadsworth, 4 November 1944. Wadsworth Papers, *Manchester Guardian* Archives, B/T19/32. Quoted in Burk, *Troublemaker*, p. 237.

116   *Time and Tide*, 23, 10, 7 March 1942, pp. 195–96. *A Personal History*, p. 166. Dame Rebecca West (1892–1983) was a journalist and distinguished author.

117   Carl Rollyson, *Rebecca West: A Saga of the Century*, London, Hodder & Stoughton, 1995, pp. 182–83 and 187–88.

118   *A Personal History*, p. 158.

119   Bogdan C. Novak, *Trieste, 1941–1954: The Ethnic, Political and Ideological Struggle*, Chicago, University of Chicago Press, 1970, pp. 1–160.

120   *A Personal History*, p. 173. Novak, *Trieste*, pp. 102–5 and 127.

121   'Trieste or Trst?', *New Statesman and Nation*, 28, 720, 9 December 1944, pp. 386–87.

122   A.J.P. Taylor, 'Postscript (1949)' to 'Trieste' in his *From Napoleon to Stalin: Comments on European History*, London, Hamish Hamilton, 1950, pp. 207–8 (with the pamphlet reproduced pp. 179–207). The pamphlet was published in London by the Yugoslav Information Office, 1945, 32 pages and a map. It was the only previously reprinted piece in Taylor, *Struggles for Supremacy*, pp. 324–46.

123   Conversation with AJPT, 29 November 1976. He did not identify the man, by then a professor, but observed: 'Not that he supplied much information for it.'

124   Wadsworth to AJPT, 24 January, 24 April and 6 May 1945. AJPT to 'AP', 23 April [1945]. Wadsworth Papers, *Manchester Guardian* Archives, B/T19/37, 43, 44 and 46.

125   AJPT to 'AP', 3 December 1944; ibid., T/19/35.

126   Sayer, *Jack*, p. 277.

127   AJPT to T. Blewitt, 28 January [1942]. T. Blewitt to AJPT, 19 February 1942. BBC Archives, AJPT Radio File 1, 1942–46 (hereafter BBC and file). Trevor Blewitt was born in Simla, India in 1900, was a newspaper correspondent in Geneva, Prague and Warsaw and translated with his wife Phyllis some 20 books from German.

128   *A Personal History*, p. 165.

129   Anne Harris to AJPT, 12 March 1942. AJPT to T. Blewitt, 14 March 1942. Memorandum by Lloyd Williams, 16 March 1942. Further questions were sent to him in small batches after being received for his second broadcast. A. Harris to AJPT, 26 March 1942. BBC Radio File 1.

130   AJPT to T. Blewitt, 4 September 1942; BBC Radio File 1.

131   T. Blewitt to AJPT, 7 December 1942; ibid. For a list of most of AJPT's radio and TV broadcasts, see Wrigley, *Taylor Bibliography*, pp. 557–604.

132   Churchill to A. Eden, 20 September 1941. Martin Gilbert, *The Churchill War Papers*, Vol. 3, London, Heinemann, 2000, p. 1238.

133   A Pók, 'British Manual on Hungary in 1944', in Pók (ed.), *The Fabric of Modern Europe*, pp. 201–7 (at p. 202).

134   *A Personal History*, p. 171. In about 1977 he asked me to look out for a copy in the Public Record Office (when I was preparing the bibliography).

135   This follows Pók, 'British Manual', pp. 203–4. Carlile Aylmer Macartney (1895–1978) served in the First World War and married Nedella Mamarchev,

daughter of a Bulgarian colonel. He was acting Vice-Consul in Vienna, 1921–25, worked in the Intelligence Department of the League of Nations, 1928–36, was Research Fellow at All Souls, 1936–65 and Montagu Burton Professor of International Relations, Edinburgh University, 1951–57. He was author of many books on Hungary and on the Habsburg Empire and was highly critical of Taylor's second edition of *The Habsburg Monarchy*. He became a Fellow of the British Academy in 1965.

136   *Time and Tide*, 23, 44, 31 October 1942, p. 873.

137   A.J.P. Taylor, 'Horthy-Culture', a review of *October Fifteenth: A History of Modern Hungary 1929–1945*, 2 vols., in *New Statesman and Nation*, 53, 1360, 6 April 1957, and reprinted in Taylor, *British Prime Ministers and Other Essays*, pp. 306–8.

138   F.L. Carsten, 'From Revolutionary Socialism to German History', in Peter Alter (ed.), *Out of the Third Reich: Refugee Historians in Britain*, London, I.B. Tauris, 1998, pp. 31–32. Burk, *Troublemaker*, p. 181. Francis Ludwig Carsten (1911–98) was Senior Demy (Foundation Scholar on half a Fellow's salary), Magdalen College, 1942, taught at London University from 1947, and was Masaryk Professor of Central European History, 1961–78.

139   Major General West's minute on memorandum, 11 October 1944. File on the German handbook (in a series originally called ABC Booklets), 1943–44. National Archives, FO 898/480. A.J.P. Taylor's review of E.J. Passant, *A Short History of Germany 1815–1945*, in *New Statesman*, 57, 1460, 7 March 1959. Ernest James Passant (1890–1959) was a Fellow and Lecturer in History at Sidney Sussex College, Cambridge, 1919–46, served in the Intelligence Division of the Admiralty, 1941–45, was Head of the German section of the Research Department of the Foreign Office, 1945–46, and then Director of Research, Librarian and Keeper of the Papers at the Foreign Office. Sir Denis William Brogan (1900–74) was a Fellow and tutor at Corpus Christi College, Oxford, then Professor of Political Science, Cambridge University, 1939–68, and author of many books on French and US politics.

140   On Rowse, see Ollard, *Man of Contradictions*, pp. 174–75 and 179–80.

141   AJPT to H. Hamilton, 11 March 1944. Hamish Hamilton Papers, University of Bristol Library. Quoted in Burk, *Troublemaker*, p. 250. He referred to W.C. Sellar and R.J. Yeatman, *1066 and All That*, London, Methuen, 1930, the long-popular spoof on British history.

142   A good example of his careful pursuit of an attractive author was his signing of Georges Simenon in early 1954. Pierre Assouline, *Georges Simenon: A Biography*, London, Chatto & Windus, 1998, pp. 292–93.

143   AJPT to H. Hamilton, 17 May and 13 September 1944; Hamish Hamilton Papers.

144   AJPT to Daniel Macmillan, 20 October 1944. Macmillan Archives. Quoted in Burk, *Troublemaker*, p 241.

145   Review of *Deutschtum im Völkerraum*, Vol. 1, *International Affairs*, 18, 6, November–December 1939, p. 856.

146   *Oxford Magazine*, 61, 1, 15 October 1942. Partly quoted in Wrigley, *Taylor Bibliography*, pp. 15 and 286, and in Burk, *Troublemaker*, pp. 250–51. George Peabody Gooch (1873–1968), like Alan Taylor, combined academic writing with a commitment to take history to a wider audience. He was president of the Historical Association 1922–25 and, for very long, chairman of its Central London branch.

147   On British propaganda, see, for example, M.L. Sanders and P.M. Taylor, *British Propaganda during the First World War*, London, Longman, 1982, and, on 'Prussianism' in occupied Belgium, see John Horne and Alan Kramer, *German*

Atrocities 1914: A History of Denial, New Haven and London, Yale University Press, 2001.

148   A.L. Rowse, 'What is Wrong with the Germans', reprinted in his *The End of an Epoch*, London, Macmillan, 1947, pp. 181–92. Alfred Leslie Rowse (1903–97) was born in Cornwall, a Fellow and Emeritus Fellow of All Souls College, Oxford, from 1925, Fellow of the British Academy, 1958, and Companion of Honour, 1997. He was Labour parliamentary candidate for Penryn and Falmouth, 1931 and 1935.

149   Rohan Butler, *The Roots of National Socialism 1783–1933*, London, Faber & Faber, 1941, pp. 9–10 and 294–99. Rohan D'Olier Butler (1917–96) was a Fellow of All Souls, 1938–84, and then Emeritus Fellow. He worked for the Ministry of Information, 1939–41 and 1942–44. He was an editor of the inter-war Documents on British Foreign Policy, 1945–65, and British Policy Overseas, 1973–82.

150   A.J.P. Taylor, review of *Germany's Three Reichs*, in *Oxford Magazine*, 63, 31, 1, March 1945, pp. 183–84. He reviewed Edmond Vermeil, *La Racisme Allemande*, in *International Affairs*, 18, 4 July–August 1939, p. 571. Rowse reprinted his reviews of Vermeil's 1938 and 1941 books in 'Germany: The Problem of Europe', in Rowse, *The End of an Epoch*, pp. 193–203. F.A. Hayek reviewed Vermeil's *Germany's Three Reichs* in *Time and Tide*, 24 March 1945. Vermeil went to the USA. A sociological approach was taken by Norbert Elias (1897–1990) in his 1939 German edition of *The Civilizing Process* and in his 1989 German edition of *The Germans*, Oxford, Polity Press, 1996.

151   *A Personal History*, p. 172. Eckart Kehr (1902–33) was based in Berlin and died in Washington, DC, on a research visit. Professor Albert Sorel (1842–1906) was secretary-general to the President of the French Senate 1876–1902 and a historian of international reputation. Namier repeatedly praised Sorel to his students, so he may have encouraged Taylor to read him; D.A. Farnie to CJW, 19 April 2005.

152   In 1941 essays reprinted in Lewis Namier, *Conflicts*, London, Macmillan, 1942. Colley, *Namier*, pp. 37–40. Sisman, *A.J.P. Taylor*, pp. 153–54.

153   *Manchester Guardian*, 29 December 1944, p. 3.

154   *Manchester Guardian*, 29 and 30 March 1944, both at pp. 4 and 8. Reprinted in Taylor, *From Napoleon to Stalin*, pp. 83–88 and *Europe: Grandeur and Decline*, Harmondsworth, Penguin, 1967, pp. 121–26. It is one of his slighter pieces.

155   A.J.P. Taylor, 'East Prussia: Is It a 'Junker Stronghold'?', *Manchester Guardian*, 18 July 1944, pp. 4 and 8.

156   Reviews of Karl Otten, *A Combine of Aggression*, and Julius Braunthal, *Need Germany Survive?*, in *Manchester Guardian*, 17 June 1942, p. 3, and 25 June 1944, p. 3.

157   Review of Thomas Mann, *Order of the Day*, and S.H. Steinberg, *A Short History of Germany*, in *Manchester Guardian*, 25 August 1943, p. 3, and 18 October 1944, p. 3.

158   Taylor, *The Course of German History*, London, Hamish Hamilton, 1945, p. 208.

159   Ibid., p. 160.

160   Ibid., p. 110.

161   Ibid., p. 70, 87 and 169. AJPT to H. Hamilton, 27 December 1944; Hamish Hamilton Papers.

162   Taylor, *The Course of German History*, p. 177.

163   Ibid., p. 163.

164   Ibid., p. 67, 70 and 114. A.J.P. Taylor, *The Struggle for Mastery in Europe 1848–1918*, Oxford, Clarendon Press, 1954, p. xxv. In December 1938 he had made Clapham's third volume of his *Economic History of Great Britain* (1938)

his first choice as book of the year, stating 'no greater work of scholarship has been produced in our time'. *Manchester Guardian, Gift Book Supplement*, 1938, p.xvii.

165   Taylor, *The Course of German History*, p.68.

166   AJPT to H. Hamilton, 17 May and 13 September [1944]; Hamish Hamilton Papers. He kept pressing on the issue of maps in December, January and February.

167   AJPT to H. Hamilton, 15 February 1945; ibid.

168   Review in *Sunday Times*, July 1945; reprinted in Rowse, *The End of an Epoch*, pp.213–16.

169   AJPT to H. Hamilton, 9 July 1945; loc. cit.

170   Lewis Namier, 'Dream-Play of the German Century: Power for Power's Sake', *Times Literary Supplement*, 2278, 29 September 1945, pp.457–59. The review, omitting all but the first fifteen and last fourteen words of this quotation was reprinted in L.B. Namier, *Facing East*, London, Hamish Hamilton, 1947, pp.25–40.

171   R. Birley in *International Affairs*, 22, 1 January 1946, pp.136–37. Sigmund Neumann in *American Historical Review*, 52, 4, July 1947, pp.730–33. Wrigley, *Taylor Bibliography*, pp.38 and 74–75.

172   H. Russell Williams, 'A.J.P. Taylor', in H.A. Schmitt (ed.), *Historians of Modern Europe*, Baton Rouge, Louisiana State Press, 1971, pp.78–94. Cole, *Traitor at the Gate*, p.102.

173   This is vividly recalled in the autobiography of the British historian Donald Read (1930–), who was president of the Historical Association, 1985–88, *A Manchester Boyhood in the Thirties and Forties: Growing up in War and Peace*, Lampeter, Edwin Mellen Press, 2003, pp.125–29.

174   The most influential critique of the *Sonderweg* thesis was by David Blackbourn and Geoff Eley in 1980, translated into English under the title *The Peculiarities of German History*, Oxford, Blackwell, 1984. Also influential and notably lucid and incisive are Richard J. Evans, *In Hitler's Shadow: West German Historians and the Attempt to Escape the Nazi Past*, London, I.B.Tauris, 1989; *Rethinking German History*, London, Harper Collins Academic (notably Part 1); and *Rereading German History 1800–1996*, London, Routledge, 1997 (especially 'Whatever Became of the Sonderweg?'). In another approach to the debate, David Calleo, *The German Problem Reconsidered*, Cambridge, Cambridge University Press, 1978, pp.58–59 and 212–13, aspects of Alan Taylor's work were discussed favourably.

175   There is a large literature on the Fischer debate. For recent reflections on it and its impact, see James Retallack, 'Wilhelmine Germany', and Holger H. Herwig, 'Industry, Empire and the First World War', in Gordon Martel (ed.), *Modern Germany Reconsidered 1870–1945*, London, Routledge, 1992, pp.33–53 and 54–73, and Stefan Berger, *The Search for Normality: National Identity and Historical Consciousness in Germany since 1800*, Oxford, Berghahn Books, 1997, Chapter 3.

176   Points made, for instance, by Hans-Ulrich Wehler in 'Like a Thorn in the Flesh' ('Wei ein Stachel im Fleisch'), *Die Zeit*, 24 May 1996, p.40. For a fascinating collection of the responses by Wehler and other German critics, see Robert R. Shandley, *Unwilling Germans? The Goldhagen Debate*, Minneapolis, University of Minnesota Press, 1998 (with Wehler's translated essay at pp.93–104). For a powerful critique, see Richard J. Evans, 'Anti-Semitism, Ordinary Germans and the "Longest Hatred"', in his *Rereading German History*, pp.149–81.

177   Wehler, 'Like a Thorn', p.98.

178   Ibid., p.98. R.J. Evans, 'Wilhelm II's Germany and the History', in his *Rethinking German History*, pp.26 and 50–51.

179   AJPT to Éva Haraszti, 4 December 1970 and 22 April 1973. A.J.P. Taylor, *Letters to Éva*, pp.24 and 124.
180   Stefan Berger, *The Search for Normality*, p.235. *Daily Telegraph*, 24 April 1996, quoted and commented on by Evans, 'Anti-Semitism, Ordinary Germans', pp.167–68.
181   AJPT to H. Hamilton, 1 September [1945]; Hamish Hamilton Papers.
182   B. Disraeli to his sister Sarah, 23 June 1834; J.W. Gunn, J. Matthews, D.M. Schurmann and M.G. Wiebe, *Benjamin Disraeli Letters*, Vol. 1, Toronto, Toronto University Press, 1982, p.416.
183   AJPT to H. Hamilton, 3 July [1945]; Hamish Hamilton Papers.
184   *A Personal History*, pp.171–72. Sir Heinz Koeppler (1912–79) worked for the Political Intelligence Department of the Foreign Office, 1940–42, and the Political Warfare Executive, 1943–45, and was Warden of Witton Park, 1946–77. He wrote, with Mark Garnett, *A Lasting Peace* (1940).
185   AJPT to Mr Smith, 25 September (1943), and 10 February 1944 to Trevor Blewitt; BBC Archives.
186   At the end of 1944 9,602,137 households held radio licences. Asa Briggs, *The History of Broadcasting in the United Kingdom*, Vol. 3, *The War of Words 1939–1945*, Oxford, Oxford University Press, 1970, pp.47, 290–91, 503, 507–9 and 666, and Vol. 4, *Sound and Vision*, Oxford, Oxford University Press, 1979, p.581.
187   AJPT to Trevor [Blewitt], 15 January 1945; BBC Archives. Briggs, *The War of Words*, p.508. Ruth Dudley Edwards, *The Pursuit of Reason: The Economist 1843–1993*, London, Hamish Hamilton, pp.482 and 485. Donald McCullough (1901–78), not MacCullough, was a public relations officer to the Ministry of Agriculture before becoming question master of the Brains Trust. Local Brains Trusts sprang up all over Britain and McCullough wrote *How to Run a Brains Trust* (1947). Barbara Ward, later Lady Jackson (1914–82), was a university extension lecturer, 1936–39, assistant editor of *The Economist*, 1939–50, a governor of the BBC, 1946–50, and later Schweitzer Professor of International Economic Development, Columbia University.
188   Blewitt to AJPT, 13 February 1945; BBC Archives. Arnot Robertson was involved in the production of the programme.
189   *A Personal History*, pp.172–73. Blewitt to AJPT, 21 August 1944 and 13 February 1945, and AJPT to Blewitt, 23 August 1944; BBC Archives. Wrigley, *Taylor Bibliography*, p.15.
190   A.P. Wadsworth to AJPT, 15 May 1944. AJPT to Wadsworth, 19 May [1944]; *Manchester Guardian* Archives. Partly quoted, Sisman, *A.J.P. Taylor*, p.156.
191   A.J.P. Taylor, 'A Feudal Society', *Manchester Guardian*, 23 March 1944, p.4 (a leader is an editorial statement).
192   Published as 'What Shall We Do with Germany?', Parts 1–3, in *The Listener*, 19 and 26 October and 7 December 1944. Robert Gilbert Vansittart, 1st Baron (1881–1957), was Permanent Under-Secretary of State for Foreign Affairs 1930–38, and was sidelined by Neville Chamberlain to Chief Diplomatic Adviser to the Foreign Secretary, 1938–41. His *Black Record* (1940) was a condemnation of Germans and Germany.
193   Transcript, as broadcast 19.30–20.05 hours, 1 December 1944, p.5; BBC Archives.
194   AJPT to Wadsworth, 5 October [1944]; *Manchester Guardian* Archives. Quoted in Sisman, *A.J.P. Taylor*, p.150.
195   Edwards, *The Pursuit of Reason*, pp.482–83. Barbara Ward's critique of Nicolson was in *The Economist*, 27 March 1943.
196   AJPT letter to *New Statesman and Nation*, 28, 16, 714, 28 October 1944, p.245. The first passage is quoted in Wrigley, *Taylor Bibliography*, p.16. C.A. Smith

lived at 81 Arcadian Gardens, London N22, and was an expert on European social democracy.

197 C.A. Smith to *New Statesman and Nation*, 28, 17, 4 November 1944, p.303.

198 AJPT to *New Statesman and Nation*, 28, 18, 11 November 1944, p.321.

199 C.A. Smith to *New Statesman and Nation*, 28, 19, 18 November 1944, p.336. Sisman, *A.J.P. Taylor*, p.151.

200 Kingsley Martin to AJPT, 21 and 22 November 1944; Kingsley Martin Papers. Sisman, *A.J.P. Taylor*, pp.151–52.

201 The review of *Maisky* was in the *Manchester Guardian*, 3 May 1944, p.3. Wadsworth to AJPT, 28 May 1944; Wadsworth Papers, *Manchester Guardian* Archives. George Bilainkin (1903–81) was an author and journalist, who had been a Special Correspondent in Moscow in 1942.

202 The third of the series was recorded on 2 November and broadcast on 1 December 1944. Transcript, pp.11, 12 and 14; BBC Archives.

203 In the series 'Friday Discussion: Questions in the Air', transmitted 7.30–8.00pm, 12 April 1946. Transcript, pp.8, 14–5, 17 and 21; BBC Archives. Rt. Hon. Sir Hugh Charles Patrick Joseph Fraser (1918–84) was MP for Stone and later Stafford, 1945–84, and first husband of Antonia Pakenham.

204 A.P. Wadsworth to AJPT, 7 August, 13 September and 9 October 1945. *Manchester Guardian* Archives, B/T19/55, 56 and 60. Sisman, *A.J.P. Taylor*, p.163.

205 AJPT to A.P. Wadsworth (no date but early December 1945). Ibid., B/T19/63.

206 AJPT to A.P. Wadsworth, 8 June [1946]. Ibid., B/T19/73.

207 A.J.P. Taylor, *A Personal History*, pp.182–83. Sisman, *A.J.P. Taylor*, pp.163–64.

208 AJPT to A.P. Wadsworth, 13 July [1946]. *Manchester Guardian* Archives, B/T19/74.

209 A.P. Wadsworth to AJPT, 21 July 1946. Ibid., B/T19/74. His final sentence was amended to 'If our international economic policy is negative we shall drive all Central Europe (and most of Western Europe too) into the arms of the Communists'. The essays were published in the *Manchester Guardian*, 24, 25 and 29 July 1946, pp.4 and 6 in each issue. They are reprinted as 'Czechoslovakia Today (July 1946)' in Taylor, *Struggles for Supremacy*, pp.347–55.

210 *A Personal History*, pp.186–87.

211 Trevor Blewitt to AJPT, 5 April 1945, BBC Archives. AJPT to Blewitt, 10 June 1945. The fourth speaker was the chairman, Edward Montgomery.

212 Transcript of 'Do Alliances Help World Peace?', broadcast 19.30–20.00 hours on BBC Home Service, 20 July 1945; BBC Archives.

213 A.J.P. Taylor, 'Crusading Civil Servant', review of Norman Rose, *Vansittart*, London, Heinemann, 1978, in *Observer*, 17 September 1978, p.34.

214 *Daily Telegraph*, 7 March 1977.

215 Record of telephone call by Dr Massey, 24 September 1945. Memorandum by R.A. Rendall, 24 September 1945. BBC Archives, Taylor Radio File 1, 1942–47. Alan Taylor was fascinated when I showed him 40 sides of notes of this and other BBC records relating to his broadcasts and we drafted carefully a letter on 6 October 1978 to secure permission to quote this material in the introduction to Wrigley, *Taylor Bibliography* (published at pp.19–22). See also Sisman, *A.J.P. Taylor*, pp.169–71, and Burk, *Troublemaker*, pp.377–80.

216 G.R. Barnes memorandum, 1 October 1945. R.A. Rendall memorandum, 30 October 1945. BBC Archives. *A Personal History*, p.185.

217 Transcript of 'What Is a Great Power?', 20 March 1946; BBC Archives.

218 AJPT to Trevor Blewitt, 14 February 1946. Trevor Blewitt to Assistant Controller (Talks), 15 February 1946. BBC Archives.

219   Transcript of 'World Affairs: The Middle East', pp.3, 4 and 6–7, broadcast 21.15–21.30 hours.

220   Memorandum by Trevor Blewitt, 20 May 1946; BBC Archives.

221   AJPT to Trevor Blewitt, 25 October 1946; BBC Archives.

222   A.J.P. Taylor, 'The Need for Controversy' and 'Britain's relations with the United States' in *The Listener*, 36, 935, 12 and 19 December 1946, pp.834–35, 873 and 889.

223   House of Commons Debates, 431, 11 December 1946, cols. 1237–40 and 1285. Henry George Strauss, 1st Baron Conesford (1892–1974), was MP for Norwich and then Norwich South, 1935–45 and 1950–55, and for the Combined Universities, 1946–50. Anthony Montague Browne, *Long Sunset*, London, Cassel, 1995, p.45.

224   AJPT to Harman Grizewood, 4 and 22 January 1947; BBC Archives, Taylor Radio File 2, 1947–49. Burk, *Troublemaker*, pp.379–80.

225   He visited Prague on the way back. AJPT to A.P. Wadsworth, 16 March [1947]; Wadsworth Papers, *Manchester Guardian* Archives, B/T19/81.

226   *A Personal History*, p.186.

227   A.P. Wadsworth to AJPT, 13 and 14 May 1947; Wadsworth Papers, *Manchester Guardian* Archives, B/T19/85 and 86.

228   A.J.P. Taylor, 'Impressions of Yugoslavia', in *Manchester Guardian*, 8 and 9 May 1947, p.6 (both issues).

229   'Yugoslavia in 1947' in the series 'European Scene', first broadcast on the African Service, 9 June 1947. Transcript, BBC Archives.

230   *A Personal History*, p.183. Conversation with Margaret Taylor, 20 December 1976. On Myra Hess and the National Gallery concerts, see Angus Calder, *The People's War* (London, Jonathan Cape, 1959), Panther paperback, 1971, p.431, and Robert Hewison, *Under Siege: Literary Life in London 1939–45* (London, Weidenfeld & Nicolson, 1977), Quartet paperback, 1979, pp.161 and 166. Dame Julia Myra Hess (1890–1965).

231   AJPT to Malcolm Muggeridge, 10 July 1945; Muggeridge Papers.

232   *A Personal History*, pp.177–78.

233   Fitzgibbon, *Life of Dylan Thomas*, p.276. Thomas and Tremlett, *Caitlin*, pp.98–99. Sisman, *A.J.P. Taylor*, pp.164–67. Burk, *Troublemaker*, pp.188–91.

234   Caitlin's frank account of her tumultuous marriage with Dylan Thomas was published posthumously. Caitlin Thomas, *Double Drink Story: My Life with Dylan Thomas*, New York, Viking, 1997, and London, Virago, 1998.

235   *A Personal History*, pp.184–85. Dylan Thomas to John Arlott, 22 July 1946, in Paul Ferris (ed.), *Dylan Thomas: The Collected Letters*, London, Macmillan, 1985, p.596.

236   Dylan Thomas' letter with his comments on her verse (no date) is published in Ferris (ed.), *Collected Letters*, pp.578–79 and 929–33.

237   Dylan Thomas to his parents, 11 April 1947, and to Edith Sitwell, 11 April 1947, in Ferris (ed.), *Collected Letters*, pp.621–24. C. Thomas, *Double Drink Story*, p.108.

238   *A Personal History*, p.185. Trevor Blewitt considered her script but rejected it on 28 June 1947; BBC Archives.

239   Dylan Thomas to Margaret Taylor, 12 April and 4 June 1947 in Ferris (ed.), *Collected Letters*, pp.625–26 and 634–36.

240   Thomas and Tremlett, *Caitlin*, pp.102–5. *A Personal History*, pp.191–92. James Nashold and George Tremlett, *The Death of Dylan Thomas*, London, Mainstream, 1997, p.78. In 1948 Dylan Thomas earned £2482 but this did not help Caitlin nor stop him scrounging money from others. Lycett, *Dylan Thomas*, p.257.

241   These days it is the blackest crime of biography not to discuss such matters at great length. However, it is beyond proof now. Caitlin Thomas thought it improbable. Margaret Taylor was convincing to at least one friend some twenty years later in confirming Caitlin's view, but any view now is speculation as to the likely truth of any remembered comment. Thomas and Tremlett, *Caitlin*, p. 99. Private information. For a similar view, see Lycett, *Dylan Thomas*, p. 250.

Chapter 5

1   CJW discussion with K.H.D. Haley, 9 March 1978, and John Grigg, 21 January 1993. A. Gollin to CJW, 4 February 1977. Kenneth Harold Dobson Haley (1920–97) taught at Sheffield University, 1947–82, being Professor of Modern History, 1962–82. John Edward Poynder Grigg (1924–2001) was a journalist, editor, historian and politician. Alfred M. Gollin (1926–2005) was official historian of the *Observer*, and Professor of History, University of California, Santa Barbara, 1967–94.

2   AJPT to Trevor Blewitt, 18 October 1945; BBC Archives, Taylor Radio File 1.

3   *A Personal History*, pp. 178–79. Burk, *Troublemaker*, p. 183. Thomas Sherrer Ross Boase (1898–1974) was Professor of the History of Art and Director of the Courtauld Institute, 1937–47, and President of Magdalen College, 1947–68.

4   Wrigley, *Taylor Bibliography*, pp. 122 and 353. Review of Bullock's *Hitler: A Study in Tyranny*, in *Manchester Guardian*, 28 October 1952, p. 4.

5   *Manchester Guardian*, 1 December 1939, *Gift Books Supplement*, p. vii. *Time and Tide*, 23, 30, 25 July 1942, p. 604. *Manchester Guardian*, 24 July 1942, p. 3.

6   W.P. Crozier to AJPT, 19 July 1942. AJPT to Crozier, 21 July [1942]; *Manchester Guardian* Archives, B/T19/2 and 3.

7   *Manchester Guardian*, 5 April 1946, p. 4, and 10 January 1948, p. 4.

8   Isaac Kramnick and Barry Sheerman, *Harold Laski: A Life on the Left*, London, Hamish Hamilton, 1993, pp. 279–80. *A Personal History*, p. 189.

9   AJPT to George Barnes, 4 November 1947. Anna Kallin to AJPT, 22 December 1947; BBC Archives, Taylor Radio File 2.

10   Transcript of 'An Exercise in Contemporary History', 13 January 1948; BBC Archives.

11   L.B. Namier, *Diplomatic Prelude 1938–1939*, London, Macmillan, 1948, pp. v–vi. Linda Colley, *Namier*, p. 28.

12   *Manchester Guardian*, 23 November 1946, pp. 4 and 6; 29 March 1947, p. 4; 19 August 1947, p. 4; 13 February 1948, p. 4; and 23 June 1948, p. 4. *Critique*, 2, 10 March 1947, pp. 240–51, and 3, 4, 29 October 1948, pp. 920–30. A.P. Wadsworth to AJPT, 14 January 1947; *Manchester Guardian* Papers B/T19/80. CJW discussion with AJPT about his publications, 29 November 1976. AJPT to CJW, 25 March 1977. Georges Bataille (1867–1962) worked as French literary agent for Hamish Hamilton for several months in 1948. Michael Surya, *Georges Bataille*, London, Verso, 2002, p. 565.

13   *New Statesman and Nation*, 41, 1058, 16 June 1951, p. 686. *Manchester Guardian*, 19 August 1947, p. 4.

14   *Manchester Guardian* 15 May 1948, p. 4.

15   Review of E.L. Woodward and Rohan Butler (eds.), *Documents on British Foreign Policy*, Second Series, Vol. 1, in *Times Literary Supplement*, 235, 12 April 1947, pp. 165–66. Reprinted in Taylor, *Struggles for Supremacy, Diplomatic Essays*, pp. 161–67.

16   Llewellyn Woodward's almost manic hostility to Taylor is witnessed by his response to Taylor's acknowledgement to him in *The Struggle for Mastery in Europe* (1954) in much correspondence in the Oxford University Press Archives. See Sisman, *A.J.P. Taylor*, pp.224–25, Burk, *Troublemaker*, pp.270–74, and Wilson, 'Governments, Historians and "Historical Engineering"', pp.1–27. AJPT to CJW, 12 May 1978. *A Personal History*, p.180. Sisman, *A.J.P. Taylor*, p.180. Nicholas Barker, *Stanley Morison*, London, Macmillan, 1972, pp.41–46. D. May, *Critical Times: The History of the Times Literary Supplement*, London, Harper Collins, 2001, pp.295–97. Butterfield to AJPT, 2 August 1949; quoted in C.T. McIntire, *Herbert Butterfield: Historian as Dissenter*, New Haven and London, Yale University Press, 2004, p.170 (and see also pp.168–70). Sir Herbert Butterfield (1900–79) was a Fellow of Peterhouse College, Cambridge, 1923–55, and its Master, 1955–68, Professor of Modern History, 1944–63, Regius Professor of Modern History, 1963–68, and Vice-Chancellor of Cambridge University, 1959–61.

17   Review of the German diplomatic documents, Series D, 1, 1937–39, in *New Statesman and Nation*, 38, 980, 17 December 1949, p.730. Reprinted in Taylor, *Struggles for Supremacy*, pp.185–87.

18   Review of German diplomatic documents, Series D, 2, 1937–38, in *New Statesman and Nation*, 39, 997, 15 April 1950, pp.434 and 436. Wrigley, *Taylor Bibliography*, pp.39–40.

19   AJPT to Mr King, 28 December [1945], and to Hamilton, 4, 12 and 19 January [1946]; Hamish Hamilton Papers.

20   AJPT to Hamilton, 30 January [1946]; ibid.

21   AJPT to Hamilton, 9 October [1946]; ibid.

22   AJPT to Hamilton, 3 and 8 November [1946]; ibid.

23   AJPT to A.P. Wadsworth, 11 August [1947]; *Manchester Guardian* Archives B/T19/93. AJPT to Hamilton [postcard of August 1947]. Hamilton to AJPT, 18 February 1948. AJPT to Hamilton, 19 February [1948]. AJPT to Roger Machell, 25 March 1947; Hamish Hamilton Papers.

24   AJPT to Hamilton, 8 November [1946]; ibid.

25   AJPT to Hamilton, 25 February 1948; ibid. Sisman, *A.J.P. Taylor*, p.177. See also Burk, *Troublemaker*, pp.241–45.

26   AJPT to Hamilton, 18 March 1948; Hamish Hamilton Papers.

27   *The Habsburg Monarchy*, 1941, p.16 and the 1948 version (Peregrine paperback), p.25 and Preface; also Wrigley, *Taylor Bibliography*, pp.70–71.

28   'The Austrian Empire', *Times Literary Supplement*, 2456, 26 February 1949, p.132 (by Henry Wickham Steed). C.A. Macartney, in *History*, 37, 125, October 1950, pp.273–74. Wrigley, *Taylor Bibliography*, pp.71–72.

29   Taylor often used the Gladstone quotation in lectures as well as in print; *The Struggle for Mastery in Europe*, p.284. Ilsa Barea, *Vienna: Legend And Reality*, London, Secker & Warburg, 1966; Pimlico paperback, 1992, pp.261 and 264. On the historiography of whether the Habsburg monarchy was doomed, see Steven Bellair, *Francis Joseph*, London, Longman, 1996.

30   Alan Sked, *The Decline and Fall of the Habsburg Monarchy 1815–1918*, 2nd edition, London, Longman, 2001, pp.6 and 278–323. Alan Sked (1945–) was the founder of the United Kingdom Independence Party (1993) and is a leading European historian at the London School of Economics.

31   AJPT to Hamish Hamilton, 4 April 1946; Hamish Hamilton Papers.

32   A.P. Wadsworth to AJPT, 2 May 1946; *Manchester Guardian* Archives, B/T19/70. *Faith in France: A Selection of Leading Articles published in the Manchester Guardian between June 1940 and September 1944*, Manchester, John Sherratt, 1946,

pp. 214–16. Stewart A. Weaver, *The Hammonds. A Marriage in History*, Stanford, Stanford University Press, 1997, p. 250. John Lawrence Le Breton Hammond (1872–1949) was a journalist and an outstanding historian.

33 In conversation with CJW, 14 June 1977 and also 9 January 1978, after the historian Peter Clarke had asked him which leaders he had written for the *Manchester Guardian*. AJPT to P. Clarke, 20 January 1978. P. Clarke to AJPT, 24 January 1978. Taylor Papers, HRRC, Austin, Texas. See also P.F. Clarke, *Liberals and Social Democrats*, Cambridge, Cambridge University Press, 1978, p. 333, and Wrigley, *Taylor Bibliography*, pp. 169–72.

34 AJPT to Hamilton, 7 January [1947]; Hamish Hamilton Papers.

35 AJPT to A.P. Wadsworth, 16 March, 15 May and 17 September [1947]. Wadsworth to AJPT, 26 September 1947.

36 AJPT to Hamish Hamilton, 13 March [1949], and to Machell, 24 and 28 May 1947; ibid.

37 AJPT to Machell, 16 July [1947]; ibid.

38 A.J.P. Taylor, *From Napoleon to Stalin: Comments on European History*, London, Hamish Hamilton, 1950, p. 9.

39 Entry for 13 April 1948. Bright-Holmes (ed.), *Like It Was*, p. 267. On Orwell and his list of 135 names, see D.J. Taylor, *Orwell: The Life*, London, Chatto & Windus, 2003, pp. 409–10, and also Gordon Bowker, *George Orwell*, London, Little, Brown, 2003.

40 Kathy Burk prints what may be a transcript of his speech, *Troublemaker*, pp. 193–94. A good account is George Weidenfeld, 'The Wroclaw Congress: A Watershed', chapter 9 of *Remembering My Good Friends*, London, Harper Collins, pp. 174–85. W.J. West, *The Quest for Graham Greene*, London, Weidenfeld & Nicolson, 1997, pp. 152–53. See also the contemporary accounts by Taylor, 'Intellectuals at Wroclaw: A Strange Congress' in *Manchester Guardian*, 2 September 1948, p. 4, and reprinted as 'Intellectuals Betray Liberty at Wroclaw' in *Sydney Morning Herald*, 9 September 1948, p. 2, and by Kingsley Martin, 'Hyenas and Other Reptiles', *New Statesman and Nation*, 36, 913, 4 September 1948, pp. 187–88 (which also contains Taylor's and the dissenting minority's letter, p. 195). See also *A Personal History*, pp. 192–93; Wrigley, *Taylor Bibliography*, pp. 21–22; and Sisman, *A.J.P. Taylor*, pp. 188–91.

41 'The Western Tradition: Totalitarianism', broadcast 7 July 1948 in English on the BBC radio European Service and also in Portuguese and Spanish on the Latin American Service. Published as 'Ancestry of the "New Democracies"' in *The Listener*, 40, 1016, 15 July 1948, pp. 92–93.

42 *Times*, 17 September 1948, p. 5.

43 Diary entry for 27 August 1948 in Bright-Holmes (ed.), *Like It Was*, p. 295. A.P. Wadsworth to AJPT, 7 September 1948 and 28 March 1949, AJPT to Wadsworth, 27 March 1949 and 29 July [1950]; *Manchester Guardian* Archives, B/T19/95, 141, 142a and 186. Ilya Ehrenburg (1891–1967) lived in Paris for many years between 1909 and 1940 and was awarded the Order of Lenin in 1961. Taylor described his speech at Wroclaw as 'a sophisticated performance'.

44 A.J.P. Taylor, 'Introduction' to Reginald Reynolds (ed.), *British Pamphleteers*, Vol. 2, London, Allan Wingate, 1951, p. 14. John Middleton Murry, *The Price of Leadership*, London, Macmillan, 1939.

45 'A New Voice for Culture' (*Encounter*), *Listener*, 50, 1284, 8 October 1953, pp. 596 and 599. Wrigley, *Taylor Bibliography*, pp. 359–60. Sisman, *A.J.P. Taylor*, p. 215. Taylor, *From Napoleon to Stalin*, p. 10. 'An Unstable World', in *Spectator*, 184, 6364, 16 June 1950, pp. 830 and 832. Elizabeth Wiskemann (1901–71) was

a distinguished writer on contemporary history and Montague Burton Professor of International Relations, Edinburgh University, 1958–61. 'Comments On Modern Europe', *Times Literary Supplement*, 2527, 7 July 1950, pp.413–14. Edward Hallett Carr (1892–1982) worked in the Foreign Office 1916–36, was Wilson Professor of International Relations, University College of Wales, Aberystwyth, 1936–47, and Fellow of Trinity College, Cambridge, 1955–82.

46   Hamilton to AJPT, 16 November 1949; Hamish Hamilton Papers.

47   Almost certainly written by Roger Machell and approved by Taylor. *Rumours of Wars* was still in print in 1964.

48   'Contentious but Creative;', *Spectator*, 190, 6516, 15 May 1953, pp.639–40. Robert James Martin Wight (1913–72) was, earlier, on the staff of Chatham House, 1936–38 and 1946–49, and, later, Professor of History, University of Sussex, 1961–72. *American Historical Review*, 69, 3, April 1954, pp.590–91. 'Mr Taylor Rides Again', *New Statesman and Nation*, 44, 1135, 6 December 1952, p.698. Wrigley, *Taylor Bibliography*, pp.80–81. Sidney Bradshaw Fay (1876–1967) was Professor of History at Dartmouth College, 1902–14, Smith College, 1914–29, and Harvard University, 1929–46. His publications included *Origins of The World War*, 2 volumes, 1928, which doubted German war guilt.

49   'History and Journalism', *Times Literary Supplement*, 2655, 19 December 1952, p.847.

50   A.J.P. Taylor, 'Rational Marxism', *Manchester Guardian*, 13 June 1950, p.4; 'Beyond Good and Evil', *New Statesman and Nation*, 40, 1032, 16 December 1950, p.628; and 'Mr Carr Backs a Winner', *The Twentieth Century*, 150, 15 November 1951, pp.407–15 (yet he commended *The New Society* in the *Sunday Pictorial*, 30 September 1951, p.6).

51   Jonathan Haslam, *The Vices of Integrity: E.H. Carr 1892–1982*, London, Verso, 1999, pp.201–2; an outstanding biography.

52   In his Introduction to the fortieth anniversary edition of E.H. Carr, *What Is History?*, London, Palgrave, 2001, pp.xxiii–xxiv.

53   In 'History and Biography' in 1937 and 'History and Politics' 1939 in *Manchester Guardian*, 3 December 1937, p.xvii, and 1 December 1939, p.273. A.J.P. Taylor, 'Revolution in Practice', *New Statesman and Nation*, 43, 1098, 22 March 1951, p.350. Wrigley, *Taylor Bibliography*, pp.260, 273–74, 336 and 347.

54   Ignatieff, *Isaiah Berlin*, pp.174–75. Carr to Isaac Deutscher, 22 February 1954, quoted in Haslam, *Vices of Integrity*, p.168. His comment was probably influenced by Taylor reading extracts from Carlyle on the BBC's Third Programme on 4 July 1953 (with publication in *The Listener*, 50, 1272, 16 July 1953, pp.108–9).

55   'Modern European History', Oxford University Press memoranda of 8 April and 25 November 1947, 20 January and 3 June 1948. AJPT to D. Davin, 24 May [1949]; File OHME General, 1947–61, OUP Archive. For detailed accounts of OUP's dealings with Taylor on this book, see Sisman, *A.J.P. Taylor*, pp.218–25, and Burk, *Troublemaker*, pp.257–63.

56   AJPT to Davin, 16 October [1949]. Davin to Deakin, 21 October 1949; File OHME General, 1947–61, OUP Archive. Sir William Deakin (1913–2005), whose Second World War service included leading the first British Military Mission to Tito, 1943, was a Fellow and Tutor of Wadham College, Oxford, 1936–49, and Warden of St Antony's College, Oxford, 1950–68.

57   Dan Davin to A.C. Poole, 21 October 1953. Memorandum of Oxford History of Modern Europe meeting, 15 December 1955. File OHME General, 1947–61; OUP Archive.

58   Memorandum of Oxford History of Modern Europe meeting, 7 January 1955. Sir Llewellyn Woodward to Colin Roberts, 23 November 1954. Ibid. For more

details of Woodward's pressure on the OUP, see Sisman, *A.J.P. Taylor*, pp. 224–25, and Burk, *Troublemaker*, pp. 270–71.

59 A.J.P. Taylor, 'The Rise and Fall of "Pure" Diplomatic History', *Times Literary Supplement*, 2810, 6 January 1956, Supplement 'Historical Writing', pp. xxviii and xxx. Reprinted without the word 'Pure' in 1956, 1967 and 1993 collections of his essays.

60 Review of two diplomatic histories in *Time and Tide*, 23, 48, 28 November 1942, pp. 955–56.

61 Taylor, *The Struggle for Mastery in Europe*, pp. 111 and 273.

62 AJPT to Éva Haraszti, 18 October 1974. Taylor, *Letters to Éva*, p. 206. *A Personal History*, p. 198. Much of the second half of his autobiography was written in 1974–75.

63 AJPT to Dan Davin, 16 October 1949; OUP Archive. *A Personal History*, p. 197.

64 Review in *International Affairs*, 15, 6, November–December 1936, pp. 926–27.

65 *A Personal History*, pp. 207 and 240.

66 Asa Briggs, 'Before the Ball Was Over', *New Statesman and Nation*, 48, 1235, 6 November 1954, pp. 586 and 588. C.W. Crawley, review in *History*, 61, 141–43, 1956, pp. 263–64. Charles William Crawley (1899–1992) was a university Lecturer in History, Cambridge University, Vice Master of Trinity Hall, 1950–66. E.H. Carr, 'European Diplomatic History', *Times Literary Supplement*, 2756, 26 November 1954, pp. 749–50. Wrigley, *Taylor Bibliography*, pp. 83–84. Haslam, *Vices of Integrity*, pp. 206–7.

67 E.H. Carr, *What Is History?*, London, Macmillan, 1961, p. 47.

68 A.J.P. Taylor, 'Bismarck: The Man of German Destiny', *Manchester Guardian*, 30 July 1948, p. 4; reprinted in *From Napoleon to Stalin* (1950), pp. 71–74, and in *Europe: Grandeur and Decline* (1967), pp. 87–90.

69 Broadcast in the 'London forum' series twice on the General Overseas Category and also on the Pacific and on the North American Services, 16 and 17 July 1950. Transcript, BBC Written Archives. AJPT to Bill Ash (of BBC radio), 15 June 1950; AJP Taylor File 3, 1950–52. Hon Sir Harold George Nicolson (1886–1968), diplomat, National Labour MP for West Leicester 1930–45, biographer, historian and diarist. Review of Herbert Butterfield, *History and Human Relations* in *New Statesman and Nation*, 42, 1081, 24 November, pp. 594 and 596; reprinted as 'History without Morality' in A.J.P. Taylor, *Rumours of Wars* (1952), pp. 9–13.

70 A.J.P. Taylor, 'Singing History'. Review of Cornwell Rogers, *The Spirit Of Revolution in 1789* in *New Statesman and Nation*, 38, 961, 6 August 1949, p. 151.

71 'History in England', *Times Literary Supplement*, 2534, 25 August 1950, Supplement, pp. iv–v; reprinted in Taylor, *Rumours of Wars*, pp. 1–8.

72 'Moving with the Times'. Review of E.H. Carr, *What Is History?*, in the *Observer*, 22 October 1961, p. 30; reprinted in A.J.P. Taylor, *Politicians, Socialism and Historians*, London, Hamish Hamilton, 1980, pp. 53–55. 'How History Should Be Written' transcript, 1950.

73 AJPT to Hamish Hamilton, 21 May and 26 December 1947 and 21 January 1948; Hamish Hamilton Papers. Trevor Blewitt memorandum (regarding her proposed radio script on Yugoslavia), 26 June 1947; BBC Written Archives, A.J.P. Taylor Radio File 2, 1947–49.

74 Angela Lambert interview with Eve Crosland, 'My husband, his other wives, and Me', *Independent on Sunday*, 7 July 1991. Mary Evelyn Raven Crosland (25 December 1920–27 November 2000) was second daughter and third child of Joseph and Jesse Crosland. She qualified as a piano teacher in 1940 and

graduated in history at Westfield College, University of London, 1944. Daniel R. Taylor, 'Eve Crosland 1920–2000' (memorial leaflet), 5 December 2000.

75 AJPT to Roger Machell, 8 April [1948]. Hamish Hamilton Papers.

76 Malcolm Muggeridge diary, 21 December 1949; quoted in Sisman, *A.J.P. Taylor*, p.193. He asked Bill Ash to communicate with him via Eve's phone number in a letter, 1 August 1950; BBC Written Archives, A.J.P. Taylor Radio File 3, 1950–52.

77 Taylor tried hard to interest Hamish Hamilton in publishing two of Megret's novels, including *C'Était Écrit*. AJPT to Hamilton, 6 January [1949]. He also recommended Norman Cameron's wife, Elfrida, for checking German translations; ibid., 1 July 1949.

78 Sisman, *A.J.P. Taylor*, pp.198–99.

79 Daniel Taylor, 'Eve Crosland', p.2. Interviews with Sebastian Taylor, 27 June 2000, and Giles Taylor, 24 September 1999.

80 Burk, *Troublemaker*, p.200.

81 Angela Lambert interview, 'My Husband, His Other Wives, and Me', p.19. CJW discussion with John Grigg, 18 September 1990.

82 Alan Taylor was the youngest of these: Bertrand Russell (1872–1970), Sir Mortimer Wheeler (1890–1976), F.R. Leavis (1895–1978) and Lord Kenneth Clark (1903–83).

83 AJPT to Peter Laslett, 22 February 1948; BBC Written Archives, A.J.P. Taylor Radio File 2, 1947–49.

84 Peter Laslett to AJPT, 4 December 1947. AJPT to Laslett, 11 December [1947]. Lord Vansittart to Ronald Lewin, 28 December 1947, and to Mr Birch, 12 January 1948. BBC Written Archives, A.J.P. Taylor Radio File 2, 1947–49, and Vansittart Radio File 2, 1946–57. I am grateful to Richard Bird for drawing my attention to this file.

85 William Collin Brooks (1893–1959) was editor of the *Sunday Dispatch* and wrote of the 1930s in *The Devil's Decade* (1947). Henry Wilson Harris (1883–1955) was editor of the *Spectator*, 1932–53, and independent MP for Cambridge University, 1945–50. AJPT to Anna Kallin, 19 and 22 October 1949. Anna Kallin to AJPT, 9 November 1949. BBC Written Archives, A.J.P. Taylor Radio File 2, 1947–49. Crossman (ed.), *The God that Failed*. As well as Spender, the contributors were Arthur Koestler, Ignazio Silone, André Gide, Louis Fischer and Richard Wright. Of the last, an African-American author, Taylor commented: 'someone I've never heard of'.

86 There are excellent accounts of 'In the News' in Grace Wyndham Goldie, *Facing the Nation: Television and Politics*, London, Bodley Head, 1977, pp.68–78, and Asa Briggs, *The History of Broadcasting in the United Kingdom*, Vol. 4, *Sound and Vision*, Oxford, Oxford University Press, 1979, pp.599–616.

87 AJPT to Mrs Mary Adams, 13 December 1949. Grace Wyndham Goldie to AJPT, 6 January 1949 (in fact 1950). BBC Written Archives, A.J.P. Taylor, Television Talks File 1, 1949–62. Sisman, *A.J.P. Taylor*, pp.195–96. Burk, *Troublemaker*, p.383. Leonard Miall, *Inside the BBC: British Broadcasting Characters*, London, Weidenfeld & Nicolson, 1994, pp.72 and 138–39. Grace Wyndham Goldie (née Nisbet) (1900–86) was Assistant Head of Talks Television, 1954–62, and Head of Talks and Current Affairs, Television, 1962–63.

88 So AJPT told CJW on 3 October 1977. Michael Foot confirmed this in a conversation, 1 December 1990. Michael Foot (1913–) was editor of *Tribune*, 1948–52 and 1955–60, a Labour MP, 1945–55 and 1960–92, Secretary of State for Employment, 1974–76, Lord President of the Council and Leader of the House of Commons, 1976–79, and Leader of the Labour Party, 1980–83.

89   Peter Laslett to AJPT, 8 November 1948; BBC Written Archives, ibid.

90   John Grist on McGivern, discussion with CJW, 27 August 2003. Also Briggs,
        Sound and Vision, pp.223–24 and 599–605. Cecil McGivern (1907–63) was
        Controller of Television Programmes, 1950–56, and Deputy Director of
        Television Broadcasting, 1956–61. Norman Richard Collins (1907–82) was
        Controller of Television, 1947–50, and later Deputy Chairman, Associated
        Television Corporation, and a very successful novelist.

91   *Observer*, 18 December 1955, p.9. By 'trephined' he presumably meant Taylor's
        arguing was like having someone make a hole in your head. Randolph
        Churchill, 'Critic for a Week', *Evening Standard*, 19 December 1955, p.5. A.J.P.
        Taylor, 'I Say What I Please', *Daily Herald*, 21 December 1955, p.4. Wrigley,
        Taylor Bibliography, p.25.

92   Dingle Foot, 'Brother Michael', *Sunday Express*, 29 September 1974, pp.8–9.
        Robert John Graham Boothby, Baron Boothby of Buchan and Rattray Head
        (1900–86), was Conservative MP for East Aberdeenshire, 1923–36, and created
        a life peer in 1958. William John Brown (1894–1960) was general secretary of
        what became the Civil Service Clerical Association, 1919–42, a Labour MP
        1929–31, and an independent MP, 1942–50.

93   Goldie, *Facing the Nation*, pp.69–78. John Grist on Barnes, discussion with CJW,
        27 August 2003. Wrigley, *Taylor Bibliography*, pp.24–25. Sir George Reginald
        Barnes (1904–60) was BBC Director of Television, 1950–56, and Principal of
        the University College of North Staffordshire, 1956–60.

94   Harriet Lane, 'Victoria's Secrets' (an interview with Victoria Wood), *Observer
        Magazine*, 9 January 2005, pp.12–13 and 15–16.

95   AJPT to Barnes, 13 May 1952; BBC Written Archives, A.J.P. Taylor Television
        Talks File 1, 1949–62, and quoted in Sisman, *A.J.P. Taylor*, p.207.

96   AJPT to Barnes, 9 October, and Barnes to AJPT, 17 October 1952; BBC
        Written Archives, ibid.

97   The most detailed account is by Peter Black in the *Daily Mail*, 15 November
        1952. *Manchester Guardian*, 15 November 1952. See also Briggs, *Sound and Vision*,
        p.603, and Sisman, *A.J.P. Taylor*, p.206. The Conservative MPs were Stephen
        James McAdden (1907–79), MP for Southend East, 1950–79, and knighted,
        1962, and Anthony Marlowe (1904–65), MP for Brighton, 1941–50, and Hove,
        1950–65. The panel was chaired by the Liberal, Frank Byers (1915–84), MP for
        North Dorset, 1945–50, and created a life peer in 1964.

98   John Irwin, 'The Taylor Incident', memorandum to Barnes, 15 November
        1952; BBC Written Archives, A.J.P. Taylor Television Talks File 1, 1949–62.
        Briggs, *Sound and Vision*, p.603.

99   *Sunday Pictorial*, 22 July 1951. BBC Board of Management decision, 1 December
        1952. Memorandum by George Barnes of agreement with Cecil McGivern and
        Edgar Lustgarten (the programme's editor), 28 November 1952; ibid.

100   Barnes to AJPT, 15 December 1952, and a copy of that letter with one to
        Barbara Wootton, 18 December 1952; ibid.

101   AJPT to Barnes, 23 February, and Barnes to AJPT, 25 February 1952 (Barnes
        defending himself by saying Taylor's public comments suggested he was no
        longer interested). 'Note of lunch with AJPT, 22 April 1953'; ibid., Briggs,
        Sound and Vision, p.603.

102   *Daily Herald*, 30 May 1953. Gilbert Harding (1907–60) was a star of many
        television quiz programmes. Miall, *Inside the BBC*, pp.113 and 120.

103   AJPT to A. Miller Jones, 8 July [1953]. Miller Jones to AJPT, 20 and 27 July
        1953; BBC Written Archives, A.J.P. Taylor Television Talks File 1, 1949–62.
        Miller Jones was more successful with the programme 'Panorama', launched by

him that autumn. Sir Peter Henry Berry Otway Smithers (1913–2006) was Conservative Mp for Winchester, 1950–64, and at Magdalen College, Oxford, had gained First-Class Honours for History. His London address was 30 Wilton Crescent, Knightsbridge. Marghanita Laski (1915–88) was a novelist, critic, journalist and an early television personality. Sir John Hubert Newson (1910–71) was an educationist, author and publisher.

104   *Daily Herald*, 24 October 1953. A.J.P. Taylor, 'Freedom of Speech and Television', *Contemporary Review*, December 1953; quoted in Briggs, *Sound and Vision*, p. 913.

105   Barnes to AJPT, 26 November 1953; BBC Written Archives, A.J.P. Taylor Television Talks File 1, 1949–62.

106   Briggs, *Sound and Vision*, p. 604.

107   AJPT to Barnes, 25 July 1953; BBC Written Archives, A.J.P. Taylor Television Talks File 1, 1949–62.

108   AJPT to Barnes, 27 September 1946; BBC Written Archives, A.J.P. Taylor Radio File 1, 1942–46. Quoted in Wrigley, *Taylor Bibliography*, p. 27.

109   AJPT to Harman Grisewood, 21 October, and Grisewood to AJPT, 7 November 1946; ibid. Albert Sorel (1842–1906) wrote *L'Europe et la Révolution Française* (1885). Heinrich von Treitschke (1834–96) wrote on nineteenth-century Germany and was deemed a prophet of German unification.

110   Burk, *Troublemaker*, p. 381 (and, more generally on these talks, pp. 380–82).

111   Barnes to AJPT, 16 May, and AJPT to Barnes, 17 May 1947; BBC Written Archives, A.J.P. Taylor Radio File 1, 1942–46. Quoted in Wrigley, *Taylor Bibliography*, p. 28. His two talks were reprinted in *From Napoleon to Stalin*, pp. 111–22, and several later collections.

112   AJPT to Anna Kallin, 28 September 1950; BBC Written Archives. A.J.P. Taylor Radio File 3, 1950–52.

113   Published as 'Tito and Stalin: The Revolt from Within', *The Listener*, 41, 1043, 20 January 1949, pp. 86–88, and reprinted in *From Napoleon to Stalin*, pp. 208–17.

114   Transcript of 'Benjamin Constant: The Liberal Intellectual'; BBC Written Archives. Henri Benjamin Constant de Rebecque (1767–1830) was a French author and politician.

115   AJPT to Anna Kallin, 27 July [1951]. A Kallin to AJPT, 31 July and 12 November 1951. BBC Written Archives, A.J.P. Taylor Radio File 3, 1950–52. 'The Man of December' was published in *The Listener*, 46, 1188, 6 December 1951, pp. 961–62, and reprinted in several collections of his essays.

116   AJPT to Anna Kallin, 19 March 1952. A. Kallin to AJPT, 1 April 1952; ibid. The John Bright lecture was given at the John Rylands Library, Manchester.

117   Keith Kyle to CJW, 1 October 2003.

118   CJW discussion with John Grist, 6 August 2003. John Frank Grist (1924–) had a lengthy broadcasting career with the BBC, including being Controller of English Regions, 1972–77.

119   'The Question of Trieste' in the series 'London Commentary', recorded and transmitted 15 September 1953; transcript, BBC Written Archives. Wrigley, *Taylor Bibliography*, pp. 576–92.

120   *Sunday Pictorial*, 11 February, 24 June, 1 July and 13 May 1951, p. 5. *Sunday Pictorial*, 1 April and 19 August 1951. On his contract, AJPT discussion with CJW, 9 January 1978. Philip Zec (1909–) was the *Daily Mirror* cartoonist who enraged Churchill during the Second World War and assisted Labour's 1945 general election campaign. He was editor of the *Sunday Pictorial* 1949–52. Hugh Kinsman Cudlipp, Lord Cudlipp (1913–98), was a leading figure in the Mirror Group of newspapers and was editor of the *Sunday Pictorial*, 1937–40, 1946–49 and 1952–63.

121 *Daily Herald*, 27 April 1955, 18 February and 22 April 1954, 1 August 1953, 2 March 1955, 7 March 1956, 10 October 1953, 26 October 1955, 28 March and 14 February 1953, 2 November 1955 and 28 February 1953.

122 *Daily Herald*, 24 January 1953, 8 April 1954 and 9 May 1956. *Sunday Express*, 13 January 1963, p.16.

123 '1952: Right Turn', *Picture Post*, 58, 3 January 1953, pp.4–6. *Daily Herald*, 22 July 1954, 11 and 25 April, 13 and 20 June and 23 May 1956. *John Bull*, 99, 2598–2600, 14, 21 and 28 April 1956.

124 *Daily Herald*, 4 July, 16 May, 9 May and 31 January 1953.

125 *Daily Herald*, 25 April 1953, 5 and 25 March 1954 and 15 August 1953.

126 AJPT discussions with CJW, 9 January 1978 and 1 September 1980. *Reynolds News*, 21 and 28 October and 4 November 1956. *Sunday Graphic*, 10 November and *News Chronicle*, 29 November 1957.

127 *Manchester Guardian*, 8 April 1944. AJPT to Wadsworth, 17 October, and Wadsworth to AJPT, 20 October 1947. *Manchester Guardian* Archive, B/T19/98 and 99.

128 *Manchester Guardian*, 1 January, 24 February, 13 March, 2 June, 2 December, 30 July and 18 September 1948. Also 11 October 1949, 7 March 1950, 20 January 1951, 22 August 1953, 27 March 1954, 11 August, 13 September and 31 October 1956.

129 AJPT discussion with CJW, 9 January 1978.

130 *Manchester Guardian*, 31 August 1957 and 11 February, 3 and 30 September 1958. *Guardian*, 1 July 1961. AJPT discussion with CJW, 9 January 1978.

131 Arthur Crook discussion with CJW (by telephone), 27 January 1978. Arthur Charles William Crook (1912–2005) was assistant editor of the *Times Literary Supplement* 1951–59 and editor 1959–74. Norman Rose, *Harold Nicolson*, London, Cape, 2005, p.271.

132 *History Today*, January, p.10, February, pp 23–31, and July 1951, pp.35–41, and April, pp.387 and 289, and May 1952, pp.366–67. Other early contributors included Lewis Namier, Sir M. Powicke, Sir P. Magnus, Hugh Trevor-Roper, Alan Bullock, Asa Briggs, J.H. Plumb, Michael Brock, G.D.H. Cole, W.G. Hoskins, J.D. Chambers and Sir Kenneth Clark.

133 Historical Association, *Annual Report for 1952–3*, pp.30–31; *Annual Report for 1955–6*, pp.24 and 35; *Annual Report for 1956–7*, pp.21, 25 and 27; *Annual Report for 1957–8*, pp.20 and 36; and *Annual Report for 1958–9*, pp.23–24. His other branch lectures of this period included Reading (early 1953) and Medway and Watford (both autumn 1958). On Bolton, John and Margaret Bate discussion with CJW, 9 January 1999. J.H.D. Bate was secretary of the Bolton branch (1956–63) while Margaret Hamer had been treasurer. Frederick Richard Poskitt CBE (1900–83) was headmaster, 1933–66, and president of the HA branch 1933–66.

134 *Daily Herald*, 7 January 1956.

135 Alistair Parker discussion with CJW, 12 October 1993. Michael Aidin heard similar lectures in 1952–53. M. Aidin to CJW, 30 October 1998. (Alastair) Robert Alexander Clarke Parker (1927–2001) was a Fellow and Tutor of Queen's College, Oxford, 1957–97, whose major books included three on the Second World War and on appeasement.

136 Bill Rodgers, *Fourth Among Equals*, London, Politico's, 2000, p.26. William Thomas Rodgers, Lord Rodgers of Quarrybank (1928–), was general secretary of the Fabian Society, 1953–60, MP for Stockton-on-Tees, 1962–83, and Secretary of State for Transport, 1976–79.

137 David Perkin conversations with CJW, 22 July 1977 and 8 June 1978. The Rev. David Perkin was a university chaplain, Warden and Lecturer at Loughborough University and later a vicar of a London parish.

138 This stems from several former students of the early 1950s. I am grateful, *inter alia*, to Professor James Campbell for an informal discussion, 12 October 1993. James Campbell (1935–), was Lecturer, then Reader, 1958–96, then Professor of Medieval History, 1996–, at Oxford University.

139 Henry Loyn discussion with CJW, 12 October 1978. Henry Royston Loyn (1922–2000) was Professor of Medieval History, Cardiff University, 1969–77, Professor of History, Westfield College, London University, 1977–87, and president of the Historical Association, 1976–79. For Professor Butterfield's unhappy TV experiences, see McIntire, *Butterfield*, pp. 364–65.

140 Rodgers, *Fourth among Equals*, p. 27. Francesca Wilson's account, 5 August 1949 (she was staying with friends while at the summer school). Francesca Mary Wilson (1888–1981) had recently written *Aftermath: France, Germany, Austria and Yugoslavia 1945 and 1946*, West Drayton, Penguin, 1947.

141 *Manchester Guardian*, 10 December 1943 and 17 November 1953. Ollard, *A Man of Contradictions*, p. 252. R. Ollard (ed.), *The Diaries of A.L. Rowse*, London, Allen Lane, 2003, p. 365.

142 A.P. Wadsworth to AJPT, 18 November 1953. AJPT to Wadsworth, 18 November [1940]. *Manchester Guardian* Archives, B/T19/239 and 240.

143 AJPT to Trevor Blewitt, 10 February [1944]. BBC Written Archives, A.J.P. Taylor Radio File 1.

144 Stanley Parker, 'A.J.P. Taylor or My Waterloo', *Oxford Mail*, 17 June 1943, p. 2.

145 Ollard (ed.), *The Diaries of A.L. Rowse*, p. 202. A.L. Rowse, *Oxford in the History of the Nation*, London, Weidenfeld & Nicolson, 1975, p. 29, and *Historians I Have Known*, London, Duckworth, 1995, pp. 128–36.

146 The lead review in *Time and Tide*, 13 December 1952, p. 1498. On Namier resenting a Beloff review, see Sisman, *A.J.P. Taylor*, p. 243. Max Beloff (1913–99), from 1981 Baron Beloff of Wolvercote was Assistant Lecturer in History, Manchester University, 1939–46, Fellow of Nuffield College, 1947–58, Gladstone Professor of Government and Public Administration and Fellow of All Souls, Oxford, 1957–74, and Principal of the University College at Buckingham, 1974–79.

147 'Balance of Power', *Time and Tide*, 13 November 1954, p. 1517, and Crosland to his mother, 10 November 1954; both quoted in Burk, *Troublemaker*, pp. 270–71. On the resulting row with Woodward, see earlier in this chapter.

148 AJPT wrote entries on Beaverbrook, Sir Stafford Cripps, Lloyd George, and the First and Second World Wars; Wrigley, *Taylor Bibliography*, p. 127. For recollections of Taylor's editorial role by Gerald Howat, see Burk, *Troublemaker*, pp. 332–33.

149 G.N. Clark to AJPT, 5 October 1964; Clark Papers, quoted in Burk, *Troublemaker*, p. 304.

150 AJPT in discussion with CJW, 21 February 1979 and 6 February 1984.

151 AJPT in discussion with CJW, 21 November 1979.

152 Review of Eric Eyke, *Bismarck*, Vol. 1, Erlenbach-Zurich, Eugen Rentsch, 1941, in *English Historical Review*, 58, 229, January 1943, pp. 113–15. Eric Eyck was a German lawyer and historian who took refuge in England from the Nazis.

153 Reviews of Vol. 2 (1943) and Vol. 3 (1944) (both again German-language editions) in *English Historical Review*, 61, 239, January 1946, pp. 109–12 and 62, and 244, July 1947, pp. 390–93. The book on Marx was L. Schwarzchild, *The Red Prussian*, reviewed in *Manchester Guardian*, 16 January 1948.

154   Review of I.F.D. Morrow, *Bismarck* (1943) in *Oxford Magazine*, 62, 10, 27 January
      1944, p.135. AJPT to Wadsworth, *Manchester Guardian* Archives, B/T19/113,
      and quoted in Sisman, *A.J.P. Taylor*, p.177.
155   On his negotiations, see Burk, *Troublemaker*, pp.277–78. For Rowse, see his
      Historians I Have Known, p.132.
156   AJPT to Wadsworth, 13 August [1953]; *Manchester Guardian* Archives,
      B/T19/234. Margaret Taylor discussion with CJW, 20 December 1976.
157   Review of M. Foot, *The Pen and the Sword*, in *New Statesman*, 54, 1394,
      30 November 1957, p.743. Wrigley, *Taylor Bibliography*, pp.30–31.
158   Translation by Willie and Barbaba Klau, 1961, with introduction by A.J.P. Taylor,
      pp.7–9.
159   A.J.P. Taylor, *Bismarck*, London, Hamish Hamilton, 1955, pp.11–12.
160   Theodore S. Hamerow, *Otto von Bismarck: A Historical Assessment*, Lexington,
      D.C. Heath & Co., 1962, p.13. Otto Pflanze, *Bismarck and the Development of
      Germany*, 3 vols., Princeton, Princeton University Press, 1963–90; quotation
      from the revised Vol. 1 (1990), 'Introduction', p.xxix.
161   Meinecke, quoted by Pflanze, ibid., p.xvii. *Bismarck*, pp.129 and 70.
162   Taylor, *Bismarck*, p.70. The death of Frederick VII of Denmark reopened
      the issue of Schleswig and Holstein (whether they should be Danish or
      German).
163   Michael Howard, 'The Iron Chancellor', *New Statesman and Nation*, 50, 1270,
      9 July 1955, pp.47–48. Gordon A. Craig, 'Devoted Opportunist', *Saturday Review*,
      38, 19 November 1955, p.35. Gordon A. Craig (1913–2005), born in Glasgow,
      was Professor of History successively at Yale, Princeton and Stanford Universities.
      'Maker of an Empire', *Times Literary Supplement*, 2785, 15 July 1955, pp.389–90.
      For these and two others, see Wrigley, *Taylor Bibliography*, pp.86–87. Sir Michael
      Eliot Howard (1922–) was Professor of War Studies, King's College, London,
      1963–68, Fellow of All Souls College, 1968–80, Chichele Professor of the
      History of War, 1977–80, and Regius Professor of Modern History and Fellow
      of Oriel College, Oxford, 1980–89.
164   *Observer*, 3 July 1955, p.11.
165   Bruce Waller, *Bismarck*, Oxford, Blackwell, 1985.

Chapter 6

1   AJPT to Wadsworth, 28 May [1953], and Wadsworth to AJPT, 29 May 1953;
     Manchester Guardian Archives, B/T19/226 and 227.
2   AJPT to Wadsworth, 22 November [1954]; *Manchester Guardian* Archives, and
     quoted in Sisman, *A.J.P. Taylor*, p.232.
3   Anna Kallin to AJPT, 8 and 15 March 1955. AJPT to Anna Kallin, 4 November
     [1955]. BBC Written Archives, A.J.P. Taylor Radio File 4, 1953–57. He nego-
     tiated his fee up from 240 guineas.
4   Anna Kallin to AJPT, 16 April 1956; ibid. The lectures were broadcast weekly
     from 4 April 1956 (and each repeated five or six days later).
5   Sebastian Taylor interview, 27 June 2000.
6   A point he made several times, including in 'Accident Prone', pp.1–18, and
     when signing my copy, 3 October 1977.
7   Taylor, *The Trouble Makers*, pp.190 and 15.
8   Ibid., p.13.
9   Ibid., p.14, 17, 23 and 32.
10   Ibid., pp.54 and 55.

11   B. McFarlane to G. Hariss, 8 February 1956; K.B. McFarlane, *Letters to Friends 1940–1966*, Oxford, Magdalen College, 1997, p.126 and quoted in Burk, *Troublemaker*, p.156.

12   AJPT to Hamish Hamilton, 28 November and Hamish Hamilton to AJPT, 29 November 1956; Hamish Hamilton Papers and quoted in Burk, *Troublemaker*, pp.295–96. Much later, in 1993, it was published as a Pimlico paperback with an introduction by Paul Addison.

13   'Political Dissent', *Times Literary Supplement*, 2866, 21 June 1957, p.382. C. Sykes, 'Agin the Government', *Time and Tide*, 29 June 1957, pp.817–18. W.L. Neumann review, *American Historical Review*, 63, 3, April 1958, p.723. Earl Attlee, 'The Dissidence of Dissent', *Spectator*, 198, 6731, 28 June 1957, p.836. Kingsley Martin, 'Dissenters', in *New Statesman and Nation*, 53, 1369, 8 June 1957, pp.740–41. For these and three other reviews, Wrigley, *Taylor Bibliography*, pp.92–94. D. May, *Critical Times*, London, Harper Collins, 2001, p.351.

14   *A Personal History*, pp.210–11. Taylor, *The Trouble Makers*, p.22.

15   *A Personal History*, pp.211 and 189.

16   *A Personal History*, pp.206–7 and 214–17; Sisman, *A.J.P. Taylor*, pp.246–49; and Burk, *Troublemaker*, pp.207–11. Alic Halford Smith (1893–1958) was Warden of New College and Vice-Chancellor of Oxford University, 1954–57. Sir John Cecil Masterman (1891–1977) was a Student (i.e. Fellow) of Christ Church, 1919–46, Provost of Worcester College, 1946–61, and Vice-Chancellor of Oxford University, 1957–58. Hugh Redwald Trevor-Roper, Lord Dacre of Glanton (1914–2003), was Student (i.e. Fellow) of Christ Church, 1946–57, Regius Professor of Modern History, Oxford University, 1957–80, and Master of Peterhouse, Cambridge, 1980–87.

17   *A Personal History*, p.216. CJW discussion with Alistair (RAC) Parker, 16 November 1993.

18   *A Personal History*, p.216. R. Pares and A.J.P. Taylor, *Essays Presented to Sir Lewis Namier*, London, Macmillan, 1956. Julia Namier, *Lewis Namier: A Biography*, p.307. A.P. Wadsworth to AJPT, 17 April 1956; *Manchester Guardian* Archives.

19   AJPT conversation with CJW, 3 October 1977. If his recollection was accurate, he referred to an earlier review of *Europe in Decay* (*Manchester Guardian*, 7 March 1950) or perhaps if he reviewed *Personalities and Powers* (1955) to that, or even to Taylor's 'The Namier View of History' (*Times Literary Supplement*, 2691, 28 August 1953).

20   Taylor, *The Trouble Makers*, pp.22, 17 and 40. *Manchester Guardian*, 16 November 1956, p.8.

21   Burk, *Troublemaker*, p.211; quoting H. Trevor-Roper to Wallace Notestein, 25 July 1957.

22   'Good King George', *Observer*, 17 November 1957, p.8. 'Old Namier', *Manchester Guardian*, 21 February 1958.

23   Burk, *Troublemaker*, pp.210–11; quoting Trevor-Roper to Notestein, 25 July 1957.

24   *A Personal History*, p.217. A.J.P. Taylor, 'A Corner In Rationality', *New Statesman*, 54, 1388, 19 October 1957 and quoted in Wrigley, *Taylor Bibliography*, p.402.

25   *Critique*, 3, 4 20 January 1948. 'The Bunker Revisited', *New Statesman and Nation*, 40, 1009, 8 July 1950, p.44. 'The Twilight of the God', *Times Literary Supplement*, 2740, 6 August 1954, Special Supplement, p.xxv, and reprinted in his *Englishmen and Others* (1956) and other collections. 'Stuck in the Mud', *New Statesman and Nation*, 46, 1165, 4 July 1953, p.357. AJPT to Jamie, 28 September 1956; Hamish Hamilton Papers.

26   AJPT conversation with CJW, 21 November 1979. A publicly made critical comment in 1986 is reported in the final chapter.

27   AJPT conversation with CJW, 31 July 1985.

28   AJPT, 'Tribute to Trevor-Roper', *London Review of Books*, 3, 20, 5–18 November 1981, pp. 9–10. Hugh Trevor-Roper to AJPT, 12 November 1981 and 15 January 1984. There is also warm correspondence between them for 1974 and 1976 in the Taylor Papers, HRRC, Austin, Texas.

29   *A Personal History*, pp. 198–99 and 222–25. At Worcester Isaiah Berlin was also approached. A. Danchev, *Oliver Franks: Founding Father*, Oxford, Clarendon Press, 1993, p. 157.

30   William Roger Louis (1936–) held various Chairs in the USA, notably Kerr Professor of English History and Culture at University of Texas, Austin, since 1985; discussion with CJW, August 1992. CJW discussion with Dr David Cuthbert, 5 July 1998. Paul Addison, 'Wizard of Ox', *London Review of Books*, 12, 21, 8 November 1990, pp. 3–4. AJPT to P. Jalland, 15 October 1979 (draft copy). AJPT to Brian Harrison, 14 July 1972.

31   AJPT discussion with CJW and Éva Haraszti-Taylor, 31 July 1985.

32   Dr Geoff Matthews later taught history at Loughborough University; discussion with CJW, 11 May 1978. Edgar Wind (1900–1971) was educated in Germany and after Chairs in the USA was the first Professor of the History of Art at Oxford University, 1955–67. Dr Colin Bonwick was later Professor of American History at Keele University; discussion with CJW, 29 June 1991. Dr Robert Houlton was later Principal of the Co-operative College, Stanford-on-Soar; discussion with CJW, 19 October 1977. (Walter) Patrick Jackson (1929–) was Under-Secretary, Department of Transport, 1981–89, then wrote biographies of the Victorian Cabinet ministers Forster, Hartington and Harcourt; conversation with CJW, 8 July 1998.

33   Michael Aidin to CJW, 30 October 1998.

34   Professor Henry Colin Gray Matthew (1941–99) was a Fellow of St Hugh's, 1978–99, Professor of Modern History, 1992–99, editor of the Gladstone diaries and of the *Oxford Dictionary of National Biography*; conversation with CJW, 7 July 1998. Ann Wagstaff (née Schove) to CJW, 26 November 1998.

35   BBC Controller of TV's meeting, 21 October 1958; BBC Written Archives, A.J.P. Taylor Television Talks File 1, 1949–62.

36   Bernard Sendall, *Independent Television*. In *Britain*, Vol. 1, London, Macmillan, 1982, pp. 13–14 and 20–21. *New Statesman and Nation*, 43, 112, 28 June 1952. Wrigley, *Taylor Bibliography*, pp. 27 and 55.

37   Fred Cooke, 'It's the Great Experiment – Taylor Vision!', *Reynolds News*, 26 May 1957, p. 8.

38   A.J.P. Taylor, *The Russian Revolution*, London, Associated Television Limited, n.d. [1958]. Norman Swallow quoted in Sendall, *Independent Television*, pp. 350–51.

39   'What Would You Like Me to Talk About?', *TV Times*, 7 February 1958, p. 15. '(Un)Quiet Flows the Don: Alan Taylor Starts a "Revolution" on ITV', *TV Times*, 9 August 1957, p. 12. Wrigley, *Taylor Bibliography*, pp. 26–27.

40   The publicity for the series 'PM Power' on Wednesday evenings at 20.45 from 22 August 2001 referred to 'a collection of hitherto unknown recordings of AJP Taylor's university lectures'; e.g., *Guardian*, 22 August 2001, p. 16.

41   John Irwin message to Mr Hood, 8 May 1961; BBC Written Archives, A.J.P. Taylor Television Talks File 1, 1949–62.

42   AJPT to Kenneth Adam, 16 October [1958]; BBC Written Archives, A.J.P. Taylor Television Talks File 1, 1949–62.

43   Internal memoranda by Leonard Miall, February 1958 and 19 May 1961. Memorandum by Edna Button, 23 October 1961. John Heyman to S. Hood, 9 October 1961. Ibid. Rowland Leonard Miall (1914–2005) worked for the

BBC, 1939–74, including as Head of Talks, 1954–61, and then as Assistant Controller, Television, 1961–64.

44   AJPT to Hamish Hamilton, 6 February [1962]; Hamish Hamilton Papers. 'The Twenties' lectures were printed in *The Listener* and all but 'The Depression' reprinted in *The First World War and Its Aftermath*, pp. 326–74, the third volume of A.J.P. Taylor, *A Century of Conflict 1848–1948*, 5 vols., ed. C.J. Wrigley, London, Folio Society, 1998. Paul Einzig, 'The Financial Crisis of 1931', in M. Gilbert (ed.), *A Century of Conflict 1850–1950*, London, Hamish Hamilton, 1966. A.J.P. Taylor 'Received with thanks', *Observer*, 20 November 1966, p. 26. Wrigley, *Taylor Bibliography*, p. 476. Paul Einzig (1897–1973) was London correspondent of the *Commercial and Financial Chronicle*, New York, 1945–73, and political correspondent, *Financial Times*, 1945–56.

45   John Irwin memorandum to Leonard Miall, 19 June 1962; BBC Written Archives, A.J.P. Taylor Television Talks File 1, 1949–62.

46   The series was heralded as 'Men of 1862' in the *Radio Times* but when published in *The Listener* was entitled 'Men of the 1860s'. They were reprinted in A.J.P. Taylor, *From Napoleon to the Second International*, London, Hamish Hamilton, 1993, pp. 274–325.

47   Roger Machell to AJPT, 12 June and 15 July 1963. Hamish Hamilton Papers.

48   AJPT to Kenneth Adam, 16 February [1963]. Donald Baverstock memorandum, 1 March 1963. John Irwin memorandum to Donald Baverstock, 4 June 1963. AJPT to Alasdair Milne, 16 June [1961]. BBC Written Archives, A.J.P. Taylor Television Talks File 1, 1949–62.

49   The lectures on Britain, Russia and the US as well as the final one, 'The Cold War Spreads', were published as a pamphlet, *World War*, London, Rediffusion Television, n.d. [1966]. A.J.P. Taylor, 'Six Angles on One War', *TV Times*, 21 July 1966, p. 13.

50   Sean Day-Lewis, 'A.J.P. Taylor's Skill is Compelling', *Daily Telegraph*, 15 July 1978, p. 15. Wrigley, *Taylor Bibliography*, p. 29.

51   Chris Wrigley, 'Introduction', p. xx, to Taylor, *From Napoleon to the Second International*.

52   Simon Schama, 'Television and the Trouble with History', and Ian Kershaw, 'The Past on the Box: Strengths and Weaknesses', in D. Cannadine (ed.), *History and the Media*, London, Palgrave, 2004, pp 24 and 120. Dr Niall Campbell Douglas Ferguson (1964–), Fellow and Tutor of Jesus College, Cambridge, since 1992. Professor Simon Michael Schama (1945–) is currently at Columbia University. Dr David Starkey (1945–), taught at the London School of Economics, 1972–98, and subsequently has been Visiting Fellow, Fitzwilliam College, Cambridge.

53   F. Taunton discussion with CJW, 9 January 1999. P. Waymark to CJW, 10 August 2003. Professor George Boyce, for instance, has recalled how Taylor's zest for history made him a hero to George and many of his school friends; discussion, 8 July 1998. Such other later historians as Dr Stefan Collini, Dr Trevor James and Professor John Shepherd were also among the audiences in the studio when the programmes were recorded.

54   AJPT to Kenneth Adam, 30 January (probably 1960). BBC Written Archives, A.J.P. Taylor Television Talks File 1, 1949–62.

55   Lord Boothby to AJPT, 30 April 1984. He doubled the length of time they performed together in discussion programmes.

56   Interview with Elizabeth Longford, 3 November 1991. The Bevanites were supporters of Aneurin Bevan, the leader of the Labour Left from 1951. Mark Jenkins, *Bevanism: Labour's High Tide*, Nottingham, Spokesman, 1979, pp. 155

and 175. D.E. Butler, *The British General Election of 1955*, London, Macmillan, 1955, p.138.

57   On BBC radio, Home Service, in 'World Affairs: A Weekly Survey', entitled 'San Francisco and the Atom Bomb', 24 September 1945; printed in *The Listener*, 34, 873, 14 October 1945, pp.381–82. The MPs were Richard Law and Raymond Blackburn. 'There's no Dodging the Bomb', *Daily Herald*, 29 April 1954, p.4. Wrigley, *Taylor Bibliography*, pp.33 and 191.

58   A.J.P. Taylor, 'Campaign Report', *New Statesman*, 55, 1423, 21 June 1958, pp.799–800. A.J.P. Taylor's paper on CND, Institute of Historical Research, London, 24 May 1978.

59   'Campaign Report', pp.799–800. Peggy Duff, *Left, Left, Left*, London, Alison & Busby, 1971, pp.160–61. Interview with Giles Taylor, 24 September 1999.

60   For the background of CND and the Central Hall meeting, see Richard Taylor, *Against The Bomb: The British Peace Movement 1958–65*, Oxford, Clarendon Press, 1988, pp.5–29 and also Frank Parkin, *Middle Class Radicalism*, Manchester, Manchester University Press, 1968.

61   His paper on CND, 24 May, 1978. See also *A Personal History*, pp.226–28.

62   Rodgers, *Fourth Among Equals*, pp.27–28.

63   Roy Jenkins conversation with CJW, 19 April 1997. Sir Albert Raymond Maillard Carr (1919–) was Fellow of All Souls College, 1946–53, and New College, 1953–64, Director of the Latin America Centre, 1964–68, and Warden of St Antony's College, 1968–87. He succeeded Alan Taylor to the Special Lectureship at Oxford.

64   Wrigley, *Taylor Bibliography*, p.34. I compiled the list from advertisements of meetings, so it is probably not comprehensive.

65   Taylor, 'Accident Prone', pp.1–18. AJPT conversation with CJW, 1 April 1986.

66   His paper on CND, 24 May 1978. AJPT discussion with CJW, 6 February 1984. Interviews with Sebastian Taylor, 27 June 2000, and Dr Ray Challinor, 19 February 1991. The Rev. Canon Leslie John Collins (1905–82) was Canon of St Paul's Cathedral, 1948–81, chairman of Christian Action, 1946–73, and chairman of CND, 1958–64. Edward Palmer Thompson (1924–93) taught in Extra-Mural Department, Leeds University, 1948–65, was Reader in Social History, Warwick University, 1965–71, and campaigned against nuclear weapons. Dorothy Thompson to CJW, 13 February 2006.

67   Diana Collins, *Partners in Protest: Life with Canon Collins*, London, Victor Gollancz, 1988, p.371.

68   Alfred Gollin conversation with CJW, 8 August 1992. Michael Foot in 'The Man Who Wanted to Get Things Done', *The Listener*, 88, 2259, 13 July 1972, pp.44–47. *A Personal History*, p.222. Beaverbrook to AJPT, 28 July 1958. Eve Taylor to Beaverbrook, 12 September [1960]. Beaverbrook to AJPT, 12 July 1960. Beaverbrook Papers, House of Lords Record Office (HLRO).

69   Beaverbrook to AJPT, 2 March 1955. AJPT to Beaverbrook, 5 March [1955]; Beaverbrook Papers, HLRO.

70   A.J.P. Taylor, 'Sound and Fury' and 'Lord Beaverbrook is Historian', *Observer*, 26 February and 28 October 1956. 'The Man Who Wanted to Get Things Done', pp.44–47. Wrigley, *Taylor Bibliography*, pp.42, 385 and 391–92.

71   'Why Must We Soft Soap the Germans?', *Sunday Express*, 27 October 1957. *A Personal History*, p.214.

72   Burk, *Troublemaker*, pp.401–2. Memorandum, dated 14 September 1961. Beaverbrook to AJPT, 3 September 1963. Beaverbrook Papers, HLRO.

73   Beaverbrook to AJPT, 31 May and 16 June 1962. AJPT to Beaverbrook, 12 June [1962].

74   'Big Beast at Bay', *New Statesman*, 65, 1669, 8 March 1963, pp.341–42. 'Why Do I Write for this "Awful Newspaper"' and 'The Man Who Deals in Sunshine', *Sunday Express*, 27 May 1962 and 24 May 1964. *History Today*, 23, 8, August 1973, pp.546–53. 'The Man Who Never Stood Still', *Daily Express*, 25 May 1979, p.8. Martin Gilbert (ed.), *A Century of Conflict 1850–1950*, London, Hamish Hamilton, 1966, pp.3–5. Sir Martin Gilbert conversation with CJW, 25 March 1986. *New Statesman*, 92, 2388, 31 December 1976, p.902.

75   'Why Not Ban these Dawdling Drivers?' 'Why Pick on the Private Motorist?' 'The Nonsense of Making Us All Go Slow', 'October 9 Could Be a Day of Danger' (when the breathalysers came in). 'Has the Time Come to Ban All Drink for Drivers?' and 'Must the Motor Be Our Master?', *Sunday Express*, 2 August and 6 December 1964, 27 August and 1 October 1967 and 28 December 1969. For summaries of his 1957–78 articles, see Wrigley, *Taylor Bibliography*, pp.209–48.

76   *A Personal History*, p.214. For earlier scepticism about the Common Market in a left-wing newspaper, see 'What Is Europe?', *Daily Herald*, 3 June 1954, p.4.

77   'Will Menzies Speak for Britain?', 'Has Heath Given the Show Away?' and 'How Much More Must We Take from de Gaulle?', *Sunday Express*, 9 September 1962, 15 September 1963 and 26 November 1967. He also repeated the 'kith and kin' phrase in 'The Path to Ruin', 11 July 1971. 'Going into Europe', *Encounter*, 19 December 1962, p.62. Peter Osborne (ed.), *Professor A.J.P. Taylor on Europe: The Historian Who Predicted the Future*, London, Bruges Group, 1997, reprints five other *Sunday Express* articles of 1962–71.

78   *A Personal History*, p.229. Wrigley, 'Five Faces and the Man', pp.225–38.

79   AJPT conversation with CJW, 26 April 1978. Interview with Sebastian Taylor, 27 June 2000.

80   G.M. Thomson, *Evening Standard*, 16 June 1957.

81   A.J.P. Taylor, *The Origins of the Second World War*, 2nd edition, Harmondsworth, Penguin, 1963, pp.265–66 and 335–36. AJPT to Hamish Hamilton, 6 August 1960. Hamish Hamilton Papers and quoting Sisman, *A.J.P. Taylor*, p.293. Wrigley, 'Alan John Percivale Taylor 1906–1990', pp.510–12.

82   H. Trevor-Roper, 'A.J.P. Taylor, Hitler and the War', *Encounter*, 18, July 1961, pp.88–96. A.J.P. Taylor, 'How to Quote: Exercises for Beginners', *Encounter*, 19, 3 September 1961, pp.72–73. Alan Fox, 'Was Hitler Guilty?', *Socialist Commentary*, June 1961, pp.5–7. Alan Fox (1920–2002) was an outstanding scholar of industrial relations at Oxford University.

83   Burk, *Troublemaker*, p.288. Of course, he may simply have forgotten to list it – though that seems unlikely.

84   Norman J.W. Goda, 'A.J.P. Taylor, Adolf Hitler and the Origins of the Second World War', *International History Review*, 23, 1, March 2001, pp.97–124.

85   T.W. Mason, 'Some Origins of the Second World War', *Past and Present*, 29, December 1964, pp.67–87.

86   Anna Kallin to Michael Stephens, 8 June 1961; BBC Written Archives, A.J.P. Taylor Radio File 5, 1958–62.

87   C.F.O. Clarke to J.F. Camacho, memorandum, 22 June 1961. J.F. Camacho to A. Kallin, n.d. Wrigley, *Taylor Bibliography*, pp.57 and 565. Burk, *Troublemaker*, pp.286–87.

88   Sisman, *A.J.P. Taylor*, p.295.

89   William Carr, *Poland to Pearl Harbor: The Making of the Second World War*, London, Edward Arnold, 1985, pp.36–37.

90   R.J. Overy, *The Origins of the Second World War*, London, Longman, 1987. R.J.B. Bosworth, *Explaining Auschwitz and Hiroshima: History Writing and the*

Second World War 1945–1990, London, Routledge, 1993, p.43. A.J. Crozier, *The Causes of the Second World War*, Oxford, Blackwell, 1999, pp.231–32.

91   E.M. Robertson (ed.), *The Origins of the Second World War*, London, Macmillan, 1971. It was supplemented by R. Boyce and E.M. Robertson (eds.), *Paths to War: New Essays on the Origins of the Second World War*, London, Macmillan, 1989 and R. Boyce and J.A. Maiolo, *The Origins of World War Two: The Debate Continues*, Basingstoke, Palgrave, 2003. W.R. Louis (ed.), *The Origins Of The Second World War*, New York, John Wiley & Sons, 1972, p.8. [Louis] G. Martel (ed.), *The Origins of the Second World War Reconsidered*, London, Allen & Unwin, 1986, p.2, and 2nd edition, London, Routledge, 1999.

92   Goda, 'A.J.P. Taylor, Adolf Hitler', p.97.

93   Sir Ian Kershaw (on his having two versions of his talk), at British Academy colloquium, Sheffield, 16 March 2002. Interview with Giles Taylor, 24 September 1999. Historical Association, *Annual Reports 1958–59* (1960), to *1965–66* (1969) and also *1969–70* (1971). Most probably not all his lectures were listed; also, in some instances, such as the Medway Towns and also Watford, in 1958–59, and Cambridge, March 1965, the topics of his lectures were not recorded.

94   AJPT to Patrick Cormack, 17 May and 19 November [1962]. Doreen Hallewell to CJW, 10 January 1997.

95   Sir Patrick Cormack to CJW, 13 January 2005.

96   Jack Yates and Henry Thorold, *Lincolnshire: A Shell Guide*, London, Faber & Faber, 1965, p.100. Susan and Michael Simpson discussion with CJW, 27 January 2000.

97   Recollections of Graham Newbon, a former student of the grammar school, John Keily, his former accountant, David Robinson, John Baker, Eleanor Bennett, Jean Howard and Ken Patience at Louth Naturalists' Antiquarian and Literary Society, 8 October 2002. On Betjeman and Yates, see Bevis Hillier, *John Betjeman: New Fame, New Love*, London, John Murray, 2002, pp.343 and 363–67. D. Cuppleditch to CJW, 25 September 2002.

98   Doreen Hallewell to CJW, 10 January 1997. AJPT to Edward Trevitt, 9 February 1977, and to Jane Francis, 19 September 1977.

99   Hamish Hamilton to AJPT, 9 April and 15 May 1956. AJPT to Hamish Hamilton, 17 May [1956]. Hamish Hamilton Papers.

100   *Observer*, 21 October 1956, p.7. 'Rogue Elephant', *New Statesman and Nation*, 52, 1338, 3 November 1956, pp.560–61. 'History without a Philosophy', *Times Literary Supplement*, 2857, 30 November 1956, p.706. Theodore Philip Toynbee (1916–81), novelist and journalist for the *Observer*, 1950–81. Ralph Partridge was an author and a member of the Bloomsbury circle.

101   AJPT conversation with CJW, 10 May 1978. Roger Machell memorandum to Hamish Hamilton, 11 February 1964. AJPT to Roger Machell, 12 February [1964]. Hamish Hamilton Papers.

102   'Lloyd George's Hour', *Observer*, 20 September 1964, p.24. 'The History of A.J.P. Taylor', *New York Review of Books*, 4, 7, 6 May 1965, pp.24–26. 'Thus Spake Hitler', *Times Literary Supplement*, 2605, 4 January 1952, pp.1–2. May, *Critical Times*, p.344. Wrigley, *Taylor Bibliography*, pp.101–2 and 345. Professor Sir Francis Harry Hinsley (1918–96) was Professor of the History of International Relations, 1969–83, Master of St John's College, 1979–89, and Vice-Chancellor, Cambridge University, 1981–82.

103   Alfred Gollin to CJW, 4 February 1977. K.O. Morgan, 'People's Historian' (review of K. Burk, *Troublemaker*), *Oxford Magazine*, 181, Michaelmas Term 2000, pp.15–16.

104   Donald Read, *A Manchester Boyhood in the Thirties and Forties: growing up in War and Peace*, Lampeter, Edwin Mellen Press, 2003, p.139.

105 Sisman, *A.J.P. Taylor*, p.306. AJPT to David Higham, 23 March 1961 and 7 May 1963. David Higham Papers, HRRC, Austin, Texas.

106 Beaverbrook to AJPT, 28 October 1963; Beaverbrook Papers, HLRO.

107 A.J.P. Taylor, *The First World War. An Illustrated History*, London, Hamish Hamilton, 1963, pp.9 and 13.

108 'Historian's View of a War', *Times Literary Supplement*, 3225, 5 December 1963, p.1013. Geoffrey Barraclough, 'Goodbye to All That', *New York Review of Books*, 2, 7, 14 May 1964, pp.3–4. Alan Clark, 'History: Instant or Interpretative?', *Spectator*, 211, 7063, 8 November 1963, pp.604–5. Alan Kenneth McKenzie Clark (1928–99) was a Conservative MP, 1974–92 and 1997–99, a minister, historian and diarist. Captain Cyril Bentham Falls (1888–1971) was Chichele Professor of the History of War and Fellow of All Souls, Oxford, 1946–53.

109 H. Jackson, *Guardian*, 20 April 1963. J. Ardagh, *Observer*, 23 June 1963. I have benefited from Ruth Wilson's undergraduate dissertation on the history of the play.

110 Joan Littlewood, *Joan's Book*, London, Methuen, 1994, p.633. AJPT to Hamish Hamilton, 23 September [1963]. Hamish Hamilton Papers. Historical Association, *Annual Report for 1963–4* (1965), p.24. *A Personal History*, p.243. Joan Maud Littlewood (1914–2002) was the dynamic force behind the Theatre Workshop Company, which she co-founded in 1945.

111 Sisman, *A.J.P. Taylor*, p.350. *A Personal History*, p.243.

112 A.J.P. Taylor, 'Introduction' to Len Deighton, *Fighter: The True Story of the Battle of Britain*, London, Jonathan Cape, 1977, pp.xv–xxi. Len Deighton to AJPT, 20 October and 18 November 1980.

113 Len Deighton to AJPT, 17 May 1978. Len Deighton to CJW, 17 December 1990. Sir Maurice Oldfield (1915–81) gained First-Class Honours in History, Manchester University, 1938, worked for the Foreign Office, 1947–77, and was Security Co-ordinator, Northern Ireland, 1979–80.

114 Roger Louis to CJW, 4 May 1977. R.C.K. Ensor to G.N. Clark, 29 September 1956. Sir G.N. Clark to D. Davin, draft letter (not sent), 12 March 1957 and memorandum, 15 March 1957. Sir G.N. Clark Papers, Bodleian Library, Oxford. C.J. Wrigley, 'Introduction' to *English History 1914–45*, London, Folio edition, 1997, pp.xxvi–xxix.

115 *A Personal History*, pp.221 and 237–38.

116 AJPT to Hamish Hamilton, 19 April 1958; Hamish Hamilton Papers. AJPT to Clark, 23 December 1961. Clark Papers.

117 AJPT to Clark, 7 December 1962, 9 February and 13 June 1964. Clark Papers.

118 AJPT to Clark, 7 December 1965. Clark Papers.

119 *A Personal History*, pp.237 and 245. A.J.P. Taylor, *From Sarajevo to Potsdam*, London, Thames & Hudson, 1966, pp.7–8.

120 JW (Amen House) to D. Davin, 30 July 1965. Davin to JW, 2 October 1965. AJPT to Colin Roberts, 26 September 1965. Oxford University Press Archives.

121 Burk, *Troublemaker*, p.308. *A Personal History*, p.244.

122 A. Bullock, 'England from Asquith to Attlee', *Observer*, 24 October 1965, p.26. N. Annan, 'Historian of the People', *New York Review of Books*, 5, 9, 9 December 1965, pp.10 and 12. 'History Taylor Made', *Times Literary Supplement*, 3329, 16 December 1965, pp.1169–70. H. Pelling, 'Taylor's England', *Past and Present*, 33, April 1966, pp.149–58. C.L. Mowat, 'England in the Twentieth Century', *History*, 51, 2, June 1966, pp.188–96. For these and others, see Wrigley, *Taylor Bibliography*, pp.103–5. Henry Mathison Pelling (1920–97) was a Fellow of Queen's College, Oxford, 1949–65, and St John's College, Cambridge, 1966–80, and Reader in Recent British History, 1976–80.

123   *A Personal History*, p. 244. Paul Addison, *The Road to 1945: British Politics and the Second World War*, London, Jonathan Cape, 1975, p. 10. Dr Robert McKay to CJW, 6 January 1999. David Cannadine, 'I Wish I'd Written', *Guardian Saturday Review*, 15 August 1998.

Chapter 7

1   John Grigg, 'Less of a Crook than a Rogue, Beaverbrook as Mischief-Maker and Man of Power' (review of Chisholm and Davie's biography), *Times Literary Supplement*, 9 October 1992, p. 5. Lord Blake, 'The Species *Salientia*', in Logan Gourlay (ed.), *The Beaverbrook I Knew*, London, Quartet Books, 1984. Alfred Gollin in discussion with CJW, Santa Barbara, California, 11 August 1992. A. Marder to AJPT, 13 November 1972. Taylor Papers, HRRC, Austin, Texas.

2   *A Personal History*, p. 246.

3   Chris Wrigley, 'Foreword' to Chris Wrigley (ed.), *Warfare, Diplomacy and Politics: Essays in Honour of A.J.P. Taylor*, London, Hamish Hamilton, 1986, pp. 1–2. Taylor wrote of the library's holdings and mentioned the research seminar in 'The Beaverbrook Library', *History*, 59, February 1974, pp. 47–54. He also spoke about it on the BBC World radio broadcast 'Outlook' on 26 November 1967.

4   Nicholas Barker, *Stanley Morison*, London, Macmillan, 1972, p. 497. AJPT to Éva Haraszti, 13 August 1970 and 4 October 1971, in Taylor, *Letters to Éva*, pp. 15 and 44. AJPT to J. Gordon, 7 August 1972. Taylor Papers, HRRC, Austin, Texas.

5   N.J. Crowson, *Fleet Street, Press Barons and Politics: The Journals of Collin Brooks, 1932–1940*, Camden 5th Series, 11, Cambridge, Cambridge University Press, 1999. Her father and A.J.P. Taylor were both on 'The Brains Trust' on 31 October 1948.

6   AJPT to Roger Machell, 14 October 1968; Hamish Hamilton Papers. On the seminars, conversations with CJW, 17 June and 20 December 1976.

7   A.J.P. Taylor, *Lloyd George: Twelve Essays*, London, Hamish Hamilton, 1971. Reprinted, with an introduction by C.J. Wrigley, Aldershot, Gregg Revivals, 1994.

8   AJPT to Roger Machell, 24 September 1970; Hamish Hamilton Papers. The scale of the unexpected costs was financially embarrassing to at least one younger contributor and I believe one contributor refused outright to pay.

9   AJPT to David Higham, 13 and 31 March 1970; David Higham Papers. HRRC, Austin, Texas.

10   *A Personal History*, p. 252.

11   A.J.P. Taylor, *Beaverbrook*, London, Hamish Hamilton, pp. 607 and 616–18.

12   Francis Wheen, *Tom Driberg*, London, Chatto & Windus, 1990, pp. 284–86. Anne Chisholm and Michael Davie, *Beaverbrook: A Life*, London, Hutchinson, 1992, pp. 480–83.

13   Driberg, *Ruling Passions*, 1977, p. 224.

14   Tom Driberg, *Beaverbrook: A Study in Power and Frustration*, London, Weidenfeld & Nicolson, 1956, pp. 305–11. Chisholm and Davie in their admirable book go too far in suggesting that Driberg was not hostile.

15   C.M. Vines, *A Little Nut-brown Man*, London, Frewin, 1969.

16   Taylor, *Beaverbrook*, p. 677.

17   See also C. Armstrong and H.V. Nelles, *Southern Exposure: Canadian Promoters in Latin America and the Caribbean, 1896–1930*, Toronto, University of Toronto Press, 1988.

18   Taylor, *Beaverbrook*, p. xvii.

19   Sisman, *A.J.P. Taylor*, p. 356.

20 AJPT to William Thomas, 6 October 1967. AJPT to Lucia Biocca, 25 January 1972.

21 AJPT to Éva Haraszti, 28 May 1972. A.J.P. Taylor, *Letters to Éva*, pp.77–78.

22 Ronald Blythe, 'Eager Beaver', *New York Review of Books*, 20, 3, 8 March 1973, pp.29–30.

23 Kenneth O. Morgan in *History*, 58, 194, October 1973, pp.475–76.

24 Tom Driberg, 'In the Sight of the Lord', *New Statesman*, 83, 2154, 30 June 1972, pp.908–9.

25 Eddie Mirzoeff to Richard Crossman, 2 November 1972. Crossman Papers, Modern Records Centre, Warwick Mss 154/3/BR/6/13. The other guests in the first series were Enoch Powell, Harold Wilson, W.H. Auden, Cecil King, Lord Hailsham and Baroness (Evelyn) Sharp. A second series had as guests Roy Jenkins, Jeremy Thorpe, Lord (R.A.) Butler, Jack Jones, Grace Wyndham Goldie and Ralf Dahrendorf. The programme was broadcast late on Sunday evenings, the time deemed least likely to attract a big audience.

26 Transcript of the programme. Crossman Papers, 154/3/BR/6/34.

27 AJPT to Éva Haraszti, 6 and 20 January and 18 February 1973. Taylor, *Letters to Éva*, pp.109, 111 and 115. 'Crosstalk', *The Listener*, 89, 2288, 1 February 1973, pp.148–49.

28 They were referring to Dudley W.R. Bahlman (ed.), *The Diary of Sir Edward Walter Hamilton, 1880–1885*, 2 vols., Oxford, Oxford University Press, 1972.

29 John Richardson to Crossman, 9 January 1973, and Helen Adutt to Crossman, 10 January 1973. Crossman Papers 154/3/BR/6/24 and 73.

30 'Richard Crossman: Chronicler of the Cabinet', *The Listener*, 5 April 1979, pp.473–75. The 'Reputations' programme, the first in the series, was broadcast on Wednesday, 4 April 1979 between 20.20 and 21.00 hours.

31 Peter Fraser, 'Lord Beaverbrook's Fabrications in *Politicians and the War 1914–1916*', *Historical Journal*, 35, 1, 1990, pp.33–70. J.O. Stubbs, 'Beaverbrook as Historian: *Politicians and the War 1914–1916* reconsidered', *Albion*, 14, 2, 1982, pp.235–253.

32 Taylor, *Letters to Éva*, p.288. Conversations with CJW, 17 April 1975 and 21 February 1979. A.J.P. Taylor (ed.), *Lloyd George: A Diary by Frances Stevenson*, London, Hutchinson, 1971. A.J.P. Taylor (ed.), *My Darling Pussy: The Letters of Lloyd George and Frances Stevenson 1913–1941*, London, Weidenfeld & Nicolson, 1975.

33 A.J.P. Taylor (ed.), *W.P. Crozier, Off the Record: Political Interviews 1933–1943*, London, Hutchinson, 1973.

34 AJPT to CJW, 3 October 1978. *A Personal History*, p.256.

35 AJPT to Éva Haraszti, 24 January 1972. Taylor, *Letters to Éva*, p.59.

36 AJPT to Éva Haraszti, 30 October 1972. Taylor, *Letters to Éva*, p.96.

37 AJPT to Éva Haraszti, 3 March 1973. Taylor, *Letters to Éva*, p.118.

38 'Churchill: The Statesman' has most recently been reprinted in A.J.P. Taylor, *From the Boer War to the Cold War*, London, Hamish Hamilton, 1995 and 'Daddy, What Was Winston Churchill?' in A.J.P. Taylor, *British Prime Ministers and Other Essays*, 1999.

39 AJPT conversation with CJW, 24 October, 1979.

40 'Surprise Party', *New York Review of Books*, 15, 3, 13 August 1970, p.236. 'How Much More Must We Take from de Gaulle?', *Sunday Express*, 26 November 1967.

41 'Will Germany Be the Next to Explode?' and 'Wilson's Blunder over Berlin', *Sunday Express*, 2 June 1968 and 16 February 1969.

42 'Labour's First Year: A Review of the Government's Record', *New Statesman*, 70, 1805, 15 October 1967, p.557.

43   'Man with the Olive Branch', *Sunday Express*, 30 January 1972. Alger Hiss, a US
      diplomat, was a major victim of McCarthyism. He was accused of being a
      communist (which he possibly was), and after denying that he was a member,
      was sent to prison for perjury. Richard Nixon was one of the prosecutors of Hiss.
44   'You Want the Best Scandals? We Have Them!', *Sunday Express*, 22 July 1973.
45   *Sunday Express*, 27 August, 9 October and 24 December 1967, 28 December
      1968, 10 January 1971, 24 June and 2 December 1973 and 17 August 1975.
46   *Sunday Express*, 10 March and 11 August 1968, 12 October 1969, 22 February
      1970, 31 October 1971 and 28 December 1975.
47   *The Author*, 80, 4, Winter 1969, pp. 155–57. On Captain Swing, conversation
      with CJW, 17 December 1975.
48   Historical Association, *Annual Report for 1967–8* (1969), pp. 24, 28, 40 and 43.
49   Historical Association, *Annual Report for 1968–9* (1970), pp. 42, 43 and 45,
      Annual Report for 1969–70 (1971), pp. 23, 28, 41 and 43, *Annual Report for
      1970–71* (1972), pp. 27 and 31, *Annual Report for 1971–2* (1973), pp. 33 and 36,
      Annual Report for 1972–3 (unpaginated).
50   CJW interview with Joan Lewin, OBE, 23 July 1997 (telephone).
51   CJW interview with Joan Lewin, OBE, at Luton University, 24 July 1997.
52   CJW interview with Joan Lewin, OBE, 23 July 1997 (telephone).
53   Interview with Sebastian Taylor, 27 June 2000. *A Personal History*, pp. 250–51
      and 257–58. AJPT to I. Sutton, 18 July 1975. Y. Menuhin to AJPT, 28 November
      1977. AJPT to Y. Menuhin, 30 November 1977. Taylor Papers, HRRC, Austin,
      Texas.
54   Éva Haraszti-Taylor, *Remembering Alan*, London, privately published, 1995,
      p. 16. Éva Haraszti-Taylor, *Choices and Decisions: A Life*, London and Budapest,
      E.H. Taylor (Astra Press), 1997, pp. 149–52.
55   Haraszti-Taylor, *Remembering Alan*, p. 22.
56   *A Personal History*, p. 262.
57   Haraszti-Taylor, *Remembering Alan*, pp. 34–35.
58   Haraszti-Taylor, *Choices and Decisions*, pp. 150 and 160–61. Haraszti-Taylor,
      Remembering Alan, p. 32.
59   Haraszti-Taylor, *Choices and Decisions*, pp. 210–12.
60   Haraszti-Taylor, *Choices and Decisions*, p. 18.
61   Haraszti-Taylor, *Remembering Alan*, p. 85.
62   AJPT to Éva Haraszti, 19 August 1971; Taylor, *Letters to Éva*, p. 40.
63   *A Personal History*, p. 247. She began working at the library under her married
      name, Wheeler.
64   Conversation with Della Hilton, London, 17 June 1976.
65   AJPT to Éva Haraszti, 3 March 1973.
66   AJPT to Karin Wood, 5 December 1974. She was the daughter (born 1910) of
      Kathleen Thompson and Gustav Juhlin. She married Harold Wood, from the
      Orkneys; they had two children, Richard and Kristin, and farmed in Cheshire.
      She died in her late sixties.
67   AJPT to Éva Haraszti, 18 October and 3 November 1974; Taylor, *Letters to
      Éva*, pp. 204–5 and 208–9.
68   Conversation with AJPT, 18 April 1975.
69   Haraszti-Taylor, *Choices and Decisions*, p. 217.
70   Conversation with AJPT, 20 December 1976. Sir Thomas Blackburn had long
      worked for Beaverbrook, his career including managing the *Evening Standard*
      and being company chairman of Beaverbrook Newspapers (from 1955 until
      after Beaverbrook's death).
71   Conversation with AJPT, 31 July 1985.

Chapter 8

1   Éva Haraszti-Taylor (1923–2005), *Remembering Alan*, p. 35.
2   AJPT to Bob Cole, 14 July 1975. To CJW, December 1976.
3   AJPT to Éva, 2 February 1974; Taylor, *Letters to Éva*, p. 166.
4   *The Last of Old Europe: A Grand Tour with A.J.P. Taylor*, London, Sidgwick and Jackson; New York, Quadrangle Books/New York Times Co., 1976. *The Russian War*, London, Jonathan Cape, 1978 (at p. 11).
5   Private information, 1976.
6   Burk, *Troublemaker*, p. 397. Sisman, *A.J.P. Taylor*, p. 380.
7   At a question and answer session with Alan and Éva Taylor organised by Juliet Gardiner on behalf of *History Today* and Channel 4 Television, 6 May 1983.
8   Conversation with CJW, 17 June 1976.
9   Conversation with CJW, 17 June 1976.
10 Private information, 7 December 1976.
11 An edited version was published as 'From Disraeli to Callaghan: Britain 1879–1979', *Historian*, 55, 1997, pp. 22–25 (with an introduction, 'A.J.P. Taylor and the Historical Association', by CJW, pp. 21–22).
12 Della Hilton telephone conversation with CJW, 17 September 1976. The resulting book, Wrigley, *A.J.P. Taylor: A Complete Bibliography*, is 607 pages long.
13 AJPT to CJW, 23 July 1979.
14 Haraszti-Taylor, *Remembering Alan*, p. 116.
15 CJW conversation with AJPT, 21 November 1979.
16 A.J.P. Taylor, *Politicians, Socialism and Historians*, London, Hamish Hamilton, 1980. He included the Toynbee anecdote as a preface to his Geyl essay, pp. 42–45. The Shaw essay is printed pp. 131–34. I rather doubt that Geyl believed Taylor's *Origins* was 'true', even if he politely responded: 'That is so.'
17 John Terraine, 'Making historians sit up', *Daily Telegraph*, 5 July 1979, p. 15. For expressions of admiration for his lecturing skill by Dirk Bogarde, see J. Coldstream, *Dirk Bogarde: The Authorised Biography*, London, Weidenfeld & Nicolson, 2004, p. 522.
18 AJTP to CJW, 16 January 1979.
19 Jeremy Isaacs, *Storm over 4: A Personal Account*, London, Weidenfeld & Nicolson, 1989, pp. 53–55. Isaacs' accounts of memorable programmes not surprisingly does not include 'How Wars End'.
20 CJW conversation with AJPT, 31 July 1985.
21 J. Betjeman telegram to AJPT, 17 September 1976. Taylor Papers, HRRC, Austin, Texas. AJPT to CJW, 28 July 1979.
22 Éva Haraszti-Taylor in conversation with CJW, 28 November 2002.
23 Diary entry, 8 June 1980. Haraszti-Taylor, *A Life with Alan*, p. 111.
24 *A Personal History*, pp. 268–70. Scripts of 'Edge of Britain' appeared in the *Spectator*, 20 September–11 October 1980 (the programmes being broadcast between 18 September and 9 October), and were reprinted in Taylor, *From Napoleon to the Second International*, pp. 402–22.
25 Diary entries, 8 and 14 June 1980. Haraszti-Taylor, *A Life with Alan*, pp. 112–13.
26 Zorba was played memorably by Anthony Quinn in the 1965 film version of the novel by Nikos Kazantzakis.
27 *Times*, 22 January 1980.
28 Broadcast, 31 January 1979. Sue MacGregor to CJW, 26 September 2003.
29 Crossman Papers, Modern Record Centre, Warwick University, Mss. 154/3/BR/6/13.
30 *Parkinson*, broadcast 22.50–23.50 hours, 25 February 1981.

31   *New Statesman*, 95, 2447, 10 February 1978, p. 182.

32   *An Phoblacht, Bealtaine* 14, 1976, pp. 1 and 4. AJPT conversation with CJW, Josie Howie and others, 9 March 1983.

33   The programme was broadcast between 23.10 and 23.55 hours on BBC1 on 22 March 1981 (CJW notes). Robert Jacob Alexander Skidelsky (Lord Skidelsky, 1939–) was Associate Professor at John Hopkins University, 1970–76, Head of History, North London Polytechnic, 1976–78, Professor of International Studies, Warwick University, 1978–90, and was created a life peer, 1991.

34   *Observer*, 5 November 1978, p. 30.

35   In his essay 'Lancashire', *Vogue*, 116, 5, mid-March 1960, pp. 89–90, 93–94 and 164–65, and reprinted in A.J.P. Taylor, *From the Boer War to the Cold War*, London, Hamish Hamilton, 1995, pp. 444–50.

36   AJPT conversation with CJW, 9 March 1983.

37   Dr (later Professor) John Ramsden (1947–) was at Queen Mary College, London University, and published *The Age of Balfour and Baldwin 1902–1940*, London, Longman, 1978 and subsequently other volumes in the *History of the Conservative Party*.

38   Dr (later Professor) Brian Bond (1936–), Department of War Studies, Kings College, London University, published *Liddell Hart: A Study of His Military Thought*, London, Cassell, 1977.

39   One exception was 10 May 1978. She noted in her diary that she did not go, as 'the subject did not interest me. Alan said he thought people went to seminars to add to their knowledge.' (The topic was 'The government and industrial relations 1910–21', by CJW.) Haraszti-Taylor, *A Life with Alan*, p. 12.

40   Dr (later Professor) Peter Clarke (1942–), then at University College, London University, and later at Cambridge University, published *The Keynsian Revolution in the Making*, Oxford, Oxford University Press, 1988.

41   John Grigg (1924–2002) published four volumes of his life of David Lloyd George, 1973–2002.

42   Published by the German Historical Institute as a pamphlet. Reprinted in Taylor, *Struggles for Supremacy*, pp. 300–13. Éva Taylor's paper on 1948 was published in *Acta Historica Academiae Scientarium Hungaricae*, 27, 1981, pp. 189–205.

43   Haraszti-Taylor, *Remembering Alan*, p. 97.

44   *Personal History*, p. 267.

45   AJPT conversation with CJW, 29 November 1978. Information from Professor R.B. McKean, the then secretary of the Stirling branch of the Historical Association, 14 December 2002.

46   Norman Gash (1912–) was Professor of Modern History at Leeds, 1953–55, then Professor of History at St Andrews, 1955–80, and an authority on the Conservative Party in the period of Liverpool, Wellington and Peel (1812–46).

47   Haraszti-Taylor, *A Life With Alan*, pp. 43–44.

48   John Fines conversation with CJW, 19 March 1998. Dr John Fines (1933–98) was a distinguished educationist, a president of the Historical Association (1994–6) and honorary archivist of Chichester Cathedral (1998).

49   Éva Haraszti-Taylor's notes. See also her *A Life with Alan*, p. 148. Diary entry 11 March 1981.

50   Lord Longford, *Diary of a Year*, London, Weidenfeld & Nicolson, 1982, p. 198.

51   Burk, *Troublemaker*, pp. 335–36. CJW's notes taken at the 1968 UCL lectures indicate they were very close to the book.

52   A.J.P. Taylor, *War by Timetable*, London, MacDonald, 1969, pp. 32 and 121. A.J.P. Taylor, 'War in our Time', *London Review of Books*, and reprinted in A.J.P. Taylor, *An Old Man's Diary*, London, Hamish Hamilton, 1984, pp. 53–61.

53   Sisman, *A.J.P. Taylor*, p. 380. A.J.P. Taylor, 'London Diary', *New Statesman*, 92, 2386, 10 December 1976, p. 836. AJPT conversation, 20 December 1976. Robert Skidelsky, 'A.J.P. Taylor' (obituary), *Independent*, 8 September 1990, p. 14. His diary for 17–30 June 1982, *London Review of Books*; reprinted in Taylor, *An Old Man's Diary*, p. 87. Seminar on 9 May 1984.

54   Sisman, *A.J.P. Taylor*, pp. 389–93. AJPT to CJW, 11 July 1980. Dr Marjorie Reeves discussion with CJW, 6 April 1993. AJPT conversations with CJW, 24 October and 21 November 1979 and 1 April 1986. Marjorie Ethel Reeves (1905–2001) was Vice-Principal, St Anne's College, Oxford, 1951–62 and 1964–67.

55   Taylor, *Letters to Éva*, p. 405. Sisman, *A.J.P. Taylor*, pp. 390–91.

56   *A Personal History*, p. 195 (where the further Boothby comments were omitted). Robert Rhodes James, *Bob Boothby: A Portrait*, London, Hodder and Stoughton, 1991, pp. 114–20.

57   John Gross, 'Media Star and Major Historian', *New York Review of Books*, 25 September 1983; quoted in Sisman, *A.J.P. Taylor*, p. 399. A. Quinton, 'Socialist at high table', *Sunday Telegraph*, 29 May 1983, p. 17. M. Muggeridge, 'Extreme views weakly held', *Sunday Times*, 29 May 1983, p. 42. S. Ross, 'The gadfly of history', *Observer*, 29 May 1983, p. 30. Extracts from the autobiography were serialised in the *Observer*, 15, 22 and 29 May 1983.

58   AJPT to CJW, 28 November 1983. Sisman, *A.J.P. Taylor*, p. 400. Henderson also recalled the occasion on the BBC2 documentary 'A.J.P. Taylor: An Unusual Type of Star' (in its series *Reputations*), 22 January 1995.

59   Éva Taylor conversation with CJW, 9 December 2004. He had earlier had a prostate operation in July 1982. AJPT conversation with CJW, 6 February 1984. AJPT to Freddy Hurdis-Jones, 3 April 1984.

60   Giles and Janet Taylor interview, 24 September 1999. AJPT conversations with CJW, 6 March and 31 July 1985.

61   CJW interview with Ferencz Hudecz, 7 April 1992. Discussion with Éva Haraszti-Taylor, Istvan ('Pisti') and Christine Hudecz, 7 July 1992. Ferencz Hudecz (1952–) was later Professor of Chemistry and Pro-Rector of Estvös University, Budapest. Istvan Hudecz (1955–) is a successful Hungarian architect.

62   Duncan Fallowell interview, 'Historian at Home', *Irish Times*, 21 June 1983; quoted in David Krause (ed.), *The Letters of Sean O'Casey*, Vol. 3, *1955–1958*, Washington, DC, Catholic University of America, 1989, pp. 236–37. Ferencz Hudecz interview, 7 April 1992.

63   AJPT discussion with CJW, 30 July 1984. Taylor, *An Old Man's Diary*. Éva Haraszti-Taylor, *Hush, I Become Eighty: My Diary for 2003*, Nottingham, Astra Press, 2004, p. 36.

64   AJPT discussion with CJW, 31 July 1985, A.J.P. Taylor, 'When You Have Life Don't Waste It', *Mail on Sunday*, 23 March 1986, and reprinted in his *British Prime Ministers and Other Essays*, pp. 371–73.

65   He also enjoyed a family eightieth birthday party. He received a third *Festschrift*: Chris Wrigley (ed.), *Warfare, Diplomacy and Politics*, London, Hamish Hamilton, 1986. AJPT discussion with CJW, 1 April 1986.

66   AJPT conversation with CJW, Alan Sked and Alan Hankinson, 17 December 1986. Terence Kevin Kilmartin (1922–91) was Literary Editor of the *Observer*, 1952–86, and an author on French literary subjects.

67   Katherine Bligh conversation with CJW, 30 January 1991. K.O. Morgan, 'People's Historian', *Oxford Magazine*, 181, Michaelmas Term 2000, p. 16. Éva Haraszti-Taylor conversations with CJW, 7 August, 25 and 28 September 1990. M.R.D. Foot conversation with CJW, 7 July 1998. Michael Richard Daniell

Foot (1919–), after teaching and research posts at Oxford University, 1947–67, was Professor of Modern History, Manchester University, 1967–73.

68   'A.J.P. Taylor: popular historian', *Financial Times*, 9 September 1990, p. 4. 'A.J.P. Taylor', *Daily Telegraph*, 8 September 1990, p. 17. 'A.J.P. Taylor', *Times*, 8 September 1990, p. 14. Robert Skidelsky, 'A.J.P. Taylor', *Independent*, 8 September 1990, p. 14. Burk, *Troublemaker*, pp. 408–9.

69   In addition there was the 1982 Sussex Tape 'Path to World War II', six volumes in the Folio Society's editions and his edited Lloyd George collection of essays.

70   M. Mazower, 'Will the State survive?' (review of D. Reynolds, *One World Divisible*), *Times Literary Supplement*, 6 October 2000, p. 6.

71   Arthur Marwick, *The Nature of History*, London, Macmillan, 1970 (3rd edition, 1989), p. 103. Peter Burke, 'Introduction', pp. 1–10, *History and Historians in the Twentieth Century*, Oxford, Oxford University Press, 2002. It is notable that in this British Academy publication to mark its centenary AJPT appears only for his anti-German writing (p. 66).

72   AJPT to R. Cole, 13 May 1967.

73   Max Beloff, 'The great narrator' (review), *Times Literary Supplement*, 10 March 1995, p. 13. Michael Foot, 'Alan Taylor', in C.J. Wrigley (ed.), *Warfare, Diplomacy and Politics*, pp. 3–13.

INDEX